T0201769

A Practical Guide to Digital Forensics Investigations

Dr. Darren R. Hayes

PEARSON

221 River St. Hoboken, NJ, 07030, USA

A Practical Guide to Digital Forensics Investigations

ISBN-13: 978-0-7897-5991-7
ISBN-10: 0-7897-5991-8

Library of Congress Control Number: 2020906041

78 2024

Trademarks

Warning and Disclaimer

Special Sales

For information about buying this title in bulk quantities, or for special sales opportunities (which may include electronic versions; custom cover designs; and content particular to your business, training goals, marketing focus, or branding interests), please contact our corporate sales department at corpsales@pearsoned.com or (800) 382-3419.

For government sales inquiries, please contact governmentsales@pearsoned.com.

For questions about sales outside the U.S., please contact intlcs@pearson.com.

Editor-in-Chief
Mark Taub

Director, ITP Product Management
Brett Bartow

Senior Editor
James Manly

Development Editor
Christopher Alan Cleveland

Managing Editor
Sandra Schroeder

Project Editor
Mandie Frank

Copy Editor
Kitty Wilson

Indexer
Ken Jhonson

Proofreader
Betty Pessagno

Technical Editors
Lorne Dannenbaum
Aamir Lakhani

Publishing Coordinator
Cindy Teeters

Designer
Chuti Prasertsith

Compositor
codeMantra

Credits

Figure 1-1   Screenshot of File metadata © Microsoft 2020

Figure 2-3   Screenshot of View advanced system settings © Microsoft 2020

Figure 2-4   Screenshot of System Properties dialog box © Microsoft 2020

Figure 2-5   Screenshot of Performance Options dialog box © Microsoft 2020

Figure 2-6   Screenshot of Performance Options dialog box with paging file size © Microsoft 2020

Figure 2-7   Screenshot of The ASCII text display © 1995-2014 BreakPoint Software, Inc.

Figure 2-8   Screenshot of The file slack © 1995-2014 BreakPoint Software, Inc.

Figure 2-9   Screenshot of Viewing the BIOS © Microsoft 2020

Figure 2-10   Screenshot of Adding the drive to the Evidence Tree © Copyright 2020 AccessData

Figure 2-11   Screenshot of Expand button © Copyright 2020 AccessData

Figure 2-12   Screenshot of Partition 1 selected © Copyright 2020 AccessData

Figure 2-13   Screenshot of NTFS highlighted © Copyright 2020 AccessData

Figure 2-14   Screenshot of Master File Table displayed in the hex editor © Copyright 2020 AccessData

Figure 2-15   Screenshot of Prefetch Files © Microsoft 2020

Figure 2-16   Screenshot of Registry Editor © Microsoft 2020

Figure 2-17   Screenshot of Two of the data types © Microsoft 2020

Figure 2-18   Screenshot of Using Disk Defragmenter © Microsoft 2020

Figure 2-19   Screenshot of The Event Viewer © Microsoft 2020

Figure 2-20   Screenshot of AutoPlay dialog box © Microsoft 2020

Figure 2-21   Screenshot of The Backup and Restore Center © Microsoft 2020

Figure 2-22   Screenshot of System Restore © Microsoft 2020

Figure 2-23   Screenshot of USB drive information © Microsoft 2020

Figure 2-24   Screenshot of USBDeview © Microsoft 2020

Figure 2-25   Screenshot of Sticky Note © Microsoft 2020

Figure 2-26   Screenshot of InPrivate Browsing with Internet Explorer © Microsoft 2020

Figure 2-27   Screenshot of Pictures Library © Microsoft 2020

Figure 2-28   Screenshot of Windows 8 Start screen © Microsoft 2020

Cover

"Wherever he steps, whatever he touches, whatever he leaves, even unconsciously, will serve as a silent witness against him. Not only his fingerprints or his footprints, but his hair, the fibers from his clothes, the glass he breaks, the tool mark he leaves, the paint he scratches, the blood or semen he deposits or collects. All of these and more bear mute witness against him. This is evidence that does not forget. It is not confused by the excitement of the moment. It is not absent because human witnesses are. It is factual evidence. Physical evidence cannot be wrong, it cannot perjure itself, it cannot be wholly absent. Only human failure to find it, study, and understand it can diminish its value."

CKA /Shutterstock

Kirk, P. L. (1974) in Thornton, J. I. (ed.) Crime Investigation, 2nd ed, John Wiley & Sons, New York, p. 2.

"fully customizable tool allows your on-the-scene agents to run more than 150 commands on a live computer system." "provides reports in a simple format for later interpretation by experts or as supportive evidence for subsequent investigation and prosecution."

Computer Online Forensic Evidence Extractor (COFEE), Microsoft Corporation

"There's no chance that the iPhone is going to get any significant market share." "We believe in touch."

Quote by Microsoft CEO Steve Ballmer

§ Managerial competence § Integrity § Quality § Efficiency § Productivity § Meeting organizational expectations § Health and safety § Security § Management information systems § Qualifications § Training § Maintaining employee competency § Staff development § Environment § Communication § Supervision § Fiscal § Conflict of interest § Response to public needs § Professional staffing § Recommendations and references § Legal compliance § Fiscal responsibility § Accountability § Disclosure and discovery § Work quality § Accreditation § Peer certification § Peer organizations § Research § Ethics

The American Society of Crime Laboratory Directors

"fat ass who should stop eating fast food, and is a douche bag."

Quoted by Donny Tobolski, Mesa Verde High School, in California

"Tor is free software and an open network that helps you defend against traffic analysis, a form of network surveillance that threatens personal freedom and privacy, confidential business activities and relationships, and state security"

Quote taken from The Tor Project

(1) In general - A provider of wire or electronic communication services or a remote computing service, upon the request of a governmental entity, shall take all necessary steps to preserve records and other evidence in its possession pending the issuance of a court order or other process. (2) Period of retention - Records referred to in paragraph (1) shall be retained for a period of 90 days, which shall be extended for an additional 90-day period upon a renewed request by the governmental entity.

18 U.S. Code, Section 2703 (f), Required disclosure of customer communications or records

(a) In General - Not Automatically Objectionable. An opinion is not objectionable just because it embraces an ultimate issue. (b) Exception - In a criminal case, an expert witness must not state an opinion about whether the defendant did or did not have a mental state or condition that constitutes an element of the crime charged or of a defense. Those matters are for the trier of fact alone.

Opinion on an Ultimate Issue', Federal Rules of Evidence, Rule 704.

(B) Witnesses Who Must Provide a Written Report. Unless otherwise stipulated or ordered by the court, this disclosure must be accompanied by a written report - prepared and signed by the witness - if the witness is one retained or specially employed to provide expert testimony in the case or one whose duties as the party's employee regularly involve giving expert testimony. The report must contain: (i) a complete statement of all opinions the witness will express and the basis and reasons for them; (ii) the facts or data considered by the witness in forming them; (iii) any exhibits that will be used to summarize or support them; (iv) the witness's qualifications, including a list of all publications authored in the previous 10 years; (v) a list of all other cases in which, during the previous 4 years, the witness testified as an expert at trial or by deposition; and (vi) a statement of the compensation to be paid for the study and testimony in the case.

Disclosure of Expert Testimony in the Federal Rules of Civil Procedure, Federal Rule 26(2)(B).

The judicial Power shall extend to all Cases, in Law and Equity, arising under this Constitution, the Laws of the United States, and Treaties made, or which shall be made, under their Authority; to all Cases affecting Ambassadors, other public Ministers and Consuls; to all Cases of admiralty and maritime Jurisdiction; to Controversies to which the United States shall be a Party; to Controversies between two or more States; between a State and Citizens of another State; between Citizens of different States; between Citizens of the same State claiming Lands under Grants of different States, and between a State, or the Citizens thereof, and foreign States, Citizens or Subjects.

Article III, section 2 of the U.S. Constitution.

In all criminal prosecutions, the accused shall enjoy the right to a speedy and public trial, by an impartial jury of the State and district wherein the crime shall have been committed, which district shall have been previously ascertained by law, and to be informed of the nature and cause of the accusation; to be confronted with the witnesses against him; to have compulsory process for obtaining witnesses in his favor, and to have the Assistance of Counsel for his defense.

Sixth Amendment of the U.S. Constitution

It has no declaration of rights.

George Mason, author of the Virginia Declaration of Rights

Congress shall make no law respecting an establishment of religion, or prohibiting the free exercise thereof; or abridging the freedom of speech, or of the press; or the right of the people peaceably to assemble, and to petition the Government for a redress of grievances.

First Amendment of the U.S. Constitution.

"It can hardly be argued that either students or teachers shed their constitutional rights to freedom of speech or expression at the schoolhouse gate." "materially and substantially disrupt the work and discipline of the school."Tinker v. Des Moines Independent Community School District (No. 21), 393 U.S. 503 (1969).

the reach of school authorities is not without limits…. It would be an unseemly and dangerous precedent to allow the state in the guise of school authorities to reach into a child's home and control his/her actions there…we therefore conclude that the district court correctly ruled that the District's response to Justin's expressive conduct violated the First Amendment guarantee of free expression.	United States Court of Appeals for the Third Circuit, February 2010
"jamfest is cancelled due to the douchebags in central office— here is a letter to get an idea of what to write if you want to write something or call her [school superintendent] to piss her off more." "created a foreseeable risk of substantial disruption"	Doninger v. Niehoff, 527 F.3d 41 (2d Cir. 2008)
The right of the people to be secure in their persons, houses, papers, and effects, against unreasonable searches and seizures, shall not be violated, and no Warrants shall issue, but upon probable cause, supported by Oath or affirmation, and particularly describing the place to be searched, and the persons or things to be seized.	Fourth Amendment of the Constitution
"One who occupies [a telephone booth], shuts the door behind him, and pays the toll that permits him to place a call is surely entitled to assume that the words he utters into the mouthpiece will not be broadcast to the world."	Katz v. United States, 389 U.S. 347 (1967)
The right of the people to be secure in their persons, houses, papers, and effects,[a] against unreasonable searches and seizures, shall not be violated, and no Warrants shall issue, but upon probable cause, supported by Oath or affirmation, and particularly describing the place to be searched, and the persons or things to be seized.	Fourth Amendment of the Constitution
We accept the reality that such over-seizing is an inherent part of the electronic search process and proceed on the assumption that, when it comes to the seizure of electronic records, this will be far more common than in the days of paper records. This calls for greater vigilance on the part of judicial officers in striking the right balance between the government's interest in law enforcement and the right of individuals to be free from unreasonable searches and seizures.	U.S., Plaintiff-Appellant, v. Comprehensive Drug Testing, Inc., Defendant-Appellee. United States Court of Appeals, Ninth Circuit. (26 Aug, 2009).
Those circumstances that would cause a reasonable person to believe that entry (or other relevant prompt action) was necessary to prevent physical harm to the officers or other persons, the destruction of relevant evidence, the escape of a suspect, or some other consequence improperly frustrating legitimate law enforcement efforts.	United States v. McConney, 728 F.2d 1195, 1199 (9th Cir.)
names, telephone numbers, ledger receipts, addresses, and other documentary evidence pertaining to the sale and distribution of controlled substances.	United States v. Carey, No. 14- 50222 (9th Cir. 2016).
Controlled substances, evidence of the possession of controlled substances, which may include, but not be limited to, cash or proceeds from the sales of controlled substances, items, substances, and other paraphernalia designed or used in the weighing, cutting, and packaging of controlled substances, firearms, records, and/or receipts, written or electronically stored, income tax records, checking and savings records, records that show or tend to show ownership or control of the premises and other property used to facilitate the distribution and delivery [of] controlled substances.	United States of America, Plaintiff- Appellee, v. Russell Lane WALSER, Defendant-Appellant. No. 01-8019

"When (the) defendant sat down at the networked computer…he knew that the systems administrator could and likely would monitor his activities," "Indeed, the undercover agents told (Gorshkov) that they wanted to watch in order to see what he was capable of doing." "the agents had good reason to fear that if they did not copy the data, (the) defendant's co-conspirators would destroy the evidence or make it unavailable."

John C. Coughenour of Seattle, U.S. District Judge

Monitoring the beeper signals did not invade any legitimate expectation of privacy on respondent's part, and thus there was neither a "search" nor a "seizure" within the contemplation of the Fourth Amendment. The beeper surveillance amounted principally to following an automobile on public streets and highways. A person traveling in an automobile on public thoroughfares has no reasonable expectation of privacy in his movements.

U.S. v. Knotts 460 U.S. 276 (1983)

[t]he undercarriage is part of the car's exterior, and as such, is not afforded a reasonable expectation of privacy.

United States of America, Plaintiff- Appellee, v. Christopher McIVER, Defendant-Appellant, Nos. 98- 30145, 98-30146. Decided: August 06, 1999

is only a semiprivate area.

United States v. Magana, 512 F.2d 1169, 1171 [9th Cir. 1975]

undercarriage of a vehicle, as part of its exterior, is not entitled to a reasonable expectation of privacy

United States of America, Plaintiff- Appellee, v. Juan PINEDA- ORENO, Defendant-Appellant. No. 08-30385. Decided: January 11, 2010

The Court explicitly distinguished between the limited information discovered by use of the beeper—movements during a discrete journey—and more comprehensive or sustained monitoring of the sort at issue in this case…. Most important for the present case, the Court specifically reserved the question whether a warrant would be required in a case involving twenty-four hour surveillance, stating, "if such dragnet-type law enforcement practices as respondent envisions should eventually occur, there will be time enough then to determine whether different constitutional principles may be applicable."

United States of America, Appellee v. Lawrence Maynard, Appellant, Consolidated with 08- 3034

What motivated the Fourth Amendment historically was the disapproval, the outrage, that our Founding Fathers experienced with general warrants that permitted police indiscriminately to investigate just on the basis of suspicion, not probable cause, and to invade every possession that the individual had in search of a crime.

Justice Sonia Sotomayor, U.S. Supreme Court

With computers around, it's now so simple to amass an enormous amount of information. How do we deal with this? Just say nothing has changed?"

Justice Samuel Alito, Associate Justice of the Supreme Court of the United States

We decide whether the attachment of a Global Positioning-System (GPS) tracking device to an individual's vehicle, and subsequent use of that device to monitor the vehicle's movements on public streets, constitutes a search or seizure within the meaning of the Fourth Amendment.

United States v. Jones 615 F. 3d 544.

Technological advances have produced many valuable tools for law enforcement and, as the years go by, the technology available to aid in the detection of criminal conduct will only become more and more sophisticated. Without judicial oversight, the use of these powerful devices presents a significant and, to our minds, unacceptable risk of abuse. Under our State Constitution, in the absence of exigent circumstances, the installation and use of a GPS device to monitor an individual's whereabouts requires a warrant supported by probable cause.

The People of the State of New York, Respondent, v. Scott C. WEAVER, Appellant. Decided: May 12, 2009.

Johnson did not produce any evidence that demonstrated his intention to guard the undercarriage of his van from inspection or manipulation by others….. Supreme Court precedent has established not only that a vehicle's exterior lacks a reasonable expectation of privacy, but also that one's travel on public roads does not implicate Fourth Amendment protection against searches and seizures.

State v. Johnson 944 N.E.2d 270 (Ohio Ct. App. 2010)

"I think there was an expectation of privacy that the defendant had for his BlackBerry, that there were not sufficient grounds to authorize the deputy to open that BlackBerry up and, therefore, anything that was discovered as a result of that activity would be suppressed…."

People v. Nottoli, 199 Cal. App.4th 531 (Cal. Ct. App. 2011)

"a routine inventory search of an automobile lawfully impounded by police for violations of municipal parking ordinances," "standard police procedures,"

South Dakota v. Opperman (1976) 428 U.S. 364 [96 S.Ct. 3092]

"the deputies were justified in searching the vehicle's passenger compartment and, 'any containers therein,' In sum, it is our conclusion that, after Reid [Nottoli] was arrested for being under the influence, it was reasonable to believe that evidence relevant to that offense might be found in his vehicle. Consequently, the deputies had unqualified authority under Gant to search the passenger compartment of the vehicle and any container found therein, including Reid's cell phone. It is up to the US Supreme Court to impose any greater limits on officers' authority to search incident to arrest.

People v. Nottoli, 199 Cal. App.4th 531 (Cal. Ct. App. 2011) People v. Nottoli, 199 Cal.App.4th 531 (Cal. Ct. App. 2011)

"I am returning Senate Bill 914 without my signature" "courts are better suited to resolve the complex and case-specific issues relating to constitutional search-and-seizures protections."

Jerry Brown, California Gov.

"ample time for the law enforcement officials to secure a warrant in order to make this significant intrusion"

People v Spinelli, 35 NY2d 77, 81

"Tracking a person's past movements through CSLI partakes of many of the qualities of GPS monitoring considered in Jones. In fact, historical cell-site records present even greater privacy concerns than the GPS monitoring considered in Jones: They give the Government near perfect surveillance and allow it to travel back in time to retrace a person's whereabouts, subject only to the five-year retention policies of most wireless carriers." "Government did not obtain a warrant supported by probable cause before acquiring Carpenter's cell-site records. It acquired those records pursuant to a court order under the Stored Communications Act, which required the Government to show "reasonable grounds" for believing that the records were "relevant and material to an ongoing investigation." 18 U. S. C. §2703(d). That showing falls well short of the probable cause required for a warrant. Consequently, an order issued under §2703(d) is not a permissible mechanism for accessing historical cell-site records."

United States v. Jones, 565 U. S. 400

No person shall be held to answer for a capital, or otherwise infamous crime, unless on a presentment or indictment of a Grand Jury, except in cases arising in the land or naval forces, or in the Militia, when in actual service in time of War or public danger; nor shall any person be subject for the same offense to be twice put in jeopardy of life or limb; nor shall be compelled in any criminal case to be a witness against himself, nor be deprived of life, liberty, or property, without due process of law; nor shall private property be taken for public use, without just compensation.

Fifth Amendment of the U.S. Constitution

You have the right to remain silent. Anything you say or do can and will be held against you in a court of law. You have the right to speak to an attorney. If you cannot afford an attorney, one will be appointed for you. Do you understand these rights as they have been read to you?

Miranda v. Arizona, 384 U.S. 436 (1966).

In all criminal prosecutions, the accused shall enjoy the right to a speedy and public trial, by an impartial jury of the State and district wherein the crime shall have been committed, which district shall have been previously ascertained by law, and to be informed of the nature and cause of the accusation; to be confronted with the witnesses against him; to have compulsory process for obtaining witnesses in his favor, and to have the Assistance of Counsel for his defense.

Sixth Amendment of the U.S. Constitution

in all criminal prosecutions, the accused shall enjoy the right...to be confronted with the witnesses against him.

Sixth Amendment of the U.S. Constitution

Section 2511 of Title 18 prohibits the unauthorized interception, disclosure, and use of wire, oral, or electronic communications. The prohibitions are absolute, subject only to the specific exemptions in Title III. Consequently, unless an interception is specifically authorized, it is impermissible and, assuming existence of the requisite criminal intent, in violation of

Federal Wiretap Act (18 U.S. Code § 2511), Interception and disclosure of wire, oral, or electronic communications prohibited 18 U.S.C. § 2511.

"combat fraud and theft of service." (A) any temporary, intermediate storage of a wire or electronic communication incidental to the electronic transmission thereof; and (B) any storage of such communication by an electronic communication service for purposes of backup protection of such communication.

Federal Wiretap Act (18 U.S. Code § 2511 (2)(a)(i)), Interception and disclosure of wire, oral, or electronic communications prohibited Federal Wiretap Act (18 U.S. Code § 2510(17))

"having knowingly accessed a computer without authorization or exceeding authorized access, and by means of such conduct having obtained information that has been determined by the United States Government pursuant to an Executive order or statute to require protection against unauthorized disclosure for reasons of national defense or foreign relations, or any restricted data, as defined in paragraph y. of section 11 of the Atomic Energy Act of 1954, with reason to believe that such information so obtained could be used to the injury of the United States, or to the advantage of any foreign nation willfully communicates, delivers, transmits, or causes to be communicated, delivered, or transmitted, or attempts to communicate, deliver, transmit or cause to be communicated, delivered, or transmitted the same to any person not entitled to receive it, or willfully retains the same and fails to deliver it to the officer or employee of the United States entitled to receive it;"

Corporate Espionage (18 U.S. Code § 1030 (a)(1)). Fraud and related activity in connection with computers

"records of session times and durations," "any temporarily assigned network address."

USA PATRIOT Act (18 U.S. Code § 2703 (c)(2)). Required disclosure of customer communications or records

§ Title I: The "WIPO Copyright and Performances and Phonograms Treaties Implementation Act of 1998," implements the WIPO treaties. § Title II: The "Online Copyright Infringement Liability Limitation Act" creates limitations on the liability of online service providers for copyright infringement when engaging in certain types of activities. § Title III: The "Computer Maintenance Competition Assurance Act" creates an exemption for making a copy of a computer program by activating a computer for purposes of maintenance or repair. § Title IV: Contains six miscellaneous provisions, relating to the functions of the Copyright Office, distance education, the exceptions in the Copyright Act for libraries and for making ephemeral recordings, "webcasting" of sound recordings on the Internet, and the applicability of collective bargaining agreement obligations in the case of transfers of rights in motion pictures.

President Bill Clinton, The Digital Millennium Copyright Act (DMCA), 1998, www. copyright.gov/ legislation/ dmca.pdf.

Anonymity is a shield from the tyranny of the majority [that] exemplifies the purpose [of the First Amendment]: 'to protect unpopular individuals from retaliation…at the hand of an intolerant society.'

McIntyre v. Ohio Elections Comm'n, 514 U.S. 334, 357 (1995)

Just when a scientific principal or discovery crosses the line between the experimental and demonstrable stages is difficult to define. Somewhere in this twilight zone the evidential force of the principle must be recognized, and while courts will go a long way in admitting expert testimony deduced from a well-recognized scientific principle or discovery, the thing from which the deduction is made must be sufficiently established to have gained general acceptance in the particular field in which it belongs. (emphasis added).

Frye v. United States, 293 F. 1013 (D.C. Cir 1923).

scientific, technical, or other specialized knowledge.

Rule 702, Testimony by Expert Witnesses, Federal Rules of Evidence

If scientific, technical, or other specialized knowledge will assist the trier of fact to understand the evidence or to determine a fact in issue, a witness qualified as an expert by knowledge, skill, experience, training, or education, may testify thereto in the form of an opinion or otherwise, if (1) the testimony is based upon sufficient facts or data, (2) the testimony is the product of reliable principles and methods, and (3) the witness has applied the principles and methods reliably to the facts of the case.

Rule 702, Testimony by Expert Witnesses, Federal Rules of Evidence

§ (i) A complete statement of all opinions the witness will express and the basis and reasons for them; § (ii) The facts or data considered by the witness in forming them; § (iii) Any exhibits that will be used to summarize or support them; § (iv) The witness's qualifications, including a list of all publications authored in the previous 10 years; § (v) A list of all other cases in which, during the previous 4 years, the witness testified as an expert at trial or by deposition; and § (vi) A statement of the compensation to be paid for the study and testimony in the case.

Rule 26 (2)(B) & (3)(A), Duty to Disclose; General Provisions Governing Discovery, Federal Rules of Civil Procedure

§ (i) The name and, if not previously provided, the address and telephone number of each witness—separately identifying those the party expects to present and those it may call if the need arises; § (ii) The designation of those witnesses whose testimony the party expects to present by deposition and, if not taken stenographically, a transcript of the pertinent parts of the deposition; and § (iii) An identification of each document or other exhibit, including summaries of other evidence—separately identifying those items the party expects to offer and those it may offer if the need arises.

Records of regularly conducted activity. A memorandum, report, record, or data compilation, in any form, of acts, events, conditions, opinions, or diagnoses, made at or near the time by, or from information transmitted by, a person with knowledge, if kept in the course of a regularly conducted business activity, and if it was the regular practice of that business activity to make the memorandum, report, record or data compilation, all as shown by the testimony of the custodian or other qualified witness, or by certification that complies with Rule 902(11), Rule 902(12), or a statute permitting certification, unless the source of information or the method or circumstances of preparation indicate lack of trustworthiness. The term "business" as used in this paragraph includes business, institution, association, profession, occupation, and calling of every kind, whether or not conducted for profit.

Rule 803, Exceptions to the Rule Against Hearsay, Federal Rules of Evidence "the by-product of a machine operation which uses for its input 'statements'entered into the machine" "was generated solely by the electrical and mechanical operations of the computer and telephone equipment."

State v. Armstead, No. 82-KA- 0896, May 23, 1983.

regular practice of that business activity

Rule 803, Exceptions to the Rule Against Hearsay, Federal Rules of Evidence

The requirement of authentication or identification as a condition precedent to admissibility is satisfied by evidence sufficient to support a finding that the matter in question is what its proponent claims.

Rule 901, Requirement of Authentication or Identification, Federal Rules of Evidence

Facts are stubborn things; and whatever may be our wishes, our inclinations, or the dictates of our passion, they cannot alter the state of facts and evidence.

John Adams, Second President of the United States (1797-1801).

§ Maintain a Cybersecurity Program § Cybersecurity Policy § Role of the CISO § Pen Testing & Vulnerability Assessment § Audit Trail § Access Privileges § Application Security § Risk Assessment § Qualified Personnel & Intelligence § Third Party Service Provider § Multi-Factor Authentication § Limitations on Data Retention § Training & Monitoring § Encryption of Non-Public Information § Incident Response Plan § Notices to Superintendent

The New York State (NYS) Department of Financial Services (DFS), Section 500, 2017

§ Airports, aircraft and airlines; § Banks and authorized foreign banks; § Inter-provincial or international transportation companies; § Telecommunications companies; § Offshore drilling operations; and § Radio and television broadcasters.

Canada Personal Information Protection and Electronic Documents Act (PIPEDA), 2000

(2) Whereas data-processing systems are designed to serve man; whereas they must, whatever the nationality or residence of natural persons, respect their fundamental rights and freedoms, notably the right to privacy, and contribute to economic and social progress, trade expansion and the well-being of individuals

Directive 95/46/EC of the European Parliament and of the Council

"Photographs" includes "still photographs, X-ray films, video tapes, and motion pictures." An "original" can include a negative or a print from the negative. A "duplicate" is "a counterpart produced by the same impression as the original, or from the same matrix, or by means of photography, including enlargements and miniatures, or by mechanical or electronic re-recording." "other output readable by sight"

Article X, Federal Rules of Evidence (FRE), Rule 1001: Contents of Writings, Recordings and Photographs

Secure Enclave is Secure Enclave is a coprocessor fabricated within the system on chip (SoC). It uses encrypted memory and includes a hardware random number generator. The Secure Enclave provides all cryptographic operations for Data Protection key management and maintains the integrity of Data Protection even if the kernel has been compromised.

Product security certifications, validations, and guidance for SEP: Secure Key Store, Apple Inc.

I came across this website called Silk Road. It's a Tor hidden service that claims to allow you to buy and sell anything online anonymously. I'm thinking of buying off it, but wanted to see if anyone here had heard of it and could recommend it. I found it through silkroad420. wordpress.com, which, if you have a tor browser, directs you to the real site at http://tydgccykixpbu6uz.onion. Let me know what you think... the best and brightest IT pro in the bitcoin community [to] be the lead developer in a venture-backed bitcoin startup company

Quoted by Ross William Ulbricht, American convict

"anybody know someone that works for UPS, FedEX, or DHL?"

Quoted by Ross William Ulbricht, American convict, April 2012

How can I connect to a Tor hidden service using curl in php? I'm trying to connect to a tor hidden service using the following php: $url = 'http://jhiwjjlqpyawmpjx.onion/' $ch = curl_init(); curl_setopt($ch, CURLOPT_URL, $url); curl_setopt($ch, CURLOPT_RETURNTRANSFER, true); curl_setopt($ch, CURLOPT_PROXY, "http://127.0.0.1:9050/"); curl_setopt ($ch, CURLOPT_PROXYTYPE, CURLPROXY_SOCKS5); $output = curl_exec($ch); $curl_error =curl_error($ch); curl_close($ch); print_r($output); print_r($curl_error); when I run it I get the following error: Couldn't resolve host name However, when I run the following command from my command line in ubuntu: curl -v --socks5-hostname localhost:9050 http://jhiwjjlqpyawmpjx.onion I get a response as expected the php cURL documentations says this: --socks5-hostname Use the specified SOCKS5 proxy (and let the proxy resolve the host name). I believe the reason it works from the command line is because Tor (the proxy) is resolving the .onion hostname, which it recognizes. When running the php above, my guess is that cURL or php is trying to resolve the .onion hostname and doesn't recognize it. I've searched for a way to tell cURL/php to let the proxy resolve the hostname, but can't find a way. There is a very similar question here: CURL request using socks5 proxy fails when using PHP but works through the command line

Stack Exchange Inc. "How can I connect to a Tor hidden service using cURL in PHP?" http://stackoverflow. com/ questions/15445285

"(1) obtain subscriber information associated with the Subject Server; (2) collect routing information for communications sent to and from the Subject Server, including historical routing data from the prior 90 days; and (3) covertly image the contents of the Subject Server."

United States of America v. Ross William Ulbricht. S1 14 Cr. 68 (KBF) (S.D.N.Y., 2014).

"failed to submit anything establishing that he has a personal privacy interest in the Icelandic server or any of the other items imaged and/ or searched and/or seized."

United States of America v. Ross William Ulbricht. No. 18-691 (2d Cir. Jan. 24, 2019)

I am creating a year of prosperity and power beyond what I have ever experienced. Silk Road is going to become a phenomenon and at least one person will tell me about it, unknowing that I was its creator. I felt compelled to reveal myself to her. It was terrible.

Quoted by Ross William Ulbricht, American convict

I told her I have secrets. She already knows I work with bitcoin wich [sic] is terrible. I'm so stupid. Everyone knows I am working on a bitcoin exchange. I always thought honesty was the best policy and now I don't know what to do. I should have just told everyone I am a freelance programmer or something, but I had to tell half-truths. It felt wrong to lie completely so I tried to tell the truth without revealing the bad parts, but now I am in a jam. Everyone knows too much, dammit.

§ Conspiracy to commit acts of terrorism transcending national boundaries § Conspiracy to commit aircraft piracy § Conspiracy to destroy aircraft § Conspiracy to use weapons of mass destruction § Conspiracy to murder United States employees § Conspiracy to destroy property of the United States

United States District Court for the Eastern District of Virginia

[The] authentication information (such as the MD5 message digest and other accepted computer forensic methods) is critical as without it, it is impossible to verify that the duplicate hard drives are an exact copy of those that exist on the original systems. Likewise, without such information it is impossible to determine if the material retrieved from the hard drives is accurate.

United States v. Zacarias Moussaoui, Criminal No. 01-455-A, United States District Court, E.D. Virginia, Jun 18, 2002

"NIST does not 'approve' any computer forensic tools. Instead, it merely reports the results of its testing. Moreover, Mr. Allison wrongly identifies Linux dd as the 'only one method…approved by [NIST].'" "there would not ordinarily be any MD5 or SH-1 hash values to disclose to the defense for any computer drives imaged with SafeBack or a Logicube disk duplicator."

United States v. Zacarias Moussaoui, Criminal No. 01-455-A, United States District Court, E.D. Virginia, Jun 18, 2002

"any comment, request, suggestion, proposal, image, or other communication which is obscene or child pornography, with intent to annoy, abuse, threaten, or harass another person."

U.S. Code Title 47. TELECOMMUNICATIONS. Section 223. Obscene or harassing telephone calls in the District of Columbia or in interstate or foreign communications

"Jumping off the gw bridge, sorry." "making out with a dude." "Anyone with iChat I dare you to video chat me between the hours of 9:30 and 12. Yes, it's happening again." "Watch out, he may come for you when you're sleeping." "It keeps the gays away."

State of New Jersey vs. Dharun Ravi, Supreme Court of New Jersey

We disapproved the wholesale seizure of the documents and particularly the government's failure to return the materials that were not the object of the search once they had been segregated. Id. at 596-97. However, we saw no reason to suppress the properly seized materials just because the government had taken more than authorized by the warrant.

United States v. Comprehensive Drug Testing, Inc., United States Court of Appeals, 513 F.3d 1085 (9th Cir. 2008)

"Given the important First Amendment and privacy implications at stake, the warrant should be quashed unless the Court finds that the State has met its heightened burden for compelled production of such materials".

State of Arkansas v. James A. Bates, Case No. 2016-370-2 (Ark. Cir.), Feb. 17, 2017

"Starting May 1, the App Store will no longer accept new apps or app updates that access the UDID; please update your apps and servers to associate users with the Vendor or Advertising identifiers introduced in iOS 6"

Using Identifiers in Your Apps', March 21, 2013, © 2020 Apple Inc.

"may also collect the precise location of your device when the app is running in the foreground or background"

Uber Privacy Notice', February 28, 2020, © Uber Technologies Inc

"Uber collects your location (i) when the app is open and (ii) from the time of the trip request through five minutes after the trip ends"

Uber Technologies Inc

"improve pickups, drop-offs, customer service, and to enhance safety"

Uber Technologies Inc

§ Phone number analysis § IMSI number analysis § IMEI number analysis § SIM number analysis § ISPC number analysis

Quote from International Numbering Plans, 'Number analysis tools'

No actions performed by investigators should change data contained on digital devices or storage media that may subsequently be relied upon in court.

Quote from Association of Chief Police Officers, 'ACPO Good Practice Guide for Digital Evidence', March 2012.

Step 1. Securing and Evaluating the Scene: Steps should be taken to ensure the safety of individuals and to identify and protect the integrity of potential evidence. Step 2. Documenting the Scene: Create a permanent record of the scene, accurately recording both digital-related and conventional evidence. Step 3. Evidence Collection: Collect traditional and digital evidence in a manner that preserves their evidentiary value. Step 4. Packaging, Transportation, and Storage: Take adequate precautions when packaging, transporting, and storing evidence, maintaining chain of custody.

Quote from U.S. Department of Justice, 'Electronic Crime Scene Investigation: A Guide for First Responders', 2008.

§ Article File: Records on stolen articles and lost public safety, homeland security, and critical infrastructure identification. § Gun File: Records on stolen, lost, and recovered weapons and weapons used in the commission of crimes that are designated to expel a projectile by air, carbon dioxide, or explosive action. § Boat File: Records on stolen boats. § Securities File: Records on serially numbered stolen, embezzled, used for ransom, or counterfeit securities. § Vehicle File: Records on stolen vehicles, vehicles involved in the commission of crimes, or vehicles that may be seized based on federally issued court order. § Vehicle and Boat Parts File: Records on serially numbered stolen vehicle or boat parts. § License Plate File: Records on stolen license plates. § Missing Persons File: Records on individuals, including children, who have been reported missing to law enforcement and there is a reasonable concern for their safety.

Source: https://www.fbi.gov/ services/cjis/ncic

§ Foreign Fugitive File: Records on persons wanted by another country for a crime that would be a felony if it were committed in the United States. § Identity Theft File: Records containing descriptive and other information that law enforcement personnel can use to determine if an individual is a victim of identity theft of if the individual might be using a false identity. § Immigration Violator File: Records on criminal aliens whom immigration authorities have deported and aliens with outstanding administrative warrants of removal. § Protection Order File: Records on individuals against whom protection orders have been issued. § Supervised Release File: Records on individuals on probation, parole, or supervised release or released on their own recognizance or during pre-trial sentencing. § Unidentified Persons File: Records on unidentified deceased persons, living persons who are unable to verify their identities, unidentified victims of catastrophes, and recovered body parts. The file cross-references unidentified bodies against records in the Missing Persons File. § Protective Interest: Records on individuals who might pose a threat to the physical safety of protectees or their immediate families. Expands on the U.S. Secret Service Protective File, originally created in 1983. § Gang File: Records on violent gangs and their members. § Known or Appropriately Suspected Terrorist File: Records on known or appropriately suspected terrorists in accordance with HSPD-6. § Wanted Persons File: Records on individuals (including juveniles who will be tried as adults) for whom a federal warrant or a felony or misdemeanor warrant is outstanding. § National Sex Offender Registry File: Records on individuals who are required to register in a jurisdiction's sex offender registry. § National Instant Criminal Background Check System (NICS) Denied Transaction File: Records on individuals who have been determined to be "prohibited persons" according to the Brady Handgun Violence Prevention Act and were denied as a result of a NICS background check. (As of August 2012, records include last six months of denied transactions; in the future, records will include all denials.) § Violent Person File: Once fully populated with data from our users, this file will contain records of persons with a violent criminal history and persons who have previously threatened law enforcement.

Sometimes you will see the following messages in DHCP logs

R. Droms, Network Working Group, March 1997. https://www.ietf.org/rfc/rfc2131.txt

Contents at a Glance

Table of Contents

About the Author

Dr. Darren R. Hayes is a leading expert in the field of digital forensics and computer security. He is the Director of Digital Forensics and Associate Professor at Pace University, and he has been named one of the Top 10 Computer Forensics Professors by Forensics Colleges. He was selected as the recipient of the *2020 Homeland Security Investigations New York Private Sector Partnership Award.*

During his time at Pace University, Hayes developed a Digital Forensics track for the University's Bachelor of Science in Information Technology degree in addition to his development of digital forensics graduate courses. He also created, and now manages, the Pace University Digital Forensics Research Laboratory, where he devotes must of his time to working with a team of students to support the efforts of law enforcement and the University's students. As part of his research and promoting this scientific field of study, he has fostered relationships with the New York Police Department, New York County D.A., Westchester County D.A., Homeland Security Investigations, National Crime Agency and numerous other agencies.

Hayes is not only an academic, however—he is also a practitioner. He has been an investigator on both civil and criminal investigations and frequently consults on cases for law firms. In fact, he has been declared an expert witness in U.S. federal court.

In New York City, Hayes has been working with six to eight public high schools to develop a curriculum in computer forensics and cybersecurity. He collaborates on computer forensics projects internationally and served as an extern examiner for the MSc in the Forensic Computing and Cybercrime Investigation degree program at University College Dublin for four years.

Hayes has appeared on CNBC, Bloomberg Television, MSNBC and Fox News and been quoted by *Associated Press, CNN, Wall Street Journal, The Guardian (UK), The Irish Independent, Japan Times, Investor's Business Daily, MarketWatch, Newsweek, SC Magazine, Silicon Valley Business Journal, USA Today, Washington Post*, and *Wired News*. His op-eds have been published by Homeland Security Today, USA Today, and The Hill's Congress Blog. In addition, he has authored a number of peer-reviewed articles in many prominent academic journals. Hayes has been both an author and reviewer for Pearson Prentice Hall since 2007.

About the Technical Reviewers

Lorne Dannenbaum has been working in digital forensics since 2004. He is an experienced Cyber-Security Analyst with a demonstrated history of working in the information technology and services industry. Skilled in Digital Forensics and Incident Response, he performed examinations of systems regarding incidents such as intrusions, data loss protection, malware, and fraud. He uses skills such as memory analysis, file system, and artifact analysis to conduct digital forensic examinations using a wide variety of tools.

Aamir Lakhani is a leading senior security strategist. He is responsible for providing IT security solutions to major enterprises and government organizations. Mr. Lakhani creates technical security strategies and leads security implementation projects for Fortune 500 companies. He has designed offensive counter-defense measures for the Department of Defense and national intelligence agencies, as well as Global 100 organizations. He has also assisted organizations with safeguarding IT and physical environments from attacks perpetrated by underground cybercriminal groups. Mr. Lakhani is considered an industry leader for creating detailed security architectures within complex computing environments. His areas of expertise include cyber defense, mobile application threats, malware management, Advanced Persistent Threat (APT) research, and investigations relating to the Internet's dark security movement. He is the author or contributor of several books and has appeared on FOX Business News, National Public Radio, and other media outlets as an expert on cybersecurity.

Dedication

This book is dedicated to my loving wife, Nalini, and my children, Shay, Fiona, Aine, and Nicolai.
I also dedicate this book to law enforcement, first responders, and our military veterans, who risk their lives to protect our safety.

Acknowledgments

I should begin by acknowledging my supportive and patient wife, Nalini, who is my best friend. Long hours working on a book mean sacrifices for everyone in the family, and my children, Nicolai, Aine, Fiona, and Shay, have been brilliant. My parents, Annette and Ted, have been mentors throughout my life, and I will always be in their debt.

We Want to Hear from You!

As the reader of this book, *you* are our most important critic and commentator. We value your opinion and want to know what we're doing right, what we could do better, what areas you'd like to see us publish in, and any other words of wisdom you're willing to pass our way.

We welcome your comments. You can email or write to let us know what you did or didn't like about this book—as well as what we can do to make our books better.

Please note that we cannot help you with technical problems related to the topic of this book.

When you write, please be sure to include this book's title and author as well as your name and email address. We will carefully review your comments and share them with the author and editors who worked on the book.

Email: feedback@informit.com

Visit our website and register this book at www.pearsonitcertification.com/register for convenient access to any updates, downloads, or errata that might be available for this book.

Introduction

The field of digital forensics has grown immensely and diversified over the past few years for a number of reasons. Therefore, this book addresses these changes in a number of new and existing chapters. The proliferation of IoT devices, wearable technologies and other new technologies, like 5G, are explained in detail in Chapter 14 because their impact on digital forensics will be profound. The chapter also discusses how new technologies are changing policing and the safety of law enforcement officers. The chapter also discusses the growing field of vehicle forensics.

There has been no slowdown in the number of network breaches globally; therefore, the need for digital forensics examiners in incident response is greater than ever. Therefore, Chapter 8 is focused on developing the skills of incident responders and highlighting indicators of compromise.

Mobile forensics continually changes and these changes are addressed in numerous chapters, including Chapter 7, when some Supreme Court landmark decisions have changed the rules for law enforcement. Chapter 9 provides an introduction to Mobile Forensics but also explains the changes in Android devices and methods of examination. Chapter 12 explains how iPhone examinations have changed dramatically and shows how full file system extractions are now available with a recently discovered exploit. Mobile applications (apps) save an immense amount of personal information and pretty much every investigation includes at least one mobile device. Therefore, Chapter 10 is a new chapter that provides investigators with forensic techniques to perform both a static and a dynamic examination of mobile apps. Furthermore, this chapter explains how real-time intelligence can be gathered from many popular apps.

Every chapter has been updated extensively to incorporate many recent changes in technology and newly discovered techniques to obtain digital evidence.

This book assumes no prior knowledge of the subject matter, and I have written it for both high school and university students and professional forensics investigators. Additionally, other professions can clearly benefit from reading this book—it is useful for lawyers, forensic accountants, security professionals, and others who have a need to understand how digital evidence is gathered, handled, and admitted to court. The book places a significant emphasis on process and adherence to the law, which are equally important to the evidence that can ultimately be retrieved.

The reader of this book should also realize that comprehensive knowledge of computer forensics can lead to a variety of careers. Digital forensics examiners and experts work for accounting firms, software companies, banks, law enforcement, intelligence agencies, and consulting firms. Every major company has an incident response team and many have a threat intelligence team or department. This book will certainly benefit those in that profession or perhaps those considering a career change. The growth of social media and open source data and tools creates a wealth of information for investigators and these are discussed in the book. Some are experts in mobile forensics, some excel in network forensics, and others focus on personal computers. Other experts specialize in Mac forensics or reverse engineering malware. The good news for graduates with computer forensics experience is that they have a variety of directions to choose from: the job market for them will remain robust, with more positions than graduates for the foreseeable future.

This book is a practical guide, not only because of the hands-on activities it offers, but also because of the numerous case studies and practical applications of computer forensics techniques. Case studies are a highly effective way to demonstrate how particular types of digital evidence have been success-fully used in different investigations.

Finally, this book often refers to professional computer forensics tools that can be expensive. You should realize that academic institutions can take advantage of significant discounts when purchasing these products. The book makes a point of mentioning many free or low-cost forensics tools that can be just as effective as some of the expensive tools. You can definitely develop your own program or laboratory in a budget-conscious way.

Register this book to unlock the data files that are needed to complete the end-of-chapter projects.

Follow the steps below:

1. Go to www.pearsonITcertification.com/register and log in or create a new account.

2. Enter the ISBN: 9780789759917.

3. Click on the "Access Bonus Content" link in the Registered Products section of your account page, to be taken to the page where your downloadable content is available.

The Scope of Digital Forensics

Learning Outcomes

After reading this chapter, you will be able to understand the following:

- The definition and importance of digital forensics;
- Different types of digital evidence and how they are used;
- The skills, training, and education required to become a computer forensics investigator;
- Job opportunities in the field of computer forensics;
- The history of computer forensics; and
- Agencies in the U.S. and internationally involved in computer forensics investigations.

Digital forensics is the retrieval, analysis, and use of digital evidence in a civil or criminal investigation. Ironically, digital forensics (or computer forensics) is not limited to computers as the source of evidence. Any medium that can store digital files is a potential source of evidence for a computer forensics investigator. Therefore, digital forensics involves the examination of digital files.

Digital forensics is a science because of the accepted practices used for acquiring and examining the evidence and its admissibility in court. Additionally, the tools used to retrieve and analyze digital evidence have been subjected to scientific testing over many years. In fact, the word **forensics** means "suitable for a court of law". This definition infers that digital evidence used in an investigation needs to be retrieved, handled, and analyzed in a forensically sound manner. *Forensically sound* means that, during the acquisition of digital evidence and throughout the investigative process, the evidence must remain in its original state. Moreover, everyone who has been in contact with the evidence must be accounted for and documented in the **chain of custody** form.

Computer forensics sometimes yields incriminating evidence used in criminal cases; this evidence is often referred to as **inculpatory evidence**. However, digital evidence can be used as **exculpatory evidence**, or evidence used to prove the innocence of a defendant.

Popular Myths about Computer Forensics

Many people think that computer security and computer forensics are the same but they are not. This is one of several misconceptions about computer forensics. Computer security is proactive, with a focus on protecting computer systems and sensitive data, which can include intellectual property. Computer forensics is reactive, and the focus is investigative in nature—meaning that a crime might have been committed. The intersection between computer security and computer forensics often occurs in incident response. Some serious incidents, like a network breach, will require the expertise of a digital forensics investigator who will seek to determine what happened, the damage that occurred, and potentially identify the perpetrator. Computer forensics skills and techniques are often used for intelligence gathering, where the intention may not be to prosecute (for example, examining a mobile device to identify whether a nation-state is using an app to profile individuals). Moreover, digital forensics techniques are often used to monitor and collect intelligence on the use of social media services by known or potential terrorist groups. The following sections introduce some of the common misconceptions about computer forensics.

Myth 1: Computer Forensics Is the Same As Computer Security

Computer security is proactive, involving protecting computers and their data from being stolen or being misused. Conversely, computer forensics is reactive and involves a search for digital evidence after a crime has been committed, in an attempt to solve a case and convict a criminal. Computer forensics can complement computer security, particularly in the area of incident response. Note, however, that the National Academy of Sciences has identified digital forensics as a subset of cybersecurity.

Myth 2: Computer Forensics Is about Investigating Computers

Future chapters of this book demonstrate that any device that stores files can be a medium for computer forensics investigators to examine. For example, a cellphone SIM card is not a computer but may contain important digital evidence.

Myth 3: Computer Forensics Is about Investigating Computer Crime

A popular misconception is that computer forensics is only used to solve computer crime or cybercrime. However, computer forensics is often equally important in murder, embezzlement, and corporate espionage investigations. For example, on April 16, 2007, Seung-Hui Cho killed 32 people and wounded many more on the campus of Virginia Polytechnic. He subsequently committed suicide. Computer forensics investigators examined Cho's computer to reconstruct the events that led up to the murder investigation. They investigated his email account, Blazers5505@hotmail.com, and his user activity on eBay, under the username blazers5505. Computer forensics investigators were able to assess whom Cho was communicating with and also what he was searching for and purchasing online. Examiners also investigated his cellular telephone. One of the reasons for the rapid response by computer forensic examiners was the need to quickly ascertain whether Cho had an accomplice in this sordid act.

When federal agents searched Enron offices in late 2001, they found that employees had been shredding a large number of documents. Computer forensic examiners were needed to retrieve evidence from computer hard drives. The amount of digital data recovered was estimated to be equivalent to 10 times the size of the Library of Congress.

Myth 4: Computer Forensics Is Really Used to Resurrect Deleted Files

The primary purpose of computer forensics is to retrieve and analyze files with computer forensics hardware and software, utilizing a scientific methodology that is acceptable in a court of law. Computer forensics goes well beyond the ability to resurrect deleted files; numerous other files that are not easily accessible can be retrieved using computer forensic tools. Additionally, computer forensic tools have highly effective search and filtering capabilities. Moreover, many professional tools provide password-cracking and decryption capabilities. For example, AccessData's FTK and its Password Recovery Toolkit (PRTK) provide these capabilities.

In Practice

Locard's Exchange Principle

Dr. Edmond Locard (1877-1966), a forensic scientist at the University of Lyon, developed a theory known as *Transfer of Evidence* whose premise was that whenever a criminal comes into contact with his environment, a cross-transference of evidence occurs:

> Wherever he steps, whatever he touches, whatever he leaves, even unconsciously, will serve as a silent witness against him. Not only his fingerprints or his footprints, but his hair, the fibers from his clothes, the glass he breaks, the tool mark he leaves, the paint he scratches, the blood or semen he deposits or collects. All of these and more bear mute witness against him. This is evidence that does not forget. It is not confused by the excitement of the moment. It is not absent because human witnesses are. It is factual evidence. Physical evidence cannot be wrong, it cannot perjure itself, it cannot be wholly absent. Only human failure to find it, study, and understand it can diminish its value.

This theory also applies to computer forensics, where the investigator must be conscious of the entire environment that the criminal has been in contact with. In other words, it is important for the investigator to not just focus on a laptop found inside an apartment but to also think about connections from the laptop, including router connections, external hard drives and Cloud storage. Thumb drives or CDs in the dwelling might also contain important evidence. Login names and passwords could be written on pieces of paper in the apartment and might be critical to accessing a suspect's system, files, or Internet services, such as email. A DVR, which is used to record television shows, is a storage medium that may also store important evidence. opentext's EnCase software supports the imaging and analysis of files stored on a DVR. EnCase is a bit-stream imaging tool. A **bit-stream imaging tool** produces a bit-for-bit copy of original media, which includes files marked for deletion.

Naturally, the investigator must ensure that evidentiary files are maintained in their original state as when they were first acquired. In later chapters it will become clear how computer forensics investigators use processes, hardware, and software to ensure that evidence remains unchanged.

Types of Digital Forensic Evidence Recovered

Practically every type of file can be recovered using computer forensics—from system files to user-created files, such as spreadsheets. The following sections list some of the most important files that can be recovered and used in criminal investigations. Many of these files can often be retrieved regardless of whether the user has tried to delete them.

Electronic Mail (Email)

Email is arguably the most important type of digital evidence. It is very important for a number of reasons, including the following:

- Control, ownership, and intent
- Chain of events
- Prevalence
- Endurance (tampering with evidence)
- Admissibility
- Accessibility

Control, Ownership, and Intent

In computer forensics, establishing control, ownership, and intent is critical in making the evidence incriminating. Sometimes nothing is more personal than email. Email can show the intentions of the suspect and victim. In the case of Sharon Lopatka, who was murdered by Robert Glass, email was the most important evidence in the murder trial. Glass and Lopatka exchanged numerous emails prior to their rendezvous in North Carolina, where Glass tortured and strangled Lopatka. The emails supported the disturbing claims that the torture and murder were consensual.

In cases involving the possession of child pornography, the defendant commonly claims that he was unaware that images were stored on his computer. The prosecution must prove that the defendant knew of their existence and that the pictures were of minors. Email evidence often shows that the suspect's images were shared, by the suspect, with other pedophiles. Ultimately, this helps prove the suspect's guilt and makes it possible to prosecute the individual for the possession of child exploitation images and using a computer to distribute illegal images. A process known as MD5 hashing can be used to verify that an image from one computer is the same as an image file found on another computer.

Chain of Events

Reconstructing the events that led up to a crime being committed is an important aspect of presenting a case. Often one email file contains a chain of conversations over a number of days and includes the times, dates, email sender, and recipient. This can aid in establishing a chain of events.

Prevalence

Electronic mail is very important because we use it so much to communicate. Therefore, it is pervasive in both personal and business communications. In the Enron investigation, tens of thousands of emails were acquired and investigated. In some cases, accounting firms, with a computer forensics unit, will have a separate unit with a group of analysts who spend every day just working on email evidence.

Endurance: Tampering with Evidence

Tampering with evidence is defined as the concealment, destruction, alteration, or falsification of evidence. It is a serious crime that carries a felony charge in many states. In the case of *Mattel v. MGA Entertainment, Inc.*, U.S. District Judge Stephen Larson ruled that the jury could hear testimony by Mattel that its former employee, Carter Bryant, had used an application called Evidence Eliminator to tamper with evidence before releasing his computer to lawyers in 2004.

Email is very valuable to investigators because even if the defendant tries to tamper with email on his or her computer, it is still accessible from other sources. For example, email files can potentially be found on the recipient's computer as well as on the suspect's computer. An email service can also be served a subpoena or search warrant to turn over email files stored on its email servers. Email files can also often be acquired from smartphones, like iPhones, and on other computing devices, like an iPad or a MacBook.

Admissibility

Judges and courts have accepted electronic mail as admissible evidence for a number of years. Interestingly, in one case, *Rombom et al. v. Weberman et al.*, the judge accepted email printouts as evidence; the plaintiff testified that he had received emails from the defendant and printed them.

Accessibility

Unlike many other sources of evidence, access to an individual's email is not necessarily subject to a search warrant. The Department of Justice has argued that after email has been opened, it is no longer protected by the Stored Communications Act (SCA). Although a judge has already rejected the government's petition for a warrantless search, the government has continued to argue that when email resides in the Cloud the government has the right to freely access that email. Under the SCA, stored communications, such as emails that are less than 180 days old, require law enforcement to obtain a warrant. Companies like Yahoo!, Google, and Microsoft have combined as a group, called the Electronic Frontier Foundation, to vigorously oppose the government's efforts in this area. However, some analysts believe that the law could change in favor of the government.

Nevertheless, what is clear is that an employee's company email is the property of the individual's employer. Therefore, a company can search an employee's email without the consent of the individual. In 2009, in the case of *Stengart v. Loving Care Agency, Inc.*, the New Jersey Superior Court, Appellate Division, reiterated that an employer may access and read an employee's email without the employee's consent when the employee uses the company's technology to access email. Therefore, gaining access to email communications is often easier than gaining access to other methods of communication.

Images

There are numerous image file types in existence. The most widely used formats are BMP (Windows bitmap), JPEG (Joint Photographic Experts Group), TIFF (Tagged Image File Format), and PNG (Portable Network Graphics). Images are especially important in child exploitation cases. Photographs have even greater importance today than they did 20 years ago. This is because digital photographs provide details about the type of camera used to take a picture (proving ownership) and often contain **GPS (Global Positioning System)** data, thereby identifying the location of the device (e.g. smartphone) and when the photograph was taken. This metadata is frequently found with photographs taken with a smartphone. Generally, the file metadata of a digital photograph can identify the make and model of the camera used to take the photograph, which is valuable information for investigators. **File metadata** (see Figure 1.1) is information about a file and can include the creation, modified and last access dates, and sometimes details about the user who created the file.

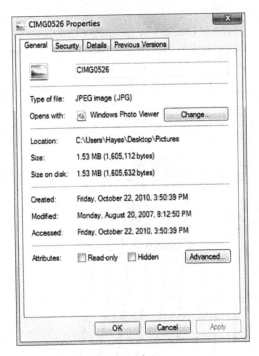

FIGURE 1.1 File metadata

Most professional computer forensics imaging and analysis software, including AccessData's FTK application, contains a user interface that can filter by file type and also separate images. These image files are grouped together and include image files that the software carved away from other files. For example, if an email or a Microsoft Word document contained an image, the application would remove (or "carve") the image and group it with other image files that it found.

X-Ways Forensics software and other forensic tools allow an investigator to filter all images by using a skin tone ratio. The result is that, for the most part, only images of people are displayed after the search is run. Photographs have been used for many years in the courtroom, but digital images today provide more information than traditional film photography. Often, many online services strip the metadata from digital photographs, so an investigator may need to subpoena the service to obtain images of interest in their original format (that is, complete with metadata). Chapter 11, "Photograph Forensics", discusses the examination of digital photographs in greater detail.

Video

Video evidence can be found on many different types of devices, including computers, digital cameras, and cellular telephones. Surveillance video today is mostly stored on computers and therefore falls under the domain of computer forensics. Surveillance video is often associated with the burglary of banks and convenience stores, but it is also being used for a much wider array of criminal activity.

The use of skimmers at automated teller machines (ATMs) has resulted in the theft of millions of dollars worldwide. A **skimmer** (see Figure 1.2) is a device used to capture the data stored on the magnetic stripe of an ATM card, credit card, or debit card. Surveillance video can be critical to the successful capture of these criminals.

FIGURE 1.2   Skimming device

Closed-circuit television (CCTV) is the use of video transmitted to a particular location. In the city of London, for example, there are more than 600,000 CCTV cameras. These cameras have been used to investigate tourists who have been robbed of their possessions or high-profile cases like the poisoning of former Russian spy Alexander Litvinenko in 2006.

Computer forensics investigators have a variety of forensic tools to choose from, including some that enhance the quality of video being analyzed. Other tools provide customizable stills at predetermined points in a video. These image stills are valuable because they can be included in an investigator's report. More importantly, these tools provide the investigator with an efficient method of identifying when in the video the important incriminating evidence exists, eliminating the need to watch the video from start to finish. Moreover, if the video content is disturbing, the investigator does not have to be subjected to watching the entire distressing video.

Ultimately, in the courtroom, video evidence can be the most compelling type of evidence for a jury to convict a criminal.

Websites Visited and Internet Searches

The debate continues in law enforcement about whether the plug on a computer should be pulled to maintain the evidence in its original state or whether a live computer should stay switched on when found. With advancements in encryption and the nature of the evidence that is lost if the plug is pulled, most investigators agree that a live system should be forensically examined while it is turned on. **Encryption** is the process of scrambling plaintext into an unreadable format using a mathematical formula known as an algorithm. Evidentiary files and data related to Internet searches and websites visited are more readily available while the computer is turned on. This is because much of a user's current activity, including Internet activity, is stored in Random Access Memory (RAM). RAM is often referred to as short-term memory or volatile memory because its contents largely disappear when the computer is powered down. It is important to understand that when a website is visited, a client computer makes a request to a web server. The client computer actually downloads an HTML document and related resources from the website, like images, to the memory on the computer.

As Figure 1.3 shows, the **client computer** is a computer that requests a resource from a server computer. The primary purpose of a **web server** is to deliver HTML documents and related resources (like images) in response to client computer requests. The easiest way to remember what a client and a server do is to think of a client as a customer and a server as providing a service. Most professional computer forensics tools can image the contents of RAM effectively while the computer is powered on. A number of open source RAM analysis tools are also available.

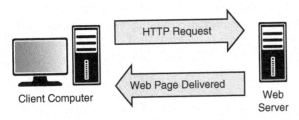

FIGURE 1.3   Communication between a client and a web server

Cellphone Forensics

The field of cellular telephone forensics, or mobile forensics, is growing exponentially as the capabilities of these mobile devices continue to expand. A cellphone can tell you who the suspect knows (contacts), appointments (calendar), who the suspect has been speaking to (call logs), and what the person has been saying (text messages). Other mobile devices can provide image and video evidence (device camera), places visited (GPS), online purchases, and websites visited (Internet-enabled smartphones).

Cellular telephones are often used to track down suspects. In the murder investigation of Fred Jablin, Detective Coby Kelley obtained a warrant for suspect Piper Rountree's cellular telephone records. Because cellular telephone towers (cell sites) keep track of a user's cellular telephone as the user moves from one cell (area) to another, this particular detective was able to locate the suspect in Richmond, Virginia, as she was heading east on I-64 toward the Norfolk airport. Later, the cellular telephone was found transmitting from Baltimore, Maryland. After further investigation, it was discovered that Rountree had booked a flight from Baltimore to Texas, using her sister's name. Piper Rountree maintained that she had never left Houston, Texas, but the cellphone records proved otherwise, and this evidence was critical to establishing Rountree's guilt.

For more information about the use of cellular telephones in computer forensics investigations, see Chapter 9, "Mobile Forensics".

IoT Forensics

Over the past few years, we have experienced significant advances in artificial intelligence (AI) systems for our homes. Furthermore, these AI-enabled devices can be controlled by our smartphones and integrated with smart home devices— from home thermostats to home surveillance devices to home lighting. Thus, being cognizant about these new ecosystems, and the digital trail that these devices save locally or in the cloud, is now a critical consideration for digital forensics investigators. We discuss IoT forensics in greater detail in Chapter 14, "Internet of Things (IoT) Forensics and Emergent Technologies".

What Skills Must a Digital Forensics Investigator Possess?

It is important to understand that computer forensics is a multidisciplinary field that draws upon skills from the fields of computer science, criminal justice, law, mathematics, writing, forensic science, and linguistics.

Computer Science Knowledge

In terms of computer science, it is important to develop a strong knowledge of both operating systems and their associated file systems. A strong foundation in this subject matter will allow the investigator to know where files are stored and determine their value to prosecutors in a criminal case. Knowledge of operating systems provides an understanding about how hardware and software interact with one another. This information is vital to reconstructing the actions of a user on a computer. For example, **BitLocker**, an encryption tool that was introduced with the Ultimate and Enterprise editions of Microsoft Windows Vista, allows for encryption at the file, folder, or drive level. Turning off a computer that has BitLocker enabled activates BitLocker encryption. Therefore, a knowledgeable computer forensics investigator who encounters this operating system on a live computer will clearly understand the potential hazards of shutting down the computer.

Simply locating and retrieving the evidentiary files is not enough. An expert computer forensics examiner must have extensive investigative abilities, which will allow her to associate that evidence with an individual; the examiner should be able to use digital evidence to demonstrate control, ownership, and intent. For example, an investigator must be able to prove that a suspect was in control of a computer when the files were stored in memory. An example of control, in this scenario, is if the user used a login and password to access the computer. Ownership is another important factor when trying to prove guilt. This can be proved when the investigator can demonstrate that the suspect created a file, modified a file, or emailed the file to someone. Finally, intent is generally vital to the successful prosecution of a criminal. In computer forensics, defendants might argue that they did not intend to visit a particular website or that they inadvertently downloaded images but never viewed them. Therefore, the computer forensics investigator is also obligated to prove that a website was accessed multiple times or perhaps that an image was viewed on a number of occasions and subsequently distributed to others, to prove intent.

Legal Expertise

Knowledge of the law is extremely important, especially when it comes to computer forensics. Gaining access to a suspect's computer may be the first challenge to an investigator. If a suspect's computer is located at the person's residence, then knowledge of the Fourth Amendment, which deals with search and seizure, is imperative. To gain access to the computer, investigators must convince a judge that a crime has been committed and that there is a reasonable expectation that key evidence is present at a particular location; law enforcement must show "probable cause" or "reasonable cause to believe" that a crime has been committed.

Communication Skills

The importance of writing skills must never be underestimated in the field of computer forensics. Ultimately, the investigator must document the investigative process and findings. Moreover, the report must be written in such a way that those involved in the case, who do not possess the technical expertise of the computer forensics examiner, can comprehend the report's findings. If a criminal case goes to trial, the computer forensics investigator could be asked to testify as an expert witness. The investigator will then have to effectively communicate her findings to a judge and jury who have a limited knowledge of computers or computer forensics.

Linguistic Abilities

Crime today has a greater international presence, facilitated by the proliferation of the Internet. With the growth of cybercrime and the adoption of technology by international terrorists, the need for bilingual investigators has grown. Therefore, a bilingual computer forensics investigator has the ability to contribute more to certain investigations.

Continuous Learning

An effective computer forensics investigator will continually learn new skills. However, there will always be skills that are critical but difficult to measure. Abstraction, or the ability to think outside the box, is imperative because every crime is different and the evidence varies. Therefore, computer forensics investigators need to continually develop new tactics and new solutions. This ability to be flexible and continuously learn new skills is particularly important given how rapidly technology changes. Rapid changes in technology also means changes in the nature of crime. Another intangible is related to psychology. Being able to understand the criminal provides a better understanding of that person's actions and can make it possible to quickly find answers in an investigation. For this reason, we need experts who can profile serial killers and other criminals.

Programming

Although it is not necessary for a computer forensics investigator to have extensive programming knowledge, some programming ability goes a long way. More specifically, knowledge of Linux can assist an investigator with Linux servers, making a clone of a volume, Android device examinations, Android app analysis, and networking; AppleScripts can be used for scraping websites or brute-forcing PINs on a Mac computer; Python can be used for automated scraping of websites; EnScripts are customizable scripts that are used by investigators using EnCase; PowerShell *cmdlets* and scripts can be used to retrieve critical evidence from different operating systems, including Windows.

An Appreciation for Confidentiality

Finally, the ability to keep information confidential is imperative. Only those who need to know about an investigation should know—the fewer, the better. If the suspect finds out, then you risk the suspect fleeing and also risk **spoliation of evidence**, which is the hiding, altering, or the destruction of evidence related to an investigation. Leaks to the media are also a concern, and the jury pool can be contaminated in high-profile cases.

The Importance of Digital Forensics

Computer forensics has grown in importance because more of our lives are being captured by technology. Information about our lives is being recorded on our computers, on our cellular telephones, and across the World Wide Web, especially through social networking websites. Facebook, for example, has close to two billion members and provides a wealth of information for investigators—from photographs, to clues about a user's password, to gaining knowledge about a suspect's networks of friends or accomplices.

Criminal investigators are typically required to reconstruct the events of a crime. Technology has facilitated this reconstruction process. A suspect can be tracked through use of an MTA MetroCard, linked to a credit card, in the New York City subway or through an E-Z Pass tollbooth payment. In early 2014, Queens County prosecutors in New York charged a taxi driver, Rodolfo Sanchez, with grand larceny, theft of service, and possession of stolen property for a scheme, after an E-Z Pass transmitter and its records showed that the driver had evaded paying numerous MTA (Metropolitan Transportation Authority) bridge and tunnel tolls. A suspect can also be easily tracked by their cellular telephone usage.

Job Opportunities

The Bureau of Labor Statistics has recognized the importance of computer forensics and security. It estimates that, between 2018 and 2028, information technology job opportunities will increase by 12%; that is, approximately 546,200 new jobs will be created. The increase in employment opportunities will occur partially in response to increased criminal activity on the Internet, such as identity theft, spamming, email harassment, and illegal downloading of copyrighted materials.

Computer forensics investigation occupations exist in law enforcement at local, county, state, federal, and international levels. However, the private sector also has extensive opportunities for computer forensics examiners. Most accounting firms have a computer forensics laboratory, and the major firms have multiple laboratories nationwide. Corporations often procure the services of an accounting firm's computer forensics division in their investigations. Much of their business is derived from **eDiscovery** (electronic discovery), which refers to the recovery of digitally stored data. The need for this recovery could be necessitated by litigation with another corporation or could be in response to a request for information from the Securities and Exchange Commission (SEC). eDiscovery services are generally associated with civil litigation.

Skilled computer forensics examiners also have job opportunities within private investigation firms. These firms, like CODEDETECTIVES LLC, are often retained by individuals who are involved in litigation. Other times they are retained by individuals going through divorce proceedings that involve a contested settlement or accusations of infidelity, This is especially true when a contentious custody battle ensues. It could be argued that the growth of mobile forensics was prompted by people investigating suspected spousal infidelity.

As computer forensics grows in importance, and as we embrace new technologies, continuing needs arise for new software and hardware solutions. Software and hardware companies, like AccessData, opentext, Cellebrite, and Paraben, employ individuals skilled in both computer science and investigations. Some of the larger law firms around the world have employed computer forensics investigators or have contracted the services of computer forensics consultants as the need for this type of expertise increases. Moreover, in many cases, computer forensics examiners have been called to the stand at trials to testify as expert witnesses.

Financial systems around the world also rely heavily on electronic communications and the digital storage of customer account information. Credit card fraud, wire fraud, and other instances of financial fraud have quickly pushed financial institutions to develop and invest in the field of computer forensics so as to capture and convict criminals. This capability provides financial institutions with a greater knowledge of criminal activity and strategies and tactics for improving computer security.

Other organizations that hire or engage the services of computer forensics investigators are Department of Defense agencies, including the United States Air Force, Army, and Navy. The Internal Revenue Service (IRS) is one of the government agencies that has been involved in computer forensics the longest. Federal agencies, including the Federal Bureau of Investigation (FBI), Department of Homeland Security (DHS), Immigration and Customs Enforcement (ICE), Drug Enforcement Agency (DEA), and U.S. Secret Service also have computer forensics laboratories. For the FBI, this knowledge is critical, whether they are investigating white-collar crime involving money laundering or perhaps the electronic communications of Al-Qaida terrorist operatives. The Secret Service also increasingly utilizes computer forensics in its investigations, including counterfeiting investigations.

In October 2001, President Bush signed the USA PATRIOT Act (H.R. 3162) into law. One of the provisions of the act was to establish a nationwide network of Electronic Crimes Task Forces. The network consists of federal, state, and local law enforcement, in addition to prosecutors, academia, and private industry. This group is charged with the protection of the United States' critical infrastructure. Moreover, the expertise of computer forensics examiners is imperative to the successful investigation of attacks on critical infrastructure, including the financial system and the power grid.

Clearly, jobs for computer forensics investigators are available in many sectors of the economy, propelled by the digitization of our personal information. Theft of our personal information and attacks on our critical infrastructure will only increase, so there is a continued need for expertise in the field of computer forensics. The scope of this discipline has expanded so much that specialized positions have emerged. Some examiners are trained to seize digital devices and then forensically image those devices. These images are then transferred to another area of the laboratory, where the images are searched for files that are specifically linked to the investigation. Later, another team might be responsible for writing the report and making the evidence available through a secure website. The latter is a procedure known as discovery, whereby both defense and prosecution lawyers can view the evidence.

Specialization within the field of computer forensics is also apparent when it comes to different types of devices. For example, mobile forensics investigators focus on cellular telephone evidence, while Mac forensics specialists focus on Apple computers and devices such as iPads and iPods.

A History of Digital Forensics

Originally, computer forensics was developed to help investigate computer crimes. In the 1950s, 1960s, and 1970s, there were phone phreakers, who used a range of techniques to make free long distance and international calls. Steve Jobs and Steve Wozniak, founders of Apple, allegedly sold a box that allowed people to make these free calls using some telecommunication hacks. These phone phreaks are referred to some as early hackers who would later inspire computer hackers in the 1980s.

1980s: The Advent of the Personal Computer

Although crimes involving computers have existed for many years, crime began to really grow with the advent of the personal computer (PC) in the 1980s. IBM was at the forefront of PC development initially, and in 1981, the company introduced the 5150 PC. In the 1980s, IBM competed with other PC manufacturers, including Atari, Commodore, Tandy, and Apple. Apple was extremely successful in the personal computer market in the 1980s. In 1984, Apple introduced the Macintosh 128K machine, with a built-in black-and-white display. Apple soon followed with the Macintosh 512K Personal Computer that same year. This computer supported productivity software, including Microsoft Excel. The Macintosh SE became one of the most popular personal computers when it launched in 1987. Interestingly, around this time, the first electronic bulletin boards emerged and facilitated communication between hackers. Subsequently, hacking groups, like the Legion of Doom in the United States, emerged. The 1983 film *War Games* introduced the public to the concept of hacking with a personal computer in order to gain access to government computers. In 1984, Eric Corley (with the handle *Emmanuel Goldstein*) published *2600: The Hacker Quarterly*, which facilitated the exchange of hacking ideas. Kevin Mitnick, one of the earliest hackers, was convicted in 1989 of stealing firmware (software) from DEC and access codes from MCI. In the wake of numerous high-profile system break-ins, Congress passed the Computer Fraud and Abuse Act in 1986. The act has subsequently been amended several times.

Federal Bureau of Investigation (FBI)

In 1984, the FBI established the Magnetic Media Program, which subsequently became known as the **Computer Analysis and Response Team** (CART). The group was responsible for computer forensics examinations. Special Agent Michael Anderson, in the criminal investigation division of the IRS, has sometimes been referred to as the Father of Computer Forensics.

National Center for Missing and Exploited Children (NCMEC)

In local and county law enforcement, computer forensics investigators generally spend a large proportion of their time working on child endangerment cases, especially those involving the possession and distribution of child pornography. In 1984, the U.S. Congress established the National Center for Missing and Exploited Children (NCMEC). **NCMEC** is mandated to help locate missing children and combat the (sexual) exploitation of children. It acts as a central repository for documenting crimes against missing children, including victims of child endangerment.

1990s: The Impact of the Internet

With the advent of web browsers, like Netscape in the 1990s, access to the Internet became much easier. Access to the Internet no longer meant using a command-line interface to reach Internet resources because now there was a user-friendly, aesthetically pleasing interface. Web browsers prompted a massive migration of computers to the Internet. Equally important was the fact that computers, which previously could not communicate with one another, like a PC and a Mac, could now communicate with relative ease, thanks to the establishment of a common communication Internet protocol known as HyperText Transport Protocol (HTTP). Electronic mail (email) was also created around this time, although initially it was used as a method of communicating within organizations. Multinational companies could dramatically reduce their telephone costs by establishing an email network. New uses of technology for communication meant that there was greater value put on digital evidence. In 1993, the first International Conference on Computer Evidence took place.

Department of Defense (DoD)

In 1998, the Defense Reform Initiative Directive #27 directed the U.S. Air Force to establish the joint Department of Defense Computer Forensics Laboratory, which would be responsible for counter-intelligence, criminal, and computer evidence investigations. Simultaneously, a computer forensics training program was created, known as the Defense Computer Investigations Training Program. The training program became an academy that was later accredited by the American Council of Education. The Department of Defense Cyber Crime Center, or DC3, was composed of the academy and laboratory and was later joined by the Department of Defense Cyber Crime Institute (DCCI) in 2002. DC3 partnered with Oklahoma State University's Center for Telecommunications and Network Security (CTANS) to develop and operate the National Repository for Digital Forensic Intelligence (NRDFI), which subsequently developed several forensic tools.

U.S. Internal Revenue Service

The IRS dates back to the American Civil War, when President Lincoln created the position of Commissioner of Internal Revenue. Today the IRS is a division of the Department of the Treasury. As computer usage has increased over the years, so has the need for use of computer forensics in IRS investigations. The IRS Criminal Investigation Division Electronic Crimes Program funded Elliott Spencer to develop a computer forensics tool known as ILook. The IRS Criminal Investigation Division (IRS-CID) began using ILook in 2000 to facilitate financial investigations. The ILook Suite was historically available to local and state law enforcement free of charge.

United States Secret Service (USSS)

We often think of the United States Secret Service (USSS) as solely providing protection for the Commander in Chief—the President of the United States. However, this federal agency has a relatively long and distinguished history in the field of computer forensics. This is because the USSS has field agents across the United States working on criminal investigations, including crimes involving money laundering and currency counterfeiting. In the 1994 Crime Bill, Congress mandated that the USSS apply its forensic and technical knowledge to criminal investigations connected to missing and exploited children. Thus, the Secret Service works closely with NCMEC. In 1996, the USSS established the New York **Electronic Crimes Task Force (ECTF)**, a center used to collaboratively investigate cybercrimes.

In 2001, the USA PATRIOT Act mandated that the United States Secret Service expand its successful New York Electronic Crimes Task Force (ECTF) and establish ECTFs nationwide. The following year, in response to a lack of coordination of law enforcement agencies prior to the events of September 11, 2001, the Department of Homeland Security (DHS) was formed. Its primary responsibility was to protect the United States from terrorist attacks and also to effectively respond to natural disasters. The Secret Service then became an agency within the DHS. In April 2003, the PROTECT Act (also known as the Amber Alert Bill) gave full authorization to the USSS to manage investigations involving child abuse and provided greater funding and resources to these efforts. In 2007, the agency established the National Computer Forensics Institute (NCFI) as a partnership between the USSS and the DHS, the Alabama District Attorneys Association, the State of Alabama, and the city of Hoover, Alabama. NCFI provides computer forensics training to law enforcement, prosecutors, and judges. The NCFI facility is comprised of high-technology classrooms, a computer forensics laboratory, and a mock courtroom. In reality, the USSS is typically less involved with child exploitation cases, given its focus on financial crimes. The FBI, DHS-ICE, and the Postal Inspector's Service are more involved in child abuse cases.

The need for international collaboration, especially cooperation with law enforcement in Europe, has become more important since the events of September 11, 2001. Therefore, in 2009 the USSS established the first European Electronic Crimes Task Force, based in Rome, Italy. The following year, the USSS established the United Kingdom Electronic Crimes Task Force.

International Collaboration

International collaboration on investigations is extremely important because, generally, the larger the crime, the larger the scope geographically. Criminals tend to use the Internet to effectively communicate both on an intrastate level and internationally. In 1995, the International Organization on Computer Evidence (IOCE) was formed. The organization facilitates the exchange of information for law enforcement internationally. In 1998, G8 appointed IOCE to create standards for digital evidence handling.

INTERPOL

In terms of international efforts and collaboration, INTERPOL has taken a central role in applying digital evidence to criminal investigations. **INTERPOL** is the world's largest international police organization, representing 188 member countries. In 1989, the General Secretariat was moved to Lyon, France. In 2004, an INTERPOL liaison office was established at the United Nations, and in 2008, a special representative was appointed to the European Union in Brussels.

INTERPOL's Incident Response Team (IRT) has provided computer forensics expertise on a number of high-profile international investigations. In a 2008 report, computer forensics examiners from law enforcement in Australia and Singapore examined 609 GB of data on eight laptops, two external hard drives, and three USB thumb drives at the request of the Colombian authorities. The hardware and software belonged to the *Fuerzas Armadas Revolucionarias de Colombia* (FARC). FARC is an anti-government terrorist organization in Colombia, which is largely funded through its control of illegal drug trafficking—primarily the trafficking of cocaine. Colombian investigators contacted INTERPOL to examine the seized laptops in an effort to have unbiased investigators view the digital evidence to corroborate the government's assertions that the digital evidence had been handled in a forensically sound manner.

At the 2008 ICPO-INTERPOL General Assembly in St. Petersburg, Russia, approval was provided for the creation of an INTERPOL Computer Forensics Analysis Unit. This unit provides training and assistance for computer forensics investigations and has been charged with the development of international standards for the search, seizure, and investigation of electronic evidence.

INTERPOL has worked for many years on fighting crimes against children. Similar to NCMEC, since 2001, INTERPOL has maintained a database of exploited children, referred to as the INTERPOL Child Abuse Image Database (ICAID). Subsequently, in 2009, ICAID was replaced by the International Child Sexual Exploitation image database (ICSE DB). The database is accessible to law enforcement in real-time around the world. This powerful database incorporates image comparison software to link victims with places. INTERPOL also works with other agencies worldwide to fight child abuse, including the COSPOL Internet Related Child Abuse Material Project (CIRCAMP) and the Virtual Global Taskforce. CIRCAMP is a European law enforcement network that monitors the Internet to detect child exploitation. The Virtual Global Taskforce has the same purpose and mission but is a global network of law enforcement agencies fighting online child abuse.

INTERPOL has been successful in coordinating international efforts to apprehend suspected pedophiles. Following a 2006 police raid on Internet predators in Norway, investigators discovered a laptop containing nearly 800 horrific images of young boys. Nearly 100 of the images depicted a middle-aged, white male watching these boys being abused. The authorities requested the assistance of INTERPOL to track down the unknown predator. INTERPOL initiated a massive manhunt and solicited help from the public through the media. Within 48 hours of an appeal for help, INTERPOL and U.S. Immigration and Customs Enforcement (ICE) arrested 60-year-old Wayne Nelson Corliss of Union, New Jersey.

Regional Computer Forensics Laboratory

In 1999, the first **Regional Computer Forensics Laboratory (RCFL)** was established in San Diego, California. In 2000, the second RCFL in the United States was opened in Dallas, Texas. An RCFL is an FBI-sponsored laboratory, used to train law enforcement in the use of computer forensics tools. The laboratories are also used for law enforcement personnel, from different agencies, to collaborate on criminal investigations. Smaller law enforcement agencies often do not have the budget and resources for an effective computer forensics laboratory. RCFLs provide smaller police departments with the opportunity to send one or two officers to a laboratory where they can be trained or can work on their investigations. The types of crimes investigated include terrorism, child pornography, theft or the destruction of intellectual property, Internet crimes, property fraud, and financial fraud. Today there are 14 RCFLs in the United States and 2 in Europe.

Fusion Centers

Established in 2003, fusion centers in the United States are central repositories for collecting intelligence at the state and local levels, with the goal of preventing terrorist attacks. The project is a joint initiative between the Department of Homeland Security (DHS) and the Department of Justice (DOJ). More than 70 fusion centers operate around the country. The locations of these centers are classified. However, a group, known as Public Intelligence, has disclosed the physical locations of most of these centers. The buildings have no signs and no street addresses and are only associated with a "P.O. Box". For example, the address of the fusion center located in West Trenton, New Jersey, is P.O. Box 7068 instead of listing a street address.

Reports, after the events of 9/11, cited the lack of information sharing between government agencies— including the National Security Agency (NSA), Central Intelligence Agency (CIA), and Federal Bureau of Investigation (FBI)—as being a major impediment to preventing the terrorist attacks. For example, Ziad Jarrah hijacked United Airlines Flight 93 on September 11, 2001—the flight that crashed in Pennsylvania that day. Jarrah was actually stopped by local police, for speeding, on September 9, 2011. This particular state trooper had no intelligence that could have been used to detain Jarrah and did not know that he was being tracked by the FBI.

Local law enforcement collects information of interest and then contributes this information to fusion centers. The type of information collected includes surveillance camera footage, license plate numbers, and suspicious activity reports (SARs). Suspicious activity reports can include reports about individuals taking photographs of government buildings, making maps, or holding unusual group meetings.

These fusion centers reportedly maintain databases of information for just about every American— information that includes unlisted cellular telephone numbers, drivers' license information, and insurance claims. Fusion centers also collect information from relatively unknown data mining companies such as Entersect. Entersect provides information to human resources about potential hires and their criminal records, litigation and bankruptcy histories, education, and employment references. It also provides a service to law enforcement known as Entersect Police Online. According to its website (entersect.net), they can provide law enforcement with access to billions of online records covering most of the U.S. population. Fusion centers also utilize other commercial database vendors, like Lexis-Nexis.

As a result of their secrecy and the amount of personal information collected, fusion centers have been shrouded in controversy. Civil liberties organizations, like the American Civil Liberties Union (ACLU), have frowned upon their zeal for collecting personal information and their lack of oversight. These fusion centers are a combination of both law enforcement and corporate personnel. Some have questioned the role of local law enforcement in monitoring suspicious activity. For example, in 2008, Duane Kerzic was arrested by Amtrak Police at Penn Station in New York after he was spotted on a train platform taking a photo of a train. He was handcuffed in a holding cell. It transpired that Kerzic was actually trying to win Amtrak's annual photo contest.

Although the role of fusion centers can be largely categorized as counterterrorism, they do play a critical role in some computer forensics investigations. Fusion centers provide a clear indication of the type of digital information that is currently being collected and stored.

2000s: Virtual Currencies, IoT, Encryption, and the Edward Snowden Effect

In May 2010, Laszlo Hanyecz bought two pizzas in Jacksonville, for 10,000 Bitcoin (BTC). Bitcoin at the time was worth less than $0.01. Ten years later, those 10,000 BTC would be worth over $77 million. Although many virtual currency owners are hard-working people, these currencies have undoubtedly facilitated millions of payments to criminals. Most notable is the use of cryptocurrencies on Dark Web marketplaces, which have included The Silk Road, AlphaBay, HonestCocaine, and other sites where the currency of choice for illicit purchases has been Bitcoin or Ethereum, given the anonymity that these cryptocurrencies provide. The Silk Road, which was run by Ross Ulbricht, was a Dark Web marketplace that was only accessible with the Tor browser. Ironically, even with the successful take-down of the Silk Road, its success in facilitating anonymous drug transactions brought about the creation of other Dark Web marketplaces operated by nefarious actors. Other Dark Web marketplaces emerged and many of their creators, administrators, and vendors were prosecuted in the 2000s. Nevertheless, these types of marketplaces are likely to continue to flourish. Cryptocurrencies are currencies of choice for drug traffickers as they eliminate the need to smuggle cash across borders and they reduce the paper trails associated with transactions through traditional financial institutions.

As previously mentioned, IoT devices, in conjunction with AI-enabled home smart devices, have rapidly become more pervasive in the 2000s. AI devices, like Alexa, or home surveillance systems, like The Ring, have provided greater potential for digital evidence.

The 2000s also marked an era where encryption has become the norm rather than a choice for consumers. More specifically, full-disk encryption has changed from being an option to becoming the default. Nowhere has this become more apparent than with smartphone developers (both Android and iPhone). Additionally, improvements with two-factor authentication (2FA) have made this security protocol more popular with companies like Apple and Microsoft; more and more, companies are requiring additional authentication via email or SMS (text message) when registering new devices or in the case of an application that is being accessed from an unrecognized device or location. These advances in encryption and authentication have undoubtedly posed tremendous challenges for digital forensics investigators.

In May 2013, Edward Snowden suddenly left the National Security Agency (NSA), taking many classified files with him. As a whistleblower, he disclosed information about how large technology companies had been transmitting vast quantities of data to the NSA, GCHQ (Government Communications Headquarters), and, in general, the Five Eyes, to support surveillance programs; **Five Eyes** is a collaborative partnership of intelligence agencies from the USA, UK, Canada, Australia, and New Zealand. Whether or not you support the actions of Edward Snowden, it has negatively impacted law enforcement's ability to collect data from third-party services, when in possession of a subpoena or a warrant. For example, some companies, like Twitter, now maintain a policy that they will inform customers if they are being investigated, unless a judge has directed otherwise. It seems that other companies have moved faster to encrypt software and hardware to protect the privacy of their customers from government surveillance and not just in an effort to improve security.

Training and Education

There are a number of ways to become a computer forensics investigator. An indirect way into the profession, for many, has been through law enforcement. Many of these professionals began their careers as police officers and later became successful investigators. Subsequently, their aptitude for computing, in addition to the needs of their department in investigating cases with digital evidence, provided them with the opportunity to become skilled computer forensics examiners. Formal training in computer forensics is still a relatively recent concept.

Law Enforcement Training

As previously noted, Regional Computer Forensic Laboratories (RCFL) are used by law enforcement to share resources, collaborate on criminal investigations, and improve their skills as computer forensics investigators. RCFLs also provide formal training classes to RCFL and FBI CART examiners. Training includes seizing and handling evidence, as well as learning about operating systems and their associated file systems.

Carnegie Mellon's Computer Emergency Response Team (CERT) has developed a number of computer forensics tools exclusively for law enforcement. Training on these tools has been available through CERT's Federal Virtual Training Environment (FedVTE).

Headquartered in Glynco, Georgia, the **Federal Law Enforcement Training Center (FLETC)** is an interagency law enforcement training organization for more than 80 federal agencies nationwide. One of the programs it provides is the Seized Computer Evidence Recovery Specialist (SCERS). FLETC also provides training in topics such as Mac forensics and network forensics.

The **National White Collar Crime Center (NW3C)** is an agency that delivers training and investigative support to law enforcement and those who prosecute criminal cases. NW3C hosts classes in various domains of computer forensics, including cellphone forensics, online investigations, operating systems, file systems, and the acquisition and handling of digital evidence. The Secure Techniques for Onsite Preview (STOP) class is one of its well-recognized courses. The class is for probation/parole officers, detectives, and officers who perform spot checks or home visits and need to quickly check a computer in a forensically sound manner. For example, a parole officer might need to check for images on the home computer of a convicted sex offender.

INTERPOL has provided computer forensics investigative support globally for law enforcement. In April 2009, University College Dublin (UCD) and INTERPOL launched an e-crime investigation training initiative. Not only did this initiative provide training, but it also facilitated academic exchanges in the field of computer forensics to further the skills of computer forensics examiners. UCD has a prestigious Master of Science in Forensic Computing and Cybercrime investigation degree program that is exclusively available to law enforcement worldwide.

Another organization committed to the exchange of ideas and practices, in computer forensics, is the **Computer Technology Investigators Network (CTIN)**. CTIN membership is open to law enforcement, corporate security professionals, and members of the academic community. Finally,

InfraGard is a public-private agency of the FBI, which promotes the exchange of information between the private and public sectors on issues related to terrorism, intelligence, and security matters. InfraGard has established local chapters nationally, and membership is open to all U.S. citizens. Applicants are subject to an FBI background check.

High School Training

A number of high schools around the United States have adopted a computer forensics curriculum for both law and technology track students. One example is the New York City Department of Education, which I have worked with for more than a decade to create a computer forensics and cybersecurity curriculum for high school students. A computer forensics curriculum is a marvelous way to teach high school students about the intricacies of investigations involving digital evidence.

University Training

Many universities have created classes for both undergraduate and graduate degree programs in computer forensics. Three of the earliest and most prestigious third-level institutions to develop degree programs are Champlain College, Purdue University, and Carnegie Mellon University. Carnegie Mellon and Purdue University work with local law enforcement in the field of computer forensics. Another notable computer forensics degree programs is offered at Bloomsburg University. Tracks in computer forensics are offered at other academic institutions, like Pace University, which also works closely with law enforcement.

Professional Certifications

Achieving a degree in computer forensics, information technology, or even information systems can provide a strong foundation in computer forensics. A degree supplemented by certifications provides greater competencies in the field and makes a candidate even more marketable to a potential employer. This is because many certification classes are taught by industry professionals and include hands-on training with professional tools.

The following sections describe the computer forensics certifications available that are beneficial to legitimizing the credentials of a computer forensics examiner. However, the list is not an exhaustive one.

Professional Certifications Available to the General Public

The International Association of Computer Investigative Specialists (IACIS) is a nonprofit organization dedicated to educating law enforcement in the field of computer forensics. One of the most recognized industry certifications is the Certified Forensic Computer Examiner (CFCE), which is offered by IACIS.

John Mellon was an active member of IACIS before he founded the International Society of Forensic Computer Examiners (ISFCE). He developed a certificate known as the Certified Computer

Examiner (CCE), which was first awarded in 2003. The ISFCE has four testing centers and provides a proficiency test for the American Society of Crime Laboratories Directors/Laboratory Accreditation Board (ASCLD/LAB), which is recognized as the pinnacle of certifications for forensic laboratories. ASCLD is a nonprofit, professional society of crime laboratory directors and forensic science managers who seek to promote excellence in the field of forensic science, including computer forensics. The United States Secret Service and many other law enforcement computer forensics laboratories are accredited by ASCLD/LAB, which is a testament to the prestige that this certification carries.

Many other vendor-neutral certifications are available to the public. The Certified Computer Forensics Examiner (CCFE) certification is offered by the Information Assurance Certification Review Board (IACRB). To attain the CCFE, the candidate must successfully demonstrate a mastery of the following domains:

- Law, ethics, and legal issues
- The investigation process
- Computer forensics tools
- Hard disk evidence recovery and integrity
- Digital device recovery and integrity
- File system forensics
- Evidence analysis and correlation
- Evidence recovery with Windows-based systems
- Network and volatile memory forensics
- Report writing

The Certified Forensic Consultant (CFC) certification, awarded by the American College of Forensics Examiners International (ACFEI), focuses on the legal aspects of computer forensics in the United States. The program educates students in the following areas:

- The litigation process
- Federal rules of evidence
- The discovery process
- Note taking
- Site inspection
- The written report
- The retainer letter

- Types of witness

- The expert witness report

- Preparing for deposition

- What to expect at deposition

- Preparing for trial

- Testifying at trial

- What to bring to court

- The business of forensic consulting

The ACFEI also provides training and assessment for the Certified Forensic Accountant (CrFA) certification. A **forensic accountant** is an individual who has an accounting background and is involved with financial investigations.

Since its formation in 1989, the SANS (SysAdmin, Audit, Network, Security) Institute has provided training to security professionals in both the public and private sectors. SANS also provides training in computer forensics and hosts a class called Computer Forensic Investigations and Incident Response. This course provides the training required to achieve the GIAC Certified Forensic Analyst (GCFA) certification. Founded in 1999, the Global Information Assurance Certification (GIAC) provides skills assessments for security professionals.

Professional Certifications Offered to Security Professionals

Although computer security and computer forensics are two different disciplines, they are two disciplines that complement each other. Therefore, many professional computer forensics examiners have computer security certifications. Both security professionals and computer forensics experts can be involved in handling security incidents, which can be network breaches. Security professionals can provide information about the type of security breach that occurred and the scope of the attack, whereas a computer forensics examiner can often determine the trail of evidence left by the perpetrator of the attack.

The Certified Security Incident Handler (CSIH) program is an excellent course for a computer forensics investigator to take. The certificate program is offered by CERT (Computer Emergency Response Team) and is a division of the Software Engineering Institute (SEI), at Carnegie Mellon University. SEI is a federally funded research and development center, sponsored by the Department of Defense (DoD). CERT provides training to network administrators and other technical support staff. The training includes the identification of existing and potential threats to networks. Moreover, CERT trains security professionals on how to handle security breaches. CERT has a renowned forensics team that works closely with law enforcement on research projects for gap areas not addressed by commercial tools for computer forensics investigators.

It is quite common for a computer forensics investigator, particularly in the private sector, to earn the Certified Information Systems Security Professional (CISSP) certification. This certification is offered by the International Information Systems Security Certification Consortium (ISC)[2]. The CISSP certification has been formally approved by the DoD in its Information Assurance Technical and Managerial categories. This important well-regarded certification is achieved after successful completion of an examination of the Common Body of Knowledge (CBK), which covers the following security domains:

- Access control
- Application development security
- Business continuity and disaster recovery planning
- Cryptography
- Information security governance and risk management
- Legal, regulations, investigations, and compliance
- Operations security
- Physical security
- Security architecture and design
- Telecommunications and network security

To pass the CISSP examination, the examinee must score at least 700 out of 1,000 points from 250 multiple-choice questions. A CISSP applicant must prove that he has a minimum of five years' experience in 2 or more of the 10 domains. The applicant is also subject to a criminal background check and must abide by the CISSP Code of Ethics. Once approved for the certification, a CISSP must attain Continuing Professional Credits (CPE) to maintain his certification.

Another recognized security certification, often held by computer forensics examiners, is the Certified Information Security Manager (CISM). Like the CISSP certification, the CISM certification is for security professionals. It differs from the CISSP, however, because the CISM is a certification for information security managers with experience in the following areas:

- Information security governance
- Information risk management
- Information security program development
- Information security program management
- Incident management and response

As with the CISSP certification, anyone with CISM certification has a continuing professional education requirement so that they stay up-to-date with the latest knowledge in information security management.

Professional Certifications Offered by Digital Forensics Software Companies

Most computer forensics software vendors offer certification classes. Some prominent digital forensics imaging software vendors are Cellebrite/BlackBag, AccessData, opentext, and X-Ways Forensics:

- BlackBag Technologies provides a variety of Mac and Windows forensics bootcamps. One of their more popular certifications is the BlackLight Certified Examiner (BCE).

- AccessData provides an AccessData Bootcamp and classes in Windows Forensics, Mac Forensics, Internet Forensics, and Mobile Forensics. Its best-known certification is the AccessData Certified Examiner (ACE). The exam tests the user's competencies with the FTK Imager, Registry Viewer, and PRTK tools.

- opentext also provides training and assessment for computer forensics examiners. A student who can demonstrate proficiency with EnCase can become an EnCase Certified Examiner (EnCE).

- X-Ways Forensics provides regular training and assessment with the X-Ways Forensics bit-stream imaging tool and also with the WinHex product. Typically, an X-Ways instructor conducts a 5-day class, beginning with a 2-day session on file systems. The remaining days focus on the forensic tools.

The BCE, ACE and EnCE certifications, as well as X-Ways Forensics training, are open to professionals from both the private and public sectors.

Summary

Digital forensics (or computer forensics) is the use of digital data to solve a crime. It is a scientific discipline, and, as with any area of forensics, close adherence to the law is imperative. Digital forensics has been used in many different types of criminal investigations but can also be used in civil litigation or as part of incident response to a network intrusion. A computer forensics investigator uses many different types of hardware and software to extract and analyze files, including a bit-stream imaging tool that produces a bit-for-bit copy of the suspect's device. Finding the evidence is not always enough—it is important to establish control, ownership, and intent by the suspect. Digital evidence can include emails, images, videos, websites visited, and Internet searches.

An effective computer forensics investigator should possess skills in a number of areas, including computer science, criminal justice, law, mathematics, writing, forensic science, and linguistics. These skills can be gained through various avenues, such as on-the-job training (common in law enforcement), degree programs at university or college, or certification courses. Those who want to pursue a career in computer forensics will have many opportunities in both the private and public sectors.

The advent of the personal computer in the 1980s increased computer usage in the home and prompted an increase in computer-related crime. Subsequently, government agencies began to devote resources to computer forensics, evidenced by the establishment of the Computer Analysis and Response Team (CART) at the FBI. The introduction of web browsers, in the 1990s, stimulated a huge migration of personal computer users to the Internet and ultimately made the Internet a valuable resource for finding information about suspects and also provided a source of incriminating evidence. Many agencies, within the Department of Homeland Security (DHS), use computer forensics. For example, the Internet has facilitated international criminal networks, so INTERPOL has greatly enhanced its computer forensics capabilities. The need for international collaboration between DHS and other countries already exists but will continue to grow, especially in the field of computer forensics.

Table 1.1 provides a brief historical perspective of developments in computer forensics and notable developments in technology that have influenced this field.

TABLE 1.1   A Brief History of Computer Forensics & Major Events in IT

Year	Event
1981	IBM introduced the 5150 PC.
1984	The FBI established the Magnetic Media Program, later known as CART.
1984	The National Center for Missing and Exploited Children (NCMEC) was founded.
1986	The USSS established the Electronic Crimes Task Force (ECTF).
1986	Congress passed the Computer Fraud and Abuse Act.
1993	The first International Conference on Computer Evidence took place.
1994	Congress passed the Crime Bill, and the USSS began working on crimes against children.
1994	Mosaic Netscape, the first graphical web browser, was released.
1995	The International Organization on Computer Evidence (IOCE) was formed.

Year	Event
1996	The USSS founded the New York Electronic Crimes Task Force (ECTF).
1998	Europol was founded.
1999	The First Regional Computer Forensics Laboratory (RCFL) was established in San Diego.
2000	The IRS Criminal Investigation Division (IRS-CID) began using ILook.
2001	The USA PATRIOT Act directed the USSS to establish ECTFs nationwide.
2001	INTERPOL developed a database of exploited children (ICAID).
2002	The Department of Homeland Security (DHS) was formed.
2003	The PROTECT Act was passed to fight against child exploitation.
2003	Fusion centers were established.
2003	Europol established the European Cybercrime Centre (EC3)
2004	Facebook was founded.
2007	The National Computer Forensics Institute (NCFI) was established.
2008	The formation of an INTERPOL Computer Forensics Analysis Unit was approved.
2009	The first European ECTF was formed (Italy).
2009	The Bitcoin Ledger began recording transactions.
2010	The second European ECTF was formed (United Kingdom).
2011	The PATRIOT Sunsets Extension Act was enacted.
2013	Edward Snowden fled to Russian following a classified data leak at the NSA.
2015	The trial of The Silk Road ends with the conviction of its creator, Ross Ulbricht.
2015	The Cybersecurity Information Sharing Act was enacted.
2016	Introduction of the Investigatory Powers Act in the U.K.
2017	APFS introduced, by Apple, with iOS 10.3.
2018	Introduction of the General Data Protection Regulation (GDPR)

Key Terms

algorithm: A set of steps used to solve a problem.

BitLocker: An encryption tool that was introduced with the Ultimate and Enterprise editions of Microsoft Windows Vista, which allows for encryption at the file, folder, or drive level.

bit-stream imaging tool: A tool that produces a bit-for-bit copy of original media, including files marked for deletion.

chain of custody: Documentation of each person who has been in contact with evidence, from its seizure, to its investigation, to its submission to court.

client computer: A computer that requests a resource from a server computer.

closed-circuit television (CCTV): Use of video that is transmitted to a particular location.

Computer Analysis and Response Team (CART): A unit within the FBI that is responsible for providing support for investigations that require skilled computer forensics examinations.

computer security: Prevention of unauthorized access to computers and their associated resources.

Computer Technology Investigators Network (CTIN): An organization committed to the exchange of ideas and practices in computer forensics.

digital forensics: The retrieval, analysis, and use of digital evidence in a civil or criminal investigation.

eDiscovery: The recovery of digitally stored data.

Electronic Crimes Task Force (ECTF): A network of nationwide centers that collaboratively investigate cybercrimes.

encryption: The process of scrambling plaintext into an unreadable format using a mathematical formula.

exculpatory evidence: Evidence used to prove the innocence of a defendant.

Federal Law Enforcement Training Center (FLETC): An interagency law enforcement training organization for more than 80 federal agencies nationwide.

file metadata: Information about a file that can include the creation, modified, and last access dates, and also the user who created the file.

Five Eyes: A collaborative partnership of intelligence agencies from the USA, UK, Canada, Australia, and New Zealand.

forensic accountant: An individual who has an accounting background and is involved with financial investigations.

forensics: Suitable for a court of law.

GPS (Global Positioning System): A device that receives communications from orbiting satellites to determine geographic location.

inculpatory evidence: Incriminating evidence often used to convict a criminal.

InfraGard: A public-private agency of the FBI that promotes the exchange of information between the private and public sectors on issues related to terrorism, intelligence, and security matters.

INTERPOL: The world's largest international police organization, representing 188 member countries.

National Center for Missing and Exploited Children (NCMEC): An agency mandated to help locate missing children and combat the (sexual) exploitation of children.

National White Collar Crime Center (NW3C): An agency that delivers training and investigative support to law enforcement personnel and those who prosecute criminal cases.

Random Access Memory (RAM): Often referred to as short-term memory or volatile memory because its contents largely disappear when the computer is powered down. A user's current activity and processes, including Internet activity, are stored in RAM.

Regional Computer Forensics Laboratory (RCFL): An FBI-sponsored laboratory that trains law enforcement personnel in the use of computer forensics tools and collaboratively works on criminal investigations.

skimmer: A device used to capture the information stored in the magnetic strip of an ATM card, credit card, or debit card.

spoliation of evidence: Hiding, altering, or destroying evidence related to an investigation.

tampering with evidence: The concealment, destruction, alteration, or falsification of evidence.

web server: Delivers HTML documents and related resources in response to client computer requests.

Assessment

CLASSROOM DISCUSSIONS

1. How can you become a computer forensics investigator?

2. What is computer forensics, and how is it used in investigations?

3. What types of criminal activities take place on Dark Web marketplaces, and why have they been so successful?

MULTIPLE-CHOICE QUESTIONS

1. Which of the following statements best defines computer forensics?

    A. Computer forensics is the use of evidence to solve computer crimes.

    B. Computer forensics is the use of digital evidence to solve a crime.

    C. Computer forensics is only used to find deleted files on a computer.

    D. Computer forensics is only used to examine desktop and laptop computers.

2. A chain of custody (CoC) form is used to document which of the following?

    A. Law enforcement officers who arrest and imprison a criminal suspect

    B. A chain of letters or emails used in an investigation

    C. Anyone who has been in contact with evidence in a case

    D. None of the above

3. Which of the following can be of evidentiary value to a computer forensics examiner?

    A. A SIM card

    B. An Xbox

    C. A digital camera

    D. All of the above

4. Which of the following statements best describes a bit-stream imaging tool?

    A. A bit-stream imaging tool produces a bit-for-bit copy of the original media.

    B. A bit-stream imaging tool often provides the examiner with deleted files.

    C. Neither A nor B is correct.

    D. Both A and B are correct.

5. Which of the following are benefits of email evidence?

    A. Email evidence generally exists in multiple areas.

    B. It can often be found easier than other types of evidence.

    C. It has been accepted as admissible evidence in a number of cases.

    D. All of the above.

6. Which of the following statements is not true about photo images?

    A. Images can possess evidence of where the suspect has been.

    B. Images cannot be easily found using bit-stream imaging tools such as FTK.

    C. An image can identify the make and model of the digital camera.

    D. Basically just one type of digital image is used today.

7. Which of the following terms best describes the hiding, altering, or destroying of evidence related to an investigation?

    A. Spoliation of evidence

    B. Manipulation of evidence

    C. Inculpatory evidence

    D. Exculpatory evidence

8. The Computer Analysis and Response Team (CART) is a unit of which government agency?

    A. USSS

    B. FBI

    C. CIA

    D. ICE

9. Which of the following acts established the Department of Homeland Security and mandated that the United States Secret Service establish Electronic Crime Task Forces nationwide?

    A. Health Insurance Portability and Accountability Act

    B. Children's Online Privacy Protection Act

    C. The PROTECT Act

    D. The USA PATRIOT Act

10. Which of the following statements is not true about Regional Computer Forensics Laboratories (RCFLs)?

    A. RCFLs can be used by criminal defense lawyers.

    B. The establishment of RCFLs has been sponsored by the FBI.

    C. RCFLs not only are used for investigations, but also provide computer forensics training.

    D. RCFLs exist in both the United States and Europe.

FILL IN THE BLANKS

1. A(n) _____ is a set of steps used to solve a problem.

2. Computer _____ is the use of digital evidence in a criminal investigation.

3. Computer _____ is the prevention of unauthorized access to computers and their associated resources.

4. A defendant can prove his innocence with the use of _____ evidence.

5. The process of scrambling plain text into an unreadable format using a mathematical formula is called _____.

6. The world's largest international police organization is called _____.

7. Short-term, volatile memory, the contents of which disappear when a computer is powered down, is called _____ Access Memory.

8. A(n) _____ is a device used to capture the information stored in the magnetic strip of an ATM, credit, or debit card.

9. A(n) _____ server delivers HTML documents and related resources in response to client computer requests.

10. _____ is a public-private agency of the FBI, which promotes the exchange of information between the private and public sectors on issues related to terrorism, intelligence, and security matters.

PROJECTS

Investigate a Crime

You are a computer forensics investigator in local law enforcement and have been assigned to a criminal investigation. The suspect, Michael Murphy, worked as the director of product development for a computer software company. He was questioned about a number of expensive international telephone calls. Further inspection of his telephone records revealed that he had been calling a software development competitor based in China with offices here in the United States. When confronted, he stated that he would need to consult with his lawyer and had no further comment. He did not show up for work the next day. The local authorities were contacted the following day. Murphy was caught trying to board a one-way flight to Beijing two days after being questioned about his contact with a competitor. At the airport, TSA officials discovered a bag filled with CDs, three SATA hard drives, and five USB thumb drives.

Detail potential types of digital evidence you will need for this investigation.

Research Employment Prospects for Computer Forensics Investigators

Describe why the need for computer forensics examiners will be in demand over the coming years. Include in your answer statistics detailing the growth of certain crimes.

Research Federal Agencies

Create an organizational chart detailing all of the federal agencies involved in computer forensics. Begin with the Department of Homeland Security at the top, and then provide the name of each agency and include its computer forensics unit name where appropriate.

Silk Road

Review the news reports and court proceedings from The Silk Road trial. Write a report detailing the use of digital evidence by the FBI and DHS, which ultimately led to the successful conviction of Ross Ulbricht.

Chapter | 2

Windows Operating and File Systems

Learning Outcomes

After reading this chapter, you will be able to understand the following:

- Explain what an operating system does;
- Explain binary, decimal, and hexadecimal and how to convert from each notation;
- The physical structure of a hard drive and how files are stored and retrieved;
- The boot process;
- Windows file systems; and
- The different features of each Windows operating system and their implications for investigators.

A strong foundation in operating systems is an important building block to becoming a highly effective computer forensics investigator. The evidence that computer forensics investigators work with are files. The organization of these files, the data they contain, and their locations will vary according to the operating system and associated file system that exists on the suspect's computer or digital device. Moreover, the type of operating system and file system will determine the way that digital evidence is acquired and analyzed in terms of both forensic software and hardware. A **file system** is a hierarchy of files and their respective directories.

This chapter begins by outlining the important concept of logical versus physical storage, which is important when discussing how we all view files on our computers through File Explorer on a PC versus how files are actually physically stored on a hard drive. A file on a computer is merely a physical impression on a metal platter, as you will learn later in this chapter. Therefore, computer scientists represent the underlying data on the hard drive in a number of ways—sometimes in binary format or hexadecimal or decimal. This chapter explains these various numbering systems in detail and shows you how to translate from one numbering system to another. This is important because most computer forensics analysis tools provide a "natural" view of the file but also enable the investigator to view a hexadecimal view of the file, which reveals far more information about the file (the file header, metadata, and other helpful information).

An understanding of operating systems is also important because different types and versions of operating systems have different features and knowing these features will assist the investigator in understanding where on the computer the most valuable evidence resides and what tools to use. Moreover, most computer forensics imaging tools give the investigator access to a variety of operating system files; the examiner must be familiar with them and be able to explain them.

When analyzing evidence from a hard disk drive, the computer forensics software displays files associated with the booting up process (when the computer is powered on). Therefore, an investigator should be familiar with these files. In fact, an investigator should be familiar with both system and user files and should be able to account for changes to these files. This is the case for all computing devices. For example, a defense attorney may state that some file changes occurred from when the suspect last used a computer, and the investigator must account for these changes.

The chapter continues by outlining all file systems that are supported by Windows operating system. This is key because the type of file system impacts the value of the evidence and the investigator's ability to view that evidence. For example, FAT12 files are not encrypted, whereas NTFS files can possess strong encryption and could be unreadable. Nevertheless, a FAT12 file has less valuable metadata than an NTFS file, and file backups are generally more probable than with FAT12. Therefore, understanding the characteristics of each file system is important for the investigator.

A recurring theme throughout this book is the importance of placing the suspect behind the keyboard and re-creating the events leading up to a crime. The Windows Registry records any kind of configuration change to a system, which provides a tremendous wealth of information related to a user's wireless connections and Internet activity. Therefore, this chapter delves into the Windows Registry to see what information we can ascertain about a suspect or victim.

The chapter then discusses the file systems supported by Microsoft. The type of file system determines the way files are stored and retrieved in memory. Moreover, the file system defines the limits on file size. The evidentiary value of a file will differ from file system to file system. There are a multitude of reasons for this. For example, the longevity of a file can vary; deleting a file on a Macintosh computer is a different process than deleting a file on a Windows personal computer running NTFS. Metadata, or the attributes of a file, are often critical to associating a criminal with evidence but the nature of this evidence differs from one file system to another. Encryption is yet another variable, and it generally becomes a more difficult proposition for forensic examiners to contend with as vendors continue to improve the quality of their file systems' security.

A file system is also responsible for determining allocated and unallocated storage space. **Allocated storage space** is the area on a volume where a file or files are stored. When a file on a personal computer is deleted, it is not physically erased from the volume (disk) but now becomes available space. When a file is deleted, it is still physically stored on a volume. However, that space is now available to be overwritten. This available file storage space is referred to as **unallocated storage space**.

Users can look to certain tools to securely delete a file. There are, however, search methods that a forensic examiner can use to check to see if a secure delete tool has been used. An examination of Windows Events will help to determine if an application was installed. Unallocated storage space can generally be used to create a primary partition on a volume. A **partition** is a logical storage unit on a disk. In computer forensics, we often hear this notion of physical versus logical when it comes to file storage or files retrieved from a computer or media storage. Therefore, it is critical for an investigator to know the difference and be able to explain that difference to non-technical people.

Physical and Logical Storage

Understanding the physical and logical storage aspects of file systems is important because computer forensics imaging software provides a quite different view of the data stored on a computer. Forensic imaging software is also known as bit-stream imaging software because it captures every bit stored on a computer's hard drive. Unlike Microsoft's Windows File Explorer, forensic imaging software displays every file stored in a computer's memory, including files from the operating system.

Physical versus *logical* can also refer to the difference between how the operating system refers to the location of a file and the physical location of a sector on a disk relative to the storage media. Physical storage is discussed in greater detail later in this chapter.

File Storage

An investigator should understand how files on a computer are stored. With this understanding comes the realization that users cannot determine the physical location where a file is stored and, therefore, cannot control the deletion of that file evidence from a hard drive. File storage and recording is largely controlled by the operating system.

A **byte** is comprised of 8 bits and is the smallest addressable unit in memory. A **sector** on a magnetic hard disk represents 512 bytes, or 2048 bytes on optical discs. More recently, some hard drives contain 4096 byte sectors. Usually a disk has bad sectors, which computer forensics software can identify. A **bad sector** is an area of the disk that can no longer be used to store data. Bad sectors can be caused by viruses, corrupted boot records, physical disruptions, and a host of other disk errors. A **cluster** is a logical storage unit on a hard disk that contains contiguous sectors. When a disk volume is partitioned, the number of sectors in a cluster is defined. A cluster can contain 1 sector (512K) or even 128 sectors (65,536K). **Tracks** are thin, concentric bands on a disk that consist of sectors where data is stored. Computer forensic tools allow the investigator to easily navigate to specific sectors on a disk image, even if a sector is part of the operating system. Figure 2.1 shows the physical layout of a hard disk, although it should be noted that solid state drives (SSDs) have become more pervasive.

FIGURE 2.1 The physical layout of a hard disk

Because most files are comprised of 512-byte blocks, it is important to understand that an 800-byte file uses two 512-byte sectors on a magnetic disk. **File slack** refers to the remaining unused bytes in the last sector of a file. It is necessary to understand what file slack is because data can be hidden in this area. In our example of an 800-byte file, the physical size of the file is 1024 bytes (two sectors), whereas the logical size of the file is 800 bytes. File Explorer displays the logical file size. The **physical file size** is the actual disk space used by a file. The **logical file size** is the amount of data stored in a file. Table 2.1 shows the physical layout of an 800-byte file. To be more specific about slack, RAM slack is the slack at the end of the logical file or sector, and file slack refers to the remaining sectors at the end of the cluster.

TABLE 2.1 Physical Layout of an 800-Byte File

Sector 1	Sector 2	
File Data	File Data	File Slack
512 Bytes	288 Bytes	224 Bytes

Computer forensics investigators typically spend most of their time examining hard disk drives. A **platter** is a circular disk made from aluminum, ceramic, or glass that stores data magnetically. A hard drive contains one or more platters, and data can usually be stored on both sides of this rigid disk. A **spindle**, at the center of the disk, is powered by a motor and is used to spin the platters. An arm sweeps across the rotating platter in an arc. This **actuator arm** contains a read/write head that modifies the magnetization of the disk when writing to it. There are generally two read/write heads for each platter because a platter usually contains data on both sides. The arm and head are nanometers from the platter. Therefore, hard drives must be handled very carefully; any impact on the hard drive could render the read/write head useless. Additionally, the examiner must be very careful not to let any magnetic device near a hard drive. A cellular telephone, for example, contains a battery, and that battery contains a magnet. Sometimes hotel guests will deactivate their hotel room key when they place the key in their pocket with their cellular telephone. This is because the magnetic charge from the telephone corrupts the data on the key. Figure 2.2 shows the layout of a hard drive.

A Track

Track Sector

Disk Sector

Platters

FIGURE 2.2   The layout of a hard drive

A **cylinder** is the same track number on each platter, spanning all platters in a hard drive. **Disk geometry** refers to the structure of a hard disk in terms of platters, tracks, and sectors. The capacity of a hard disk drive can be calculated using the following formula:

Number of cylinders × Number of heads × Number of sectors × Number of bytes per sector

Therefore, an HDD with 16,383 cylinders and 16 heads and 63 sectors (512 bytes per sector) is calculated thus:

= 16,383 × 16 × 63 × 512

= 8,455,200,768 bytes, or 8GB (8 gigabytes)

A gigabyte can be quantified as 10^9. See Table 2.2 for a byte conversion table.

TABLE 2.2 Byte Conversion Table

Name	Symbol	Value
Kilobyte	KB	10^3
Megabyte	MB	10^6
Gigabyte	GB	10^9
Terabyte	TB	10^{12}
Petabyte	PB	10^{15}
Exabyte	EB	10^{18}

Paging

Virtual memory is a feature of most operating systems, including Windows. When we think of virtual memory we often think about RAM (Random Access Memory). Many new computers come with configurations of 4GB/8GB/16GB/32GB/64GB/128GB of RAM. In terms of speed and efficiency, RAM is far superior to a hard disk drive, yet it is expensive and comparatively much smaller in size. Therefore, when there are numerous applications running simultaneously, RAM requirements can exceed what is physically available and therefore a solution is required to expand virtual memory. Thus, the Windows operating system facilitates the use of the hard drive to extend the functionality of RAM. The **page file** is the area on a hard disk that stores an image of RAM. **Pagefile.sys** stores frames of data that have been swapped from RAM to the hard disk.

Let's Get Practical!

How to View Settings for the Pagefile.sys

1. Find a computer running Windows 10, which you have permission to use.

2. Press the ⊞ + S and then type `advanced`. **View advanced system settings** will display under **Best match**, as shown in Figure 2.3.

3. Click **View advanced system settings**, and the **System Properties** dialog box will display, as shown in Figure 2.4.

4. On the **Advanced** tab of the **System Properties** dialog box, click the **Settings** button in the **Performance** section to display the options shown in Figure 2.5.

5. In the **Performance Options** dialog box, on the **Advanced** tab, under **Virtual memory**, notice that the **Total paging file size** is displayed, as shown in Figure 2.6.

It is recommended that you do not change or meddle with the Pagefile.sys and its settings. Page files have a .*SWP* file extension.

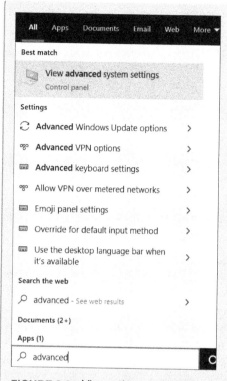

FIGURE 2.3   View advanced system settings

FIGURE 2.4   System Properties dialog box

FIGURE 2.5 Performance Options dialog box

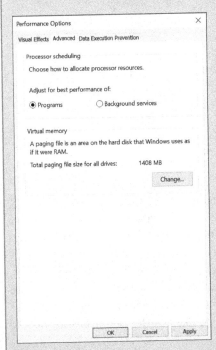

FIGURE 2.6 Performance Options dialog box with paging file size

RAM, Pagefile.sys, or any type of virtual memory, is invaluable to investigators given that it may contain information about running processes, passwords, and Web browsing artifacts. Given that live memory forensics is a critical part of incident response, RAM and Pagefile.sys will be covered in more detail in Chapter 8, "Network Forensics and Incident Response".

File Conversion and Numbering Formats

Computer forensics investigators need to be able to convert between different numbering formats because the forensics software that we use displays system and user data in different formats. Moreover, some files or data on a computer are in a format like binary, and you might need to convert that data before you can interpret it as information.

Conversion of Binary to Decimal

Binary is the language that computers understand. Binary is comprised of bits. **Bits** can only be one of two values, where a 1 is a positive charge and a 0 is a negative charge. Binary can be easily converted to decimal with a scientific calculator. However, we can use Table 2.3 to convert the following binary number: 1011 1111.

TABLE 2.3   Binary-to-Decimal Conversion Example

Binary	1	0	1	1	1	1	1	1
Base 2	2^7	2^6	2^5	2^4	2^3	2^2	2^1	2^0
Total	128	64	32	16	8	4	2	1

$$= (1 \times 128) + (0 \times 64) + (1 \times 32) + (1 \times 16) + (1 \times 8) + (1 \times 4) + (1 \times 2) + (1 \times 1)$$

$$= 128 + 0 + 32 + 16 + 8 + 4 + 2 + 1$$

$$= 191$$

Hexadecimal Numbering

Hexadecimal is yet another numbering system that can be found in forensics software tools, like FTK or X-Ways. An investigator sometimes comes across binary files on a computer and may need to use a hex editor to read the content or may perhaps convert the file to an ASCII format. Some configuration files, for example, are in a binary format. As we mentioned, binary uses 2 symbols (0,1). Decimal uses 10 symbols (0 to 9). **Hexadecimal** is a numbering system that uses 16 symbols (base 16), which includes numbers 0 to 9 and letters A to F. It is necessary to understand hexadecimal because most computer forensics imaging software includes a hex editor. A **hex editor** enables a forensics examiner to view the entire contents of a file. Some hex editors, like WinHex, allow investigators to manipulate hex values, which can be helpful in making unreadable files readable. Table 2.4 illustrates the conversion from binary to decimal to hexadecimal.

TABLE 2.4 Hexadecimal Conversion Table

Binary	Decimal	Hexadecimal
0000	00	0
0001	01	1
0010	02	2
0011	03	3
0100	04	4
0101	05	5
0110	06	6
0111	07	7
1000	08	8
1001	09	9
1010	10	A
1011	11	B
1100	12	C
1101	13	D
1110	14	E
1111	15	F

Conversion of Hexadecimal to Decimal

A **nibble** is one digit of a hexadecimal (hex) value, which represents 4 bits. Therefore, 7DA2 represents 2 bytes (4 bits × 4 = 16 bits, or 2 bytes). To differentiate hexadecimal numbers from other numbers, we use *0x* before hex numbers. To convert 0x7DA2 to decimal, we can use Table 2.5.

TABLE 2.5 Conversion of 7DA2 to Decimal

Hex	7	D	A	2
Conversion	7	13	10	2
Base 16	16^3	16^2	16^1	16^0
Total	4,096	256	16	1

$$= (7 \times 4{,}096) + (13 \times 256) + (10 \times 16) + (2 \times 1)$$

$$= 28{,}672 + 3{,}328 + 160 + 2$$

$$= 32{,}162$$

Conversion of Hexadecimal to ASCII

Knowing how to convert hex to ASCII (American Standard Code for Information Interchange) is more important than converting hex to decimal. Table 2.6 outlines the conversion of hexadecimal to ASCII.

TABLE 2.6   Hexadecimal-to-ASCII Conversion Table

ASCII	Hex	Symbol	ASCII	Hex	Symbol	ASCII	Hex	Symbol
0	00	NUL	43	2B	+	86	56	V
1	01	SOH	44	2C	,	87	57	W
2	02	STX	45	2D	-	88	58	X
3	03	ETX	46	2E	.	89	59	Y
4	04	EOT	47	2F	/	90	5A	Z
5	05	ENQ	48	30	0	91	5B	[
6	06	ACK	49	31	1	92	5C	\
7	07	BEL	50	32	2	93	5D	]
8	08	BS	51	33	3	94	5E	^
9	09	TAB	52	34	4	95	5F	_
10	0A	LF	53	35	5	96	60	`
11	0B	VT	54	36	6	97	61	a
12	0C	FF	55	37	7	98	62	b
13	0D	CR	56	38	8	99	63	c
14	0E	SO	57	39	9	100	64	d
15	0F	SI	58	3A	:	101	65	e
16	10	DLE	59	3B	;	102	66	f
17	11	DC1	60	3C	<	103	67	g
18	12	DC2	61	3D	=	104	68	h
19	13	DC3	62	3E	>	105	69	i
20	14	DC4	63	3F	?	106	6A	j
21	15	NAK	64	40	@	107	6B	k
22	16	SYN	65	41	A	108	6C	l
23	17	ETB	66	42	B	109	6D	m
24	18	CAN	67	43	C	110	6E	n
25	19	EM	68	44	D	111	6F	o
26	1A	SUB	69	45	E	112	70	p
27	1B	ESC	70	46	F	113	71	q
28	1C	FS	71	47	G	114	72	r
29	1D	GS	72	48	H	115	73	s
30	1E	RS	73	49	I	116	74	t
31	1F	US	74	4A	J	117	75	u

ASCII	Hex	Symbol	ASCII	Hex	Symbol	ASCII	Hex	Symbol
32	20	(space)	75	4B	K	118	76	v
33	21	!	76	4C	L	119	77	w
34	22	"	77	4D	M	120	78	x
35	23	#	78	4E	N	121	79	y
36	24	$	79	4F	O	122	7A	z
37	25	%	80	50	P	123	7B	{
38	26	&	81	51	Q	124	7C		
39	27	'	82	52	R	125	7D	}
40	28	(	83	53	S	126	7E	~
41	29	)	84	54	T	127	7F	
42	2A	*	85	55	U			

Some of the symbols in Table 2.6 are not intuitive. For example, in Table 2.6, Hex 10 has a symbol of DLE (Data Link Escape). **Data Link Escape** is a communications control character that specifies that the proceeding character is not data but rather a control code. A **control character** begins, modifies, or terminates a computer operation and is not a written or printable symbol. The first 32 codes in Table 2.6 are control characters. Another example from Table 2.6 is the symbol ACK (Hex: 06), which is a transmission control character affirmation (or acknowledgment) that a transmission was received.

Many free hex converters are available online. We use Table 2.7 here to convert the sentence Hi there!

TABLE 2.7 Conversion of Hi there! to Hex

ASCII	H	i		t	h	e	r	e	!
Hex	48	69	20	74	68	65	72	65	21

Let's Get Practical!

Download and Use a Hex Editor

Many different hex editors are available, and most computer forensics tools include one. Hex Workshop is a hex editor created and distributed by BreakPoint Software. A free download of the tool is available from www.hexworkshop.com. Download the software and then go through the following steps:

1. Start the Hex Workshop application.
2. Click **File** and then click **Open**.
3. Navigate to your student data files and open the file Introduction to Operating Systems.doc.

The file opens in the hex editor window.

4. Using the scrollbar, scroll down until you see the ASCII text display (see Figure 2.7).

FIGURE 2.7   The ASCII text display

5. Scroll all the way to the bottom of the file to the file type and version, as shown in Figure 2.8. In the hex editor, the zeros (00) denote the file slack.

6. **Exit** Hex Workshop.

FIGURE 2.8   The file slack

Using Hex to Identify a File Type

The file header identifies the type of file you are examining. This is important because if a suspect tries to hide a file by changing its extension, it probably will not open from File Explorer, but forensic tools will generally display the file even if the file extension has been manually changed. The hex value for a particular file type often remains consistent, as you can see in Table 2.8.

TABLE 2.8 Conversion of Hex to File Type

File Type	Hex Value	ASCII Value
Excel (.xls)	D0 CF 11 E0	
JPEG	FF D8 FF E1	
JPEG	FF D8 FF E0	JFIF
JPEG	FF D8 FF FE	JFIF
PPT	D0 CF 11 E0	
PDF	25 50 44 46	%PDF
Word (.doc)	D0 CF 11 E0	
ZIP	50 4B 03 04	PK

Unicode

Frequently, an investigator comes across the term *Unicode* and should understand what the term means. **Unicode** is an international encoding standard that supports various languages and scripts from across the world. For example, the Cyrillic alphabet, used in the Russian language, and Arabic script are supported by Unicode. This means that computers today have broader appeal because they support regional characters. Each letter, character, or digit is assigned a unique number. Unicode can be found in operating systems and in certain programming languages.

Operating Systems

An **operating system** is a set of programs used to control and manage a computer's hardware and system resources. Forensic software tools display many different files from the operating system, on a suspect's or victim's computer. Therefore, investigators must know how to recognize these files. Moreover, a user's interaction with a computer is often evident through an examination of the operating system. When a user starts (or "boots") a computer or inserts a CD, the computer's operating system records these events.

The Boot Process

The **kernel** is at the core of the operating system and is responsible for communication between applications and hardware devices, including memory and disk management. When a computer is powered on, the computer executes code stored in ROM, referred to as the BIOS. The **Basic Input/Output System (BIOS)** starts an operating system by recognizing and initializing system devices, including the hard drive, CD-ROM drive, keyboard, mouse, video card, and other devices. **Bootstrapping** is the process of running a small piece of code to activate other parts of the operating system during the boot process. The bootstrap process is often contained in the ROM chip. **Read-only memory (ROM)** is non-volatile storage that is generally not modified and is used during the boot process. In some computers, UEFI has replaced the BIOS in personal computers. **Unified Extensible Firmware Interface (UEFI)** is software that links a computer's firmware to the operating system. Thus, the boot process is different on computers installed with UEFI instead of a traditional BIOS.

In many examinations, a computer forensics investigator removes the suspect's hard drive, and that hard drive is then cloned or imaged. It is important for the investigator to also document information about the system and its specifications. Therefore, the investigator will power on the computer, with the hard drive removed, to prevent changes to the hard drive.

Remember that a user might have password-protected the BIOS, which can cause problems for the investigator. However, some solutions are available on the Internet to deal with BIOS passwords.

Let's Get Practical!

View the BIOS

1. Press the **power** button to start your computer.

During an actual investigation, the hard drive would have already been disconnected and removed from the computer.

2. Press the **F2** button on your keyboard several times to prevent the BIOS from loading.

On some computers, F4 is the function key that stops the BIOS from loading. Another key also might be used to access the BIOS.

3. Use the **down arrow** key to scroll down to the **BIOS**. Compare your screen with Figure 2.9.

The sequence of how the input/output devices are initialized is listed on your screen.

4. Press the **power** button once to shut down your computer.

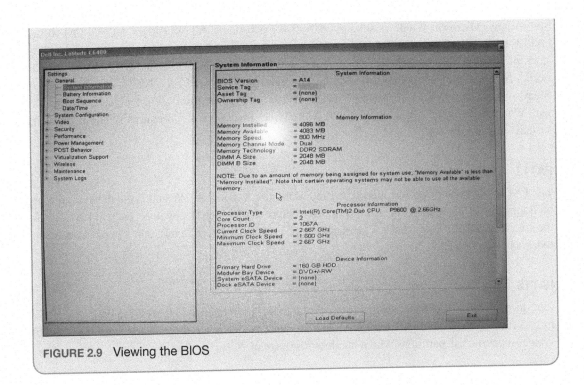

FIGURE 2.9 Viewing the BIOS

Master Boot Record (MBR)

The first sector on a hard disk (Sector 0) is known as the Master Boot Record. The **Master Boot Record (MBR)** is involved in the boot process and stores information about the partitions on a disk, including how many exist and their locations. A floppy disk has no MBR because the first sector on a floppy disk is the boot sector. When a computer is powered on and the BIOS initiates the boot process, the BIOS always looks at Sector 0 for instructions on how to load the operating system. The MBR is comprised of the Master Partition Table, Master Boot Code, and Disk Signature. The **Master Partition Table** contains descriptions about the partitions on a hard disk. There is only enough room in this table for four descriptions, so there is a maximum of four physical partitions on a hard drive. If a user wants to create an additional partition, then it must be a logical partition with a link to a primary partition (physical partition). The BIOS uses the **Master Boot Code** to start the boot process. The **Disk Signature** identifies the disk to the operating system. The **End of Sector Marker** is a two-byte structure found at the end of the MBR.

Windows File Systems

Windows is a series of operating systems with a graphical user interface (GUI), developed by Microsoft. This GUI was introduced in 1985 in response to the highly successful Macintosh (Mac) GUI, which was released in 1984. Although Apple's macOS continues to grow in market share, Windows is still the dominant operating system worldwide.

Surprisingly, Microsoft Windows supports only five file systems: NTFS, FAT64, FAT32, FAT16, and FAT12. **FAT (File Allocation Table)** is a file system developed by Microsoft that utilizes a table to store information about where files are stored, where file space is available, and where files cannot be stored. **NTFS (New Technology File System)** subsequently replaced FAT. NTFS was developed by Microsoft and introduced with Windows NT. NTFS is the primary file system that has been included with Windows since the advent of Windows 2000. Windows 2000 and subsequent Windows operating systems still support FAT.

FAT12

The **FAT12** file system was introduced in 1980 as the first version of FAT and is the file system found on floppy disks. Initially, FAT12 was developed to support 5.25-inch floppy disks but was later used for the smaller 1.44MB floppy disks. Practically every operating system running on a personal computer today still supports FAT12.

FAT16

Introduced in 1987, **FAT16** is a 16-bit file system that was developed for use with MS-DOS. Filenames in FAT16 are limited to eight characters, and the file extensions are three characters long. This file system supports disk partitions with a maximum storage of 2GB.

FAT32

FAT32 is a 32-bit version of FAT that uses smaller clusters, thereby allowing for a more efficient utilization of space. The operating system determines the cluster sizes. This file system was introduced with Windows 95 and has a maximum file size of 4GB.

FAT64

The **FAT64** file system, also referred to as exFAT (Extended File Allocation Table), was developed by Microsoft. This file system was introduced with Vista Windows Service Pack 1, Windows Embedded CE 6.0, and Windows 7 operating systems. Interestingly, macOS, like Snow Leopard (10.6.5), can recognize exFAT partitions. Therefore, it is a practical file system to use when transferring files from a personal computer (running Windows) to a Mac. However, this file system does not possess the security or journaling features found in NTFS.

FATX

FATX is a file system developed for use on the hard drive of Microsoft's Xbox video game console, as well as any associated memory cards. It is worth mentioning the FATX file system because computer forensics investigators have found incriminating evidence on video game consoles. Nevertheless, the FATX file system cannot be viewed natively on a Windows PC.

NTFS (New Technology File System)

NTFS is the latest file system developed by Microsoft for use with Windows operating systems. Unlike FAT, NTFS supports advanced file encryption and compression. **File compression** allows the user to reduce the number of bits in a file, which allows for faster transmission of a file. NTFS also supports a 16-bit Unicode character set for filenames and folders, which has more international appeal. File and folder names can also have spaces and use printable characters (except for "/\:<>|"?). NTFS added security to its file system with the introduction of access control lists. An **access control list** is a list of permissions associated with a file and details the users and programs granted access to the file. A forensic examiner should know who has access to certain files. NTFS files also have potentially negative implications for an investigator because of the potential for encryption. NTFS files can be very large, with a maximum file size of 16EB (16×1024^6 bytes).

Unlike its predecessor FAT32, NTFS also utilizes journaling. **Journaling** is a form of file system recordkeeping that records changes made to files in a journal. The **journal** uses tracked changes to files for fast and efficient restoration of files when a system failure or power outage occurs. The NTFS log, with the filename $LogFile, records these changes.

NTFS maintains an update sequence number (USN) change journal. Prior to Windows Vista, this feature was not available by default. Whenever a change is made to a file or directory on a volume, the $UsnJrnl file is updated with a description of the change and the corresponding file or directory. Thus, the NTFS journal can be tremendously important for incident responders seeking to identify changes to files and directories on a volume. Here is a summary of the types of changes that are recorded:

- Time of change
- Reason for the change
- File/directory's name
- File/directory's attributes
- File/directory's MFT record number
- File record number of the file's parent directory
- Security ID
- Update Sequence Number of the record
- Information about the source of the change

The $UsnJrnl file is also used to recover indexing after a computer or drive failure. The actual location of the change journal can be found at $Extend\$UsnJrnl, and the actual journal entries can be retrieved from the $UsnJrnl:$J alternate data stream. When a NTFS file/directory is added, deleted, or modified, these changes are entered in streams.

NTFS also introduced alternate data streams into the file system. An **alternate data stream (ADS)** is a file's set of attributes. NTFS allows files to have multiple data streams that can be viewed only by accessing the Master File Table. For example, Windows File Explorer details a music file's logical path in a file system. However, the media provider might also use an additional data stream to update information about the album that the music file is derived from or associate the music file with an existing music download from the same artist. Hackers can use alternate data streams to hide data, including rootkits associated with viruses. Therefore, it is important for investigators to know about ADS.

Table 2.9 provides a summary of Windows file system features.

TABLE 2.9   Windows File System Comparison

File System	Year Introduced	Max File Size	Max Filename Length	Max Volume Size	Access Control Lists	Alternate Data Streams	Encrypting File System	Journaling
FAT12	1980	4GB	255B	32MB	No	No	No	No
FAT16	1987	4GB	255B	2GB	No	No	No	No
FAT32	1996	4GB	255B	2TB or 8TB or 16TB	No	No	No	No
FAT64	2006	16EB	255B	64ZB	Yes	No	No	No
NTFS	1993	16EB	255B	8PB*	Yes	Yes	Yes	Yes

Windows 10

Master File Table

In NTFS, the **Master File Table (MFT)** maintains file and folder metadata in NTFS, including the filename, creation date, location, size, and permissions for every file and folder. Other file properties, like compression or encryption, are found in the MFT. The MFT also tracks when files are deleted and indicates that the space can be reallocated.

Every file/directory on an NTFS volume has a file record in the MFT, and the default size for each of these entries is 1024 bytes. The MFT header accounts for the initial 42 bytes of the record, and the remaining bytes are dedicated to attributes. Attributes can be either resident (content stored in the MFT record) or non-resident (content stored in external clusters).

Timestamps are an important part of NTFS metadata. It is important to understand that these timestamps can be manipulated or simply wrong. Therefore, using corroborating time and date information is a necessary protocol to follow. Sometimes malware can overwrite timestamps, which creates a challenge for an investigator seeking to craft a timeline from a suspect's PC. However, the $MFT file contains two sets of timestamps for files/directories: Standard Information (SIA) and Filename Attribute (FNA). While the SIA may have been altered, the FNA may not, and therefore comparing the two timestamps is important to determine if a change was made.

Table 2.10 details the NTFS system filenames, functions, and locations.

TABLE 2.10 NTFS System Files

Position	Filename	Function
0	$MFT	Contains one file record for each file and directory on the volume.
1	$MFTMirr	A duplicate of the first four entries of the MFT.
2	$LogFile	Tracks metadata changes. It is used for system restoration.
3	$Volume	Contains information about the volume, including the file system version and volume label.
4	$AttrDef	Records file attributes and numeric identifiers.
5	$	The root directory.
6	$Bitmap	Indicates which clusters are used and which are free and available to allocate.
7	$Boot	Contains the bootstrapping code.
8	$BadClus	Lists clusters that have errors that are unusable.
9	$Secure	The ACL database.
10	$UpCase	Converts uppercase characters to lowercase Unicode.
11	$Extend	Contains optional extensions, such as $Quota or $Reparse.
12...23	$MFT extension entries	

Let's Get Practical!

Use FTK Imager

FTK Imager is a professional computer forensics bit-stream imaging tool that is available for free.

1. Find a personal computer running Microsoft Windows.

2. Go to https://accessdata.com/product-download and download *FTK Imager*. Once it is downloaded, start FTK Imager.

3. Click **File** and then, from the displayed menu, click **Add Evidence Item**.

4. In the displayed **Select Source** dialog box, verify that **Physical Drive** is selected and click **Next**.

Clicking the down arrow displays the different physical drives available to be imaged.

5. With **\\.\PHYSICALDRIVE0...** selected, click **Finish**. Compare your screen with Figure 2.10.

Notice that \\.\PHYSICALDRIVE0 was added to the Evidence Tree.

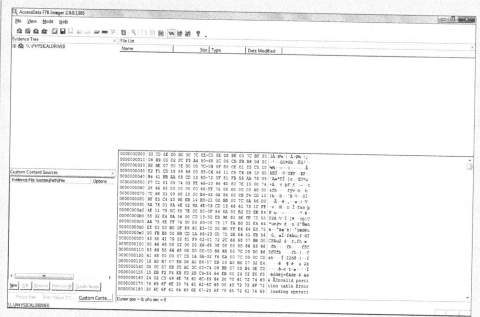

FIGURE 2.10 Adding the drive to the Evidence Tree

6. Click the \\.\PHYSICALDRIVE0 ⊞ (see Figure 2.11).

Your screen will be slightly different, based on the number of partitions on your system.

7. Click **Partition 1** and then compare your screen with Figure 2.12.

Notice that the name of the file system (NTFS) is displayed in the hex editor.

8. In the first row of the hex editor, using your mouse, highlight the values **4E 54 46 53**. Compare your screen with Figure 2.13.

Notice that NTFS is highlighted on the right.

9. Using Table 2.6, verify that 4E 54 46 53 does translate to NTFS.

10. Click the Partition 1 ⊞, and then click the **[root]** directory.

FIGURE 2.11 Expand button

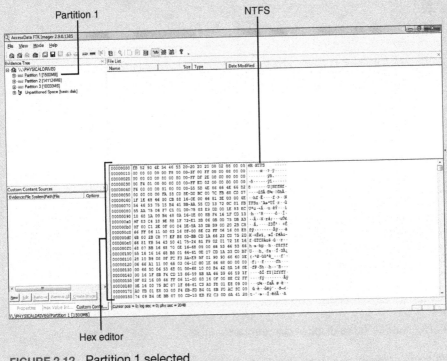

FIGURE 2.12 Partition 1 selected

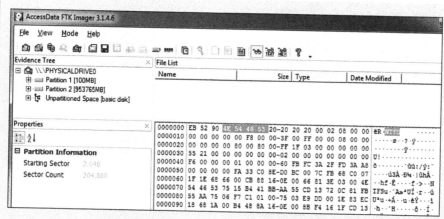

FIGURE 2.13   NTFS highlighted

11. In the **File List**, scroll down to see all the files. Click **$MFT**, and then compare your screen with Figure 2.14.

Notice that the hex editor displays the first entry in $MFT as FILE0.

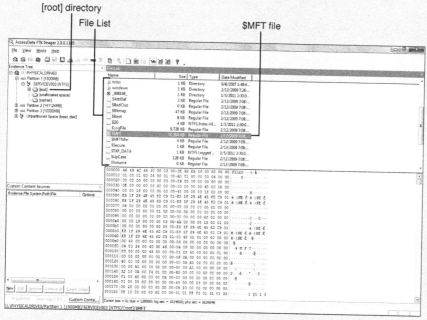

FIGURE 2.14   Master File Table displayed in the hex editor

12. Explore some of the other system files. Exit FTK Imager.

Prefetch Files

Introduced with Windows XP, **Prefetch files** contain information about an application (executable), how many times it has been run, and when it was run. The purpose of Prefetch is to increase performance with the application startup process. From a forensics perspective, an investigator can examine Prefetch files to determine what applications were run and when they were run. For example, this information might dertermine a program that was installed and run to remove incriminating evidence files from a system. The Registry key for Prefetch can be found here:

```
HKEY_LOCAL_MACHINE\SYSTEM\CurrentControlSet\Control\Session Manager\Memory Manage-
ment\PrefetchParameters
```

Prefetch files are stored here:

```
<Root>/Windows/Prefetch
```

A Prefetch file contains the name of the executable, the run count (number of times the program has run), volume path and serial number, size of the Prefetch file, and files and directories associated with a particular executable. This is important because an incident responder could see a known file execute from a temp folder instead of the recognized Windows systems folder.

A Prefetch file will have the extension *.pf*. The Prefetch file will also contain two different timestamps: (1) time that the executable was last run and (2) volume creation time, where the Prefetch file has been saved. From Windows 8 onwards, Prefetch files can maintain up to eight timestamps that indicate when the application was last run. There are a number of applications available that will parse out Prefetch files, including Magnet Forensics' AXIOM and Eric Zimmerman's free PECmd tool. Figure 2.15 shows some examples of Prefetch files on a PC

PC > Windows (C:) > Windows > Prefetch

Name	Date modified	Type	Size
ReadyBoot	9/3/2018 10:19 AM	File folder	
7Z.EXE-97CB5A9B	9/13/2018 11:58 AM	PF File	3 KB
7Z1805-X64 (1).EXE-875B3B4A	9/13/2018 11:57 AM	PF File	7 KB
7ZFM.EXE-56DE4F9A	9/13/2018 11:58 AM	PF File	9 KB
7ZG.EXE-F49B3D46	9/13/2018 12:00 PM	PF File	9 KB
69.0.3497.92_68.0.3440.106_CH-B24274F6	9/13/2018 7:28 AM	PF File	17 KB
ADDINUTIL.EXE-38D7B022	9/13/2018 8:07 AM	PF File	17 KB
ADOBEARM.EXE-F9223367	9/9/2018 11:29 AM	PF File	15 KB
ADOBEARMHELPER.EXE-FA58E1EF	9/9/2018 11:29 AM	PF File	10 KB
AgAppLaunch	6/9/2018 9:13 PM	Data Base File	327 KB

FIGURE 2.15   Prefetch files

SuperFetch Files

SuperFetch was introduced with Windows Vista and works with the memory manager service to increase performance by reducing the time required to launch an application. Unlike Prefetch, Super-Fetch analyzes memory usage patterns of executables over time to optimize performance.

SuperFetch data is collected by the Service Host process (`<Root>\System32\Svchost.exe`) and is located here on a Windows computer:

```
<Root>\System32\Sysmain.dll
```

The files are stored in the Prefetch directory, and the beginning of each file contains the prefix `Ag` and ends with a `.db` file extension.

The format of Prefetch files changed with the introduction of Windows 10.

ShellBags

ShellBag information provides user viewing preferences for Microsoft's File Explorer. This information can provide information about the user's sizing and positioning of a folder window on a PC and also tracks information about when folders were viewed by a user. ShellBag information is tracked by the Windows operating system for recovery purposes but, as you can imagine, it can be invaluable to investigators who can prove that a user accessed a particular folder at a particular point in time. Moreover, the information contained in ShellBag keys can assist incident responders because they provide historical information on recently accessed or mounted volumes and deleted folders. Given that ShellBag information relates to user preferences, this information is stored in keys, within the Registry.

If a suspect claims that he was unaware of illicit photographs on his hard drive, then an examination of ShellBag information can show if the suspect did in fact access a specific folder. ShellBag data resides in several Registry hives, and the important information can be found in the following locations:

```
HKEY_USERS\<USERID>\Software\Microsoft\Windows\Shell
HKEY_USERS\<USERID>\Software\Microsoft\Windows\ShellNoRoam
```

ShimCache

ShimCache contains a record of binaries that have executed on a system and also tracks executables that have been viewed through `explorer.exe` that have not been executed. As you can imagine, ShimCache can provide a wealth of evidence for criminal investigators and incident responders. On a Windows XP computer, ShimCache will contain a maximum of 96 entries, while a Windows 7 machine can maintain 1,024 entries. The cache stores file metadata that may include the following:

- File Full Path
- File Size
- Process Execution Flag (in later versions of Windows only)

- ShimCache Last Updated time

- $Standard_Information (SI) Last Modified time

To forensically examine ShimCache, the SYSTEM file, which is located in c:\windows\system32\config, can be imaged, or the Registry file can be exported. On a Windows XP computer, the data structure is stored in the following Registry key:

```
HKLM\CurrentControlSet\Control\Session Manager\AppCompatibility\AppCompatCache
```

In more recent Windows systems, the ShimCache data is stored here:

```
HKLM\SYSTEM\CurrentControlSet\Control\Session Manager\AppCompatCache\AppCompatCache
```

Prefetch files can potentially be found in the Application Compatibility Database (AppCompatCache), which is also extremely important to incident responders, especially in cases involving malware. Amcache.hve (<volume>\Windows\AppCompat\Programs\Amcache.hve) is yet another Registry file that can yield valuable evidence to an incident responder examining malware.

There are a number of tools available for examining ShimCache and arguably the more well-known tool is ShimCacheParser, which was developed Mandiant (now FireEye). When a system is powered off, the data structure is copied to these file registries:

```
HKLM\SYSTEM\CurrentControlSet\Control\Session Manager\AppCompatibility\AppCompatCache
```
or:

```
HKLM\SYSTEM\CurrentControlSet\Control\Session Manager\AppCompatCache\AppCompatCache)
```

ShimCacheParser will find the registry paths and output the content to a .csv file.

Windows Registry

Windows Registry is a hierarchical database that stores system configuration information. It maintains files used to control the operating system's hardware and software and keeps track of the system's users. In terms of evidence, the Windows Registry can provide a wealth of information, including Internet searches, sites visited, passwords, and user activity.

The Registry is comprised of two elements: keys and values. Keys are akin to folders and are easily identified by noting the folder icon. Most keys contain subkeys (or folders). These subkeys can contain multiple subkeys. The Windows Registry has five basic hives, each of which plays an important role.

CAUTION

Do not make any changes to Windows Registry. Changes may cause serious problems, which may require you to reinstall your operating system.

Let's Get Practical!

Explore Windows Registry

For this exercise, find a computer running Windows XP, Window Vista, Windows 7, 8, 9, or 10.

1. Click **Start** and then type **regedit**. If the **User Account Control** dialog box displays, click Yes. Compare your screen with Figure 2.16.

The Registry Editor dialog box displays.

Hives

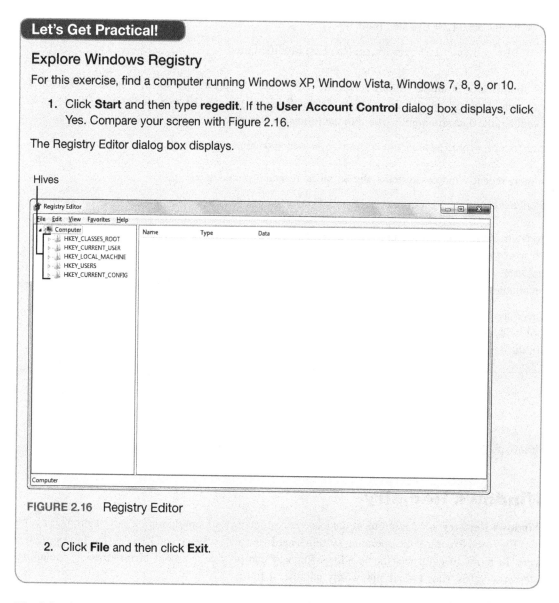

FIGURE 2.16   Registry Editor

2. Click **File** and then click **Exit**.

The following is a detailed explanation of the five major hives in the Registry:

- **HKEY_CLASSES_ROOT (HKCR):** Contains filename extension associations like `.exe`. Also contained in this hive are COM objects, Visual Basic programs, and other automation. The **Component Object Model (COM)** allows nonprogrammers to write scripts for managing Windows operating systems.

- **HKEY_CURRENT_USER (HKCU):** Contains the user profile for the current profile that is logged in to the system when viewed. This profile changes each time the user logs in to the system. A user profile includes desktop settings, network connections, printers, and personal groups. This hive contains very little data but acts as a pointer to HKEY_USERS.

- **HKEY_LOCAL_MACHINE (HKLM):** Contains information about the system's settings, including information about the computer's hardware and operating system.

- **HKEY_USERS (HKU):** Contains information about all of the registered users on a system. Within this hive are a minimum of three keys. The first key is .DEFAULT, which contains a profile when no users are logged in. There is also a key containing the SID for the current local user, which could look something like S-1-5-18. There is also a key for the current user with _Classes at the end—for example, HKEY_USER S\S-1-5-21-3794263289-4294853377-1685327589-1003_Classes.

- **HKEY_CURRENT_CONFIG (HKCC):** Contains information pertaining to the system's hardware that is necessary during the startup process. Within this hive are screen settings, screen resolution, and fonts. Information about the plug-and-play BIOS is also found in this hive.

Registries are an important source of information for an investigator, and the user profile information is invaluable in linking a particular suspect to a machine.

Registry Data Types

The Registry uses several different data types. Figure 2.17 shows two data types. REG_SZ is a fixed-length text string. REG_DWORD is data represented by a 32-bit (4-byte) integer.

FIGURE 2.17 Two of the data types

FTK Registry Viewer

Although the five primary Registry keys are very similar in each version of the Windows operating system, the keys within each hive vary in location. Many forensic tools enable an examiner to export, search, and view the contents of the Registry. AccessData's FTK includes a tool called Registry Viewer that enables the user to access the Registry's encrypted Protected Storage System Provider, which can contain usernames and passwords, Internet searches, and Internet form data.

Microsoft Office

Microsoft Office requires a different license than Microsoft Windows. However, we usually see it installed on a Windows PC and often on an Apple Mac computer. The functionality of Office is slightly different on a Mac, however. Furthermore, Microsoft Access is not available for Mac. Microsoft Office contains the following applications:

- Word
- Excel
- PowerPoint
- Access
- Outlook

While the content of user-created documents can be important to the forensics investigator, the file metadata can be equally important in proving ownership and helping to re-create a sequence of events. Microsoft Office metadata includes the following:

- Title (may be different from the file name)
- Subject
- Author
- Created
- Modified (time and date that file was last saved)
- Accessed (time and date that file was last opened)
- Printed (time and date that file was last printed)
- Last saved by (author who last saved file)
- Revision number (number of times file has been saved)
- Total editing time (number of minutes of editing since file was created)
- Statistics (includes number of characters and words in document)

- Manager
- Company
- Keywords
- Comments
- Hyperlink base (file path or URL to document)
- Template
- Save preview picture (a picture of the first page of the document is saved)

It should be noted that some of this metadata could be manipulated by the user. Therefore, corroborating evidence, like Windows Event Viewer, is critical for a thorough examination.

Microsoft Windows Features

The nature of some forensics evidence will change from one version of an operating system to another. Therefore, an investigator must understand these changes and how these changes will impact the investigation. When Microsoft introduced Windows Vista, it introduced a whole host of changes.

Windows Vista

Microsoft released Vista to the public in November 2006. It was not one of the more popular versions of Windows, given its hardware requirements. This RAM-intensive operating system had a slower response rate to commands than its predecessor, Windows XP.

Microsoft's Vista was a dramatic departure from previous versions of the vendor's operating systems in terms of security and file systems. Microsoft's technical advances in security have created problems for law enforcement and other computer forensics investigators. The proceeding section details the major features that were introduced with this operating system and explores the implications for forensic investigators.

Vista was made available in a 32-bit or 64-bit operating system version. The 32-bit version supported up to 4GB of RAM; the 64-bit version could support a maximum of 128GB.

When examining a computer running Vista, the first NTFS partition begins at Sector 2048. Previously, the first NTFS partition was located at Sector 63. While Microsoft no longer supports security updates for Windows Vista it is important to understand the raft of changes implemented with this operating system; investigators will still encounter unsupported versions of Windows.

Defragmentation in Vista

Defragmentation is the process of eliminating the amount of fragmentation in a file system to make file chunks (512K blocks) closer together (more contiguous) and increase free space areas on a disk.

Fragments of files are not always stored contiguously on a hard drive but are often scattered. This defragmentation process can improve the read/write performance of the file system.

The defragmentation program on Vista is different than in previous versions of Windows. Most importantly, defragmentation in Vista is set to automatically run once a week. We know that some defragmentation occurs periodically in previous versions of Windows, unbeknownst to us. A defragmentation can also be executed manually in Vista, if necessary. Either way, it works in the background at a low priority without a graphical display. Defragmentation can also run from an administrative command prompt.

Why is this important? Its importance stems from the fact that, with the advent of automatic defragmentation, computer forensics investigators will face a significant decrease in evidentiary data.

Let's Get Practical!

Use Disk Defragmenter

1. Find a personal computer running Microsoft Windows Vista or higher.

2. Click **Start** and then, in the search box, type `defrag`.

3. Under Programs, click **Disk Defragmenter** and then compare your screen with Figure 2.18.

In the displayed Disk Defragmenter dialog box, a list of your computer's drives and attached drives will display. Notice that a schedule for defragmentation has already been set up by default.

4. Click **Close**.

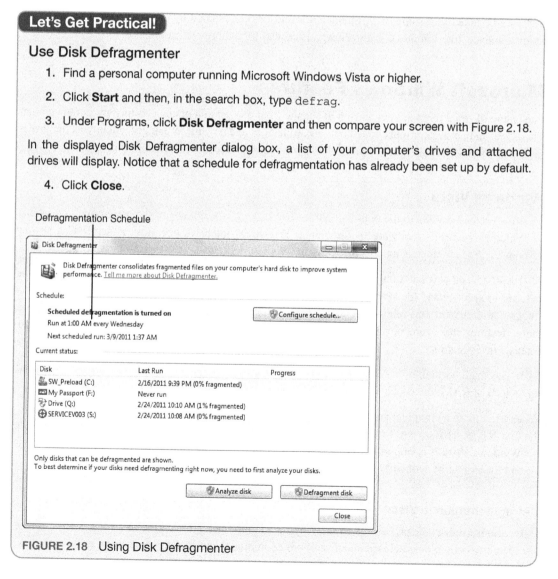

FIGURE 2.18   Using Disk Defragmenter

Event Viewer in Vista

An investigator working the scene of a crime needs to re-create the events that led up to the crime being committed. Moreover, the investigator must prove that certain actions transpired, especially actions that involved the victim(s) and perpetrator(s). The same is true for a computer forensics investigator. One way in which an investigator can reconstruct events is by examining the event logs. An **event** is a communication between one application and another program or user on a computer. **Event Viewer** is a Windows application used to view event logs. An event can include the following occurrences: successful authentication and login of a user on a system, a defragmentation, an instant messaging chat session, or the download of an application. In certain cases, prosecutors have used event logs to demonstrate that a suspect installed an application to remove file registries or Internet activity, in an effort to tamper with evidence after receiving a subpoena.

Let's Get Practical!

Use Event Viewer

1. Find a personal computer running Microsoft Windows Vista or higher.

2. Click **Start** and then, in the search box, type `event.`

3. Under Programs, click **Event Viewer**. If necessary, maximize the **Event Viewer** dialog box, and then compare your screen with Figure 2.19.

In the displayed Event Viewer dialog box, notice the **Overview and Summary** window in the center of your screen.

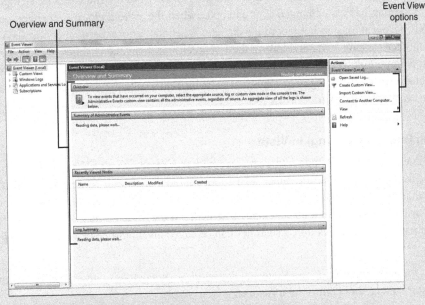

Overview and Summary

Event View options

FIGURE 2.19 The Event Viewer

4. Click **File** and then click **Exit**.

The Event Viewer on computers running Windows Vista or later is noticeably different from previous versions of the application. The GUI changed and included a preview pane for a selected event located beneath the event list. Event logs now have a `.evtx` extension and are in an XML format. **XML (Extensible Markup Language)** is a standardized language that is compatible for use on the Internet. These event logs, found in `C:\Windows\System32\winevt\Logs\`, can be viewed using Windows Event Viewer. When you click the Start button on your Windows machine, simply type `eventvwr` to access the application. Because Vista event logs are XML based, an investigator can simplify searches of event logs by using **XPath (XML Path Language)**, a powerful query language used for searching XML documents. XPath queries can be executed through the Event Log command-line interface or through a user interface in Event Viewer.

Prior to Windows Vista, event logging had issues dealing with an expanding Event Log. More memory is available in more recent versions of Windows. In fact, a greater array of attributes, associated with each event log, is available. Prior to Vista, only two attributes for each event were available: `EventID` and `Category`. More recent versions of Windows provide the following attributes: `event time`, `process ID`, `thread ID`, `computer name`, and `security identifier (SID)` of the user, along with the `EventID`, `Level`, `Task`, `Opcode`, and `Keywords` properties. As mentioned in Chapter 1, "The Scope of Digital Forensics", associating a user with actions on a computer is particularly important when demonstrating control. Therefore, the SID is significant if multiple users, each using a different login and password, are using a system.

Event logging has been around since Windows NT. However, the structure of the event logs has undergone significant changes in recent versions of Windows. Not only has the file structure changed, but the actual event logging has also changed. For example, when the system clock is changed on a machine running XP, the event logs do not record the change. When the same experiment is carried out with a personal computer running Vista and above, the Event Viewer notes the changes to the system clock. Therefore, it is important to understand that Windows operating systems will have major variations from version to version. Event logging is not just valuable on the client side, but it can provide important evidence on Windows servers.

Windows Search Engine (Indexing) in Vista

The Windows search engine and indexing feature changed with the introduction of Vista. Indexing has existed in Windows for more than a decade. Since Vista, indexing in Windows is turned on by default, which is different than in previous versions. The indexing feature allows for searches of numerous file types and can locate files based on their metadata, text within a file, or even files within a file (for example, an attachment to an email). A user's searches can be saved and could be of value later to the investigator.

The default settings for indexing in Windows Vista and newer are advantageous to investigators seeking to ascertain ownership, intent, and control by a suspect.

ReadyBoost and Physical Memory in Vista

ReadyBoost is a tool first introduced with Vista that allows a user to extend a system's virtual memory through the use of a USB drive. The purpose of ReadyBoost is to make a computer and its processes run faster. When attaching a USB drive, the option to run ReadyBoost displays (see Figure 2.20).

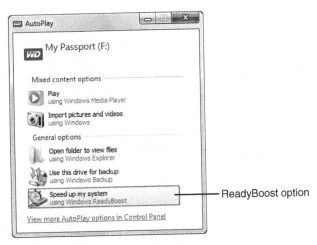

FIGURE 2.20   AutoPlay dialog box

Note that when ReadyBoost has been activated, any data stored on the USB device has been encrypted with AES-128 encryption. **Advanced Encryption Standard (AES)** is an encryption standard used by the U.S. government.

ReadyBoost is an important feature for an examiner to be cognizant of, especially because USB memory has become so pervasive in recent times that it can now be used as an extension of a system's volatile memory, and the file footprint for a USB drive has changed with Vista.

File Metadata

As mentioned, file metadata is an important element of digital evidence. In Vista, when a file is opened, the last access date is not updated, which was the case with previous versions of Windows. As previously noted, dates are a significant source of information for investigators. For example, it is not enough to simply find contraband images stored on the computer of a suspect facing child endangerment charges. The prosecution must also demonstrate intent, with accurate information pertaining to file access times.

Volume Shadow Copy Service

Volume Shadow Copy Service is a backup infrastructure for volumes that was developed by Microsoft for Windows XP and Windows Server 2003. Two types of shadow copy exist: (1) a complete copy or clone of the volume and (2) copies only of the changes to the volume. Two data images are created with the original volume, which has read-write capabilities, and the shadow copy volume, which is read-only. Changes at the block level are found in the System Volume Information folder. We will provide more practical uses of Volume Shadow Copy (VSC) later in the book when we discuss network forensics and incident response in Chapter 8, "Network Forensics and Incident Response".

Hyberfil.sys

The Hiberfil.sys is a file that contains a copy of the contents of RAM and is saved to a computer's hard drive when the computer goes into hibernate mode. Because the Hyberfil.sys file is a mirror image of the contents of RAM, the size of this file is generally equal to the size of the computer's RAM. When the computer is restarted, the contents of Hiberfil.sys are reloaded into RAM.

Remember that RAM can be of great importance to a forensic investigator because it often contains Internet searches, a history of websites visited, and other valuable evidence. This file is found in the root directory of the drive where the operating system is installed.

Vista Summary

Windows Vista can be viewed as more problematic for investigations involving the use of digital evidence. The problems encountered are mainly a result of enhancements made to encryption, through Vista's Encrypted File System (EFS), BitLocker Drive Encryption with Trusted Platform Module (TPM), and electronic mail encryption in Windows Mail. It appears that Microsoft has sought to remove the user from many housekeeping tasks associated with operating systems, such as file restoration and defragmentation. On the one hand, shadow copy and file restoration features are beneficial to examiners. On the other hand, the introduction of automatic defragmentation poses new problems for data recovery.

Windows 7

Windows 7 is no longer supported by Microsoft. Nevertheless, it is worth discussing since an investigator may still encounter this operating system. Windows 7 was released to the public in July 2009. The 32-bit version requires a minimum of 1GB of RAM, and the 64-bit version requires a minimum of 2GB of RAM. For most 32-bit versions of Windows 7, there is a physical memory (RAM) limit of 4GB.

The changes in Windows 7 are not as great as the changes that emerged with Windows Vista. Nevertheless, Microsoft has embraced changes in our technical environment that are manifested through advances in biometric authentication, file backups, and consumer growth in removable memory and touch-screen computing. Arguably, the greatest challenges Windows 7 poses include file backups to networks, encryption of USB devices using BitLocker To Go, and touch-screen computing. Changes to the operating system's registries are also noteworthy to computer forensics examiners because the locations for many of these files have changed.

Biometrics

Connecting a criminal suspect with incriminating evidence is a challenge in computer forensics. The investigator must be able to prove that a suspect had control of a computer when files were created, accessed, modified, or deleted. The use of biometric authentication when accessing a system is one way in which a prosecutor can link a suspect to a series of events and the associated digital footprint left by the suspect. Biometric authentication is different in Windows 7 with the introduction of Windows Biometric Framework (WBF). Previous versions of the Windows operating system worked with fingerprint devices; the vendor was required to provide its own drivers, software development kits (SDKs), and applications. Windows 7 provides native support for fingerprint biometric devices through WBF, which was not a feature of its predecessor, Microsoft Vista.

JumpLists

Introduced with Windows 7, **JumpLists** are a Windows taskbar feature that allows the user to quickly access recently used files or actions. A Windows user can also configure JumpList settings based on personal preferences. From a forensics perspective, JumpLists can be parsed, and the evidence from this artifact can be used to determine how an individual interacted with a system's files. The JumpList files can be accessed here:

```
\Users\<username>\AppData\Roaming\Microsoft\Windows\Recent\
```

When a user opens an application or a file, information about that activity can be found here:

```
\Users\<username>\AppData\Roaming\Microsoft\Windows\Recent\AutomaticDestinations-ms
```

There is an application ID (AppID) associated with each file. For example, d00655d2aa12ff6d is the AppID for Microsoft Office PowerPoint x64, and a0d6b1b874c6e9d2 is the AppID for the Tor Browser 6.0.2.

When a user "pins" a file to the taskbar or Start menu, the file can be found here:

```
\Users\<username>\AppData\Roaming\Microsoft\Windows\Recent\CustomDestinations-ms
```

Backup and Restore Center

It is well documented that bit-stream imaging tools like Autopsy, FTK, EnCase, and X-Ways can retrieve files that have been marked for deletion. If a file cannot be recovered or can be only partially recovered, a computer forensics investigator might resort to searching for backup copies of files. Therefore, it is important to understand changes to the backup and restoration of files in Windows 7. Most importantly, this operating system supports backups to a shared network space or to an external drive.

The Windows Backup and Restore Center (see Figure 2.21) can be accessed through the Start menu search feature or through the Control Panel. The Backup and Restore Center displays the drive selected to be your backup, available memory, the space being utilized by Windows Backup, and whether a backup is currently running. You can view the breakdown of space utilization by choosing Manage

Space from the main Backup and Restore window. Windows 7 Backup gives you access to previous system image files marked for deletion and shows exactly how much space each of its backup components is using. After the first backup, the tool copies only the changed bits in files. The tool also provides a comprehensive view of the space required to make available for the backup.

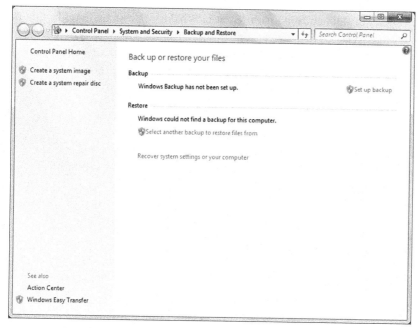

FIGURE 2.21   The Backup and Restore Center

Windows Vista replaced the tape-oriented Windows NT Backup Wizard with a new backup system optimized for external hard disks; some editions also included disaster recovery. However, Vista's Backup and Restore Center was missing some functionality, including the inability to create a recovery environment disc to boot your system. File and folder backup, in addition to system image backup, were performed with different programs. Moreover, Home Premium users who needed an image backup were required to purchase a third-party program. Windows 7 builds on features developed in Windows Vista's backup and addresses the aforementioned shortcomings.

Microsoft's goal with Windows 7 Backup and Restore was to provide usable image and file backup services for users of external hard disks, DVD drives, and network shares without third-party solutions. Unlike Windows Vista, Windows 7 uses a single backup operation to perform both file and image backup. Every edition of Windows 7 includes file and image backup support. Unlike Windows XP, Windows 7 provides disaster recovery, without requiring the reinstallation of the operating system first.

Windows 7 Backup is designed to use the advanced features of NTFS, which is the default file system used by Windows XP, Vista, and Windows 7. When you use an NTFS-formatted drive as a backup target, you can create scheduled backups that record changes to the system image and changes to individual files. Moreover, Windows 7 Backup backs up only NTFS-formatted drives. Windows 7 does not include the Removable Storage Service (RSS) used by NTBackup, the backup tool used in Windows 2000 and XP. However, if the backup does not reside on tape or removable media, the user can copy NTBackup files to the Windows 7 system and run NTBackup to restore files directly to Windows 7.

It is important for computer forensics investigators to understand how files are being backed up because attached devices could contain important evidence and permission to access backup servers. A court-issued warrant could be critical.

Restoration Points

Restoration points have been a feature of Windows operating systems for a number of years. However, there are some changes to this feature in Windows 7. Unlike Windows Vista, Windows 7 provides a few options for configuring the System Restore option. For example, the user can prevent System Restore (see Figure 2.22) from backing up the Registry, meaning that restore points will not consume as much disk space. This has implications for forensic investigators because Registry files are often an important source of evidentiary data in investigations. Furthermore, the user can eliminate all of the restore points by pressing the Delete key, which has the potential to reduce the amount of data available for forensic investigators.

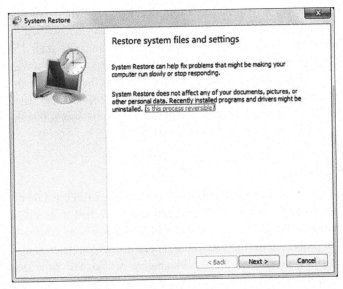

FIGURE 2.22   System Restore

Backing Up to a Network

A computer forensics investigator not only needs to be concerned about backups to external devices but also needs to be cognizant of a system's ability to back up to a network. Windows 7 Starter,

Home Basic, and Home Premium editions only support backups to local drives, whereas Windows 7 Professional, Ultimate, and Enterprise editions also support backups to network locations. Therefore, an investigator must also consider that a system's imaging and analysis could also include external devices and a network. This will certainly impact the scope of an investigator's search warrant.

BitLocker To Go

BitLocker was a tool introduced with Windows Vista. The tool was developed to encrypt at the file and folder level, or even encrypt an entire hard drive. BitLocker To Go is a more advanced tool that debuted in Windows 7. What sets this tool apart from its predecessor is that the encryption tool encrypts removable USB storage devices. Files written to USB devices that are AES encrypted can be decrypted in previous versions of Windows (XP and Vista). XP and Vista provide read-only access until the files are copied to another drive. The application BitLocker To Go Reader (bitlockertogo.exe) allows the investigator to view the files from a USB drive using XP or Vista. Simply removing the USB device activates the encryption, so an examiner needs to be cognizant of this. This has serious implications for computer forensics examiners because the perpetrator of a crime might not have used BitLocker To Go simply to encrypt the hard drive; she also might have encrypted associated removable memory with the same encryption algorithm. A user who wants to encrypt a drive is required to either enter a "strong password" or use a smart card. Windows 7 provides the option to save the recovery key to a file or to print it, which is of note to an investigator.

COFEE (Computer Online Forensic Evidence Extractor) is a tool developed by Microsoft that is made available exclusively to law enforcement to work on systems running BitLocker. According to Microsoft, this "fully customizable tool allows your on-the-scene agents to run more than 150 commands on a live computer system". Microsoft also states that it "provides reports in a simple format for later interpretation by experts or as supportive evidence for subsequent investigation and prosecution." COFEE has also been developed for Windows 7 and is used by law enforcement when working with a system running BitLocker To Go. The major disadvantage with using the tool is that the system must be live and will not work if the suspect has powered down the computer.

Establishing Ownership of a USB Device

Establishing ownership of a USB flash memory device can be critical for a computer forensics investigator. Interestingly, these devices leave a timestamp and other metadata when attached to a system running Windows 7. The metadata includes the unique serial number or identification code originally assigned to the USB device. A record of when the device was last connected to a computer is also recorded in the metadata. However, not all of these devices leave a signature behind. For those that do leave a signature, law enforcement can link the usage of those devices to the suspect's computer. The information about USB devices is stored in the Registry key called HKEY_LOCAL_MACHINE\ System\CurrentControllerSet\Enum\USB. Figure 2.23 displays the contents of this hive.

The contents of this Registry key can be parsed using a freeware utility called USBDeview, which was created by NirSoft (www.nirsoft.net). An examiner can generally determine the device manufacturer through the vendor ID, a unique identifier with the serial number displayed along with the product ID, which identifies the make and model of the device. The tool can also provide information about when the device was last attached to the computer. Figure 2.24 illustrates the various types of USB devices that were connected to a computer using the USBDeview application.

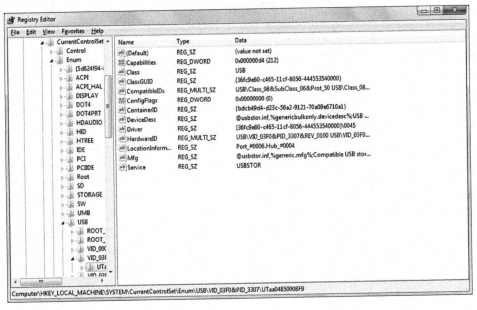

FIGURE 2.23 USB drive information

FIGURE 2.24 USBDeview

Touchscreen Computing in Windows 7

Demand for touchscreen computing has clearly been very strong, and the number of touchscreen devices will continue to grow. From smartphones to the iPhone, touchscreens are pervasive. Interestingly, in April 2007, Microsoft CEO Steve Ballmer stated, "There's no chance that the iPhone is going to get any significant market share." Ballmer had a change of heart in 2009 when he stated, "We believe in touch." This belief was followed by conviction when Microsoft released Windows 7 with integrated touchscreen technology. Previously, touchscreen operating systems in the personal computer market were associated with tablet PCs. Windows 7 operating system supports touchscreen computing natively, allowing the user to move and size application windows, for example, with the use of a touch-enabled screen. The user now has the ability to use an onscreen keyboard to type Internet searches or URLs, or even draw the letters. There is no question that evidence pertaining to Internet communications is extremely important to criminal investigations but integrating new touchscreen features into Windows 7 has noteworthy implications for forensic examiners and prosecutors. Potentially, an investigator will not be able to use a traditional keystroke logger, which relies on keyboard input, for the same method of evidence capture. Computer forensics tools will, of course, be able to track sites visited, but capturing login and password information, which is often captured with a keystroke logger, could be problematic. Notorious hackers Alexey Ivanov and Vasiliy Gorshkov were convicted based on evidence obtained by the FBI using a keystroke logger. The user can use fingers or a pen to write, which implies that handwriting analysis might need to be carried out and the computer screen may need to be dusted for fingerprints to find corroborating evidence to prove ownership of the computer system.

Sticky Notes

Sticky Notes (see Figure 2.25) are a feature of Windows 7, in the Home Premium, Professional, and Ultimate editions of the operating system.

FIGURE 2.25   Sticky Note

Sticky Notes were available in Vista, but these notes had more advanced features with Windows 7, including the ability to format text, resize, and flip through open Sticky Notes. Sticky Notes support pen and touch input if the user is using a pen or a touchscreen. Sticky notes may contain important evidence for a case, but more importantly may assist the investigator in placing the suspect in front of the computer and prove ownership and control. This argument is further strengthened if the suspect used a pen with the Sticky Notes. A handwriting analyst could potentially be asked to testify with the computer forensics examiner. Sticky Notes files have an `.snt` file extension and, by default, are saved to the following location: `C:\Users\YourName\AppData\Roaming\Microsoft\Sticky Notes`.

An `.snt` file can be viewed in Microsoft Word. However, the commercial tool Structured Storage Extractor allows for a forensic examination.

Registry Analysis in Windows 7

As mentioned earlier, the Windows Registry lies at the core of the operating system and can be a tremendous resource for evidence for a computer forensics investigator. It stores the settings and options for the entire system and therefore can provide a wealth of information.

Although the Registry viewed by standard Registry Editor (`regedit.exe`) appears to be a single database, it is in fact a highly integrated collection of files. The following list details the Registry hives and associated file paths in Windows 7:

```
HKLM\System File path: C:\Windows\System32\config\SYSTEM
HKLM\SAM File path: C:\Windows\System32\config\SAM
HKLM\Security File path: C:\Windows\System32\config\SECURITY
HKLM\Software File path: C:\Windows\System32\config\SOFTWARE
HKU\User SID File path: C:\Users\<username>\NTUSER.DAT
HKU\Default File path: C:\Windows\System32\config\DEFAULT
```

This is the `HKLM\Components*` file path:

```
C:\Windows\System32\config\COMPONENTS
```

This is the `Usrclass.dat*` file path:

```
C:\Users\<username>\AppData\Local\Microsoft\Windows\usrclass.dat
```

As with Vista, Windows 7 does not automatically record the last access time on the NTFS volume. By default, Microsoft disabled the update to reduce performance overhead, which in turn caused examiners to lose a very important source of evidence. The value accountable for that setting is found in the following location:

```
HKEY_LOCAL_MACHINE\SYSTEM\CurrentControlSet\Control\FileSystem>NtfsDisableLastAccess
Update
```

Registry Paths and Corresponding Files in Windows 7

Establishing the sequence of events to create a timeline using the operating system is crucial to a computer forensic investigation. Registry keys contain information pertaining to events and the associated system's time.

In addition to establishing the system's time, registries can provide an examiner with the LastWrite time for a particular key. Although the timestamp for each value is not recorded, it can still be helpful to know that the key was changed, especially when a Registry key has a single value. Moreover, the timestamp from the Registry key can be compared against other timestamps on a system.

Event Viewer in Windows 7

When a computer running Windows 7 is shut down unexpectedly, an event is automatically created. That event is subsequently escalated to the category of *Error*. Moreover, when the metadata of the event log is observed, it provides the time when the system was shut down. An additional event log, with a new Event ID, is created when the system is restarted; the system documents that an unexpected system shutdown occurred due to a possible loss of power. This event creates a unique power button timestamp.

When the system date and time are changed, a log event, with the designation of *Security State Change*, is created. Moreover, the previous date and time and the changed date and time are recorded. This metadata is stored in XML format, and the event viewer GUI provides an option to view this content in either an XML format or in a user-friendly text format.

Understanding how system time changes are recorded is important because an attorney might question an examiner's methods of reconstructing events. Events differ from one operating system to another, as does file metadata.

Web Browsers

The U.S. version of Windows 7 is bundled with Internet Explorer 8. This browser introduces a new way to display HTML pages on the Web. It is important to note that there are substantial changes in Internet Explorer 8, which provides new challenges for forensics investigators.

InPrivate Browsing, a feature of Windows Internet Explorer 8 (see Figure 2.26), helps to protect data and privacy by preventing the browsing history, temporary Internet files, form data, cookies, and usernames/passwords from being stored or retained locally by the browser, leaving virtually no evidence of the user's browsing or search history. However, during an InPrivate Browsing session, files that are saved to the hard disk and websites that are added to the user's Favorites are preserved. The most successful retrieval of Internet forensics always comes from a live system because Internet files and search information often reside in RAM, which is volatile memory.

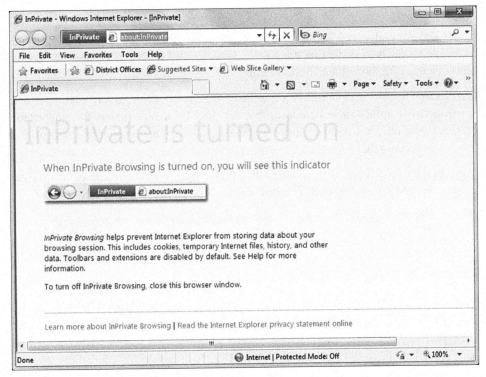

FIGURE 2.26   InPrivate Browsing with Internet Explorer

InPrivate Browsing has an impact on a forensic analysis because it may cause the investigator to lose more evidence related to the suspect's online activities. Internet activity is especially important in child pornography and online fraud cases. An InPrivate Browsing session in Internet Explorer 8 can be initiated from the Safety menu by selecting Start InPrivate Browsing from a New Tab page. Once initiated, a new Internet Explorer 8 window opens with an InPrivate indicator displayed to the left of the address bar. The behavior of the browser changes only for the InPrivate session. Therefore, if the user had the standard window open, the browser history would be stored as normal, whereas the activity within the InPrivate mode window would be discarded. Other competing browsers, like Firefox and Chrome, have similar privacy modes.

When searching for Internet activity, it is not only necessary to check for multiple users but to also recognize that a user may use multiple web browsers, which could also include Tor. Nowhere is this more evident than in the investigation of Casey Anthony. Apparently, investigators retrieved 17 vague searches related to Internet Explorer but failed to recover more than 1,200 Google searches performed using Firefox, including searches for "fool-proof suffication". The defense attorneys knew about the Firefox browser evidence and were surprised that they never came to light during the trial.

File Grouping

Windows 7 introduced more advanced "library" functionality, which allows users to view all their files in one logical location, even though the files are physically distributed randomly across a PC or even across a network. Figure 2.27 shows the Pictures Library.

The folder that is added to a library has an index attached to it, thereby allowing for faster searching, which can be particularly helpful to investigators as they can use FTK to look for any file mapped to a particular index. A parole officer making a house call to a sex offender on probation may also want to use this feature to view picture files expeditiously, although this cannot be considered a forensic search.

Indexing is a prerequisite for a folder to be added to the library. Indexed locations can be investigated to determine user-specified places. They are recorded in the following Registry key:

```
HKLM\Software\Microsoft\Windows Search\CrawlScopeManager\Windows\SystemIndex\Working-
SetRules
```

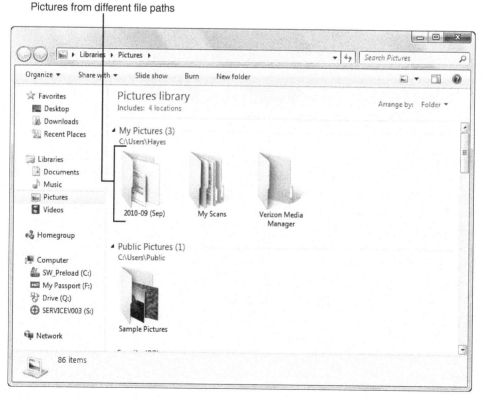

FIGURE 2.27   Pictures Library

Windows Federated Search

Windows Search 4.0 was introduced with Windows Vista as an update. However, the introduction of the libraries feature extended the usefulness of this search feature. The Libraries can be accessed based on different metadata criteria encapsulated within the files. Microsoft introduced Windows Federated Search, which allows a user to query external data sources, including databases and even content from the Web, if they support OpenSearch technology. Search connector files exist for many popular websites and services, like YouTube and Google Photos. The most important field in the file is the `<domain>` tag because it displays a suspect's website searches. A computer forensics examiner needs to understand that a suspect may have retrieved information from the Internet without a web browser by utilizing the search features of Federated Search. With Windows 7, the computer forensics examiner has to observe these `*.osdx` search connector files for Web searches. There is arguably less intent by the suspect to access Web content. Here is an example of the content output from a connector file:

```
<?xml version="1.0" encoding="UTF-8"?>
<searchConnectorDescription xmlns="http://schemas.microsoft.com/windows/2009/ search-
Connector">
    <description>Search deviations on DeviantArt.com</description>
    <isSearchOnlyItem>true</isSearchOnlyItem>
    <domain>http://backend.deviantart.com</domain>
<supportsAdvancedQuerySyntax>false</supportsAdvancedQuerySyntax>
    <templateInfo>
      <folderType>{8FAF9629-1980-46FF-8023-9DCEAB9C3EE3}</folderType>
    </templateInfo>
    <locationProvider clsid="{48E277F6-4E74-4cd6-BA6F-FA4F42898223}">
      <propertyBag>
          <property name="LinkIsFilePath" type="boolean"><![CDATA[true]]></property>
          <property name="OpenSearchShortName"><![CDATA[DeviantArt]]></property>
          <property name="OpenSearchQueryTemplate"><![CDATA[http://backend.deviantart.
[ic:ccc]com/rss.xml?q=boost%3Apopular+{searchTerms}&offset={startIndex}]]></property>
          <property name="MaximumResultCount" type="uint32"><![CDATA[100]]></property>
      </propertyBag>
    </locationProvider>
</searchConnectorDescription>
```

Windows 8.1

The first thing that you notice about Windows 8 and 8.1 is the change in the user interface. By default, you are brought to the *Start screen*, which has a series of *tiles* and each tile represents an application, as shown in Figure 2.28.

FIGURE 2.28   Windows 8 Start screen

This is a departure from the user desktop being the default landing place after the computer's initial bootup. You can quickly access the desktop from the Start screen by clicking the Desktop tile. As you can see in Figure 2.29, the most notable change is that there is no Windows Start button on the lower left of the screen.

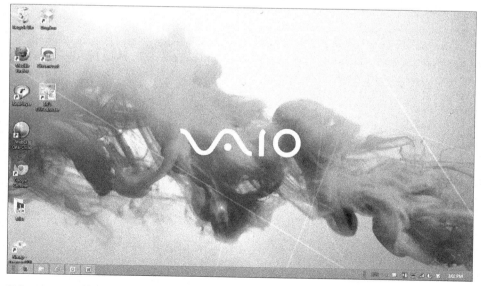

FIGURE 2.29   Windows 8 Desktop

To access applications and programs or to change the computer's settings, you need to use the Start screen. The Windows interface on a PC has a similar interface to a tablet running Windows 8, which is also similar to a smartphone running Windows (as does the Xbox One). These devices create a Windows ecosystem, while a Windows Live account can seamlessly join the user experience across various devices. This is a similar strategy to what Apple has already successfully created.

New Applications

Some new applications come standard with Windows 8. Mail enables the user to combine all email accounts into one app. Videos is an app that enables the user to browse and watch movies on their PC or play them on their television. The People app enables users to communicate with their contacts on email, Twitter, Facebook, and other apps. Other apps on Windows 8 include Maps, Games, Food + Drink, Weather, Sports, Health + Fitness, Travel, and News. Many of the changes to Windows 8 reflect its focus on its support of touchscreen.

Gathering Evidence

The Recycle Bin has seen no major changes, although the interface has changed slightly. Deleted files are found in the $Recycle.Bin folder. If the investigator wishes to find information about connected USB devices, not much has changed—this information can be retrieved from the Registry Editor at HKEY_CURRENT_CONFIG\System\CurrentControlSet\Enum\USB (see Figure 2.30).

FIGURE 2.30   USB connection history in the Registry Editor

It is possible to use the application USBDeview and other forensics software, such as EnCase, to recover this information.

Security in Windows 8.1

A major change in Windows 8/8.1 is Picture Password. This feature allows a user to select a photo to lock the computer. The computer is then unlocked with a series of gestures on the screen. For example, a user may decide to draw two circles on a specific portion of a photo.

Windows 10

Windows 10 was released on July 29, 2015, for use with personal computers. It introduced the idea of universal apps, whereby apps on your PC would have the same look and feel as the apps on other Windows-enabled devices, like tablets, smartphones, Xbox, and Surface. Microsoft introduced support for fingerprint and facial recognition with Windows 10, but they also introduced several feature changes, including Notifications, the Edge web browser, and Cortana.

Notifications

The Notifications center in Windows 10 allows programs to display messages, which may provide valuable evidence to the investigator. These messages can be retrieved from the appd.dat file in an XML format. The file is located here:

```
<volume>\Users\<UserName>\AppData\Local\Microsoft\Windows\Notifications
```

Edge Web Browser

Microsoft's Edge was introduced with Windows 10 as a replacement for Internet Explorer. This browser claims to use less battery life than competitors, like Firefox, and also blocks more phishing websites than competitors, like Chrome. Unlike Internet Explorer, where browsing files were stored in index dat, Web browsing artifacts, associated with Windows 10, are stored in the WebCacheV01. dat file. Browsing history files for both Internet Explorer (IE) and Edge can be found here:

```
<volume>\Users\<UserName>\AppData\Local\Microsoft\Windows\WebCache\
```

Cortana

Cortana is a digital personal assistant that was introduced with Windows 8.1 and was later integrated with the Windows 10 desktop operating system. Cortana can search for files, assist with calendar reminders, or use artificial intelligence to answer questions.

As you can imagine, questions and searches performed by the user and facilitated by Cortana can be invaluable for an investigator seeking to prove that a specific user was operating a PC. Evidence related to Cortana searches is stored in an Extensible Storage Engine (ESE) database format. The two files associated with Cortana, `IndexedDB.edb` and `CortanaCoreDb.dat`, are in the following locations:

```
<volume>\Users\<UserName>\AppData\Local\Packages\Microsoft.Windows.Cortana_xxxx\
AppData\Indexed DB\
<volume>\Users\<UserName>\AppData\Local\Packages\Microsoft.Windows.Cortana_xxxx\
LocalState\ESEDatabase_CortanaCoreInstance\
```

The first database contains data relating to information indexed by Cortana, while the second database contains data related to the interaction between Cortana and the user. In reference to the second database, time values are in a Google Chrome Value format. DCode, from Digital Detective, is a utility that can assist with calculating these date and time values. The *CortanaCoreDb.dat* is the most valuable file as it can provide contacts, reminders, attachments, geofences (longitude/latitude), and important information.

Microsoft Office 365

In recent times, Microsoft has pushed consumers to adopt more subscription-based services, like Xbox Live, OneDrive, Skype, and Microsoft 365. The need for consumers to access Microsoft Office documents on their mobile devices, coupled with the need for more cloud storage, has prompted more consumers to subscribe to Microsoft 365 and seamlessly access files from multiple devices. Therefore, investigators are gradually relying more on sending court orders (or warrants) to Microsoft to obtain cloud-based files and evidence.

Summary

An operating system is responsible for managing a computer's resources, which includes the computer's hardware. It is important to understand how an operating system works because much of the interaction between a user and a computer can be viewed through changes to the operating system. A computer forensics examiner will also encounter a variety of different file systems on computers and storage media. Each file system will vary in terms of file size, metadata, encryption, and permissions. The type of evidence, the weight of evidence, and the accessibility and location of the evidence all differ based on the type of operating system and file system running on a suspect's computer. Professional computer forensics tools generally include a view of files in hexadecimal format, and therefore it is important for a computer examiner to understand how to read hexadecimal code. These tools also display a physical view of files stored on a hard drive, so it is helpful to understand the physical layout of a hard drive. Windows Registry can provide a treasure trove of evidence for a forensic investigator. Much of the user's activity, such as installing an application or logging on to the system, can be ascertained through an examination of the registries. Registries are particularly important when multiple users are utilizing a computer and you need to differentiate each user's activity.

Microsoft's Windows Vista introduced many notable changes and was a dramatic departure from previous versions of the operating system. Of note, the XML file format for system events and robust querying abilities are available with the use of XPath. Sometimes an investigator will rely on file backups for evidence, and Volume Shadow Copy in Vista means that the nature of file backups has changed. The biggest challenge for a forensic examiner encountering a system running Vista is BitLocker, a tool used to encrypt at the file, folder, or drive level. Windows 7 added to this challenge by enabling USB devices to be encrypted. Windows 7 introduced new features, which will surely impact investigations. The operating system now natively supports biometric authentication and also allows for the use of a touch screen monitor without downloading any additional drivers. Windows 7 enables a user to back up the system and files to a network, and this feature provides an indication of future issues for investigators to deal with, including cloud computing.

Microsoft 365 has major implications for investigators because a user subscription means that the same file may reside on multiple devices. Furthermore, a subscription includes cloud services in the form of OneDrive. Therefore, even without a PC or a suspect's mobile device, Microsoft could be subpoenaed for evidence in the Cloud.

The introduction of Windows 10 can present both challenges and problems for investigators. With an increased emphasis on biometrics for accessing a PC (facial recognition and fingerprint), a judge could in theory force a criminal suspect to open a device with a biometric. Conversely, case law generally indicates that a suspect cannot be forced to enter a password or PIN (Fifth Amendment and self-incrimination). With the introduction of the personal assistant, Cortana, there is a new source of potential evidence.

Key Terms

access control list: A list of permissions associated with a file that details the users and programs granted access to the file.

actuator arm: The part of a hard drive that contains a read/write head that modifies the magnetization of the disk when writing to it.

Advanced Encryption Standard (AES): An encryption standard used and approved by the U.S. government.

allocated storage space: The area on a volume where a file or files are stored.

alternate data stream (ADS): A file's set of attributes.

bad sector: An area of a disk that can no longer be used to store data.

Basic Input/Output System (BIOS): Set of instructions that starts an operating system by recognizing and initializing system devices, including the hard drive, CD-ROM drive, keyboard, mouse, video card, and other devices.

binary: The language that computers understand, consisting of 0s and 1s.

bits: Can only be one of two values, where a 1 is a positive charge and a 0 is a negative charge.

bootstrapping: The process of running a small piece of code to activate other parts of the operating system during the boot process. The bootstrap process is contained in the ROM chip.

byte: Comprised of eight bits and is the smallest addressable unit in memory.

COFEE (Computer Online Forensic Evidence Extractor): A tool developed by Microsoft that is made available exclusively to law enforcement to work on systems running BitLocker.

cluster: A logical storage unit on a hard disk that contains contiguous sectors.

Component Object Model (COM): Allows nonprogrammers to write scripts for managing Windows operating systems.

control character: Begins, modifies, or terminates a computer operation and is not a written or printable symbol.

Cortana: A digital personal assistant that was introduced with Windows 8.1 and was later integrated with Windows 10 desktop operating system.

cylinder: The same track number on each platter, spanning all platters in a hard drive.

Data Link Escape: A communications control character that specifies that the proceeding character is not data but rather a control code.

defragmentation: The process of eliminating the amount of fragmentation in a file system to make file chunks (512K blocks) closer together and increase free space areas on a disk.

disk geometry: Refers to the structure of a hard disk in terms of platters, tracks, and sectors.

disk signature: Identifies the disk to the operating system.

End of Sector Marker: A two-byte structure found at the end of the MBR.

event: A communication between one application and another program or user on a computer.

Event Viewer: A Windows application used to view event logs.

FAT (File Allocation Table): A file system developed by Microsoft that utilizes a table to store information about where files are stored, where file space is available, and where files cannot be stored.

FAT12: Introduced in 1980 as the first version of FAT. It is the file system found on floppy disks.

FAT16: A 16-bit file system that was developed for use with MS-DOS.

FAT32: A 32-bit version of FAT that uses smaller clusters, allowing for more efficient utilization of space.

FAT64: A file system, also referred to as exFAT (Extended File Allocation Table), that was developed by Microsoft.

FATX: A file system developed for use on the hard drive of Microsoft's Xbox video game console, as well as associated memory cards.

file compression: A process that allows the user to reduce the number of bits in a file, which in turn allows for faster transmission of the file.

file slack: Refers to the remaining unused bytes in the last sector of a file.

file system: A hierarchy of files and their respective directories.

FTK Imager: A professional computer forensics bit-stream imaging tool that is available for free.

hex editor: Application that enables a forensics examiner to view the entire contents of a file.

hexadecimal: A numbering system that uses 16 symbols (base 16), which includes the numbers 0 to 9 and letters A to F.

journal: Tracks changes to files for fast and efficient restoration of files when there is a system failure or power outage.

journaling: A file system record keeping feature that records changes made to files in a journal.

JumpLists: A Windows taskbar feature that allows the user to quickly access recently used files or actions.

kernel: At the core of the operating system, this is responsible for communication between applications and hardware devices, including memory and disk management.

logical file size: The amount of data stored in a file.

Master Boot Code: Code used by the BIOS to start the boot process.

Master Boot Record (MBR): Involved in the boot process and stores information about the partitions on a disk, including how many exist and their location.

Master File Table (MFT): Maintains file and folder metadata in NTFS, including the filename, creation date, location, size, and permission for every file and folder.

Master Partition Table: Contains descriptions about the partitions on a hard disk.

nibble: One digit of a hexadecimal (hex) value, which represents 4 bits.

NTFS (New Technology File System): Developed by Microsoft and introduced with Windows NT.

operating system: A set of programs used to control and manage a computer's hardware and system resources.

Pagefile.sys: Stores frames of data that has been swapped from RAM to the hard disk.

page file: The area on a hard disk that stores an image of RAM.

partition: A logical storage unit on a disk.

physical file size: The actual disk space used by a file.

Prefetch files: Contain information about an application (executable), how many times it has been run and when it was run.

read-only memory (ROM): Non-volatile storage that is generally not modified and is used during the boot process.

ReadyBoost: A tool first introduced with Vista that allows a user to extend a system's virtual memory through the use of a USB drive.

sector: On a magnetic hard disk, represents 512 bytes; on an optical disk, represents 2048 bytes.

ShellBag: This information provides user viewing preferences for Microsoft's Windows Explorer.

ShimCache: Contains a record of binaries that have executed on a system and also tracks executables that have been viewed through explorer.exe that have not been executed.

spindle: Found at the center of the disk, this is powered by a motor and used to spin the platters.

SuperFetch: A feature introduced with Windows Vista that works with the memory manager service to increase performance by reducing the time required to launch an application.

tracks: Thin, concentric bands on a disk that are comprised of sectors, where data is stored.

unallocated storage space: Available file storage space.

Unicode: An international encoding standard that supports various languages and scripts from around the world.

Unified Extensible Firmware Interface (UEFI): Software that links a computer's firmware to the operating system.

Volume Shadow Copy Service: A backup infrastructure for volumes developed by Microsoft for Windows XP and Windows Server 2003.

Windows: A series of operating systems with a graphical user interface (GUI), developed by Microsoft.

Windows Registry: A hierarchical database that stores system configuration information.

XML (Extensible Markup Language): A standardized language that is compatible for use on the Internet.

XPath (XML Path Language): A powerful query language used for searching XML documents.

Assessment

CLASSROOM DISCUSSIONS

1. Why is it important to learn about hexadecimal?

2. How can the type of operating system influence the work of a computer forensics examiner?

3. If you were an incident responder, and you wanted to find out what a hacker had changed on a client computer, what files would you look at and what forensic tools would you use?

MULTIPLE-CHOICE QUESTIONS

1. Which of the following values are found in binary?

    A. 0 or 1

    B. 0–9 and A–F

    C. 0–9

    D. A–F

2. Which of the following values are found in hexadecimal?

   A. 0 or 1

   B. 0–9 and A–F

   C. 0–9

   D. A–F

3. A nibble represents how many bits?

   A. 2

   B. 4

   C. 8

   D. 16

4. Which of the following best describes an actuator arm on a hard disk?

   A. It is an area of the disk that can no longer be used to store data.

   B. It is a circular disk made from aluminum, ceramic, or glass where data is stored magnetically.

   C. It is found at the center of the disk, is powered by a motor, and is used to spin the platters.

   D. It contains a read/write head that modifies the magnetization of the disk.

5. What is the name of the non-volatile storage that can generally not be modified and is involved in the boot process?

   A. RAM

   B. Flash memory

   C. Partition

   D. ROM

6. Which of the following refers to the rigid disk where files are stored magnetically?

   A. Cylinder

   B. Actuator

   C. Spindle

   D. Platter

7. Which of the following file systems was developed for use on the Xbox?

   A. FAT12

   B. FAT16

   C. FAT32

   D. FATX

8. Which of the following contains the permissions associated with files?

    A. Journal

    B. Alternate data stream

    C. Access control list

    D. BIOS

9. Which of the following best describes the information contained in the MFT?

    A. File and folder metadata

    B. File compression and encryption

    C. File permissions

    D. All of the above

10. Which of the following Windows features allows the user to extend virtual memory using a removable flash device?

    A. BitLocker

    B. Volume Shadow Copy

    C. ReadyBoost

    D. Backup and Restore

FILL IN THE BLANKS

1. A(n) _____ can possess one of two values: 1 or 0.

2. _____ is the base 16 numbering system, which includes numbers 0 to 9 and letters A to F.

3. A(n) _____ is comprised of eight bits and is the smallest addressable unit in memory.

4. The Master Boot _____ is used by the BIOS to start the boot process.

5. _____ refers to the structure of a hard disk in terms of platters, tracks, and sectors.

6. _____ file system was introduced in 1980 as the first version of FAT and is the file system found on floppy disks.

7. The _____ uses tracked changes to files for fast and efficient restoration of files when there is a system failure or power outage.

8. _____ is a hierarchical database that stores system configuration information. The Registry is comprised of two elements, keys and values.

9. _____ is the process of eliminating the amount of fragmentation in a file system to make file chunks (512K blocks) closer together and increase free space areas on a disk.

10. _____ is a Windows application used to view event logs.

PROJECTS

Create a Guide to Navigating the Registry

Choose a Windows operating system and then create an investigator's guide to navigating through the Registry for that system. Highlight in a table what you believe to be the most important keys for the investigator to focus on.

Explain the Boot Process

Detail the process that occurs when the power button on a personal computer is pressed to start a system.

Use Event Viewer

Find a computer running Windows XP or later. Using that computer's Event Viewer, document the events that occurred from an investigator's perspective.

Explain File Storage

Explain the process that occurs when saving a Word document that is 1500 bytes in size. Include how the computer physically stores the file and also detail how the operating system keeps track of the new file being created.

Submit USB Evidence

Download the free USBDeview program to a computer running Windows. Run the application to determine the types of USB devices that were attached to the computer. Submit your report as directed by your instructor.

Incident Response

Write an investigator's guide to Windows features and file registries that may contain evidence as part of a network intrusion. Consider how an investigator might identify if malware was used as part of an attack on a client computer.

Chapter | **3**

Handling Computer Hardware

Learning Outcomes

After reading this chapter, you will be able to understand the following:

- The importance of being able to recognize different types of computer hardware;
- The various disk drive interfaces that an investigator can encounter;
- The types of devices used to forensically extract data from different storage devices;
- The variety of storage media used and how this evidence should be handled and analyzed; and
- The use of storage media in actual investigations.

As an aspiring computer forensics investigator, you should develop an understanding of computer hardware, for several reasons. The first reason is that certain types of systems and hardware will only support certain types of software, in terms of operating system, file system, and applications. For example, it is important to understand that an Intel-based Macintosh computer can support macOS and its related APFS or HFS+ file system and that same computer can also support a Windows operating system and related NTFS file system when Boot Camp is running. **Boot Camp** is a utility that is included with macOS that enables a user to run a Windows operating system on an Intel-based Mac.

Being cognizant of the diversity of computer hardware is also necessary because you need to know how systems can be connected to external devices, like routers or external hard drives. These connected devices, like routers, will often contain digital evidence and may need to be seized if a warrant permits. The investigator might also need to be able to reconstruct the computer and its devices when she returns to the laboratory.

Computer hardware, operating system(s), and applications also determine the kind of computer forensics tools necessary to acquire evidence from that system. For example, BlackLight software might be better suited to image (a strategy you learn about later in this chapter) a MacBook Pro running macOS, while Guidance Software's EnCase can be used to image a computer running Windows. Knowing that a computer is running Windows may not always be enough, however, because the version of the operating system may influence an investigator's decision regarding the type of forensic software to use. Additionally, the type of investigation determines the value of different types of evidence and guides the investigator to choose the most appropriate forensic tool. For example, in a case against an alleged sex offender, a computer forensics investigator might choose to use X-Ways Forensics, which has a particularly effective filtering feature for searching images for skin tones. Realistically, though, many local police departments simply do not have the budget to purchase the full array of forensic tools and thus do not have the luxury of selecting the most appropriate tool. Moreover, even if they could purchase some of these tools, they do not have the training budget to support their usage.

Proper planning for an investigation is critical. This entails knowing about different computer hardware, like hard drives and other devices, in order to purchase the appropriate equipment. As you will learn in this chapter, many of the connections and related forensic hardware cannot be purchased at a local Staples stationary store if you need something; much of the forensic hardware is specialized and is only available from a very limited number of suppliers.

Finally, the way in which computer hardware is handled, during an investigation, has legal ramifications. Evidence must be seized and handled in accordance with standard operating procedures that follow the law in that jurisdiction. Ultimately, the process by which you acquired the evidence is just as important as the evidence itself.

Hard Disk Drives

In Chapter 2, "Windows Operating and File Systems", we discuss the components of a computer's hard disk drive and also describe how files are physically saved and retrieved. It is, however, necessary now to discuss the various types of hard disk drive interfaces that a computer forensics investigation will encounter.

Small Computer System Interface (SCSI)

Small Computer System Interface (SCSI) is a protocol for both the physical connection of devices and the transfer of data. SCSI devices can include hard disks, tape drives, scanners, and CD drives. It is important to understand that SCSI also refers to a command protocol. Larry Boucher is credited with much of the SCSI development and advances, which began at Shugart Associates. It was developed as a vendor-neutral protocol for devices and therefore enabled the same device to work on either a personal computer or on an Apple Macintosh computer. SCSI devices can also be connected to UNIX systems. The benefits of using SCSI are not limited to its compatibility with various systems; it also enables high rates of data transfer. Another tremendous advantage introduced with SCSI is that several devices can be connected in a chain to a single SCSI port.

Forensic Investigations Involving SCSI

From an investigator's point of view, it is important to understand that there are still computers that utilize devices with SCSI connectors (see Figure 3.1). Therefore, you may need older systems in your lab to operate these devices, and you must also think about the relevant drivers that will need to be installed. SCSI hard disk interfaces are uncommon today. However, there are still forensic imaging devices that can be used with SCSI hard disks. For example, the RoadMASSter 3 Mobile Computer Forensics Data Acquisition and Analysis Lab is a system that supports the SCSI interface.

FIGURE 3.1   SCSI connector

Integrated Drive Electronics (IDE)

Integrated Drive Electronics (IDE) is a drive interface, connector, and controller, which is largely based on IBM PC standards, for devices like hard disk drives, tape drives, and optical drives. The disk (or drive) controller is built into the drive itself. The **disk controller** facilitates communication between a computer's central processing unit (CPU) and hard disks (or other disk drives). See Figure 3.2.

FIGURE 3.2   IDE interface on a hard disk

The IDE interface was developed by Western Digital, and IDE drives were first installed in Compaq computers in 1986. This initial version of IDE can be referred to as ATA/ATAPI (Advanced Technology Attachment with Packet Interface). IDE and EIDE have been retrospectively called Parallel ATA or PATA.

Western Digital later introduced Enhanced IDE (EIDE) in 1994. IDE and EIDE connectors typically have 40 pins, although there are 80-pin versions, and the cable is generally 3.5 inches wide (see Figure 3.3).

FIGURE 3.3 IDE 40-pin connector

Serial ATA (SATA)

Serial ATA is an interface that connects devices like hard disk drives to host bus adapters. SATA provides higher data transfer rates than Parallel ATA (PATA). SATA was introduced to the market in 2003 and largely replaced EIDE devices. A SATA drive is generally the most common hard disk drive interface that an investigator will encounter, whether it is a desktop or a laptop, or an iMac or a MacBook. Figure 3.4 shows a SATA data cable for desktop, server, and laptop computers.

FIGURE 3.4 SATA data cable

The SATA power cable is a wider, 15-pin connector, distinguished by red and black wires (see Figure 3.5).

FIGURE 3.5   SATA power cable

In some investigations, an investigator may come into contact with eSATA connections. Therefore, eSATA connectors should also be a part of the computer forensic investigator's toolbox. **eSATA** is a variation of SATA that is used for external drives. See Figure 3.6.

FIGURE 3.6   eSATA connector

SATA disk drives come in different sizes. For example, Figure 3.7 displays a 1.8-inch hard drive. There are significantly smaller hard drives found in Dell D420 and Dell 430 laptops. Toshiba manufactures these hard drives for Dell. The significance for an investigator is that the ZIF cable (see Figure 3.8) and adapter are very specialized and can be difficult to source.

FIGURE 3.7   1.8-inch Hitachi hard disk drive

FIGURE 3.8   ZIF cable

Cloning a PATA or SATA Hard Disk

There are two processes used by computer forensics examiners for making a bit-for-bit copy of a hard drive:

- A **disk clone** is an exact copy of a hard drive and can be used as a backup for a hard drive because it is bootable just like the original.

- A **disk image** is a file or a group of files that contain bit-for-bit copies of a hard drive but cannot be used for booting a computer or for other operations.

The image files can also be different because they can be compressed, unlike a disk clone, which is not compressed. When cloning, the bit-for-bit copy is transferred to a second hard drive that is of equal size or larger than the source drive. Another difference is that specialized software, like EnCase, X-Ways, or FTK, is needed to view the contents of the image files. In general, image-viewing software is read-only, and files cannot be added. Nevertheless, some applications allow image files to be edited; WinHex, which is produced by X-Ways Forensics, is one such example.

Cloning Devices

The process of cloning a hard drive is a faster process than imaging a hard drive. The time difference between the two processes is substantial. Therefore, when a computer forensics examiner is working undercover or perhaps needs to obtain a copy of a hard drive and leave the computer with the custodian, then cloning the drive is more practical. On average, successfully cloning a SATA drive takes less than an hour. Of course, the time to clone depends on the size of the source hard drive and the cloning equipment being used.

One forensic cloning device used in investigation is the Disk Jockey PRO Forensic Edition (see Figure 3.9). The device is write-protected and allows the user to copy directly from a SATA or IDE hard disk drive to another SATA or IDE hard disk drive. *Write-protected* refers to the fact that it can copy the device storage without writing to the drive or volume.

FIGURE 3.9   Disk Jockey PRO Forensic Edition

Before the investigation, all harvest disk drives must be sanitized. The Disk Jockey PRO has a function that performs a Department of Defense (DoD)–approved seven-pass secure erase. When a new hard drive is removed from its packaging, it should be securely erased because an attorney might question a forensic investigator on this. Later, when we discuss evidence admissibility, we will emphasize the importance of establishing crime scene and forensic lab protocols for handling and examining evidence so that best practices are established to defend against potential objections from counsel. Other devices, like the WipeMASSter Hard Disk Sanitizer from Intelligent Computer Solutions, are used solely to securely erase hard disk drives.

Before embarking on an investigation, it is also helpful to identify the specifications of a suspect's machine (the make and model), where possible. This enables the investigator to research the computer that they will be working on and learn how to remove the hard drive. This might sound like common sense, but removing a hard drive from a Dell Inspiron 6400 laptop for cloning is very different from removing the drive from a Dell Latitude D430. The equipment required to clone each of these hard drives is also very different. A Dell Inspiron 6400 is relatively easy to remove, and then you can connect a SATA data cable and a SATA power cable. For a Dell Latitude D430 (or D420) laptop, the battery must be removed. Then a thin cable must be removed from the hard drive and a rubber casing around the drive also must be removed. A special ZIF cable, ZIF adapter, and IDE interface cable are necessary to connect the 1.8-inch SATA hard drive to the Disk Jockey PRO, as shown in Figure 3.10. If possible, also try to predetermine the target computer's operating system.

FIGURE 3.10   Cloning a hard disk drive with Disk Jockey PRO Forensic Edition

A simple Internet search for "removing the hard drive dell 430" will result in helpful documentation (including pictures) that Dell has made available online. In fact, Dell maintains a web page for most of its computer models that details hard disk drive removal. For other computers, manufacturers provide similar documentation. Removing the hard drive from an iMac is a very involved process that requires some unique tools. Apple provides comprehensive instructions on the removal of hard drives from iMacs. YouTube also hosts numerous helpful videos to assist the investigator. The website ifixit.com also provides helpful tips for teardowns of Macs and PCs. Nevertheless, you should initially refer to either your own internal guidelines for hardware devices and also other agency best practice guides. The National Institute of Justice provides a number of best practice guides, for example.

The Disk Jockey has both a "Disk Copy" function and a "Disk Copy (HPA)" cloning function. An investigator should first attempt to use the "Disk Copy (HPA)" clone function. This function makes a copy of the disk that includes the Host Protected Area (HPA). The **Host Protected Area (HPA)** is a region on a hard disk that often contains code associated with the BIOS for booting and recovery purposes. Manufacturers use the HPA to assist in the recovery process, and this feature replaces the need for a consumer recovery CD. An investigator should try to make a copy of this area because criminals have been known to hide incriminating evidence in this region of the disk. Sometimes the Disk Jockey PRO is unable to recognize and copy the HPA. When an error message appears on the Disk Jockey PRO's LCD display, the investigator must then use the Disk Copy function instead of Disk Copy (HPA).

Let's Get Practical!

Standard Operating Procedures for Operating the Disk Jockey PRO

Preparation

1. Connect the new hard drive to the right side of the Disk Jockey labeled Destination Disk.

2. Press the **POWER/START** button. With DATA ERASE DoD selected, press the **POWER/START** button. Record this action, with date and time, in your investigator notes.

This process could take up to two hours, depending on the size of the hard drive that you need to sanitize.

The Investigation

In a real investigation, you would have paperwork to fill out at this point, including a chain of custody form. See Chapter 6, "Documenting the Investigation", for a copy of this form.

1. Remove the hard disk drive from the suspect's computer. Take a photograph of the suspect's computer, the computer's serial number, and the hard drive, while ensuring that you capture the serial number of the hard drive in the photograph.

2. With the hard disk drive removed, turn on the suspect's computer and then press **F2** or **F4** to enter the BIOS; some computers require a different function key or key combination. You should then transcribe the BIOS information from the computer into the computer worksheet form (see Chapter 6). The most important information to record is the computer's system time. You should then record the actual time (perhaps from a cellular telephone with the accurate current time). Note any time differences in your investigator report.

3. Connect the suspect's hard drive on the left side of the Disk Jockey, where you see the words "Source Disk".

4. Connect your new sanitized hard drive (harvest drive) on the right, where you see the words "Destination Disk". Take a photograph of the harvest drive. Compare your screen with Figure 3.11.

   Note that, if available, you should place a rubber mat under the Disk Jockey and the two hard drives to eliminate any possibility of electromagnetic interference.

5. Press the **POWER/START** button. Turn the Mode button clockwise until DISK COPY (HPA) displays, and then press the **POWER/START** button; compare your screen with Figure 3.12. Record this action, with date and time, in your investigator notes.

If an error message displays, redo step 5, but this time select DISK COPY and then press the **POWER/START** button.

6. When the cloning process is complete, the Disk Jockey PRO automatically shuts down. You should then record the date and time the disk copy process ended in your investigator notes.

7. Connect your harvest drive to a forensic write-blocker, which should then be connected to the USB port on your laptop. Then access the harvest drive to verify that you successfully created a copy of the suspect's hard drive.

FIGURE 3.11   Configuration of hard drives connected to the Disk Jockey PRO

FIGURE 3.12   Disk copy process initialized

Alternative Copy Devices

The ImageMASSter Solo IV Forensic is a much more expensive device than the Disk Jockey PRO, but it has the ability to image two devices simultaneously. The investigator can select either a Linux DD file or an E01 image file.

Solid State Drives

A solid state drive (SSD; see Figure 3.13) is a non-volatile storage device found in computers. Unlike on a hard drive, files on a solid state drive are stored on memory chips in a stationary layout of transistors, and not on metal platters. In other words, a solid state drive has no moving parts—no read/write heads or spinning disks. Most solid state drives are flash memory NAND devices. It is important to know about these drives because they are growing in importance; they can be found in Chromebooks, the MacBook Air/Pro, and numerous personal computers today.

FIGURE 3.13   Solid state drive

In a single-level cell (SLC) NAND flash, each cell in the SSD has 1 bit. In a multi-level cell NAND flash, each cell has two or more bits. An MLC has higher density but generally requires more voltage than an SLC.

There are more than 80 SSD manufacturers, while there are very few hard disk drive manufacturers. There are numerous controller manufacturers who have different manufacturing requirements for SSD manufacturers. Therefore, this complicates the life of a computer forensics investigator, i.e., an SSD from one manufacturer can have different controllers with varying firmware. The proprietary firmware associated with the controller affects garbage collection, caching, wear-leveling, encryption, compression, bad block detection, and more.

Consider the following examples of SSD controller manufacturers:

- Marvell
- Hyperstone
- SandForce
- Indilix

- Phison
- STEC
- Fusion-io
- Intel
- Samsung

In many ways, solid state drives are a more efficient alternative to hard disk drives, given their more efficient use of power, faster retrieval and storage of files, and greater resistance to environmental factors, including heat and vibration. Nevertheless, solid state drives suffer from ware-leveling. **Ware-leveling** is the process by which over time areas of a storage medium become unusable.

From a file storage perspective, solid state drives are very different from hard disk drives, and they do not use the traditional 512-byte storage sectors.

In terms of computer forensics, recovering deleted files on a solid state drive is more challenging as a result of the garbage collection process. **Garbage collection** is a memory-management process that removes unused files to make more memory available. Garbage collection is rather unpredictable with solid state drives and is particularly problematic from a forensics perspective. Changes to files stored on a solid state drive can occur without warning, regardless of the best efforts of a computer forensics examiner. Garbage collection and other automated functions associated with an SSD mean that once a hash is forensically created for a hard drive, and then another hash is generated, on the same drive, the two hashes might not match, which is different with a HDD.

Unlike a hard disk drive, with an SSD, data must be erased before a write can occur. Writes are completed in large blocks with high latency. Another difference is that the operating system does not keep track of the physical location of files; the File Translation Layer (FTL) is responsible for this. The File Translation Layer (FTL) maps a logical block address to a physical block address. TRIM is an operating system function that informs a solid state drive which blocks are no longer in use, and this allows for greater write performance. TRIM runs immediately after the Recycle Bin is emptied. However, there are a couple of important points that should be made. First, techniques have been developed to prevent the TRIM function and garbage collection from operating, which can be explored in recently published academic literature. Secondly, there are many instances in digital forensics today where one copy of a volume is not an exact match to another, based on the MD5 or SHA-1 verification process. This is largely because of the introduction of NAND flash storage in smartphones and hard drives, which is more volatile. Nevertheless, we know from case law that this evidence is still admissible.

Random Access Memory (RAM)

Random Access Memory (RAM) is volatile memory that is used for processes currently running on a computer. Please see Figure 3.14, which display some sample RAM. Its volatile nature comes from the fact that, when a computer is powered off, the contents of RAM are generally erased. However, if a system is powered on, RAM can provide a forensics examiner with a treasure trove of information, which can include Internet searches, websites visited, and possibly even passwords. There are numerous forensics tools, including Volatility, which can perform a RAM capture (acquisition).

FIGURE 3.14   RAM chip

Redundant Array of Independent Disks (RAID)

A Redundant Array of Independent (or Inexpensive) Disks (RAID) is commonly referred to with the acronym RAID. A **RAID (Redundant Array of Independent Disks)** is where two or more disks are used in conjunction with one another to provide increased performance and reliability through redundancy (see Figure 3.15). In the case of a RAID, reliability refers to **fault tolerance**, which means that if one component in a system, like a hard disk drive, fails, then the system will continue to operate. This kind of reliability is worth the investment for many critical systems in an organization. More recently, organizations have installed RAIDs to increase storage. Although RAID contains multiple hard disks, the operating system views the RAID as one logical disk with the use of hardware controllers.

From a computer forensics perspective, it is important to know that a computer may have multiple hard drives connected to it, all of which have evidentiary value. It is also important for an investigator to note the order in which each drive was added to the RAID and which drive adapter is connected to which drive, as this can be confusing.

FIGURE 3.15 RAID

Removable Memory

Today, it is rare for an investigator to simply seize a laptop computer and then only analyze that computer's hard drive. The investigator must also consider the myriad of removable storage devices that are so pervasive today because of the low cost of removable memory. It is important to consider all potential storage when drafting a warrant and when conducting a search. You must understand how these devices are connected to the computer, understand trace evidence, and know the types of files that may be stored on these devices. This is easier said than done, given that removable memory has become smaller and more varied, with more wireless capabilities. This section provides some helpful advice on how to deal with removable memory.

FireWire

FireWire is the Apple version of IEEE 1394, which is a serial bus interface standard for high-speed data transfer. FireWire (see Figure 3.16) provides for higher data transfer speeds than USB wire, with speeds up to 400Mbps (megabits per second). FireWire 400 (1394-1995) can transfer data between devices at speeds ranging from 100, 200, or 400 megabits per second full duplex, and the cable length can measure up to 14.8 feet. FireWire 800 (1394b-2002) can transfer data at rates of 782.432 megabits per second full duplex. Apple, which has been largely responsible for the development of FireWire, has been slowly phasing out this protocol in favor of its Thunderbolt interface. Chapter 12, "Mac Forensics", details how helpful FireWire can be for acquiring a forensic image from an Apple Mac using an Apple Mac.

FIGURE 3.16   FireWire cables

USB Flash Drives

As noted in Chapter 2, each time a device is connected to a computer, information about that device is recorded in Windows File Registry. Figure 3.17 shows exactly where in the Registry USB device connections are recorded.

These file registry entries are important in showing a history of what devices were connected to a computer. Every USB device has a serial number that is recorded in the subkey for that USB registry.

Access to files on a USB is not a forgone conclusion, however, because many of these storage devices have built-in utilities. For example, Ironkey USB devices use AES 256-bit encryption to protect files on the device. These devices protect the user and enterprise from theft of intellectual property. After a series of unsuccessful attempts to access the device, the device automatically reformats the drive.

The file system found on a USB flash memory device is usually a version of FAT, which is a file system that most computers recognize, although the device can be formatted to support other file systems.

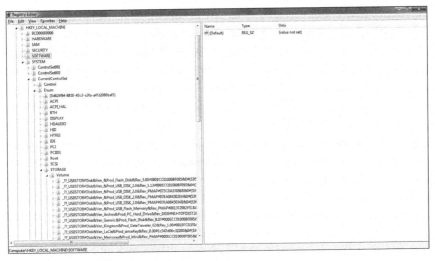

FIGURE 3.17   Registry Editor

External Hard Drives

There are generally two types of external hard drives: a USB-powered hard drive and an external drive that uses the USB interface for data transfer while using an adapter to power the drive. Housed within the casing, an investigator usually finds a Serial ATA hard disk drive. This is important to know because if there is a limited amount of time to acquire evidence or the external hard drive cannot be removed from the premises, then it is probably advisable to remove the hard disk drive from the outer casing. By removing the drive from the casing, a cloning device can be used to make a copy of the external drive. If the hard disk drive is not removed from its casing, then the drive must be imaged using a write-blocker connected to a laptop. The Western Digital external hard disk drive in Figure 3.18 houses a 2.5-inch drive. A mini USB port is used for both power and data transfer to a computer.

FIGURE 3.18   Western Digital (WD) external hard drive

In some cases, a cloning device may not be feasible, so an investigator should always carry a write-blocker (including a USB write-blocker). For imaging and validating the drive, an investigator can bring FTK Imager Lite on a USB or another imaging tool. Imaging a 250GB drive, with verification, using FTK Imager Lite could take many hours, whereas cloning that same drive could take approximately 40 minutes. When cloning or imaging a hard drive, it is proper protocol to place the source and destination hard drives on an antistatic, rubberized mat to avoid any electromagnetic interference. Hard drives should also be transported in antistatic bags.

External hard drives are mostly used today for backups or as an extension to a computer's memory. An examiner should be aware that an external hard disk drive could contain any number of file systems, including NTFS (Windows) or APFS (Mac). More importantly, if the external drive is connected to a PC with Windows 10 installed and BitLocker Drive Encryption is running, then disconnecting the drive from the computer can make it problematic to subsequently decrypt an external drive. In other words, think before you remove any USB device that is connected to a live system. Of course, external drives can also be eSATA. Newer drives may also have software installed for backing up the drive, perhaps to a cloud service. It is important to check for all installed software utilities on the suspect's drive and note that backup software and other data integrity utilities can be present on a separate partition.

MultiMediaCards (MMCs)

A **MultiMedia Card** is storage memory that was developed by Siemens AG and SanDisk for use in portable devices, like cameras. MMCs are not as popular as they once were because they have largely been replaced by secure digital (SD) cards. An MMC has a standard size of 24mm × 32mm × 1.4mm. MultiMedia Cards replaced SmartMedia cards, which Toshiba developed in 1995, and had a storage capacity of 16 MB–128 MB. As you can see in Figure 3.19, a SmartMedia card is very similar in appearance to an SD card.

FIGURE 3.19   SmartMedia card

Secure Digital (SD) Cards

A **Secure Digital (SD)** card is a file storage device that was developed for use in portable electronics, like cameras. The association that developed SD cards and set the standard for this memory is a joint venture between Matsushita Electrical Industrial Co., Ltd. (Panasonic), SanDisk Corporation, and Toshiba Corporation.

The standard size for an SD card is 24mm wide and 32mm long, with a thickness of 2.1mm (see Figure 3.20). This standard size SD card has often been used in digital cameras, and many laptops come with an SD card slot and reader as standard. SDHC (Secure Digital High Capacity) cards have also still sold. SDHC cards generally go up to around 32GB. More recently, 64GB cards began to appear with the emergence of SDXC (Secure Digital eXtended Capacity). Micro SDXC cards are now available with 1TB of storage. Secure Digital cards are formatted with the FAT32 file system.

FIGURE 3.20   Secure Digital card

Note that some SD cards are Wi-Fi enabled with preinstalled utilities. Some of these utilities can automatically send photos to a mobile device, upload files to social media sites, or even add files to a cloud service. Generally, a logo on the SD card indicates that the card is Wi-Fi enabled, but this might not always be the case. The investigator should be cognizant of potential wireless capabilities.

If you encounter an SD card during an investigation, it is proper protocol to set the write-protect switch to on, when present on the card, to prevent any data from being written to this memory. Of course, the investigator will use a write-blocker before examining any removable memory, like an SD card.

A miniSD is 20 mm wide and 21.5 mm long. The microSD format was developed by SanDisk. A microSD card can be used in a Standard Digital card reader with the use of an SD adapter. microSD cards are sometimes found in cellular telephones, and therefore they can be a valuable source of evidence. Additionally, many cellphone forensic imaging or cloning devices cannot read the contents of the microSD card, so the card may have to be removed and imaged separately.

CompactFlash (CF) Cards

CompactFlash (see Figure 3.21) is a memory card that was first developed by SanDisk for use in portable electronics, like digital cameras. A CompactFlash (CF) can have two different dimensions: (a) Type I is 43mm × 36mm × 3.3mm, and (b) Type II is 43mm × 36mm × 5mm. CompactFlash cards are not as popular today as Secure Digital cards, but they do have an effective file storage system and can potentially support up to 1TB of memory.

FIGURE 3.21   CompactFlash

Memory Sticks

A **Memory Stick** (see Figure 3.22) is Sony's proprietary memory card that was introduced in 1998. Unlike many other flash memory manufacturers, Sony also produced many of the electronic devices that support its memory card. Sony manufactures televisions, laptops, cellular telephones, digital cameras, video recorders, game consoles, MP3 players, and numerous other electronic devices, all of which often supported additional memory through the use of a Memory Stick. The original Memory Stick was replaced by the Memory Stick PRO in 2003, to enable a greater storage capacity. The PRO series utilized FAT12, FAT16, and FAT32 file systems. The Memory Stick Duo was a smaller memory card that was developed to fit well into small handheld devices. Other versions of the Memory Stick were developed to increase memory capabilities and to support high-definition video capture.

The Memory Stick XC (Extended High Capacity) series was released by Sony and SanDisk. These memory cards have the potential to store up to 2TB of memory. The XC series uses the exFAT (FAT64) file system. This series has maximum data transfer rates up to 160 Mbps and 480Mbps depending upon the XC model.

The important point for investigators to note is that if a suspect owns Sony products, Memory Sticks could be present in these devices. For example, a Sony television might have a Memory Stick inserted. Moreover, that memory card will probably contain files uploaded from a computer.

FIGURE 3.22 Memory Stick

xD Picture Cards

Introduced in 2002, **xD (Extreme Digital) Picture Cards** were developed by Olympus and Fujifilm for digital cameras and some voice recorders. These memory cards have been slowly phased out by Olympus and Fujifilm in favor of the more popular SD cards.

Hardware for Reading Flash Memory

There are a few ways to securely view the contents of flash memory cards. One tool is Digital Intelligence's UltraBlock Forensic Card Reader and Writer (see Figure 3.23). This device is connected to a computer via the USB port (2.0 or 1.0) and can read the following media:

- CompactFlash
- MicroDrive
- Memory Stick
- Memory Stick PRO
- Smart Media Card
- xD Picture Card
- Secure Digital Card (SD and SDHC)
- MultiMediaCard

A regular memory card reader could be used in addition to a USB write-blocker to ensure that the data is viewed forensically. A write-blocker is a hardware device that allows an individual to read data from a device, like a hard drive, without writing to that device. An investigator could connect a media card reader to Digital Intelligence's UltraBlock USB Write Blocker, which would be connected to a computer, where the media card's contents would be viewed or acquired.

FIGURE 3.23   UltraBlock Forensic Card Reader and Writer

Let's Get Practical!

Read the Contents of a Secure Digital Card

If you do not have write-blockers available, you can use another method as only a last resort. Find a laptop with a Secure Digital slot or a computer and a media card reader. Then go through the following steps:

1. Start the FTK Imager application.

On the Secure Digital card, slide the protective lock-switch to the **Lock** position, as shown in Figure 3.24.

2. Insert the Secure Digital card into the card reader. If you are not using a card reader, simply insert the card into the Secure Digital slot on your computer.

3. Click **File** and then click **Add Evidence Item**.

FIGURE 3.24   Secure Digital Card with lock on

4. In the displayed **Select Source** dialog box, with the **Physical Drive** option selected, click **Next**.

5. Click the drop-down menu and then select the Secure Digital drive.

6. Click **Finish**.

7. In the **evidence tree**, click to expand the physical drive until you file the folder named DCIM. This is the folder that will contain any photographs that you have taken.

Notice that the file system on the SD card is FAT32.

8. Click **File** and then click **Exit**.

Compact Discs

A **compact disc (CD)**, also known as an optical disc, is a polycarbonate plastic disc with one or more metal layers, used to store data digitally. A CD is usually 1.2mm thick and weighs 15–20 grams. Aluminum is generally used for the metallic surface. Data is stored to the disc and read from the disc using a laser. The laser that writes data to a disc reaches a temperature of 500–700 degrees Celsius. Because the data is stored using a laser, CDs are not vulnerable to electromagnetic charges. The high temperatures used in storing the data cause the metal alloy to liquefy, and the reflective state changes. **Lands** are the reflective surfaces on a CD burned flat by a laser. **Pits** are the less reflective surfaces on a CD that have not been burned by a laser. The differences between the reflective and less reflective surfaces can be translated to binary (0s, 1s).

CDs were initially developed by Sony and Philips to store and play audio files. Later the CD-ROM was developed for data storage. A CD-R allows data to be stored once. Because a CD-R can only have data written to it once, handling this type of CD in a forensically sound manner does not require a write-blocker. A CD-RW, on the other hand, allows data to be written multiple times to the disc. Today a standard CD generally has a storage capacity of 700MB.

ISO 9660, introduced in 1988, refers to the standard for optical discs and their file system. ISO 9660 is also called CDFS (Compact Disc File System), and it was created to support different operating systems, like Windows and macOS. Other file systems that can also be supported by CDs include Joliet, UDF, HSG, HFS, and HFS+. Joliet allows for longer filenames, which are associated with more recent versions of Windows. Because other file systems can exist on a CD, it is important to remember that a CD used in a Windows computer may show that it is invalid if an HFS+ file system resides on the disc. This means that specialized tools may be required to access the files stored on a CD. IsoBuster, for example, is a data recovery tool for CD, DVD, and Blu-ray. InfinaDyne's CD/DVD Inspector is a specialized tool for a forensic acquisition of files from CDs and DVDs. It should be noted that an .iso file, which is an image of an optical disc, may be saved on the hard drive of a suspect's computer or on another storage device.

The International Standardization Organization (ISO) in Geneva, Switzerland, has created this standard to facilitate the use of CDs on Windows, Macintosh, and UNIX computers. **Frames** consist of 24 bytes and are the smallest unit of memory on a CD-ROM. A sector on a CD-ROM consists of 98 frames (2352 bytes).

Compact Disc–Rewritable (CD-RW)

A CD-RW usually stores less data than a CD (570MB instead of 700MB). A **track** on a compact disc is a group of sectors that are written to at one time. A **session** on a compact disc is a group of tracks recorded at the same time. The **table of contents (TOC)** records the location of the start address, the session number, and track information (music or video) on a compact disc. The TOC is an example of a session, and every session contains a TOC. If the TOC cannot be read by the computer's CD-ROM drive, then the compact disc will not be recognized. A full erase of a CD-RW deletes all data on a disc. However, a quick erase will only remove all references to tracks and sessions, leaving the land and pits unchanged. Nevertheless, the CD-RW will not be recognized because the sessions have been removed.

CnW Recovery is a tool that claims to recover disc data that has been through the quick erase process. Ultimately, when a quick erase has been performed, it is possible to recover the data on a CD-RW. When a full erase has been executed, the data cannot be recovered.

Case Study

State of Connecticut v. John Kaminski

In 2004, John Kaminski was interrogated by the New Britain, Connecticut, police following a complaint about his alleged sexual abuse of a 14-year-old girl. After obtaining a search warrant of Kaminski's home, police confiscated his computer, his digital camera, and a number of compact discs. It quickly became obvious that Kaminski had erased a considerable amount of evidence from his computer's hard drive, as well as the compact discs that had been seized. The suspect had run a quick erase on the CD-RW disc. In this particular case, investigators were able to create a new compact disc and retrieve the evidence from the suspect's CD-RW. Adaptec's CD Creator was used to begin the burn process to create a new session on the disc's lead-in. The burn process was then aborted right after the table of contents (TOC) was created. With a new session created, the evidence on the CD-RW could then be read. Obviously, no experimentation was conducted directly on the suspect's disc. A copy of the disc would be used in the reassembly process.

It is important to know that, in this case and many other cases, extensive scientific testing was conducted to ensure that the CD burn process to make the CD-RW data recognizable did not affect any other data stored on the CD. Conducting tests to demonstrate consistent results is extremely important to ensure that evidence will stand up to any objections by a defense attorney.

In this particular case, the reassembled CD-RW contained six videos of Kaminski sexually abusing and torturing three children who had been drugged. Faced with this evidence, Kaminski accepted a plea bargain and was sentenced to 50 years in prison.

DVDs

A **Digital Video (or Versatile) Disc (DVD)** is an optical disc with a large storage capacity that was developed by Philips, Sony, Toshiba, and Time Warner. A single-sided DVD generally has a capacity of 4.7GB. Other DVD formats can store more than 17GB of data. Their large storage capacity makes them ideal for storing video files, which are often very large in size. A DVD player uses a red laser (650 nanometers [nm]) to read data from a DVD disc.

Blu-ray Discs

A Blu-ray disc (BD) is a high-capacity optical disc that can be used to store high-definition video. A single-layer disc has a storage capacity of 25GB, while dual-layer disc can store 50GB of data. Also available are 3D Blu-ray players and discs. A firmware upgrade available for Sony's PlayStation 3 facilitates 3D Blu-ray playback as well. The name of this storage media comes from the blue laser (405nm) used to read the disc. This laser enables more data to be stored than the red laser used in DVDs. Standards for these optical discs have been developed and are maintained by the Blu-ray Disc Association (www.blu-raydisc.com).

From a forensics perspective, Blu-ray discs have limited value because both the Blue-ray burner and recordable discs can be prohibitively expensive for the average consumer. A suspect is more likely to store video on a hard drive or burn video files onto a DVD. Nevertheless, there are two different recordable formats. A BD-R disc can be written to once, while a BD-RE can be used for re-recording.

Companies like Digital Forensics Systems produce devices for imaging and analyzing CDs, DVDs, and BDs.

Floppy Disks

While floppy disks have been replaced by other storage media, it is not inconceivable that an investigator could still encounter these. A **floppy disk** is a thin, flexible, plastic computer storage disc that is housed in a rigid plastic rectangular case. Files are stored on the disk magnetically. These disks have historically come in 8-inch (see Figure 3.25), 5¼-inch, and 3½-inch (see Figure 3.26) sizes. Initially, these disks were used to store a computer's operating system. Subsequently, they were used for general file storage purposes. The 3½-inch disk was introduced in 1987 and its storage capacity ranged from 720KB to 1.4MB.

IBM invented the floppy disk drive, which was used to store and read data from floppy disks.

Floppy disks have been largely replaced by flash memory, optical disks, and external hard drives. An investigator who encounters floppy disks during an investigation is more likely to find the PC-compatible 1440KB format. Floppy disks are formatted with the FAT12 file system. All of these disks will only have either one or two clusters.

FIGURE 3.25   8-inch floppy disk

FIGURE 3.26 3½-inch floppy disk

A forensic image of a floppy disk can be made by using the following Linux command:

```
# dd if=/dev/fd0 of=/evidence/floppy1.img bs=512
```

In this command, `/dev/fd0` refers to the floppy disk drive, and `bs=512` refers to the block size (`bs`), which is 512 bytes.

Of course, prior to inserting any disk, you should make sure that the disk is set to write-protected. You should then make a bit-for-bit copy of the floppy disk and lock the original disk in an evidence locker, away from any potential magnetic interference. To view the files on the disk, you can use the following command:

```
# ls /dev/fd0
```

Case Study

The BTK Killer

Between 1974 and 1991, the BTK (bind, torture, kill) Killer was responsible for the murder of 10 people. Police were baffled for many years about the identity of the BTK Killer. In 2004, letters and packages, some containing items belonging to the victims, were sent to the local media. A cereal box containing items belonging to a victim was left in the bed of a pickup truck at a Home Depot. The owner of the truck discarded the box before anyone discovered it. When the killer, who had not yet been identified as the BTK Killer, asked the media about the package, no one had any knowledge of it. He subsequently went back and retrieved the box from the trash. This was a fatal error. The police were later able to review surveillance camera footage and identify the suspect with a black Jeep Cherokee in the parking lot of the Home Depot as the one retrieving the cereal box.

The BTK Killer later asked the police if he sent them a floppy disk, would it be possible to trace the computer's owner? In the *Wichita Eagle Newspaper*, the police responded to the suspect's request, stating that it was okay to use a floppy disk. A translucent purple Memorex disk was then sent to the police. The 1.44MB floppy disk was analyzed using Guidance Software's EnCase. Randy Stone, a 39-year-old Desert Storm veteran, was the investigator from the Forensic Computer Crime Unit, of the Wichita police, and he conducted the analysis of the floppy disk. Stone found one file on the disk, named `Test A.rtf`. The metadata from this document identified "Dennis" as the author and also displayed "Wichita's Christ Lutheran Church", An Internet search for "Lutheran Church Wichita Dennis" displayed the result "Dennis Rader, Lutheran Deacon". Police began surveillance of Dennis Rader and found a black Jeep Cherokee parked outside his residence. It was the same vehicle identified in the surveillance camera footage at Home Depot. A pap smear from his daughter was accessed from the medical clinic at the University of Kansas. The DNA was a match to DNA found under the fingernails of one of the BTK Killer's victims.

It took many years to find the BTK Killer because of a lack of evidence and because serial killer profiling did not help; Rader was a father, a Cub Scout leader, and president of the Congregation Council at Zion Lutheran Church.

Digital evidence was ultimately a key piece of evidence in the case. Rader was eventually arrested in 2005. In June 2005, Rader pleaded guilty and was sentenced to 10 consecutive life sentences for the 10 murders. He could not be sentenced to death because the murders occurred prior to when the death penalty was introduced in 1994. He was imprisoned in the El Dorado Correctional Facility.

Zip Disks

A **zip disk** is a removable storage medium that was developed by Iomega in the early 1990s. Zip disks originally came with a 100MB capacity and subsequently increased to 750MB. They were introduced as a higher-capacity alternative to floppy disks. A zip drive, in which zip disks are loaded, can be either an internal drive or an external drive. Zip drives and their disks have largely been replaced by CDs and the more popular, smaller, flash memory devices.

Magnetic Tapes

Magnetic tape is a thin plastic strip with a magnetic coating that is used for storing audio, video, and data. Because data is stored magnetically, an investigator must be careful to keep magnetic tapes away from all types of magnetism. Magnetic tapes are unique in the way that data is retrieved because they must be read in a linear fashion, from the start of the tape through the end of the tape. This often makes the process of acquiring data from magnetic tape quite time-consuming.

The use of audio tapes in investigations has become less important than it once was. The same is true of videotapes used in video cassette recorders (VCRs).

Magnetic Tapes (Data Storage)

Forensic imaging and analysis of magnetic tapes (see Figure 3.27) used for data storage on servers is challenging. Many different proprietary server systems exist, which makes a single solution impossible. An analysis of the physical surface can be conducted using a complicated process known as magnetic force microscopy. This method can be used to uncover wiped or overwritten data.

FIGURE 3.27   Magnetic tape for data storage

Generally, data is recorded to a magnetic tape in blocks. Data at the block level can be accessed using the **dd** command. In computer investigations, dd is a UNIX command that produces a raw data image of a storage medium, like a hard drive or magnetic tape, in a forensically sound manner. The dd command is written in such a way that the image is copied to a hard drive, which allows for better search capabilities. A magnetic tape has no hierarchical file system because files are stored sequentially or in a tape partition. Partitions on magnetic tapes allow users to group files in "tape directories", When a sector is only partially used by a file, the remainder of the sector is referred to as memory slack, buffer slack, or RAM slack. Similar to hard disks, file slack on magnetic tape can contain remnants of data from previously existing files.

Summary

It is important for computer forensics investigators to understand the vast array of digital devices that they may encounter at a crime scene. This knowledge is essential because each device needs to be handled differently, and investigators must maintain and update different power and data cables over time. Moreover, with each device, there are different types of evidence associated with each device, and a different methodology is required to acquire evidence from these devices.

Hard disk drives are a primary source of evidence for investigators. There are different types of hard disk drives, which are mainly differentiated by their drive controllers and connections. There are Small Computer System Interface (SCSI) hard disk drives and Integrated Drive Electronic (IDE) hard disk drives. However, Serial ATA (SATA) hard disk drives have become more prevalent. Hard disk drives are cloned rather than imaged when a hard disk drive needs to be copied quickly. Solid state drives have gained market share in recent times but present significant challenges for computer forensics investigators, given the unstable nature of these drives compared to traditional hard disk drives. Occasionally, an investigator will encounter a computer with multiple hard disk drives, referred to as a Redundant Array of Independent Disks (RAID).

USB thumb drives and other kinds of flash memory continue to grow in significance as they become cheaper and provide greater memory capacity. However, cloud storage has become even more important. Interestingly, though, connecting USB devices to a computer leaves a digital footprint in the Windows computer's Registry, which the investigator then can view. This digital footprint is also often available on Mac and UNIX systems.

Key Terms

Blu-ray disc (BD): A high-capacity optical disc that can be used to store high-definition video.

Boot Camp: A utility included with macOS that enables a user to run a Windows operating system on an Intel-based Mac.

compact disc: A polycarbonate plastic disc with one or more metal layers that is used to store data digitally.

CompactFlash: A memory card that was first developed by SanDisk for use in portable electronics such as digital cameras.

dd: A UNIX command that produces a raw data image of a storage medium, such as a hard drive or magnetic tape, in a forensically sound manner.

Digital Versatile Disc (DVD): An optical disc with a large storage capacity that was developed by Philips, Sony, Toshiba, and Time Warner.

disk clone: An exact copy of a hard drive that can be used as a backup for a hard drive because it is bootable, just like the original.

disk controller: Facilitates communication between a computer's central processing unit (CPU) and hard disks (or other disk drives).

disk image: A file or a group of files that contain bit-for-bit copies of a hard drive but cannot be used for booting a computer or other operations.

eSATA: A variation of SATA that is used for external drives.

fault tolerance: The ability of a system to continue to operate if one component in a system, such as a hard disk drive, fails.

File Translation Layer (FTL): Maps a logical block address to a physical block address.

FireWire: The Apple version of IEEE 1394, which is a serial bus interface standard for high-speed data transfer.

floppy disk: A thin, flexible, plastic computer storage disk that is housed in a rigid plastic rectangular case.

frame: The smallest unit of memory on a CD, consisting of 24 bytes.

garbage collection: A memory-management process that involves removing unused files to make more memory available.

Host Protected Area (HPA): The region on a hard disk that often contains code associated with the BIOS for booting and recovery purposes.

Integrated Drive Electronics (IDE): A drive interface, largely based on IBM PC standards, for devices such as hard disk drives, tape drives, and optical drives.

lands: The reflective surfaces on a CD that are burned flat by a laser.

magnetic tape: A thin plastic strip with a magnetic coating that is used for storing audio, video, and data.

Memory Stick: Sony's proprietary memory card that was introduced in 1998.

MultiMediaCard: Storage memory that was developed by Siemens AG and SanDisk for use in portable devices such as cameras.

pits: The less reflective surfaces on a CD that have not been burned by a laser.

RAID (Redundant Array of Independent Disks): Two or more disks used in conjunction with one another to provide increased performance and reliability through redundancy.

Random Access Memory (RAM): Volatile memory that is used for processes that are currently running on a computer.

Secure Digital card: A file storage device that was developed for use in portable electronics such as cameras.

Serial ATA: An interface that connects devices such as hard disk drives to host bus adapters.

session (on a compact disc): A group of tracks recorded at the same time.

Small Computer System Interface (SCSI): A protocol for both the physical connection of devices and the transfer of data.

solid state drive (SSD): A nonvolatile storage device found in computers.

table of contents (TOC): Records the location of the start address, the session number, and track information (music or video) on a compact disc.

track (on a compact disc): A group of sectors that are written to at one time.

TRIM: An operating system function that informs a solid state drive which blocks are no longer in use to allow for high write performance.

wear-leveling: The process by which areas of a storage medium become unusable over time.

write-blocker: A hardware device that allows an individual to read data from a device such as a hard drive without writing to that device.

xD (Extreme Digital) Picture Card: Memory storage developed by Olympus and Fujifilm for digital cameras and some voice recorders.

zip disk: A removable storage medium that was developed by Iomega in the early 1990s.

Assessment

CLASSROOM DISCUSSIONS

1. Under what circumstances is a computer forensics investigator required to conduct an investigation onsite instead of removing a computer for analysis back at the lab?

2. What major challenges do investigators face in regards to removable memory?

MULTIPLE-CHOICE QUESTIONS

1. Which of the following facilitates the communication between a computer's CPU and hard disks?

    A. Actuator arm

    B. ROM chip

    C. Disk controller

    D. FireWire

2. Which of the following is true of a disk clone?

   A. It is a bootable copy.

   B. It can be used as a hard drive backup.

   C. Neither A nor B is true.

   D. Both A and B are true.

3. Which of the following is true of solid state drives?

   A. They have no moving parts.

   B. Files are stored on metal platters.

   C. It is volatile memory.

   D. None of the above are true.

4. Which of the following is volatile memory that is used for processes that are currently running on a computer?

   A. RAM

   B. ROM

   C. Hard disk drive

   D. Flash

5. Which of the following refers to two or more disks used in conjunction with one another to provide increased performance and reliability through redundancy?

   A. RAM

   B. SCSI

   C. IDE

   D. RAID

6. FireWire is based on which of the following standards?

   A. 802.11

   B. ANSI N42

   C. IEEE 1394

   D. ISO 9660

7. Which of the following memory cards is most likely to be found in Sony electronics?

   A. Secure Digital card

   B. CompactFlash

   C. MultiMediaCard

   D. Memory Stick

8. The reflective surfaces on a CD that are burned flat by a laser are referred to as which of the following?

   A. Lands

   B. Pits

   C. Mirrors

   D. Craters

9. Which of the following is a high-capacity optical disc that can be used to store high-definition video?

   A. CD

   B. DVD

   C. BD

   D. VCD

10. Which of the following is a UNIX command that produces a raw data image of a storage medium such as a hard drive or magnetic tape in a forensically sound manner?

    A. aa

    B. bb

    C. cc

    D. dd

FILL IN THE BLANKS

1. Boot _____ is a utility included with Mac OS X 10.6 (Snow Leopard) that enables the user to run a Windows operating system on an Intel-based Mac.

2. Integrated Drive _____ is a drive interface, connector, and controller that is largely based on IBM PC standards for devices such as hard disk drives, tape drives, and optical drives.

3. _____ ATA is an interface that connects devices such as hard disk drives to host bus adapters.

4. A disk _____ is actually one file or a group of files that contain bit-for-bit copies of a hard drive but cannot be used for booting a computer or for other operations.

5. The Host _____ Area is a region on a hard disk that often contains code associated with the BIOS for booting and recovery purposes.

6. _____ collection is a memory management process that involves removing unused files to make more memory available.

7. Fault _____ means that if one component in a system, such as a hard disk drive, fails, the system will continue to operate.

8. A(n) _____ is a hardware device that allows an individual to read data from a device such as a hard drive without writing to that device.

9. The less reflective surfaces on a CD that have not been burned by a laser are called _____.

10. A(n) _____ disk is a thin, flexible plastic computer storage disk that is housed in a rigid plastic rectangular casing.

PROJECTS

Work with a Dual-Boot System

Find an Apple Mac computer running a dual-boot system or install Boot Camp and Microsoft Windows on an Apple Mac with macOS currently running. Create standard operating procedures to help computer forensics investigators identify whether a Mac computer is running more than one operating system and determine how to acquire digital evidence from this type of machine.

Identify Changes in Computer Hardware

Write an essay that discusses how computer hardware and memory are likely to be transformed over the next 5 years. Include in your discussion how computer forensics practices will have to change to keep pace with changing technology.

Identify the Use of RAID

Find out how an investigator can identify whether a suspect's computer is running RAID. How should RAID be forensically examined?

Work with Volatile Memory

Random Access Memory (RAM) can provide an extraordinary amount of evidence. What computer forensics tools can be used to image RAM? Are there any issues with using RAM as a source of evidence in an investigation?

Explain USB Flash Memory

Explain the physical makeup of a USB flash drive. Include in your explanation how files are stored and organized on this type of storage device.

Reference

James Wardell and G. Stevenson Smith, "Recovering Erased Digital Evidence from CD-RW Discs in a Child Exploitation Investigation", *International Journal of Digital Forensics & Incident Response* 5 (no. 1–2), 2008.

Chapter 4

Acquiring Evidence in a Computer Forensics Lab

Learning Outcomes

After reading this chapter, you will be able to understand the following:

- Requirements for a certified computer forensics laboratory;
- Best practices for managing and processing evidence in a computer forensics laboratory;
- Structuring a computer forensics laboratory;
- Computer forensics laboratory requirements for hardware and software;
- Best practices for acquiring, handling, and analyzing digital evidence;
- Methods for investigating financial fraud; and
- How to use UNIX commands to search files for particular information of interest.

The process by which an investigator acquires evidence is just as important as the evidence itself. Remember that the term *forensic* means "suitable for a court of law". Evidence can only be brought to trial if it was legally obtained using a search warrant, approved by a court magistrate or a judge, or if appropriate consent to a search was granted. Certain forms are necessary when handling evidence, including the chain of custody form. Additionally, because forensics is a science, the process by which the evidence was acquired must be repeatable, and produce the same results. As previously noted, the increased volatility of storage media means that some results may change. It is, however, important to understand that individual user-created data or files are likely to remain unchanged. Furthermore, in Chapter 9, "Mobile Forensics", you will learn that advances in mobile device encryption have prompted investigators to use more invasive techniques for examining mobile devices. These techniques include chip-off, which renders the device unusable for the future and the technique is generally not repeatable for the same device.

Lab Requirements

The creation of a computer forensics laboratory, with all of the necessary equipment, is critical to evidence handling, acquisition, and analysis. Moreover, there are important management considerations to be aware of. Although notable differences might exist between one computer forensics laboratory and another, there are still similarities in the basic requirements and guidelines for forensics laboratories. These requirements ensure that certain standards are maintained in terms of equipment used and that industry standards for utilizing that equipment are maintained. Many fields, related to computer science, are bereft of standards to guide us. However, in computer forensics, standard practices do exist, and they are assessed and certified by an independent body known as the American Society of Crime Laboratory Directors.

American Society of Crime Laboratory Directors (ASCLD)

ASCLD is a non-profit organization that provides a set of guidelines and standards for forensic labs. The organization not only promotes excellence in forensic practices, but also encourages innovation in the forensic practitioner community. ASCLD is not an accrediting body and should not be confused with ASCLD/LAB. More information can be found on their website at ascld.org.

American Society of Crime Laboratory Directors/Lab Accreditation Board (ASCLD/LAB)

ASCLD/LAB was originally a committee, within ASCLD, when it was created in 1981. Since 1982, however, it has been accrediting crime labs. In 1984, ASCLD/LAB became a separate non-profit entity with its own board of directors. It currently certifies labs for federal, state, and local agencies, as well as some crime labs based outside the United States. The certification process of crime labs includes computer forensics labs. As an impartial entity, ASCLD/LAB strives to maintain certain standards for forensics labs, including standards that govern the behavior and practices of lab employees and their managers. In other words, those who work in a forensics lab must be always mindful of the law and continually adhere to proper scientific practices. Moreover, ASCLD/LAB also promotes a code of ethics for lab staff and management.

ASCLD/LAB Guidelines for Forensic Laboratory Management Practices

Laboratory managers are advised to act with integrity and create an environment of trust and honesty. A forensics laboratory should also have quality controls and maximize the use of laboratory resources in an efficient manner, to effectively manage the laboratory's casework. A laboratory manager is also accountable for maintaining the health and safety of those who work in the lab. Furthermore, maintaining the security of the laboratory, particularly with respect to access, is also a responsibility of the manager. The manager must also ensure that she hires highly qualified staff and also encourages research and continuous training, including staff certifications. The following list summarizes the proper laboratory management practices, as outlined by ASCLD/LAB (https://www.ascld.org/wp-content/uploads/2018/07/Guidelines-for-Forensic-Laboratory-Management-Practices-2018.pdf):

- Managerial competence
- Integrity
- Quality
- Efficiency
- Productivity
- Meeting organizational expectations
- Health and safety
- Security
- Management information systems
- Qualifications
- Training
- Maintaining employee competency
- Staff development
- Environment
- Communication
- Supervision
- Fiscal
- Conflict of interest
- Response to public needs
- Professional staffing
- Recommendations and references
- Legal compliance
- Fiscal responsibility
- Accountability
- Disclosure and discovery
- Work quality
- Accreditation

- Peer certification

- Peer organizations

- Research

- Ethics

Many law enforcement agencies strive to attain ASCLD/LAB certification, but most never secure this certification. It might not always be necessary to realize this certification, but agencies should still try to adhere to many of the principles outlined by ASCLD/LAB, including maintaining best practices and industry protocols, proper documentation, and ongoing training for lab personnel.

ISO/IEC 17025:2017

ISO/IEC 17025:2017 are the "General requirements for the competence of testing and calibration laboratories". These international standards can apply to any type of laboratory that carries out calibration and testing activities, which may include digital forensics laboratories. Formed in 1946, the International Organization for Standardization (ISO) is an independent, non-government organization, which is comprised of 162 national standard bodies. ISO provides guidance on many standards in technology, from certifications to hardware and software standards. For example, ISO 9660 provides guidance for the Compact Disc File System (CDFS) and the hardware for optical disc manufacturers. Thus, a music CD purchased in Ireland can work on a CD player in Canada.

ISO/IE 17025 may be used in conjunction with ASCLD/LAB. The version, released in 2017, replaces the previous guidelines that were released in 2005. The latest version provides a greater emphasis on information technology, through the use of computer systems, electronic results, and reporting. While the standards outlined in ISO/IEC 17025:2017 have been primarily adopted by traditional scientific laboratories (biology, chemistry, medical, etc.), in theory, these standards could be adopted by a digital forensic laboratory.

Scientific Working Group on Digital Evidence (SWGDE)

The **Scientific Working Group on Digital Evidence (SWGDE)** is a committee dedicated to sharing research and setting standards for investigators working with digital and multimedia evidence. The group was formed in 1998 and subsequently began working with ASCLD/LAB in 2000. Later in 2003, the field of digital evidence was added to the ASCLD/LAB accreditation program.

Federal, state, and local law enforcement officers, who do not have any commercial interests, are invited to join as regular members. Additionally, educators, and those from the private sector, can join as associate members. SWDGE is a marvelous resource for computer forensics research on topics that range from investigations involving various operating systems to best practices in mobile phone examinations (www.swgde.org).

SWGDE is well-respected and provides best practices for computer forensics examinations, digital evidence collection, image authentication and much more. Their publications are continually updated to incorporate the latest advances in technology. For example, with a dramatic increase in full disk encryption on computer systems, SWGDE emphasizes the importance of forensically imaging live systems, especially volatile memory (primarily RAM).

Private-Sector Computer Forensics Laboratories

Computer forensics labs exist in the private sector for many reasons. Sometimes a lab is developed to make a profit through client consulting services. Meanwhile, other large organizations maintain labs to investigate internal fraud or fraud suffered by their customers. Banks and credit card companies often have their own internal computer forensics practitioners. All major accounting firms maintain sophisticated computer forensics laboratories that are primarily used to support investigations requested by their clients. Most of these investigations are not criminal investigations but are electronic discovery (eDiscovery) investigations. **eDiscovery** is the detection of electronic data for the purposes of litigation. For example, when a company sues another company, the plaintiff may request certain electronically stored information (ESI). A **plaintiff** is the party that makes a claim against another party and initiates a lawsuit. **Electronically stored information (ESI)** can include email, Word documents, spreadsheets, databases, or any other type of digitally stored information. Under the Sarbanes–Oxley Act, publicly traded companies must maintain all electronic information for a specific period of time. Retention times for documents are dependent upon the type of document and the industry. U.S. companies that handle personal data for European citizens must also comply with data retention rules embodied in the General Data Protection Regulation (GDPR). Sometimes the Securities and Exchange Commission (SEC) will issue a *10-day notice* to a publicly-traded company. This notice directs a company to produce certain documents, pertaining to an investigation, within 10 days. For many companies, which may have tens of thousands of hard drives, finding specific historical information may be impractical given their limited IT resources and the imposed time constraint. Therefore, many companies will employ the services of accounting firms to quickly find the information requested by SEC investigators.

eDiscovery generally requires the expertise of computer forensics investigators, information technology (IT) staff, and corporate lawyers. The IT staff generally coordinates with computer forensics investigators to determine the location of the evidence (servers or employee computers), and the computer forensics investigators ensure that all evidence acquired is done so in a scientific manner and ultimately is available as court-admissible evidence. The lawyers will determine the value of the evidence extracted. In summary, the corporate IT staff members act as liaisons between the computer forensics examiners and the firm's lawyers.

At large accounting firms, several different laboratories make up the computer forensics department. Although there are differences from company to company, the following is an outline of the different types of laboratories. Moreover, the skills the staff members possess can differ according to the area in which they work.

Evidence Acquisition Laboratory

An evidence acquisition laboratory is responsible for extracting evidence from hard drives, flash drives, and other storage devices to create read-only forensic image files. The staff members in this laboratory need to be skilled in imaging software like FTK, EnCase, and X-Ways. Additionally, they will often have to crack passwords using tools like AccessData's Password Recovery Toolkit (PRTK), perhaps with the addition of rainbow tables. **Rainbow tables** are password hashes used for a dictionary attack on a file or even a volume. Files, folders, and drives may also need to be decrypted. Laptop hard drives and associated removable flash memory or external drives often utilize an encryption tool such as Credant, and therefore a computer forensics examiner will need a decryption key. Often, decryption is nearly impossible or impossible when a suspect has used Pretty Good Privacy (PGP) encryption or has activated full-disk encryption using FileVault or FileVault2 on a Mac.

Email Preparation Laboratory

Email evidence is arguably the most important type of evidence that can be retrieved from a computer. Email often reveals our most innermost thoughts and the most incriminating evidence. Because of the tremendous importance of email in investigations, some computer forensics departments have a laboratory dedicated to email examinations, where staff will parse email files to make them easier to view by attorneys involved in a case.

Inventory Control

Sometimes an investigation involves thousands of hard drives and storage media. Moreover, the sources can vary greatly, from magnetic tapes, to hard disk drives, to zip disks, to thumb drives. Therefore, proper management and control of this storage media is critical. A laboratory is often devoted to the management and storage of evidence.

Large corporate investigations create vast amounts of evidentiary data. For example, the collapse of Enron, due to corporate malfeasance, necessitated the use of numerous computer forensics examiners, who sifted through thousands of emails and other digital data. The investigation generated 31 terabytes of data (10^{12} bytes), which is the equivalent of 15 academic libraries. More paper was generated for this one investigation than exists in the Library of Congress.

Laboratory Information Management Systems

Using an off-the-shelf product will reduce the time to develop and manage case management and may be necessary if system developers are not available or cannot be factored into a budget. Lima Forensic Case Management, by IntaForensics, is one option for a digital forensics laboratory. ASCLD/LAB also provides guidance about case management. Nevertheless, if information technology developers are available, then it is recommended that a custom information management system be developed. This is because the needs of each laboratory are different. For example, the needs of an eDiscovery firm are very different from a high technology crime laboratory for a district attorney's office. A larger district attorney's office may maintain a scheduling system for prosecutors to meet with forensic examiners. The crime laboratory may also maintain a special intake area for evidence so that a prosecutor does not need to enter the crime laboratory. With larger laboratories, an information management system is critical so that cases are managed appropriately and are prioritized. Furthermore, an information management system should have a comprehensive reporting system so that case metrics can be reported and to help senior management identify how the purchase of forensic tools and training programs may be justified.

Web Hosting

Once evidence has been extracted, analyzed, and parsed into a readable format, it needs to be made available to a company's lawyers. Simply emailing the evidence to legal counsel is often not feasible. Therefore, a computer forensics department or consulting firm may provide a web hosting service, where authorized individuals can access the evidence for an investigation through a secure website. **Discovery** is the period leading up to a trial when each party involved in civil litigation can request evidence from the other party. Hence, web hosting can provide a safe and effective way to display evidence to the plaintiff and defense counsels. Of course, discovery can not only include evidence from a computer but also evidence in the form of depositions or subpoenas from entities not party to a lawsuit.

The technical skills of staff members, assigned to this area of a computer forensics department, are certainly different than in other areas of the department. Website designers are required (at least, during the initial phase) to create the site, and web developers are needed to organize the information. Additionally, staff skilled in database design, development, and management are required to create a database that will not only contain searchable evidence and reporting features, but also will manage access to relevant information in a secure manner. Additionally, staff are needed to continually upload and maintain the evidence online for various investigations.

Computer Forensics Laboratory Requirements

Computer forensics labs vary greatly from region to region, but there are certain standards and requirements that every lab must maintain. This section details the basic layout, equipment, and standards that a legitimate computer forensics lab must adhere to.

Laboratory Layout

The layout of your laboratory will be determined by your investigative needs, the number of staff who will be involved in investigations, and the resources that you have available. Figure 4.1 is a diagram of a relatively small computer forensics laboratory.

Key

A – Equipment Closet
B – Evidence Locker
C – PC Workstation
D – Mac Workstation
E – Workbench

FIGURE 4.1   Compact computer forensics laboratory

Workstations

The workstations in a computer forensics laboratory are used for investigators to acquire evidence in the form of read-only image files. With the proliferation of Apple Macintosh computers, it is now more commonplace to find Macintosh workstations. All workstations should be password protected and should ideally use biometric authentication to gain access. All case files should be password protected. Many forensic tools, like FTK, require a good processor, more volatile memory (RAM) and large storage space because of indexing and necessary database storage. Therefore, investing in a workstation with the best processor, at least 32GB of RAM and at least 2TB of disk space are essential. The process of imaging a hard drive takes a long time today, and therefore obtaining a powerful system will increase examiner productivity on cases. One potential solution, which is scalable, is the FRED (Forensic Recovery of Evidence Device) Workstation. Digital Intelligence produces these forensic workstations. What is convenient about these powerful systems is that storage can easily be swapped in and out of the workstation through a series of drive bays on the front of these computers.

Workbench

A **workbench** is used to prepare hardware devices for investigative analysis. When cloning a device, the computer's case is opened to remove the hard drive. On the area where hard drives will be cloned, there should be rubber mats to ensure that no static electricity from a metal surface will interfere with the suspect's drives. If an Apple iMac needs to be opened to retrieve the hard drive, a lot of space is required to ensure that the screen is dismantled safely (without damage). As with all electronic evidence, the area needs to be well lit—not only to work safely with evidence, but also photograph all evidence.

Mobile Device Examination Workbench

Generally, every investigation today involves at least one smartphone. Now that full-disk encryption has become the default for most smartphones, more invasive techniques, which require taking the device apart, have become the norm. Therefore, maintaining a workbench for investigators to dismantle mobile devices and perform soldering with the aid of a microscope is important. Chapter 9 discusses these invasive techniques, including JTAG, chip-off, and ISP. Table 4.1 outlines some equipment that should be considered for a mobile device examination workbench.

TABLE 4.1   Mobile Device Examination Workbench Hardware and Software

Mobile Forensics Hardware	Mobile Forensics Software (Android & iOS)
Cellebrite UFED Touch2	Cellebrite Physical Analyzer
GreyKey (unlocks iPhones – only available to law enforcement)	Oxygen Forensics
MFC Dongle (some iPhones)	BlackLight (iOS & macOS), BlackBag.
RIFF Box 2 (JTAG burner phone or Windows phone examinations)	
ORT Box (JTAG burner phone examinations)	
ZRT3 (www.fernico.com/ZRT3.aspx) (manual burner phone examinations)	
Ramsay Box STE6000 (Faraday box)	
Paraben Stronghold Bags (Faraday).	

Field Kit Storage Unit

When space permits, a high technology crime laboratory should maintain a field kit storage unit or a workbench. Many forensic investigators are also sworn law enforcement and may be required to execute warrants and perform onsite collections as a Crime Scene Investigator (CSI). The hardware and software required for a crime scene will often differ from the tools used in the laboratory. For example, a CSI will often need to perform triage at the crime scene, and this may include imaging a live system. Table 4.2 provides a list of some hardware and software that a CSI may take with her when executing a warrant.

TABLE 4.2   Field Kit Storage Hardware, Software, and Miscellaneous Tools

Hardware	Software	Miscellaneous
Sanitized Hard Drives (at least 4 drives with each duplicator, for example 2 x 2TB and 2 x 4TB. More is always better)	X-Ways dongle and portable USB SSD drive with X-Ways Forensics installed	Forms (chain of custody, custodian consent, Server/HDD/computer worksheets, etc.)
Powerful laptop (to test collected images and to potentially collect evidence over the network, e.g. F-Response)	Large capacity (128/256 GB) USB flash drive, with RAM capture tools such as DUMPIT, Magnet RAM Capture, etc.	Evidence bags
Cellebrite UFED (cellphones always appear when executing a search warrant)	Large capacity (128/256 GB) USB flash drive with FTK Imager Light, Magnet Encrypted Disk Detector, Web Page Saver	IFIXIT kit
Faraday Bags	F-Response Dongles (https://www.f-response.com)	Multi-tip screwdriver
External USB HD FAT32 formatted (at least 2 x 2TB, used for CCTV, DVR footage collections).	Mouse Jiggler (phony mouse input).	Flashlight
Sanitized Hard Drives (at least 4 drives with each duplicator, for example, 2 x 2TB and 2 x 4TB. More is always better)		Camera (or smartphone)
		Leatherman multi-tool
		Sharpie markers
		Wet cell phone emergency drying kit
		Pens
		Sticky notes

Faraday Room

Faraday rooms and Faraday boxes at high technology crime laboratories have become more commonplace with the exponential growth of smartphones. A Faraday room will enable an investigator to conduct an analysis of a mobile device, without being concerned about the device connecting to a network. An investigator is not only concerned with network connections changing the original state of the device, and its files, but a bigger concern is a suspect sending a remote wipe command to his mobile device and leaving no evidence on the device. This concern is especially true for iPhones and MacBook computers.

Evidence Locker

An **evidence locker** is a metal cabinet with individual compartments that can be locked individually. These cabinets are often made of steel with tamper-resistant padlocks. A high-end door lock, like a Simplex lock, should be used with other physical security measures. Figure 4.2 shows an image of the door to an evidence room, and Figure 4.3 shows digital evidence stored in the evidence room.

FIGURE 4.2   Evidence locker

FIGURE 4.3   Digital evidence

Cabinets

When planning the development of a computer forensics lab, provision should be made for at least two large closets (cabinets). One cabinet is needed to store reference materials. These reference materials should include textbooks, professional journals, binders with articles, and training manuals. Reference materials should also include laboratory operating procedures, legal reference materials, and standard operating procedures for investigations. A second cabinet can be used to store forensic equipment.

Hardware

A number of hardware devices must be budgeted for when developing a computer forensics laboratory. The following sections highlight the most important items that should be purchased.

Cloning Devices

Every computer forensics laboratory should have a forensic disk duplicator (cloning device) for forensically cloning hard disk drives at the crime scene or in the laboratory. Many different types of hard disk duplicators exist. They generally provide a feature to sanitize a harvest drive, which is an important process in preparing for an investigation. However, when purchasing a disk cloner, the purveyor should ensure that the device is a "forensic" device. Higher-end hard disk cloners have the ability to create multiple copies simultaneously. The investment is worthwhile if the laboratory handles large quantities of suspect hard drives. Disk cloners typically support both SATA and IDE hard disk drive connections.

Write-Blockers

As noted in Chapter 3, "Handling Computer Hardware", a write-blocker is a hardware device that allows an individual to read data from a device, such as a hard drive, without writing to that device. In general, a write-blocking kit will include a number of different write-blockers, power adapters, and cables, which will connect to eSATA, SATA (see Figure 4.5), IDE, Serial Attached SCSI, USB (see Figure 4.7), and FireWire (see Figure 4.6) devices. A lab should also maintain a write-blocking card reader (see Figure 4.8) for Secure Digital cards, xD cards, Memory Sticks, and so on, as well as a ZIF hard drive adapter and cables. The latter is used for imaging or cloning 1.8-inch ZIF hard disk drives, manufactured by Toshiba, Samsung, and Hitachi. These hard disk drives can be found in Dell Latitude D420 and D430 laptops. When the ZIF adapter and ZIF cable are connected between the suspect's 1.8-inch ZIF hard disk drive and the IDE connection, cloning the drive can often fail, so be prepared to image the drive through the USB connection on the laptop (with a write-blocker of course). Any failure to clone or image a drive should be included in the investigator's notes.

FIGURE 4.4   2.5-inch IDE hard drive adapter

FIGURE 4.5   UltraBlock SATA/IDE write-blocker

FIGURE 4.6   UltraBlock FireWire 800 + USB 2.0 SCSI bridge (write-blocker)

FIGURE 4.7   UltraBlock USB write-blocker

FIGURE 4.8   UltraBlock forensic card reader

SIM Card Readers

Cellular telephones that operate on the Global System for Mobile (GSM) Communications network contain a Subscriber Identity Module (SIM) card, which will need to be forensically examined using a SIM card reader (see Figure 4.9). Chapter 9 provides more information on this topic.

FIGURE 4.9   SIM card reader

Harvest Drives

Harvest drives are hard disk drives that act as receptacles for evidence acquired from the suspect's hard disk drive. A computer forensics laboratory often uses thousands of SATA drives annually. Remember, in most cases, two copies of each of the suspect's hard drive are made. The same type of SATA hard disk drives can be used to clone the hard disk drives of both Macintosh computers (Macs) and personal computers (PCs), regardless of whether they are desktops or laptops. As previously noted, harvest drives should be sanitized (wiped clean) when initially purchased. Naturally, a variety of sizes of hard disk drives should be purchased, and an investigator should always have hard drives with the latest capacities available to ensure that they can cope with the latest technologies. An investigator should also always carry extra harvest drives to an investigation because the cloning process can fail and there may be no time to sanitize the harvest drive (or destination drive) again and restart an acquisition. USB-powered hard disk drives (see Figure 4.10) should also be part of the investigator's collection of harvest drives because direct drive-to-drive cloning may not be possible.

FIGURE 4.10   USB-powered hard drive

Toolkits

Every computer forensics examiner needs a computer toolkit similar to the one depicted in Figure 4.11. The tools are primarily screwdrivers used for removing hard drives from desktops, laptops, and the enclosures surrounding external hard drives. Other tools should also be considered, including a snips to remove cable fasteners and pliers to hold or bend wires and other objects.

FIGURE 4.11   Computer toolkit

Flashlights

An investigator sometimes requires the use of a good flashlight for locations where the lighting is poor and inadequate. Moreover, there are times when a suspect may try to hide digital devices and therefore a flashlight is required.

Digital Cameras

An investigator's notes are key to effectively documenting an investigation. Photographing devices that are seized is critical to properly documenting an investigation. An investigator should take photographs of where the devices are located. Additionally, the configuration of devices or how they are connected should be carefully photographed and documented. This is important because the investigator may need to re-create how a number of devices were connected, especially with an unusual setup that is unfamiliar to the investigator.

When photographing a computer, the investigator must photograph the computer, its drive bays (CD/DVD, etc.), ports (serial, USB, etc.), and the serial number of the computer. The serial number format varies on different computers; sometimes there will be "S/N" before the number, and on Dell computers, the serial number is called the Service Tag. When the cover on a desktop is removed to display the hard disk drive, be sure to look for multiple hard disk drives. The investigator should photograph the drives before they are removed and then note the order in which each hard disk drive was located. Each drive should be differentiated by the serial number of the hard disk drive. Each hard disk drive should be photographed, and the investigator should verify that the serial number in each photograph is clearly visible. Finally, it is always important to bring replacement batteries for the digital camera.

Evidence Bags

Evidence bags (see Figure 4.12) come in many shapes and sizes, but they all serve the same purpose: to prevent tampering evidence and to record the chain of custody. This means that an evidence bag will have a tamper-resistant device, like an adhesive closure strip, so that the evidence cannot be accessed surreptitiously. **Antistatic polyethylene evidence bags** are designed to protect electronic devices from static electricity, and a computer forensics examiner should always have these when going onsite (crime scene).

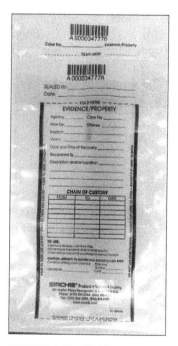

FIGURE 4.12   Evidence bags.

Evidence Labels

All drive bays should be sealed with an evidence label, and computers should be wrapped with tape to ensure that the evidence is not tampered with.

Software

A computer forensics laboratory should purchase and download different types of software. The laboratory should have computers running Windows and Mac operating systems. There should also be licenses for Microsoft Office and other applications that may be required to view files. A laboratory not only needs bit stream imaging tools, but must also have password-cracking software tools, an MD5 program for evidence verification, antivirus software, and virtual machine software. The list that follows illustrates the wide range of software requirements for a computer forensics laboratory. Chapter 9 covers the software requirements for mobile forensics.

Computer Forensic and Bit-Stream Imaging Software

Many forensic imaging tools can be considered for use in a computer forensics laboratory. A combination of imaging tools is ideal because each tool has its own strengths in terms of recognizing partitions, the type and number of files recovered, filtering, and decryption. Using different tools on the same drive frequently recovers varying amounts of evidence, and it is good practice to use multiple tools and log these differences in the case notes for the investigation.

Many of the tools discussed here have 30-day trials available, which makes it easier to determine which tools are most suitable. The pricing for each of the tools listed varies, but discounts are often available for those in law enforcement, government agencies, and academia. The tools also have notable differences in features, and some companies, like opentext, will build customized programs for their clients.

The following is a list of differences between computer forensic tools that should be noted when considering which tool to purchase:

- File systems supported
- Password cracking and decryption
- Hardware requirements to run the tool
- Cost
- Customer support*
- File filtering
- Evidence file backups

---

* Customer support can include software setup, hardware configuration, use of programmers for customized add-ons, and even the availability of an expert witness to testify in court.

- GUI (user interface)

- Reporting features

- Security of evidence files created.

Some organizations will purchase a tool, like EnCase or FTK, so that they can avail of an expert witness, from the vendor, should a case ultimately go to trial. Forensic tools that have been noted and accepted in court proceedings are arguably better to use in an investigation. To reiterate, there will often be differences in the level of evidence acquired by each tool, and therefore multiple tools should be used when gathering and analyzing the same devices and evidence. The following is a list of forensic imaging and analysis tools that you may consider for use in a digital forensics lab:

- **The Sleuth Kit (TSK) and Autopsy Forensic Browser**—The Sleuth Kit is an open source computer forensics tool that is comprised of a group of command-line tools. The tool allows an investigator to examine file systems and a hard disk drive's volume. This tool supports NTFS, FAT, exFAT, YAFFS2, UFS 1, UFS 2, Ext2, Ext3, Ext4, Ext2FS, Ext3FS, HFS and ISO 9660 file systems. Raw dd images can also be analyzed using the tool. Autopsy is a graphical user interface (GUI) that is used in conjunction with The Sleuth Kit. These tools can be used on either Windows or UNIX systems. Further information about this tool is available at www.sleuthkit.org.

- **ILook**—The ILook Investigator suite of tools was developed by Elliot Spencer in conjunction with the IRS Criminal Investigation Electronic Crimes Program. Further information about this tool can be found at www.ilook-forensics.org.

- **DriveSpy**—This forensic tool provides detailed information about a hard disk drive, including DOS and non-DOS partitions, slack space, allocated and unallocated disk space, and many other features. The tool logs when files are added or deleted from a location. More importantly, the tool allows the investigator to create a disk-to-disk forensic duplicate. The downside to using this tool is that it uses a DOS command-line interface instead of a nice user-friendly interface.

- **X-Ways Forensics**—This tool is a well-recognized forensic imaging tool. It supports numerous file systems (FAT12, FAT16, FAT32, exFAT, TFAT, NTFS, Ext2, Ext3, Ext4, Next3, CDFS/ISO9660/Joliet, and UDF). The tool has a particularly effective file-filtering feature, which is important for analyzing hundreds of thousands of files.

- **WinHex**—Like X-Ways Forensics, this software is produced by X-Ways Software Technology AG. This is not a forensic tool because it has write capabilities. Sometimes files are recovered by a forensic tool but cannot be viewed in their natural format because the file is damaged or has been marked for deletion. WinHex comes with a hex editor that allows the user to recover files. In other words, editing a file with a hex editor might make an unreadable file viewable.

- **F-Response**—The tool is used to conduct a live forensic acquisition, perform data recovery or eDiscovery over an IP network. The tool can obtain a full-disk image, perform a RAM capture, or pull cloud data.

- **PALADIN**—Produced by SUMURI, this is a Linux (Ubuntu) distribution, which is open-source.
  It is used for triage and the examination of Mac, Windows, Android, and Linux systems. PALADIN is a suite of forensic tools that includes Autopsy, from Basis Technology.

- **Mobilyze**—The tool is produced by BlackBag Technologies and is used for triage on iOS and Android mobile devices. In January 2020, it was announced that Cellebrite acquired BlackBag Technologies.

- **AXIOM**—Produced by Magnet Forensics, the tool is used for digital evidence recovery and analysis from computers, smartphones, IoT devices, and cloud services.

- **FTK**—Forensic Toolkit (FTK) is bit-stream imaging and analysis software produced by AccessData. The software has been well documented in many court trials, including the Scott Peterson murder trial.

A free version of the software, called FTK Imager, is also available. It can be downloaded to a USB flash drive or burned to a CD. This tool allows the user to create a forensic image of a storage device and view the contents of the file system using the built-in hex editor. Beyond that, it has very few capabilities.

The full version of FTK is not free, but it has many other features, including comprehensive reporting, file decryption, and file carving. **File carving** is the process of identifying a file by certain characteristics, like a file header or footer, rather than by the file extension or metadata. For example, a suspect could try to hide images from investigators by changing the file extension of a picture from .jpg to .dll. When conducting a search using File Explorer, you will not be able to find the file, and even trying to open the file will be unsuccessful because the association between the file and the appropriate application has been broken. Nevertheless, in our example, the file is still a picture. The file header for the picture will not have changed. A JPEG file generally shows "JFIF" in the file header, which is the equivalent of "4A 46 49 46" in the hex editor. Tools, like FTK, can identify the true file type and classify it as a picture. The file carving option also extracts files embedded within other files. For example, a picture sent with an email can be viewed within the email using FTK and also as a picture listed with other pictures listed under that category. FTK also facilitates drive indexing. This is the process of taking categories of files, like emails, and creating a list of words found in each file. These words can then be used for keyword searches or even for password cracking. As you can imagine, this indexing function means that the investigator does not have to spend valuable time performing keyword searches by opening one file at a time.

Let's Get Practical!

Image a USB Drive Using FTK Imager

1. Download and open the FTK Imager application.

2. Find a USB drive that you have used before, and then plug it into your computer.

The smaller the memory size, the better; imaging a 2GB USB thumb drive takes a lot less time than imaging a 32GB thumb drive.

3. Click **File**, and then from the displayed menu, click **Add Evidence Item** (see Figure 4.13).

FIGURE 4.13   Add Evidence Item selected

4. In the displayed **Select Source** dialog box, make sure that the **Physical Drive** option is selected, as in Figure 4.14, and then click **Next**.

5. Click the drop-down menu and then select the USB drive, as displayed in Figure 4.15.

You will be able to recognize the drive by noting the size of the drive.

6. Click **Finish**.

7. In the **Evidence Tree** window, click the **Expand** button (icon) and then compare your screen to Figure 4.16.

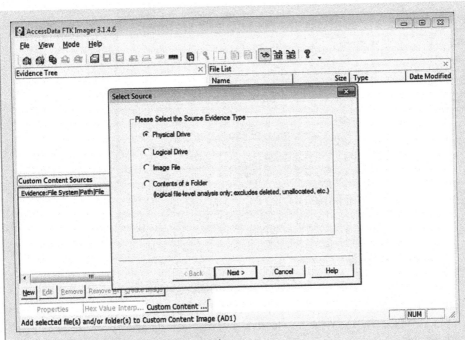

FIGURE 4.14 Physical Drive selected

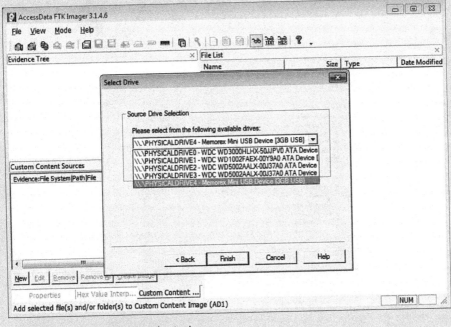

FIGURE 4.15 USB drive selected

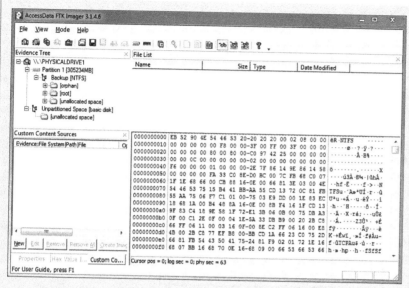

FIGURE 4.16   FTK Imager user interface

8. Click to further expand the drive and folders. You can also double-click a folder to open that folder.

If you have deleted any files or folders on your drive, they will display with a red X, as in Figure 4.17.

FIGURE 4.17   FTK Imager user interface showing deleted files

9. Click to select a file. Click **Mode**, and then click **Hex**. Compare your screen with Figure 4.18.

Notice from the file selected that the file type is noted as .xml.

FIGURE 4.18   FTK Imager user interface

10. Click **File** and then click **Exit**.

The pay-per-license version of FTK also contains a tool called Password Recovery Toolkit (PRTK), which can recover passwords from applications. These passwords can then be used to access to files, folders, and drives that a user password protected.

FTK provides a Windows-based tool for examining Macintosh computers.

AccessData provides training at various locations throughout the United States and internationally, as well as online. The company also provides the opportunity to become certified with the tool by successfully completing a proficiency test to become an AccessData Certified Examiner (ACE):

- **EnCase**—This forensic software was developed by Guidance Software (now opentext) and is comparable to FTK in terms of functionality, reputation, and expert witnesses. Customers can request that opentext create special add-on programs. **EnScript** is a programming language, developed by opentext, that allows EnCase users to create their own customized functions and features in EnCase. There are numerous websites where EnCase users make EnScripts freely available to other users.

  Guidance Software (now called opentext) also created its own file type: **E01**, a forensic disk image file format. Interestingly, many competitors also utilize this file format as an option in their software. The three primary forensic image file formats are E01, AD1 (AccessData), and dd (or RAW). Computer forensics examiners also sometimes use the SMART file format. **SMART files** are forensic disk image files (compressed or uncompressed). **Advanced Forensics Format (AFF)** is an open source format, which was developed by Simson Garfinkel, and is supported by Autopsy and The Sleuth Kit forensics software. There are many other forensic image file formats that can be used by computer forensics investigators. opentext markets a tool called EnCase Enterprise that companies can use for network-based investigations, including investigations on internal computers and incident handling involving network attacks external to the organization. EnCase Enterprise allows for remote imaging of host computers, servers, and smartphones and tablets on a network. The software also facilitates the imaging of multiple drives simultaneously.

- **Mac Marshal**—Developed by ATC-NY, Mac Marshal is macOS forensic imaging software. Mac Marshal Forensic Edition is used by the investigator on a Mac workstation to retrieve evidence from Mac machines. The software is currently available to law enforcement in the United States for free. Outside the United States, law enforcement and private-sector agencies can purchase the software.

- **BlackLight**—This tool, produced by BlackBag Technologies, is available to the general public. It is used to image Apple Macintosh computers, iPhones, and iPads. More specifically, the tool can image computers running macOS operating systems. The tool can also work to analyze Windows and Android.

Chapter 9 documents the necessary hardware and software for forensically examining cellular telephones.

Virtual Machine Software

Sometimes investigators need to use virtual machine software in an investigation, especially if they think there could be malware on a suspect's machine. A **virtual machine** is a computer running software that allows for an instance of an operating system, or multiple operating systems, without making any changes to the user's computer. In other words, after the user terminates a virtual machine session, the computer's configuration remains unchanged. If a criminal uses virtual machine software to perpetrate criminal activities, this makes the work of the computer forensics examiner difficult because little or no evidence relating to the suspect's activities then can be found on the computer.

VMware is well-known virtual machine software that an investigator can use to reverse-engineer malware. This software is ideal for examining malware because the investigator's computer's settings will remain unaffected by the malware. Examining the malware code is helpful because the programming code for viruses can be compared to identify whether malware code found on victims' computers was authored by the same hacker. Additionally, the virus code may include the IP address of the hacker's computer, which was used for command and control (C&C), so reverse-engineering malware can be extremely helpful in solving a crime. Many malware programs can, however, detect the presence of a virtual machine and in such an instance would not execute.

Antivirus Software

When examining a suspect's machine, an examiner should recognize that viruses could be present on the machine. Having antivirus software running on the investigator's computer should help mitigate the threat of malware.

Password-Cracking Software

A computer forensics examiner commonly encounters computers that are password protected. The entire system may require a password to access the desktop, files, and folders. A separate password may be required for administrator access, which allows for certain access, like installing software. A computer may also have a separate firmware password. **Firmware** refers to programs that control electronic devices like hard disk drives, game consoles, or mobile telephones. Therefore, with the proliferation of numerous types of passwords, effective password-cracking software is necessary.

As previously noted, AccessData's fee-based version of FTK comes with a tool called Password Recovery Toolkit (PRTK). Many law enforcement agencies purchase rainbow tables that contain thousands, or even millions, of different hash values that are used to try to crack passwords. Other notable password-cracking tools include John the Ripper and Cain and Abel. John the Ripper is a free tool that works with Windows, UNIX, and many other operating systems. The Cain and Abel tool is also free and works with Windows to execute brute-force, dictionary, and cryptanalysis attacks. A **brute-force attack** checks all possible keys to decrypt data. A **dictionary attack** uses a predetermined list of words to decrypt data or authenticate a user. **Cryptanalysis** attempts to target weaknesses in protocols and cryptographic algorithms to try to break a system or gain access to data. Passware and ElcomSoft are other companies that provide popular commercial password-cracking tools.

It is important to note, however, that sometimes password-cracking software is not needed because investigators have techniques to circumvent the password system or locate a file containing a system's password.

Photo Forensics

The importance of photos to investigations is clear because they are so personal and they are so prevalent. To give you an example of their importance, an estimated 6 billion photos are uploaded to Facebook every month. Photos can be used in all types of investigations, but child abuse is certainly the most important in terms of relying on evidence to convict a suspect. Photos are also quite important to cases involving intellectual property and copyright issues. Chapter 11, "Photograph Forensics", provides more detailed information about photo forensics.

Photo File Formats

JPEG is the most popular picture file format and is supported by most systems and photo-enabled devices. Many other picture file formats exist, however. Websites can contain JPEG, GIF, and PNG picture formats. Cameras use JPEG and RAW formats. The Adobe Digital Negative (DNG) format also is used, and Microsoft has its proprietary BMP format. All of these images are **raster-based graphics** that are rectangular pictures based on pixels.

Photo files are sometimes compressed. There are two types of compression: (i) **lossy compression** where the picture is made smaller with some image quality compromise and loss of data and (ii) **lossless compression** where unneeded data is eliminated from a file without loss of original data. JPEG photos use lossy compression.

Photo Metadata

As previously noted, EXIF data (see Figure 4.19) is the metadata found in images that can contain the date and time that a photo was taken, the make and model of the camera that took the picture, and an embedded thumbnail of the image. EXIF data can also contain the geographic location (longitude and latitude) of where the photograph was taken. Sometimes the serial number of the camera may also be stored in a photograph. The user may of course also add a personalized description to an image.

Filename	Date	Time	Camera Manufacturer & Model	Width x Height	Size of image file	Exposure (1/sec)	Aperture	ISO	Was flash used?	Focal length
DSCN0029.JPG	2012:09:09	13:10:00	NIKON COOLPIX L810	3456x4608	3507668	1/320	f4.2	80	No	13
DSCN0031.JPG	2012:09:09	13:10:25	NIKON COOLPIX L810	3456x4608	3397764	1/320	f4.2	80	No	13
DSCN0035.JPG	2012:09:09	14:20:17	NIKON COOLPIX L810	3456x4608	3468599	1/400	f4.0	80	No	11
DSCN0039.JPG	2012:09:09	14:21:07	NIKON COOLPIX L810	3456x4608	4021210	1/160	f10.6	80	No	5

FIGURE 4.19   Sample EXIF data

Photo Evidence

Most forensic imaging tools, like FTK, EnCase, and X-Ways, can efficiently find and display photo images in a separate category. More photo images can be found by carving pictures that are embedded in other files, like emails for example. Photo files have now become so large that they are often fragmented across a hard disk drive. When fragmentation occurs, reconstructing these images can be problematic. If a fragment is overwritten, then reconstruction is virtually impossible, which is in contrast to many other file types.

Adroit Forensics

Adroit Forensics is a photo forensics tool developed and distributed by Digital Assembly. Adroit uses a process called SmartCarving, which enables the investigator to reconstruct a photograph when file fragments of the picture are located in non-contiguous sectors on a hard disk. The tool can also categorize photographs by date and by camera. Filters can be applied to search for skin tones and, more specifically, child faces.

Energy Requirements

Computer forensics investigators require more electricity to complete their work than the average employee. This is because an investigator may be cloning, or sanitizing, hard drives while also using a workstation to image a hard drive, while simultaneously using his workstation to build case files. Moreover, some forensic imaging software is optimally run using a quad core processor with a lot of RAM. A FRED Workstation will require even more electricity. Therefore, the workstation alone will utilize more energy than the average workstation. Some workstations are loaded with Graphics Processing Units (GPUs), are dedicated to password-cracking, and consume energy (electricity) at a rapid rate—primarily due to the cooling system required. Additionally, large hard drives are often imaged overnight because of the time the process takes to complete, which makes this occupation different. Many organizations that create computer forensics laboratories fail to understand that the energy utilization is very different from other departments. A licensed electrician may be needed to upgrade the electric box and connections to facilitation greater power consumption. Labs also need an **uninterruptible power supply (UPS)**, a power supply that contains a battery that will maintain power in the event of a power outage. Some UPS for computers are designed so that a backup will automatically be triggered if there is a power outage.

Laboratory Safety

An increase in energy requirements for a computer forensics laboratory introduces an increased risk of electrical fire. Dry chemical fire extinguishers should be strategically placed inside and outside the laboratory. An ABC fire extinguisher is probably the most appropriate for a laboratory. An **ABC fire extinguisher** uses a dry chemical extinguishing solution called monoammonium phosphate powder and ammonium sulfate and is suitable for electrical fires. It is called an ABC extinguisher because it can be used on Class A fires (standard combustibles), Class B fires (flammable liquids), and Class C fires (electrical equipment). According to National Fire Protection Association (NFPA) standards, rechargeable fire extinguishers must be recharged every 10 years and disposable fire extinguishers must be replaced every 12 years. Smoke detectors should also be installed throughout the laboratory and checked every six months.

The health and safety of employees should also include the use of ergonomics. Some suggested purchases include the following for examiner workstations:

- Aeron chair (Herman Millar)
- Antiglare screens
- Adjustable keyboard
- Wrist rests

Budget

Developing a fully functional computer crime laboratory is expensive. For many local law enforcement agencies, it is cost prohibitive. This is why the growth of Regional Computer Forensics Laboratories (RCFLs) across the United States, managed by the FBI and staffed by local law enforcement, has become so important. In January 2011, an RCFL was opened in Orange County, California, at a cost of $7 million.

Setup costs for a computer forensics laboratory are high. Nevertheless, maintenance costs are also exceedingly high for a crime lab. Apart from staff salaries, the costs for maintaining software licenses must be calculated. Continuous education for laboratory staff must also be included in the budget. A computer forensics investigator will also go through an inordinate number of hard disk drives (harvest drives) during criminal investigations. Finally, new electronic devices must be continually purchased and tested with forensic software. For example, new versions of the iPhone, iPad, Samsung Galaxy, and other devices need to be purchased and benchmark tested before suspect devices arrive at the laboratory. Remember, benchmark testing involves the scientific testing of tools on different devices to determine the effectiveness of that forensic tool.

An effective method for budgeting a computer forensics laboratory is to keep copious notes about each criminal investigation. The primary points to document are as follows:

- **Crime category:** For example, identity theft, child pornography, or murder.
- **Investigative hours:** That is, crime scene investigation, lab hours, and report writing.
- **Resources utilized:** That is, software to retrieve the evidence and hardware used to store the evidence, e.g., harvest drives and server space.
- **Suspect devices:** Detail the types of devices seized and examined. This is necessary to justify forensic software and hardware purchases and maintenance fees.

Laboratory Management

The American Society of Crime Laboratory Directors Laboratory Accreditation Board (ASCLD/LAB) provides extensive guidelines on best practices for managing a forensics laboratory. Many people view the ASCLD/LAB certification as the ultimate approval of a forensics laboratory. Most laboratories will never be ASCLD/LAB certified, but many labs still adhere to the principles outlined by ASCLD/LAB. Some forensics laboratory managers believe that attaining this certification will benefit their standing in the courtroom as experts who follow proper protocols. Thus, it is important to outline some of these guiding principles in the proceeding sections.

Laboratory Access

Restricting access to a computer forensics laboratory is extremely important and should be part of your physical security plan. Ideally, only those who handle evidence and manage the laboratory should have access to the room or building where your equipment and evidence are held. Access to a laboratory can be controlled using the following methods:

- Picture identification card
- Biometric authentication
- Security guard
- Closed-circuit television (CCTV)
- Keypad with access code

To prevent unauthorized access, other precautions should be put in place. The laboratory manager can perform a background check, with the assistance of the human resources department, to make sure that employees have nothing in their background, such as a criminal record, that would preclude employment in the laboratory. Naturally, the laboratory manager should also undergo a background check before employees are assigned to the laboratory. Unfortunately, many employers do not continue to monitor the activities of their laboratory employees after they are hired.

Data Access

When making an assessment of laboratory access, it is critical to also review access to the laboratory's data and evidence. Strict controls should govern who has access to certain workstations and who has access to particular cases under investigation. Forensic software, like AccessData's FTK, has an effective means to password-protect certain cases and can allow an investigator to only view certain files in an investigation. Access to files varies because both an investigator and her supervisor may need access to the case. Additionally, prosecutors may require access, as do defense attorneys upon request.

Access to data also includes access to the server rooms where the evidence is backed up. Restricting employee access to these servers is vital. A digital forensics laboratory should maintain a server for backups onsite. However, a lab manager should consider secure cloud storage to store old case evidence.

Data access in an organization can also occur through Wireless Fidelity (Wi-Fi) connections. Ideally, there should be no wireless accessibility in a computer forensics laboratory, but Wi-Fi should be used intermittently for software updates and patches. Removal of wireless connectivity should not be limited to Internet access but should also include removing access to other radio frequencies, including cellular frequencies. **Cellular telephone jammers** are devices that prevent cellular telephone users from connecting with other cellular telephones. The Federal Communications Commission (FCC) has recently warned many organizations about the illegal use of signal jammers, and some computer forensics laboratories have stopped using these devices. The alternative today is the use of a Faraday box or Faraday room for more secure examinations.

Physical Security

In terms of physical security, there should be no openings in any of the walls. For example, the walls should reach the ceilings. If there is a drop-down ceiling, you should ensure that the walls of the laboratory go all the way up to the true ceiling so that access cannot occur from an adjacent room. A laboratory should not have any windows because they are a potential access point.

Laboratory Access Auditing

An audit of those who access the computer forensics laboratory is necessary. Preferably, a system is in place that can automatically record anyone who enters the laboratory, possibly by recording entry automatically when a person uses his or her identification card to enter the laboratory. This audit could hopefully be backed up with CCTV surveillance. At a minimum, there should be a clipboard, by the entry point, where staff and visitors are required to sign in and out of the laboratory with the date and time. Figure 4.20 shows a sample sign-in sheet.

Computer Forensics Laboratory Sign-In

Date	Full Name (CAPS)	Signature	Organization	Time In	Time Out	Approval Signature

Supervisor Signature:_____

Date:_____

FIGURE 4.20   Sample forensics lab sign-in sheet

Location of a Laboratory

A computer forensics laboratory should be located in a secure area that is monitored continuously. Often a laboratory is located in the basement of the building. If this is the case, provision should be made to keep the area dry and cool. The laboratory should also allow for server scalability. In other words, evidence files should be backed up every evening on the laboratory's servers. Over time, more servers will need to be added, and room will need to be allocated to these. When possible, a backup site should be maintained in case the computer forensics laboratory needs to be evacuated. This backup can be planned for in the organization's Disaster Recovery Plan. On 9/11, valuable evidence acquired by law enforcement and stored at the World Trade Center as part of ongoing investigations was destroyed.

Extracting Evidence from a Device

Investigators use three primary methods to extract evidence from a device. The first method involves using a hardware device such as a Talon forensic hard disk drive duplicator. The second method involves using vendor software, such as FTK or EnCase. Finally, another method involves using a line-command interface. This third method involves running Linux commands both to acquire evidence and to search and filter evidence. The Talon and other professional tools, such as EnCase, are expensive, so in the next section, we explain the dd utility, which is a free and accepted tool in the courtroom.

Using the dd Utility

As previously noted, dd is a UNIX command-line utility used to copy data from a source location to a destination. From a computer forensics perspective, dd is important because it is an accepted file format for forensic imagining and because of its versatility. In addition, dd is versatile because it can be used to image very specific data, the user can verify images by using the MD5 algorithm, and images can be sourced from a specific computer on a network and that image sent to a network location.

The basic format of a dd command follows:

```
dd if=<source> of=<destination> bs=<byte size>
```

In the example above, if is short for input file and of is short for output file. The byte size is often set at 512 bytes but differs according to the file system you are working with and how quickly you want to copy the source data.

As noted earlier, a destination drive should be sanitized before acquiring data. dd can be used to forensically clean a drive using the following command:

```
dd if=/dev/zero of=/dev/
```

In the example above, `dev` is short for device. When executed, the drive will have zeros written to it. This command confirms that the drive now just contains zeros:

```
dd if=/dev/sda | hexdump -C | head
```

In the previous example, `sda` refers to the hard disk, which is the source of data you want to copy. Here is a list of other devices you might want to copy from:

- **sr0:** CD-ROM

- **fd0:** Floppy disk

- **sdb1:** USB volume

The following command would then create a copy of the source file:

```
dd if=/dev/ of=/dev/ bs=512 conv=noerror
```

In the previous expression, `conv=noerror` is used to skip blocks with bad data.

A major benefit of using the `dd` utility is the ability to image a file across a network. In UNIX, we can use a utility called netcat to copy files over a network. We use the command `nc`, which is used for netcat. Following is the structure of `dd` over a network:

```
dd if (input file) | nc (NetCat) <Target-IP Address> <Port>
```

Here is an example of a `netcat` command:

```
dd if=/dev/hda bs=512 | nc 192.166.2.1 8888
```

In the previous example, `192.166.2.1` is the IP address of the target computer and `8888` is an arbitrary port number that we will use to transmit the file.

It is also possible to conduct remote imaging of a hard drive over a network using SSH, which can prevent sniffing by a third party (https://www.linode.com/docs/migrate-to-linode/disk-images/copying-a-disk-image-over-ssh/).

Using Global Regular Expressions Print (GREP)

Many computer forensics tools today have become so user-friendly that some people have termed them "push-button forensics". While using these tools can be nice, relying on them too much could mean that an investigator fails to understand the science behind these tools. This is problematic when an investigator is called on to be an expert witness and must explain how these tools work. Additionally, when we have a better understanding of concepts like Global Regular Expressions Print (GREP) and know Linux commands, we gain more control over how we conduct an investigation and become more competent.

Most of the computer forensics imaging tools available contain advanced search features, one of which is GREP. **Global Regular Expressions Print (GREP)** is a powerful set of UNIX expressions used for pattern matching. When using GREP, each line from a file is copied to the buffer, is compared against a search string (or expression), and then, if there is a match, outputs the result to the screen. GREP can be used not only to search through files, but also to search through the output of a program. GREP allows an investigator to search evidence files for key terms or numbers using specialized expressions.

Amazingly, very few computer forensics books cover GREP, even though this powerful search feature can be found in forensic tools like EnCase. Similarly, GREP provides tremendous search capabilities from the command line.

Here is a list of commands used in GREP:

- c Does not print the keyword, but instead details the number of times the keyword displays.

- -f searches a particular file for a keyword.

- -i is not case sensitive, meaning that it ignores the case of the search term.

- -l Outputs the filenames of the matches.

- -n Provides details about which lines in a file contain a match.

- -v Displays the lines that do not contain the keyword.

- -x Outputs only exact matches.

- $ is used to search lines that end in a certain character.

Imagine a file containing the following data:

```
Secluded
Sector
Sect
Sects
$ect
```

The following simple GREP expression searches each line for any word containing Sect in the file test.txt:

```
# grep "Sect" test.txt
```

The following result then prints onscreen:

```
Sector
Sect
Sects
```

To specify the line when the match was made, you use the following:

```
# grep -n "Sect" test.txt
```

The following result then prints onscreen:

```
2:Sector
3:Sect
4:Sects
```

To search for an exact match, use the following command:

```
# grep -x "sect" test.txt
```

The following result prints onscreen:

Nothing is printed to the screen because `Sect` in the file is not an exact match with `sect`.

To find keywords that end with the letter `r`, you use the following expression:

```
# grep "r$" test.txt
```

The following result prints onscreen:

```
Sector
```

Extended Global Regular Expressions Print (EGREP) allows for the additional use of operators not found in basic GREP. The following shows EGREP notation:

Union/or |

Kleene star   *

Kleene plus   +

May or might not appear   ?

The use of ? means that the previous character may or not be in the keyword. Take a look at this example:

```
# grep "Sects?" test.txt
```

The following result prints onscreen:

```
Sect
Sects
```

In EGREP, a | is known as a pipe. On the PC keyboard, hold down the Shift key and then press the key above the Enter key. A pipe functions as an "or" command. Here is an example of an EGREP expression using a pipe:

```
# egrep "Sect|Sects" test.txt
```

the following result prints onscreen:

```
Sect
Sects
```

The same result prints to the screen. Thus, you should remember that GREP and EGREP will often provide multiple expression connotations to produce the same output.

Finally, there is FGREP. **Fast Global Regular Expressions Print (FGREP)** is a UNIX search utility that does not use regular expressions but interprets characters literally and is therefore faster than GREP. Consider an FGREP expression:

```
# fgrep "$ect" test.txt
```

The following result prints onscreen:

```
$ect
```

We can now take a look at a more practical example of how an investigator might use GREP. In this example, a detective has been tipped off about a Word document on a suspect's machine. The file is called bank.docx. The investigator does not know the name of the file or its contents, but we know:

```
Dave,
Here's the stolen credit card details that I told you about.
Have fun!
J-Man

1. James Colgan
Card# 6011-0001-0001-0001-0001
CVV: 444
Expiration: 12/14
Telephone: (212) 555-0879
SS# 123-45-6789

2. Francis Bolger
Card# 53690001000100010001
CVV: 444
Expiration: 0113
Telephone: 6095551111
```

An informant told the detective that the suspect had accessed the Word document (.docx) within the past three days. The following GREP expression can find all Word documents accessed in the past three days:

```
# find . -name '*.docx' -atime -3
```

Here is a breakdown of that command:

- # is automatically added in UNIX and indicates that this is the root user.
- find is the search function in FGREP.
- . refers to all files being searched.
- -name refers to a search for a filename.
- * is the Kleene star, which means that anything can display before the proceeding file extension.
- .docx refers to the file extension we are searching for.
- -atime refers to the access time.
- -3 refers to three—in this case, three days.

If the detective knew the approximate modify date, then -mtime (Modified Date) could have been used instead of -atime (Access Date).

The following are some additional helpful GREP expressions for investigators.

City, State, Zip Code

```
'[a-zA-Z]*, [A-Z][A-Z][0-9][0-9][0-9][0-9][0-9]'
```

Email Address

```
'[a-z0-9\.]*@[a-z0-9\.]*\.[a-z][a-z][a-z]+'
```

The + indicates that there could be either two or three letters at the end of the email address.

The following GREP expression will find an IP address:

IP Address

```
'[0-9]*\.[0-9]*\.[0-9]*\.[0-9]*'
```

This regular expression is for IPv4 addresses. The * looks for any number of characters between 0 and 9 digits long. The \. indicates that a period follows.

FTK and EnCase tools have their own versions of GREP, so understanding the GREP commands listed previously is extremely helpful.

Financial Fraud

The criminal investigation noted above involved financial fraud and, more specifically, credit card theft. Before continuing with GREP searches of the file listed previously, it is prudent to understand some basic information about credit cards to make your GREP searches more efficient. Moreover, credit card fraud is a huge problem in the Western world.

There are distinctive groups of bank and credit cards. Certain cards, like American Express, MasterCard, and Visa, are issued through banks. These can be in the form of credit, debit, or prepaid (or gift) cards. Other cards, like Discover, are issued direct to the customer without a secondary bank. Capital One is in a separate category, as it is a bank that issues its own credit cards.

When searching for credit card numbers on a computer, it is helpful to know how the numbering system works. The **Major Industry Identifier (MII)** refers to the first digit of a credit card number. Figure 4.21 shows some issuer categories.

MII	Category	Card Issuers
3	Travel & Entertainment & Banking/Financial	American Express, Diner s Club
4	Banking & Financial	Visa
5	Banking & Financial	MasterCard
6	Merchandising & Banking/Financial	Discover

FIGURE 4.21   MII chart

The Issuer Identification Number (IIN) refers to the first six digits of a credit card number. A credit card number can range from 12 digits to 19 digits. Figure 4.22 shows a list of some of the major credit card issuers and their IINs.

Issuer	IIN Range	No. of Digits
American Express	34, 37	15
Discover Card*	6011, 6440-6599	16
MasterCard	51-54	16
Visa	4	16

*Diners Club International operates on the Discover Network.

FIGURE 4.22   IIN matrix

Based on the information in the preceding matrices and the data in the `bank.docx` file, it is clear that the credit card belonging to James Colgan is a Discover card, whereas Francis Bolger owns a MasterCard. This is helpful because if we wanted to search for MasterCard on a computer, we know that the first two digits range between `51` and `54` and that the credit card has a total of 16 digits.

A simple GREP search for a 16-digit credit card with five groups of four digits and dashes could be written as follows:

```
# grep "[[:digit:]]\{4\}-[[:digit:]]\{4\}-[[:digit:]]\{4\}-[[:digit:]\{4\}-
[[:digit:]]\{4\}" bank.docx
```

Result(s): 6011-0001-0001-0001-0001

However, we can see from the `bank.docx` file that Bolger's credit card number is listed without dashes. Therefore, to find both matches, an EGREP command can be used:

```
# egrep "[[:digit:]]\{4\}-?[[:digit:]]\{4\}-?[[:digit:]]\{4\}-?[[:digit:]\{4\}-
?[[:digit:]]\{4\}" bank.docx
```

The `?` in the previous command denotes that the dash may or may not appear for it to be a positive match and print to the screen.

Result(s): 5369000100010001 and 6011-0001-0001-0001-0001

The following GREP search on `bank.docx` finds numbers with 20 digits and no dashes:

```
# grep "[[:digit:]]\{20\}" bank.docx
```

Result(s): 5369000100010001

The following GREP command finds credit cards that begin with a 4 or 5 or 6. In other words, a Visa card, MasterCard, or Discover card could be a match, but an American Express would not be a match because it begins with a 3.

```
# egrep "[[:digit:]][456]\{3\}-?[[:digit:]]\{4\}-?[[:digit:]]\{4\}-?[[:digit:]\{4\}-
?[[:digit:]]\{4\}" bank.docx
```

Result(s): 5369000100010001 and 6011-0001-0001-0001-0001With the previous expression run on the `bank.docx` file, both credit cards would be a match and would be output to the screen. `[456]` in GREP is the equivalent of the series `{4,5,6}`.

The `bank.docx` file also contains telephone numbers that might be of interest to us. The following GREP search looks for a 10-digit telephone number with no spaces:

```
# grep "^[0-9][0-9][0-9][0-9][0-9][0-9][0-9][0-9][0-9][0-9]$"
```

Result: 6095551111

It is important to note that, as with Word, Microsoft Office documents are actually a file bundle. Therefore, another program needs to be run before a GREP search can be performed. Likewise, a direct GREP search cannot be performed on an entire hard drive, although FTK and EnCase make the GREP search process easier.

One cannot underestimate the importance of knowing Linux as a computer forensics investigator. The importance of knowing Linux becomes even more apparent when we cover Android forensics, as discussed in Chapter 9, "Mobile Forensics". There are numerous wonderful resources available online, including the following for Bash Shell Scripting (http://www.tldp.org/LDP/abs/html/).

Check Fraud

Another important type of investigation is check fraud. An investigator might want to run a GREP search to find ABA numbers. An **American Bankers Association (ABA)** number is found on checks and indicates how this financial instrument is to be routed through the banking system. The first two digits of the ABA relate to a corresponding Federal Reserve Bank. Figure 4.23 lists these banks.

First Two Digits of ABA	Federal Reserve Bank
01	Boston
02	New York
03	Philadelphia
04	Cleveland
05	Richmond
06	Atlanta
07	Chicago
08	St. Louis
09	Minneapolis
10	Kansas City
11	Dallas
12	San Francisco

FIGURE 4.23   ABA Federal Reserve Bank reference list

An investigator can quickly ascertain the exact bank and branch for a check by checking online websites like *Bank Routing Numbers* (routingnumber.aba.com).

GREP and EGREP searches can be used for any alphanumeric search, including searches for IP addresses, Social Security numbers, email addresses, picture files, and many other important searches.

Skimmers

A **skimmer** is an electronic device used to capture the data from the magnetic stripe on a debit, credit, or prepaid card. These devices will often be examined in a computer forensics laboratory. Skimmers have reached epidemic proportions and are used by identity thieves worldwide. They are generally battery operated, and although they are illegal in the United States, they can be easily purchased in Canada. They are also available on the Internet. For a comprehensive report on skimmer fraud, see www.accaglobal.com/content/dam/acca/global/PDF-technical/other-PDFs/skimming-surface.pdf.

Criminals use various types of skimmers. A **parasite** is a point-of-sale skimmer. In 2011, Michael's Stores discovered that skimmers had been installed in many of their point-of-sale (POS) terminals and ended up replacing 7,200 terminals. Criminals also use different types of parasites. With one type, a terminal is compromised. With another type, a phony terminal is installed. This type merely captures the data from the customer's credit or debit card but does not function as a payment system. Some POS skimmers are homemade. The last type of skimmer is a do-it-yourself (DIY) kit used to modify an existing POS. These DIY kits work with POS terminals produced by VeriFone, Ingenico, Xyrun, and TechTrex. POS skimmers can have a Bluetooth board installed, which enables the criminal to download consumer POS data using a Bluetooth-enabled computer or cellphone. This has the added benefit of enabling the criminal to inconspicuously capture the data wirelessly. Typically, the device has a fake, paper-thin keypad that sits under the legitimate keypad on the POS and is used to capture PINs.

An **ATM skimmer** is used to capture data from the magnetic stripe on credit cards or ATM cards. The ATM has a false front to capture this data (as shown in Figures 4.24 and 4.25)—in other words, a false card reader is placed over the real one. A tiny camera is then usually hidden close to the ATM to capture the PIN number. The camera is sometimes hidden in a false leaflet box attached to the ATM or is placed in other areas like a false smoke detector. Sometimes a false PIN pad can be added, instead of using a camera.

IBM created the magnetic stripe (or magstripe) in 1960. Data is stored in magnetized iron particles. Whereas skimmers are illegal in the United States, magstripe encoders are not. A **magstripe encoder** is a device used to transfer data onto a plastic card with a magnetic stripe (see Figure 4.26).

FIGURE 4.24 ATM fake card slot overlay

FIGURE 4.25 Back of ATM card slot overlay with skimmer device

FIGURE 4.26 Magstripe reader

There are sophisticated technologists/programmers who have the ability to manufacture credit cards that look legitimate and work exactly like the original card. A computer programmer typically downloads consumer card information from the skimmer by connecting it to a computer. The data is acquired through a computer port or by connecting pins to the EEPROM. Many skimmers are password-protected, and therefore cooperation from a criminal suspect may be required to bypass this protection. Interestingly, sometimes these devices will be password-protected or contain encrypted skimmed data—not to evade law enforcement, but to prevent their own criminals from taking and using the stolen credit card data. After a criminal technologist has his or her henchmen gather the skimmer devices and he or she downloads the data, the technologist can create fake credit cards using a special printer to make the blank white cards look like real credit cards. The magstripe encoder is then used to add the customer data to the cards. After the credit cards have been prepared, a number of "shoppers" are sent out to make purchases with the fraudulent cards. These purchased goods might end being sold on websites such as eBay.

The United States Secret Service and the FBI are very involved with skimmer investigations in the United States. These investigations generally have the cooperation of the affected financial institutions and assistance from local law enforcement. Software is available for examining these skimmers—primarily Exeba-COMM Law Enforcement Version, which can forensically analyze and decode skimmers and their skimmed data. Laws have now been adopted to deal with the skimmer epidemic. The New York State Penal Code now contains a law pertaining to the unlawful possession of a skimmer device.

Steganography

Steganography is the process of concealing data, like an image or a file or a message within a file. The concealed data can be stored in either plaintext or can be encrypted. It is problematic finding a file that contains hidden data, and often the only way to know is to notice that a file is unusually larger than normal. **Steganalysis** is the process of identifying the use of steganography in a file and extracting the concealed data. Steganalysis tools, used for detection, include stegdetect, StegSpy, and Stego Watch. Extracting the concealed data is also challenging since you generally need the application used to secrete the information to also perform the extraction. There are numerous steganography tools available, including the following examples:

- Hide and Seek

- JPEG-JSTEG

- Pretty Good Envelope

- StegoDos

- Stegano Wav

- PGP Stealth

- StegHide

Very few investigators have ever encountered steganography, although it is unclear whether this is because they have not been looking for concealed data within a file. It should still be a consideration. Uses of steganography can include secret messages between extremists or criminals selling codes for the illegal use of software licenses.

Summary

The development and maintenance of a computer forensics laboratory plays a critical role in both the discovery of evidence and the ability to process that evidence in a way that makes it admissible in court. The American Society of Crime Laboratory Directors/Lab Accreditation Board (ASCLD/LAB) is an independent, non-profit organization that provides guidelines on lab management and also certifies labs. ISO/IEC 17025:2017 are the "general requirements for the competence of testing and calibration laboratories", which could also be applied to a digital forensics laboratory.

A computer forensics lab must contain equipment that will be used in the field, as well as equipment that will be used in the laboratory. The tremendous range of digital devices, especially mobile devices, means that the hardware and software used for evidence acquisition has become greater and the cost for these solutions has increased over the past few years. Creating a lab budget is important when creating and maintaining a computer forensics lab. There are energy requirements, there are safety and security concerns, and the general management of the lab must be addressed.

A computer forensics laboratory is not just used for criminal investigations. In the private sector, these labs are used for eDiscovery and often civil litigation. All large accounting firms typically have a computer forensics lab and provide eDiscovery services to their clients.

Photo forensics is important because these images can provide information about where the suspect was at a particular point in time. The importance of photos can be seen with how prolific they are on the Web, especially on social networking sites. Photos are particularly important when it comes to child exploitation cases. Chapter 11, "Photograph Forensics", discusses photo forensics in depth.

Numerous computer forensics tools are available today, but not all are expensive. dd is a UNIX command utility that can create a forensic image—even remotely on a network. Global Regular Expressions Print (GREP) is a set of UNIX expressions used to search for key terms or for patterns, like credit card or Social Security numbers.

Skimmers are devices used to capture personal and financial data from the magnetic strip of credit, debit, prepaid, and gift cards. Law enforcement is often called upon to examine and retrieve evidence from these devices in a computer forensics laboratory.

Finally, although steganography is not widely used, an investigator should consider the potential for a suspect hiding data within a file.

Key Terms

ABC fire extinguisher: A fire extinguisher that uses a dry chemical extinguishing solution called monoammonium phosphate powder and ammonium sulfate and is suitable for electrical fires.

Advanced Forensics Format (AFF): An open source file format developed by Simson Garfinkel and supported by Autopsy and The Sleuth Kit forensics software.

American Bankers Association (ABA) number: A number on a check that denotes how the financial instrument is to be routed through the banking system.

antistatic polyethylene evidence bags: Bags that are designed to protect electronic devices from static electricity.

ASCLD: The American Society of Crime Laboratory Directors, a non-profit organization that provides a set of guidelines and standards for forensics labs.

ASCLD/LAB: The American Society of Crime Laboratory Directors/Lab Accreditation Board, an organization that accredits crime labs that was originally a committee within ASCLD.

ATM skimmer: A device used to capture data from the magnetic stripe on credit cards or ATM cards.

brute-force attack: An attack that involves checking all possible keys to decrypt data.

cellular telephone jammer: A device that prevents cellular telephone users from connecting with other cellular telephones.

cryptanalysis: The process of attempting to target weaknesses in protocols and cryptographic algorithms to try to break a system or gain access to data.

dictionary attack: A type of attack that involves using a predetermined list of words to decrypt data or authenticate a user.

discovery: The period leading up to a trial during which each party involved in civil litigation can request evidence from the other party.

E01: A forensic disk image file format developed by Guidance Software.

eDiscovery: The detection of electronic data for the purposes of litigation.

electronically stored information (ESI): Digitally stored information, including email, Word documents, spreadsheets, databases, and any other types of digitally stored information.

EnScript: A programming language developed by Guidance Software that allows EnCase users to create their own customized functions and features in EnCase.

evidence locker: A metal cabinet with individual compartments that can be locked individually.

Extended Global Regular Expressions Print (EGREP): Allows for the additional use of operators not found in basic GREP.

Fast Global Regular Expressions Print (FGREP): A UNIX search utility that does not use regular expressions but interprets characters literally and is therefore faster than GREP.

file carving: The process of identifying a file by certain characteristics, like a file header or footer, rather than by the file extension or metadata.

firmware: Programs that control electronic devices like hard disk drives, game consoles, or mobile telephones.

Global Regular Expressions Print (GREP): A powerful set of UNIX expressions used for pattern matching.

Issuer Identification Number (IIN): The first six digits of a credit card number.

lossless compression: A process that eliminates unneeded data from a file without loss of the original data.

lossy compression: A process that makes a picture smaller, with some image quality compromise and loss of data.

magstripe encoder: A device used to transfer data onto a plastic card with a magnetic stripe.

Major Industry Identifier (MII): The first digit of a credit card number.

parasite: A point-of-sale skimmer.

plaintiff: The party that makes a claim against another party and initiates a lawsuit.

Rainbow tables: Password hashes used for a dictionary attack on a file or even a volume.

raster-based graphics: Rectangular pictures that are based on pixels.

Scientific Working Group on Digital Evidence (SWGDE): A committee dedicated to sharing research and setting standards for investigators working with digital and multimedia evidence.

SMART files: Forensic disk image files (compressed or uncompressed) originally developed by ASRData's Expert Witness.

steganalysis: The process of identifying the use of steganography in a file and extracting the concealed data.

steganography: The process of concealing data, like an image or a file or a message within a file.

uninterruptible power supply (UPS): A power supply containing a battery that maintains power in the event of a power outage.

virtual machine: A computer running software that allows for an instance of an operating system, or multiple operating systems, without making any changes to the user's computer.

workbench: A work surface that is used to prepare hardware devices for investigative analysis.

Assessment

CLASSROOM DISCUSSIONS

1. Explain the process by which you would plan, create, and maintain a successful computer forensics lab.

2. How can GREP be used in computer forensics investigations?

3. Detail the type of equipment that a computer forensics examiner in law enforcement would need to bring to a crime scene.

4. Why have skimmers become such a huge problem worldwide?

MULTIPLE-CHOICE QUESTIONS

1. Which of the following fire extinguishers are suitable for electrical fires?

   A. AFF

   B. FAC

   C. DBA

   D. ABC

2. Which of the following indicates the routing information for a bank branch?

   A. ABC

   B. AFF

   C. ABA

   D. ESI

3. Which UNIX search utility does not use regular expressions but interprets characters literally and is therefore faster than GREP?

   A. FGREP

   B. GREP

   C. EGREP

   D. XGREP

4. Which of the following best describes using a predetermined list of words to decrypt data or authenticate a user?

   A. Dictionary attack

   B. Brute-force attack

   C. EGREP

   D. Cryptanalysis

5. Which of the following formats is the forensic disk image file format developed by Guidance Software?

   A. AFF

   B. dd

   C. AD1

   D. E01

6. Which of the following formats is the forensic disk image file format developed by ASRData's Expert Witness?

   A. AFF

   B. E01

   C. SMART

   D. RAW

7. Which of the following best describes what electronically stored information (ESI) can include?

   A. Email

   B. Spreadsheets

   C. Databases

   D. All of the above

8. Which of the following organizations is an independent body that provides forensics lab guidelines and certification?

   A. ASCLD

   B. ASCLD/LAB

   C. ESI

   D. SWGDE

9. Which of the following refers to the first six digits of a credit card number?

   A. Issuer Identification Number

   B. Major Industry Identifier

   C. Electronically stored information

   D. Sequential identification number

10. Which of the following is not a forensic file image format?

   A. dd

   B. E01

   C. SMART

   D. UPS

FILL IN THE BLANKS

1. The open source file format developed by Simson Garfinkel and supported by Autopsy and The Sleuth Kit forensics software is called _____ Forensics Format.

2. An ATM _____ is used to capture data from the magnetic strip on credit cards or ATM cards.

3. A cellphone _____ is a device that prevents cellular telephone users from connecting with other cellular telephones by blocking all radio signals.

4. The programming language developed by Guidance Software that allows EnCase users to create their own customized function and features in EnCase is called _____.

5. File _____ is the process of identifying a file by certain characteristics, such as a file header or footer, rather than by the file extension or metadata.

6. When unneeded data is eliminated from a photo, this is referred to as _____ compression.

7. A(n) _____ machine is a computer running software that allows for an instance of an operating system, or multiple operating systems, without making any changes to the user's computer.

8. _____ power supply is a power supply containing a battery that will maintain power in the event of a power outage.

9. A(n) _____ is a point-of-sale skimmer.

10. An evidence _____ is a metal cabinet with individual compartments that can be locked individually.

PROJECTS

Design the Ultimate Lab

You have been tasked with designing a computer forensics laboratory for a local law enforcement agency. Imagine that you have a $1 million budget for your new laboratory. Create a graphical layout of the laboratory and, based on what you have learned in this chapter, draw up a list of the items (software, hardware, and so on) that you would like to purchase for the laboratory.

Create a Plan for a Forensics Lab

Using both NIST publications and ASCLD/LAB guidelines related to best practices in computer forensics, create a plan for a new computer forensics laboratory. Be sure to include important concepts such as physical security, auditing, benchmarking testing tools, management, and ongoing training.

Chapter | **5**

Online Investigations

Learning Outcomes

After reading this chapter, you will be able to understand the following:

- How to gather personal data about a suspect from a variety of online sources;
- Databases available to law enforcement to profile a suspect;
- Different types of online crime and how criminal investigations are conducted online; and
- How to capture Internet communications, video, images, and other content to add to an investigative report.

When I ask my college students about conducting an online investigation and trying to find personal information about an individual, they generally suggest using the Google search engine. However, searching for information by simply using Google will yield numerous unfocused search results. An investigator could take hours gleaning through these results to find the specific personal information about a suspect that he is trying to find. This chapter highlights how to find targeted information about an individual, how to covertly communicate with a suspect online, and, ultimately, how to comprehensively document an investigator's findings and communications.

When we think about online investigations, it conjures up ideas of undercover detectives interacting with suspects online. However, we should also remember that companies continually conduct online investigations, especially when a company considers hiring a new employee. Moreover, there are numerous incidents involving employees who post incendiary comments about their employers online. Companies are now more vigilant about monitoring what their employees post on blogs and on social media websites. In fact, many companies have rewritten their Internet policies as a result of employees commenting about their employers online. In one example, Dawnmarie Souza was fired by her employer, American Medical Response, for derogatory comments that she posted about a coworker on Facebook. The National Labor Relations Board (NLRB) and Souza saw things differently and ended up in court. The NLRB and Souza felt that her Constitutional right to freedom of speech had been violated, especially because Souza's comments were posted using her home computer on her own time. The NLRB believed that the company's Internet and social media policy violated employee rights. Ultimately, there was a settlement between the company and Souza, and the company changed its blogging and Internet use policies so as not to prohibit employees from posting their personal opinions about the company online.

In another example, at Mesa Verde High School, in California, Donny Tobolski was suspended for posting rude comments about a teacher on his Facebook account. The boy posted that his biology teacher was a "fat ass who should stop eating fast food, and is a douche bag", The American Civil Liberties Union (ACLU) argued that the school violated the student's state and federal Constitutional rights, as well as the California Education Code.

This chapter details a number of online resources, some of which are free and some of which are paid premium services, to create an online profile while investigating criminal activity. Sometimes this fake online profile is called a "sockpuppet". This chapter also describes databases that are regularly used by international, federal, state, and local agencies to gather and share intelligence on the general public.

> **Note**
>
> All online resources in this chapter were correct at the time of writing, but of course websites are subject to change without notice.

Working Undercover

An **undercover investigation** is the process used to acquire information without the individual or suspect knowing the true identity of the investigator. Prior to any interaction with a suspect, an investigator will perform reconnaissance on the individual. This background search involves building a profile about the suspect. The profile will include various types of personal data discussed in this chapter and will also include profiling the suspect's behavior. It is important that the investigator performs this reconnaissance incognito. As more of our personal data, attitudes, communications, and general behaviors are captured on the Web, online reconnaissance has become extremely important. Additionally, the Internet has facilitated the growth of certain types of criminal activities. It is easier for a criminal to dupe a victim into handing over credit card information online than to steal someone's wallet. Pedophiles have gravitated to the Internet as they have found it easier to find similar deviants online and even use the Internet to help plan their activities. However, the Internet also provides advantages for undercover detectives; it is relatively easy to convince a pedophile that a 40-year-old detective is a 14-year-old girl when chatting online. During the reconnaissance phase, a detective may gain access to the suspect's email account or user groups or gather information from social networking websites, if the law permits.

Following a background check of the suspect, surveillance of the suspect can begin. Detectives may begin monitoring the suspect's residence, movements, and daily routine and generally build a profile of his behavior. Similarly, online the detective will monitor the suspect's activities in chat rooms and in user groups. During this phase of the investigation, the investigator plans how detectives will record the suspect's activities, which can include video and audio, decide whether any warrants need to be requested, and plan how the interaction between the detective and the suspect will occur.

The next phase of an investigation involves a more formal monitoring and recording of the suspect's activities. This step of the investigative process might include acting on court-approved warrants, whether search warrants or wiretaps.

Finally, there is a sting operation. This step of the investigation is designed to catch the criminal in the act of committing or planning to commit a crime. A detective might pose as an accessory to a criminal act, or in the case of a child endangerment investigation, the investigator might pose as a child and speak with the criminal suspect. The Internet makes the process easier now because an actual child does not have to be used as "bait" to capture the suspect. In many cases, the suspect believes that he has been able to lure a child to a parking lot, where, in reality, police have lured the suspect for a rendezvous.

Generating an Identity

When working undercover, an investigator often needs to create a *sockpuppet*, which is a fake online persona created to interact with a person of interest. The investigator may need to create a Gmail or Yahoo! account, and the verification process will require an established email account and telephone number. ProtonMail (protonmail.com) or Tutanota (tutanota.com) are services that will allow you to create disposable email accounts for verification. We will discuss disposable email in more detail in the next section.

Blur (abine.com) is a tool that allows you to obfuscate your email information. You can also create email accounts for use on the Dark Web, using services like Mail2Tor (mail2tor.com or mail-2tor2zyjdctd.onion) or Secmail Tor (sigaintevyh2rzvw.onion). Regarding SMS verification, for new online accounts, you can use free services, like TextNow (textnow.com) or Talkatone (talkatone.com), or you could use a burner phone.

Sometimes an investigator will need to use Bitcoin in an investigation and ensure that the Bitcoin address is untraceable or close to being untraceable. Bitcoin Laundry (bitcoin-laundry.com) may be a good solution, if approved by your department. A Bitcoin ATM is another option, and these ATMs can be located at Coin ATM Radar (coinatmradar.com). Another option is to use a prepaid debit card, which does not require that the purchaser provide a name and address. A OneVanilla prepaid Visa card may be an appropriate option (onevanilla.com). This Visa card can then be linked to a PayPal account, if needed.

When interacting online with a suspect, it is important that your identity remains a secret and that your computer is protected against malware. Therefore, you may consider using a paid VPN service. Algo VPN (github.com/trailofbits/algo) allows you to create your own VPN service. There are paid VPN services too, like NordVPN (nordvpn.com) and RSocks (rsocks.net). You might also consider using the Tor browser (www.torproject.org) with the Tails OS (tails.boum.org) to remain anonymous online.

Realistically, it is not difficult for a detective to create an undercover identity. Nevertheless, there is a service that allows the user to quickly generate a false identity. Fake Name Generator (www.fakenamegenerator.com) is a free online service that allows the user to generate an ad hoc identity (see Figure 5.1). Moreover, the service allows the user to select gender (male/female), name set (American, Chinese, Hispanic, etc.), and country (Australia, Italy, United States, etc.). Once these three criteria have been submitted, a phony name, address, email address, telephone number, credit card number, Social Security number, weight, height, and other personal data are generated. Of course, sometimes the investigator may decide to tailor an undercover identity for a specific type of investigation—perhaps posing as a young girl when chatting online with a suspected pedophile. One problem for undercover investigators is the use of photographs to create a fake persona. The website thispersondoesnotexist.com creates realistic-looking computer-generated photos of people.

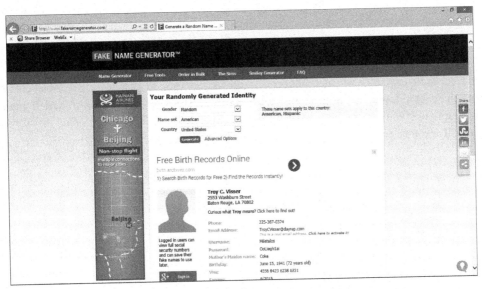

FIGURE 5.1   Fake Name Generator website results

Generating an Email Account

When working undercover, creating a temporary email account can be necessary to start a new service that will be utilized during an investigation. For example, when creating a new Gmail account, an email address is required to validate the user when setting up a new account. There are several disposable email services that allow the user to create an ad hoc email account with an inbox. Once the browser is closed, the email account is eliminated. Gmail accounts are particularly useful with undercover investigations because Google obfuscates the originating IP address from the email headers.

GuerrillaMail (www.guerrillamail.com) allows a user to create a temporary email address, which does not require any type of registration (see Figure 5.2). Your temporary email address will not have the @guerrillamail.com extension. The GuerrillaMail email address will last for 60 minutes.

FIGURE 5.2   Guerrilla Mail website

Another service, *mail expire* (www.metafilter.com), allows the user to create a disposable email account that can be set to last up to three months (see Figure 5.3). However, unlike Guerrilla Mail, mail expire does require that you register and enter an existing email address. It should be noted that some disposable email accounts are blocked by some services as a method of verification.

FIGURE 5.3   mail expire website

Another disposable email service that does not require any type of registration is Mailinator (mailinator. com; see Figure 5.4). Interestingly, you can select your own username with this service. For example, you could select the email address hipster@mailinator.com.

FIGURE 5.4 Mailinator website

All of these aforementioned disposable email services are advertised as beneficial to users who wish to avoid spam. Nevertheless, they provide an effective means for detectives to utilize services without providing any (genuine) personally identifiable information.

In summary, an investigator can create a phony profile for an undercover investigation. A Gmail, or other email account, can be created using the phony profile. The email required by the Gmail registration process would be a disposable email created on-the-fly by a service like mailinator. Once a confirmation email appears in the mailinator Inbox, the detective can then click the confirmation link to finalize the Gmail account setup.

Masking Your Identity

Detectives have numerous methods at their disposal to remain anonymous online. Bluffmycall.com is one service that enables the user to (1) change her caller ID to any number, (2) disguise his voice, or (3) record his calls (see Figure 5.5). SpoofCard (www.spoofcard.com) is a similar service, which is also popular.

FIGURE 5.5   Bluffmycall.com website

Spy Dialer (www.spydialer.com) is a free online service that allows a user to contact a cellphone number to hear who answers the telephone, without identifying the number of the caller (see Figure 5.6). The service can also be downloaded as an app to a smartphone.

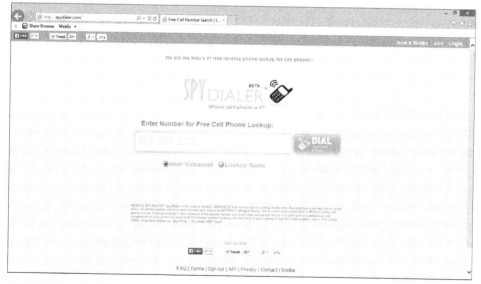

FIGURE 5.6   SpyDialer.com website

Law enforcement can use a service called LEAP (Local Number Portability Enhanced Analytical Platform) to track criminals who try to evade investigation by switching telephone carriers. See lawen forcement. numberportability.com for more information about the service. It is also possible to find the carrier name associated with a telephone number by performing a reverse lookup with FoneFinder (fonefinder.net). Neustar (www.home.neustar) can then be used to see if the user of a number has ported it to another carrier.

It is important to note that law enforcement requires a wiretap to record telephone conversations. Laws differ from state to state about whether a recorded telephone conversation can be admitted as evidence; in New York State, only one party is required to consent to being recorded, whereas in California, both parties must consent. In New York State, the interception of a telephone call without consent or permission from a judge is eavesdropping, which is a felony. However, in New York you may record a call with one-party consent, when that party is part of a conversation. In many other states, all parties must consent to being recorded. This was clear in 1999, when Linda Tripp was indicted on charges of wiretapping, under Maryland law, after she recorded Monica's Lewinsky's confessions about her relationship with President Clinton. In this case, each wiretap violation carried a maximum penalty of five years in prison, a fine of $10,000, or both.

A user's identity (more specifically, the IP address) can be masked by use of an online proxy. With an *online proxy*, a user utilizes another computer to communicate with a third party, with the result that the third party cannot recognize the IP address of the originating communication. Online proxy services include VIP Socks (vip72.com), Megaproxy (megaproxy.com; see Figure 5.7), Ion by Anonymizer (anonymizer.com), and The Cloak (the-cloak.com). In the case of Sarah Palin's email account being hacked in 2008, David Kernell, using the handle "Rubico", utilized a proxy service, but investigators were able to quickly identify the originating IP address. Kernell also left his email address (rubico10@yahoo.com) after posting Palin's emails to 4chan, which is a website for anonymously posting information, including sensitive stolen data.

FIGURE 5.7   Megaproxy website

Many of these anonymizers (online proxies) are used by criminals to carry out their cybercriminal activity. Moreover, many of the computers being used as proxies are being used without the consent of the users and are a part of a botnet. Therefore, these proxy services and their servers generally operate outside the United States, especially in countries where the United States has little or no legal influence—countries like Russia or the Ukraine. Often U.S. investigators also encounter difficulties with accessing data from servers within the European Union because their privacy laws can stifle an investigation.

Dark Web Investigations

The World Wide Web (WWW), sometimes referred to as the "Clear Web", is easy to use with traditional web browsers, like Safari, Edge, or Firefox. This is because regular websites, on the World Wide Web, are indexed and therefore searchable with search engines, like Bing and Google. There is, however, an unindexed part of the Web: The Dark Web.

The Dark Web is an encrypted network that utilizes the public Internet. Among the various overlay networks, the most widely used is Tor Routing. Tor was originally developed as part of a secure communication effort of the U.S. Naval Research Laboratory, as a means to protect and anonymize traffic by passing it through multiple layers of encrypted relays. The Dark Web is purposely hidden using a peer-to-peer (P2P) network. Dark Web sites are primarily accessed using the Tor Browser, which is a user-friendly browser that protects the anonymity of the user and can be important for individuals seeking to overcome censorship, ensure their privacy, or by criminals who seek to obfuscate their identity. According to the Tor Project's website, "Tor is free software and an open network that helps you defend against traffic analysis, a form of network surveillance that threatens personal freedom and privacy, confidential business activities and relationships, and state security". The success of the Dark Web can be attributed to concerns about privacy, especially in a post-Snowden era.

OSINT Framework

A tremendous resource for finding open source intelligence (OSINT) is OSINT Framework (osintframework.com). This website can, for example, help an investigator search for Dark Web websites of interest. Figure 5.8 displays the type of online resources available related to the Dark Web.

Tor

Tor is free, open source, software and an open network that enables a user to surf the Internet with anonymity. A user can download the Tor Browser Bundle, thereby enabling the user to proxy through numerous host computers on the Tor network, throughout the world, while remaining anonymous. Tor also allows users to publish websites without disclosing their location and which are only available to Tor users. This is often referred to as the Dark Web because these websites are not searchable with a traditional browser, like Microsoft's Edge. Many of these sites are hosted by criminal actors.

Tor is problematic for investigators because the identities of users on the Tor network are obfuscated, and there are numerous websites with hidden locations. Furthermore, the proprietors of nefarious sites conduct their criminal activities with numerous unknown users. Tor can also be a breeding ground for malware. The Silk Road is one example of a website on the Dark Web. This site, with close to

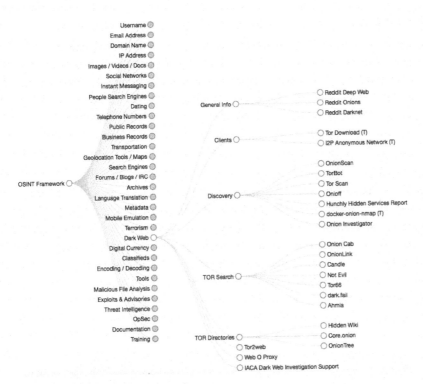

FIGURE 5.8 OSINT Framework

one million registered users, was founded by William Ulbricht, also known as Dread Pirate Roberts, in 2011. The site facilitated criminal transactions: drug trades in LSD, cocaine, heroin, and more. To facilitate anonymity even further, transactions were conducted using Bitcoin. Over the space of 2 ½ years, 9.5 million Bitcoins changed hands (equivalent to $1.3 billion at the time), and Silk Road's commissions totaled $85 million.

Although it is difficult, or even impossible, to determine the identities of users online, once a user's computer has been seized, law enforcement can gather some evidence about a user's activity on Tor, which is derived from the Tor browser bundle. If the suspect's computer is turned on, then some Tor browser activity can be retrieved from RAM or from the `hiberfil.sys` file—a file, which is a copy of RAM that is stored on the hard drive when the computer goes into hibernate mode on a PC. When performing a GREP search, the following statement can be used to find Tor sites, which possess a `.onion` extension:

```
http.{5,100}\.onion
```

If the user used Tor in conjunction with Tails, the task becomes challenging. **Tails** (short for TheAmnesicIncognitoLiveSystem) is a live operating system that provides anonymity for the user using virtualized sessions with Tor. It can be run from a USB, SD card, or DVD on virtually any computer. Tor is just one type of Darknet. Another is I2P, which we will discuss next.

Invisible Internet Project

The Invisible Internet Project (I2P) is another tool available for secure communications and anonymous Internet surfing. This network uses public/private key encryption, and, like Tor, websites are hosted anonymously. On the suspect's computer, the `router.config` file contains some information about I2P connectivity by the user. The investigator can also search for files with an `.i2p` extension on the suspect's computer.

Freenet

Released in 2000, Freenet is a peer-to-peer (P2P) network. Freenet is a networked data store where users on that network can store files in an encrypted format on your computer. The user must be willing to dedicate a minimum of 256MB to the P2P community. The more space that you contribute, the faster your connection on the network (in theory). There are two modes of sharing and communication: "Opennet", where the user is automatically connected with another host on the network, and "Darknet", where the user manually selects a specific host on a network that they trust. Like Tor, the goal is to provide anonymity and protect freedom of speech. Like Tor, Freenet attracts pedophiles who wish to share images and videos of abused children.

SecureDrop

Although we sometimes associate Tor and other proxy services with hackers or criminals, there are situations where there is a need for these proxy services. For example, a journalist working with a corporate whistleblower or a political dissident may need to preserve anonymity for fear of death or oppression. Of course, whistleblowers can be tremendously controversial, as seen with Edward Snowden and Chelsea Manning. SecureDrop is an open source submission system, funded by the Freedom of the Press Foundation, which allows whistleblowers to anonymously communicate with journalists.

Dark Web Marketplaces

An investigation of Dark Web marketplaces typically begins with a search on the World Wide Web. One helpful resource for finding these marketplaces is TheDarkWebLInks (thedarkweblinks.com). Websites like pastebin.com can also be used to find these marketplaces. A user could enter the following search, for example:

```
site:pastebin.com ".onion" "hidden wiki"
```

The user can then limit the search to the previous week.

Dark Web sites can be scraped using Python or AppleScript, and then later analyzed by the investigator. Given that most of the listings on these marketplaces are narcotics, the investigator should have a dictionary of names of each drug or perhaps create one. For example, the drug fentanyl is also referred to as the following:

- Apache
- China Girl

- Goodfellas

- Jackpot

- Tango and Cash

- TNT

The Silk Road

The Dark Web has gained notoriety, in more recent times, because of the exponential growth of Dark Web marketplaces after the rise (2011) and fall (2013) of the Silk Road. The Silk Road was a Dark Web marketplace that facilitated vendors (often criminals) to surreptitiously sell drugs, counterfeit documents and other illegal items, anonymously to consumers, using Bitcoin as the crypto-currency of choice for buying and selling these illicit commodities. Bitcoin provides vendors, and their clients, with an extra layer of security on the Dark Web by leaving virtually no paper trail. This extraordinarily successful marketplace was devised and administered by Ross Ulbricht until he, and the Silk Road site, were taken down by the Federal Bureau of Investigation (FBI) and Homeland Security Investigations (HSI). This infamous marketplace was arguably so successful because of its enormous selection of drugs, which included new psychoactive substances. Many consumers were impressed by the professionalism of its customer support and the fact that they felt safe shopping there. Several other marketplaces have spawned since then, and different studies have analyzed how the number of vendors and sales, on Dark Web marketplaces, have evolved, while the majority of marketplaces have shown year-over-year increases.

PlayPen

In 2015, the FBI were responsible for taking down the PlayPen website, which was operating on the Dark Web. The website was responsible for distributing sexually explicit images of minors to its more than 200,000 subscribers. According to the FBI website, 25 producers of child pornography in the USA were prosecuted, 51 child abusers were prosecuted, 55 children were successfully identified or rescued in the USA and many more internationally. This take-down also led to 350 arrests in the USA and 548 international arrests. For some, the case was controversial because allegedly the FBI was in control of the PlayPen server for two weeks as they identified its subscribers. It appears that during these two weeks the FBI installed malware or a "NIT" (network investigative technique) onto computers that visited the PlayPen website, in an effort to identify visitors. Federal Prosecutor Annette Hayes wrote in a court filing that the government was forced to decide between disclosing its secret NIT and dismissing the case, and ultimately the Department of Justice decided to dismiss the case rather than disclose.

Operation Bayonet

In 2017, a multinational law enforcement operation, which included Homeland Security Investigations (HSI), Federal Bureau of Investigation (FBI), and Europol, shut down two of the most notorious Dark Web marketplaces: AlphaBay and Hansa.

Alexandre Cazes, a 26-year-old Canadian, who allegedly founded AlphaBay, was arrested. He never went to trial because he was found dead in his cell, several days after his arrest in Thailand. At the time that the site was shut down, it had approximately 400,000 users and around 369,000 listings.

According to a government complaint, Cazes used his own personal email (pimp_alex_91@hotmail. com) account when contacting some of the marketplace users. Investigators also found records of Cazes' assets, totaling over $23 million, on a computer.

In the case of Hansa, the Dutch police received a tip-off from some security researchers who had discovered a development version of the marketplace. Police subsequently discovered old IRC chat logs that detailed the full names and addresses of the Hansa site administrators.

Virtual Currencies

Fiat currency is legal tender that is backed by a government or governments. The U.S. dollar and the Euro are examples of fiat currency. There are literally hundreds of virtual currencies worldwide. In fact, some might say that most transactions are virtual because many of us use credit cards and use mobile payments for most financial transactions. What has changed is the recent introduction of crypto-currencies, whereby a non-state-sponsored currency is sent from a computer or a smart device to another user and the payment is only transferred once an algorithm (mathematical computation) is solved. This mathematical computation is solved by a middle-man, or miner. Subsequently, a public ledger of transactions, in theory, assures the integrity of the transaction. However, not all virtual currencies are crypto-currencies. For example, Second Life, which is a virtual world, allows users to buy buildings and artwork from other users using Linden dollars. There are many other virtual payment systems, including WebMoney, PerfectMoney, Yandex, and SolidTrust Pay, to name but a few.

CoinMarketCap (coinmarketcap.com) is a website that displays the market cap for crypto-currencies as well as a current quote for each currency.

Virtual currencies do carry tax consequences in different jurisdictions. For example, the Internal Revenue Service (IRS) in the United States, provides guidance about virtual currencies in Notice 2014-21. Those who facilitate the transfer of crypto currency, through mining (solving a mathematical algorithm), also have reporting requirements. These requirements are outlined by the Department of the Treasury, Financial Crimes Enforcement Network (FinCEN), in FIN-2014-R001 (www.fincen. gov/sites/default/files/administrative_ruling/FIN-2014-R001.pdf). For example, this would mean that a Bitcoin miner in the US would be deemed a money services business (MSB). Knowledge of these regulations may be important when prosecuting a suspect in the United States.

Bitcoin

Bitcoin is a crypto-currency, which is a decentralized, peer-to-peer, virtual currency. Bitcoin was invented by Satoshi Nakamoto, which is a pseudonym for an unknown identity. Satoshi means "wisdom" or "reason" and Nakamoto means "central source". Some say that Bitcoin is a libertarian concept, given its decentralized, non-government system. Crypto-currencies, like Bitcoin, are not illegal in the USA, although they are sometimes used by nefarious actors given its innate anonymity. Bitcoin can be used to book flights, book hotels, order pizza, and buy many other products worldwide.

When a Bitcoin owner sends Bitcoin to another person, the currency is sent from a Bitcoin wallet to another Bitcoin wallet on a computer or on a smart device. A **Bitcoin wallet** stores a user's Bitcoin currency. There are numerous Bitcoin wallets to choose from, and this wallet can be encrypted and password-protected. The wallet often uses SHA-256-bit encryption with a public and private key. The public key is displayed on blockchain.info. The wallet address is usually 34 alpha-numeric characters in length. Payment can also be made using a QR code. This QR code can also be used to buy or sell Bitcoin at special Bitcoin ATMs. An investigator will typically search for the **wallet.dat** file on a suspect's computer or smartphone to find the Bitcoin wallet. WalletExplorer.com is one website that investigators can use to search for bitcoin addresses, wallet IDs, and other identifiers.

A **Bitcoin miner** will solve a mathematical problem before forwarding the Bitcoin currency to the recipient. In return, the miner will receive a small percentage of Bitcoin for solving the algorithm. Bitcoin mining requires tremendous computing power, and corporations are now dealing with the issue of some miners using their networks to mine Bitcoin.

The **Blockchain** (blockchain.info) is an electronic public ledger that keeps track of all Bitcoin transactions or blocks. Anyone can view these blocks in real time. However, determining who is responsible for each transaction is problematic without knowing the date and time of a transaction and knowing the identities of the people. Additionally, each block can be a combination of user transactions. To complicate matters further, a criminal can use a Bitcoin tumbler. A **Bitcoin tumbler** service is used to mix up Bitcoin transactions and make it ever harder to link Bitcoin to a specific transaction on the Blockchain. Thus, Bitcoin is the currency of choice for criminals on Dark Web marketplaces. Furthermore, many sellers operating on these marketplaces will convert the Bitcoin that they receive and quickly convert this crypto-currency into another crypto-currency, like Monero, Ethereum, or Dash. A criminal may exchange Bitcoin for Monero because Monero, unlike bitcoin, does not have a public ledger, and therefore examining these transactions are more challenging for investigators.

The **Genesis Block** was the first block in the Blockchain. It was created on or after January 3, 2009, and this Genesis Block can never be used again.

Venmo and Vicemo

There are numerous peer-to-peer payment services. Venmo (venmo.com) is one service that allows users to send money to other people, make deposits to a bank or even make purchases. Vicemo (vicemo.com) is a website that displays users who are allegedly buying drugs, alcohol, and sex on Venmo. Although the actual transactions should be verified, Vicemo is yet another potential source of open source intelligence for law enforcement.

Website Evidence

Websites change their content continuously, and sometimes by the time a computer forensics investigator becomes involved in an online investigation, a website of interest has changed.

Website Archives

Interestingly, there is a website that allows users to view a website at a particular point in history. At www.archive.org, the user can utilize the WayBackMachine utility (see Figure 5.9) to enter a URL and run a search to view historical snapshots of a website.

FIGURE 5.9   Historical view of www.apple.com (on 8/19/04) using the WayBackMachine

Website Statistics

Sometimes an investigator will need to find statistics about a particular website. Netcraft (news. netcraft.com) provides a range of comprehensive statistics about a website, such as the IP address, how long the website has been active, the mailing address for the domain owner, the web server's operating system, and many other helpful site statistics (see Figure 5.10).

FIGURE 5.10   Netcraft statistics on www.pace.edu

The Pirate Bay

The Pirate Bay (thepirate-bay.org) is a website that claims to be the world's largest BitTorrent tracker. **BitTorrent** is a file-sharing protocol that facilitates the dissemination of large files. The website is notorious for sharing stolen confidential information, like the sensitive data stolen by a hacktivist group, AntiSecurity (or "AntiSec"), from Booz Allen Hamilton, which is a high-profile government security contractor. The group uploaded seven files containing 90,000 stolen military emails and passwords.

Alexa

Alexa (www.alexa.com/siteinfo) is another website that provides an array of statistics about various websites (see Figure 5.11).

FIGURE 5.11   Alexa website

Background Searches on a Suspect

Online reconnaissance of personal information can vary greatly according to the needs of the investigator. Several online resources are available to assist in ascertaining the following personal information:

- Personal information
- Personal interests and membership in user groups
- Contribution to blogs

- Presence on social networking websites
- Professional networks
- Public records
- Location

Finding Personal Information

Many websites provide basic information on individuals, like their address and telephone number. Most of these websites make money by selling the site users more extensive personal information under "premium" services, which can include information about an individual's assets. Employers sometimes utilize the services of the following websites, and detectives also use them. It is important to note that searches by name generally provide multiple results, some of which are duplicates for the same person because old addresses may be listed.

Zaba Search

Zaba Search (www.zabasearch.com) enables the user to conduct a search based on a cellular telephone number (see Figure 5.12). The free service also provides a Google Earth map of the individual's location.

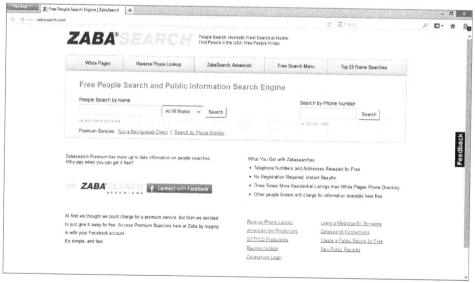

FIGURE 5.12   Zaba Search website

US SEARCH

US SEARCH (www.ussearch.com) is yet another online resource for finding personal information (see Figure 5.13). The results identify a list of relations, where possible. The value of this website is limited unless the investigator is willing to pay for additional information.

FIGURE 5.13   US SEARCH website

Searchbug

SearchBug (www.searchbug.com) is a free service on the Web that allows text messages to be sent to any cellular telephone free of charge (see Figure 5.14).

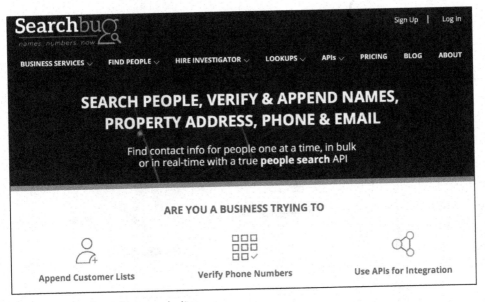

FIGURE 5.14   Searchbug website

Skipease

Skipease (www.skipease.com) allows the user to enter the zip code and a name to search for a person. Search results show additional information from sponsored websites (see Figure 5.15).

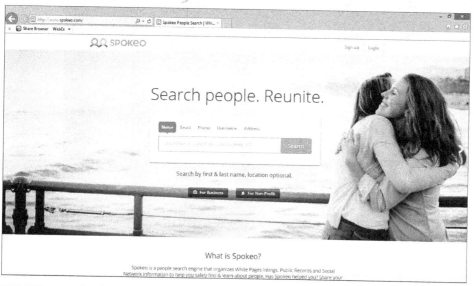

FIGURE 5.15   Skipease website

Spokeo

Spokeo (www.spokeo.com) allows a user to search for individuals (see Figure 5.16). It also allows individuals to have their information removed from the site's search engine. In addition, this site can help ascertain membership in social networking sites (although there may be charges associated with such searches).

FIGURE 5.16   Spokeo website

pipl

The pipl website (www.pipl.com) provides search results for other personal data, which includes websites like Been Verified or White Pages (see Figure 5.17).

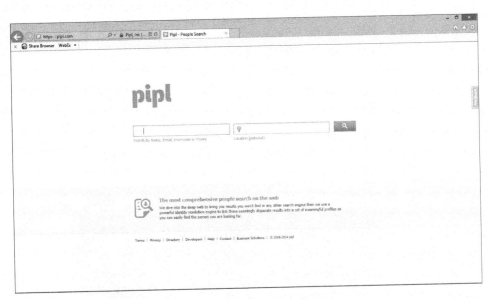

FIGURE 5.17   pipl website

Numerous other personal data providers operate online, including PeopleFinders (peoplefinders.com) and Intelius (www.intelius.com), but most of these websites provide very limited information unless you are willing to pay for their premium services.

Personal Interests and User Groups

In June 2009, Swiss police announced that they had identified an Internet child pornography network that spanned 78 countries, involving more than 2,000 IP addresses. The police had received a tip-off from INTERPOL about a supposed hip-hop music website that was actually being used to disseminate videos of children being abused. The investigation led to numerous arrests and convictions. The Internet continually facilitates the dissemination of contraband, including illicit video and images of children. Pedophiles are also found in user groups, sharing images and ideas about how to groom children to succumb to their abhorrent demands. More importantly, once a user group is found, law enforcement can take down an entire network of pedophiles because these criminals are notorious for networking with like-minded deviants. Many of these pedophile networks pose as a legitimate service to disguise their underground activities. In one case, local law enforcement and the FBI uncovered a website that purported to assist abused children but was actually used to lure underage children.

Al-Qaeda has effectively used the Internet—and user groups in particular—to share its message of hatred and recruit new members. Law enforcement frequently visits these user groups to identify who they should be monitoring and ascertain whether there is any impending danger to the community at large. In 2011, it was claimed that 10,000 jihadist groups were using *vBulletin*, a group discussion platform. Today, these jihadist groups and numerous right-wing paramilitary groups spread their propaganda across thousands of channels on Telegram. Telegram is an application that allows users to communicate on a channel as a group, via a cellphone or via a web browser. Telegram can also be used to directly message individuals. It has become extremely popular with extremist groups because of its strong, proprietary encryption and the fact that the company does not facilitate law enforcement investigations. SocialNet and OIMonitor, from ShadowDragon (shadowdragon.io) are tools that can be used to copy data from Telegram.

User groups are generally a great source of personal data when it comes to profiling an individual's behavior. There are many excellent resources that can speed up the work of an investigator.

The HootSuite social media management site (hootsuite.com) is an integration system that collates a variety of social media sites and is a valuable tool for investigators (see Figure 5.18).

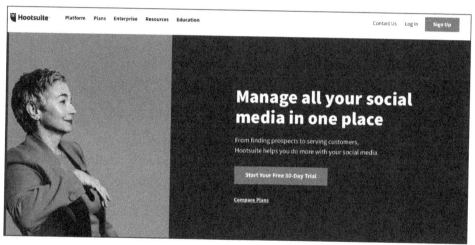

FIGURE 5.18   HootSuite website

Social Searcher (social-searcher.com) is another helpful website for searching for social media accounts, using identifiers like usernames. Another similar website is knowem? (knowem.com).

Searching for Stolen Property

The Internet has made it easier for thieves to profit from their crimes, but the Internet has also made it easier to search for stolen goods. SearchTempest (www.searchtempest.com) is a website that allows the user to search for goods listed in classifieds from multiple websites, including eBay and Amazon. Of course, investigators also should check eBay and Craigslist directly. Searching these websites for stolen property is challenging, but a search can be effective for unique items.

LeadsOnline (leadsonline.com) is a service for law enforcement, eBay, and other resellers that provide a searchable database of stolen property.

Sometimes an investigator will want to establish ongoing surveillance for a suspect, which may include an associated telephone number or email address. Monster Crawler (www.monstercrawler.com), Search.com, and Google Alerts (www.google.com/alert) are effective for searching across multiple search engines and alerting an investigator to online activity by a suspect. It is also possible to use RSS feeds on eBay to be alerted to certain telephone numbers. This is especially important when seeking to identify drug dealers. Investigators can also use keywords to find drug users and dealers, with terms like 420YNOT, PIFF, and MJ. When searching for gang activity, there are keywords, like blood, crip, and cokeboys, that will assist the investigator.

Instant Messaging (IM)

Instant messaging has been transformed recently from merely providing text messaging to including more advanced video, VoIP, and video communications. Most computers come with an integrated webcam as standard, and data transfer rates have dramatically increased with improvements in broadband communications, thereby making video a more viable option. Therefore, applications like Skype, FaceTime, and Google Hangouts have become more prominent.

Internet Relay Chat (IRC) is a text-to-talk tool for communicating with other people online, and it is synonymous with instant messaging. IRC can be used for one-to-one communication or to chat with a group of people in a chat room. IRC can also be used to share files. In addition, the IRC protocol can be used maliciously to send commands to another computer, making it a zombie computer. Port 6667 is often associated with malware being sent to IRC users.

Mibbit is a website (see Figure 5.19) that provides a search engine for chat groups. The website monitors more than 6,000 IRC networks, and users can search these networks based on category.

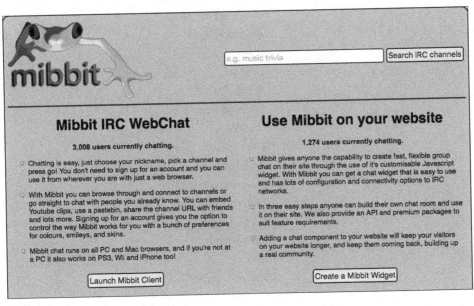

FIGURE 5.19   Mibbit website

IRC is extremely important to law enforcement because many criminals use it to communicate with other criminals, co-conspirators, or potential victims. Terrorists, pedophiles, credit card thieves, and cyberbullies have all frequented chat rooms. From a computer forensics perspective, the most important source of information are the IRC servers, more than the computers using the service. However, investigators must act quickly because companies do not maintain their users' chat logs for very long—perhaps seven days, at most, in many cases.

The importance of instant messaging evidence can be seen in the cyberbullying case of Ryan Halligan. On October 7, 2007, the middle school student committed suicide after being bullied online. Halligan and his friends conversed using AIM (AOL Instant Messenger). The boy's conversations were inadvertently recorded and archived because Halligan had installed *DeadAIM*. **DeadAIM** was a freeware program, created by JDennis, to disable advertising and enable tabbed browsing. Ryan's father discovered archived folders that DeadAIM had created on Ryan's computer. The archived folders contained transcripts of conversations from AIM that revealed that a girl called Ashley pretended to like Ryan but later called him a loser. She pretended that she liked Ryan so that she could obtain personal information about him to later share and to embarrass him in front of his friends.

One issue that investigators have to deal with when investigating chat logs is the use of slang and acronyms. Table 5.1 defines some acronyms often used on IM and in cellphone text messages. Naturally, I have chosen to eliminate many acronyms that are inappropriate to print here, but those are readily available online.

TABLE 5.1   Common IM Acronyms

Chat Acronym	Meaning
BF	Best friend/boyfriend
BFF	Best friends forever
BG	Be good
CUL8R	See you later
def	Definitely
GF	Girlfriends
GGN	Gotta go now
huh	What?
K	OK
KPC	Keeping parents clueless
LOL	Laughing out loud
MOS	Mom over shoulder
NP	No problem
OMG	Oh my God
peeps	People
PIR	Parent in room
PLZ	Please

Chat Acronym	Meaning
POMS	Parent over my shoulder
pron	Pornography
PRW	Parents are watching
pw	Password
r	Are
R U there?	Are you there?
RBTL	Read between the lines
RN	Right now
S2U	Same to you
sec	Wait a second
shhh	Quiet
srsly	Seriously
sup	What is up?
SWF	Single white female
TOM	Tomorrow
TOY	Thinking of you
TTFN	Tata for now
W8	Wait
WD	Well done!
XLNT	Excellent
XOXO	Hugs and kisses
XTC	Ecstasy

> **Note**
>
> Urban Dictionary (www.urbandictionary.com) is a great resource for acronyms and terms young people use today when communicating on social media.

Instant Messaging Evidence

Forensic tools, like FTK, allow the user to search for instant messenger chat logs on a suspect's computer. Different instant messaging applications store user logs in different locations on a computer: registries, AppData folders, Program Files, and also in Documents and Settings.

The primary instant messenger protocols are IRC, ICQ, and XMPP. Attackers have targeted Internet Relay Chat (IRC) because of its use of unencrypted connections. IRC was historically used by AOL, although it now uses OSCAR (Open System for Communication in Realtime). ICQ was initially developed by Mirabilis but was then purchased by AOL, who subsequently sold it to Mail.ru Group in 2010. **Extensible Messaging and Presence Protocol (XMPP)**, formerly known as Jabber, is an instant messaging protocol based on XML which was developed by the open source community.

Discord, with more than 250 million users worldwide, is yet another messaging service that is worth mentioning. An examination of the associated SQLite database renders a wealth of evidence, including photos and chats. Slack is also an important messaging platform, which is primarily used in a business environment.

AIM Phoenix

Numerous types of instant messaging applications are available. What complicates the job of a computer forensics investigator is that the file formats also vary. AIM messages are stored in an HTML format, while other services store messages as plaintext. By default, AIM messages are not stored automatically. These files can be recognized by their `.aim` file extension. AIM had the largest market share for instant messaging in North America.

Skype

Conversely, Skype text messages are saved by default. The bad news is that Skype files are not easily readable. Skype files can be recognized by their `.dbb` file extension. SkypeLogView is a freeware application that can read Skype log files. These log files include chat messages, incoming and outgoing calls, and file transfers. There are also other tools, including Skyperious and SkypeBrowser. Many other Skype applications, such as Skype Recorder, can automatically record your audio conversations. This is helpful to know because an undercover detective may need to communicate with a suspect using Skype and then could record the conversation. On a Windows computer, the location of Skype log files depends on the operating system version, but here is a good location to begin searching:

```
<root>:\Documents and Settings\[Username]\AppData\Roaming\Skype\[Skype Username].
```

In Windows 10, you locate Skype chat logs here:

```
%localappdata%\Packages\Microsoft.SkypeApp_*\LocalState\<SkypeUserName>\skype.db
```

On a Mac, you can access these logs here:

```
~/Library/Application Support/Skype/<SkypeUserName>/main.db
```

Google Hangouts

Google Hangouts, formerly known as GoogleTalk, has grown in market share as an alternative to Skype because it is bundled with many Android operating system devices, including tablets. **Android** is an operating system, owned by Google, which was developed for use on mobile devices, like cellular telephones and tablet personal computers. Google Hangouts evidence can be located in the Hangouts.json file, the contents of which can then be viewed using a JSON converter. JSONBuddy is one tool that a forensics investigator might consider using. Google Takeout is a tool, produced by the Google Data Liberation Front, which allows Google users of Google applications to export their data to an archive file for review and analysis. Investigators may also opt to use this tool.

Usenet Groups

Whether a detective is looking for a pedophile or a terrorist suspect, usenets are a good place to begin. Binsearch is a website (see Figure 5.20) that can assist investigators in locating particular groups or suspects on usenets. A **usenet** is an online distributed discussion board that allows users to post messages and read postings. Usenets, sometimes called *newsgroups*, first appeared in 1980 and are similar to bulletin board systems or Internet forums. Usenets groups are notorious for attracting pedophiles, political dissidents, terrorists, and others because there is no central host web server—thus, anyone can set up a web server for their own purposes.

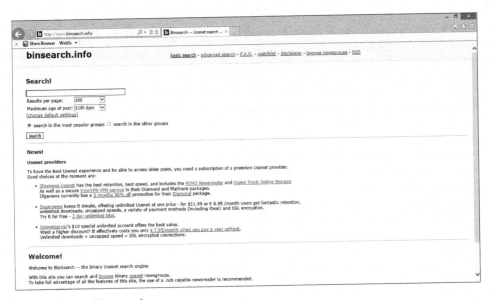

FIGURE 5.20   Binsearch

Google Groups

Another way to search for a suspect on a usenet is by using Google Groups (see Figure 5.21). The website allows users to search the archives of millions of usenet postings over a number of years.

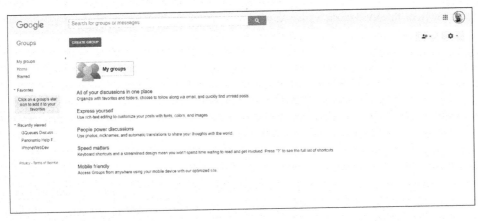

FIGURE 5.21   Google Groups

Blogs

Monitoring blogs and accumulating information about a suspect on blogs is important. Moreover, there are some types of crimes that have a particular attraction for certain kinds of criminals. Pedophiles are notorious for their use of blogs and chat rooms as they seek to network with their own kind. Terrorists also frequent blogs and share their hatred and conviction to a particular cause with like-minded individuals.

In the wake of the Norwegian killing spree in 2011, police searched blogs to find out if there had been any postings by the murderer, Anders Behring Breivik. It is customary for police to search blogs after a serious crime has been committed, especially after a killing spree, to assess the motivation for an attack and, more important, ascertain whether the perpetrator had an accomplice.

You can use the Blog Search Engine (www.blogsearchengine.org, see Figure 5.22) to search for blog content.

FIGURE 5.22   Blog Search Engine

Militant Jihadists, especially Al-Qaeda and Islamic State (IS), have successfully used blogs to recruit and motivate sympathetic individuals. For example, Samir Khan was a prolific radical pro-Al-Qaeda blogger while he was a student at a community college in Charlotte, North Carolina. He was later killed, along with the notorious Al-Qaeda leader Anwar al-Awlaki, by a U.S. drone attack in Yemen.

Social Networking Websites

The proliferation of social networking websites means that they are a tremendous source of information to investigators. Access to sites like Facebook is ubiquitous. Moreover, users can quickly take photos with smartphones, like a Samsung Galaxy, and upload them within seconds. Those with a tablet or iPad can also quickly upload images or post comments.

Geodata

Geolocational data, available from websites like Facebook, Twitter, and Foursquare, has grown in importance. In other words, users of these services provide a tremendous amount of information about their location, either intentionally or unintentionally. For example, geographical positioning is often available by default from devices, like an iPhone. Today, this geographical positioning information is not enabled on the device by default. Smartphones running on the Android operating system also capture geographic positioning data.

Photographs taken with certain cameras, and also photographs taken with smartphones, like an iPhone, will contain a geotag if Location Services are enabled. A **geotag** is digital image metadata containing the latitude and longitude of the geographic location where the picture was captured.

Geolocational data can be associated with numerous applications, including Instagram, YouTube, Facebook, and Twitter. It is possible to subpoena MapQuest for the IP address associated with searches on its website.

Although geotags and geographic locational data can help law enforcement locate and apprehend wanted suspects and convicted criminals, criminals can also use geographic data to identify where individuals are located in order to stalk them or rob their homes. For example, a user posting tweets to Twitter or checking in to locations with Facebook can make it simple for a criminal to learn the routine of the individual and determine when the person has left home. Websites like Please Rob Me (pleaserobme.com) use social networking data to reveal where a person has been and where he or she currently is. Geofencing, which enables investigators to subpoena Google to determine users who have been in a specific area, is also an extremely important source of geolocation information that can narrow a pool of suspects.

Creepy (geocreepy.com) allows an investigator to find the location of a user based on geolocation data culled from Twitter, Facebook, and other social networking websites. While the tool is still available, it is not maintained with new updates.

Facebook

Facebook has more than 2.6 billion active users. A large number of these users access their profiles from mobile devices. Facebook has been used by identity theft criminals to profile their victims. Additionally, Facebook has been used by investigators to find and apprehend criminals on the lam and even by victims who post photos of home invaders. Conversely, it has been used by thieves to target homes, as a result of people posting status updates, like "I'm on vacation".

Facebook can be used as a search engine for user profiles and content. For example, a search on Facebook could begin "Photos of people who live in…" or "People who live in <location> who like drugs".

As mentioned, photos today contain geolocation information, so an investigator may be able to determine where a photograph was taken. In recent times, fugitives have been caught because photographs they posted on Facebook contained geolocation information (geotag) that ultimately led police to their place of hiding. Although Facebook now strips out geotag data from images that its users upload, prior to making the pictures available online, the company does keep a record of location data. Law enforcement can generally gain access to this geotag data with an appropriate search warrant.

Facebook also has thousands of groups in existence. Law enforcement has embraced Facebook groups, especially in Canada. A group called Canada's Most Wanted Criminals can be found on Facebook and is dedicated to making the public aware of known criminals who are wanted by the law. The Royal Canadian Mounted Police (RCMP) uses Facebook extensively to raise public awareness of its initiatives and crime in general. The RCMP on Prince Edward Island (PEI), Canada's smallest province, has used Facebook to keep track of where kids are having parties during prom season and to prevent kids from drinking and driving. PEI RCMP also maintains an AMBER Alert Facebook profile to help in quickly locating abducted children. **AMBER** is the acronym for America's Missing: Broadcasting Emergency Response, although the name is in memory of Amber Hagerman, a 9-year-old who was abducted and murdered in Texas.

Incidentally, an organization called Wireless AMBER Alerts enables users to sign up and assist with missing children (https://amberalert.ojp.gov/resources/wireless-emergency-alert). The FBI has also developed the Child ID app, where guardians can register information about their children and promptly send those details to law enforcement in time of emergency.

The FBI has also used Facebook to try to apprehend wanted criminals and has even developed an iPhone application called FBI Wanted. The FBI has used Facebook, Twitter, and YouTube to raise public awareness about its most wanted criminals, and some credit can be attributed to social media in the apprehension of James "Whitey" Bulger, the Bostonian mobster on the lam for 16 years. A YouTube video was posted by the FBI, who targeted Bulger's girlfriend—Catherine Greig (see Figure 5.23).

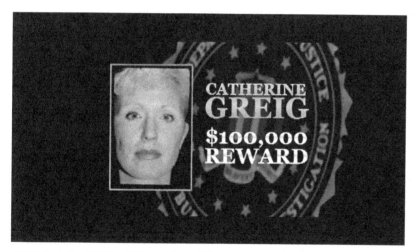

FIGURE 5.23   FBI YouTube video of Catherine Greig (Bulger's girlfriend)

Twitter

Twitter can be a marvelous resource for helping an investigator re-create the events that led up to a crime or the behavior of the criminal. The site enables users to tweet (upload a message) to show where they are and what they are doing. Some Twitter accounts also have been used to evade law enforcement; drivers in California were using Twitter to alert other drivers about sobriety checkpoints.

The URL twitter.com/explore will enable an investigator to find out which users are discussing a particular topic on Twitter. A search can be specific to a location: "near:boston lego".

There are a number of Twitter analytics tools that use Twitter's APIs. An **Application Programming Interface (API)** is a computer program that facilitates the interaction between two computer applications or programs.

Foller.me is a tremendous tool for Twitter analytics. It details a user's connections, topics, and URLs, as well as the mode of posting tweets; for example, postings were performed using an iPad. Foller. me provides information about a user and when he or she joined. This tool also provides highlights of topics discussed by that user. The number of tweets and retweets are noted for a user. The website followerwonk.com allows a user to log into his Twitter account and analyze his followers, getting information about where they are located and when they tweet. Another tool, TweetDeck (tweetdeck. twitter.com), facilitates real-time tracking of Twitter accounts in a convenient manner.

MySpace

MySpace is a social networking website that is very similar to Facebook but that has many fewer users. A user can create a profile and befriend individuals and groups. The average user tends to be younger than a Facebook user, and music is an important part of the site.

Professional Networks

Investigators often think about using social networking websites to profile a suspect or apprehend a criminal. However, they should also consider searching through professional networking websites.

LinkedIn

More than 460 million professionals use LinkedIn (www.linkedin.com; see Figure 5.24). Information about a user's network of friends and professional colleagues can also be gleaned by searching the site. An investigator can also determine an individual's interests, based upon their membership of the many professional groups and organizations available. LinkedIn facilitates the use of other social networking services, like Twitter, as well. A user can link a LinkedIn account to a Twitter account and can post tweets through LinkedIn. When searching for user profiles, it is important to remember that a user can identify who has viewed a profile. Therefore, a search can be conducted through google.com and it is preferable to search using a sockpuppet profile.

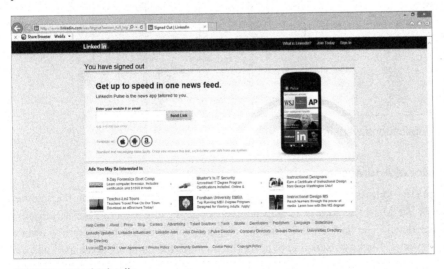

FIGURE 5.24   LinkedIn

In addition, these websites can also provide information about professionals and the organizations that they are associated with:

- Xing (www.xing.com)

- Spoke (www.spoke.com)

- D&B Hoovers (www.dnb.com)

Public Records

Many different public records containing personal information are available on the Web. Some of these records involve legal actions and are profiled here.

BRB Publications, Inc.

BRB Publications (www.brbpub.com; see Figure 5.25) provides detailed background information on individuals for a fee. The requested report includes information like criminal offenses, bankruptcies, liens, real estate records, and business ownership.

FIGURE 5.25   BRB Publications website

Using Internet Protocol Addresses

An **Internet Protocol** (IP) address is a 32-bit number that uniquely identifies a host on the Internet using Internet Protocol Version 4 (IPv4) or a 128-bit number for IPv6. In Chapter 8, we will discuss IP addresses in greater detail. The host can be a client computer, a web server computer, or even a shared resource like a printer. Luckily, users do not need to remember the numbers associated with an IP address.

Websites like WebToolHub.com allow you to enter an IP address in text format and convert it to its numeric value, and vice versa.

A **dynamic IP address** is an IP address assigned by an Internet service provider (ISP) each time one of its clients connects to the Internet. A static IP address is an IP address that an ISP assigns for a fixed period of time or permanently.

Numerous websites provide information to investigators about the location of a suspect or even a victim. Here is a list of IP lookup websites:

- American Registry for Internet Numbers (www.arin.net)
- IP Chicken (www.ipchicken.com)
- MaxMind (www.maxmind.com)
- Geo Data Tool (www.geodatatool.com)
- WhatIsMyIPAddress (whatismyipaddress.com)

Another tool with more expanded capabilities than some of the tools listed here is CentralOps.net. This website provides a tremendous wealth of information about domains.

Searches Using Metadata

Fingerprinting Organizations with Collected Archives (FOCA), from Eleven Paths (www.elevenpaths.com), is a tool that uses metadata hidden within documents to locate similar documents across the Web. The tool can be used to identify if documents have been leaked from a company and identify websites where they are located. This link analysis tool is very effective in searching for files across the Internet with similar metadata, including the same author.

Locating a Suspect

Creepy (www.geocreepy.com) is a free tool that integrates with the Application Programming Interface (API) of social media applications, including Twitter. The tool can be used to track where a person of interest has been based on their social media postings, while their location services function is enabled on their mobile device.

Using Router Forensics

As previously noted, finding a live system and retrieving evidence from the computer while it is still switched on is very important. Investigating a computer while it is turned on is called *live forensics* or *triage forensics*. A greater amount of Internet activity is generally available from a live system because investigators can retrieve the contents of RAM. The same is true with routers. Unfortunately, many investigators focus on retrieving the suspect's computer and neglect the potential evidence available from a router.

Default router passwords can be found online at websites such as RouterPasswords.com. Law enforcement can access a suspect's router directly with a search warrant or consent and can document the settings by printing each page to a PDF (perhaps by using a tool such as CutePDF, at cutepdf.com) or by taking screenshots.

Law Enforcement Access to Personal Information

A review of the events on September 11, 2001, found an information gap in intelligence gathering that might have prevented the terrorist attacks. In other words, intelligence agencies and law enforcement were not sharing information about persons of interest and criminal suspects. In the wake of the 9/11 attacks, the Department of Homeland Security (DHS) was formed. Although the system is not perfect, local, state, and federal law enforcement agencies have better access to information, and with less bureaucracy.

Local Law Enforcement

Each local authority maintains its own databases of known criminals. In New York, there is a center for maintaining this information, known as the Real Time Crime Center. The **Real Time Crime Center (RTCC)** is a data warehouse developed and used by the New York Police Department's more than 35,000 police officers to track and apprehend known and suspected criminals. The databases maintain criminal records, criminal complaints, arrests, and telephone calls made to 911 and 311 services. Police officers even record the nicknames and tattoos of suspects that are arrested and store this information in their databases at the RTCC. The agency has also developed a sophisticated geographic information system (GIS) that includes satellite imagery to help officers quickly find and apprehend suspects.

Federal, State, and Local Information Exchange

Fusion centers across the United States rely on both government databases and commercial data repositories to collect and retrieve personal information. *Entersect* is a commercial data broker that at one time claimed that it maintained billions of records on virtually all Americans. Entersect has provided these personal records to fusion centers. As previously noted, fusion centers are a joint initiative of the Department of Homeland Security (DHS) and the Department of Justice (DOJ).

The DHS is responsible for **Homeland Security Information Network State and Local Intelligence Community Interest (HSIN-SLIC)**, which is used for disseminating sensitive but non-classified intelligence between federal, state, and local authorities. The **Homeland Security Data Network (HSDN)** was a network developed by Northrup Grumman and contains top-secret, classified, and unclassified information. Fusion centers can also rely on intelligence gathered by the **National Counterterrorism Center (NCTC)**, a government agency that is part of the Office of the Director of National Intelligence (ODNI) and gathers top secret information related to counterterrorism efforts.

The primary mission of fusion centers is to facilitate information gathering and dissemination at the federal, state, and local law enforcement levels, and to provide that intelligence in hopes of both preventing crimes and solving criminal offenses. A **Terrorism Liaison Officer (TLO)**, employed by a fusion center, has the primary responsibility to facilitate and coordinate information sharing among numerous agencies. This function involves coordinating **record management systems (RMS)**, which are local databases often found at the local law enforcement level. Local, state, and federal law enforcement also have access to other databases, like the Department of Motor Vehicles (DMV), which provides investigators with information relating to driving violations and other personal information. TLO online services are available for free to law enforcement but can be accessed by those in the private sector for a fee. Interestingly, companies like Jiffy Lube also maintain extensive personal records.

Founded in 1967, the **National Crime Information Center (NCIC)** is an extremely important crime database utilized by law enforcement nationwide to apprehend fugitives, recover stolen goods, identify terrorists, and locate missing persons. According to the FBI, by the end of 2015, NCIC contained more than 12 million active records and averaged 12.6 million active transactions per day. The database can be used to identify a sex offender, locate a gang member, or find out whether a seized gun was stolen. During a routine traffic stop, police can access NCIC to identify any warrants against the driver or see if the car has been reported stolen. Of importance to digital forensics investigators are stolen electronics, like computers, tablets and smartphones, which can often be found in the FBI's database (NCIC).

Other government agencies have their own proprietary networks with searchable databases, like the FBI's secure FBINET. **Threat And Local Observation Notice (TALON)** is a secure counter-terrorism database that the U.S. Air Force has maintained since the 9/11 terrorist attacks.

International Databases

INTERPOL is the most prolific international law enforcement agency that gathers and disseminates intelligence on known and suspected criminals. It maintains international databases on everything from stolen art, to suspected terrorists, to lost travel documents, to child abuse victims. **MIND/FIND (Fixed Interpol Network Database and Mobile INTERPOL Network Database)** are online and offline databases maintained by INTERPOL to protect borders by enabling travel document searches.

Access to Personal Data in the European Union

The European Union (E.U.) has developed privacy laws that have drastically reduced the amount of personal data that companies can maintain and make available to third parties. This is in contrast to the United States, where privacy laws are much more relaxed in terms of personal data collection and storage. Concerted efforts are underway to improve the exchange of personal data between the United States and the European Union, but there are major differences in how information is collected, from airline passenger data to hotel registration information. These differences can severely hamper the work of collaborative international investigations. E.U. online privacy laws, which have reduced the amount of personal information collected, limit the amount of digital evidence available to investigators. You can learn more about this, and the General Data Protection Regulation (GDPR), in Chapter 7, "Admissibility of Digital Evidence". In July 2020, a European Court of Justice ruling invalidated a commonly-used E.U.-U.S. sharing agreement, referred to as Privacy Shield.

Online Crime

The Internet is a tremendous resource for thieves to obtain personal information and carry out their attacks. Criminals can find new ways to mask their identity, social engineer, and bilk people and corporations out of millions of dollars. Identity theft and payment card fraud has grown to unprecedented levels as a result of the Internet.

Identity Theft

In terms of gathering personal information, a criminal can use a variety of the online websites, noted earlier, to determine someone's telephone number, address, and net worth by paying for an in-depth search. Moreover, a criminal can view a person's residence (using a site like Zillow, www.zillow.com) and quickly decide on a plan to rob that house, if necessary, through the use of Google Earth.

Hackers do not even need to work out a user's password today but can simply reset a password by answering challenge questions from the email service provider. For example, a challenge question might be to enter the city where you were born or to enter your pet's name. The answers to these questions are frequently available from a person's profile on Facebook or similar social networking website. Alaska Governor Sarah Palin had her Yahoo! email account hacked, and her personal emails were subsequently posted online. Apparently, the email account hack did not require much technical skill; the password was reset using Palin's date of birth, zip code, and information about where she met her husband—questions easily found through Google searches. Two-factor authentication (2FA) has helped to mitigate some of these vulnerabilities. For example, an authorization code may be texted to the user's smartphone before a password can be reset.

Access to user accounts, like online banking and email accounts, frequently occurs through keystroke loggers. Law enforcement officials also can use these keystroke loggers to capture criminals. An example of this was the capture of Alexey Ivanov and Vasily Gorshkov, notorious hackers who plied their trade in extortion. The FBI ultimately brought down the hackers through the use of a keystroke logger. Chapter 13, "Case Studies", provides more details about this case.

Credit Cards for Sale

Credit card theft is a huge problem worldwide. The Internet has enabled credit card theft to grow. Crime in some areas has moved from the streets to the Web. Simply type the word "fullz" into any search engine, and you can see a list of websites that offer stolen credit card numbers for sale, including the CVV number that so many believe provides security to the user. A stolen credit card number can cost as little as $1.50. Many credit cards have been stolen from individuals because of malware like Zeus. **Zeus** was a Trojan horse virus that used a keystroke logger to steal bank and credit card information.

Electronic Medical Records

In August 2014, Community Health Systems, a general hospital healthcare provider, reported that 4.5 million healthcare records were stolen. Mandiant (now called FireEye) believed that Chinese hackers were responsible. The Health Information Technology for Economic and Clinical Health Act (HITECH Act) was enacted as part of the American Recovery and Reinvestment Act. This act mandated the move from paper records to electronic health records (EHR). Although this act was designed to increase efficiency in the healthcare industry, moving so many records to a digital format and storing them on a network has enticed hackers to attack healthcare providers. This mandate required the movement of all medical records to an electronic format by January 2015. The act cost billions of dollars, and, unfortunately, compliance was often the primary focus rather than computer security.

The growth in this type of crime has been phenomenal—for one clear reason: while a stolen Social Security or credit card number can sell for as little as $1, a patient EHR can sell for $20 or more on the black market. An EHR can fetch a larger sum of money because it contains more personally identifiable information (PII), which criminals can then use for a whole range of fraudulent activity.

Counterfeit and Counter-proliferation Investigations (CPI)

The are many types of investigations that can involve examining shipping information. For example, trade in counterfeit goods or counter-proliferation investigations (CPI) can benefit from this type of information. **Counter-proliferation** refers to efforts to prevent the export of weapons and proprietary technologies to foreign nations or terrorist groups. Port Examiner (portexaminer.com) is an online resource that allows an investigator to examine U.S. Customs records. VesselFinder (vesselfinder.com) is a website that allows you to track shipping vessels just about anywhere across the globe. Marine-Traffic (marinetraffic.com) allows an investigator to track active and decommissioned marine vessels across the globe. Google Street View and Google Earth could be used to take a closer view of shipping ports and warehouses to gather reconnaissance. When investigating counterfeit goods on a website, many unauthorized websites and counterfeit listings use photos of real products and images taken from legitimate websites. There are websites, like TinEye (tineye.com), that can perform a reverse image lookup to show where that photo image appears on other websites.

Cyberbullying

Cyberbullying continues to be a problem worldwide and has received a great deal of media attention, particularly in the high-profile cases of Ryan Halligan, Phoebe Prince, Megan Meier, and Tyler Clementi. Prosecutors must rely heavily on digital evidence from online sources from the victim's computer, suspects' machines, and Web service providers. Unfortunately, the laws in many jurisdictions have yet to be updated to criminalize cyberbullying.

Social Networking

As discussed earlier in this chapter, law enforcement, criminals, and companies can use social networking to find out about individuals. Social networking websites have also been a hotbed of criminal activity. Facebook, for example, has been used to launch phishing apps (applications). One example is a fraudulent notification about a comment to a user's post. The hyperlink in the notification may then lead to a phishing website.

Another case highlights the problems associated with social networking websites. Recently, a college resource company posted phony high school class profiles on Facebook. The phony profiles showed a high school student from a class looking to connect with other students from the same graduating class. A marketing company was setting up the profile so it could use the connections to market colleges to high school students.

The U.S. Department of Defense has been of two minds about whether to permit military personnel access to social networking sites. On one hand, social networking can boost troop morale, enabling those stationed abroad to maintain contact with family and friends. On the other hand, military secrets could potentially be leaked to the public. In Israel, a military raid was scrubbed after an Israeli soldier posted information about the raid on Facebook.

The social networking site Twitter has also been in the news. In 2010, the Twitter accounts of U.K. cabinet ministers were hacked. Similarly, during the Russia–Georgia conflict over Ossetia in 2008, Twitter accounts were hacked and the website of the Georgian president was subjected to a distributed denial-of-service attack (DDoS).

Online criminal activity is no longer simply motivated by money or just a challenge of wits. Online criminal activity has changed in recent times to include religious propaganda by groups, like Al-Qaeda and Islamic State, and is also politically charged with the emergence of hacktivists like Anonymous, AntiSec, and LulzSec. Junaid Hussein, a British-born hacker, rose to the highest ranks of the Islamic State and carried out a global cyber-attack that compromised the identity of U.S. military personnel.

Capturing Online Communications

Computer forensics investigators often need to capture online content either in real time or retroactively. The content captured online can be HTML pages, the IP address of a computer on the Internet, voice, video, and instant messages. Some tools are well-suited to capturing online content and communications, including AXIOM.

Magnet Forensics is the developer of AXIOM. The tool is popular with investigators because it forensically acquires Internet artifacts from computers and smart devices. The tool can effectively parse out cookie data, websites visited, and temporary Internet files.

Using Screen Captures

Many different types of screen capture software are available. Whether you are using a personal computer or an Apple Mac, capturing what is displayed onscreen is relatively simple. On a PC, there is a Print Screen button. On a Mac, this is a little more involved.

Let's Get Practical!

Make Screen Captures Using a Mac
Capture the Entire Screen Using a Mac

1. Open the web browser on your Mac.

2. Press and hold the **Apple** key, **Shift** key, and number **3** key and then release all three keys.

3. Navigate to the **Desktop**, where you see the screen capture image.

Capture a Portion of the Screen Using a Mac

1. Open the web browser on your Mac.

2. Press and hold the **Apple** key, the **Shift** key, and the number **4** key and then release all three keys.

   Crosshairs now display.

3. Drag the crosshairs across and down to select the area of the screen that you want to capture.

4. Navigate to the **Desktop**, where you see the screen capture image.

Capture an Application Window Using a Mac

1. Open an application on your Mac.

2. Press and hold the **Apple** key, the **Shift** key, and the number **4** key and then release all three keys.

   Crosshairs now display.

3. Press the **Spacebar** once.

   A camera displays.

4. Click the application you want to capture.

5. Navigate to the **Desktop**, where you see the screen capture image.

6. Press the **Apple** key and **Q** to exit the application.

Windows 10 now includes the Snipping Tool, which can easily capture an entire screen, a smaller window, or a small portion of a screen. In the Search bar, on your Windows Desktop, simply type **snip** and then press **Enter** to open the application.

Using Video

Investigators will often come into contact with video content on the Internet. It is important to possess a tool that can capture that video content.

Investigators today do not need to view videos in their entirety to understand the content, especially if the video is particularly graphic and disturbing. Autopsy Video Triage enables an investigator to view thumbnail images instead of streaming the video. The investigator can predetermine the intervals for creating thumbnails. An additional advantage of creating thumbnails is that the images can simply be copied to the report instead of having to create DVDs of the video for the defense and prosecution.

SaveVid.org is yet another tool to capture online video from YouTube and other hosts in a variety of video file formats.

Real Player is available for free from real.com. What sets it apart from other tools is how user-friendly it is. When viewing a video, you do not have to open the application; you can simply move the mouse over the right top corner to find the button Download This Video.

A number of other video recording tools are available, including WM Recorder (wmrecorder.com).

Viewing Cookies

A **cookie** is a text file sent from a web server to a client computer for the purposes of identification and authentication. A **persistent cookie** is a text file identifying an Internet user that is sent to the browser and then stored on a client computer until the expiration date stored in the cookie is reached. Generally, persistent cookies are used to record websites that a user visits and are spyware. Nevertheless, cookies are not malware. A **session cookie** is a text file sent to a browser that is stored on a computer and used to identify and authenticate an Internet user; it is removed when the user's browser is closed. Online banks use session cookies to authenticate users during a browser session, when requests are made, to prevent man-in-the-middle attacks. If a hacker attempts to take over an online session, the web server should be able to know that the intruder is impersonating the legitimate user because the intruder does not have a cookie issued by the bank. An analogy is an adult paying to enter a county fair and receiving a green wristband, the equivalent of a cookie. If a teenager attempts to buy beer (equivalent to a hacker) and has a yellow wristband, the vendor (equivalent to a web server) would deny service to the individual. Yet another type of cookie is a flash cookie. A **flash cookie**, also referred to as a Local Shared Object (LSO), stores data on a user's system and is pushed out by websites running Adobe Flash. These cookies can be used to track a user online.

Microsoft Edge stores cookies randomly in a variety of folders, in an effort to fend off hackers. Examiners working with systems running Microsoft Vista, Windows 7/8/10 can find cookies in `<root>\Users\<username>\AppData\Roaming\Microsoft\Windows\Cookies\`

The cookie text file clearly identifies the website(s) that the user has visited, as shown in this example:

```
__qca P0-170859135-1366509561547 livefyre.com/ 2147484752 559795968 30403767
3611057200 30293555 * __utma 218713990.303107170.1366509562.1366509562.13665095
62.1 livefyre.com/ 2147484752 3363037824 30440406 3612307241 30293555 * __utmb
218713990.1.10.1366509562 livefyre.com/ 2147484752 130586240 30293560 3612307241
30293555*__utmz 218713990.1366509562.1.1.utmcsr=msn.foxsports.com|utmccn=(referral)
|utmcmd=referral|utmcct=/nhl/story/new-york-islanders-beat-florida-panthers-041613
livefyre.com/ 2147484752 2471084672 30330268 3612307241 30293555*
```

In a move to improve system security further, Internet Explorer 9.0.2 randomly assigned an alphanumeric name to each cookie text file. The contents of the cookie files remained the same, although investigators could no longer associate the cookie filename with websites.

Using Windows Registry

An investigator can determine the websites a user has visited by accessing Windows Registry. The following Registry location displays websites that the user has visited:

HKEY_CURRENT_USER\Software\Microsoft\Internet Explorer\TypedURLs

From here, the investigator can export the registries as a text file and then open the entries with an application like Notepad. Of course, other applications, like AccessData's Registry Viewer application, provide a comprehensive way to access file registries.

A history of websites visited can also be retried from a hidden file called index.dat. The file index.dat is a collection of files created by Microsoft Internet Explorer and contains websites visited and Internet searches. The file also includes cookies and cache saved on a user's computer. The file actually contains a large amount of historical Internet information, and the good news for investigators is that the file is linked to the user who has logged in; the user has very little control over how the file stores information. According to the Microsoft website, the file never increases in size, even when the user deletes Internet history and clears the browser cache, and it is never deleted.

The index.dat database of files is not readable without the use of a special viewer. The following exercise introduces you to a free application that enables you to view the contents of index.dat.

Let's Get Practical!

View the Contents of index.dat (for a PC with Internet Explorer)

1. Download **Index.dat Viewer** from the website https://www.pointstone.com/products/index.dat-Viewer/.

2. From the folder where you downloaded the application, double-click the **Index.dat Viewer** application.

   A list of websites visited displays on the screen.

3. Exit Index.dat Viewer.

If you are using the Edge Web Browser, then try using WebCacheV01.dat Internet History Decoder instead for this practical. (Download: https://www.guidancesoftware.com/app/webcachev01.dat-internet-history-decoder)

Edge Web Browser

Microsoft's Edge was introduced with Windows 10 as a replacement for Internet Explorer. This new browser claims to use less battery life than competitors, like Firefox, and also blocks more phishing websites than its competitors, like Chrome. The **WebCacheV01.dat** file contains web browsing artifacts for Microsoft Edge. Browsing history files for both Internet Explorer (IE) and Edge, on a Windows 10 computer, can be found here:

```
<volume>\Users\<UserName>\AppData\Local\Microsoft\Windows\WebCache
```

Summary

The rise of social networking websites has provided investigators with a wealth of information about suspects. Pedophiles and other criminals use the Internet as a resource to carry out their criminal activities. Therefore, it is important for an investigator to know the user groups frequented by these criminals and also be aware of online resources that can mask an investigator's identity while working undercover.

The contents of RAM on a suspect's computer can be a valuable source of evidence for retracing an individual's Internet activity. Nevertheless, there are other sources of evidence. For example, the **index. dat** file is a database of files that document websites an individual visits; on a Windows 10 computer the corresponding file is **WebCacheV01.dat**. Windows Registry can also provide invaluable information about a user's Internet activity. Some Internet communication services, like Skype, save text messages on a user's computer by default. Yahoo! Messenger stores messages on a user's computer using a simplistic encryption algorithm. It is important for an investigator to be familiar with the digital footprint left by instant messaging applications and know the tools available to view these files.

With the rise of the Internet, there has been a rise in online crime. Online criminal activity includes the possession and distribution of child exploitation images, identity theft, stolen credit card retailing, cyberbullying, and social networking scams.

Online investigations require the investigator to acquire digital evidence from a variety of sources, including computers (victims and suspects), mobile devices, websites (HTML documents), web server logs, IP addresses, digital images, and sound and video content.

Key Terms

AMBER: Acronym for America's Missing: Broadcasting Emergency Response, although the name is in memory of Amber Hagerman, a 9-year-old who was abducted and murdered in Texas.

Android: An operating system owned by Google that was developed for use on mobile devices like cellular telephones and tablet personal computers.

Application Programming Interface (API): A computer program that facilitates the interaction between two computer applications or programs.

Bitcoin: A crypto-currency, which is a decentralized, peer-to-peer, virtual currency.

Bitcoin miner: Solves a mathematical problem before forwarding the Bitcoin currency to the recipient.

Bitcoin tumbler: A service used to mix up Bitcoin transactions and make it harder to link Bitcoin to a specific transaction on the Blockchain.

Bitcoin wallet stores a user's Bitcoin currency.

BitTorrent: A file-sharing protocol that facilitates the dissemination of large files.

Blockchain: An electronic public ledger that keeps track of all Bitcoin transactions or blocks.

cookie: A text file sent from a web server to a client computer for the purposes of identification and authentication.

counter-proliferation: Efforts to prevent the export of weapons and proprietary technologies to foreign nations or terrorist groups.

DeadAIM: A freeware program created by JDennis to disable advertising and enable tabbed browsing.

dynamic IP address: An IP address assigned by an Internet service provider (ISP) each time one of its clients connects to the Internet.

Extensible Messaging and Presence Protocol (XMPP): Formerly known as Jabber, an instant messaging protocol based on XML that was developed by the open source community.

Fiat currency: Legal tender that is backed by a government or governments.

flash cookie: Also referred to as a local shared object (LSO). Stores data on a user's system and is pushed out by websites running Adobe Flash. These cookies can be used to track a user online.

Genesis Block: The first block in the blockchain.

geotag: Digital image metadata containing the latitude and longitude of the geographic location where the picture was captured.

Homeland Security Data Network (HSDN): A network developed by Northrup Grumman that contains top-secret, classified, and unclassified information.

Homeland Security Information Network State and Local Intelligence Community Interest (HSIN-SLIC): A network that is used for disseminating sensitive but non-classified intelligence between federal, state, and local authorities.

index.dat: A collection of files generated by Microsoft Internet Explorer that contains websites visited and Internet searches.

Internet Protocol (IP) address: A 32-bit or 128-bit number that uniquely identifies a host on the Internet.

Internet Relay Chat (IRC): A talk-to-text tool for communicating with other people online.

MIND/FIND (Fixed INTERPOL Network Database and Mobile Interpol Network Database): Online and offline databases maintained by INTERPOL to protect borders by enabling travel document searches.

National Counterterrorism Center (NCTC): A government agency that is part of the Office of the Director of National Intelligence (ODNI) and is responsible for gathering top secret information related to counterterrorism efforts.

National Crime Information Center (NCIC): An extremely important crime database utilized by law enforcement nationwide to apprehend fugitives, recover stolen goods, identify terrorists, and locate missing persons.

online proxy: A computer used to mask a user's identity so that the third party cannot recognize the IP address of the originating communication.

persistent cookie: A text file identifying an Internet user that is sent to the browser and then stored on a client computer until the expiration date stored in the cookie is reached.

Real Time Crime Center (RTCC): A data warehouse developed and used by the New York Police Department's more than 35,000 police officers to track and apprehend known and suspected criminals.

record management systems (RMS): Local databases often found at the local law enforcement level.

session cookie: A text file sent to a browser and stored on a computer in order to identify and authenticate an Internet user. It is removed when the user's browser is closed.

Tails: A live operating system that provides anonymity for the user, through virtualized sessions with Tor.

Terrorism Liaison Officer (TLO): A person employed by a fusion center whose primary responsibility is facilitating and coordinating information sharing among numerous agencies.

Threat And Local Observation Notice (TALON): A secure counterterrorist database maintained by the U.S. Air Force since the 9/11 terrorist attacks.

Tor: Free open source software and an open network that enables a user to surf the Internet with anonymity.

undercover investigation: A process used to acquire information without an individual or a suspect knowing the true identity of the investigator.

usenet: A distributed online discussion board that allows users to post messages and read postings.

WebCacheV01.dat: A file containing Web browsing artifacts for Microsoft Edge

Zeus: A Trojan horse virus that uses a keystroke logger to steal bank and credit card information.

Assessment

CLASSROOM DISCUSSIONS

1. In this chapter, you have learned that numerous online resources can assist investigators in gathering personal information about a suspect. Conversely, the abundance of personal information available online may be providing criminals with information that can assist them with identity theft, burglary, and other serious crimes. Some countries have sought to provide greater protection for consumers and limit the amount of personal information available online. Is there enough protection for consumers and their personal information?

2. Say that you are a detective, who has been asked to investigate a website suspected of selling counterfeit Microsoft and Adobe applications. What would you do to find out about the website and document the content and website statistics for your investigation report?

3. There is a benefit to investigators to have access to geotags and other geolocational information to locate and apprehend suspects and convicted criminals. Conversely, the availability of this information puts many individuals in danger of being stalked or robbed. Is greater public awareness more important than the digital evidence that it provides investigators?

MULTIPLE-CHOICE QUESTIONS

1. Which of the following can be used to share large files with other Internet users?

    A. BitTorrent

    B. XOR

    C. TALON

    D. Zeus

2. IRC is the acronym for which of the following?

    A. Internet Recipient Chat

    B. Instant Response Communication

    C. Internet Response Communication

    D. Internet Relay Chat

3. Jabber is the old name for an instant messaging protocol that is now called what?

    A. DeadAIM

    B. iChat

    C. XMPP

    D. XML

4. Which of the following is an operating system developed by Google for use on mobile devices?

    A. Linux

    B. Android

    C. iOS

    D. Windows

5. Which of the following includes the longitude and latitude of where a digital photograph was taken?

   A. Geotag

   B. LatLongTag

   C. Metatag

   D. Cookie

6. AMBER is the acronym for which of the following?

   A. Alert Motorists Broadcast Emergency Relay

   B. America's Missing: Broadcast Electronic Relay

   C. Automatic Monitoring: Broadcasting Emergency Response

   D. America's Missing: Broadcasting Emergency Response

7. What is the name of the unique identifier assigned by an internet service provider (ISP) each time one of its clients connects to the Internet?

   A. Session cookie

   B. Persistent cookie

   C. Dynamic IP address

   D. Router

8. Which of the following is the name of the Trojan horse virus that uses a keystroke logger to steal bank and credit card information?

   A. Poseidon

   B. Zeus

   C. Apollo

   D. Hermes

9. Which of the following could be considered spyware?

   A. Persistent cookie

   B. Session cookie

   C. Cache

   D. Dynamic IP address

10. Which of the following is a file that contains a history of websites visited using Microsoft Edge on a Windows 10 personal computer?

    A. WebCacheV01.dat

    B. IE.dat

    C. Index.dat

    D. WebCache.dat

FILL IN THE BLANKS

1. A(n) _____ is the process used to acquire information without the individual or suspect knowing the true identity of the investigator.

2. _____ (short for theamnesicincognitolivesystem) is a live operating system that provides anonymity for the user using virtualized sessions with Tor.

3. _____ currency is legal tender that is backed by a government or governments.

4. Sometimes referred to as newsgroups, a(n) _____ is an online distributed discussion board that allows users to post messages and read postings.

5. The Real Time _____ is a data warehouse developed and used by the New York Police Department's more than 35,000 police officers to track and apprehend known and suspected criminals.

6. The _____ Security Data Network is a network developed by Northrup Grumman that contains top-secret, classified, and unclassified information.

7. A _____ cookie is also referred to as a local shared object (LSO). It stores data on a user's system and is pushed out by websites running Adobe Flash.

8. A(n) _____ Programming Interface is a computer program that facilitates the interaction between two computer applications or programs.

9. A(n) _____ address is a 32-bit or 128-bit number that uniquely identifies a host on the Internet.

10. A(n) _____ cookie is a text file sent to a browser that is stored on a computer and used to identify and authenticate an Internet user; it is removed when the user's browser is closed.

PROJECTS

Conduct a Criminal Investigation

You are a computer forensics investigator in local law enforcement who has been assigned to an identity theft case. The suspect has set up a website that purports to be a technology blog, but trusted users can log in to a secure area of the website and buy stolen credit card numbers.

Detail how you would conduct your investigation in terms of profiling the suspect, working undercover, and capturing incriminating evidence online.

Perform Online Reconnaissance

Use the online resources documented earlier in this chapter to report on the accuracy of the information listed about you. Provide details about the type of information you find. You do not need to provide personal details; just note the type of information available. You do not need to pay for any services for this exercise.

Write an Essay about the Silk Road

Prosecutors in the case against Ross Ulbricht relied on a combination of traditional investigative techniques and digital evidence. Write an essay detailing the use of digital evidence in this case.

Investigating a Local Incident

Imagine that you are traveling home one evening and the streets, close to your home, are blocked by law enforcement and emergency responders. There is no information from media outlets, on the radio or on television, about what is happening in the area. Write an essay about how you could use OSINT to (1) determine the street and/or building where the incident is taking place and (2) identify the type of emergency.

Write an Essay about Consumer Privacy Online

Over the years, legislators have faced challenges, in the US Capitol, with introducing legislation that protects the privacy of Internet users. The revelations about the data collection practices of Cambridge Analytica, leveraging Facebook's consumers, caused consternation and prompted some to reconsider privacy legislation. Some have argued that the European Union and other countries take online privacy more seriously than the United States.

Write an essay comparing consumer privacy protection for Internet users in the United States compared to the European Union and other countries. Include references to legislation being discussed or passed, especially the General Data Protection Regulation (GDPR).

Documenting the Investigation

Learning Outcomes

After reading this chapter, you will be able to understand the following:

- How to obtain evidence from a service provider;
- How to document a crime scene;
- The process for seizing evidence;
- How to document and handle evidence;
- Forensic tools for documenting an investigation;
- Report writing;
- The role of an expert witness; and
- Standard operating procedures.

Writing a detailed comprehensive investigative report can be the key to successfully prosecuting a criminal. The report should be detailed enough to withstand the defense counsel's objections, including claims that protocols were not followed, or issues arising from media that were not examined with enough care and consideration, or concerns that certain important files were missed. The report should be comprehensive, which means that someone with no technical background must be able to understand important concepts and the value of the evidence being presented. This chapter explains how to obtain data from third parties, explores how to properly document the crime scene, illustrates how to retrieve files from various computing devices, and discusses the implications of that evidence. This chapter also provides guidelines on the role of the examiner's report and the expert witness at trial.

Obtaining Evidence from a Service Provider

According to CTIA (ctia.org), trillions of text messages are sent annually, 85% of photographs taken in 2017 were taken with a smartphone, and 89% of people always have their smartphone within arm's reach. With the introduction of 5G, smartphone usage will only continue to grow. It is therefore hardly surprising that telecom companies do not maintain text messages (SMS) or multimedia (MMS) messages for a long period of time, given the high costs associated with storing the vast quantity of communications. Consequently, the retention time for these communications is only a few days. The retention policy for communications varies from company to company. The Department of Justice provides law enforcement with guidelines about the retention policy for each telecom company and for each type of communication (SMS, MMS, email, etc.). Law enforcement usually needs a couple of days to obtain a warrant or a subpoena requesting the electronic communications of a suspect. However, law enforcement can request that communications relating to a suspect be retained pending the approval of a warrant or a subpoena. Title 18 of the U.S. Code deals with federal crimes and criminal procedure. 18 U.S. Code § 2703: *Required Disclosure Customer Communications of Customer Communications or Records* is a part of the Stored Communications Act (SCA), which is part of the Electronic Communications Privacy Act (ECPA) of 1986.

Companies, like Facebook, Google, and Verizon, are bound by federal laws, including the ECPA and the SCA. This means that they must comply with government requests for information, which have been approved by the court. Each company provides specific guidance about how law enforcement must request business records related to a particular person. At time of writing, the process for obtaining this information, from Apple, could be found here: https://www.apple.com/legal/privacy/law-enforcement-guidelines-us.pdf Apple, and some other companies have actually publicly reported the number of government requests for this information, broken down by country and the type of request, including the approval percentage (https://www.apple.com/legal/transparency/us.html).

A **preservation order** is a request to a service provider to retain records relating to a suspect. The guidelines for obtaining a preservation order are embodied in Title 18 U.S.C. § 2703(f):

> (1) In general—A provider of wire or electronic communication services or a remote computing service, upon the request of a governmental entity, shall take all necessary steps to preserve records and other evidence in its possession pending the issuance of a court order or other process.

> (2) Period of retention—Records referred to in paragraph (1) shall be retained for a period of 90 days, which shall be extended for an additional 90-day period upon a renewed request by the governmental entity.

To summarize, law enforcement can request that communications be preserved for 90 days, and a subsequent request can be made to extend that order for an additional 90 days. This gives law enforcement close to six months to obtain a signed warrant from a judge or magistrate. Investigators must remember, however, that they should inform the service provider not to inform the suspect that such a request has been made, or else the suspect is likely to know that the information is being shared with law enforcement. Much has changed in the wake of Edward Snowden because many service providers, like Twitter, have decided to inform users that they are being investigated. Therefore, an investigator is now more likely to ask a judge to request that the service provider not inform the suspect that he or she is being investigated in the subpoena.

Documenting a Crime Scene

According to the U.S. Department of Justice (NIJ) guidelines, in the *Electronic Crime Scene Investigation: A Guide for First Responders*, an investigator should secure the crime scene, ensure the safety of those around, and protect potential evidence. Protecting digital evidence is a relatively new phenomenon for many crime scene investigators. Unlike other evidence, digital evidence cannot simply be boxed or bagged up. A microSD card, for example, is smaller than an adult fingernail and can be easily missed. Likewise, pulling the plug on a computer will annihilate critical evidence, like passwords and Internet activity, from volatile memory and may also encrypt a computer and associated devices. Hypothetically, a suspect could set up a dead man's switch with an Ethernet connection so that a system becomes inoperable when that cable is unplugged, or the suspect could launch a remote attack on the computer and wipe the drive or encrypt the drive. The issue of remotely controlling devices is an important consideration. For example, a suspect could remotely wipe a device, like an iPhone, which can potentially finish an investigation. Some suspects purposely hide networking devices. For example, suspects have hidden routers behind walls, in ceilings, and in attics. There are other important considerations, like maintaining the battery life of a device after it has been seized. Therefore, crime scene investigators should seriously consider waiting for a computer forensics examiner before removing evidence.

A computer forensics examiner should always photograph and document everything found at the crime scene. Particularly important at this point is the need to photograph the connections between devices. These can be quite complex, and photographs help the examiner, back at the lab, to see how devices were configured and connected. A home network can contain so many connected devices, cables, and adapters that creating an evidence list from a crime scene is critical. Figure 6.1 is a sample evidence list:

EVIDENCE LIST

SUSPECT			CASE #	
INVESTIGATOR			PAGE #	
ITEM #	DATE	MANUFACTURER	MODEL #	
		SERIAL #	ITEM DESCRIPTION	
	BARCODE	CUSTODIAN	LOCATION OF ACQUISITION	
ITEM #	DATE	MANUFACTURER	MODEL #	
		SERIAL #	ITEM DESCRIPTION	
	BARCODE	CUSTODIAN	LOCATION OF ACQUISITION	
ITEM #	DATE	MANUFACTURER	MODEL #	
		SERIAL #	DESCRIPTION	
	BARCODE	CUSTODIAN	LOCATION OF REMOVAL	

FIGURE 6.1 Evidence list

When documenting the crime scene, the *Electronic Crime Scene Investigation—A Guide for First Responders* guide also notes that the investigator should document both digital-related and conventional evidence. After all, a computer forensics examiner might also be very interested in non-digital evidence. For example, investigators who seize a computer should also seize other digital devices, cables, adapters, and boxes from these articles, along with manuals. Post-it Notes, lying around, might have important passwords written on them. It should also be noted that some people wear USB drives like jewelry or can mask them as a toy.

Seizing Evidence

Finding incriminating evidence on a computer or a device is worthless if standard operating procedures are not followed. These protocols must be followed from the crime scene, to the forensics laboratory, to the courtroom. Defense counsel often spends much of its time questioning the actions taken by investigators instead of focusing on the actual digital evidence. There are several options for learning about best practices for crime scene investigations, seizure of evidence, evidence extraction, analysis, and reporting. Luckily, there are a number of publicly available best practice guides. While some are several years old, the basic principles still hold. Here are some examples:

- **U.S. Department of Justice:** *Forensic Examination of Digital Evidence: A Guide for Law Enforcement*

- **U.S. Department of Justice:** *Electronic Crime Scene Investigation: A Guide for First Responders*

- **Massachusetts Digital Evidence Consortium:** *Digital Evidence Guide for First Responders*

- **United States Secret Service:** *Best Practices for Seizing Electronic Evidence*

- **Association of Chief Police Officers (ACPO):** *Good Practice Guide*

- **Department of Homeland Security (DHS):** *Cybersecurity Engineering: A Guide to Securing Networks for Wi-Fi*

Crime Scene Examinations

Crime scene investigators must carry a notebook and take copious notes about any equipment they find. They also must inform first responders about what to do if they encounter digital evidence. If a computer is powered on, it should be left on. If the monitor shows activity, such as instant messaging, it should be photographed. Under no circumstances should an inexperienced police officer or investigator review evidence at the crime scene; this includes watching a video and reviewing photos. First responders should let the digital forensics examiner analyze the evidence in the lab. Of course, some extenuating circumstances can come into play, such as after a kidnapping or before a terrorist threat, when time is of the essence.

Computers, hard drives, and other digital devices should be tagged with identifying information, including make, model, serial number, and assigned investigator. Proper identification helps with an accurate logging in of evidence at the precinct or crime lab and facilitates efficient inventory control. Although solid state drives are becoming more prevalent, most drives are still SATA hard disk drives in which files are magnetically stored on metallic platters (disks). Therefore, antistatic bags should be used to contain computing devices and prevent any type of evidence contamination. Evidence tape should be wrapped around computers to ensure that only a lab technician has accessed the device. Drive bays and trays should have white tape applied and display the signature of the crime scene investigator.

Crime Scene Investigator Equipment

The equipment that a computer forensics crime scene investigator (CSI) carries is different from that of a traditional CSI. Here is a list of equipment typically carried by a computer forensics CSI:

- Notebook
- Laptop (preloaded with forensics software)
- Wireless access device (e.g., MiFi device)
- Camera
- Extra batteries for camera
- Extra SD card for camera
- Sanitized USB flash drive
- Flashlight
- Computer toolset
- USB with forensic tools for live forensics (triage)
- Sanitized hard drives
- Write blockers
- Antistatic bags
- Stronghold bags for smartphones and tablets
- Faraday box
- Evidence tape
- Drive bay labels

Other equipment may include a field kit for onsite hard drive imaging or a field kit for smartphones and tablets. If a computer is still turned on, it is advisable for an investigator to perform triage and image both RAM and potentially the hard drive. Encryption may be enabled for the hard drive, and therefore imaging the volume before the system is shut down is advisable. Additionally, RAM can be a treasure trove of evidence, including user passwords, Internet activity, running processes, and other important evidence. Therefore, an investigator might want to bring a tool, like Magnet RAM Capture for a PC or MacQuisition for a MacBook, to capture the contents of RAM.

Documenting the Evidence

Certain open source tools are available to image a hard drive, but one of the reasons for using a licensed product, like BlackLight, is to take advantage of the comprehensive reporting feature that comes with it. These tools enable you to tag evidence files and add them to a report so that the defense and jury do not need to wade through thousands of files. These tools also allow the investigator to add notes to tagged evidence files, take screenshots, and record other steps taken during the examination. In other words, licensed forensics tools provide expanded features for analyzing hard drives, memory, and image files. Figure 6.2 illustrates tagged files in a case.

FIGURE 6.2   Tagged evidence

Completing a Chain of Custody Form

When handling evidence and documenting an investigation, the assumption must always be that the evidence will end up in court. Each item must therefore be handled in accordance with the law.

Evidence should be legally obtained through a court order, subpoena, or search warrant or with consent of the owner. A subpoena is a type of court order, whereby a person is ordered to come to court to testify. A court order is an order generally issued by a judge. As you will later learn (Chapter 7), a warrant necessitates that certain requirements be met, like probable cause, as outlined in the Fourth Amendment. These parameters change for business owners who obtain evidence from an employee who is a suspect. After the evidence has been seized, the investigator needs to possess and maintain a chain of custody form (see Figure 6.3).

Defense attorneys will thoroughly examine the chain of custody form and try to find mistakes, to render evidence inadmissible. More mistakes can occur with digital evidence than with other types of evidence, like a gun or a dress. For example, when making two copies of a suspect's hard drive, there are now multiple hard drives that must be accounted for on the chain of custody form. In our example here, two copies of the suspect's drive need to be added to the chain of custody form, and then both are released to the investigator to be examined. You can imagine how complex this form becomes if the examiner images a RAID with five hard drives and the investigator makes two copies of each drive. In this case, a total of 15 different hard drives needs to be properly accounted for on the chain of custody form. Mistakes are easy to make. The examiner also needs to photograph how the drives are configured before they are removed from the computer, so that they are appropriately put back in the computer casing later. Piecing together all these RAID images after they are forensically imaged, with a tool like RAID Recovery, only adds to the complexity of the examination.

SUSPECT:		CASE #		
EXAMINER:		PAGE #		
ITEM #	MANUFACTURER / MODEL	SERIAL #	DESCRIPTION	
	RELEASED BY	SIGNATURE	DATE	TIME
	RECEIVED BY	SIGNATURE	DATE	TIME
ITEM #	MANUFACTURER / MODEL	SERIAL #	DESCRIPTION	
	RELEASED BY	SIGNATURE	DATE	TIME
	RECEIVED BY	SIGNATURE	DATE	TIME
ITEM #	MANUFACTURER / MODEL	SERIAL #	DESCRIPTION	
	RELEASED BY	SIGNATURE	DATE	TIME
	RECEIVED BY	SIGNATURE	DATE	TIME

FIGURE 6.3   Chain of custody form

Completing a Computer Worksheet

An investigator should complete a separate computer worksheet for each computer that is analyzed. The following details should be noted on this worksheet:

- Suspect and/or custodian

- Case number

- Date

- Location

- Investigator

- Make

- Model

- Serial number

- CPU

- RAM

- BIOS version

- BIOS boot sequence

- Operating system

- Drives (CD/CD-RW, etc.)

- BIOS system time and date

- Actual time and date

- Ports (USB, USB-C, IEEE 394 FireWire, etc.)

As with all hardware evidence, each item should be photographed, and then the serial number should be photographed up close. These images can be added to the investigator's report. Figure 6.4 provides an example of the type of images that can be used.

FIGURE 6.4   Computer evidence photograph

Completing a Hard Disk Drive Worksheet

A separate worksheet should be completed for each hard drive that is analyzed. Remember that some systems, such as RAID systems, have multiple hard drives. The following details should be noted on this worksheet:

- Suspect and/or custodian

- Case number

- Date

- Location

- Investigator

- Make

- Model

- Serial number

- Drive type (SATA, PATA, SCSI, etc.)

- Capacity

This form should also have notes detailing the forensic acquisition (imaging or cloning) process. These notes should describe the hardware (for example, Logicube Forensic Dossier) or software (for example, Raptor) used during the acquisition process. The investigator should also provide details about the destination or receptacle drive, which includes the following:

- Acquisition start and end times

- Acquisition verified (yes/no)

- Sanitized (yes/no)

- Make

- Model

- Serial number

The investigator should make note of any error messages that the forensic hardware or software displayed, and whether the process needed to be restarted. As always, the investigator should be specific about the versions of hardware and software that were used to perform an analysis. When cloning a drive, the investigator should try to first include the host protected area (HPA). If an error displays, the process should continue without copying the contents of the HPA. When imaging a drive, the investigator should note whether compression or encryption was used during the examination.

Completing a Server Worksheet

An investigator should complete a separate server worksheet for each server analyzed. The following details should be noted on this worksheet:

- Suspect and/or custodian
- Case number
- Date
- Location
- Investigator
- Make
- Model
- Serial number
- CPU
- RAM
- BIOS
- BIOS boot sequence
- Operating system
- Drives
    - Number
    - Type
    - Size
- System time and date
- Actual time and date
- System state (on/off)
- Shutdown method (hard/soft/left running)
- Cables
- Backups
- Drive mapping
- Server type (file/email/web/DNS/backup/virtualized/other)
- Protocol (TCP/IP or VPN, etc.)

- Domain

- Domain IP address(es)

- DNS

- Gateway IP address

- Passwords

- Logging

    - Enabled— (yes/no)

    - Types of logs

- IT staff consulted

- Name

    - Position

    - Email address

    - Telephone

- Image verified (yes/no)

Occasionally, an investigator might not have direct access to a host computer on a network, yet have the option, and permission, to remotely access that computer. After permission has been granted, an investigator can actually image a suspect's hard drive remotely using a network tool called netcat (`nc` command). Of course, the investigator needs to know the IP address for the host computer. Another helpful tool is netstat (network statistics). This line-command tool shows network connections, protocol statistics, and other valuable information. Of course, the investigator must be aware that a suspect could also be listening on that network—especially if the suspect is a systems administrator.

Using Tools to Document an Investigation

As mentioned earlier in this chapter, professional computer forensics tools include a report-writing feature. Nevertheless, an investigator can simply use Microsoft Word, and later create a PDF of the document. Some of the tools noted here are available for download online. There are other apps that can be purchased from Google Play or from Apple's App Store.

FragView

FragView allows for fast and easy viewing of HTML, JPG images, and flash files. The tool is available from Simple Carver (www.simplecarver.com).

Helpful Mobile Applications (Apps)

Google Play and the Apple App Store offer a number of free and fee-based applications that can assist a computer forensics investigator in the field and in the lab. The following is a good selection of apps, but it is important to continually check for new helpful applications.

Network Analyzer

Both computer forensics investigators and security professionals can use Network Analyzer. The app is available for both iPhone and iPad from the App Store. When activated, the app can scan for Wi-Fi connections, and within these access points, the investigator can determine the name and IP addresses for all connected devices. Tools such as `traceroute` (with geodata) and `ping` are available with the app. The software comes in both a free and a fee-based version. For more information, visit https://techet.net/netanalyzer.

System Status

The System Status app, also available from https://techet.net/sysstat, provides in-depth information about an iPhone or iPad, including CPU usage, battery, memory, network connections, and router tables. From a forensics perspective, it provides a list of running processes, which is helpful because processes could be running on a suspect's or victim's cellphone in stealth mode, meaning that no icon appears for the installed app.

The Cop App

The Cop App was designed for law enforcement investigators to capture information in the field. The app can create an investigator's report, facilitate note-taking, take photos, and make audio recordings (up to 60 seconds). The report is then uploaded online in an HTML format that can easily be converted into a PDF. For more information, visit www.thecopapp.com.

Lock and Code

The Lock and Code app, produced by The International Association of Computer Investigative Specialists, is a reference guide for the digital forensics lab technician. It is a helpful resource for referencing sectors on a hard drive, including the operating system, and it maps the file registries on Windows PCs. The guide also has an evidence seizure guide for first responders who perform onsite triage. For more information, visit www.lockandcode.com.

Digital Forensics Reference

The Digital Forensics Reference app, available from Google Play, is a reference guide for computer forensics investigators and incident response professionals. The guide covers a variety of operating systems, including Windows, Android, Mac, and iOS.

Federal Rules of Civil Procedure (FRCP)

The FRCP app, from Tekk Innovations, is a helpful reference guide for the Federal Rules of Civil Procedure (FRCP). Of course, every investigator should learn about the law and the rules behind how trials are conducted.

Federal Rules of Evidence

The Federal Rules of Evidence app, from Tekk Innovations, is a helpful reference guide for the Federal Rules of Evidence, which comes from the appendix of U.S.C. 28. This app and FRCP are helpful for investigators to learn about evidence that is admissible in court and the rules for conducting a federal trial. Chapter 7, "Admissibility of Digital Evidence", discusses these rules in more detail.

Writing Reports

The purpose of a computer forensics investigator's report is to detail findings, not to convey an opinion or convince a jury that a suspect is guilty. The report is a statement of facts, and the jury must decide on the issue of guilt. An investigator must not only state findings but also provide full details about the process of the investigation, which must always include mistakes investigators made or the failings of an inquiry.

Recording the Use of Forensic Tools

As previously mentioned, an investigator must use multiple tools during an investigation of digital media. The lab technicians must have benchmark-tested all forensic tools, while the investigator should know these findings, including known error rates. In relation to this last point, the investigator should note limitations of the examination, such as areas of storage media that were unreadable. This may include negative sectors on a hard disk drive, bad blocks, files that failed to open, or any other inaccessible data. Being proactive should mitigate some awkward questions by defense attorneys.

Time Zones and Daylight Saving Time (DST)

Obviously, dates and times are extremely important. The investigator must note the current time and the source of the current time (for example, iPhone 11, cellular service provided by Verizon, time set to auto-adjust based on current location). All system times for the devices being examined must be noted and compared to the investigator's time. The website timeanddate.com can assist you with date and time formats when working out time zones and can answer other important questions you may have. For example, you can check the time in another state or another country today or at a date in the future.

Daylight Saving Time (DST)

Ireland is 5 hours ahead of New York, but there are exceptions; the 1-hour adjustment of Daylight Saving Time and subsequent corrections do not occur on the same weekend. **Daylight Saving Time (DST)** is the practice of advancing time by one hour in the spring and then decrementing time by one hour in the fall. In the United States, DST was written into federal law in 1966. However, a state may choose not to observe DST.

Observing DST primarily occurs in Europe and the United States. DST is one of the most problematic practices for investigators to deal with when synchronizing times from varying computers and devices across the United States and internationally. The growth of cloud computing has meant that servers are even more scattered and likely to be located in multiple time zones for an organization. DST is simply not an international issue because there are domestic disparities with DST. Additionally, if an incident occurred over a weekend when the changeover to DST happened, times are even more difficult to determine.

Mountain Standard Time (MST)

Mountain Standard Time (MST) is a time zone in the United States that includes Arizona, Utah, Colorado, New Mexico, Wyoming, Idaho, and Montana. MST is seven hours behind UTC.

Arizona does not observe Daylight Saving Time and remains in MST. Therefore, during DST, the time in Arizona is the same time as in California, but at other times of the year, Arizona is one hour ahead of California and other states in Pacific Standard Time (PST). To make this scenario even more interesting, consider the fact that the Navajo Nation, in Northern Arizona, observes DST. This might seem of little consequence looking at the big picture, but even though your investigation does not involve a Native American, some computer servers reside in these areas. DST is also not practiced in Hawaii, American Samoa, Guam, Puerto Rico, and the Virgin Islands.

Coordinated Universal Time (UTC)

Coordinated Universal Time (UTC) is an international time standard that is based on longitude and uses a 24-hour clock format. UTC is calculated from 0 degrees longitude, which runs through the Royal Observatory in Greenwich, England. UTC uses an atomic clock to maintain accuracy and account for leap seconds. A **leap second** is a second that is added to clocks to allow for inconsistencies between the Earth's rotation and the time recorded by our everyday devices (watches, computers, etc.). The **Leap Second Bug** refers to computer glitches that can occur as a result of a leap second that is added to atomic clocks in order to coordinate with the Earth's rotation. There are 24 time bands that run east and west of Greenwich, and each band accounts for 1 hour (or time zone).

Greenwich Mean Time (GMT)

Greenwich Mean Time (GMT) is the time recorded at 0 degrees longitude. All time zones around the world are coordinated with this time. GMT does not recognize Daylight Saving Time. UTC is important for investigators because the system clock on a computer is based on UTC. When creating a new investigation file, most professional computer forensics tools ask the investigator to stipulate the time zone to synchronize evidence files. UTC and GMT are the same time. However, unlike GMT, UTC is not a time zone but rather an atomic time scale that is used in computing.

Creating a Comprehensive Report

Every detail in the report must be technically precise, yet the report also needs to be comprehensive so that someone with limited technical knowledge can understand the investigator's actions and the report findings. Computer scientists talk a different language with their peers, as do doctors and lawyers. Therefore, the report should not have acronyms unless they are explained earlier in the report (for example, instead of using *NIST*, use *National Institute of Standards and Technology*) and also should not use shortened words (such as *apps* instead of *applications*) or technical terms without an explanation. For example, instead of saying, "We made a hash of the disk", but rather say, "We used the MD5 algorithm to create an alphanumeric code, or hash, that uniquely identifies the hard disk drive from the computer. Creating an MD5 hash is a standard for computer forensics investigators to ensure that the copy they are working from is unaltered from the original media seized from the suspect's computer", You could also include a separate section for technical definitions. If you have conducted a prudent investigation and publish the facts of the case, you should have nothing to worry about. Remember, you have a duty to be fair to both the prosecution and the defense.

No ambiguity should surround anything stated in the report. Have someone else review your report for accuracy and potential inconsistencies, to identify confusion, and determine if someone with no technical background can understand it. Ultimately, in theory, your report should be detailed enough for someone to use your report to re-create the same analysis and retrieve the same results.

Using Graphic Representations

A graphical representation is often superior to the written word. The saying that a picture can tell a thousand words is true. For example, a spreadsheet with a call log is far less effective than a graphic displaying a picture of the suspect with lines to contacts he or she communicated with the most, including any co-conspirators or a victim. A graphical timeline of events is also superior to a simple list. Likewise, a graphic of networked friends on a Facebook network is more appropriate than a list of friends. Additionally, the use of maps can indicate how file metadata can place the movements of a suspect, including his or her presence at the scene of a crime. Many cell site analysis tools provide this type of mapping capability for cellphone activity.

Structuring the Report

Investigative reports vary, but you might want to structure your report as follows:

- Cover Page
- Table of Contents

- Executive Summary

- Biography

- Purpose of the Investigation

- Methodology

- Electronic Media Analyzed

- Report Findings

- Investigation Details Connected to the Case

- Exhibits/Appendices

- Conclusion

- Glossary

The Cover Page

The cover page should include at least the following:

- Report title

- Author

- Department and organization

- Investigation number

- Report date

The cover page might also include the signature and date lines for those involved in the investigation.

The Table of Contents

A well-organized report should include a table of contents to assist prosecuting attorneys and defense attorneys, as well as any expert witnesses, who may be called upon to examine the report.

The Executive Summary

The executive summary portion of the report will provide a synopsis of the purpose of the examination and the investigator's major findings. In law enforcement, a separation of duties often occurs, particularly in larger computer forensics labs. This means that one officer works the investigation, and another officer performs the forensic analysis. Therefore, the work of more than one law enforcement agent is included in the report, and that must be clearly outlined in the report.

Biography

A brief biography of the investigator should be included, which highlights all relevant experience. This section should include college degrees, certifications, and any digital forensics training classes completed. An approximate number of hours of pertinent training should be noted. The investigator should also detail her investigative and professional experience. For example, include how many years of experience working in her department. Ultimately, this section should explain why the investigator was a suitable expert to conduct an investigation and produce reliable findings related to the case.

The Purpose of the Investigation

The purpose section is optional because the report writer may have explained the reason for conducting the investigation in the executive summary. To set the tone for the report, the report writer might want to explain the reason for the investigation and the scope of the warrant, which will later help to explain the types of computing devices and media that were examined, and the areas of memory/storage that were analyzed. For example, picture and video files will be important in a suspected pedophile case, whereas emails might be particularly important in a corporate insider investigation, and bank information is important in an embezzlement investigation.

The Methodology

The methodology can be included as a separate section in the report or can be included later in the report. The methodology explains the science behind the examination. It should explain the approach the forensics examiner took, which might include a rationale for the choice of software or hardware tools used. The investigator may also reference standard practices for computer forensics examinations that were used in the examination; these could be lab specific, could come from the Department of Justice, or could be recommendations from NIST.

Predictive Coding

Predictive coding is a scientific methodology used to find keywords, patterns, or relevant content on a computer. For example, in an eDiscovery case, a forensics examiner may perform searches related to a contractual dispute, which might include a keyword search for company names or key personnel involved in contract negotiations. When investigating fraud, a GREP search may be performed to search for patterns of numbers that look like credit card numbers, Social Security numbers, or ABA routing numbers. As with all tools used in an examination, the investigator should explain the use of this methodology. Furthermore, at trial, the plaintiff may be required to show how the tool works, discuss benchmark tests completed with the tool before it was used in an actual examination, and explain the "seed data sets" that were used when initially testing the tool.

The Electronic Media Analyzed

Once again, this information might be included in another section of the report. It is important, however, to describe in detail the media examined, how the storage media related to other media examined, and how these objects related to the suspect. Consider an example:

An examination of property list files on the suspect's computer indicated that other devices had been synced to his MacBook. Property list files are configuration files that show any changes to the configuration of a computer. When an iPhone, an iPod, or other device is connected to a computer, via a USB cable, the device type and a unique identifying serial number is generally recorded on the computer. This information led the investigator to request a search warrant for the suspect's iPhone, which was subsequently seized on May 17, 2020. The suspect's iPhone was then examined....Details about the suspect's iPhone found in the property list files then led the examiner to analyze the backup files on the suspect's MacBook. The backup file was located at....

All dates and times must be clearly outlined, in detail, for every step taken in the examination.

The Report Findings

As previously noted, the report should be clear about the findings related to the nature of the investigation and within the scope of all search warrants. All technical terms should be comprehensively explained. It is important for the investigator to state the facts and be careful about interpretations—that is for the attorneys and, potentially, the jury to decide. Consider an example of proper phrasing versus improper statements:

> **Improper:** Joe Doe downloaded thousands of images of children being abused.

> **Proper:** An analysis was performed on the hard disk drive removed from the Dell computer Model E6400, Service Tag 4X39P5. This computer was seized from the residence of John Doe, 123 River Road, Sterling City, New York 10028. A total of 578,239 images of children were downloaded to this computer. John Doe noted in his statement to police, dated July 27, 2020, that he was the only user of that computer at the residence. During the analysis, it was discovered from an analysis of Windows Registry that only one user was set up on that computer. The examiner also discovered a login and password on this Dell computer.

The Investigation Details Connected to the Case

This is not necessarily a separate section, but it is important to note supporting evidence, to the investigation, that is not digital. These might include statements from the suspect and witnesses.

The Exhibits/Appendices

Exhibits can include photos of seized objects, screenshots of the computer screen, tagged photographs, printed emails, and any other files of interest. Appendices can include forms, like the evidence list and the search warrant.

The Glossary

Placing a comprehensive glossary at the end (or beginning) of the report is good practice. Defense counsel often argues that they were at a disadvantage because of the lack of resources available to their investigation compared to those available to law enforcement. By assisting and cooperating with the defense counsel and including a glossary, footnotes, and other helpful resources you will diminish these arguments of inequality.

Using Expert Witnesses at Trial

When explaining evidence from a scientific perspective, it is imperative for the prosecution and defense to have an expert available who can verify the validity of an exhibit at trial or explain a scientific concept.

The Expert Witness

An **expert witness** can create an investigative report or review the findings of an investigative report and then interpret those findings based on specialized education, training, and knowledge. The expert is usually hired by an attorney to be an adviser. Ultimately, an attorney can call upon the expert witness to discredit or refute the report findings, or to draw out the importance of incriminating evidence highlighted in a report. At trial, the role of the expert witness is to educate the jury. Both the prosecution and the defense counsel can hire their own experts and ask them to testify. Of course, any expert witness that is called to testify will most certainly be cross-examined.

The role of the expert witness at trial (federal court) is also described in the Federal Rules of Evidence. FRE 704, *Opinion on an Ultimate Issue*, states the following:

> (a) In General—Not Automatically Objectionable. An opinion is not objectionable just because it embraces an ultimate issue.

> (b) Exception—In a criminal case, an expert witness must not state an opinion about whether the defendant did or did not have a mental state or condition that constitutes an element of the crime charged or of a defense. Those matters are for the trier of fact alone.

This rule clearly illustrates that although an expert cannot pass judgment on a defendant, an expert can provide opinions based on facts.

The Goals of the Expert Witness

The expert witness should educate the jury and break down complex concepts into meaningful information. For example, an algorithm can be explained using the metaphor of a cake recipe, with a list of steps to reach a particular outcome. Metaphors can really help with comprehension. The expert is also there to persuade, while weaving in important concepts can help with this. The expert should aim to imprint core concepts onto the minds of the jurors through repetition of these concepts.

> **Note**
>
> A **lay witness** testifies about his personal experience and knowledge and may not express an opinion.

Preparing an Expert Witness for Trial

In most cases, the expert witness is required to provide a written report, as noted in Rule 26(2)(B), *Disclosure of Expert Testimony in the Federal Rules of Civil Procedure*:

> (B) Witnesses Who Must Provide a Written Report. Unless otherwise stipulated or ordered by the court, this disclosure must be accompanied by a written report—prepared and signed by the witness—if the witness is one retained or specially employed to provide expert testimony in the case or one whose duties as the party's employee regularly involve giving expert testimony. The report must contain:
>
> (i) a complete statement of all opinions the witness will express and the basis and reasons for them;
>
> (ii) the facts or data considered by the witness in forming them;
>
> (iii) any exhibits that will be used to summarize or support them;
>
> (iv) the witness's qualifications, including a list of all publications authored in the previous 10 years;
>
> (v) a list of all other cases in which, during the previous 4 years, the witness testified as an expert at trial or by deposition; and
>
> (vi) a statement of the compensation to be paid for the study and testimony in the case.

The expert witness should ensure that her curriculum vitae is up-to-date and that she refreshes her memory about the contents of that document. For example, if you were an expert witness, you would have to be able to describe a job you had 10 years ago and explain any gaps in your employment history. If you had noted membership in organizations, you would have to be familiar with their by-laws and code of ethics and explain why you are a member. You would need to refresh your memory about your training because a good defense attorney often questions experts about their training on forensic tools and calculates how many hours they were trained for and how many hours of experience they had in the lab. Even if you answer with confidence and correctly, your answers could be used to illustrate how defense counsel was at a disadvantage because they could not use the same resources and expertise as the prosecution.

If you will be acting as an expert witness, the client's attorney will help you prepare for your expert testimony. An expert witness may bring a portfolio of exhibits and props to court to help explain important concepts. Of course, all exhibits or props should be cleared with your representative attorney beforehand. Also prepare a well-organized binder of notes to bring with you that you can quickly access. You do not want to seem disorganized if you are asked a question, but it is perfectly acceptable to ask to refer to your notes when a question is directed to you.

Before you enter the courtroom, the prosecuting attorney should possess the following:

- Curriculum vitae
- Authority for all searches that were performed
- Chain of custody form
- Investigative report
- Bench notes

Tips for an Expert Witness for the Prosecution

An expert witness can be asked hypothetical questions. When answering these types of questions, the answer must be rooted in facts. An expert should resist going beyond answering the question and not volunteer additional information. The expert should resist being pulled out of her realm of expertise, which could be a ploy by the defense to discredit her expertise and make her look uncomfortable and less confident.

The expert should always be courteous to everyone in the court, but especially with the court reporter and the judge. Never talk over someone else speaking in the courtroom, or the court reporter will reprimand you. You should address the judge as "Your Honor", not "Miss" or "Ma'am".

When answering questions, be clear about who did what and when. Always avoid qualifying words such as *probably*. Have the conviction to say, "I don't know—that is outside my area of expertise". When summarizing key concepts, be sure to include important facts derived from the evidence.

Be clear about units of measurement—for example, 8GB of RAM. Also pay particular attention to time zones, which defense attorneys question more and more.

Summary

Effectively documenting an investigation requires crime scene investigators and lab technicians to take copious notes on both their actions and their findings. Proper handling, containment, and examination of the evidence is just as important as the evidence found. At the crime scene, taking detailed notes and photographing all digital devices and their connections is vital. An investigator can use other means to obtain evidence as well, including requests to third-party service providers. A preservation order is a document that is a legally binding request that forces a provider to preserve data related to one of its customers. The data will subsequently be released when the service provider receives a subpoena or warrant.

When evidence is seized from a suspect or a crime scene, it is essential to document all custodians of that evidence using a chain of custody form. Digital evidence can become complicated with a chain of custody form. For example, an investigator might be working with a RAID that includes five hard disk drives, and policy is to make two copies of each drive.

One of the reasons why investigators pay a license fee is the ability to use more advanced computer forensics tools with report-writing features. However, free tools also can assist with documenting the investigation; these include CaseNotes, FragView, and VideoTriage.

The actual investigative report should include the scope of the investigation. For example, if the case involved the investigation of a doctor, a judge might allow investigators to examine only certain portions of a hard drive to avoid accessing confidential patient records. The investigator should also note the scientific methodology or approach used during the investigation. This portion of the report details methods of examination that are accepted practices in this field of science. One example is predictive coding.

The forensics examiner must be careful about accounting for time differences associated with file metadata. Synchronizing these dates is complicated by Daylight Saving Time (DST). Coordinated Universal Time (UTC) is the international time standard, which is based on longitude and is the time computer systems are based upon.

The services of an expert witness can be engaged by the court, the client, a prosecutor, a defendant—or perhaps a plaintiff, in the case of civil litigation. An expert witness is different from a lay witness because an expert may provide an opinion based on the ultimate issue of the case. An expert witness must provide an up-to-date curriculum vitae and be able to explain every entry in that document, including the code of ethics associated with memberships. Opposing counsel may use many tactics to discredit the expert's qualifications and testimony. Ultimately, a well-written report and a qualified expert, who fully comprehends the findings of a report, should be able to withstand any cross-examination.

Key Terms

Coordinated Universal Time (UTC): An international time standard that is based on longitude and uses a 24-hour clock format.

Daylight Saving Time (DST): The practice of advancing time by one hour in spring and then decrementing time by one hour in fall.

expert witness: An individual who creates an investigative report or reviews the findings of an investigative report and provides an interpretation of those findings based on specialized education, training, and knowledge.

Greenwich Mean Time (GMT): The time recorded at 0 degrees longitude. All time zones around the world are coordinated with this time.

lay witness: Someone who testifies in court about personal experience and knowledge and may not express an opinion.

leap second: A second that is added to clocks to allow for inconsistencies between the Earth's rotation and the time recorded by our everyday devices.

leap second bug: Computer glitches that can occur as a result of a leap second that is added to atomic clocks to coordinate with the Earth's rotation.

Mountain Standard Time (MST): A time zone in the United States that includes Arizona, Utah, Colorado, New Mexico, Wyoming, Idaho, and Montana.

predictive coding: A scientific methodology used to find keywords, patterns, or relevant content on a computer.

preservation order: A request to a service provider to retain the records relating to a suspect.

Assessment

CLASSROOM DISCUSSIONS

1. Explain why time differences can make or break a case for the prosecution.

2. If you had a friend who was asked to be an expert witness, what advice would you give your friend to successfully prepare for trial?

3. Detail all forms that might be required for seizing evidence from the home of a suspect.

4. Discuss why chain of custody forms are often inaccurately filled out.

MULTIPLE-CHOICE QUESTIONS

1. Which time zone in the United States includes Arizona, Utah, Colorado, New Mexico, Wyoming, Idaho, and Montana?

    A. Mountain Standard Time

    B. Pacific Standard Time

    C. Central Time Zone

    D. Greenwich Mean Time

2. Which of the following is the standard time for computer systems?

    A. Greenwich Mean Time

    B. Mountain Standard Time

    C. Eastern Standard Time

    D. Universal Time Coordinated

3. Which of the following is a request to a service provider to retain the records relating to a suspect and is valid for 90 days before it may be extended?

    A. Chain of custody

    B. Preservation order

    C. Subpoena

    D. Warrant

4. Which of the following is a scientific methodology used to find keywords, patterns, or relevant content on a computer?

    A. Java programming

    B. Analysis coding

    C. Keyword search

    D. Predictive coding

5. Which of the following refers to the practice of advancing time by one hour in spring and then decrementing time by one hour in fall?

    A. Leap second advancement

    B. Daylight Saving Time

    C. British Standard Time

    D. Mountain Standard Time

6. Which of the following witnesses will testify about personal experience and knowledge and may not express an opinion on the ultimate issue?

    A. Expert witness

    B. Lay witness

    C. Character witness

    D. Court witness

7. Which of the following witnesses will testify about personal experience and knowledge and may express an opinion on the ultimate issue?

    A. Expert witness

    B. Lay witness

    C. Character witness

    D. Court witness

8. Which of the following is added to clocks to allow for inconsistencies between the Earth's rotation and the time recorded by our everyday devices?

    A. Incremental seconds

    B. Leaping second

    C. Leap year second

    D. Leap second

9. Which of the following is the time recorded at 0 degrees longitude, with all time zones around the world coordinated with this time?

    A. British Standard Time

    B. Mountain Standard Time

    C. Greenwich Mean Time

    D. Universal Time Coordinated

10. Which of the following refers to computer glitches that can occur as a result of a leap second that is added to atomic clocks in order to coordinate with the Earth's rotation?

    A. Leap second bug

    B. Logic bomb

    C. Worm

    D. Rootkit

FILL IN THE BLANKS

1. Predictive _____ is a scientific methodology used to find keywords, patterns, or relevant content on a computer.

2. The time recorded at 0 degrees longitude is called _____ Mean Time.

3. The practice of advancing time by one hour in spring and then decrementing time by one hour in fall is called _____ Saving Time.

4. A lay _____ testifies about personal experience and knowledge.

5. A(n) _____ second is added to clocks to allow for inconsistencies between the Earth's rotation and the time recorded by our everyday devices.

6. A(n) _____ witness may create an investigative report or review the findings of an investigative report and provide an interpretation of those findings based on specialized education, training, and knowledge.

7. _____ Standard Time is the time zone in the United States that includes Arizona, Utah, Colorado, New Mexico, Wyoming, Idaho, and Montana.

8. The computer glitches that can occur as a result of a leap second that is added to atomic clocks in order to coordinate with the Earth's rotation is referred to as the leap second _____.

9. Universal Time _____ is an international time standard that is based on longitude and uses a 24-hour clock format.

10. A(n) _____ order is a request by law enforcement to maintain the records of a suspect, pending the approval of a subpoena or warrant.

PROJECTS

Conduct an Onsite Investigation

You have been called to the residence of a suspected drug dealer. At the residence, you are informed that there is a Microsoft Surface computer and a Samsung Galaxy S20. Outline the steps you will take in the possible onsite examination of these devices. You should note how to properly document and handle these devices based on published guidelines for law enforcement. Describe what other hardware, present at the home, could be of evidentiary value to the investigator. As part of your outline, write about the type of equipment the investigator should bring to the suspect's residence.

Write a Report

Based on the description of the investigation in Project 1, provide an outline for the investigative report that you will write. Describe your methodology (scientific approach) used for this examination. Include other sources of evidence that you may need to request, and describe how you will request it (*hint:* service providers). Given that you will be examining a Microsoft Surface computer and a Samsung Galaxy S20, mention the tools that you can potentially use during the lab examination. You have also been asked, as part of your investigation, to look for certain keywords related to the suspect's drug dealing activities and stolen Social Security numbers that were stored on the computer.

Synchronize Time

Based on the description of the investigation in Projects 1 and 2, it was discovered that the suspect took the following excursions from his residence in New York City:

(1) **Destination:** Rio de Janeiro, Brazil

Date: August 25–31, 2020

(2) **Destination:** Phoenix, Arizona

Date: October 24–29, 2020

(3) **Destination:** Dublin, Ireland

Date: January 2–10, 2021

(4) **Destination:** Durban, South Africa

Date: May 11–19, 2021

Detail the way in which you would synchronize these times in the report.

Chapter | **7**

Admissibility of Digital Evidence

Learning Outcomes

After reading this chapter, you will be able to understand the following:

- The structure of the legal system in the United States;
- The role of constitutional law in computer forensics;
- Principles of search and seizure of computers and other digital devices;
- Rules for the admissibility of evidence at trial;
- Case law concerning the use of digital surveillance devices by law enforcement;
- Cases of computer forensics gone wrong;
- Structure of the legal system in the European Union; and
- Data privacy and computer forensics in the European Union.

The United States legal system is one of the most complicated in the world, primarily as a result of a dual legal system that is comprised of federal and state laws and their respective court systems. This complexity also makes for arguably one of the most exciting legal systems in the world.

Like other legal systems worldwide, U.S. legislation has been complicated further by the growing importance of digital evidence in criminal investigations and trial proceedings. U.S. legislation at all levels (federal, state, and local) has been impacted by computers and other digital devices. This chapter details how traditional laws have been applied to new technologies and how traditional laws have been amended to address the admissibility of digital evidence, and how new laws have been introduced to keep up with advances in technology.

History and Structure of the United States Legal System

First and foremost, a state-based legal system predates the federal legal system in the United States. Prior to the War of Independence, each of the 13 states operated with autonomy, with their own legal system, including their own official religion. For example, Maryland was originally established as a Catholic colony, whereas the Church of England was the state religion for New York, Virginia, Georgia, North Carolina, and South Carolina. These disparate entities, formerly known as colonies, were eventually united by a common outrage: taxation by Britain without representation. Although there was some notion of a confederation, this union did not have a tremendous amount of meaning until it became apparent that states needed to be united to fight the "oppression" of taxation by the British Crown and government. Furthermore, this confederation could be effective only if states were forced to fund a Congress that could then fund a Union Army. These states would also require this Congress to establish common laws for this federation—in other words, the institution and ratification of federal laws. Understandably, it took quite some time for each of these states, with a variety of denominations, ethnicities, and values, to come to an agreement on a new legal system that would coexist with their established state system. The relationship between a federal and state system was contentious during colonial times, and this relationship was severely tested during the American Civil War, which was not as much about the abolition of slavery as it was about the supremacy of the federal government on contentious issues such as the extension of slavery. The Civil War was also about the future of the U.S. economy: the rural, agrarian economy of the South, which was a vision of the future for founding father Benjamin Franklin, versus the urban capitalist society of the North, which was the way forward for Alexander Hamilton.

What does all of this have to do with computer forensics? The answer is that both federal and state laws impact criminal investigations and court trials. Moreover, investigations and court proceedings at the state and county levels are influenced by the Constitution, which is a federal document that protects the rights of the individual. Additionally, a computer forensics investigator must abide by federal and state laws, when conducting an investigation.

Interestingly, a case can be tried in a number of different ways. For example, in a criminal investigation, a jury might find the defendant not guilty. A **jury** is a group of people put under oath to hear arguments at trial and render a verdict of guilty or not guilty. But a civil lawsuit then can ensue, with a victim seeking monetary compensation against an offender or third party for physical damage or emotional distress. The **plaintiff** is the person who initiates the lawsuit and is responsible for the cost of litigation. The **defendant** is the person who defends him- or herself in a lawsuit. O. J. Simpson was acquitted of the murders of Nicole Brown Simpson and Ronald Goldman in a criminal trial, but the families successfully secured a $33.5 million settlement against him in civil court.

The Civil War ended more than a century and a half ago, but there is still a dichotomy of laws and authority between federal and state institutions in the United States. Problems still exist today, as evidenced by certain states with different immigration laws compared to the President of the United States, and other members of Congress. This tension is also clearly illustrated by California's state law legalizing the use of marijuana for medicinal purposes, yet these distributors are operating illegally under federal law.

The United States Constitution was created on September 17, 1787, and then subsequently ratified by each state. With this ratification, the Constitution (and federal government) is supreme concerning the powers delegated to it, yet it still recognizes the sovereignty of the states and their supremacy over matters of state. The Constitution is a framework that defines the relationship between the federal government, its united states, and its citizens. The Constitution has been amended 27 times. The **Bill of Rights** refers to the first 10 amendments to the Constitution, which protects the rights of the individual.

The first three Articles of the Constitution establish the three branches of government: Article I, the Legislature (Congress), which is comprised of the House of Representatives and the Senate; Article II, the Executive (President); and Article III, the Judicial (Supreme Court and lower federal courts). In summary, Congress writes laws, the Supreme Court interprets those laws, and the President has the power to either sign into law or veto Congressional legislation.

Origins of the U.S. Legal System

The origins of the legal system in the United States are found in common law and English law. **Common law** is based on case law and precedent, with laws derived from court decisions. With **precedent**, court decisions are binding on future decisions in a particular jurisdiction. Therefore, these laws are derived not from legislation, but based on court decisions. The exception to this legal system is Louisiana, where the legal system was originally based on the Napoleonic Code. The Napoleonic Code has its origins in Roman law. Napoleon developed a written, uniform code of laws to assist in the administration of his vast empire.

The Napoleonic Code was based on civil law. **Civil law** is based on scholarly research, which, in turn, becomes a legal code, and is subsequently enacted by a legislature. There is no precedent. The Louisiana Civil Code Digest of 1808 has changed over time, and the current legal system in Louisiana is not that much different today from other states.

Three primary bodies of law exist in the United States: (a) constitutional law, (b) statutory law, and (c) regulatory law. **Constitutional law** outlines the relationships among the Legislative, Judiciary, and Executive branches, while protecting the rights of its citizens. It is also referred to as federal law. **Statutory law** is written law set forth by a legislature at the national, state, or local level. There are codified and uncodified laws in statutory law. **Codified laws** are statutes that are organized by subject matter. An example of this is the United States Code (U.S.C.). **Regulatory law** governs the activities of government administrative agencies. This body of law involves tribunals, commissions, and boards that are responsible for decision making. These decisions affect the environment, taxation, international trade, immigration, and so forth.

Overview of the U.S. Court System

It is important to explain the structure of the U.S. court system because you will then have a better understanding of the rationale for cases being tried in federal court versus those cases tried in state or county courts. A criminal prosecution might be tried in federal court because of the jurisdiction, meaning that crimes were committed across multiple states. Another reason for trying a case in federal court might be the nature of the crime. For example, the victim and perpetrator could both be located in California, but the defendant was accused of corporate espionage, which threatens national security and is therefore a federal case. Sometimes a case begins in a state court, but the case is then referred to a federal district court. This is common when the judge has determined that guilt or innocence depends on an interpretation of the Constitution; in other words, it is a constitutional matter.

In some cases, local law enforcement in multiple states collaborate. The criterion for determining where the case should be tried is often determined by deciding which of the states has tougher laws for a particular crime. Other times, one state might lack legislation for certain offenses. Figure 7.1 illustrates the basic structure of the court system.

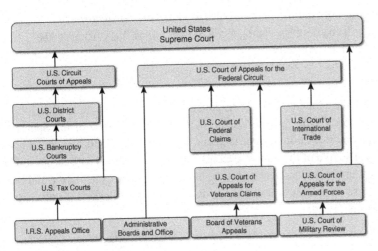

FIGURE 7.1   U.S. court system

The basic structure of federal, state, and local courts is the same. A defendant has the right to a fair trial, with the outcome determined by a jury of his or her peers. The role of the **judge** is to facilitate the trial process and ensure that the proceedings are in accordance with the law. The judge must also ensure that the proceedings are free of prejudice and that the innocence of the defendant is presumed until proven otherwise. The burden of proof is always on the prosecution. The role of the *jury* is to determine the facts of a case and render a verdict.

Appeals Courts

The U.S. court system enables its citizens to appeal a conviction. An appeals court decides whether to hear an appeal. Note that a court appeal is not a trial—there is no jury, so a panel of judges renders a decision about whether a mistake occurred in a lower court. One example might be that evidence was presented at trial that should have been deemed inadmissible. In that situation, the case is sent back to be retried, without the evidence deemed admissible. The prosecution may decide that the case is not worth retrying without a key piece of evidence deemed inadmissible or they may decide to retry the case in court. The panel of appeal judges consists of an odd number of judges and decides whether there has been a mistake of law in a previous trial.

Federal Courts

Two types of federal courts exist. The first type is derived from Article III of the Constitution. It consists of the U.S. District Courts, the U.S. Circuit Courts of Appeal, and the U.S. Supreme Court. There are two other types of Article III courts: the U.S. Court of Claims and the U.S. Court of International Trade. These special courts do not have general jurisdiction. **Jurisdiction** refers to the scope of legal authority granted to an entity.

The next category of federal court was not established by Article III but rather was created by Congress. These courts include magistrate courts, bankruptcy courts, the U.S. Court of Military Appeals, the U.S. Tax Court, and the U.S. Court of Veterans' Appeals.

Supreme Court

Under Article III, the President of the United States is responsible for appointing federal judges, which includes Supreme Court justices. Their appointment is subject to the approval of the Senate. The appointment is for life unless removed through impeachment. The Supreme Court has one chief justice and eight associate justices. The role of the Supreme Court was largely decided with the case of *Marbury v. Madison*, in 1803, when the court demonstrated its right to interpret the Constitution and be the ultimate decision-maker in congressional issues. In other words, the judiciary branch is the ultimate arbiter of the law, not Congress or the President.

Article II of the Constitution outlines the jurisdiction of the Supreme Court and other federal courts:

> The judicial Power shall extend to all Cases, in Law and Equity, arising under this Constitution, the Laws of the United States, and Treaties made, or which shall be made, under their Authority; to all Cases affecting Ambassadors, other public Ministers and Consuls; to all Cases of admiralty and maritime Jurisdiction; to Controversies to which the United States shall be a Party; to Controversies between two or more States; between a State and Citizens of another State; between Citizens of different States; between Citizens of the same State claiming Lands under Grants of different States, and between a State, or the Citizens thereof, and foreign States, Citizens or Subjects.

Federal Appellate Courts

There are 13 circuit courts of appeals, which were first established in the original 13 states of the United States. Today there are 12 regional circuit courts in several cities, as well as an additional Federal Circuit Court (13th Court) in Washington, D.C. Each of these circuits is assigned a circuit justice from the Supreme Court.

This chapter highlights many notable circuit court decisions with respect to the admissibility of digital evidence. One of the most noteworthy districts is the Ninth Circuit, which is by far the largest circuit and covers districts in Alaska, Arizona, California (Central, Eastern, Northern, Southern), Hawaii, Idaho, Montana, Nevada, Oregon, and Washington (Eastern and Western), with appellate jurisdiction over the territories of Guam and Northern Mariana Islands courts. These courts hear cases referred from lower federal district courts, known as U.S. District Courts.

Ultimately, the federal appellate courts can refer cases to the U.S. Supreme Court. Typically, three judges sit in these courts.

U.S. District Courts

There are 94 U.S. District Courts across the United States. Every state has at least one District Court, and larger states have more. For example, New York has a Southern District of New York (Bronx, Dutchess, New York, Orange, Putnam, Rockland, Sullivan, and Westchester counties), a Northern District of New York (from Ulster County and North), the Eastern District of New York (Kings, Nassau, Queens, Richmond, and Suffolk counties), and a Western District of New York. There can be multiple courthouses in each district. For example, in the Southern District of New York, there are courthouses in White Plains and New York City (Manhattan).

Most federal cases begin in a U.S. District Court. Cases in these courts can be civil or criminal. A kidnapping or intellectual property dispute case generally is the type of case tried in a U.S. District Court.

State Courts

The state court system varies from state to state. Nevertheless, there are some similarities. Local trial courts are located throughout the state and hear cases at the lower level. If the defendant is found guilty, the defendant can appeal a conviction in a state appellate court.

State Appellate Courts

Two types of state appellate courts exist. Often referred to as supreme courts or courts of appeal, these are the highest courts in the state judicial system. They have discretion over which cases they hear and are often referred cases where there could be an error in determining the law. They are confined to a particular jurisdiction and can be asked to preside over contentious decisions, like elections. Anywhere from three to nine judges can sit on a panel in a state appellate court.

Intermediate Appellate Courts

Intermediate appellate courts exist in 40 of the 50 states. The following states have no appellate courts: Delaware, Maine, Montana, Nevada, New Hampshire, Rhode Island, South Dakota, Vermont, West Virginia, and Wyoming. The number of these courts varies from state to state, as does the number of judges. Decisions from appellate courts can be appealed to the state's highest court, which is referred to as the State Appellate Court.

Trial Courts of Limited Jurisdiction

Trial courts of limited jurisdiction are limited to hearing certain types of cases. These courts include the following:

- **Probate court:** Sometimes referred to as a surrogate court, this court hears cases relating to the distribution of a deceased's assets.

- **Family court:** This court hears cases relating to family matters, including child custody, visitation, and support cases, as well as restraining orders.

- **Traffic court:** This court hears cases relating to driving violations. An individual who is cited for a traffic violation can pay the fine (plead guilty) or can appeal in traffic court. With DUI (driving under the influence) citations, the individual may be required to appear in court before a judge. DUI and DWI (driving while intoxicated) are crimes, and these cases can be tried in criminal courts in many jurisdictions.

- **Juvenile court:** In this court, minors are tried by a tribunal. The court generally hears cases against defendants who are under the age of 18. However, more serious crimes, like murder or rape crimes, that are committed by juveniles can be moved to a different court, where the defendant is prosecuted as an adult.

- **Small claims court:** The function of these courts is to settle private disputes involving relatively small monetary amounts.

- **Municipal court:** This court hears cases when a crime has occurred within their jurisdiction. These can include DUI, disorderly conduct, vandalism, trespassing, building code violations, and similar offenses.

Trial Courts of General Jurisdiction

A trial court of general jurisdiction can basically hear any kind of criminal or civil case that is not exclusive to another court.

New York Trial Courts

It is probably helpful to see an example of how the court system is set up in a particular state. For this example, let us consider New York State. In New York City, a trial by jury can be held in the following courts:

- Supreme Court

- New York City civil court

- New York City criminal court

Outside of New York City, a jury trial can be held in the following courts:

- Supreme Court
- County court
- District court
- City court
- Town and village court

A civil trial lasts for an average of 3 to 5 days; a criminal trial generally averages 5 to 10 days. The following people generally are present at trial:

- Attorneys (or Counsel)
- Court reporter
- County clerk
- Court officer
- Defendant
- Interpreter
- Jury
- Plaintiff
- Prosecutor
- Spectators
- Witnesses

In the Courtroom

It is helpful for a computer forensics examiner to understand the pretrial and trial process because they might one day become part of that trial as an expert witness. The following is an outline of the steps taken during the pretrial and trial in a civil or criminal case:

1. Jury selection
2. Oath and preliminary instructions
3. Opening statement(s)
4. Testimony of witnesses and presentation of other evidence

5. Closing arguments

6. Jury instructions

7. Deliberations

8. Verdict

9. Sentencing

The Jury

The right to a trial by jury is clearly outlined in the Sixth Amendment to the U.S. Constitution:

> In all criminal prosecutions, the accused shall enjoy the right to a speedy and public trial, by an impartial jury of the State and district wherein the crime shall have been committed, which district shall have been previously ascertained by law, and to be informed of the nature and cause of the accusation; to be confronted with the witnesses against him; to have compulsory process for obtaining witnesses in his favor, and to have the Assistance of Counsel for his defense.

Voir dire is the questioning process used in the jury selection process. During *voir dire*, lawyers and, in some cases, the judge ask potential jurors questions to determine any prior knowledge of the facts of the case or any biases that could influence their impartiality in the case. All defendants are presumed innocent until proven guilty beyond a reasonable doubt. Jurors may be required to fill out a survey prior to oral questioning. In a criminal case, *voir dire* is recorded by the court reporter and becomes part of the trial record. If used, the questionnaire and responses also become a part of the trial record. Generally, in civil trials, *voir dire* and any questionnaire would not become part of the court record.

Civil trials typically have 6 jurors and up to 4 alternates. For criminal felony trials, there are 12 jurors and up to 6 alternatives. In lesser criminal trials there may be 6 jurors and up to 4 alternates. During the trial, jury members may not discuss the trial amongst themselves or with others and may not read about the case. This is because each juror must hear all facts of the case before making a decision. A juror can be held in contempt of court if he or she discusses the trial before deliberations occur. In certain trials, particularly highly publicized trials, the jury can be sequestered in local accommodations, instead of being allowed to go home each day. **Jury sequestration** refers to isolating the jury and preventing external influences on jury decisions. **Contempt of court** means violating the rules of court procedure. The **foreperson** is usually the first juror seated and is ultimately responsible for reporting the verdict to the judge.

Opening Statements

During a criminal trial, the prosecution makes an opening statement first because the burden of proof is on the prosecution. The **burden of proof** implies that a defendant is innocent until proven guilty, the prosecution must prove guilt, and the defense must not prove anything. Under the Fifth Amendment, the defendant need not speak ever during the trial. Of course, in practice, defense counsel makes opening and closing remarks and is involved in direct examination and in cross-examination. A **direct examination** is the questioning of counsel's witness in a trial. A **cross-examination** is the questioning of the opposing side's witness in a trial.

Verdicts

Deliberations are the process whereby the jury reviews the evidence from the trial and discusses opinions about the case. A **hung jury** occurs when the jury cannot come to a unanimous decision in a criminal trial and a retrial must occur. Unlike a criminal trial, in a civil trial, the decision by the jury does not need to be unanimous. The jury also decides compensatory issues in a civil trial.

After the jury has reached a verdict, it is the responsibility of the judge to determine the sentence. Following deliberations, the foreperson informs the court officer that the jury has reached a decision and will deliver a verdict.

Criminal Trial Versus Civil Trial

Criminal charges are initiated by government prosecutors on behalf of the people. As a result, the defendant is indicted to stand trial and answer questions relating to serious crimes or provide information. A **felony** is a serious crime and generally carries a penalty of a year or more in prison. A **misdemeanor** is a less serious crime, with a possible sentence of less than a year. In a civil trial, depositions may be taken whereas in a criminal trial, they are generally not taken. A deposition is sworn witness testimony taken, prior to a trial (discovery phase), which can be presented during a civil trial. Thus, witness testimony and cross-examination are largely based on their depositions recorded during discovery. In a criminal trial the government accuses an individual of breaking the law, a statute or a penal law that appears to have been violated. In a civil case, a case is brought by an individual or organization (including corporations and the government), referred to as the plaintiff, against an individual or organization.

Civil trials generally involve disputes over money. If successful, the plaintiff is awarded money by the jury. A civil trial identifies whether an entity failed to act reasonably and prudently under a certain set of circumstances. The standard that needs to be met to win a civil trial is referred to as preponderance of the evidence. This means that most of the evidence presented indicates which party was in the right and which party was in the wrong. In a criminal trial, the burden of proof is on the prosecution to prove that the defendant is guilty. In a civil trial, the burden of proof begins with the plaintiff. However, in civil trials, the burden of proof can move to the defense to prove that he or she was not at fault. In a criminal trial, the standard to prove guilt is "beyond a reasonable doubt". This means that, regardless of the evidence, there must be no doubt in the minds of all jurors that the defendant is guilty. Of course, this is a different standard than preponderance of the evidence. Table 7.1 summarizes the differences between criminal and civil trials.

TABLE 7.1   Comparison of Criminal Versus Civil Trials

Description	Criminal Trial	Civil Trial
Deposition	No	Yes
Trial law	Statutes, penal laws, and precedent	Plaintiff claims defendant was negligent
Charges	Accused of felony or misdemeanor	Lawsuit
Voir dire	Part of trial record	Not recorded
Litigant	Government prosecutor	Plaintiff (individual or organization)
Jury members	Up to 12 jurors + 6 alternates	6 jurors + 4 alternates
Verdict	Must be unanimous	Majority rule
Sentence/Penalty	Delivered by the judge	Delivered by the jury

Evidence Admissibility

The judge is responsible for deciding whether the evidence being submitted is legally admissible. Evidence can include witness testimony. The admissibility of digital evidence is problematic because judges were originally trained to be lawyers years earlier. The prosecution and investigators are often called upon to explain to a judge why certain types of digital evidence should be admitted in a case. A judge may know what an email is but may not know what a system log is and whether it is acceptable in court. These system logs could be critical in determining the fate of a defendant. Moreover, a jury is comprised of individuals with various backgrounds and occupations. For example, a juror could include a pastry chef, a shoe salesman, a geography teacher, or a stay-at-home mother. Imagine how difficult it can be for the prosecution to explain system logs, IP addresses, file registries, and so on.

Constitutional Law

George Mason, author of the Virginia Declaration of Rights, became an opponent of the Constitution because he stated, "It has no declaration of rights". Mason's views were strongly considered, and ultimately, James Madison drafted a series of amendments to the Constitution. These amendments were based on Mason's Virginia Declaration of Rights and later became known as the Bill of Rights. The Founding Fathers originally intended for the Supreme Court to decide on the constitutionality of laws passed by Congress. However, in 1803, with the landmark case of *Marbury v. Madison*, the Supreme Court became recognized as a court for judicial review. As previously noted, cases that require an interpretation of the U.S. Constitution are handled by the federal court system, which includes the U.S. Supreme Court.

First Amendment

Surprisingly, many books and articles that detail the impact of constitutional law simply focus on the Fourth Amendment and fail to recognize the importance of other amendments, like the First Amendment.

So many cases today involve digital evidence that relate to an individual's First Amendment rights. The importance of this amendment is especially pertinent in cyberbullying cases. The First Amendment states the following:

> Congress shall make no law respecting an establishment of religion, or prohibiting the free exercise thereof; or abridging the freedom of speech, or of the press; or the right of the people peaceably to assemble, and to petition the Government for a redress of grievances.

We know that this amendment was written long before the advent of digital communications. Nevertheless, we rely on the Supreme Court and lower federal courts to interpret what protections a person posting insulting comments about an individual on a blog has, in addition to the rights of the victim. Can any opinion, no matter how disturbing, be posted on a blog? The initial answer is no—you cannot post a message that could incite a disturbance or violence. In March 2011, the Supreme Court ruled that the First Amendment protected the Westboro Baptist Church from suits seeking emotional distress caused by picketing (see *Snyder v. Phelps, 562 U.S. 443 (2011)*). The church made headlines with its protests at military funerals and its condemnations of homosexuals, Catholics, and Jews. Others waved signs with captions like "THANK GOD FOR DEAD SOLDIERS", The Supreme Court agreed to review the case following the conflicting decisions of two circuit courts in Ohio. Unfortunately, there is sometimes a difference between moral responsibility and constitutional law.

First Amendment and the Internet

The Internet is relatively new. Therefore, we rely on traditional laws and case law to guide us most of the time. One area of constitutional law that is still being explored and interpreted involves freedom of speech, the role of the school, and school control over student activities on the Internet.

It is important to begin this discussion with a landmark case that predates the Internet as we know it today. The case of *Tinker v. Des Moines Independent Community School District, 393 U.S. 503 (1969)*, was a case heard by the Supreme Court over the rights of a student to protect school policy. Two siblings, John and Mary Beth Tinker, decided to protest the Vietnam War by wearing black armbands to school. The Des Moines School District adopted a policy banning students from wearing the armbands and stated that students who did not comply would be suspended and could return only when they agreed to comply. The Tinker siblings chose not to comply by wearing the black armbands and were also joined by Christopher Eckhardt. As expected, the students were summarily suspended. The Tinker parents filed suit in U.S. District Court (under 42 U.S.C. § 1983), claiming that their First Amendment right to freedom of speech had been violated. However, the court agreed with the school's policy. When the case came to the Eighth Circuit U.S. Court of Appeals, a panel of judges was tied in its decision, which meant that the U.S. District Court decision stood. The Tinkers and Eckhardts then appealed to the Supreme Court. The Supreme Court ruled that the Tinkers' and Christopher Eckhardt's First Amendment rights had been violated and that the First Amendment does apply to public schools. The Court noted, "It can hardly be argued that either students or teachers shed their constitutional rights to freedom of speech or expression at the schoolhouse gate".

According to the Supreme Court, student expression may not be suppressed unless it will "materially and substantially disrupt the work and discipline of the school".

In the case of *Layshock et al v. Hermitage School District et al*, Justin Layshock's parents argued that their son's school violated Justin's First Amendment right to freedom of speech. Justin created a fake MySpace profile of Eric Trosch, the school principal for Hickory High School, Pennsylvania. Justin posted the following comments online:

- In the past month have you smoked? Big Blunt
- Use of alcohol? Big keg behind my desk
- Your birthday? Too drunk to remember
- Big steroid fan
- Big whore
- Big hard ass

The school asserted that Justin had been disrespectful and disruptive with his comments. Word spread around the school about the profile page. Justin attempted to delete the profile page, and he apologized to the principal. Subsequently, the school contacted MySpace to have the page removed. Justin and his father were summoned to the local police station for questioning, but no charges were filed. Justin, a 17-year-old with a 3.3 GPA, seemed destined for college. However, the school placed Justin in an alternative program comprised of students with behavior and attendance problems. The class met only three hours a day and had no assignments from regular classes. Justin was also banned from extracurricular activities, including Advanced Placement (AP) classes and the graduation ceremony.

Justin's parents filed suit in federal court, arguing that the school had overstepped its bounds with an off-campus ban. Furthermore, they argued that they were responsible for Justin outside of school. They argued that their son had created a non-threatening parody of the school's principal. The school argued that Justin's behavior was disruptive because the school's computers had to be shut down after so many students visited the profile page, which then led to class cancellations. The IT staff also needed to install extra firewall protection. The court encouraged the school and the parents to reach a settlement, which they did. Justin could return to regular classes, was allowed to participate in extracurricular activities, and could attend graduation.

In February 2010, a three-judge panel of the Third Circuit of Appeal ruled that the school had violated Justin's First Amendment rights. In its opinion:

> ...the reach of school authorities is not without limits....It would be an unseemly and dangerous precedent to allow the state in the guise of school authorities to reach into a child's home and control his/her actions there...we therefore conclude that the district court correctly ruled that the District's response to Justin's expressive conduct violated the First Amendment guarantee of free expression.

The school's principal later filed a suit claiming that Justin's actions had damaged his reputation, caused humiliation, and impaired his earnings capacity. The court ruled that Justin's statements were not malicious, and the principal was ordered to pay punitive damages.

Federal court judges have not always found in favor of a student's right to post derogatory comments online and not suffer repercussions. The case of *Avery Doninger v. Lewis Mills High School* is an interesting case related to the First Amendment rights of students in school (see *Doninger v. Niehoff, 527 F.3d 41 (2d Cir. 2008)*). Avery Doninger was a 16-year-old junior, who was class secretary and a member of the student council at Lewis Mills High School, Connecticut. In 2007, she had been planning "Jamfest" (Battle of the Bands). The event had been canceled three times and was likely to be canceled again because the school's technician was unavailable. An upset Avery sent emails to get community support and encouraged people to antagonize the principal and superintendent. Avery posted the following message to her LiveJournal blog: "jamfest is canceled due to the douchebags in central office—here is a letter to get an idea of what to write if you want to write something or call her [school superintendent] to piss her off more". When the school found out about Avery's online comments, it prevented her from running for senior class secretary. Students wore T-shirts with "Team Avery" on them, which the school banned. Even though Avery's name was not on the ballot, she still won the student election, although Avery was not permitted by the school to take office. Avery's mother filed a lawsuit, arguing that it was unconstitutional for the school to prevent her daughter from running for office, and that the school had intentionally inflicted emotional distress. The case was then moved to federal court because it was deemed to be a constitutional matter related to the First Amendment.

The court ruled that, as a student leader, Avery should have exhibited qualities of good citizenship both on and off campus. Furthermore, her comments were intended to irritate the superintendent, which was in violation of school policy. Moreover, Avery had not been barred from school office based on skin color, religion, or politics. Avery had been prevented from running from office because of the language on her blog and the risk of disruption at school. Avery was free to express her opinion, but the First Amendment does not protect the right to run for a voluntary extracurricular position. Her request for a new election was denied. The Second Circuit Court of Appeal ruled that the school did not violate Avery's constitutional rights in disciplining her because Avery's blog "created a foreseeable risk of substantial disruption" at the school.

However, there are limits on certain types of speech. In the case of *Miller v. California, 413 U.S. 15 (1973)*, the U.S. Supreme Court affirmed that obscenity is not protected by the First Amendment.

Fourth Amendment

The Fourth Amendment of the Constitution is a part of the Bill of Rights. The purpose of this constitutional amendment was not only to protect individuals against unlawful search and seizure, but also to provide a system of checks and balances in the judicial system. The amendment states the following:

> The right of the people to be secure in their persons, houses, papers, and effects, against unreasonable searches and seizures, shall not be violated, and no Warrants shall issue, but

upon probable cause, supported by Oath or affirmation, and particularly describing the place to be searched, and the persons or things to be seized.

In the landmark case of *Weeks v. United States*, 232 U.S. 383 (1914), the Supreme Court stated that a warrantless search of a private residence is a violation of a person's Fourth Amendment rights. This case was responsible for the introduction of the exclusionary rule. The **exclusionary rule** states that evidence seized and examined without a warrant or in violation of an individual's constitutional rights will often be inadmissible as evidence in court in a criminal case. An extension of the exclusionary rule is called fruit of the poisonous tree. **Fruit of the poisonous tree** is a metaphorical expression to describe evidence that was initially acquired illegally, meaning that all evidence subsequently gathered at every point from that initial search is inadmissible in court.

A number of years later, the U.S. Supreme Court heard the case of *Olmstead v. United States, 277 U.S. 438 (1928)*. Roy Olmstead was found guilty of charges relating to violating the National Prohibition Act. He challenged his conviction based on the premise that his Fourth and Fifth Constitutional Amendment rights had been violated because federal agents had tapped his private telephone calls without a court-issued warrant. The court upheld Olmstead's conviction. This decision was later overturned by the Supreme Court's decision in the *Katz v. United States* case.

It is clear that the Fourth Amendment protects people, not places. The case of *Katz v. United States, 389 U.S. 347 (1967)*, clearly illustrates this assertion. Charles Katz was accused of using a public payphone to conduct his illegal gambling business. Katz later found out that the FBI had placed a wiretap on the payphone. They then used Katz's recorded conversations as evidence at trial. Katz was found guilty and sentenced. Katz challenged his conviction and argued that his Fourth Amendment right had been violated based on unreasonable search and seizure and because he believed there was an expectation of privacy. Katz was unsuccessful in the Court of Appeals, but the Supreme Court granted certiorari. **Certiorari** is an order made by a higher court that directs a lower court or tribunal to send it court documents, related to a case, for further review. The Supreme Court ruled in favor of Katz. The Supreme Court opined: "One who occupies [a telephone booth], shuts the door behind him, and pays the toll that permits him to place a call is surely entitled to assume that the words he utters into the mouthpiece will not be broadcast to the world." Wiretapping constitutes a search and, therefore, requires a warrant. One of the issues that arises with the Fourth Amendment is the expectation of privacy. A link clearly exists between unreasonable search and seizure and the expectation of privacy, but the Supreme Court has not always been clear about the linkage. This causes confusion, and case law is the best guide for litigators.

An expectation of privacy in the workplace is still a grey area. In the case of *O'Connor v. Ortega, 480 U.S. 709 (1987)*, the Supreme Court heard the case of Magno Ortega, a California State Hospital doctor who argued that a search of his office violated his Fourth Amendment rights. Ortega's supervisors found alleged inculpatory evidence in his office during investigations into employees violating hospital policies. The case was subsequently remanded to the district court, and 11 years later, the Ninth Circuit found in favor of Ortega. With this decision, employer monitoring of employees is reduced when there is a failure to notify employees.

Search Warrants

The Fourth Amendment is arguably the most important part of the Constitution in terms of computer forensics investigations and probably all investigations. Law enforcement must obtain a warrant, issued by a judge or magistrate, before a search or arrest can be carried out. A **search warrant** is a court order issued by judge or magistrate authorizing law enforcement to search a person or place, as well as seize items or information within the parameters of the warrant. Furthermore, an investigator must demonstrate probable cause. **Probable cause** refers to the conditions under which law enforcement may obtain a warrant for a search or arrest, when it is evident that a crime has been committed. Law enforcement must show that a crime was committed and that it is more probable than not to expect that evidence exists at the place to be searched.

The case of *United States v. Leon, 468 U.S. 897 (1984)*, created a "good faith" exception to the exclusionary rule. A judge issued a search warrant to the police in Burbank, California. Later, the search warrant was found to be invalid because the police did not properly demonstrate probable cause. Nevertheless, the police were deemed to be acting in good faith when seizing the evidence initially because they believed the warrant to be valid at the time.

In the case of *United States v. Warshak, 562 F. Supp. 2d 986 (S.D. Ohio 2008)*, the Sixth Circuit of the U.S. Court of Appeals held that the government's seizure of 27,000 private emails from Steven Warshak's Internet service provider (ISP) violated his Fourth Amendment rights because the emails were acquired without a warrant. The ruling demonstrates that a federal court has recognized an expectation of privacy with emails stored on third-party servers. Nevertheless, the evidence was admissible in court because the government had relied, in good faith, on the Stored Communications Act (SCA).

Email is probably the most important type of digital evidence, and it is continually addressed in many cases. In the case of *United States v. Ziegler*, William Wayne Ziegler was accused of viewing child pornography on a computer at work. The employer decided to make copies of the suspect's hard drive and delivered them to the FBI. Ziegler filed a motion to suppress the evidence because his Fourth Amendment rights had been violated. A **motion in limine** is a request by a lawyer to hold a hearing before a trial, in an effort to suppress evidence. That evidence could include expert witness testimony. If this motion is successful, the jury will never see the evidence. The Ninth Circuit Court of Appeals agreed that the employee did have an expectation of privacy. However, warrants apply to government agents, and the employer was not acting as an agent of the government or in response to a request from a government agent.

It is important to understand that a warrant is specific to a particular crime and criminal investigation and is very specific to a geographic location. For example, if a house borders two counties, then two separate warrants are necessary to search the entire property. This specificity cannot be overemphasized. In one case, law enforcement was issued a warrant to search a house. When investigators arrived at the house, they realized that the suspect's computer was located in a shed at the back of the house. Therefore, investigators were not permitted to search the location of the computer and could not seize the computer.

The Fourth Amendment states the following:

> The right of the people to be secure in their persons, houses, papers, and effects,[a] against unreasonable searches and seizures, shall not be violated, and no Warrants shall issue, but upon probable cause, supported by Oath or affirmation, and particularly describing the place to be searched, and the persons or things to be seized.

The scope of a warrant is narrow, which means that even with probable cause, a government is limited to a specific place, person, and thing(s) to be searched. A Ninth U.S. Circuit Court of Appeal's decision in 2008, and other decisions, have made this fact clear. Federal investigators successfully obtained a search warrant from the Central District Court of California to investigate the records of 10 Major League Baseball (MLB) players suspected of taking steroids kept at Bay Area Laboratories Company (BALCO). Federal investigators subsequently searched records of steroid use involving many more MLB players. Even though investigators tried to argue that the records of other players not noted in the initial warrant were in plain view, the majority of Ninth Circuit judges ruled that the investigators went too far. The court's majority noted the following:

> We accept the reality that such over-seizing is an inherent part of the electronic search process and proceed on the assumption that, when it comes to the seizure of electronic records, this will be far more common than in the days of paper records. This calls for greater vigilance on the part of judicial officers in striking the right balance between the government's interest in law enforcement and the right of individuals to be free from unreasonable searches and seizures.

The ruling will naturally have implications for computer investigations going forward.

Warrantless Searches

Not all searches require a search warrant, however. With the passing of the USA PATRIOT Act, law enforcement has been provided with greater powers, which extends to warrantless searches when a person's life or safety may be in danger. **Exigent circumstances** allow agents to conduct a warrantless search in an emergency situation when there is risk of harm to an individual or when there is risk of possible destruction of evidence. The case of *United States v. McConney, 728 F.2d 1195, 1199 (9th Cir.)*, clearly details what is meant by exigent circumstances:

> Those circumstances that would cause a reasonable person to believe that entry (or other relevant prompt action) was necessary to prevent physical harm to the officers or other persons, the destruction of relevant evidence, the escape of a suspect, or some other consequence improperly frustrating legitimate law enforcement efforts.

The U.S. Department of Justice (DOJ) provides guidelines for warrantless searches and seizures of computers at https://www.justice.gov/criminal-ccips/ccips-documents-and-reports.

When appropriate consent is granted to a government agent, a warrant is not required. Consent can be granted when an individual waives his or her Fourth Amendment rights. However, the search is limited to the physical area of the individual's authority and is limited to a specific criminal investigation. A warrantless search is also subject to the totality of circumstances. This means that the individual granting consent must be of sound mind, must be an adult, and must be educated with a certain degree of intelligence.

Sometimes law enforcement uses a tactic known as a "knock and talk". **Knock and talk** is when law enforcement does not have sufficient evidence or cannot demonstrate probable cause to enter a residence and execute a search. Instead, law enforcement personnel go to the suspect's home and try to obtain the consent of the individual to gain entry to the home and conduct a consensual search. Sometimes this includes a non-custodial interview. This is an example of a warrantless search.

Plain view doctrine allows a government agent to seize evidence without a warrant when the officer can clearly observe contraband. To comply with this doctrine, an officer must be lawfully present in an area protected by the Fourth Amendment, the evidence must be in plain view, and the officer must immediately identify the item as contraband without further intrusion. These conditions of the plain view doctrine were affirmed in the case of *Horton v. California*.

Extending the scope of a warrant to include digital evidence in plain view can be extraordinarily difficult, however, as illustrated in the case of *United States v. Carey* (see *United States v. Carey, No. 14-50222 (9th Cir. 2016)*). Patrick Carey was under investigation for suspected possession and sale of cocaine. After a series of controlled drug purchases at his residence, police obtained an arrest warrant. Police asked Carey for consent to search his apartment. Concerned that his apartment might be trashed during a search, he signed a formal written consent. During the search, police seized drugs and two computers. Police subsequently obtained a warrant to search the computers for "names, telephone numbers, ledger receipts, addresses, and other documentary evidence pertaining to the sale and distribution of controlled substances". Detective Lewis went through the computers' files and noticed directories and files with sexually suggestive names. The detective opened an image file that was deemed to be child pornography. The detective continued with the search and downloaded 244 image files and viewed some more images of child pornography. Carey moved to suppress the images. The Tenth Circuit U.S. Court of Appeals agreed with the defendant because, after viewing one image, the detective would have had an expectation of more child pornography on the computer and, therefore, required a new warrant to investigate a different crime. The warrant the detective had obtained was for a drug investigation, not for possession of child pornography.

In this case, the detective might have successfully argued his case that evidence of a crime was in plain view if the images had been displayed in the normal course of the investigation. In this case, the detective had been performing keyword searches to find evidence supporting his investigation of illegal possession and distribution of narcotics. You obviously would not be running keyword searches on images. A search warrant never allows investigators to conduct a general search.

The case of *UNITED STATES of America, Plaintiff-Appellee, v. Russell Lane WALSER, Defendant-Appellant. No. 01-8019* is similar in nature. In June 2000, the manager of a hotel went to a guest room to check on a smoke alarm. While in the room, he noticed what he believed to be illegal drugs. He called the police, who then secured the room and obtained a search warrant for the hotel room. The warrant gave permission for the following search:

> Controlled substances, evidence of the possession of controlled substances, which may include, but not be limited to, cash or proceeds from the sales of controlled substances, items, substances, and other paraphernalia designed or used in the weighing, cutting, and packaging of controlled substances, firearms, records, and/or receipts, written or electronically stored, income tax records, checking and savings records, records that show or tend to show ownership or control of the premises and other property used to facilitate the distribution and delivery [of] controlled substances.

The police searched the room, found illegal drugs and drug paraphernalia, and seized a computer in the room. Back at the forensic laboratory, during a search of the computer by Agent McFarland, the investigator stumbled upon what he believed to be child pornography. Agent McFarland ended his search and informed an investigator more familiar with child endangerment cases. The computer was shut down immediately, and another warrant was obtained. The defendant-appellant requested that the Tenth Circuit U.S. Court of Appeals approve his motion to suppress the evidence garnered from the two searches of his computer, arguing that they lacked probable cause to do so. The court examined the case for plain error. **Plain error** arises when an appeals court identifies a major mistake made in court proceedings, even though no objection was made during the initial trial in which judgment was passed and a new trial was ordered. Under Rule 52(b), in the Rules of Criminal Procedure, a plain error that affects substantial rights may be considered even though it was not brought to the court's attention. **Rules of Criminal Procedure** are protocols for how criminal proceedings in a federal court should be conducted. The defendant argued that the investigator who opened the `.avi` file, a video file, exceeded the scope of the warrant. He argued that a video file could not possibly have contained evidence relating to an investigation of drug possession, so the investigator should not have opened the file under the conditions outlined in the warrant. Based on the fact that the agent showed restraint in continuing his search, the court opined that the search was lawful and that the evidence was admissible.

This decision was in contrast to the Tenth Circuit Court's decision earlier, in the case of *United States v. Carey*, when a police search of the suspect's computer was deemed to be overly broad. We can therefore conclude that warrants must be specific to a particular criminal investigation and if, in the normal course of an investigation, the investigator inadvertently finds contraband unrelated to the initial investigation, the investigator should immediately cease the search for new contraband and obtain a new search warrant.

Interestingly, in the case of *United States v. Mann (No. 08-3041)*, the Seventh Circuit Court upheld an earlier conviction in the case of a lifeguard instructor named Matthew Mann. He was investigated after video cameras were found in a locker room where women were changing clothes. Police obtained a warrant to search for computers and storage media. During the investigation, police found child pornography on the suspect's hard drive, and Mann was subsequently charged. Mann filed a motion to suppress this evidence, but the Seventh Circuit Court opined that the search was not overbroad, even though the images of children were specially flagged by investigators, who knew that they were now working on a different investigation. Nevertheless, given previous decisions, it does seem wise for law enforcement to err on the side of caution and obtain a warrant before continuing a search related to a different crime.

The case of *People v. Diaz* is an interesting case that deals with a warrantless search of a suspect's cellphone. The Supreme Court of California upheld the Court of Appeals decision that a warrantless search of text messages is lawful after an arrest. Diaz was arrested after selling drugs to a police informant. Upon arrest, the suspect's cellphone was seized, placed into evidence, and searched. The defense moved to suppress the cellphone evidence, but the court sided with law enforcement, citing that it was incident to arrest. A subsequent ruling, with *Riley v. California*, which was a landmark Supreme Court decision in 2014, held that a warrantless search of a cellphone, incident to arrest, is illegal. **Search incident to a lawful arrest** allows law enforcement to conduct a warrantless search after an arrest has been made. The search is limited to the individual and her surrounding area and may include a search of the suspect's vehicle (see *Arizona v. Gant, 2009*).

Law enforcement may also be able to acquire evidence without a warrant via a third-party. For example, a service provider might offer evidence for a suspect, or text messages or email could be acquired from a victim. In these situations, the suspect has no standing. **Standing** refers to a suspect's right to object to a Fourth Amendment search, as outlined by the Supreme Court.

Case Study

The Case of the Russian Hackers

Alexey Ivanov and Vasili Gorshkov were hackers from Russia. They were certainly black hat hackers because they hacked into numerous corporate networks, and then made extortion demands. On countless occasions, the duo stole a company's financial data and sensitive customer records, and then demanded that the company pay them money. Most companies paid, fearing the possible negative publicity that a breach of security could bring. One company that was compromised was an ISP called CTS Network Services. Ivanov hacked into an ISP called Lightrealm Communications. The company gave in to Ivanov's extortion demand that it hire him as a security consultant. Ivanov subsequently used his Lightrealm email account to hack into other companies.

The FBI found Ivanov's resume online and set up a sting operation. After setting up a phony security company, the FBI invited Ivanov to interview in Seattle for a job at the company. Ivanov was encouraged to bring Gorshkov with him. Unbeknownst to Ivanov, the FBI had installed a keystroke logger on a laptop at the phony company. Agents asked Ivanov to use the laptop to demonstrate his skills. The keystroke logging program recorded URLs, logins, and passwords that he typed in. The FBI arrested Ivanov and Gorshkov and then used the recorded keystrokes to log in to computers that the hackers had used in Russia and downloaded incriminating evidence.

What is interesting about this case is that Gorshkov s defense filed a motion stating that his Fourth Amendment rights had been violated. The defense argued that there was an expectation of privacy while using the computer and that the government agents illegally downloaded data from a server in Russia without a warrant. The judge, however, ruled that there is no expectation of privacy on a network. Moreover, when using a network, one must assume that a network administrator could be monitoring that network. "When (the) defendant sat down at the networked computer...he knew that the systems administrator could and likely would monitor his activities", U.S. District Judge John C. Coughenour of Seattle wrote. "Indeed, the undercover agents told (Gorshkov) that they wanted to watch in order to see what he was capable of doing."

The judge ruled that the agents could access servers in Russia because the Fourth Amendment does not apply to Russia. The agents were in the right because there was an expectation that the evidence could be destroyed. Coughenour noted that "the agents had good reason to fear that if they did not copy the data, (the) defendant's co-conspirators would destroy the evidence or make it unavailable." Moreover, the download of evidence was incident to arrest, which makes it legal. Additionally, the judge ruled that the Fourth Amendment does not apply to non-residents. The judge ruled that the 250GB of imported data was subject to the Fourth Amendment but that the agents did act appropriately because they acquired a warrant before viewing the data.

Interestingly, Russian authorities subsequently issued a warrant for the arrest of the FBI agents. FBI agents Michael Schuler and Marty Prewett were honored with the Director's Award for Excellence. Gorshkov was found guilty and was sentenced to three years in jail and ordered to pay $692,000. Ivanov was sentenced to three years, eight months, and was ordered to pay $800,000.

When Does Digital Surveillance Become a Search?

Two recent court cases bring into question the rights of an individual and the expectations of government agents during an investigation. In all but one of the following cases, the convicted criminals were involved in some appalling criminal activities.

In the case of *U.S. v. Daniel David Rigmaiden, 844 F.Supp.2d 982 (2012)*, the suspect was charged with financial fraud. Between January 2005 and April 2008, Rigmaiden allegedly acquired $4 million from fraudulently filing 1,900 tax returns. The case was tried in the U.S. District Court of Arizona. Law enforcement located the suspect using a "Stingray" device. **Stingray** is the generic name given to a device that acts like a cellphone tower to locate criminal suspects but can also be used to locate people in disaster areas, such as earthquakes. In the case of Rigmaiden, federal agents were able to locate him based on a Verizon broadband card, which operates on a cellphone network.

The defense argued that federal agents required a search warrant to use the device. In addition, they argued that they had a right to view the Stingray used to capture the suspect. The prosecution contended that the use of a pen register requires only a court order, not a warrant. A **court order** is issued by a court and details a set of steps to be carried out by law enforcement; it is easier to obtain than a warrant because probable cause need not be demonstrated. A **pen register** is an electronic device that captures telephone numbers. Pen register orders require law enforcement to show only that information retrieved is likely to assist in an ongoing investigation. Rules governing the use of a pen register can be found in 18 U.S.C., Chapter 206. A pen register is not a search, as opined by the Supreme Court in *Smith v. Maryland, 442 U.S. 735 (1979)*. The defense counsel argued that the Stingray cannot be classified as a pen register device because the device also records the location of people. The defense counsel also argued the legality of the prosecution using the device, expunging the device of evidence, and not allowing the defense to view the device. The prosecution did not want to show the device because it is a "secret device" and the evidence was regularly scrubbed from the device because the device would also record the information of innocent cellphone users. The Department of Justice later admitted that it conducted a search but still contended that, when using a cellphone (or a broadband card), there is no expectation of privacy. The prosecution also stated that a court order did allow investigators to capture real-time data from Verizon. Nevertheless, the suspect was found in his apartment. A search warrant for the apartment was later obtained.

GPS Tracking

The use of GPS tracking devices is prevalent and widespread, but only recently has the legality of these devices come to the fore. Yasir Afifi, a 20-year-old Arab-American student, was the son of an Islamic-American community leader. Afifi was surfing the Internet when he noticed a piece about GPS tracking devices. On a whim, he checked his car and noticed a wire sticking out. Afifi found the device on the undercarriage of his car and had it removed. The device, known as the Orion Guardian ST820, is manufactured by Cobham PLC.

FBI agents showed up at the student's house and demanded the expensive, secretive device back. Afifi complied with their demand. Interestingly, the Ninth Circuit Court opined that attaching the device was not illegal and did not require a warrant, even if the device was attached to the car while in a person's driveway. Afifi's driveway was not enclosed and did not pass the Dunn test for Curtilage. **Curtilage** refers to the property surrounding a house. In the case of *U.S. v. Dunn, 480 U.S. 294 (1987)*, Drug Enforcement Agency (DEA) agents used electronic tracking devices in an electric hot plate stirrer, a drum of acetic anhydride, and a phenylacetic acid container. Agents noticed from aerial photographs that the suspect backed his truck up to a barn on his ranch. The entire ranch perimeter was enclosed by a fence and barbed wire. Agents crossed a perimeter fence and an interior fence, looked through the window of a barn, and spotted a methamphetamine laboratory in the barn with the use of a flashlight. They subsequently entered the barn to confirm the existence of the laboratory. They then obtained and executed a search warrant. The Fifth Circuit Court of Appeals reversed the Dunn conviction because agents had entered the ranch without a warrant, and the barn was within the protected curtilage. The U.S. Supreme Court reversed the decision and opined that the barn was not within curtilage because it was not used for intimate activities. They stated that the agents in "open fields" were no different than being in a public place.

In a similar case, *U.S. v. Knotts 460 U.S. 276 (1983)*, Minnesota police placed a radio transmitter (beeper) inside a chloroform container. The suspect, Armstrong, was suspected of using chloroform to manufacture illicit drugs. The Federal District Court denied the defendant's motion to suppress the evidence obtained from the beeper. Later the Court of Appeals reversed the decision of the Federal District Court. The case was subsequently heard by the Supreme Court, which reversed the Court of Appeals decision and upheld the original conviction. In the majority opinion:

> Monitoring the beeper signals did not invade any legitimate expectation of privacy on respondent's part, and thus there was neither a "search" nor a "seizure" within the contemplation of the Fourth Amendment. The beeper surveillance amounted principally to following an automobile on public streets and highways. A person traveling in an automobile on public thoroughfares has no reasonable expectation of privacy in his movements.

The use of GPS tracking devices has come up numerous times in case law. In *U.S. v. McIver*, law enforcement attached a tracking device to McIver's car while it was parked in front of his garage. McIver was suspected of growing marijuana. The court deemed the car to be outside the curtilage of his home and was therefore not deemed a search. They also noted that "[t]he undercarriage is part of the car's exterior, and as such, is not afforded a reasonable expectation of privacy." The case of *U.S. v. Pineda-Moreno* was very similar, and the case was heard by the Ninth Circuit Court of Appeals. The DEA noticed the suspect purchasing large quantities of fertilizer from a Home Depot and suspected that he was using it for growing marijuana. On seven different occasions, a GPS tracking device was attached to the suspect's Jeep, once when the car was parked in the owner's driveway. Agents pulled the suspect's car over, smelled the odor of marijuana, and asked the suspect for permission to search the vehicle. The suspect allowed the agents to search the car, and they found two large trash bags filled with marijuana. The suspect was then indicted by a grand jury. Defense counsel filed a motion to suppress the evidence on the basis of a Fourth Amendment violation and entered a conditional plea of guilty with the District Court. The Ninth Circuit ruled that the car was within the curtilage of the home, which "is only a semiprivate area" (see *United States v. Magana, 512 F.2d 1169, 1171 [9th Cir. 1975]*). The court also noted that the "undercarriage of a vehicle, as part of its exterior, is not entitled to a reasonable expectation of privacy."

In the case of *United States v. Jones*, the D.C. Circuit Court was asked to hear the case of Antoine Jones, concerning a GPS tracking device that was used. Jones was suspected of distributing narcotics. Agents secured a Title III wiretap, which allows for electronic surveillance. A D.C. federal judge issued a warrant to covertly install a GPS tracking device on Jones's Jeep Cherokee within 10 days of the warrant issue date. However, agents did not install the device until the 11th day. Agents later seized 97 kilograms of cocaine and $850,000 from the suspect's home. The U.S. District Court (D.C.) found Jones guilty of conspiring to sell cocaine and he was sentenced to life in prison. However, a Court of Appeals later reversed the decision. The D.C. Circuit Court noted that the Knotts decision did not apply because Jones was under constant surveillance. The court opined:

> The Court explicitly distinguished between the limited information discovered by use of the beeper—movements during a discrete journey—and more comprehensive or sustained monitoring of the sort at issue in this case....Most important for the present case, the Court

specifically reserved the question whether a warrant would be required in a case involving twenty-four hour surveillance, stating, "if such dragnet-type law enforcement practices as respondent envisions should eventually occur, there will be time enough then to determine whether different constitutional principles may be applicable."

The case was then referred to the U.S. Supreme Court, and because the warrant had expired when the device was attached, the question became whether a warrant was necessary. During oral arguments, it was clear that this case is different from other cases involving the warrantless use of tracking devices. Justice Sonia Sotomayor stated the following:

> What motivated the Fourth Amendment historically was the disapproval, the outrage, that our Founding Fathers experienced with general warrants that permitted police indiscriminately to investigate just on the basis of suspicion, not probable cause, and to invade every possession that the individual had in search of a crime.

Justice Samuel Alito took quite a different view of the use of tracking devices, in a digital age when so much of our personal information is freely available on social networking websites:

> "With computers around, it's now so simple to amass an enormous amount of information. How do we deal with this? Just say nothing has changed?"

Justice Elena Kagan noted that times have changed and that many cities have numerous speed and surveillance cameras.

The use of GPS surveillance devices has clearly become a contentious issue, and there is a distinct lack of clarity in case law. Under *Knotts*, law enforcement may be able to install GPS tracking devices even if the installation occurs on a driveway, generally deemed by the courts to be outside of the privacy of one's home, in a semi-private area and not protected under the Fourth Amendment.

In January 2012, the Supreme Court unanimously decided that government agents violated Jones's Fourth Amendment rights. However, the justices' reasoning for doing so was split 5–4. The majority ruled that the search was illegal because they deemed that the agents had trespassed. Justice Alito, a conservative, and three other justices went as far as to say that Jones's expectation of privacy was violated, although Justice Scalia and four others did not agree.

The *U.S. v. Jones* Supreme Court decision has had repercussions for the GPS surveillance of criminal suspects. GPS tracking constitutes a search and seizure. Justice Scalia noted the following in the decision:

> We decide whether the attachment of a Global Positioning-System (GPS) tracking device to an individual's vehicle, and subsequent use of that device to monitor the vehicle's movements on public streets, constitutes a search or seizure within the meaning of the Fourth Amendment.

An interesting part of this case are the opinions of the Supreme Court justices, who appeared to be voicing the opinions of divided public opinion and considering whether it is right to sacrifice our expectation of privacy in a digital age.

GPS Tracking (State Law)

A number of states prohibit the use of GPS tracking devices without a warrant. In the case of *Oregon v. Meredith*, a transmitter was attached to a United States Forest Service (USFS) truck. The suspect was caught setting a fire and was charged with arson. In this case, the lower court agreed with the defense's motion to suppress evidence derived from the transmitter. The Supreme Court of Oregon disagreed because the defendant did not have an expectation of privacy when using the vehicle in public. Moreover, the defendant was using the employer's vehicle. The use of the monitor did not constitute a "search" under Article 1, Section 9, of the Oregon Constitution.

There was a slightly different opinion, however, in the case of *Washington v. Jackson, 150 Wash.2d 251, 76 P.3d 217 (Wash. 2003)*. Under Article 1, Section 7, of the Washington Constitution, GPS tracking is unlawful without a warrant. GPS tracking is viewed as an intrusion into someone's life. The court ruled that law enforcement did have a warrant to use GPS tracking and that it was the only reasonable way to track the two vehicles needed to track the suspect.

The New York Constitution prohibits the use of GPS tracking devices without a warrant. In the case of *New York v. Weaver*, a police officer attached a GPS device to a suspect's van bumper in connection with a series of burglaries. The defendant and code-fendant were arrested and charged with burglary in the third degree and grand larceny in the second degree. The New York Court of Appeals opined:

> Technological advances have produced many valuable tools for law enforcement and, as the years go by, the technology available to aid in the detection of criminal conduct will only become more and more sophisticated. Without judicial oversight, the use of these powerful devices presents a significant and, to our minds, unacceptable risk of abuse. Under our State Constitution, in the absence of exigent circumstances, the installation and use of a GPS device to monitor an individual's whereabouts requires a warrant supported by probable cause.

The State of Ohio has upheld the warrantless use of GPS tracking devices. In *Ohio v. Johnson*, agents attached a tracking device to the undercarriage of a suspected drug dealer's van. Police later stopped Johnson's van, and the suspect admitted that he was on his way to sell cocaine. The court opined,

> "Johnson did not produce any evidence that demonstrated his intention to guard the under-carriage of his van from inspection or manipulation by others....Supreme Court precedent has established not only that a vehicle's exterior lacks a reasonable expectation of privacy, but also that one's travel on public roads does not implicate Fourth Amendment protection against searches and seizures."

Traffic Stops

The acquisition of digital evidence during a traffic stop can appear somewhat confusing when perusing case law. Surprisingly, Michigan State Police occasionally performed warrantless searches of drivers' cellphones during traffic stops, using the Cellebrite UFED, which has the ability to capture evidence from thousands of different cellphone models. You might expect that these types of searches required a warrant, but certain types of warrantless searches can be conducted incident to arrest.

In the case of *California v. Nottoli*, policed stopped the suspect, Reid Nottoli, after speeding on a highway in his silver Acura TL. Santa Cruz County Deputy Sheriff Steven Ryan suspected that Nottoli was driving under the influence of a drug but was not driving while impaired. Nottoli's license was also expired. Ryan informed the driver that his car would be impounded. Nottoli was placed in hand-cuffs and then put in the patrol car. Ryan decided to take an inventory of the vehicle's contents before having it towed. During the search of the vehicle, he found a Glock 20 handgun with a Guncrafter Industries conversion, which meant that it should have been secured in the trunk of the car. Deputy Gonzales, who had later arrived on the scene, noticed a BlackBerry Curve cellphone in a cup holder. He pressed a button on the BlackBerry to see if it was functional and noticed a wallpaper image of a man wearing a mask holding two AR-15 assault rifles in akimbo fashion. The officer suspected that the individual in the picture was Nottoli. These rifles had been legal in California before the weapons ban, but Ryan confiscated the cellphone as evidence of possible "gun-related" criminal activity. The officer viewed pictures, emails, and text messages for approximately 10 minutes, according to court documents.

Only after this initial search did Ryan secure a search warrant for the cellphone and a second search warrant for Nottoli's residence. SWAT personnel were sent into the home based on suspected drug-related information retrieved from the cellphone. Law enforcement seized $15,000 and a large cache of weapons and discovered a marijuana-growing operation. Nottoli filed a motion to suppress the evidence based on a violation of the Fourth Amendment, a warrantless search of the cellphone. At the initial trial, the magistrate agreed that the officers did not have a right to search the cellphone without a warrant:

> I think there was an expectation of privacy that the defendant had for his BlackBerry, that there were not sufficient grounds to authorize the deputy to open that BlackBerry up and, therefore, anything that was discovered as a result of that activity would be suppressed....

In *South Dakota v. Opperman (1976) 428 U.S. 364 [96 S.Ct. 3092]*, the Supreme Court held that "a routine inventory search of an automobile lawfully impounded by police for violations of municipal parking ordinances", consistent with "standard police procedures", was reasonable under the Fourth Amendment to the U.S. Constitution.

The Court of Appeals of the State of California ruled that the deputies were justified in searching the vehicle's passenger compartment and, 'any containers therein', based upon the Supreme Court decision on *Arizona v. Gant*. The court continued, with Justice Franklin D. Elia writing for the three judge panel:

> In sum, it is our conclusion that, after Reid [Nottoli] was arrested for being under the influence, it was reasonable to believe that evidence relevant to that offense might be found in his vehicle. Consequently, the deputies had unqualified authority under Gant to search the passenger compartment of the vehicle and any container found therein, including Reid's cell phone. It is up to the US Supreme Court to impose any greater limits on officers' authority to search incident to arrest.

Many lawmakers were incensed by this decision. The California State Senate and Assembly then passed a bill requiring that a warrant be required before carrying out a search of a cellphone. Surprisingly, California Gov. Jerry Brown then vetoed the bill. Brown wrote in his message to the Senate, "I am returning Senate Bill 914 without my signature" and stated that the "courts are better suited to resolve the complex and case-specific issues relating to constitutional search-and-seizures protections."

The case of *New York v. Perez (2011 NY Slip Op 07659)*, had a different outcome. The defendant was found guilty in Suffolk County Court, New York, of criminal possession of a controlled substance in the first degree, false personation, operating a motor vehicle while using a mobile telephone (under Vehicle and Traffic Law § 1225-c(2)(a)), operating a motor vehicle without using a safety belt (under Vehicle and Traffic Law § 1229-c(3)), and failing to stay in a designated lane (under Vehicle and Traffic Law § 1128(a)). Police stopped the defendant and impounded the vehicle. While the vehicle was impounded, an officer searched the vehicle and leafed through a notebook. The notebook indicated the possible presence of narcotics in the vehicle. Police returned with a canine to help locate the suspected drugs. Police then pried open a compartment and found bundles of secreted cash. The New York State Supreme Court overturned the lower court's decision and found that the defendant's Fourth Amendment rights had been violated with an illegal search. With the car impounded, there was "ample time for the law enforcement officials to secure a warrant in order to make this significant intrusion" (*People v Spinelli, 35 NY2d 77, 81*). The defendant's statements were suppressed after the illegal search as *fruit of the poisonous tree*.

In the case of *Riley v. California, 573 U.S. 373 (2014)*, the U.S. Supreme Court ruled in 2014 that police require a warrant to search the cellphone of someone who is arrested. This was a landmark decision for law enforcement and forensics investigators because a cellphone can no longer be searched incident to arrest.

Carpenter v. United States

In the case of *Carpenter v. United States* in 2018, a 5–4 Supreme Court decision, authored by Chief Justice Roberts, stated that when the government obtains historical cellphone records that contain cell site location information (CSLI), without a warrant, then they are violating the Fourth Amendment.

The case stemmed from armed robberies at a RadioShack and a T-Mobile store in Michigan. The four thieves were caught and arrested. The FBI obtained call logs from one of the robbers, which ultimately included call logs from Timothy Carpenter, the Petitioner in this case, who was not one of the robbers. Historical cell-site location information (CLSI) data tracked Carpenter for 127 days—an average of 101 data points per day. In the Supreme Court opinion for this case, Roberts cited the previous court decision in *United States v. Jones, 565 U. S. 400*, whereby concerns were raised with GPS tracking. Again, the data derived from cell-sites could be used to track Carpenter's location over a 127-day period. The opinion stated:

> Tracking a person's past movements through CSLI partakes of many of the qualities of GPS monitoring considered in Jones. In fact, historical cell-site records present even greater privacy concerns than the GPS monitoring considered in Jones: They give the Government near perfect surveillance and allow it to travel back in time to retrace a person's whereabouts, subject only to the five-year retention policies of most wireless carriers.

Furthermore, the opinion (18 U. S. C.§2703(d)) noted:

> that the "Government did not obtain a warrant supported by probable cause before acquiring Carpenter's cell-site records. It acquired those records pursuant to a court order under the Stored Communications Act, which required the Government to show "reasonable grounds" for believing that the records were "relevant and material to an ongoing investigation." 18 U. S. C. § 2703(d). That showing falls well short of the probable cause required for a warrant. Consequently, an order issued under § 2703(d) is not a permissible mechanism for accessing historical cell-site records.

Carpenter's case was heard once again by the Sixth Circuit and he was sentenced to 116 years in prison, even with the Supreme Court ruling about the government requiring a warrant for location data, associated with cell site records. The court ruled that the FBI acted lawfully in collecting this data and therefore was not subject to the exclusionary rule.

Fifth Amendment

The Fifth Amendment is also a part of the Bill of Rights. This amendment protects the individual from self-incrimination. A defendant is not compelled to testify at trial and may "plead the Fifth". However, an **indictment** is a charge delivered by a grand jury stating that the accused must stand trial. A **grand jury** is a relatively large jury that determines whether conditions exist for criminal prosecution in a case. The wording of this amendment states that a defendant in a criminal investigation cannot be tried more than once for the same crime. Therefore, a computer forensics investigator must be sure to have gathered all the necessary evidence before the case goes to trial. This is no easy feat, considering that corroborating evidence can be gathered from a suspect's computer and cellphone, the victim's computer and cellphone, web servers, email servers, CCTV, and a multitude of other sources.

The text of the Fifth Amendment is as follows:

> No person shall be held to answer for a capital, or otherwise infamous crime, unless on a presentment or indictment of a Grand Jury, except in cases arising in the land or naval forces, or in the Militia, when in actual service in time of War or public danger; nor shall any person be subject for the same offense to be twice put in jeopardy of life or limb; nor shall be compelled in any criminal case to be a witness against himself, nor be deprived of life, liberty, or property, without due process of law; nor shall private property be taken for public use, without just compensation.

In the case of *Miranda v. Arizona*, the Supreme Court ruled that an incriminating statement by a suspect is inadmissible in court if the suspect was not advised of the Fifth Amendment right to remain silent and not give self-incriminating evidence. In addition to this, a person who is detained by a government agent has the right to counsel, as outlined in the Sixth Amendment. The Supreme Court opined that Ernesto Arturo Miranda's Constitutional rights had been violated when arrested for rape and kidnapping. Generally, the following Miranda Rights are read to a suspect upon arrest:

> You have the right to remain silent. Anything you say or do can and will be held against you in a court of law. You have the right to speak to an attorney. If you cannot afford an attorney, one will be appointed for you. Do you understand these rights as they have been read to you?

The Fifth Amendment can influence the outcome of computer forensics investigations, but the connection is rarely discussed. In the federal criminal case of *In re Boucher, No. 2:06-mj-91, 2009 WL 424718*, a suspect was stopped at the border, crossing from Canada into Vermont, and his laptop was searched. Agents found what they believed to be sexually explicit images of children on the computer, arrested the suspect, and charged him with the transportation of child pornography. Investigators imaged the hard drive but later realized that files on the hard drive were encrypted and password protected. The government issued a subpoena directing the defendant to assist with decrypting the files. A **subpoena** is an order by a court demanding a person to testify or to bring evidence to court. The defendant sought to quash the subpoena, arguing that it would violate his Fifth Amendment by being self-incriminating. The court agreed with the defendant and quashed the subpoena. This is because forcing a defendant to supply a password is forcing the defendant to provide testimony because the defendant is conveying his knowledge (a known password) to access files with incriminating evidence. This scenario is similar with a PIN on a cellphone, whereby a suspect cannot be forced to provide the PIN to access his device. Conversely, a suspect can be forced to use his finger to unlock a laptop or smartphone. Biometric access is not protected by the Constitution.

Sixth Amendment

The Sixth Amendment states the following:

> In all criminal prosecutions, the accused shall enjoy the right to a speedy and public trial, by an impartial jury of the State and district wherein the crime shall have been committed,

which district shall have been previously ascertained by law, and to be informed of the nature and cause of the accusation; to be confronted with the witnesses against him; to have compulsory process for obtaining witnesses in his favor, and to have the Assistance of Counsel for his defense.

The Sixth Amendment does not impact the work of computer forensics investigators in law enforcement very frequently, but it is important to acknowledge. In the case of *Melendez-Diaz v. Massachusetts*, the U.S. Supreme Court reversed the Massachusetts Appeals Court judgment, ruling that certificates of forensic findings should not have been admitted in court and violated the defendant's Sixth Amendment right to confront witnesses against him. The **Confrontation Clause** is a Sixth Amendment clause that states: "in all criminal prosecutions, the accused shall enjoy the right...to be confronted with the witnesses against him." Although this case did not involve digital evidence, there are obviously implications for computer forensics investigators, who previously submitted notarized testimony but are now being forced to appear in person.

Congressional Legislation

As previously mentioned, the role of Congress is to write laws, while the federal courts interpret congressional legislation and pass judgment over those who violate those laws. Changes in technology have brought about changes in legislation.

Federal Wiretap Act (18 U.S.C. § 2511)

The following is the preamble to the Federal Wiretap Act of 1968, which is often referred to as Title III:

> Section 2511 of Title 18 prohibits the unauthorized interception, disclosure, and use of wire, oral, or electronic communications. The prohibitions are absolute, subject only to the specific exemptions in Title III. Consequently, unless an interception is specifically authorized, it is impermissible and, assuming existence of the requisite criminal intent, in violation of 18 U.S.C. § 2511.

The law is clear in detailing how law enforcement is prohibited from using a wiretap without permission from a judge. In fact, law enforcement can be penalized for any unauthorized use of a wiretap. A wiretap is authorized by the Justice Department, signed off by a U.S. District Court or Court of Appeals judge, and is valid for up to 30 days. Under 18 U.S.C. § 2511(2)(a)(i), service carriers may, on occasion, monitor and intercept communications to "combat fraud and theft of service".

The Federal Wiretap Act has been amended several times to account for changes in technology. The Electronic Communications Privacy Act of 1986 (ECPA) was developed to extend the restrictions placed on law enforcement by the Federal Wiretap Act. Basically, the ECPA extended the Wiretap Act to include electronic data transmitted by a computer from merely including telephone intercepts. As part of the ECPA, Congress included the Stored Communications Act (SCA). When an individual uses an ISP or an electronic mail service provider, there are no protections under the Fourth Amendment. The Stored Communications Act was introduced to protect the rights of the individual and maintain their expectation of privacy.

"Stored communications" is defined at 18 U.S.C. § 2510(17):

(A) any temporary, intermediate storage of a wire or electronic communication incidental to the electronic transmission thereof; and

(B) any storage of such communication by an electronic communication service for purposes of backup protection of such communication.

The issue of applying SCA is somewhat problematic, however, considering that law enforcement operating in one jurisdiction is granted a search warrant but an ISP or electronic mail service provider may be headquartered in another jurisdiction, while the actual email server may be located in yet another jurisdiction. When Google introduced Gmail in 2004, it provided a tremendous amount of memory to its users and changed Internet email services forever. People now save thousands of emails for years, which is a tremendous benefit to law enforcement.

Recently, in the case of *City of Ontario v. Quon, 560 U.S. (2010)*, two police officers were disciplined when their pager text messages were examined, and sexually explicit texts were found. Jeff Quon, a police sergeant from Ontario, California, and other officers sued the city, their superiors, and the service provider in federal court and argued that their Fourth Amendment rights and federal communications privacy laws had been violated. The Supreme Court ruled that the search was reasonable, thereby reversing the Ninth Circuit's decision that a less intrusive search was warranted. This ruling means that there should be a diminished expectation of privacy, with electronic communications, in the workplace.

A similar case can be seen in *Bohach v. City of Reno*, where police officers faced an internal affairs investigation based upon stored pager messages. The officers in question tried to stop the investigation based on their rights under ECPA. The court disagreed that the search was illegal and stated that there could be no expectation of privacy because many people had access to the system where the messages were stored. Furthermore, there was no notion of an "intercept" of communications in this investigation.

In the case of *Smyth v. The Pillsbury Company*, Michael Smyth's employment with the Pillsbury Company was terminated for inappropriate comments about management that he sent in an email. Smyth filed suit against the company for unfair dismissal because the company clearly stated in its policy that emails were confidential and would not be intercepted—and, furthermore, that emails could not be used as grounds for termination. Interestingly, the court found in favor of Pillsbury. Judge Charles R. Weiner granted Pillsbury's motion to dismiss after examining common law exceptions to Pennsylvania's denial of a cause of action for the termination of an at-will employee.

Foreign Intelligence Surveillance Act (FISA-1978)

The Foreign Intelligence Surveillance Act is a congressional act that was introduced during President Carter's administration. The act outlines procedures by which electronic surveillance may be carried out to protect the United States against international espionage by foreign governments. The act was subsequently amended by the USA PATRIOT Act in 2001, which extended the scope to include terrorism, which may not be state-sponsored.

Certain portions of the act stand out when considering computer forensics investigations. One example is the use of pen registers and also trap-and-trace devices in foreign intelligence investigations (Title 50 U.S.C., Chapter 36, Subchapter III, § 1842).

The Protect America Act of 2007 amended FISA to allow for warrantless surveillance of foreign targets of intelligence gathering. This act was later repealed with the FISA Amendments Act of 2008 (Title VII of FISA).

Computer Fraud and Abuse Act (18 U.S.C. § 2511)

The Computer Fraud and Abuse Act is a part of Title 18 of the United States Code, which was passed by Congress in 1986. The early 1980s saw the growth of the personal computer, and with that growth came the emergence of the computer hacker. High-profile hackers targeted both corporate networks and government agency networks. The Computer Fraud and Abuse Act was introduced to invoke stiffer penalties for those found guilty of unauthorized access to a network. Section 814 of the USA PATRIOT Act made several amendments to the Computer Fraud and Abuse Act, including an increase in the maximum penalty for hackers, who damage protected computers, from 10 years to 20 years in prison. Moreover, the act changed to include intent to damage a computer rather than simply a type of damage. The USA PATRIOT Act also included a new offense for damaging computers used for national security or criminal justice. Some major provisions of the act are outlined shortly.

In the case of Andrew "weev" Auernheimer, the hacker was found guilty of violating the Computer Fraud and Abuse Act when he released hundreds of thousands of iPad email addresses. The Third Circuit Court of Appeals overturned his conviction after federal prosecutors wrongly filed the case against him in New Jersey, noting that none of the crimes had been perpetrated in that state.

Corporate Espionage (18 U.S.C. § 1030(a)(1))

Title 18 U.S.C. § 1030(a)(1) states:

> having knowingly accessed a computer without authorization or exceeding authorized access, and by means of such conduct having obtained information that has been determined by the United States Government pursuant to an Executive order or statute to require protection against unauthorized disclosure for reasons of national defense or foreign relations, or any restricted data, as defined in paragraph y. of section 11 of the Atomic Energy Act of 1954, with reason to believe that such information so obtained could be used to the injury of the United States, or to the advantage of any foreign nation willfully communicates, delivers, transmits, or causes to be communicated, delivered, or transmitted, or attempts to communicate, deliver, transmit or cause to be communicated, delivered, or

transmitted the same to any person not entitled to receive it, or willfully retains the same and fails to deliver it to the officer or employee of the United States entitled to receive it....

Other provisions of the Computer Fraud and Abuse Act are important:

- Computer Trespassing (18 U.S.C. § 1030(a)(2))

- Committing Fraud with a Protected Computer (18 U.S.C. § 1030(a)(3))

- Distributing Passwords of a Government/Commercial Computer (18 U.S.C. § 1030(a)(6))

- Damage to a Protected Computer (18 U.S.C. § 1030(a)(7))

Communications Assistance for Law Enforcement Act (CALEA) (47 U.S.C. § 1002)

Advancements in telecommunications have often made it more difficult for law enforcement to carry out effective electronic surveillance of a criminal suspect. The Communications Assistance for Law Enforcement Act (CALEA) was introduced to facilitate law enforcement in their surveillance activities of telecom companies. In essence, telecommunications companies were forced to redesign much of their infrastructure to become compliant with CALEA and provide improved electronic surveillance for law enforcement. In other words, there is a legal obligation for telecommunication service providers to assist law enforcement with their investigations. Cisco has actually published a *Lawful Intercept Configuration Guide*, which outlines the schematics for communications interceptions by law enforcement agencies under CALEA. You can review the Cisco guide online (www.cisco.com).

What is important to note is that VoIP operators, like Vonage or Magic Jack, are not subject to CALEA and, therefore, might not be able to assist law enforcement with investigations, like a traditional telecom company, such as Verizon, can. Moreover, serious technological challenges are associated with using a Title III wiretap with VoIP because of the absence of switches on a VoIP network.

USA PATRIOT Act

The USA PATRIOT Act was introduced in the wake of the September 11, 2001, atrocity, to provide greater powers to law enforcement in an effort to prevent terrorist attacks from happening again. The act has caused such a stir because law enforcement now has the power to conduct surveillance without judicial approval in certain circumstances. Some view this legislative change as a reduction in our Fourth Amendment rights and introduces the potential for more "big brother" warrantless surveillance.

The USA PATRIOT Act has impacted investigations involving digital forensics. For example, if law enforcement received an email from someone who had been kidnapped, then under the USA PATRIOT Act, law enforcement could act without the use of a warrant because someone's life was in danger. Before 9/11/2001, a warrant was needed to conduct a search, even when a person's life was in danger.

Section 202 of the USA PATRIOT Act provides law enforcement with the authority to intercept voice communications in computer hacking investigations. Previously, law enforcement could not apply for a wiretap order or wire intercept for violations of the Computer Fraud and Abuse Act.

Section 209 of the USA PATRIOT Act impacts law enforcement's access to electronically stored voice messages, like voicemail. Since the Electronic Communications Privacy Act, changes have been made to the electronic storage of communications. For example, with the introduction of Multipurpose Internet Mail Extensions (MIME), a government agent with a search warrant could not tell whether an unopened email contained a voice recording. Section 209 now allows law enforcement to access stored voice recordings without a Title III wiretap. In summary, recorded voice messages are no longer protected by the Fourth Amendment but have a lower standard under ECPA.

Section 210 of the USA PATRIOT Act broadens the amount of personal information that a government agent has access to with the use of a subpoena. Subsection 2703(c)(2) includes "records of session times and durations", as well as "any temporarily assigned network address". Section 210 also enables agents to obtain credit card and bank information for Internet users, which was previously unavailable without a subpoena. This is important because a user who used a false identity, but a real credit card, can now be found without the use of a warrant.

Section 210 of the USA PATRIOT Act was introduced to compel Internet Service Providers (ISPs) to assist law enforcement when there is the potential for loss of life. Section 210 also enables ISPs to voluntarily report non-content records, like a user's login records, to law enforcement to protect themselves. If a computer hacker were to hack into an email server, the service provider is now legally able to hand over complete details about the incident to law enforcement. There has, however, been some pushback by ISPs about providing this information.

Section 213 of the USA PATRIOT Act is often referred to as the "sneak and peek" warrant provision. This provision enables law enforcement to search a home or business hastily without notifying the target in advance. The section was added to prevent a criminal suspect from tipping off other criminals about an imminent search.

Section 216 amends the Pen Register and Trap and Trace Statute to extend the law from just to telephone records to now include non-content information related to the Internet. Thus, pen register and trap-and-trace searches now can include IP addresses, MAC addresses, port numbers, and user account or email addresses.

Section 217 allows an individual, whose protected computer has suffered unauthorized access by a hacker, to allow law enforcement to intercept the communications of the trespasser. The user also has the right to intercept these communications. However, the victim must meet four conditions prior to monitoring:

1. Owner or user of a protected computer must authorize the interception of communications (Section 2511(2)(i)(I));

2. The person who intercepts the communication must be lawfully engaged in the ongoing investigation (Section 2511(2)(i)(II));

3. Reasonable grounds to believe that the interception of a communication will assist in an ongoing investigation (Section 2511(2)(i)(III)); and

4. Investigators must only intercept the communications of the trespasser (Section 2511(2)(i)(IV)).

Section 220 compels ISPs to hand over email records that are outside the jurisdiction of an investigation. On occasion, judges would not provide permission for law enforcement to access email located in another jurisdiction.

Finally, *Section 816* requires the Attorney General to create regional computer forensics laboratories and to continue supporting existing laboratories.

PROTECT Act

The PROTECT Act of 2003 (PROTECT stands for Prosecutorial Remedies and Other Tools to end the Exploitation of Children Today) was codified as 18 U.S.C. § 2252(B)(b). The act was introduced to provide greater protection for children against abuse. The law eliminates waiting periods for law enforcement to begin investigating missing persons between the ages of 18 and 21. Another provision of the act is the elimination of statutes of limitations for child abuse or kidnapping. The act also prohibits computer-generated child pornography, although the First Amendment constitutionality of this provision has been questioned in case law.

Digital Millennium Copyright Act (DMCA) (17 U.S.C. § 1201)

The Digital Millennium Copyright Act (DMCA) was signed into law in 1998 by President Bill Clinton. DCMA is divided into four titles:

- **Title I:** The "WIPO Copyright and Performances and Phonograms Treaties Implementation Act of 1998" implements the WIPO treaties.

- **Title II:** The "Online Copyright Infringement Liability Limitation Act" creates limitations on the liability of online service providers for copyright infringement when engaging in certain types of activities.

- **Title III:** The "Computer Maintenance Competition Assurance Act" creates an exemption for making a copy of a computer program by activating a computer for purposes of maintenance or repair.

- **Title IV:** Contains six miscellaneous provisions, relating to the functions of the Copyright Office, distance education, the exceptions in the Copyright Act for libraries and for making ephemeral recordings, "webcasting" of sound recordings on the Internet, and the applicability of collective bargaining agreement obligations in the case of transfers of rights in motion pictures.

A copy of DCMA is available at www.copyright.gov/legislation/dmca.pdf.

The act is important because many people have been involved in litigation in civil cases that involve copyright infringement. These cases often involve subpoenas issued to online service providers and expert witness testimony from computer forensics investigators.

In the case of *Sony Computer Entertainment America v. George Hotz*, Sony filed a lawsuit against George Hotz, who was accused of violating the DCMA. Hotz provided users with a jailbreak for Sony PlayStation 3's firmware that enabled users to play games on the PlayStation console that were unauthorized by Sony. Hotz posted the jailbreak solution on his blog and in a YouTube video; Hotz also had followers on Twitter. DCMA prohibits any device that circumvents intellectual property, and this was the focus of the violation from Sony's perspective. Sony also believed that Hotz and others who used the firmware jailbreak had violated its terms of service.

Two issues stand out in this case. The first is that Sony managed to convince a magistrate to give the company permission to obtain the IP addresses and names of those who had visited Hotz's blog, viewed the YouTube video, and followed him on Twitter. The Electronic Frontier Foundation (EFF) supported Hotz financially during the case and noted in a letter to the magistrate that allowing Sony to obtain the names of Hotz's followers on the Internet was unlawful. Moreover, the foundation argued that this action would mean naming individuals who were not a part of the lawsuit and could not be present to object, in court, to their names being revealed.

It should be noted that there are some exemptions to being prosecuted under DMCA. For example, an entity seeking to find security flaws in a legitimate manner is exempt from prosecution.

The Supreme Court decision in the case of *McIntyre v. Ohio Elections Comm'n, 514 U.S. 334, 357 (1995)*, clearly protects the right to anonymity:

> Anonymity is a shield from the tyranny of the majority [that] exemplifies the purpose [of the First Amendment]: "to protect unpopular individuals from retaliation...at the hand of an intolerant society."

The case of *Sony Music Entertainment v. Does, 326 F.Supp.2d 556, 565 (S.D.N.Y. 2004)*, is more specific about protecting an individual's right to speak anonymously on the Internet. Several other cases protect the identity of online service subscribers under the First Amendment. Some have even cited the *Federalist Papers*, authored by Alexander Hamilton, James Madison, and John Jay, promoting the U.S. Constitution. This series of 85 articles was published under the pseudonym of Publius. Therefore, our Founding Fathers believed that the Constitution should protect the right of anonymous speech and reading.

The second interesting fact about the case involving *Sony v. Hotz* is that the hacktivist group Anonymous hacked into Sony's PlayStation network and compromised 24.6 million user accounts, along with credit card and bank information for many of those users. This was retribution for Sony's lawsuit against Hotz. In the group's eyes, Sony was challenging Hotz's First Amendment right to free speech.

Ultimately, Sony and Hotz reached an out-of-court settlement, but serious questions were raised about the ability of Sony to obtain IP addresses and names of Internet users who were not part of the lawsuit.

CLOUD (Clarifying Lawful Overseas Use of Data) Act

Enacted in 2018, this federal legislation obliges USA-based technology corporations to allow federal law enforcement to obtain data stored on servers domestically and internationally, with a subpoena or a warrant. This act has largely been in response to pushback by companies, including Microsoft, with servers in countries, like Ireland, which believed that servers located outside of the USA fall under the jurisdiction of other nations. This act has been viewed by some as being controversial since data stored on a server in an EU country should comply with both sovereign law (country law) and EU legislation, which is the case for other types of evidence. Conversely, it is important for law enforcement to have access to critical evidence on foreign servers, where the suspect or victim is based in the USA.

At time of writing, this law needs to also be ratified reciprocally by other countries—more specifically, in the European Union.

Rules for Evidence Admissibility

The admissibility of digital evidence will continue to be challenged. The primary issue is that the traditional science of forensics has been applied to computers and technology. In theory, evidence is gathered from a crime scene or suspect and remains unchanged when admitted to court. When a blood sample has been gathered and has undergone DNA analysis, there is still blood that remains unchanged in its chemical composition. In digital forensics, systems are often in a state of flux. For example, if a system is running, then the contents of RAM are particularly important in potentially finding a suspect's password, websites visited, processes running, and so forth. Nevertheless, while gathering the contents of RAM, the computer's memory is continually changing. The same is true when a cellular telephone has been seized. Typically, the cellphone will be powered on and system changes will occur while in custody. These continual changes make the evidence easier to challenge in court. Additionally, with rapid changes in technology, new decisions are being made in court cases. No longer do we simply rely on files retrieved from a hard disk drive, but we also need to consider evidence from social networking websites, mobile devices, and cloud computing. With the diversification of digital evidence, finding experts with strengths in numerous areas of this discipline becomes problematic.

Ultimately, when dealing with the issue of admissibility in court, we rely on case law, especially as it relates to acceptable scientific practice, and what are known as Federal Rules of Evidence. Of course, the manner by which the evidence was seized, handled, and documented in accordance with the law is critical to its acceptance by a judge.

Frye Test for Evidence Admissibility

The case of *Frye v. United States* dealt with the admissibility of evidence in a case in which James Alphonzo Frye was tried for second-degree murder. The focus of evidence credibility was a systolic blood pressure test that was a precursor to the polygraph test. This blood pressure test was not widely accepted by scientists, so it was ruled inadmissible. The case is a landmark case because the decision has subsequently influenced the admissibility of scientific evidence, particularly in reference to expert witness testimony. In 1923, the D.C. Court of Appeals opined:

> Just when a scientific principal or discovery crosses the line between the experimental and demonstrable stages is difficult to define. Somewhere in this twilight zone the evidential force of the principle must be recognized, and while courts will go a long way in admitting expert testimony deduced from a well-recognized scientific principle or discovery, the thing from which the deduction is made must be sufficiently established to have gained general acceptance in the particular field in which it belongs. (emphasis added).

In summary, the decision states that expert opinion must be derived from a thing and must be based on science that is demonstrable and not experimental.

Daubert Test for Evidence Admissibility

In some jurisdictions, the Frye test (or standard) has been supplanted by the Daubert test. In the case of *Daubert v. Merrell Dow Pharmaceuticals* in 1993, the parents of Jason Daubert and Eric Schuller sued Merrell Dow Pharmaceuticals over birth defects suffered by their children after the use of the drug Bendectin. Both parties used expert witness testimony, but the plaintiffs referenced the impact of the drug testing on animal—testing that was not yet generally accepted in the scientific community. Under the Frye standard, this evidence would be inadmissible. The U.S. District Court found in favor, and the Ninth Circuit agreed when appealed by Daubert and Schuller. The plaintiffs submitted a request for review by the Supreme Court, which they agreed to do. The plaintiffs argued that after Congress passed the Federal Rules of Evidence (FRE) in 1975, the *Frye* standard no longer applied. The Supreme Court agreed and opined that the *Frye* standard no longer applies.

The case of *Kumho Tire Co. v. Carmichael* extended the importance of the Federal Rules of Evidence over the *Frye* standard by giving equal weight to the testimony of a technician with that of a scientist. Rule 702 of FRE applies to "scientific, technical, or other specialized knowledge".

Ultimately, the impact of *Frye* and *Daubert* on investigations involving digital evidence is that computer forensics investigators must perform benchmark testing on their hardware and software tools. This testing will enable the investigator to explain known error rates.

Federal Rules of Evidence

The **Federal Rules of Evidence (FRE)** are a set of rules that determine the admissibility of evidence in both civil and criminal cases in federal court. Nevertheless, many states have adopted similar guidelines for evidence admissibility. These rules became law when Congress enacted FRE under the Act to Establish Rules of Evidence for Certain Courts and Proceedings.

Several FRE directly impact the admissibility of digital evidence and expert testimony. As noted earlier, Rule 702 deals with expert testimony:

> If scientific, technical, or other specialized knowledge will assist the trier of fact to understand the evidence or to determine a fact in issue, a witness qualified as an expert by knowledge, skill, experience, training, or education, may testify thereto in the form of an opinion or otherwise, if (1) the testimony is based upon sufficient facts or data, (2) the testimony is the product of reliable principles and methods, and (3) the witness has applied the principles and methods reliably to the facts of the case.

However, the rule noted above does not outline how to determine what "knowledge" is. When determining knowledge, we need to qualify the expertise of an expert witness.

Expert Witnesses

In general, testimony that is not firsthand is referred to as *hearsay* and is therefore inadmissible in court. An exception exists, however, for digital evidence under the Federal Rules of Evidence. Therefore, an expert witness can provide her opinion in court, and that opinion can be used as evidence. Expert testimony can be provided during a trial or in a deposition. A **deposition** is pretrial testimony given under oath, with both defense and prosecution attorneys present.

Both the defense and the prosecution can use their own expert witness and have the right to cross-examine the opponent's expert. An expert witness might also be appointed by the court. The goals of the defense are to discredit the expert, the testimony, the evidence, the tools, and the scientific methodology used, to ultimately gain concessions.

Under FRE 702, 703, and 704, all parties in a trial must disclose the witnesses that they will use at trial, which includes expert witnesses. The role of the expert witness is to educate the jury. Unlike a lay witness, an expert witness can express opinion according to FRE 704. An expert can speculate on a theory based on a theory rooted in facts. Opinion will guide the questions posed by the counsel the expert is representing. An expert may bring his own exhibits to the trial.

When seeking guidelines on the use of an expert witness at trial, we not only observe FRE guidelines, but we must also note the Federal Rules of Civil Procedure. The **Federal Rules of Civil Procedure (FRCP)** apply to civil cases in federal district courts, and these rules are promulgated by the U.S. Supreme Court. Many state courts also have adopted these rules. Under Rule 26(2) of FRCP, an expert witness who will be used at trial generally needs to provide a written report. Disclosure of an expert witness is an important part of discovery. **Discovery** is a pre-trial phase in which both parties in a civil lawsuit must share evidence when requested, by means of interrogations, depositions, documents, and subpoenas from parties not part of the lawsuit. Under Rule 26(2)(B), the expert witness's written report must contain the following:

> (i) A complete statement of all opinions the witness will express and the basis and reasons for them;

> (ii) The facts or data considered by the witness in forming them;

(iii) Any exhibits that will be used to summarize or support them;

(iv) The witness's qualifications, including a list of all publications authored in the previous 10 years;

(v) A list of all other cases in which, during the previous 4 years, the witness testified as an expert at trial or by deposition; and

(vi) A statement of the compensation to be paid for the study and testimony in the case.

As part of the pretrial disclosures, under Rule 26(3)(A), a party must provide the other party with the following information:

(i) The name and, if not previously provided, the address and telephone number of each witness—separately identifying those the party expects to present and those it may call if the need arises;

(ii) The designation of those witnesses whose testimony the party expects to present by deposition and, if not taken stenographically, a transcript of the pertinent parts of the deposition; and

(iii) An identification of each document or other exhibit, including summaries of other evidence—separately identifying those items the party expects to offer and those it may offer if the need arises.

Of course, as with any evidence (or witness testimony), there can be objections to the testimony of an expert witness both at pretrial and during the trial.

Federal Rules of Evidence (FRE) and Hearsay

Another important rule that impacts digital evidence is FRE, Rule 803(6), which states the following:

> **Records of regularly conducted activity.** A memorandum, report, record, or data compilation, in any form, of acts, events, conditions, opinions, or diagnoses, made at or near the time by, or from information transmitted by, a person with knowledge, if kept in the course of a regularly conducted business activity, and if it was the regular practice of that business activity to make the memorandum, report, record or data compilation, all as shown by the testimony of the custodian or other qualified witness, or by certification that complies with Rule 902(11), Rule 902(12), or a statute permitting certification, unless the source of information or the method or circumstances of preparation indicate lack of trustworthiness. The term "business" as used in this paragraph includes business, institution, association, profession, occupation, and calling of every kind, whether or not conducted for profit.

We can determine from this rule that emails, spreadsheets, systems logs, and so forth are records created in the normal course of business and are therefore admissible in federal court.

According to the Federal Rules of Evidence, **hearsay** is a statement other than one made by the declarant while testifying at the trial or hearing offered in evidence to prove the truth of the matter asserted. Digital evidence can be categorized as hearsay, but this is not always the case. In *State v. Armstead*, digital evidence is not hearsay when it is "the by-product of a machine operation which uses for its input 'statements' entered into the machine" and was "was generated solely by the electrical and mechanical operations of the computer and telephone equipment." Therefore, under Rule 803(6) of FRE, digital evidence that is conducted in the "regular practice of that business activity" is not hearsay. Nevertheless, there is a distinction between digital evidence of a conversation in an email versus digital evidence in the form of a system log that simply notes when an individual logged onto a computer. In other words, the hearsay rule is applied differently to content created by a person versus content created by a machine. Evidence on a computer can however be created by both the human and the computer. For example, the user may enter information into a Quicken application, but the application has a computational component built in.

Rule 901, *Requirement of Authentication or Identification*, states the following:

> The requirement of authentication or identification as a condition precedent to admissibility is satisfied by evidence sufficient to support a finding that the matter in question is what its proponent claims.

In the case of *United States v. Tank*, the defendant appealed his conviction of conspiring to receive and distribute child pornography. The appeal focused on the admissibility of chat logs saved on a computer. Tank argued that the chat logs were incomplete and that the logs from a co-conspirator could have been altered before the government seized the computer. The court stated that the issue of the completeness of the chat logs was influenced by the weight of the evidence rather than its admissibility. Riva, the co-conspirator, explained how the logs were created and stated that the printouts were an accurate representation of the chat logs. Even though the screen name on the printouts displayed "Cessna" and not "Tank", several co-conspirators stated that Tank used the name Cessna. The court accepted printouts of chat logs as authentic and admissible under Rule 903(a).

Best Evidence Rule

The **best evidence rule** states that secondary evidence, or a copy, is inadmissible in court when the original exists. Nevertheless, an exception is often made for digital evidence. When you think about it, all files physically stored on a hard disk drive are just variations in the magnetism of a metal disk. These magnetically charged areas are represented by 1s and 0s that make sense only when translated to text or some type of interpretation. Common sense shows that you cannot submit the original media and have the judge and jury look at metal platters. Therefore, printouts of information are necessary. Moreover, an investigator might need to change something or use an application to view the content of a file. As noted in Chapter 3, "Handling Computer Hardware", in the case of *State of Connecticut v. John Kaminski*, police needed to modify the media to view the contents of a compact disc. Criminals will often try to tamper with evidence or hide files and therefore investigators are forced to modify files—and sometimes even storage media—to recover incriminating evidence. Additionally, a cellphone conversation travels through many different channels, and the communication changes formation as conversations become digital data packets. Therefore, evidence will change from its original form from sender to recipient.

Criminal Defense

On March 5, 1770, five colonists were dead—shot by British regulars in an event that was to go down in history as the Boston Massacre. Their deaths were the culmination of bitterness toward the tremendous burden of taxation imposed by the British. The soldiers were brought up on criminal charges, and given the overwhelming hatred cast upon these "murderers", it was certainly not strange that the culprits of this great tragedy could not find a lawyer to defend them in court. One man reluctantly stepped forward, and to everyone's surprise, six of the soldiers were acquitted and the two soldiers, who had fired directly at the protestors, were convicted on only manslaughter charges, even though they had initially been charged with murder. That man was John Adams, who went on to persuade many colonial leaders to support and sign the Declaration of Independence. Adams later served as the second President of the United States (1797–1801). He was famously quoted: "Facts are stubborn things; and whatever may be our wishes, our inclinations, or the dictates of our passion, they cannot alter the state of facts and evidence."

It is important to note that we should respect the vital work of law enforcement and prosecutors in bringing criminals to justice. Nevertheless, we must acknowledge the vital role of defense attorneys in the judicial system. It must be remembered that, under the Sixth Amendment, all defendants must be given the right to defense counsel. At the end of the day, if expert investigators lawfully and scientifically acquired incriminating evidence and the findings are presented appropriately, the prosecution should be successful if the defendant is guilty.

A **defense attorney** is an advocate and representative for a defendant in a court case. Defense attorneys use a number of strategies to defend their clients. One important tactic is to find reasons why each evidence exhibit should not be admitted into trial. Another tactic is to question the way in which the evidence was acquired and handled. Moreover, the defense attorney will question the legality of the steps carried out by investigators during the investigation, procedural issues relating to the pretrial discovery, and also the prosecution's actions during the trial itself.

As we can see from the earlier section on the Fourth Amendment, defense attorneys first focus on whether the investigators' search and seizure of evidence was legal. For example, did law enforcement personnel need a warrant to conduct the search? If so, did they do so in accordance with the provisions of the warrant?

After the suspect is arrested, the defense attorney determines whether there was sufficient evidence to make the arrest and then ascertains whether the suspect was properly informed of his rights. In terms of rights, a suspect has the right to remain silent (Fifth Amendment) and the right to an attorney "for his defence" (Sixth Amendment). Pending the trial, bail can be granted (Eighth Amendment).

During the pretrial phase, the defense attorney has the right to examine the evidence being used by the prosecution in its case. Therefore, if a computer and USB drive of a suspect were seized, defense counsel has the right to obtain copies of the computer's hard drive and a copy of files retrieved from the USB device. Defense counsel must also be afforded ample time to review these copies by one of its computer forensics experts.

During the trial, defense counsel will raise questions about how the evidence was acquired and whether it was obtained in a forensically sound manner. Under cross-examination, a defense attorney might question the credentials of the investigator, the methods used, and knowledge about the forensic tools used, as well as ask general questions about the investigation. The search warrant is not the only legal document that the defense will scrutinize; the defense will also examine the investigators' notes and, more importantly, the chain of custody form. Any gaps of time or inconsistencies on this form will render the evidence inadmissible.

California Consumer Privacy Act (CCPA)

Signed into law in 2018, the CCPA came into effect in 2020. The law impacts for-profit businesses with exposure to the personal data of California (CA) residents. More specifically, the act impacts businesses with revenues in excess of $25 million, who handle records for 50,000 or more CA residents or businesses that derive at least 50% of revenue by selling personal information for CA residents. This act stipulates that a business must inform customers about what personal information is being collected and shared with third parties. The act also forces businesses to allow consumers to easily opt-out of the collection of personal information. Consumers under the age of 16 must not be opted-in by default. Furthermore, consent from a parent/guardian must be obtained by the business for consumers aged 13 and under.

California residents, under CCPA, will have the right to request the removal of personal information, prevent the sale of personal information, and have the right to access their personal information from businesses. Data theft or a security breach may result in a fine of $100 to $750 per CA resident or the actual cost of damages. There may also be an additional fine of $7,500 for each intentional violation or $2,500 for each unintentional violation.

CCPA and other similar privacy legislation is important for a forensics investigator to know so that she can understand required local/state/federal/regional notifications and determine what forensics data may be available and how it can be lawfully accessed.

NYS DFS Rule 23 NYCRR 500

The New York State (NYS) Department of Financial Services (DFS) Section 500 was announced in 2017, in an effort to ensure that the financial services industry create an effective cybersecurity plan to protect their networks and their customers. With fines of up to $250,000 or 1% of banking assets, banks and other financial institutions in the financial capital of the world have taken notice, and taken action, to ensure compliance. For a financial institution to comply, it needs to ensure that it has developed effective planning and policies that address the following domains:

- Maintain a cybersecurity program
- Cybersecurity policy

- Role of the CISO
- Pen testing & vulnerability assessment
- Audit trail
- Access privileges
- Application security
- Risk assessment
- Qualified personnel & intelligence
- Third party service provider
- Multi-factor authentication
- Limitations on data retention
- Training & Monitoring
- Encryption of non-public information
- Incident response plan
- Notices to superintendent

Canada Personal Information Protection and Electronic Documents Act (PIPEDA)

Introduced in April 2000, this act impacts private sector companies across Canada that collect, use, or disclose personal information. These federally regulated organizations include the following:

- Airports, aircraft and airlines;
- Banks and authorized foreign banks;
- Inter-provincial or international transportation companies;
- Telecommunications companies;
- Offshore drilling operations; and
- Radio and television broadcasters.

The act states that an organization must obtain an individual's consent when they collect or share personal information. An individual also has the right to access that information and challenge its accuracy. PIPEDA also includes mandatory breach notifications.

Private sector privacy laws, which are substantially similar to PIPEDA, also exist in Quebec (An Act Respecting the Protection of Personal Information in the Private Sector), Alberta (Personal Information Protection Act) and British Columbia (Personal Information Protection Act).

When Computer Forensics Goes Wrong

Law enforcement generally gets it right when it comes to investigations involving digital evidence. There are, however, occasions when things do not go according to plan.

Pornography in the Classroom

Julie Amero was a 40-year-old substitute teacher at Kelly Middle School in Connecticut. On October 19, 2004, Amero was teaching a seventh-grade language class when her Internet browser inexplicably began displaying pornographic images. Instead of shutting down the computer, she immediately sought help from the school's administration, which she later explained was protocol. A letter was sent to the pupils' parents explaining that Amero would never teach in the school district again. Shortly afterward, Amero was arrested and charged with multiple felonies.

At the trial, a computer crimes investigator from Norwich Police Department, Det. Mark Lounsbury, testified that Amero had been intentionally viewing pornography on the Internet during her class. The detective stated that Amero would have had to click on links to display the pornographic images. In 2007, Norwich Superior Court found Amero guilty on four counts of risk of injury to a minor or impairing the morals of a child.

The conviction followed controversy as many experts, including 28 professors, disagreed with the detective's findings. They believed that his assertions were flawed because he did not check the computer for malware, which could have enabled the pornographic pop-ups. It was later discovered that a DNS hijacking program, called NewDotNet, had been installed on the computer before the alleged crime.

On June 6, 2007, the conviction was thrown out in a New London court, and a new trial was granted. On November 21, 2008, Amero pled guilty to a charge of disorderly conduct and was fined $100. She also lost her ability to teach again, although this was a small price to pay, considering that the original charges in this case could have led to Amero facing up to 40 years in prison.

The moral of the story is that computer forensics experts need to be thorough and make no initial assumptions. An investigator should also never just rely on one forensics tool, where possible. Moreover, an investigator should exhaust all possibilities in a case and be open to getting advice from other experts.

Structure of the Legal System in the European Union (E.U.)

In this digital age, the use of digital evidence in investigations has grown exponentially. We have already discussed how the Internet necessitates more cross-border collaboration. This collaboration refers not just to interstate investigations, but also to international collaboration. The growth of cloud computing has exacerbated this phenomenon. It is important to also think about how U.S. corporations often maintain their servers, and the records of U.S. citizens, on servers located in other countries. These records then become subject to privacy and search and seizure laws in the country where the servers reside.

Increasingly, we read about INTERPOL's involvement in international investigations, especially those involving crimes against children, human trafficking, financial fraud, and drug trafficking. In addition, we are hearing about the concept of cyberwarfare as the possible precursor to an actual war.

Origins of European Law

Apart from Ireland and the United Kingdom, the legal systems of most European countries are based on Roman law. Roman law consists of three books of law: (a) people, (b) property, and (c) acquiring property. The first category refers to issues such as marriage. Property issues relate to ownership, which, in Roman times, included slaves. Acquiring property included wills and laws of succession. Under Roman law, the plaintiff was required to call the defendant, or sometimes force the defendant, to come to court. The magistrate then decided whether the case should go before the **Judex**, a group of prominent laymen, who in Roman times heard arguments, questioned witnesses, and then rendered a decision. The concept of the summons originated in Roman times, as did the role of the court in enforcing court sentences.

Structure of European Union Law

The European Union (E.U.) consists of 27 countries, each with its own sovereign laws. These countries are as follows: Austria, Belgium, Bulgaria, Croatia, Cyprus, the Czech Republic, Denmark, Estonia, Finland, France, Germany, Greece, Hungary, Ireland, Italy, Latvia, Lithuania, Luxembourg, Malta, the Netherlands, Poland, Portugal, Romania, Slovakia, Slovenia, Spain, and Sweden.

The European Union is similar to the United States because it has a dual legal system in place: each country has (1) its own laws and (2) E.U. law. However, there some notable differences in the composition of both entities. The European Union is a treaty with member states. Any state can leave this union at any time without consequence, which is certainly not the case in the United States, as demonstrated when states in the South tried to secede from the Union in 1861.

E.U. Legislature

The **E.U. legislature** is comprised of the European Parliament and the Council of the European Union. These institutions have the power to write, amend, and repeal laws. The European Commission is similar to the Office of the President of the United States, in that it is the executive body of the E.U. However, the **European Commission** has the power to propose legislation and initiate legal proceedings against member states. The **Court of Justice of the European Union** interprets European law, related to its treaties, and is the highest court in the European Union. This court is the equivalent of the U.S. Supreme Court and is made up of the Court of Justice, the General Court, and a number of specialized courts.

Data Privacy

E.U. law clearly protects the rights of an individual in terms of personal data sharing more than the U.S. legal system does. In the United States, very few laws protect an individual's personal information, especially at the federal level. The Health Insurance Portability and Accountability Act (HIPAA) gives control of personal healthcare data to the individual. The Gramm–Leach–Bliley Act is also concerned with privacy, in that financial institutions must provide consumers with a copy of their privacy policy and any amendments. Nevertheless, consumers have no right to prevent the financial institution from sharing their personal data. That is not the case in Europe, where the individual is afforded control over personal data. This presents tremendous challenges to computer forensics investigators and their access to digital evidence in the E.U.

A U.S. investigator traveling to the E.U. will notice some significant differences. For example, in some jurisdictions, employees need to be notified when an investigation of their computer will take place, which is not the case in the United States. Additionally, an investigator cannot acquire evidence from a computer in some European countries and simply bring it back to the United States for analysis. Online privacy is an individual right in the E.U., whereas this is not the case in the United States. For example, cookies have become standardized. As stipulated by the E.U., a user must choose to opt in to accept cookies on a website. Conversely, in the United States, the user generally is opted in by default. Therefore, the Internet evidence for a user differs in the E.U. from the United States. In May 2014, the European Union Court of Justice (ECJ) ruled that people on the Internet have the right to be forgotten, and therefore people can force Google to remove sensitive data about themselves. In fact, the user now has more control over searches performed, so Google and others have been gradually removing websites from searches performed by users. This may be good news for the users and their privacy, but online searches of suspects and subpoenas sent to Internet companies, like Google, will often yield fewer results for investigators, and the environment should prove even more problematic in the future. Directive 95/46/EC outlines the processing, handling, and sharing of personal data:

> (2) Whereas data-processing systems are designed to serve man; whereas they must, whatever the nationality or residence of natural persons, respect their fundamental rights and freedoms, notably the right to privacy, and contribute to economic and social progress, trade expansion and the well-being of individuals

In January 2012, the European Commission voted to overhaul the 1995 Data Protection Directive, thereby enabling Internet users to have more control over their personal information. The provisions of the new law allow people to ask firms to delete their data and notify customers when their information has been compromised.

Directive 97/66/EC protects the processing of personal data and the protection of privacy in the telecommunications sector.

General Data Protection Regulation (GDPR)

Instituted in the EU on May 25, 2018, GDPR has had a profound impact on incident response and criminal investigations involving digital data. This regulation stipulates how companies, or entities, must handle the records of European Union citizens. Thus, a U.S. company that maintains personal information for EU citizens on its servers must comply. The law does not apply to small and mid-sized companies where personal data is not core to its business and personal data is not at risk.

The reason why this law has caused fear for so many companies is the fact that (i) a fine could be as high as €20 million or 4% of global annual turnover and (ii) the law limits the amount of data that a company can collect about a consumer. The latter has huge implications for companies, like Facebook and Google, which collect vast amounts of personal data about consumers, which goes beyond the initial transactional level. For example, under GDPR, a company can only collect personal data that is necessary to complete a transaction. Therefore, a shop selling shoes can only request an email address from a customer with their explicit consent and by explaining how they intend to use that information after the purchase has been made. Personal data may not be used for another purpose later and cannot be sold to a third party.

The focus of GDPR is protection of the individual and ensuring that the individual is in control of his or her own personal data rather than corporations. These rights include:

- The right to be forgotten
- The right to access their personal data
- The right to amend incorrect personal data
- The right to transfer data from one provider to another

A company must clearly state its privacy policy and data sharing agreements in full and not links i.e. providing web links to its policies are inappropriate. A consumer must be provided with details that include the name of the Data Protection Officer (DPO) of the company, reasons why their data is being collected, categories of personal data, legal justification, and data retention policy.

What Type of Data Can Be Collected under GDPR?

A company or entity must have a specific purpose for collecting personal data ("purpose limitation"). Furthermore, you must inform the E.U. citizen as to the purpose of the data collection. Only data necessary to complete a transaction can be collected ("data minimization"). A company must ensure that the personal data collected is correct ("accuracy"). Personal data can only be used for the original purpose and not used for any additional activities. A company cannot store data longer than necessary ("storage limitation"). The company must also ensure data security ("integrity and confidentiality").

Personal Data versus Sensitive Data

GDPR makes a distinction between personal data and sensitive data. Personal data can include a consumer's name, address, email address or IP address. Sensitive data can include race or ethnicity, political opinions, religious/philosophical beliefs, trade union membership, genetics/biometrics, health records and sexual orientation. This information becomes important in terms of how a data breach is reported. Under GDPR, a data breach must be reported within 72 hours to the Data Protection

Authority (DPA). The DPA has the authority to issue warnings, reprimand, place a temporary ban on processing or a definitive ban on processing and issue a fine up to €20 million or 4% of global annual turnover. An individual may also claim compensation if his personal information has been compromised. More information about incident response and reporting requirements will be covered in Chapter 8, "Network Forensics and Incident Response".

GDPR also makes a distinction between a data controller and a data processor, which makes a difference in terms of reporting after a data breach. A data processor is an entity that processes data for a data controller, based on specific guidelines provided by the controller. The controller essentially maintains the personal information. For example, Cisco is a data controller for its employees, while a third-party payroll company would be a data processor for Cisco's employees. Hypothetically, if ADP was the payroll company for Cisco, then it would take direction from Cisco about how Cisco's employee information should be handled or processed.

Impact of GDPR on Digital Forensics Investigations

One cannot underestimate the impact of GDPR on investigations. With limitations on data collection and retention, a criminal investigator may have more limited access to personal information from corporations. The biggest impact of GDPR is on incident response (IR). For example, if a U.S. company had an employee located in Spain whose laptop was stolen, it could be problematic to check if that laptop was compliant, i.e., was encrypted. Additionally, if that same company needed to image a computer in an E.U. country, then both GDPR and local legislation impact whether that investigation must take place in-country, whether the data can be transferred back to investigators in the USA, and permission may need to be sought from the employee to investigate a laptop owned by the company.

One major shift with IR, under GDPR, is that investigations have become attorney directed, i.e., the incident responder may have to seek advice from a cyber legal attorney, country legal, and the company's data protection officer (also an attorney) during an investigation because of the potential reporting requirements. If a data breach has a reporting requirement, under GDPR, then the Data Protection Authority may ask the following questions:

- What happened?
- When did it happen?
- What data was involved?
- What data protections were in place?
- How have you mitigated the threat?
- How will you mitigate future threats?
- With regards to the inadvertent disclosure, did the employee have access to the data in the normal course of business?
- Was the data encrypted?

- Was the device encrypted?

- What type of device was the data stored on?

- Has the client been informed?

- When was the client informed?

- Has the employee been referred for consequences?

- What type of training do you provide your employees?

There are some challenges, however, associated with reporting a data breach. For example, it can be difficult for a company to pinpoint when a breach occurred. If there has been data exfiltration, and the hacker(s) encrypted the data, then the company may not be able to determine if personal data has been compromised or not.

Human Trafficking Legislation

The U.K. Modern Slavery Act is an extremely important piece of legislation. It is important because it confirms that slavery still exists in the Western World as well as in other regions of the globe. Men, women and children are being manipulated by criminals with the prospect of job opportunities in other countries and then forced into the sex industry (primarily women and children) or other forced labor, including agriculture, fishing and factories (primarily men). For example, women and children from high unemployment regions of Eastern Europe and Africa are being sold into slavery in Western countries, including Germany and France. Women and children from South American countries, like Honduras, are being enslaved in the USA – especially in lucrative cities like Las Vegas. Modern slavery is a multi-billion dollar industry. Of course, there are other countries, like India and North Korea, where slavery and human trafficking is a huge problem. Human trafficking has been rising significantly in recent years, and figures from the White House estimate that more than 25 million people are enslaved worldwide.

The criminals involved in modern slavery are investigated by agencies, including the National Crime Agency (NCA), Federal Bureau of Investigation, Homeland Security Investigations and Europol, to name but a few. One cannot underestimate the seriousness of this criminal activity and the time afforded by agencies worldwide to combat the abuse of women and children. Recently, the laws have changed in places, like New York State, where the focus of prosecution has moved to combat sex trafficking and support the victims. Some agencies have been progressive and changed laws to recognize the victims of the sex trade. Manhattan District Attorney is one organization that has recognized victims of trauma and expunged the records of many victims of the sex trade. Agencies, like Homeland Security Investigations, actively support the victims of human trafficking and raise charitable donations through the Homeland Security Philanthropy Council.

Investigatory Powers Act 2016

The Investigatory Powers Act, passed by both Houses of Parliament in 2016, details what digital data law enforcement and intelligence agencies, in the United Kingdom (U.K.), may access and what they cannot access. The goal of the Act is to improve national security (intelligence) and the capabilities of law enforcement (criminal investigations), by providing greater access to more electronic data. In particular, the act provides greater guidance about the lawful inception of communications data. The Investigatory Powers Commissioner's Office (IPCO) oversees the use of investigatory powers by law enforcement, intelligence agencies and other public authorities. IPCO's staff includes 15 Judicial Commissioners (current and retired judges) and a Technical Advisory Panel of scientific experts.

Facebook

The location of the data is always key in terms of jurisdiction. In 2011, Facebook agreed to overhaul its privacy settings for more than half a billion users following a probe by the Irish Data Protection Commissioner (DPC). Facebook Ireland handles all of Facebook's users who reside outside the United States and Canada. WhatsApp, which is owned by Facebook, maintains message servers in Ireland.

Intellectual Property

The recording industry has experienced tremendous challenges to the protection of intellectual property in the European Union. In a recent dispute between Scarlet Extended SA, an ISP owned by Belgacom, and Belgian management company SABAM (Case C-70/10), Europe's highest court, the European Court of Justice, ruled that Internet access is a human right and that the music industry could not force ISPs to block access to users illegally sharing music and videos. In a similar decision, Eircom had been questioned by the Data Protection Commission about its "three strikes" policy against users illegally downloading copyrighted files. E.U. law prevents injunctions, decided by national courts, from being imposed when requiring the ISP to install filtering systems to prevent users from illegally downloading files.

Amendment 138/46 has been highly controversial. France and the U.K. had sought to scrap the amendment as part of the Telecoms Package, which states that the Internet is a basic human right. However, a compromise was found so that countries could impose their own laws on denying Internet service to copyright violators but allow the E.U. Parliament to review such cases.

E.U. Directives on Child Pornography

The European Union has been very tough on criminals who view, possess, and distribute child pornography. Recent directives now require member states to remove child pornography websites and enact national laws prohibiting child pornography. The European Parliament has fought for tougher penalties against these criminals and has outlined penalties for approximately 20 criminal offenses. For example, those producing this type of content will face a minimum of three years, while criminals viewing this content online will face at least one year in prison.

In summary, each member state of the European Union has its own laws concerning the use of digital evidence in cases. However, the E.U. allows individuals to appeal judgments, which is similar to the U.S. Supreme Court.

Europol

Europol is the European Union law enforcement agency. It investigates more than 12,000 cases annually, from human trafficking, to drug trafficking, to cybercrime, to currency counterfeiting. In March 2012, Europol announced the establishment of the European Cybercrime Centre (EC3) at The Hague, Belgium. The new center became operational in 2013 and is supported by a team of digital forensics investigators. The focus of the center is on investigating cybercrime and online child abuse cases. In May 2017, Europol officially became the European Union Agency for Law Enforcement Cooperation. This change means that Europol has more power when it comes to counter-terrorism and cybercrime investigations.

OLAF (European Anti-fraud Office)

In January 2014, OLAF released its standard operating procedures for digital forensics investigations conducted by its agencies. These guidelines outline good practices for the identification, acquisition, imaging, collection, analysis, and preservation of digital evidence. This guide is available at https://ec.europa.eu/anti-fraud/sites/antifraud/files/guidelines_en.pdf.

ACPO Guidelines

The Association of Chief Police Officers (ACPO) in the United Kingdom has created a set of guidelines for computer forensics investigations in a report called *Good Practice Guide for Computer-Based Electronic Evidence*. The document is important because many other European law enforcement agencies have based their standard operating procedures on these guidelines.

The guidelines lay out a number of important principles of good practice. Law enforcement should maintain the digital evidence in its original format. However, in certain circumstances, when the original evidence must be accessed, it must be accessed by an expert who can clearly explain the need for his activities and be able to detail the implications of his actions on the evidence. Furthermore, all steps performed by the investigator must be meticulously documented so that a third-party could follow the same documented steps to achieve the same results. Finally, the lead investigator is responsible for ensuring that accepted scientific methods of investigation and the law are adhered to at all times.

Privacy Legislation in Asia

Internet and privacy legislation is still being developed in Asia and varies greatly from country to country.

China

China has arguably the greatest restrictions on Internet content, and the government closely monitors content that its citizens view. Censorship has become so contentious that Internet users in mainland China cannot use Google's search engine. Google moved its operations to Hong Kong in favor of reduced governmental scrutiny. Therefore, U.S. companies operating online services in China might have less information about Internet users. Conversely, India has less censorship but has instituted important privacy legislation.

India

In April 2011, India introduced new privacy legislation known as *Information Technology (Reasonable Security Practices and Procedures and Sensitive Personal Data or Information) Rules 2011*. The legislation was introduced to protect the privacy of online consumers, and it is important to know that this legislation impacts U.S. companies that outsource services to India. This legislation contains five primary tenets:

- **Privacy policy:** All organizations must maintain a privacy policy of how they process and use personal data. This policy must be posted on their website. This information can be helpful for investigators who need to find out how much information may be available about a customer that they are investigating.

- **Consent:** An individual needs to provide an organization with consent before their information is shared with a third party.

- **Consumer access and editing:** An individual has the right to access personal information being collected about them and can dispute any erroneous data.

- **Transfer of personal data:** Consent from the customer must be obtained before sensitive information is transferred to another party, and the organization must ensure that the recipient has similar standards for data privacy.

- **Security:** An organization must maintain best practices in terms of security. However, the guidelines on what exemplifies best practices are not clearly outlined.

Summary

The original legal system in the United States was primarily state based, but the move toward independence solidified the federal legal system. The U.S. Constitution was created on September 17, 1787, and was subsequently ratified by each of the colonies. The first three articles of the Constitution establish the three branches of government: (1) the legislature (Congress), which writes laws; (2) the executive (president), which approves congressional laws; and (3) the judicial branch (the Supreme Court and lower federal court), which interprets and enforces the law.

Ten amendments were added to the U.S. Constitution, which later became known as the Bill of Rights. These amendments affect individual rights and can have a tremendous impact on investigations involving computer forensics. Of particular note is the Fourth Amendment, which protects an individual from illegal searches and requires that government agents demonstrate probable cause before obtaining a warrant to conduct a lawful search. Cases that require an interpretation of the U.S. Constitution are referred to federal court.

The U.S. legal system is based on common law, also known as case law, and English law. Case decisions create a precedent and are therefore binding on future decisions in that jurisdiction. The exception to this is Louisiana, whose legal system is based upon the Napoleonic Code, which has its roots in Roman law.

A state legal system, with its own courts, co-exists with the federal legal system. State courts can provide citizens greater protections than the federal system. For example, the Supreme Court has historically ruled in favor of warrantless usage of GPS tracking devices on vehicles, whereas some states have ruled that law enforcement requires a court-issued warrant. Evidence illegally attained without a warrant is subject to the exclusionary rule, which means that it is inadmissible in court, unless the court rules that law enforcement acted in good faith.

Many criminal suspects are investigated and charged under congressional law. In terms of electronic surveillance, the Federal Wiretap Act has been amended several times to incorporate changes in technology. The Electronic Communications Privacy Act (ECPA), which includes the Stored Communications Act (SCA), was introduced to protect the rights of the individual to unlawful searches, including email searches. The Foreign Intelligence Surveillance Act (FISA) was introduced to allow for surveillance of foreign entities and has been amended several times to include electronic surveillance. Some of those changes were instituted with the introduction of the USA PATRIOT Act, which broadens the warrantless electronic surveillance powers of law enforcement.

Congressional laws have been enacted to specifically deal with computer-related crimes. Of note is the Computer Fraud and Abuse Act, which includes a provision for corporate espionage.

In terms of evidence admissibility, digital evidence needs to pass the Daubert test. Evidence is also subject to the guidelines found in the Federal Rules of Evidence (FRE). Civil cases in federal court use the Federal Rules of Civil Procedure (FRCP), which are also often used by state courts, to determine evidence admissibility. Digital evidence is not helpful to a jury in its original format, so a representation of the data is appropriate, as outlined under the Best Evidence Rule.

Over the past few years, important privacy legislation has been introduced by New York State and California, which greatly impacts digital forensics investigations. Canada and many of its territories have also implemented important privacy legislation, with important reporting requirements when it comes to data breaches. The most significant privacy legislation to impact investigations is GDPR because it limits the amount of personal information and data retention, in addition to the potential for millions in fines for violating this regulation.

Investigations involving digital forensics are different in the European Union (E.U.) because of strict E.U. privacy laws. Generally, less personal information is captured and saved electronically, so employees typically must be informed before a search of their computers can be conducted at the workplace. The E.U. has enacted tough laws with stiff penalties for anyone found possessing or distributing child pornography or endangering the safety of a minor. The Association of Chief Police Officers (ACPO) was one of the first law enforcement agencies to establish guidelines for computer forensics investigations. Many other agencies across Europe have adopted the investigative principles.

Apart from Ireland and the United Kingdom, most countries in the European Union have a legal system that has origins in Roman (civil) law.

Key Terms

Best Evidence Rule: This rule states that secondary evidence, or a copy, is inadmissible in court when the original exists.

Bill of Rights: The first 10 amendments to the Constitution that protect the rights of the individual.

burden of proof: A legal principle that implies that a defendant is innocent until proven guilty. The prosecution must prove guilt, and the defense does not have to prove anything.

certiorari: An order made by a higher court that directs a lower court or tribunal to send it court documents related to a case, for further review.

civil law: Law that is based on scholarly research, which, in turn, becomes a legal code, which is subsequently enacted by a legislature.

codified laws: Statutes that are organized by subject matter.

common law: Law based on case law and precedent, where laws are derived from court decisions.

Confrontation Clause: A Sixth Amendment clause stating that "in all criminal prosecutions, the accused shall enjoy the right…to be confronted with the witnesses against him."

constitutional law: Laws that outline the relationship among the legislative, judicial, and executive branches and also protect the rights of its citizens.

contempt of court: To violate the rules of court procedure.

Court of Justice of the European Union: Interprets European law and is the highest court in the European Union.

court order: Issued by a court and details a set of steps to be carried out by law enforcement. It is easier to obtain than a warrant because probable cause need not be demonstrated.

cross-examination: Questioning of the opposing side's witness in a trial.

curtilage: Refers to the property surrounding a house.

defendant: The person who defends himself in a lawsuit.

defense attorney: An advocate and representative for a defendant in a court case.

deliberations: The process by which the jury reviews the evidence from the trial and discusses opinions about the case.

deposition: Pretrial testimony given under oath, with both defense and prosecution attorneys present.

direct examination: Questioning of counsel's witness in a trial.

discovery: A pretrial phase in which both parties in a civil lawsuit share evidence when requested, by means of interrogations, depositions, documents, and subpoenas from parties not part of the lawsuit.

European Commission: The body that has the power to propose legislation and initiate legal proceedings against member states.

E.U. Legislature: A body comprised of the European Parliament and the Council of the European Union.

exclusionary rule: States that evidence seized and examined without a warrant or in violation of an individual's constitutional rights will often be inadmissible as evidence in court in a criminal case.

exigent circumstances: A set of conditions that allow agents to conduct a warrantless search in an emergency situation when there is risk of harm to an individual or risk of the possible destruction of evidence.

family court: Hears cases relating to family matters, including child custody, visitation, and support cases, as well as restraining orders.

Federal Rules of Civil Procedure (FRCP): A set of rules that apply to civil cases in federal district courts. These rules are promulgated by the U.S. Supreme Court.

Federal Rules of Evidence (FRE): A set of rules that determine the admissibility of evidence in both civil and criminal cases in federal court.

felony: A serious crime that generally carries a penalty of a year or more in prison.

foreperson: Usually the first juror seated and the person ultimately responsible for reporting the verdict to the judge.

fruit of the poisonous tree: A metaphorical expression to describe evidence that was initially acquired illegally, meaning that all evidence subsequently gathered at every point from that initial search is inadmissible in court.

grand jury: A relatively large jury that determines whether the conditions exist for criminal prosecution in a case.

hearsay: A statement other than one made by the declarant while testifying at the trial or hearing, offered in evidence to prove the truth of the matter asserted.

hung jury: A jury that cannot come to a unanimous decision in a criminal trial, forcing a retrial.

indictment: A charge delivered by a grand jury stating that the accused must stand trial.

Judex: A group of prominent laymen who, in Roman times, heard arguments, questioned witnesses, and then subsequently rendered a decision.

judge: A person who facilitates the trial process and ensures that the proceedings are fair and in accordance with the law.

jurisdiction: Refers to the scope of legal authority granted to an entity.

jury: A group of people put under oath to hear arguments at trial and render a verdict of guilty or not guilty.

jury sequestration: Isolating the jury and preventing external influences on their decisions.

juvenile court: A court where minors are tried by a tribunal.

knock and talk: When law enforcement does not have sufficient evidence or cannot demonstrate probable cause to enter a residence and execute a search, so they go to the suspect's home and try to get the consent of the individual to gain entry to the home and conduct a search.

misdemeanor: A less serious crime, with a possible conviction of less than a year.

motion in limine: A request by a lawyer to hold a hearing before a trial, in an effort to suppress evidence.

municipal court: Court that hears cases when a crime has occurred within its jurisdiction. Charges can include DUI, disorderly conduct, vandalism, trespassing, building code violations, and similar offenses.

pen register: An electronic device that captures telephone numbers.

plain error: When an appeals court identifies a major mistake that was made in court proceedings, even though no objection was made during the initial trial where judgment was passed. A new trial then is ordered.

plain view doctrine: Allows a government agent to seize evidence without a warrant when the officer can clearly observe contraband.

plaintiff: Person who initiates the lawsuit and is responsible for the cost of litigation.

precedent: Court decisions are binding on future decisions in a particular jurisdiction.

probable cause: The conditions under which law enforcement may obtain a warrant for a search or arrest, when it is evident that a crime has been committed.

probate court: Sometimes referred to as a surrogate court; this court hears cases relating to the distribution of a deceased's assets.

regulatory law: Governs the activities of government administrative agencies.

Rules of Criminal Procedure: Protocols for how criminal proceedings in a federal court should be conducted.

search incident to a lawful arrest: Allows law enforcement to conduct a warrantless search after an arrest has been made.

search warrant: Court order issued by a judge or magistrate authorizing law enforcement to search a person or place, as well as seize items or information within the parameters of the warrant.

small claims court: Courts that settle private disputes involving relatively small monetary amounts.

standing: Refers to a suspect's right to object to a Fourth Amendment search as outlined by the Supreme Court.

statutory law: Written law set forth by a legislature at the national, state, or local level.

Stingray: The generic name given to a device that acts like a cellphone tower to locate criminal suspects, but can also be used to locate people in disaster areas such as earthquake zones.

subpoena: A court order demanding a person to testify or to bring evidence to court.

traffic court: Court that hears cases relating to driving violations. An individual who is cited for a traffic violation can pay the fine (plead guilty) or can appeal in traffic court.

voir dire: The questioning process used in jury selection.

Assessment

CLASSROOM DISCUSSIONS

1. In this new digital age, can we assume that we have fewer protections under the Fourth Amendment?

2. What was the motivation for the Founding Fathers' creation of the Bill of Rights?

3. How could an investigation involving digital evidence be different in the European Union than in the United States?

4. Under what circumstances can a case move from a state court to federal court?

5. Under what circumstances is a warrant not required by law enforcement to conduct a search?

6. Why is the USA PATRIOT Act so contentious with the American public?

7. What is GDPR and what is its impact on investigations involving digital data?

MULTIPLE-CHOICE QUESTIONS

1. The person who initiates the lawsuit and is responsible for the cost of litigation is referred to as which of the following?

    A. Counsel

    B. Plaintiff

    C. Defendant

    D. Suspect

2. Which of the following courts hears cases relating to the distribution of a deceased individual's assets?

    A. Small claims court

    B. Municipal court

    C. Family court

    D. Probate court

3. Which of the following amendments allows an individual to freely post opinions online, as long as those opinions do not incite violence?

    A. First Amendment

    B. Second Amendment

    C. Third Amendment

    D. Fourth Amendment

4. Which of the following amendments protects the individual from government agents performing an illegal search?

    A. First Amendment

    B. Fourth Amendment

    C. Fifth Amendment

    D. Sixth Amendment

5. Which of the following best describes a court order that requires an individual to testify or make evidence available?

    A. Indictment

    B. Warrant

    C. Writ

    D. Subpoena

6. Which of the following is a set of rules that determine the admissibility of evidence in both civil and criminal cases in federal court?

    A. Federal Rules of Discovery

    B. Federal Rules of Civil Procedure

    C. Federal Rules of Evidence

    D. Federal Rules of Hearsay

7. Which of the following states that secondary evidence, or a copy, is inadmissible in court when the original exists?

    A. Exclusionary Rule

    B. Federal Rules of Evidence

    C. Hearsay Rule

    D. Best Evidence Rule

8. Which of the following entities has the power to propose legislation and initiate legal proceedings against member states?

    A. European Legislature

    B. European Commission

    C. Court of Justice of the European Union

    D. European Parliament

9. What is the name of the court that interprets European law and is the highest court in the European Union?

    A. Court of Justice of the European Union

    B. E.U. Supreme Court

    C. European State Court

    D. Council of the European Union

10. Which of the following best describes pretrial testimony given under oath, with both defense and prosecution attorneys present?

   A. Deposition

   B. Discovery

   C. Subpoena

   D. Indictment

FILL IN THE BLANKS

1. A group of people put under oath to hear arguments at trial and render a verdict of guilty or not guilty is referred to as a(n) _____.

2. The Bill of _____ refers to the first 10 amendments to the U.S. Constitution.

3. The _____ Amendment states that a defendant is not required to take the witness stand.

4. Fruit of the _____ is a metaphorical expression for evidence acquired from an illegal search.

5. _____ refers to the conditions under which law enforcement may obtain a warrant for a search or arrest when it is evident that a crime has been committed.

6. A statement other than one made by the declarant while testifying at the trial or hearing, offered in evidence to prove the truth of the matter asserted, is called _____.

7. The _____ test means that evidence does not necessarily need to have general acceptance by the scientific community but does need to meet the requirements of FRE 702.

8. _____ is the pretrial phase in which both parties in a civil lawsuit must share evidence when requested, by means of interrogations, depositions, documents, and subpoenas from parties not part of the lawsuit.

9. _____ is the name given to the property surrounding a house.

10. _____ is the generic name given to a device that acts like a cellphone tower to locate criminal suspects, but can also be used to locate people in disaster areas, such as earthquake zones.

PROJECTS

Review Court Cases of Email Evidence

Find some court cases in which email was used as evidence at trial to help convict a suspect of criminal activity.

Write an Essay about the Use of Digital Evidence

Write an essay describing how the use of digital evidence in investigations has impacted criminal cases. Include in your answer case law.

Write an Essay Detailing the Impact of Changes in Legislation

Write an essay detailing how both congressional and state legislation have changed to deal with changes in technology and the way criminal activity has changed.

Create a Chart Comparing U.S. Investigations to E.U. Investigations

Create a chart or matrix comparing how conducting an investigation is different in the U.S. from the E.U. Be as specific as possible—for example—"Cookies" would be one category.

# Chapter 8

Network Forensics and Incident Response

Learning Outcomes

After reading this chapter, you will be able to understand the following:

- The importance of network forensics;
- Hardware devices that contain network logs that are valuable to a forensic examiner;
- IPv4 and IPv6;
- The OSI Model;
- Mistakes made when investigating networks;
- Windows artifacts;
- Advanced persistent threats: perpetrators, vectors of attack, and indicators of compromise; and
- How to investigate a network intrusion.

Network forensics is extremely important, but very few people understand it. This domain of forensics is so important because of the explosion in network breaches. The Sony PlayStation breach in 2011 alone is estimated to have cost the company $170 million when more than 100 million customer records were compromised. The NotPetya ransomware attack of 2017 cost Merck as much as $1.3 billion. As a nation, we have relied on security and general information technology personnel to handle these incidents. However, with so much at stake, in terms of financial liability and bad publicity, it is imperative that organizations think more in terms of in-house forensics investigators who have the legal and technical expertise to adequately handle these breaches, especially with the risk of civil lawsuits.

The lack of expertise in the community stems from the fact that forensic examiners focus on client computers and devices during investigations and obtain server-side evidence from a variety of service providers. For example, when Hotmail email messages are required, only a court order is needed to obtain the records. The method by which this evidence is retrieved is irrelevant. Additionally, the prevalence of advanced persistent threats (APTs) means that there is a greater need for network forensics examiners. These examiners need to understand a very different file system, operating system, and type of evidence. The abbreviation *APT* includes the word *advanced*, meaning that attacks on networks are more sophisticated, with tremendous resources supporting them, and are allegedly supported by national governments, like China.

The success of economies that rely on digital information, such as the United States, will remain intact only if competent network forensics investigators are effectively trained and hired in government and corporate organizations. Universities that conduct research for the Department of Defense and other government agencies, as well as law firms that house vast quantities of intellectual property during civil litigation cases, are prime targets for government-sponsored attackers. More recently, we have read about managed service providers (MSPs) being compromised as an effective means to access related networks. A **managed service provider (MSP)** generally provides IT infrastructure services, like cloud storage, to an organization.

Finally, we should not think of network forensics as simply being associated with organizations. Home networks have grown in importance tremendously. For example, think about the "Apple Environment", which can be comprised of a Mac computer, an iPad, Apple TV, HomePod, and iCloud. A home router can be compromised to provide an attacker with a device from which to sniff traffic and modify the DNS (Domain Name System).

The subject of network forensics could take several textbooks to cover in depth. This chapter provides an overview of some of the main domains and key concepts associated with this subject.

Note

A network forensics investigator should understand the infrastructure of networks in terms of hardware and software. This knowledge will lead the investigator to know where the evidence is located.

The Tools of the Trade

There are two approaches to network forensics: (1) real-time capture and analysis, and (2) retroactive analysis of captured data. Tremendous resources are required to perform real-time analysis—you need very large storage and a lot of horsepower (RAM). To cater to the large storage requirement, you could use a RAID (redundant array of independent disks). Optimally, you will use a RAID 0, which allows for high performance, large storage, and low redundancy. Kali Linux is an open source Linux tool that is often used for real-time packet capture. However, numerous other network forensics and analysis tools also work, although many are quite expensive to purchase and maintain. These tools include the following:

- EnCase Endpoint Investigator
- RSA NetWitness
- Kibana

- Carbon Black
- Splunk

These open source tools also work well:

- tcpdump
- WinDump
- Xplico
- Wireshark
- Kismet
- TCPflow
- Ettercap
- Traceroute
- TCPtraceroute
- NGREP
- WGET
- CURL

Packet sniffers are used to capture data packets on a wireless or wired network. Wireshark and tcpdump are examples of packet sniffers. The network interface card (NIC) only responds to packets addressed to its MAC address, but a packet sniffer puts the NIC into promiscuous mode. **Promiscuous mode** enables a NIC to listen to communications broadcast on a network, regardless of the intended recipient. Packet sniffers are used in conjunction with protocol analyzers by network forensics investigators. A **protocol analyzer** is used to analyze and interpret traffic over a network.

Networking Devices

When learning about network forensics, it is imperative to learn about devices that have logging capabilities and therefore contain historical evidence for investigators. Investigators must note all of the different system times for each networking server or device. In other words, data can be routed through several networking servers, and these server timestamps will differ from one another. A defense attorney might challenge prosecutors about this on the witness stand. All of the following network devices have logging capabilities:

- Proxy servers
- Web servers

- DHCP servers

- SMTP servers

- DNS servers

- Routers

- Switches

- Hubs

- IDS

- Firewalls

Proxy Servers

A **proxy server** is a computer that relays a request for a client to a server computer. This is important to know because a suspect might actually use another user's computer, or multiple computers, as an intermediary to request information from a server. Therefore, investigators might seize a web server hosting illicit photographs of minors, but the client requests to download pages or images might show the IP addresses of unsuspecting individuals, who had their computers compromised by hackers. Squid is a caching proxy service that can be used to increase performance on a web server, by caching popular requests, and it can also cache DNS, Web, and network lookups. Web cache is of interest to forensics investigators because it can provide invaluable information about Internet activity through requests to a web server. Most proxies are web proxies. All traffic through Port 80, Port 8080, Port 80443, or Port 443 must go through a web proxy.

Web Servers

A **web server** stores and serves up HTML documents and related media resources in response to client requests. In other words, when you type a URL into your web browser, and then press Enter, a data packet is sent to that web server that includes your IP address. In turn, the webpage (HTML file and associated media files) is sent to your computer and saved in cache. For example, if you visit a friend's Facebook page, you download the HTML profile page and any photos or videos (media files) embedded on that profile page. A forensics investigator can analyze client user requests from the web server logs.

When reviewing log files on a web server, the following information can be obtained:

- Date and time

- Source IP address

- HTTP source code

- Resource requested

There are several folders on a Linux computer that will be of interest to a forensics investigation, and they are as follows:

- **/etc:** Contains system configuration files and some other file types.

- **/etc/passwd:** Configuration file that contains local user information. You can find user login information in this file. The file uses data encryption standard (DES).

- **/etc/group:** Contains user group information.

- **/etc/shadow:** You can find user login password hashes here. The file is only readable by the root user.

- **/home:** Location where all user home directories are created.

- **/.bash_history:** Logs a history of all commands that have been run in the file.

- **/etc/ssh & /.ssh:** Holds private and public keys for the host.

- **/var/log:** Contains logs of several running services. On a web server this may be Apache (a popular open source web server software) or SSH (a cryptographic network protocol for securing network communications).

- **/var/www:** Apache stores web server files and subdirectories in this folder.

- **/var/www/html:** Stores the content of a website running Apache.

Uniform Resource Identifier (URI)

A **Uniform Resource Identifier (URI)** is used to locate a resource on the Internet. The most common type of URI is a uniform resource locator (URL), which consists of the following:

- Transmission protocol (generally HyperText Transfer Protocol [HTTP])

- Colon (:)

- Two slashes (//)

- Domain name, translated to an IP address

- Resource HTML document or file, e.g., a .jpg file

Web Browsers

On the client side, a web browser is used to render the HyperText Markup Language (HTML). Before the advent of the web browser, File Transport Protocol (FTP) was used to download and upload files from servers on the Internet. Now we primarily use FTP to securely upload files to a web server. A **web browser** is used to (1) work with a DNS server to resolve DNS addresses, (2) make HyperText Transfer Protocol (HTTP) requests, (3) download resources, and (4) display the contents of the file with Browser Help Objects (BHOs). A **Browser Help Object (BHO)** is used to add functionality to a web browser; the object starts every time the user opens the browser. For example, an Adobe BHO allows users to view PDF documents within the browser window. A BHO is slightly different than a plug-in because it is specific to Internet Explorer (IE), and Microsoft provides an interface and guidelines for developers who wish to create a BHO. Microsoft Edge browser does not support ActiveX and BHO technologies.

HyperText Transfer Protocol (HTTP)

HyperText Transfer Protocol (HTTP) is a standard for requests and responses between a client and a server. HTTP contains common methods used for client-server requests. The following are referred to as "safe" methods:

- **GET:** Retrieves the resource in the requested URI.

- **HEAD:** Similar to the GET request but does not include the body of the file being requested. This can be used when testing a hypertext link.

- **OPTIONS:** Requests information about the options that are available with communications involving the URI.

Certain client methods are potentially harmful to a server and include the following:

- **POST:** Calls upon a server to accept an enclosed entity, which could be a file, in the request.

- **PUT:** Requests that an entity at a specified URI be added.

- **DELETE:** Erases a specific resource.

- **CONNECT:** Can be used to allow Transport Layer Security (TLS) communications and also can be used to create an HTTP tunnel that circumvents firewalls and intrusion detection systems.

- **TRACE:** Takes a request made by a client to be sent back by the client. However, TRACE can be used to trick a web browser into issuing a TRACE request to another site.

Status codes within HTTP inform the client about the status of a request or the server. For example, sometimes you enter a URL in your web browser and the browser displays an error code of "404", meaning that the resource being requested (the website) was not found. This is probably because the user entered an incorrect URL, or perhaps the resource has moved. A 404 error might mean that the server does not wish to disclose the reason for a resource not being found. Here are some other common HTTP status codes for client errors:

- **400:** Bad request

- **401:** Unauthorized

- **403:** Forbidden
- **405:** Method not allowed
- **406:** Not acceptable
- **407:** Proxy authentication required
- **408:** Request timeout
- **409:** Conflict
- **410:** Gone

Here are some examples of HTTP status codes on the server side:

- **500:** Internal server error
- **501:** Not implemented
- **502:** Bad gateway
- **503:** Service unavailable
- **504:** Gateway timeout
- **505:** HTTP version not supported

Scripting Language

It is important to understand how scripting languages on websites work. The vast majority of scripting languages have a legitimate purpose, like checking to see whether a client computer has an application installed (plug-in) to view embedded content, like Audacity for a sound file. Nevertheless, certain scripts can be malicious. Other scripts can be used by law enforcement to identify a suspect on a network who is using a proxy service. An investigator may be called upon to explain how scripts on a webpage were executed on a suspect's computer, or perhaps the suspect was operating a web server with malicious or illicit content.

A script can run either on the client side or on the server side. Scripting languages, like JavaScript (the most popular), JScript, or VB Script, are embedded in HTML pages to enable dynamic elements and interaction. For example, a currency or temperature converter can be created with JavaScript and is interactive because it requests a number and then converts it (output) for the client (user).

Of course, some scripts run on the server side:

- Python
- PHP (`.php`)

- PERL (`.pl`)

- Java

- Ruby

- ColdFusion Markup Language (`.cfml`)

- Active Server Pages (`.asp`/`.aspx`/`asp.net`)

DHCP Servers

Dynamic Host Configuration Protocol (DHCP) is a standard for allowing a server to dynamically assign IP addresses and configuration to hosts on a network. This dynamic addressing means that a new client can join a network without having to possess a preassigned IP address. The DHCP server assigns a unique IP address, and then after a client leaves the network, that IP address is released and can be used for a new host that enters the network. DHCP means that a network administrator does not need to manually assign IP addresses and keep track of clients using those IP addresses but can have DHCP client software perform those tasks automatically. An Internet service provider (ISP) can use DHCP to allow customers to join its networks. Similarly, on a home network, a broadband router uses DHCP to add clients to its network—these can include a PC, a smart TV, a tablet, or a smartphone. At a minimum, a DHCP server provides an IP address, subnet mask, and default gateway. A **subnet mask** facilitates the communication between segregated networks. An IP address has two parts: network and host address. A subnet mask separates an IP address into network and host addresses. We will discuss subnetting in more detail later in this chapter. The **default gateway** is the node on a network that serves as the forwarding host (router) to other networks. For example, on a home network, the default gateway might be the broadband router.

A router maintains an ARP (Address Resolution Protocol) table, which is based on ARP requests and responses. When a packet is sent across the Internet, it is sent to the MAC address of the router interface that is the default gateway. ARP binds a static IP to a MAC address in a device's ARP table. DHCP, on the other hand, always assigns the same IP address to a device. ARP is used to get the MAC address from an IP address and is primarily used on a LAN (Local Area Network).

The routing table contains the following:

- Destination network IP addresses;

- Destination gateway IP address; and

- Corresponding interface.

When the router receives a packet, it will check for the destination network IP address in the routing table. If the packet is destined for a network that is directly connected to the router, then the destination MAC address will be obtained from the ARP table. MAC addresses (Layer 2 of the OSI Model) are mapped to IP addresses (Layer 3) using ARP. ARP responses are cached on hosts that make up the LAN. The ARP cache can be queried on a Windows system to identify MAC—IP address mappings using the following command:

```
arp -a
```

You can view DHCP service activity on your personal computer by launching the Event Viewer application. As you can see in Figure 8.1, an event is created every time DHCP starts and stops.

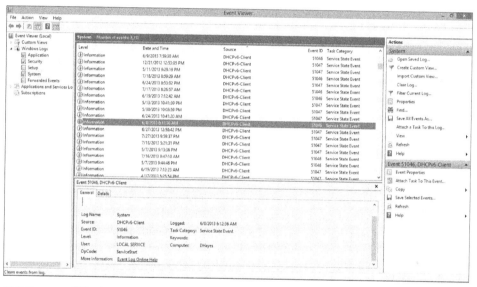

FIGURE 8.1   Windows Event Viewer: DHCP

DHCP is a client/server protocol that provides an IP host with an IP address and other configuration information, e.g. a subnet mask or default gateway. Static IP addresses are assigned to networking equipment, including routers, firewalls, and servers. Host computers, including tablets and smartphones are generally assigned a dynamic IP address.

An examination of DHCP logs will display the MAC addresses of devices that connected to a router. If an organization uses a DHCP server, then the logs, with MAC addresses, may be extensive. DHCP can be handled by a router or a server. You may be able to identify a DHCP server by monitoring traffic on Ports 67 and 68.

There are a number of known DHCP attacks, which includes DHCP poisoning and DHCP starvation. It is therefore important to understand that you might find evidence of this type of spoofing in DHCP logs. Thus, an attacker might impersonate a legitimate user, and therefore the investigator needs to be cognizant of this possibility.

Sometimes you will see the following messages in DHCP logs:

```
Message        Use
-------        ---

DHCPDISCOVER - Client broadcast to locate available servers.

DHCPOFFER    - Server to client in response to DHCPDISCOVER with
               offer of configuration parameters.

DHCPREQUEST  - Client message to servers either (a) requesting
               offered parameters from one server and implicitly
               declining offers from all others, (b) confirming
               correctness of previously allocated address after,
               e.g., system reboot, or (c) extending the lease on a
               particular network address.

DHCPACK      - Server to client with configuration parameters,
               including committed network address.

DHCPNAK      - Server to client indicating client's notion of network
               address is incorrect (e.g., client has moved to new
               subnet) or client's lease as expired

DHCPDECLINE  - Client to server indicating network address is already
               in use.

DHCPRELEASE  - Client to server relinquishing network address and
               cancelling remaining lease.

DHCPINFORM   - Client to server, asking only for local configuration
               parameters; client already has externally configured
               network address.
```

Source: https://www.ietf.org/rfc/rfc2131.txt

DHCP Logs

A DHCP server will log the following:

- Startup
- Shutdown
- DHCP leases

- DHCP assignments
- DHCP requests

On a Linux DHCP server, leases are stored in the file dhcpd.leases, which can be found here:

/var/lib/dhcp/dhcpd.leases

The configuration file is dhcpd.conf and can be found in the following directory:

/etc/

The dhcpd.conf file will provide the following information:

- Default lease time
- Maximum lease time
- Syslog* logging
- Range of dynamically allocated addresses

Syslog is used by network devices to send event messages to a logging server.

Hub

A **hub** is a hardware networking device that broadcasts data packets to all devices on a network regardless of the MAC address. A hub is a Layer 1 (OSI Model) device.

Switch

A network **switch** is an intelligent hardware device that connects devices on a network. It is also referred to as a switching hub, bridging hub, or MAC bridge. The difference between a hub and a switch is that the latter only forwards packets to the required destination device on a network. A network switch operates at the data link layer (Layer 2 of the OSI Model), although some switches can also operate at the network layer (Layer 3 of the OSI Model). Content Addressable Memory (CAM) is a type of memory used by Cisco switches, and a CAM address table may be available for an investigator to analyze.

SMTP Servers

A **Simple Mail Transport Protocol (SMTP) server** is used to send email for a client. The email is subsequently routed to another SMTP server or other email server. For example, when you use Microsoft Outlook to send an email, this email application informs an SMTP server of the sender and recipient email addresses, as well as the body of the message. When sending an email to another domain (for instance, an email from Hotmail to Yahoo!), the SMTP server communicates with a DNS server and requests the IP address of the SMTP server. The DNS then responds with the IP address or addresses for SMTP servers that Yahoo! (in this example) operates. SMTP servers communicate with one another using simple commands, like HELO (introduction), MAIL FROM: (specify the sender), RCPT TO: (specify the recipient), QUIT (quit the session), HELP (get help), VRFY (verify the address), and DATA (To, From, Subject, Body of message). Internet Message Access Protocol (IMAP) allows the user to access email from just about any type of Internet-enabled device. With IMAP, the user's email is stored on an email server, and when an email message is requested, it is only temporarily downloaded to the user's device. Post Office Protocol (POP) is a different electronic mail standard because the email is stored on the user's device, not on the server. Some email services, like Gmail, can be set as a POP or IMAP email service by the user.

Electronic Mail (Email)

Analyzing email requires some knowledge of network forensics. The following listing shows a sample email that we will analyze from a network forensics perspective. Comments explaining certain parts are explained after the example:

```
1) Received: (qmail 29610 invoked by uid 30297); 27 Jul 2013 19:13:41 -0000
2) Received: from unknown (HELO p3plibsmtp01-05.prod.phx3.secureserver.net)
[ic:ccc] ([10.6.12.128])
3) (envelope-sender <dhhayes@pace.edu>)
4) by p3plsmtp10-06.prod.phx3.secureserver.net (qmail-1.03) with SMTP
5) for <dhayes@codedetectives.edu>; 27 Jul 2013 19:13:41 -0000
6) Received: from coloutboundpool.messaging.microsoft.com ([216.32.180.188])
16) Received: from mail22-co1-R.bigfish.com (10.243.78.243) by
17) CO1EHSOBE025.bigfish.com (10.243.66.88) with Microsoft SMTP Server id
22) X-Forefront-Antispam-Report: CIP:198.105.43.6;KIP:(null);UIP:(null);IPV:NLI;H:
exchnycsmtp1.pace.edu;RD:none;EFVD:NLI
55) MIME-Version: 1.0
58) X-FOPE-CONNECTOR: Id%0$Dn%*$RO%0$TLS%0$FQDN%$TlsDn%
63) Hello
64) Dr. Sherlock Holmes | sholmes@pace.edu<mailto:sholmes@pace.edu> | Dir=
65) Assistant Professor | The Moors | (212) 555-1234=
66) | Fax (212) 555-1234 | Pace University, 163 William Street, New =
67) York, NY 10038
68) Visit Us Online: http://www.pace.edu/pace/seidenberg/
72) <html dir=3D"ltr">
73) <head>
81) 10pt;">Hello<br>
136) </body>
137) </html>
```

Line 1: This is the start of the email header. The reference to qmail refers to mail software running on UNIX. The email includes unique IDs that should correspond to IDs in the server logs.

Line 2: This lists the IP address of the receiving server, which is as follows:

```
p3plibsmtp01-05.prod.phx3.secureserver.net
```

When initiating communication, the client uses the HELO command with the SMTP server.

Line 3: This is the sender of the email.

Line 4: Once again, this indicates the name of the server receiving the email for the recipient and shows that the SMTP messaging protocol is being used in transmission of this email.

Line 5: Here you see the email address of the recipient, along with the date and time the message was received.

Line 6: The IP address 216.32.180.188 is displayed, with domain name of co1ehsobe005.messaging. microsoft.com. If you type 216.32.180.188.ipaddress.com into the browser, you can see that Microsoft hosts the server and that it is located in Chesterfield, Missouri.

Lines 16–17: You can see several references to BigFish.com, which is a Microsoft Exchange Server. You can check by visiting http://who.is/whois/bigfish.com/. You can therefore assert that the sender of the email is using Microsoft Exchange (Outlook).

Line 22: You can see that Microsoft Forefront (a cloud service to protect companies from viruses, spam, and phishing scams) software has inspected the email. You can also see that the email was sent by an email server at pace.edu (exchnycsmtp1.pace.edu), which corresponds later to the name of the sender—ddhayes@pace.edu, noted in Line 41. This is important because it appears that this email has not been spoofed by the sender.

Line 55: You can see MIME noted. **Multipurpose Internet Mail Extensions (MIME)** is an electronic email protocol that extends character sets beyond ASCII and supports email attachments.

Line 58: This line includes a reference to FOPE-CONNECTOR. Microsoft Forefront Online Protection for Exchange (FOPE) has connectors for advanced email functionality.

Lines 63–68: These lines contain the body of the email.

Lines 72–137: These lines show the body of the message in an HTML format. If the sender had sent the message in plain text, this HTML code would not have been generated.

It should be noted that the header in an email can be spoofed. DomainKeys Identified Mail (DKIM) is a tool used to authenticate that a specific sender and domain, noted in the email, did in fact actually send an email.

DNS Servers

The **Domain Name System (DNS)** is a naming system for computers and other devices connected to the Internet. One function of DNS is to convert domain names to IP addresses. For example, the IP address for the domain name www.pace.edu is actually 198.105.44.27 (IPv4), but we use letter names because it is easier to remember when surfing the Internet. DNS servers are also referred to as nameservers. A DNS server will point a client to either the company that a domain was registered to or to the company that hosts their Website. Zone files contain the domain's DNS settings.

DNS maintains different types of records. A primary "A" record is called "@" and this controls what your domain name does when a client visits your website. An "A" record provides the mappings between host names and IPv4 addresses. CNAMEs point your subdomains to a different server. "AAAA" records provide the mappings between host names and IPv6 addresses. "MX" records are mail exchange records, which are used to determine the priority of email servers for a domain. "PTR" records resolve an IP address to a domain name, which is the opposite of a client request to a server (domain name → server).

DNS is sometimes referred to as a query-response protocol. Generally, a client sends a request with a single UDP packet, and then the server responds with a single UDP packet. With larger systems, the server may respond via TCP.

As you can see in Figure 8.2, Windows Event Viewer records DNS resolution services.

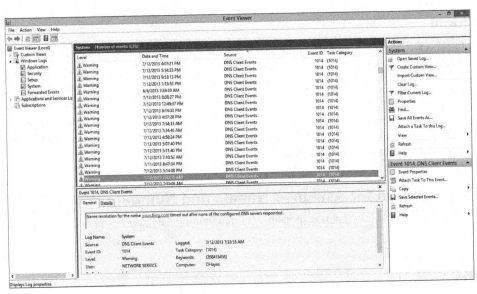

FIGURE 8.2 Windows Event Viewer: DNS resolution service

The Hosts File

The **hosts file** is a text file found on Windows that maps hostnames to IP addresses. It is an operating system file. The host name may be mapped to both IPv4 and IPv6 addresses. Thus, the domain name resolution may occur on the host side. Sometimes a systems administrator may modify this file and the IP mappings. Unfortunately, hackers have also been known to compromise this file to redirect client computers. On a Windows PC (Windows XP and up), the file can be found here:

%SystemRoot%\System32\drivers\etc\hosts

On an Apple Macintosh, a similar file can be found here:

/private/etc/hosts

With DNS domains, there is a hierarchical structure. At the top are root nodes. Then we have "top level domain" nodes, e.g. .com, .net, .org. A top-level domain contains "domain nodes", which are also referred to as "zones", e.g., google.com. Within each domain there may be "sub-domains", e.g. accounts.google.com.

DNS servers are referred to as "nameservers" and points a client to the company that controls the DNS settings, which is often the company that the domain name was registered to. Alternatively, the nameserver may be the company that hosts your website. A zone files are files that contains all of your domain's DNS settings. A record will point your domain or sub-domain name to a specific server. There is always a primary A Record called "@" and controls what actions your domain name performs when a client visits. CNAMEs point your subdomains to a different server.

DNS Protocol

DNS is sometimes referred to as a query-response protocol. The client typically sends a request with a single UDP packet, and the server response generally fits into a single UDP packet. Again, UDP is a Layer 3 protocol. If the server response is too large to fit into a single packet, then the response may be sent via a TCP connection. An example of this is when a request is made for an AXFR record, which is also known as "zone transfer". This query is basically a client request to send information about a particular domain. However, DNS over TCP Port 53 is often blocked by the administrator to prevent disclosure of DNS information to potential hackers.

Internet Corporation for Assigned Names and Numbers (ICANN)

ICANN is a non-profit organization that is responsible for maintaining databases related to namespaces on the Internet.

Traceroute

Traceroute is a tool used to track the path of IP packets from one system to another. Traceroute can be used to diagnose issues with transmitting IP packets.

Routers

A **router** is hardware that connects a network to one or more other networks and directs data packets from one node to another. The router inspects each packet, and then directs that packet based on the IP address contained in each packet. **DHCP** is a client/server protocol that provides an IP host with an IP address and other configuration information, e.g. a subnet mask or default gateway. Static IP addresses are assigned to networking equipment, like routers, firewalls, and servers. Host computers, including tablets and smartphones are generally assigned a dynamic IP address.

Secure Data Transmission

Secure Data Transmission is the process of sending data over a secure channel, whereby the channel remains secure with the use of encryption. In wireless networks, secure data transmission is facilitated with the protocol Wi-Fi Protected Access (WPA/WPA2/WPA3), while Web-based transmission often relies on Transport Layer Security (TLS). When you are on the Web, you can tell if you are using TLS because a website will have "https" at the start of the URL. The purpose of secure data transmission is to prevent eavesdropping and confidential data from being leaked to hackers.

Pretty Good Privacy (PGP) Encryption

PGP is an encryption program that is used for the secure transmission of email and encryption of files, directories, and volumes (disks). PGP is the most widely used email encryption program in the world. In 1991, Phil Zimmermann created the PGP program and made it freely available to the public. It also became popular outside of the USA. Given that PGP uses an RSA encryption algorithm, RSA Data Security sued Pretty Good Privacy for patent infringement in a licensing dispute (https://cryptome.org/jya/rsavpgp.htm). Interestingly, the United States Customs Service then initiated a criminal investigation against Zimmermann for violating the Arms Export Control Act and termed cryptographic software as "munitions". Thus, Zimmermann was suspected of "arms trafficking" and arrested at Washington's Dulles Airport by U.S. Customs agents. Fortunately for him, he was arriving into the USA. If he had been leaving the USA, with PGP encrypted files, then he could have been arrested on federal charges for exporting weapons without a license. Charges against Zimmermann were later dropped, and he was never indicted. Zimmermann later went on to work for Silent Circle, the company that created the Blackphone (encrypted smartphone).

How Does PGP Work?

PGP combines symmetric key encryption and public key encryption. The message is first encrypted with symmetric key encryption. The symmetric key is a one-time-only session key that is sent to the receiver during transmission, and the message is also encrypted with the receiver's public key. The receiver can only decrypt the symmetric (session) key with their private key. PGP also uses a digital signature, using either RSA or DSA algorithms to ensure message authentication. PGP also supports integrity checking to ensure that the message was not altered during transmission; if the message was altered, then the receiver will not be able to decrypt the message.

PGP and the Dark Web

PGP is of particular interest to investigators because it is widely used for secure email communication between Dark Web marketplace vendors and their customers; PGP is used to prevent eavesdropping by law enforcement. These vendors have made their PGP public key available on Dark Web marketplaces, like Hansa, Honest Cocaine, and AlphaBay. Kleopatra is a tool, which is available from OpenPGP, that can extract the email address used to generate a PGP key, using the public PGP key.

What Does a PGP Key Look Like?

Figure 8.3 shows an example from a Dark Web marketplace vendor:

MaryJane400,36345,8,8,March 19, 2015,698299060,No information,
MaryJane400@jwchat.org,http://ogjfsfodjgsjdfkkf.onion,{$KEY},{$DATA}

| {$KEY} | -----BEGIN PGP PUBLIC KEY BLOCK-----
Version: BCPG C# v1.6.1.0

zTEXVFSWKO0BCADA9xL1i2FlIRSDeaLS5oh8uyBFh2zVlwLGiexQ1dgT1RYiFngO
yccdhpD3a9JqnHFW0FQOYBeYetMIajkCyzJnTLjPZPidipyISeWRd+−UYI0I9bJb
k6MIKFyVs06ofM4kq43bf2g5PTSAZKo5kYuFZfn7TSR5vdTpB14oMpzy0QGb1kO/
+gCXXrA58g6EhnUiqGjIBP6hsdUh+3+g0Y4UWeJd/rqntzx8nMDWBWmLaJnshRvZ
nVRdqcqe3AtvncOV57yCdQic2C0vrj9jdPblQcPZ0wntA0+gNePRKMxV2gD439Gj
Xi5EvBY8S6HK8Dj1nIWYzfRXQY2Y−XrdP/P7ABEBAAG0FHJlZHNvbkBzYWZlLW1h
aWwubmV0iQEcBBABAgAGBQJUFijtAAoJEDgJmV8Xfj+XBRYIAJjdWz8−3GxK/GRx
zQKjWDQTxxT5WT/6UKOR5Re/Ei7T7vF2−/6C0bxQpOb7tY5qCFbJQ58fzRQlzZE−
yXZbdNe09WbDhcu+8ZtPVODwB3upbs6fG7UMm2roalo6I−i3LWaeIL+VOSd7RL0w
HCg9Fwc4mn+MTlE7qsr15yCg5z7mPzGXZze9qD+g8SsGYbMmOKaR5wE7bX7yUNRi
47yW7sVCwrgIpEbGtt34QXnm0lxLrbh855voqSayuQvc7ua9CF0dmGdC1F6YggNY
fpIWzl6NfxLWahoaOv4YJm4udCiA3+gUlZDipTAKMIV20yL6zPBmJbZphwJzvvgQ
tODm9yA=
=PeRO
-----END PGP PUBLIC KEY BLOCK----- |
| {$DATA} | ##
CONTACT ME :
SHOP : http://sdfjj.su / http://rrthdfgfdtllnoqyuu.onion
JID : MaryJane400@jwchat.org
EML : MaryJane400@safe-mail.net - MaryJane400@dotanota.de
ICQ : 598277020
|

FIGURE 8.3   Example of a PGP key

OpenPGP

Patent issues associated with using RSA encryption licensing issues have continued to be a concern. Thus, PGP Inc. approached the IETF and proposed a new standard called OpenPGP. There is now an OpenPGP Working Group, which is administered by the IETF.

IPv4

Currently, most traffic on the Internet uses IPv4. **Internet Protocol version 4 (IPv4)** is the fourth version protocol for connectionless data transmission on packet-switched internetworks. A **packet** is a block of data transmitted across a network. On the Internet, these packets are transmitted in sequence, and each packet is uniform in size and structure. An IP packet (block of data sent across the Internet) contains a header section and a data section. An IPv4 header has 14 fields, as outlined in Figure 8.4.

Octet	0				1				2				3			
Bit	0 1 2 3	4 5 6 7	8 9 10 11	12 13 14 15	16 17 18 19	20 21 22 23	24 25 26 27	28 29 30 31
0	Version	IHL	DSCP	ECN	Total Length			
32	Identification				Flags	Fragment Offset		
64	Time To Live		Protocol		Header Checksum			
96	Source IP Address							
128	Destination IP Address							
160	Options (if IHL > 5)							

FIGURE 8.4   IPv4 header

- *Version:* The version (a value of 4 bits shows that it is IPv4).

- **Internet Header Length (IHL):** The length of the header.

- **Differentiated Services Code Point (DSCP):** Differentiated Services (DiffServ) code for real-time data streaming.

- **Explicit Congestion Notification (ECN):** An optional feature that allows for notification of network congestion.

- **Total Length:** A 16-bit field that denotes the size of the packet (header and data).

- **Identification:** A unique identifier.

- **Flags:** A unique identifier used to identify fragments.

- **Fragment Offset:** A 13-bit value used to specify the offset of a fragment.

- **Time To Live (TTL):** The time that a datagram may live. A router decrements this number and discards the packet when it reaches 0.

- **Protocol:** The protocol used in the data part of the IP datagram, as defined by IANA.

- **Header Checksum:** Used for error checking by the router.

- **Source IP Address:** The sender's IP address.

- **Destination IP Address:** The recipient's IP address.

- **Options:** Infrequently used but can hold data from the IHL.

IPv4 uses 32-bit addresses, which are usually represented in four octets of dotted decimal notation—see the previous example for www.pace.edu, where 198.105.44.27 is an IPv4 address.

IPv4 uses 32-bit addresses, which are usually represented in four octets of dotted decimal notation, like the example above for www.pace.edu where 198.105.44.27 is an IPv4 address. An IPv4 address is broken into two parts: (1) Network and (2) Host. The host refers to a specific device on a network. For example, a device could be a computer, fax machine or printer. IANA (Internet Assigned Numbers Authority) is the organization responsible for assigning IP addresses (iana.org). IANA assigns blocks of IP addresses to Regional Internet Registries (RIRs), which in turn allocate IP addresses within their region:

- AfriNic (Africa)

- APNIC (Asia Pacific)

- ARIN (North America)

- LACNIC (Latin America & Caribbean)

- RIPE (Europe)

Subnet Mask

Subnetting allows an administrator to create multiple (logical) networks within a Class A, B, C network. The subnet mask is used by TCP/IP to locate a specific host on a subnet. Ultimately, the purpose of the subnet mask is to determine where the network part of an address ends and where the individual device address begins. An IP address is comprised of 32 binary bits. These 32 bits can be divided into four octets (1 octet = 8 bits). The value of each octet ranges from 0 to 255 decimal, i.e. 00000000 – 11111111 (binary).

In the first example below, we convert an octet when all bits are set to 1.

1	1	1	1	1	1	1	1
2^7	2^6	2^5	2^4	2^3	2^2	2^1	2^0
128	64	32	16	8	4	2	1

128 + 64 + 32 + 16 + 8 + 4 + 2 + 1 = **255**

Here is another example where all bits are not set to 1. As you can see, we use the same formula and multiply the binary value (top row) by the value in the third row (128, 64, …)

0	1	0	0	0	0	1	0
2^7	2^6	2^5	2^4	2^3	2^2	2^1	2^0
128	64	32	16	8	4	2	1

64 + 2 = **66**

Class A Network

For a Class A network, which has a major network address range of 1.0.0.0 - 127.255.255.255, the first octet is for the network. Octets 2, 3, and 4 (24 bits) are for the network manager to divide into subnets and hosts.

Class A network addresses have more than 65,536 hosts.

Class B Network

For a Class B network, which has a major network address range of 128.0.0.0 - 191.255.255.255, the first two octets are for the network. Therefore, octets 3 and 4 (16 bits) are for the network manager to divide into subnets and hosts.

Class B network addresses have between 256 and 65,534 hosts.

Class C Network

For a Class C network, which has a major network address range of 192.0.0.0 - 223.255.255.255, the first three octets are for the network. Therefore, octet 4 (8 bits) is for the network manager to divide into subnets and hosts.

Class C networks addresses have less than 254 hosts.

Network Masks

The default masks are as follows:

Class A: 255.0.0.0 (or 11111111.00000000.00000000.00000000 in binary)

Class B: 255.255.0.0

Class C: 255.255.255.0

An example of a Class A network that has no subnet is 8.20.15.1 255.0.0.0:

8.20.15.1 = 00001000.00010100.00001111.00000001

255.0.0.0 = 11111111.00000000.00000000.00000000

The network id (8) is in bold, and the remaining octets represent the host id (20.15.1), which is in italics.

In Table 8.1, the first column indicates the class of network, while the second column shows the IP address range. For example, an IP address that looks like 101.x.x.x is a Class A address. We will discuss the "Mask" in column three shortly, but basically it means that a Class A network may assign many more hosts/IPs on a network than a Class B or Class C network.

Column four shows the possible number of hosts for each class of IP address. Therefore, in a Class C network, only the last octet can be used for the host address.

TABLE 8.1   Network Address Classes for IP Ranges in IPv4

Class	IP Range	Mask	Addresses in Each Network
A	1–127	N.H.H.H	16,777,216
B	128–191	N.N.H.H	65,536
C	192–223	N.N.N.H	256
D	224–239	Multicasting	
E	240–255	Experimental	

N = Network, H = Host

Given that IANA has run out of IP addresses to assign, it is important to use a system called NAT. **Network Address Translation (NAT)** allows multiple network devices on a network to share a single IP address (see RFC 1631). Thus, a device, like a router, can use that one IP address, which may represent a plethora of network devices. A computer that is on an internal network can use private IP addresses in the range of 10.0.0.0–10.255.255.255 and some other ranges. Using the NAT process, the router will change the private IP address to a public IP address. The router also generates a source port number. NAT is used to overcome the shortage of IP addresses associated with IPv4. A NAT operates in a similar fashion as someone calling the main telephone number of a business, asking for a specific employee, and then being transferred to that employee.

Originally, IP addresses were allocated disproportionately because some companies were assigned Class A and Class B network IP addresses, which are not being utilized to their full potential. Class A network IP addresses were assigned in the 1990s to organizations that include General Electric (GE), IBM, Apple, Ford Motor Company, and the Department of Defense (DoD). Thus, does Ford really need more than 16 million unique addresses for their network? Probably not.

Reserved IP Addresses

There are some IP addresses that cannot be used to identify computers on a network, e.g., 127.x.x.x, e.g., 127.0.0.1 = localhost. Also, any IP address where the host portion is all 1s in binary, e.g. 255.255.255.255 (broadcast addresses). Similarly, any IP address when the network part is all 0s in binary cannot be used, e.g., 0.0.0.0.

There are also some private IP addresses that cannot be used on the Internet and these ranges are as follows:

- 10.0.0.0–10.255.255.255

- 172.16.0.0–172.31.255.255

- 192.168.0.0–192.168.255.255

- 169.254.0.0–169.254.255.255

These IP addresses are not routable but can be used on an internal network. The third category of IP addresses is used by business and home networks and can be used when a DHCP server is unavailable. The fourth category is used by different companies, including Microsoft, Apple, and Linux, who all have their own different schemes for using the IP addresses. **APIPA (Automatic Private IP Addressing)** is the scheme used by Microsoft Windows and allows DHCP to self-configure to an IP address and subnet mask when a DHCP server is unavailable.

Calculate an IP Subnet Mask

Let us take some time to determine the class of network for an IPv4 address.

1. Determine the network class (A, B or C)

    a. Class A: IP Address begins with 1-126

       1.0.0.0 - 127.255.255.255

    b. Class B: IP Address begins with 128-191

       128.0.0.0 - 191.255.255.255

    c. Class C: IP Address begins with 192-223

       192.0.0.0 - 223.255.255.255

2. Let's use Ireland.com as an example. Using mxtoolbox.com we can determine that the IP address is 193.120.44.197. We can tell that it is a Class C IP Address (begins with "193").

3. The subnet mask in a binary format is as follows:

111111111111111111111111100000000

4. To make it more readable we separate the binary string into groups of 8 bits:

11111111.11111111.11111111.00000000

5. The binary number 11111111 = 255

6. The binary number 00000000 = 0

Thus 11111111.11111111.11111111.00000000 can be represented as:

255.255.255.0

7. For a Class C IP address, the standard subnet mask will be 255.255.255.0 (see above).

How to Find the Subnet Mask on a Windows Computer

1. Go to the Run box (Windows Key + R).

2. Type **cmd** to open the Command Prompt.

3. Type the command **ipconfig /all** and press the **Enter** key.

MAC (Media Access Control) Addresses

A MAC address is a unique identifier (48-bit (6 byte) number) for network-enabled devices. These devices operate at the Data Link Layer (Layer 2). These network hardware devices can include the following:

- Router
- PC
- Smartphone
- Printer

How do I find the MAC address for a device?

Usually it is printed on the back or bottom of the device.

What does a MAC address look like?

BC:9E:EF:88:6E:0F

How do I find the MAC address on a PC?

For Windows 10:

1. Click the **Start** button.

2. In the taskbar Search box, type **cmd** and select the Command Prompt App. This will open the command window.

3. At the command prompt, type **ipconfig/all.**

4. Copy down the "physical address" (aka the MAC address) from the "Wireless LAN Adapter Local Area Connection" section (see Figure 8.5).

5. Close the Command Prompt window.

FIGURE 8.5   Finding the MAC Address on a Windows 10 PC

How do I find the MAC address on an Apple Macintosh?

1. From the **Apple** menu, select **System Preferences**.

2. In **System Preferences**, from the **View** menu, select **Network**.

3. In the left of the "Network" window that opens, click the name of your connection (e.g. Wi-Fi, AirPort, Ethernet, Built-in Ethernet).

4. Click **Advanced**, and in the sheet that appears, click the **Hardware**, **Ethernet**, or **AirPort** tab.

The address is the string of letters and numbers next to "MAC Address:", "Ethernet ID:", or "AirPort ID:"

How do I find the MAC address on an iPhone?

1. Click **Settings**.

2. Click **General**.

3. Click **About**.

4. View the "Wi-Fi Address", i.e. the MAC address.

Notice that the Bluetooth address is only one letter off the Wi-Fi MAC address. Thus, if you have one, you can determine the other.

IPv6

IPv6 is the latest version and, like IPv4, was developed by the Internet Engineering Task Force (IETF). It was developed in response to the limited number of IP addresses associated with IPv4 (4,294,967,296 available addresses). The **Internet Assigned Numbers Authority (IANA)** is responsible for the allocation of IP addresses globally. All devices operating on the Internet need an IP address.

IPv6 is a 128-bit address and, therefore, has 2^{128} addresses available. The example of 198.105.44.27 converts to 2002:C669:2C1B:0:0:0:0:0 in IPv6. As you can see from this example, an IPv6 address has eight groupings of four hexadecimal digits, and semicolons are used to separate each grouping.

NetFlow is a helpful tool for network forensics investigators because it can capture transactions for IP network traffic. Cisco developed the tool in 1996, but it works with NetFlow-compatible routers and switches. Regardless of the manufacturer, most routers are NetFlow compatible. NetFlow version 9 has become the basis for an IETF standard called Internet Protocol Flow Information eXport (IPFIX). NetFlow is particularly helpful with incident response because it can potentially capture all connection activity between nodes on a network. This network flow activity is then forwarded to a collector, a server that captures, processes, and saves these transactions. The data stored includes the source and destination IP, source and destination ports, IP protocol used, and type of service, but not the content of packets saved. NetFlow is beneficial when full packet capture is not feasible.

IDS

An **intrusion detection system (IDS)** is hardware or software used to monitor network traffic for malicious activity. An IDS can provide alerts when suspicious activity occurs and provide detailed logging information with professional reporting capabilities. An IDS is generally a sophisticated system, in that these systems can alert the network administrator to anomalies on the network relative to normal activity instead of simply being preprogrammed. An IDS can work either heuristically or with predetermined signatures. This is important because anomalies differ from network to network. For example, data being transmitted from a government facility in the United States to China may trigger an alert, whereas Internet traffic between a U.S. university and Beijing may be an everyday occurrence. The IDS monitors both inbound and outbound network traffic.

Naturally, the IDS, with its logs and reports, is one of the first items a network forensics examiner analyzes. The efficacy of an IDS or an intrusion prevention system (IPS) is diminished by encryption because of the system's inability to inspect these packets. In these cases, logs from network monitoring tools can be invaluable. FireEye provides one of these tools that checks for malware. Unfortunately, in the case of Target Stores, alerts from FireEye were largely ignored, and the data theft of millions of customers continued after the company was notified.

Many different types of IDS exist, and they all work in very different ways:

- Network intrusion detection system (NIDS)
- Network node intrusion system (NNIDS)
- Host-based intrusion detection system (HIDS)
- Intrusion prevention system (IPS)

Network Intrusion Detection System (NIDS)

The NIDS operates in promiscuous mode. Promiscuous mode means that a network adapter can capture and read all data packets on a particular network. A Network Intrusion Detection System (NIDS) is used to monitor the traffic on a subnet by matching that network traffic with known attacks. If an attack is identified, then the network administration is alerted.

Network Node Intrusion System (NNIDS)

A Network Node Intrusion System (NNIDS) is used to monitor traffic between a network and a host. One example of an NNIDS would be use for monitoring traffic connected to a VPN.

Host-Based Intrusion Detection System (HIDS)

A Host Intrusion System (HIDS) works on the premise of taking a snapshot of a system at a specific point in time and then compares the current snapshot with a previous snapshot to identify if any system-critical files were either modified or deleted. Often HIDSs are placed on critical systems to monitor changes.

Intrusion Prevention System (IPS)

An Intrusion Prevention System (IPS) is a network security tool that is placed in direct communication between the source and destination to detect attacks. Unlike the passive IDS, an IPS takes automated actions when a threat is discovered, which may include alerting the network administrator, dropping suspected malicious packets, blocking traffic, or resetting a connection.

Firewalls

A **firewall** is a software or hardware mechanism used to inspect data packets on a network and determine, based on its set of rules, whether each packet should be allowed through. The network administrator can set these rules. For example, an administrator might prohibit inbound/outbound traffic from IP addresses from China. Chinese hackers have been known to get around this by using Google Groups and other U.S. IP addresses for command and control so that they can access a network without being flagged by the firewall. The network administrator should add known malware sites to the firewall as blocked websites. These malware sites are published on websites, like www.malwaredomainlist.com, and are also available from federal law enforcement.

A firewall can perform detailed inspection at Layer 4 (TCP and ICMP), while other firewalls can inspect Layer 7 data, including FTP and DNS requests. A firewall is sometimes used to implement a Virtual Private Network (VPN).

One of the first things that a hacker may try to do is to change the firewall settings so that they can send and receive data without interruption. A network forensics examiner will check to see if the firewall rules have been changed. A firewall can be built into an operating system or could be a part of a network router.

There are different types of firewalls:

- Proxy firewalls
- Stateful inspection firewalls
- Unified threat management (UTM)
- Next-generation firewalls (NGFW)

A proxy firewall is a server and acts as an intermediary between a user and an Internet connection. Stateless firewalls monitor traffic and unblock packets based on the source and destination addresses or other predetermined values. A stateless firewall filter is often referred to as an access control list. A stateful firewall monitors traffic streams in an end-to-end fashion. These firewalls can support IP security or IPsec functions, which includes encryption and tunnels. Stateful firewalls are generally better at flagging unauthorized communications. Unified threat management (UTM) provides multiple layers of security, and its functionality includes content filtering, Web filtering, and antivirus. UTM devices are marketed as network security appliances, which can be a network hardware appliance, virtual appliance, or cloud service. Unified threat management can include intrusion detection and intrusion prevention technologies. For example, they may detect an attack, based on malware signatures or other anomalies. UTM also supports virtual private network (VPN) functionality. In terms of Web filtering for content, some UTMs can scan websites for security vulnerabilities that may be harmful to the requesting computer. Next-generation firewalls (NGFW) are third generation firewalls, which are a mix of a traditional firewall, while incorporating other security applications. This includes deep packet inspection, which is an intrusion prevention system (IPS). An NGFW goes beyond the capabilities of a stateful firewall. A next generation firewall has the ability to block high-risk applications. Thus, an NGFW may detect and block network attacks, based on protocol, port, and application levels. An NGFW can perform full packet inspection by checking both the signatures and payload of packets to detect anomalies or even malware.

Firewall Evidence

An investigator can retrieve the following evidence from a firewall:

- **Access Control Lists:** determine traffic allowed and blocked traffic;
- **Packet logs:** include the origin/destination address, timestamps, packet size, and protocols; and
- **Data content:** if it is a Layer 7 firewall.

Ports

A **port** is a communication channel that is specific to a running process or application on a computer. Ports are extremely important for network forensics investigators because ports that are typically not used by a system but have been active can indicate a compromise. The number of the port in system logs also indicates the type of application that was running on a computer. A total of 65,535 ports exist. The following is a list of commonly used ports:

- **20 and 21:** File Transfer Protocol (FTP)
- **22:** Secure Shell (SSH)
- **23:** Telnet remote login service
- **25:** Simple Mail Transfer Protocol (SMTP)
- **53:** Domain Name System (DNS) service
- **80:** Hypertext Transfer Protocol (HTTP), used on the World Wide Web
- **110:** Post Office Protocol (POP3)
- **143:** Internet Message Access Protocol (IMAP)
- **443:** HTTP Secure (HTTPS)

Port 80 is often used the most by clients because it is associated with a user's Internet activity. Most webmail today uses SSL and Port 443.

Understanding the OSI Model

The **Open Systems Interconnection (OSI) Model** is a model used to define how data is transmitted across the Internet. This standard was introduced in 1984 by the International Organization for Standardization (ISO). The ISO introduced the notion that we communicate across the Internet using seven layers. (Other groups have a different model with fewer layers.) It is important to understand the different layers of communication (see Figure 8.6) because a forensics examiner might need to explain to a jury how we can be sure that an email received by the victim did, in fact, come from the criminal suspect. To do that, you would need to explain the header information in an email and tell how that message is routed through different hardware. I can send you an email, but how can you prove that the email was actually sent from me? A helpful way to remember the layers is APSTNDP—*All People Seem To Need Data Processing* or *A Priest Saw Three Nuns Doing Pushups.*

OSI Model

| Application Layer |
| Presentation Layer |
| Session Layer |
| Transport Layer |
| Network Layer |
| Data Link Layer |
| Physical Layer |

FIGURE 8.6   The OSI model

The Physical Layer

The **Physical Layer** (Layer 1) defines the hardware or medium through which data is transmitted and the power required for transmission. That power often is in the form of electrical impulses defined by 0s and 1s (binary). Physical hardware can include the following:

- Coaxial cable
- Fiber optic
- Ethernet cable
- Network Interface Card (NIC)

The Data Link Layer

Address Resolution Protocol (ARP) is a method by which the Network Layer (Layer 3) of the OSI is linked to the Data Link Layer (Layer 2). In other words, when you are using the Internet on your home network, the request is sent with an IP address for your home network. When the web server responds and sends a message back to that IP address, the router needs to route that message to the appropriate device on that network using ARP (that is, routing the message to the appropriate MAC address for the specific device that requested the information).

Two addresses are used on a LAN, a MAC address and an IP address. At the Data Link Layer, MAC addresses are used to find a destination computer listed in a table called the ARP cache. A MAC address is stored in the network card. Applications use an IP address to find a destination computer.

A router maintains an ARP table, which is based on ARP requests and responses. When a packet is sent across the Internet, it is sent to the MAC address of the router interface that is the default gateway. ARP binds a static IP to a MAC address in a device's ARP table. DHCP on the other hand always assigns the same IP address to a device. ARP is used to get the MAC address from an IP address and is primarily used on a LAN (local area network).

The routing table contains the following:

- Destination network IP addresses;

- Destination gateway IP address; and

- Corresponding interface.

When the router receives a packet, it will check for the destination network IP address in the routing table. If the packet is destined for a network that is directly connected to the router, then the destination MAC address will be obtained from the ARP table. MAC addresses from Layer 2 are mapped to Layer 3 IP addresses using ARP. ARP responses are cached on hosts that make up the LAN. The ARP cache can be queried on a Windows system, to identify MAC to IP address mappings using the **arp –a** command.

The Network Layer

The **Network Layer** defines communications between networks or operation of the subnet and makes decisions about the physical path through which transmission should occur. At the Network Layer, logical addresses are translated to physical addresses. At this layer, routing frames between networks and frame fragmentation decisions are made.

Routers operate at this layer. A router is a hardware device with a motherboard, a central processing unit (CPU), and input/output ports. Routers also have memory, which contains startup configurations, operating system, and routing tables. A **routing table** contains information about the network and provides the most effective method of directing packets across that network.

The Transport Layer

Transmission Control Protocol (TCP) is a communication standard that is used in conjunction with the Internet. It is found in the Transport Layer (Layer 4) and is used for the reliable delivery of data over a network connection. Services like the World Wide Web (WWW), email, and FTP use this communication protocol. Applications that require faster communication, and can compromise on error checking, use User Datagram Protocol (UDP). VoIP and video often use UDP because of its speed and because it is no big deal if a data packet is sent out of order or is dropped. TCP, on the other hand, is more orderly and provides error checking to ensure that all data packets are sent in the correct sequence.

> **Note**
>
> User Datagram Protocol (UDP) is a connectionless communication protocol that has limited packet recovery functionality and operates at the transport layer.

TCP Three-Way Handshake (SYN–SYN–ACK)

TCP uses a three-message handshake, also known as SYN–SYN–ACK, to set up a TCP/IP connection (a connection over the Internet). Here is how it works:

1. Host A sends a TCP Synchronize (SYN) packet to Host B.

2. Host B then sends a Synchronize-Acknowledge (SYN–ACK) to Host A.

3. In response, Host A sends an Acknowledgment (ACK) to Host B.

4. Once Host B receives the ACK, the TCP socket connection is established.

Another three-way communication is used to "tear down" the TCP connection, once communication ends. The following protocols all use TCP and, therefore, use the three-way handshake:

- FTP
- HTTP
- HTTPS
- SMTP
- IMAP
- SSH
- POP3
- Telnet

TCP Retransmission

TCP Retransmission is a process used for error correction to TCP data packets. Retransmission will occur when the receiver determines that an error (or checksum) has occurred and subsequently does not transmit an "ACK" to the sender. The sender will then retransmit the packet. Once the recipient determines that there has been no error during transmission, an "ACK" packet will be sent to the sender. TCP retransmission also occurs if the packet was lost during transmission and no "ACK" was returned by the intended recipient.

SYN Flood Attack

A SYN flood attack occurs when a hacker sends SYN requests to a host at such a rapid rate that the server cannot handle all the requests and ultimately renders it useless. In other words, the client does not send the server the expected ACK request in the three-way handshake.

Note

The Importance of TCP

So why do we care about TCP? In network forensics, much of our work revolves around analyzing data packets. When monitoring network traffic, we might want to use a sniffer to analyze TCP/IP data packets. Most packet sniffers operate at Layer 2 or Layer 3 of the OSI Model.

A TCP/IP header includes the source port and IP address, and the destination port and IP address. For example, identifying the IP address can tell you whether there is communication with a server in China. The port number can tell you the type of service being used. For example, Internet Relay Chat (IRC) uses the TCP protocol and can be found operating on port 6667. But IRC has been used by bot herders (malicious hackers) for command and control (that is, they use your zombie computer to send out their spam). You can use the Ngrep (ngrep.sourceforge.net) tool to view IRC logs.

In summary, many network forensics examiners use TCP tools to analyze data packets on networks to see who is communicating on the network, what services they are using, and, ultimately, what mischievous activities they are conducting.

The Session Layer

As its name suggests, the **Session Layer** (Layer 5) is responsible for initiating, maintaining, and terminating processes on different systems.

The Presentation Layer

The **Presentation Layer** (Layer 6) prepares data for the Application Layer and is responsible for data conversion, compression, and encryption.

The Application Layer

The **Application Layer** (Layer 7) can be viewed as the closest to the end user and interacts with applications. Functionality at this layer includes email (SMTP), remote file access, remote printer access, File Transfer Protocol (FTP), HyperText Transfer Protocol (HTTP), and network management.

> ## Case Study
>
> ### When Network Forensics Goes Wrong
>
> Law enforcement has limited resources when it comes to computer forensics. Unfortunately, there are even fewer network forensics examiners. Therefore, it is not surprising that sometimes mistakes happen. Consider, for example, the following case of mistaken identity.
>
> On March 7, 2011, at 6:20 a.m., a resident of Buffalo, New York, was awakened by seven armed agents who had just broken down his back door. The Immigration and Customs Enforcement (ICE) agents allegedly yelled, "Get down! Get down on the ground!" and threw the suspect down the stairs. The suspect was allowed to get to his feet and get dressed in the bathroom. The agents had just captured a prolific pedophile—or so it seemed. It turned out that the IP address of the pedophile, identified on the peer-to-peer site, was a "dirty IP address", meaning that the perpetrator had hijacked an unsecured wireless connection.
>
> Investigators will find the IP address of a suspect online and then contact the ISP to confirm the owner. However, the IP address is merely a unique identifier to a router, not to the many wireless devices (computers) that use that router. Therefore, anyone in the vicinity can jump on an unsecured Wi-Fi connection and download or upload contraband without the owner's knowledge. The agents in this case were ultimately able to view the computers and devices in the home and quickly realize that they did not have their suspect. Viewing the DHCP logs on the computer attached to the router would show what devices are attached to the wireless connection at any given time. Additionally, many access points also have integrated routers, and therefore the DHCP logs are present in the router itself. A stand-alone access point may also include a table that lists attached devices.
>
> This case may seem incredible, but situations in which agents arrest the wrong suspect because of a dirty IP address have occurred numerous times. U.S. Attorney William Hochul and Immigration and Customs Enforcement special agent in charge Lev Kubiak later apologized to the innocent homeowner. Agents subsequently arrested and charged a neighbor with the distribution of child pornography.

Tools are available to help an investigator understand more about wireless access points in an area. For example, Net Analyzer, which is available for the iPhone, can identify the closest access points, and the investigator can quickly determine how many devices are connected to that access point. Net Analyzer provides not only the MAC address of the device but will also provide the name assigned to that device and the manufacturer. In this case, the device may be a laptop, a Samsung Galaxy S20, an Xbox One, a Roku, or an IP camera—basically, any Wi-Fi-enabled device. This type of Wi-Fi analysis should be performed before executing a warrant, which did not happen in the case study just detailed.

If an open wireless signal is found, the investigators must account for it. Even if a wireless network is open, there is still probable cause to believe that evidence of the crime is located within the network equipment at the location. Some criminals even leave their wireless networks open intentionally to maintain some plausible deniability. The bottom line is that just because an IP address is traced back to a location, that is not sole proof that a person at the location is responsible for the incident.

Introduction to VoIP

The recent exponential growth of mobile communication applications means that investigations involving VoIP communications continue to grow in importance.

Voice over Internet Protocol (VoIP)

Voice over Internet Protocol (VoIP) is a protocol that takes analog audio signals, e.g. voice, and converts those signals to digital data that can be transmitted across the Internet. A traditional landline telephone uses an analog signal. VoIP, however, allows a user with broadband Internet access to use VoIP. VoIP calls are facilitated via a VoIP-enabled telephone or via a computer (desktop/laptop/smartphone). If your call ends up on a traditional telephone, then the signal will be converted back to an analog signal.

VoIP is an alternative to the traditional PSTN (Public Switched Telephone Network). VoIP includes open standards, like SIP, but also includes proprietary applications, like Skype and Google Talk.

Disadvantages of VoIP

Not all VoIP services connect directly with emergency services and locating the caller can be a challenge. VoIP will not work during a power outage unless you have a battery backup. Caller ID can be easily spoofed with VoIP, and the protocol has enabled the emergence of "robocalls". The Federal Trade Commission (FTC) in the United States has initiated more than 100 lawsuits against more than 600 companies that have been responsible for billions of robocalls. The FTC has also conducted many competitions to detect and block robocalls.

PBX (Private Branch Exchange)

A **PBX (Private Branch Exchange)** is the telephone system within an organization that switches calls between users in that organization on local telephone lines, while enabling users to share a limited number of external telephone lines. The primary reason for using a PBX is the cost savings associated with sharing telephone lines, rather than paying for one telephone line for each employee. The PBX is owned and managed by the enterprise.

There are different types of PBX. For example, there is a traditional PBX with copper cables for telephone landlines attached to it. This type of PBX will accommodate a mixture of analog and digital signal transmissions. There is also a cloud-based PBX system that can be used by the enterprise.

An IP-PBX is an Internet Protocol PBX that uses digital telephone signals, rather than analog land-lines, to facilitate calls. Ethernet cables connect telephones rather than traditional phone lines.

PBX Fraud

PBX fraud often results from criminals establishing premium calling services, then breaking into companies, and using the organization's telephone lines to call premium services, thereby racking up tens of thousands of dollars in charges, often over the weekend, when office staff are at home.

How do these criminals gain access to a telephone system? When you call an office telephone number late at night, or over the weekend, the call will typically go to voicemail. Some corporate systems will enable employees to remotely access their voicemail with the use of a PIN. Sometimes the default PIN is set to the last four digits of the telephone number. On certain telephone systems, there is an option for the user to forward calls to another number. Once a criminal gains access to voicemail, she can use the call forwarding option to forward calls to a pay-per-minute premium service, which is owned by the criminal. Therefore, any call to that company telephone number is forwarded to the premium service. Consequently, the company would be billed an astronomical amount in premium call charges. The charges would only be noticed on the Monday when employees return to the office.

Most VoIP telephones lack intelligence. Thus, they require another system to function, i.e. a PBX. When someone picks up the telephone, the telephone then contacts a PBX for assistance. The PBX instructs the telephone to play a dial tone. When the user pushes a number, the telephone sends another request to the PBX. The PBX typically responds with an instruction to play a digit tone. This continues until the user pushes enough numbers for the PBX to connect the call. The PBX can however be too helpful, as it does not know who is authorized to make telephone calls. Thus, it lacks adequate security. Anyone who knows the IP address of an unsecured PBX can make phone calls that originate from that organization. Therefore, criminals that find the IP address of a PBX can make calls using a PBX. They can subsequently configure their telephone to pick up the handset and check for a dial tone. The criminal can then begin making calls to pay-per-minute premium numbers and use robotic dialers to dial hundreds of times a day, or perhaps thousands of times a week.

Unfortunately, in these situations, the company is liable for the charges. This is actually built into their contract with the telecom company, and they do not realize this until the fraud occurs. The PBX is internal for the company, and therefore if it is compromised it is viewed as negligence on the part of the company. Most companies do not have the in-house expertise to properly configure a PBX and therefore select a contractor, which may be the cheapest, and least knowledgeable, contractor.

A PBX must be on the Internet, to receive incoming calls and therefore you cannot block all incoming access to the PBX. To further complicate matters, some offices have remote workers who need to connect from home. This means that the PBX needs to be configured to facilitate calls initiated from the Internet. It is not uncommon for a company to find out on a Monday morning that calls made over the weekend total more than $30,000 and as much as $60,000.

It is often difficult for the police to investigate these cases or recoup these losses since many of these scams involve international calls to countries like Zimbabwe, Cuba, or Pakistan. Many of these crimes go unreported because companies fear the bad publicity or being found negligent. Some companies will call the FBI. However, these crimes may not reach the financial threshold to initiate an FBI investigation.

Session Initiation Protocol (SIP)

Session Initiation Protocol (SIP) is a peer-to-peer, multimedia signaling protocol developed by the Internet Engineering Task Force (IETF). The IETF develops and promotes voluntary Internet standards. SIP uses existing IP protocols, like DNS, and SDP (Static Dial Plan), and operates at the application layer control protocol. SIP is used to establish, modify and terminate multimedia sessions, i.e., voice, video, instant messaging over the Internet. SIP generally utilizes UDP or TCP.

STUN (Simple Traversal of UDP Through NATs (Network Address Translation))

STUN allows devices behind a NAT firewall or router to make telephone calls to VoIP provider hosts outside of their local network.

Incident Response (IR)

Incident response is often associated with network breaches, but it often has a much wider scope than that. Many larger organizations maintain a security operations center (SOC) and an incident response (IR) team. The SOC often focuses on information security and threat detection, which may include monitoring for unusual login attempts (multiple attempts or from a different location), malware, data exfiltration, and unusual external IP address connections attempts. The IR team may handle incidents as small as a lost/stolen smartphone to a more serious incident involving stolen credentials or a large network breach. Thus, the SOC will filter out false positive alerts, and then escalate notable incidents to IR personnel. Some incidents are low risk. For example, an encrypted iPhone with no client or customer data would be considered low risk because the primary asset is not the device but the potential data compromise. An iPhone may cost $1,000 but loss of intellectual property or client information can reach millions of dollars, as Target Corporation can attest to. Incident response is often a team response as it can involve technical digital forensics examiners, a legal team, public relations, human resources, client liaisons, and many more people.

Whether an incident is large or small, the first step is always the same – begin with triage. Triage is the initial step with incident response, and it involves mitigating the risk. Sometimes triage may involve capturing perishable data (data that quickly expires). Mitigating the risk generally means preventing the loss of data, money, or any potential threats to the organization. An example of triage would be to capture the latest state of the device (last login, last location, etc.), send a remote wipe to a stolen iPhone, inform the cellular carrier about the loss, file a police report, and have the user change her passwords to any network services that the device was used for.

Assembling the right team to deal with an incident is an important next step (after triage) and will often involve counsel (legal) staff, unless it is a low risk case. An attorney will help to assess the legal obligations of the organization. For example, different states in the United States have different laws relating to disclosures involving personally identifiable information (PII). A disclosure of health records may be impacted by the Health Insurance Portability and Accountability Act (HIPAA), while a disclosure of personal information for citizens of the European Union (EU) will be covered by the General Data Protection Regulation (GDPR) and perhaps nation state laws too.

Once triage has been performed, the team can begin an investigation. Once an investigation has concluded, a root cause analysis (RCA) report may recommend training for an employee and/or a review of processes to ensure that a similar incident will not occur. It is important to identify lessons that can be learned from incidents.

STIX, TAXII, and Cybox

Threat intelligence has become extremely important as organizations today encounter threats from hacktivists, individual hackers and nation states. Many individual industries encounter similar threats. For example, while the W32.Stuxnet malware variant targeted the centrifuges at the Iranian nuclear facility at Natanz, the Stuxnet worm impacted similar networks in Indonesia, India, and many other countries. Moreover, APT10, also referred to as Operation Cloud Hopper, targeted the managed service provider (MSP) industry, using similar types of malware. Therefore, sharing intelligence, especially within industries, and even among competitors, has become a more robust and effective strategy. As an example, we have sector-based Information Sharing and Analysis Centers (ISAC). There is a Financial Services Information Sharing and Analysis Center (FS-ISAC), one for the automotive industry, aviation and so forth. An ISAC provides actionable intelligence for security professionals. More information about the ISACs can be found on the National Council of ISACs website (www.nationalisacs.org). There are many other organizations that provide security training and provide security alerts to security professionals. The United States Secret Service hosts quarterly meetings, under the organizational name of the Electronic Crimes Task Force (ECTF). The Cybersecurity and Infrastructure Security Agency (CISA), within the Department of Homeland Security (DHS), provides extremely important security alerts for both organizational and personal security. InfraGard, a public-private organization of the FBI, also provides organizations with security alerts. Finally, Europol hosts a series of forums and provides security alerts, which are generally by invitation only.

Advanced Persistent Threats

An advanced persistent threat (APT) is a sophisticated, relentless, coordinated attack on a computer network, with the goal of stealing intellectual property. The term was first used by the U.S. Air Force in 2006. It is a well-known fact that the People's Liberation Army (PLA) has been mandated not only to protect China, but also to engage in economic development; this involves economic espionage. Mandiant (now owned by FireEye) is just one organization that has disclosed how the Chinese government employs hackers to steal intellectual property from the United States. The Mandiant report has provided details about Unit 61398 in Shanghai, which is manned by hundreds or perhaps thousands of hackers.

APT10

As previously mentioned, APT10 was a cyber espionage attack, perpetrated by hackers in China, on managed service providers (MSPs). It is understandable why MSPs would be the target of an attack, given the vast amounts of intellectual property managed by cloud service providers. According to a report by PwC UK, in collaboration with BAE Systems, APT10 attacks began as early as 2014 and continued for a number of years. During those years, APT10 used a series of malware types, from Poison Ivy to PlugX to RedLeaves to QuasarRAT. APT10 used hundreds of domains for command and control of their compromised network hosts, thereby making it difficult to blacklist certain IP addresses from communicating with a network.

As with all APT attacks, it is difficult to identify when the network was initially compromised. Moreover, it is a challenge to contain the infection of the malware since these attackers move laterally throughout the network, and it becomes even more problematic if a large number of credentials have been compromised since successful logins do not raise flags like unsuccessful logins do. Finally, it is problematic to determine what data has been compromised since the attacker may encrypt the data that is being exfiltrated from the network and will use techniques, like timestomping, to thwart the work of forensics investigators. **Timestomping** is an anti-forensics technique used to manipulate the timestamps of a file.

Cyber Kill Chain

The whitepaper "Intelligence-Driven Computer Network Defense Informed by Analysis of Adversary Campaigns and Intrusion Kill Chains" details the six stages in an advanced attack on a computer network. This Intrusion Kill Chain explains what happens during a sophisticated attack on a network, usually an attack so advanced that it is government sponsored. Figure 8.7 shows how this chain of events occurs and then gives a detailed description of each phase.

FIGURE 8.7   The intrusion kill chain

Reconnaissance

During this phase, an attacker takes some time to learn about the structure of an organization. An adversary can collect information, about a target, in many ways, as detailed in the following sections.

Job Postings

An attacker can review job openings on an organization's website or on a recruitment site like Monster. com—particularly those that relate to IT positions. Often the job requirements listed give an attacker a wealth of information related to the systems in use. The attacker then has information about the potential vulnerabilities associated with each system and application noted, including default passwords in case an administrator has not bothered to change them. The following is an example of qualifications for a database administrator posted on Monster.com:

- Bachelor's degree in computer science or equivalent years of work experience required; plus minimum of five (5) years relevant experience with Oracle 10g and 11g databases implementing RAC, ASM and DataGuard required

- Functional and technical knowledge and experience supporting Oracle E_Business Suite in an R12 environment and/or Oracle Identity Management desirable

- Experience supporting Oracle on Windows Server as well as Linux helpful

- Some experience with Microsoft SQL Server

As you can see, this information can benefit an adversary during reconnaissance.

Press Releases

Many organizations unknowingly provide information to adversaries through press releases in a variety of ways. One way would be to announce a large purchase of IT systems for an organization.

Tech Forums

It is common for IT personnel to reach out to other IT professionals to get answers to issues that they are experiencing in their organizations on tech forums. The problem is that these Internet forums are generally open to the public. An adversary can gain a lot of information about an organization's systems by reviewing postings on these forums.

Other Sources

Adversaries can also find a lot of information about an organization by reviewing social media websites, including Facebook and LinkedIn. These sites can provide invaluable information about events at an organization and also facilitate profiling key employees in that organization.

Some employees have posted sensitive information about their organization through websites, like WikiLeaks, SecureDrop, or Pastebin, which provide further information during the reconnaissance phase.

Other information that can help an adversary can be found on the company's website. In one case, it was possible to view a sample employee identification card at a large healthcare provider and get details about the company that produces these ID badges. Other sources of information can include looking up the DNS records for a company. Some free services can allow you to find out the name of the individual who registered a domain name, as well as that person's address.

Weaponization

In this phase, the adversary places malicious code into a payload. For example, the payload could be a PDF document with an embedded virus or perhaps a Trojan. A **Trojan** is a legitimate-looking application that is used to disguise malware. Other vectors of attack can also include spam, USB drives, and a hacked Wi-Fi connection.

Delivery

This phase merely involves delivery of the payload to the target. The delivery method could include SQL injection or spear phishing, using perhaps an electronic birthday card with a link to malware.

Exploitation

Exploitation is the successful execution of the payload. This could mean that an employee clicked the link in that e-card and executed malware on that machine, and the attacker now has access to that system and any network access associated with that computer.

C2 (Command and Control)

The command and control (C2) phase may or may not occur. This involves using some type of system to conduct your attack. C2 is used to obfuscate the attacker so that a request from a host or an IP address looks legitimate. If an unsuspecting host computer on a network is used to communicate with other systems on the network, this is termed a lateral attack. Sites like Twitter and Google groups have been used for command and control because the IP addresses of these sites are generally not blocked by organizations, but behind these legitimate sites is a hacker located perhaps in Russia or China. Amazon Web Services (AWS) has also been used by many hackers.

Exfiltration

Exfiltration involves the theft of data from a network. PFC Bradley Manning is a prime example of data exfiltration from a government network, and Edward Snowden is yet another obvious example. Exfiltration is the payoff for a government-sponsored attack and can provide key intellectual property, for example, from a missile defense system or cooling tiles on the NASA space shuttle.

Tactics, Techniques, and Procedures (TTP)

The terms *tactics, techniques* and *procedures* are used to describe ways to analyze an APT or a type of threat actor (hacker). Once you identify how malware was used to access a network or ways in which an adversary logged onto another computer on a network (e.g. using Remote Desktop Protocol (RDP)).

The following sections will discuss the tools and methods used to achieve their goals and ways in which to identify TTPs and remediate these threats.

YARA

YARA is an open source tool that is used to classify and identify malware variants. An examiner can also copy the MD5 hash for a file and search on VirusTotal to see whether the file has been previously identified as malware (see Figure 8.8).

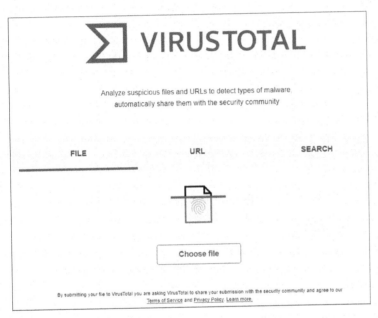

FIGURE 8.8   VirusTotal website

Persistence

Once a hacker has successfully infiltrated a network, the key to success is to remain on a compromised system using malware that is persistent. To maintain persistence, the malware installation will need to remain in a directory where it is activated every time that a host computer is powered on. Therefore, one of the first places that an investigator will examine is the start-up directory on a computer.

Dynamic-Link Library (DLL) Side-Loading

Microsoft, in an effort to make binary updates more convenient for developers, with the Windows side-by-side (WinSxS) feature, has inadvertently created a vulnerability used by APT attackers. Using this feature, hackers have successfully circumvented anti-virus tools and passed malware from computer to computer. The malicious payload actually runs in memory, rather than in the file system, where anti-virus scanners function.

Remediation

An investigator should remediate the risk once an intrusion has been identified. A computer can be easily replaced and preventing a threat and protecting the data are paramount. The investigation is secondary to nullifying the risk to a network, primarily because of the threat to intellectual property and other proprietary data. In terms of remediation, a company should follow some or all of the following steps:

1. Block malicious IP addresses;

2. Block malicious domain names;

3. Remove compromised systems from the network;

4. Generate a list of indicators of compromise (IOCs) and create a remediation and investigative process based on those IOCs;

5. Rebuild compromised systems;

6. Coordinate with cloud and service providers;

7. Enterprise password change;

8. Verify all remediation activities; and

9. Create a root cause analysis to prevent similar types of attacks in the future.

Indicators of Compromise (IOC)

The problem with APTs is that they are so advanced that many traditional security mechanisms, like firewalls, IDS, antivirus, etc., are ineffective. However, certain hallmarks of an APT attack, or indicators of compromise (IOCs), are known and can include the following:

- **Registry keys:** Windows configuration files.

- **DLL files: Dynamic Link Library (DLL) files** are Windows system files that contain procedures and drivers that are executed by a program. Multiple programs can access these shared system files. Changes might have occurred. If so, they can be identified by matching version numbers of the DLL files with the version of Windows.

- **ServiceDLL:** If the *service.dll* file is found on a personal computer, the machine could be infected with the Trojan infostealer.msnbancos.

- **svchost.eve:** This is a system process that hosts multiple Windows services. If the file `svchost.exe` is located outside the System32 directory, there has been a compromise.

- **Email:** The email SMTP IP address does not match the domain name.

- **Ports:** Regularly unused computer ports that are now used. Internet Relay Chat (IRC) is an Internet protocol for live chat. It utilizes port 6667. IRC is also used for command and control of compromised computers that are controlled by hackers.

- **$USN_Journal:** This is the Update Sequence Number Journal, which is a feature of NTFS, and keeps track of changes on a volume. This is also referred to as the Change Journal. This file should be examined by an incident responder.

- **Prefetch files:** New prefetch files might refer to new drivers or new downloaded files. **Prefetch** is a folder in the Windows system folder that contains files used in the boot process and regularly opened by other programs. The purpose of prefetch is to boot up a machine or start a program faster by keeping track of commonly used files.

- **System32:** Contains Windows system files and other program files, which are critical to the Windows operating system. The directory can be found in *C:\Windows\System32 or C:\Winnt\ system32*. The `System32` folder may also contain malicious files installed by a hacker and be an indicator of compromise. DNS and DHCP logs can also be found in the `System32` directory.

- **Master File Table (MFT):** Contains an entry for every file that is stored on an NTFS volume and includes metadata about the file, including the size, date created, date modified, last accessed date and permissions. The MFT is a critical resource for incident responders as well as for traditional forensic examiners. This is because if anti-forensics techniques were attempted with a system, such as timestomping, or an attempt was made to delete files, then the MFT can be used to identify whether a hacker or a suspect did manipulate files. Most dates can be manipulated by an attacker except for the "FN Info Creation Date".

The MFT can be parsed with most licensed forensics tools and there are free tools, such as Eric Zimmerman's MFTECmd parser tool. The MFT is located here in Windows: *%systemroot%\$MFT*.

The investigator should be very specific with search dates with an MFT parsing tool because the MFT contains a huge amount of entries. Figure 8.9 shows some sample MFT data.

Filename	Full Path	Size (bytes)	Created	Modified	Accessed	Is Deleted
[root]	Partition 1\System [NTFS]\[root]\	56	2018-Dec-01 17:53:42.013448 UT	2019-Jan-16 17:28:59.865004 UT	2019-Jan-16 17:28:59.865004 UT	no
$I30	Partition 1\System [NTFS]\[root]\$I30	4096	2018-Dec-01 17:53:42.013448 UT	2019-Jan-16 17:28:59.865004 UT	2019-Jan-16 17:28:59.865004 UT	no
$TXF_DATA	Partition 1\System [NTFS]\[root]\$TXF_DA1	56	2018-Dec-01 17:53:42.013448 UT	2019-Jan-16 17:28:59.865004 UT	2019-Jan-16 17:28:59.865004 UT	no
System Volume I	Partition 1\System [NTFS]\[root]\System Vo	160	2018-Dec-01 18:19:24.813961 UT	2018-Dec-01 18:19:25.282710 UT	2018-Dec-01 18:19:25.282710 UT	no
BOOTSECT.BAK	Partition 1\System [NTFS]\[root]\BOOTSEC	8192	2018-Dec-01 18:17:59.903866 UT	2018-Dec-01 18:17:59.903866 UT	2018-Dec-01 18:17:59.903866 UT	no
BOOTNXT	Partition 1\System [NTFS]\[root]\BOOTNXT	1	2019-Jan-16 17:28:59.865004 UT	2018-Apr-11 23:34:28.149121 UT	2019-Jan-16 17:28:59.865004 UT	no
bootmgr	Partition 1\System [NTFS]\[root]\bootmgr	407698	2018-Dec-01 18:17:59.802504 UT	2019-Jan-09 05:44:00.646920 UT	2019-Jan-16 17:28:59.802504 UT	no
Boot	Partition 1\System [NTFS]\[root]\Boot\	160	2018-Dec-01 18:17:57.685093 UT	2019-Jan-16 17:28:59.865004 UT	2019-Jan-16 17:28:59.865004 UT	no
$Extend	Partition 1\System [NTFS]\[root]\$Extend\	552	2018-Dec-01 17:53:42.013448 UT	2018-Dec-01 17:53:42.013448 UT	2018-Dec-01 17:53:42.013448 UT	no
$UpCase	Partition 1\System [NTFS]\[root]\$UpCase\	131072	2018-Dec-01 17:53:42.013448 UT	2018-Dec-01 17:53:42.013448 UT	2018-Dec-01 17:53:42.013448 UT	no
$Secure	Partition 1\System [NTFS]\[root]\$Secure\	56	2018-Dec-01 17:53:42.013448 UT	2018-Dec-01 17:53:42.013448 UT	2018-Dec-01 17:53:42.013448 UT	no

FIGURE 8.9 Sample MFT data

- **Event Logs:** were introduced in Chapter 2 as an important source of evidence for investigators. They are also important for IR. One example in incident response (IR) are Event IDs related to successful login attempts. Event ID 4624 indicates that a successful login occurred.

However, this Event ID also provides a Logon Type. If the Event ID 4624 Logon Type is 2 (Interactive: logon at keyboard and screen of system), then we might not be concerned. However, a Logon Type of 10 (Terminal Services, Remote Desktop or Remote Assistance) could be an indicator of compromise, as sophisticated hackers will often use Remote Desktop to remotely connect to other hosts on a network, as they move laterally. This particular Event ID (4624) will also provide information about the host that successfully remotely logged onto another host. Important Event IDs, associated with Remote Desktop (RDP), are Event ID 21/22 (RDP/Citrix authentications), Event ID 23/24 (RDP/Citrix logoffs), Event ID 1158 (RDP from an IP address), and Event ID 1149 (successful RDP authentication). Other important Event IDs are 7045, 7036 and 4697 to identify installed services on an infected host machine.

■ At the time of writing, the website ultimatewindowssecurity.com provides a comprehensive list of Event IDs. Figure 8.10 shows a tremendous resource for searching for Event IDs of interest.

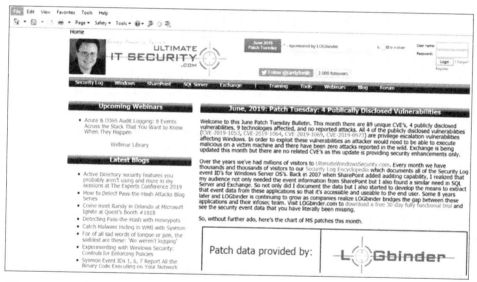

FIGURE 8.10   Ultimate IT Security website

■ **MRU (most recently used) lists:** are also a potential artifact of interest for an incident responder. These are a listing of applications and files recently used by a user. This file can be found in Windows Registry here: *HKCU\Software\Microsoft\Windows\ CurrentVersion\ Explorer\RunMRU.*

■ **PsExec:** is a Windows command-line tool that allows a user to remotely execute processes on a computer without having to install client software. As you can imagine, it could be a tool of choice for an attacker. Ironically, PsExec is also used by Windows administrators and incident responders. Event ID 540 will show a PsExec login.

- **UserAssist:** contains a list of programs that have been executed on a Windows computer, including the run count and last execution date and time. Didier Stevens has produced a tool to parse these entries. The file containing these entries is located here: *HCU\Software\Microsoft\Windows\CurrentVersion \Explorer\UserAssist*

- An IR team will typically circulate a list of IOCs for team members to search for—some of which are out highlighted above. IOCs on that list may also include IP address(es) of interest, malware name(s) and MD5 hash(es) of known malware, and a list of keywords that can be used to search through an imaged drive. A keyword list may include names of malware, IP addresses, and other search terms of interest.

Investigating a Network Attack

Network attacks and breaches are not all APTs. Some attackers simply want to cause disruption and destruction, while others want to smash and grab your money or sensitive data. Identifying a compromise can be difficult, especially because an attacker may move from computer to computer in an organization and because an indicator of a compromise can be hard to find. With regards to the latter, finding small changes in a labyrinth of registry files can be like finding a needle in a haystack. Sometimes the most efficient way to identify a compromise is to compare a potentially infected system with an uninfected system. If an organization was recently attacked, and you can find the computer of an employee who is on disability leave or on vacation, that computer might not be infected and would make identifying the compromise a lot easier. Another method of identifying a compromise on a Windows machine is to look at restore points on a system. Since the introduction of Windows Vista, Microsoft has used a file backup system called Volume Shadow Copy (VSC). There are several tools used to examine VSCs, like BlackLight and ProDiscover, which can examine versions of a computer's system at a particular point in time.

Random Access Memory (RAM)

An important indicator of compromise (IOC) is RAM. Of course, a forensic analysis of RAM requires a system to be powered on and requires special RAM live forensics tools.

AmCache

As discussed in Chapter 2, an analysis of the `AmCache.hve`, introduced with Windows 8, can be used to determine what applications were run by a malicious actor. Eric Zimmerman's AmcacheParser, which is a free open source tool, will parse out the contents of the `AmCache.hve`, which includes installation date and time, execution date and time, the Program ID (application), and the path from which the application was run. Figure 8.11 shows output from an `Amcache.hve` file.

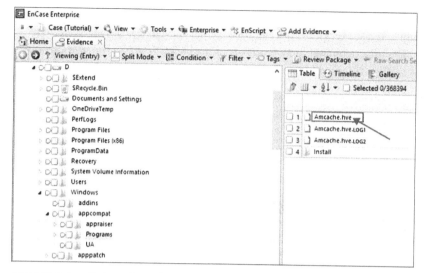

FIGURE 8.11   Output from Amcache.hve

ShimCache

In Chapter 2, we spoke in depth about the importance of ShimCache in investigations. As previously noted, ShimCache can potentially provide information about applications that were executed by a hacker on a system. ShimCache Parser is one of a number of tools that can be used to parse Shim-Cache. AppCompatCacheParser is another tool that can be downloaded for free to analyze ShimCache.

ShellBags

As previously noted in Chapter 2, ShellBags are valuable in identifying folders that were accessed by hackers or other users. ShellBags are located in several locations, including the following:

```
HKEY_USERS\<USERID>\Software\Microsoft\Windows\Shell
HKEY_USERS\<USERID>\Software\Microsoft\Windows\ShellNoRoam
```

Volume Shadow Copy

Volume Shadow Copy (VSC) Service was introduced in Chapter 2 and we discussed how a comparison of copies, between different dates, can provide investigators with an idea of what changed in the system. With an APT, the attacker may have replaced Windows DLL (service files) with malicious files, for example, and an examination of VSCs may provide some insight into small changes made by a sophisticated attacker to a system. Many tools, like BlackLight, natively support of comparison of VSCs. There are also some free, open source tools, like libvshadow 4; libvshadow was created by Joachim Metz and can perform VSC comparisons.

Endpoint Detection and Response (EDR)

Endpoint Detection and Response (EDR) is a tool for monitoring threats on network hosts and then automatically responding to certain types of attacks. The power of EDR lies in its tremendous logging capabilities, which certainly make the life of an incident responder much easier. Carbon Black is one of the most well-known EDR tools, with comprehensive logging capabilities. However, the cost of EDR can be prohibitively expensive for most companies.

Kibana

Kibana is a free, open source, data visualization tool, which can be used for log analysis and application monitoring. The tool integrates with Elasticsearch, which is a powerful analytical search engine. Kibana uses a variety of histograms, heat maps, line graphs, and other data visualization tools, to visually identify what occurred during a specific timeframe. This is easier than scanning through thousands of logs. When using Kibana, we can identify if there was a lot of activity during a time when an employee would not normally be at work. This could indicate that a hacker in Asia has been remotely active on a host computer at 2:00 am, local time, in New York, which is during daytime hours in Asia. Kibana can also display unusual connections to IP addresses in other countries that would not be expected. It should however be noted that with APT attacks, the hackers have used proxy computers in other countries to obfuscate their identities, i.e. their true Domain Name Server and IP address. An incident responder would also search for large amounts of data being transferred out of the targeted company – an indication of data exfiltration. Kibana also has the ability to quickly search for specific Event IDs for specific hosts on a network. For example, Event ID 4624 with a logon type of 10 would be of particular interest.

Log2Timeline/Plaso

Log2Timeline is an important tool for incident responders as it takes log files and parses different types of logs, from a variety of Registry files, and creates a timeline of system logs. The tool is typically used on an infected computer once the security team has narrowed down some potential dates of compromise for a host on a network. Given the thousands of system logs that can be generated by a host each day, it is important to narrow the scope of time when an attack occurred as quickly as possible. You may want to consider adding the following files to Log2Timeline for further analysis:

- \Windows\AppCompat\Programs\Amcache.hve
- \Windows\system32\config\SAM
- \Windows\system32\config\SECURITY
- \Windows\system32\config\SOFTWARE
- \Windows\system32\config\winevt

SANS SIFT Workstation

The SIFT is a free suite of forensics tools, which are available from SANS Institute (www.sans.org). The tool integrates with VMWare Player, which is also a free download. The SIFT can be used to mount images and then perform different types of analysis, using the many tools included, in a virtual box, i.e., each session of the SIFT will have no impact on your personal computer. Figure 8.12 shows the SANS SIFT user interface. Learning to use virtual machines is an important skill to obtain in digital forensics and cybersecurity positions, especially when working with a system potentially infected with malware.

FIGURE 8.12   SANS SIFT Workstation

The SIFT supports the following file systems:

- NTFS (NTFS)
- iso9660 (ISO9660 CD)
- hfs (HFS+)
- raw (raw data)
- swap (swap space)
- memory (RAM data)
- fat12 (FAT12)

- fat16 (FAT16)

- fat32 (FAT32)

- ext2 (EXT2)

- ext3 (EXT3)

- ext4 (EXT4)

- ufs1 (UFS1)

- ufs2 (UFS2)

- vmdk

The SIFT Workstation includes the following open source tools:

- Log2timeline (Timeline Generation Tool)

- Rekall Framework (Memory Analysis)

- Volatility Framework (Memory Analysis)

- autopsy

- dc3dd

- libevt

- libevtx

- libvshadow

- lightgrep

- log2timeline

- RegRipper and plug-ins

- Sleuth Kit

A basic knowledge of Linux is required since the Workstation does use a line command interface.

Windows Registry

In Chapter 2, we introduced Windows Registry and learned that the registries contain changes to a computer's configuration. Generally, all 32-bit and 64-bit Windows programs store configuration and preference data in the Registry. As discussed earlier, the Registry also stores information about Plug and Play hardware configuration. For example, information about USB devices that were connected to a system are stored in *HKLM\SYSTEM\ControlSet00x\Enum\USBSTOR*

The Registry can also provide us with detailed information about what a hacker was doing. This is different from other investigations where the user-created files, like photos or Office documents, are of importance. A sophisticated attacker may access a host on your network, copy data and then use anti-forensics techniques. **Anti-forensics** is a concerted effort to manipulate files on a system to cover up a hacker's activity. For example, a hacker may try to change the system clock on a host or change a file extension or mimic the activity of a regular user. However, a seasoned network examiner can use Windows Registry and Windows Event Viewer to identify when an intrusion occurred and gain some insight into what the hacker sought to do. We could write an entire book on the registries but in this section, we will focus on some of the most important hives and files related to incident response. Figure 8.13 shows the Registry hives.

FIGURE 8.13   Registry hives in Registry Editor

RegRipper is a free, open source tool that can be used to parse different registry files for a personal computer. After the investigator/responder forensically images a computer, e.g. with FTK Imager, the SYSTEM, SOFTWARE, SAM and SECURITY hives (Registry) can be copied from the image copy, copied and pasted into the folder, where you installed RegRipper and then parsed out by the tool. RegRipper is a Windows, command-line tool. Knowledge of some basic Linux commands is required to process the Registry files. We shall now discuss some important hives in more detail.

HKEY_CLASSES_ROOT (HKCR)

This registry hive stores information about applications, including file name extension associations and COM class information. This hive also includes information about program shortcuts and the user interface.

HKEY_CURRENT_USER (HCR)

This registry contains information about the user that is currently logged in to the system, which includes their desktop settings and user folders.

HKEY_CURRENT_USER\Software\Microsoft\ActiveSetup\InstalledComponents

HKEY_LOCAL MACHINE (HKLM)

HKEY_LOCAL_MACHINE stores settings that apply to all users on a system. *HKEY_LOCAL_ MACHINE/SOFTWARE* stores information about Wi-Fi networks, including SSID and MAC address. You may also find malware, installed and uninstalled programs in this hive. You may also be able to retrieve saved passwords for a user here. ShellBag information is also found in this hive and indicates which folders a user accessed and when they were accessed. You will also find prefetch files here and these files will show you how many times an application has been executed. These files have a .pf extension. Prefetch is a feature that allows a system to run faster by preloading some code that is frequently used by a user.

ImagePath is yet another potential IOC, and this is a back door found in the following registry key:

```
HKEY_LOCAL_MACHINE\SOFTWARE\Microsoft\ActiveSetup\InstalledComponents
```

HKEY_USERS (HKU)

This registry contains information about all users, regardless of who is currently logged in. This information does not have to be accessed via the Registry but can be accessed here:

Documents and Settings\User Profile\NTUSER.DAT

The NTUSER.DAT file is very important for incident response as it contains the profile of a specific user. You can identify which applications were executed on a particular computer for a specific user.

The file *NTUSER.DAT\Software\Microsoft\Windows\CurrentVersion\ Explorer\RecentDocs Interpretation* contains the last 150 files or folders opened by a specific user.

HKEY_CURRENT_CONFIG (HCU)

This registry contains configuration information for the user currently logged in to the system being examined.

Summary

Numerous network forensics tools exist, many of which are expensive, like EnCase Enterprise, but there are also numerous highly effective free, open source tools, like Wireshark and tcpdump. Networking devices, including intrusion detection systems, routers, and firewalls, can yield a tremendous amount of evidence about hosts on a network. Network forensics differs from traditional forensics because both client and internal server computers are examined. One of the most important types of server is a web server, which not only contains webpages but also contains logs relating to client computer requests. Therefore, an investigator does not have to simply rely on a suspect's computer for Internet activity. The investigator can also subpoena a web server proprietor to obtain client requests for webpages. Internet Protocol version 4 (IPv4) is the most pervasive Internet addressing protocol today, but the inevitable exhaustion of IP addresses has necessitated the move to longer IPv6 addresses. Applications on the Internet use IP addresses to find a destination host on a network.

On a LAN, a MAC address is used to identify a host on a network and is used at the Data Link Layer of the OSI Model. The OSI Model is used to explain how data is routed from one host on the Internet to another host. Investigators must understand the different layers of the OSI so that they can explain how communications are transformed as they move from one layer to another, while also demonstrating that they can prove that a suspect was responsible for a particular communication. The Transport Layer of the OSI Model is arguably the most important because many of the tools that analyze TCP/IP traffic are invaluable to investigators, particularly when identifying network intrusions by hackers.

An investigator whose knowledge is limited to examining client computers, and who does not understand the network or networks that it is connected to, runs the risk of missing important evidence. This can actually lead to the arrest of the wrong individual, as noted in an earlier case study.

Advanced persistent threats (APTs) are a major concern for the United States and illustrate how important it is for organizations to hire network forensics investigators instead of relying on existing IT security personnel. These threats are so sophisticated that many traditional methods of security are unreliable. APTs are developed using months of planning. Many organizations do not realize that they publicly provide information that gives an attacker a wealth of information about their network infrastructure. This information can be gleaned from job postings, press releases, corporate websites, and a variety of other sources.

Incident Response (IR) requires a knowledge of both network and computer forensics. IR is very different from traditional forensics because (1) many more computers on a network must be examined, (2) the investigation is generally performed internally within an organization, (3) rates of prosecution are much lower since the actor is often remotely accessing a host and the chances of extraditing the perpetrator are extremely low, and (4) system logs are the focus of the investigation rather than user-created documents. There are numerous indicators of compromise, and an examination of Event IDs are critical to identify how an attacker logged onto a system and determine what services were installed. In terms of identifying which programs were executed, the examiner can review the following forensics artifacts: AmCache, Prefetch, ShimCache and RecentFileCache.bcf. Eric Zimmerman has developed numerous free, open source tools to assist incident responders with examining Windows operating system artifacts.

Key Terms

Address Resolution Protocol (ARP): A method by which the Network Layer (Layer 3) of the OSI is linked to the Data Link Layer (Layer 2).

advanced persistent threat (APT): A sophisticated, relentless, coordinated attack on a computer network, with the goal of stealing intellectual property.

anti-forensics: A concerted effort to manipulate files on a system to cover up a hacker's activity.

Application Layer: The closest layer to the end user. Interacts with applications.

Browser Help Object (BHO): Adds functionality to a web browser. The object starts every time the user opens the browser.

default gateway: The node on a network that serves as the forwarding host (router) to other networks

Domain Name System (DNS): A naming system for computers and other devices connected to the Internet.

Dynamic Host Configuration Protocol (DHCP): A standard for allowing a server to dynamically assign IP addresses and configuration to hosts on a network.

Dynamic Link Library (DLL) files: Windows system files that contain procedures and drivers that are executed by a program.

firewall: Software or hardware mechanism used to inspect data packets on a network and determine, based on a set of rules, whether each packet should be allowed through.

hosts file: A text file found on Windows that maps hostnames to IP addresses.

Hub: A hardware networking device that broadcasts data packets to all devices on a network regardless of the MAC address.

HyperText Transfer Protocol (HTTP): A standard for requests and responses between a client and a server.

Internet Assigned Numbers Authority (IANA): Organization that is responsible for the allocation of IP addresses globally.

Internet Protocol version 4 (IPv4): The fourth version protocol for connectionless data transmission on packet-switched internetworks.

intrusion detection system (IDS): Hardware or software used to monitor network traffic for malicious activity.

managed service provider (MSP): A company that generally provides IT infrastructure services, like cloud storage, to an organization.

Multipurpose Internet Mail Extensions (MIME): An electronic email protocol that extends character sets beyond ASCII and supports email attachments.

Network Address Translation (NAT): A protocol that allows multiple network devices on a network to share a single IP address (see RFC 1631).

Network Layer: Defines communications between networks or operation of the subnet and makes decisions about the physical path through which transmission should occur.

Open Systems Interconnection (OSI) Model: A model used to define how data is transmitted across the Internet.

packet: A block of data transmitted across a network.

packet sniffers: Used to capture data packets on a wireless or wired network.

PBX (Private Branch Exchange): A telephone system, within an organization, that switches calls between users in that organization on local phone lines and enables users to share a limited number of external phone lines.

Physical Layer: Defines the hardware or medium through which data is transmitted and the power required for transmission.

port: Communication channel that is specific to a running process or application on a computer.

Prefetch: A folder in the Windows system folder that contains files used in the boot process and also files regularly opened by other programs.

Presentation Layer: Prepares data for the Application Layer and is responsible for data conversion, compression, and encryption.

promiscuous mode: Enables a NIC to listen to communications broadcast on a network, regardless of the intended recipient.

protocol analyzer: Used to analyze and interpret traffic over a network.

proxy server: A computer that relays a request for a client to a server computer.

router: Hardware that connects a network to one or more other networks and directs data packets from one node to another.

routing table: Contains information about the network and provides the most effective method of directing packets across that network.

Secure Data Transmission: The process of sending data over a secure channel, whereby the channel remains secure through the use of encryption.

Session Layer: Responsible for initiating, maintaining, and terminating processes on different systems.

Simple Mail Transport Protocol (SMTP) server: Used to send email, for a client, and the email is then routed to another SMTP server, or other email server.

subnet mask: Facilitates the communication between segregated networks.

switch: An intelligent hardware device that connects devices on a network.

Timestomping: An anti-forensics technique used to manipulate the timestamps of a file.

Traceroute: A tool used to track the path of IP packets from one system to another.

Transmission Control Protocol (TCP): A communication standard that is used in conjunction with the Internet.

Trojan: A legitimate-looking application used to disguise malware.

Uniform Resource Identifier (URI): Used to locate a resource on the Internet.

User Datagram Protocol (UDP): A connectionless communication protocol that has limited packet recovery functionality and operates at the Transport Layer.

Voice over Internet Protocol (VoIP): A protocol that takes analog audio signals, e.g., voice, and converts those signals to digital data that can be transmitted across the Internet.

web browser: Used to (1) work with a DNS server to resolve DNS addresses, (2) make HTTP requests, (3) download resources, and (4) display the contents of the file with browser help Objects (BHO).

web server: Stores and serves up HTML documents and related media resources in response to client requests.

Assessment

CLASSROOM DISCUSSIONS

1. How is the job of a network forensics examiner different from that of a traditional computer forensics examiner?

2. What difficulties are associated with investigating APTs?

3. Discuss indicators of compromise (IOCs) that an investor should look for in a network intrusion investigation.

MULTIPLE-CHOICE QUESTIONS

1. Which of the following best describes malware that is disguised as a legitimate application or program?

    A. Worm
    B. Virus
    C. Trojan
    D. Logic bomb

2. Which of the following has a primary function of serving up HTML documents?

    A. Web server

    B. Proxy server

    C. SMTP server

    D. Virtual server

3. What is the name of the folder in the Windows system folder that contains files used in the boot process and regularly opened by other programs?

    A. User

    B. Journal

    C. svchost

    D. Prefetch

4. Which layer of the OSI Model can be viewed as closest to the user view?

    A. Session Layer

    B. Application Layer

    C. Presentation Layer

    D. Transport Layer

5. Which layer of the OSI Model defines the wires that electrical impulses flow through that are involved in Internet communication?

    A. Transport Layer

    B. Session Layer

    C. Data Link Layer

    D. Physical Layer

6. Which of the following is a protocol for connectionless data transmission on packet-switched internetworks? Its header has 14 fields. This protocol uses 32-bit addresses, which are usually represented in four octets of dotted decimal notation.

    A. IPv2

    B. IPv4

    C. IPv6

    D. IPv8

7. Which of the following enables a NIC to listen to communications broadcast on a network, regardless of the intended recipient?

    A. Proprietary mode

    B. Passive mode

    C. Promiscuous mode

    D. Active mode

8. Which of the following defines the standard format for electronic mail?

   A. IRC

   B. ICMP

   C. SMTP

   D. HTTP

9. Within the OSI Model, this layer is responsible for initiating, maintaining, and terminating processes on different systems.

   A. Transport Layer

   B. Session Layer

   C. Data Link Layer

   D. Physical Layer

10. Which of the following organizations is responsible for the allocation of IP addresses globally?

    A. ISO

    B. IEEE

    C. IANA

    D. NIST

FILL IN THE BLANKS

1. A(n) _____ is a block of data used in communications across the Internet.

2. Transmission _____ Protocol is a communication standard that is used in conjunction with the Internet.

3. A(n) _____ detection system is hardware or software used to monitor network traffic for malicious activity.

4. User _____ Protocol is a connectionless communication protocol that has limited packet recovery functionality and operates at the Transport Layer.

5. Address _____ Protocol is a method by which the Network Layer (Layer 3) of the OSI Model is linked to the Data Link Layer (Layer 2).

6. A(n) _____ Help Object is used to add functionality to a web browser. The object starts every time the user opens the browser.

7. Dynamic _____ Library files are Windows system files that contain procedures and drivers that are executed by a program.

8. An advanced _____ threat is a sophisticated, relentless, coordinated attack on a computer network, with the goal of stealing intellectual property.

9. Packet _____ are used to capture data packets on a wireless or wired network.

10. HyperText _____ Protocol is a standard for requests and responses between a client and a server.

PROJECTS

Research Internet Crimes

Conduct a search for crimes on the Internet that you believe would require the skills of a network forensics investigator. Detail the nature of the network evidence that would have been helpful to the investigation.

Write a Report Detailing Evidence Types Found on a Computer

Write a report detailing the type of evidence that can be found on a client computer relating to a user's network activity.

Create an Investigation Guide on Device Types

Create a guide for investigators that details the type of devices in a home or business network that may contain valuable evidence.

Log2Timeline/RegRipper

Create an E01 file image of a Windows personal computer, using FTK Imager. Download either Log2Timeline or RegRipper. Use the files from your image, to examine the registry files, and then report what you find. Include in your report data from the NTUSER.DAT file.

SANS SIFT Workstation (Advanced)

Create an E01 file image of a Windows personal computer, using FTK Imager. Register and then download a copy of the SANS SIFT Workstation from www.sans.org. Download VMWare Player (free version). With some direction from your teacher/professor, try some of the many tools from the suite of applications contained in the SIFT workstation.

Chapter | 9

Mobile Forensics

Learning Outcomes

After reading this chapter, you will be able to understand the following:

- The evolution and importance of cellphone forensics;
- How cellular networks operate;
- The type of evidence available from cellphone carriers;
- Retrieving evidence from smartphones;
- Conducting SIM card forensics;
- Different mobile operating systems;
- Legal considerations associated with cellphone investigations;
- Tablets, GPS, and other mobile device forensics; and
- How to document a cellphone investigation.

The field of mobile forensics has grown immensely in recent times and is now one of the most important areas of research. There are several reasons for this. First and foremost, the capabilities of cellphones have been greatly enhanced, and these mobile devices are arguably more important than desktop or laptop computers because they are generally always turned on and continually record the user's location in a variety of ways. Therefore, they continually record our movements, our activities, and provide tremendous insight into our behavior. Communication on a cellphone is very different compared to a traditional computer, and criminals will often say or text things on a cellphone that they would never communicate using a traditional computer.

Cellphone forensics has not always been taken seriously, and even in 2008 if you had asked someone in law enforcement about investigating cellphones, you would have typically heard someone say that nobody in their laboratory worked on cellphones or that they did not hold anything of value. In fact, some say that the only reason that there was cellphone forensic software was that some suspicious spouses would buy the software to see if their partner was cheating. Hardware imaging devices have also been used for several years but were not originally used for investigations. Cellebrite sold their hardware to cellphone retailers who needed a device to copy the contents of a customer's cellphone and its SIM card to another cellphone—usually when the customer wanted to upgrade to a new cellphone. When law enforcement became involved in cellphone investigations, Cellebrite made some minor modifications and began selling many more devices.

Cellphone forensics was always important but not many people realized its importance. It is not surprising because the available cellphone forensics software could not work with the vast majority of cellphones. Once Internet capabilities were added to cellphones, their importance to investigations grew. With this demand came better forensics software. Suddenly, more evidence was available, which included email, Internet searches, and social networking activity. Today, just about every computer forensics laboratory has cellphone forensics capabilities. Additionally, there has been a separation of duties in larger laboratories. For example, one investigator may be responsible for extracting evidence from the cellphone, while another investigator might be responsible for much of the paperwork, including subpoenas to cellphone carriers, while another investigator may be responsible for gathering and analyzing data from Base Transceiver Stations. A **Base Transceiver Station (BTS)** is the equipment found at a cell site that facilitates the communication of a cellphone user across a cellular network.

Cellphone forensics has tremendous challenges, however. There are still a huge number of cellphones that cannot be imaged. Only the most popular cellphones will be supported by forensic software and hardware. Full disk encryption means that many mobile devices cannot be accessed, which has created a backlog of criminal cases that rely on accessing a particular device. Furthermore, while a judge may force a suspect to unlock a device, using his biometric, a suspect may not be forced to unlock the device if it has been PIN or password protected. This is because entering a PIN or password has been viewed in a number of cases as self-incrimination, which is protected under the Fifth Amendment.

Hundreds of new cellphones come to market each year, many of which will never be supported by forensic tools. Compounding all these problems for investigators is the plethora of operating systems running on cellphones today. An investigator working with a laptop is generally going to encounter a Microsoft Windows operating system or Apple's macOS (operating system). An investigator who obtains a cellphone, on the other hand, could encounter other mobile device operating systems, like Android.

A major challenge for law enforcement today, particularly in Europe, is the purchase of encrypted smartphones by criminals. Encrypted devices are important for security and privacy and many of these producers provide a vital service to the government. These companies include BlackBerry, Boeing, Bull Atos, GSMK CryptoPhone, Silent Circle, Sikur, Sirin Labs, Turing Robotic Industries and Thales Group. These crypto-phone manufacturers have however attracted the interest of organized criminal gangs, who are willing to pay a premium to obfuscate their criminal enterprises and activities. For example, in the U.K. and other European countries, organized criminals paid approximately $1,870 every six months to run EncroChat on repurposed Android devices; EncroChat is an encrypted instant messaging service.

In looking to the future, our dependency on cellphone forensics will only increase, and the number of vendor-supported cellphones and tablets will expand. The strong market for Android and iOS devices means that the investigator must look outside the device more and more—to the synced computer, to the synced devices in the home and at work, and in the Cloud. Cellphones continue to have a growing dependence on cloud computing, which means that investigators will increasingly rely on evidence that goes beyond the scope of the network carrier. Mobile applications, like Facebook, WhatsApp, Instagram, and others will continue to be an extremely important source of evidence, although advances in encryption mean that investigators now rely more on subpoenas to third parties and less on being able to extract the evidence from the device itself.

This chapter is called "Mobile Forensics" and not "Cellphone Forensics" because this chapter will discuss other mobile devices that can store or generate incriminating evidence, including tablets, personal media players, and GPS devices. Additionally, even without possession of a suspect's mobile device, there are numerous sources of mobile device evidence available, as you will learn in this chapter.

The Cellular Network

A **cellular network** is a group of cells. A **cell** refers to a geographic area within a cellular network. A **cell site** is a cell tower located in a cell. When you make a call with your cellphone, you connect with a cell tower. The communication is then transmitted to the Mobile Switching Center. A **Mobile Switching Center (MSC)** is responsible for switching data packets from one network path to another on a cellular network. If the user is calling a user on a cellular network, managed by another carrier, then the call will be routed from the MSC to the Public Switched Telephone Network. The **Public Switched Telephone Network (PSTN)** is an aggregate of all circuit-switched telephone networks. The purpose of the PSTN is to connect all telephone networks worldwide, and this is where tolls for connecting calls across different networks are calculated. Figure 9.1 details the path of a cellphone call.

Cellular Telephone Network

FIGURE 9.1   Cellular network

Base Transceiver Station

A cell site, also known as a cell tower, can be a stand-alone tower or be attached to a building or other structure. The cell tower generally has an antenna with three panels on each side. Typically, there are three sides on each antenna. Usually the middle panel is a transmitter and the two outer panels are receivers. The cell tower is generally over 200 feet high. A tower can contain multiple antennae, which are owned by different carriers, as illustrated in Figure 9.2. An antenna can either be located on a cell tower or be placed on the side or top of a building.

FIGURE 9.2   Cell tower

Let's Get Practical!   Locate Local Cell Towers and Antennae

Understanding the location of cell towers and antennae is helpful to know and there are resources to help.

1. **Start** your Web browser and then navigate to www.antennasearch.com.

2. In the **Street Address** field type 100 Fifth Avenue in City type New York in **State** type NY in **Zip** type 10011 and then click **Go**.

3. Click **Process**, and then compare your screen to Figure 9.3.

4. Click the **Download Records** link under View Tower Results.

5. In the displayed **File Download** dialog box, click **Open**.

The unformatted results will display in Excel.

6. Save the file as directed by your instructor, and then Exit Excel.

7. On the antennasearch.com website, click **View Tower Results**.

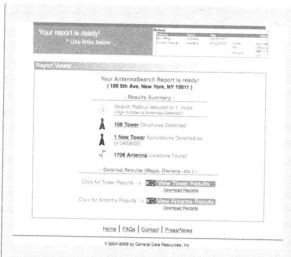

FIGURE 9.3   Search results

A Google map displays. You can also click the *Satellite* button or *Hybrid* button for a different view. You can also use the control to zoom in on a tower.

8.   Click one of the cell tower links, and then compare your screen with Figure 9.4.

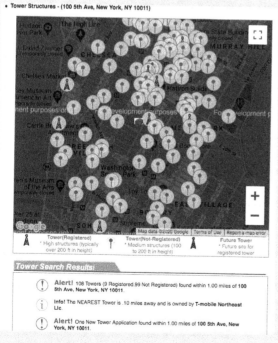

FIGURE 9.4   Map of cell tower locations

9.   Close your web browser.

As previously noted, the Base Transceiver Station (BTS) is the equipment, at the cell site, that facilitates communication between the cellphone user and the carrier's network. A **Base Station Controller (BSC)** manages the radio signals for base transceiver stations, in terms of assigning frequencies and handoffs between cell sites. When moving through an area, your cellphone call may be handled by several base transceiver stations, i.e., there will be a handoff from one BTS to another. There are two types of handoff. A **soft handoff** is when a cellular communication is conditionally handed off from one base station to another and the mobile equipment is simultaneously communicating with multiple base transceiver stations. The handoff is conditional because the signal strength on a new BTS will be adjudicated. A **hard handoff** means that the communication is only handled by one base transceiver station at a time with no simultaneous communication.

BTS Evidence

From a computer forensics perspective, it is important to understand how a cellular network is structured so that the investigator can realize the type of evidence that can be retrieved from the carrier's network, even without access to the suspect's handset. Law enforcement can request cell site records from a carrier, for a particular cellphone user, which is data retrieved from the BTS. It is important for the investigators to specify the format that they wish the evidence to be in; obtaining the information in a spreadsheet is generally more helpful because the data can be easily sorted and analyzed. Figure 9.5 shows sample data from a BTS.

Call Type	Call Start Date/Time	Duration (Mins: Seconds)	Calling Number	Called Number	First Cell ID	Last Cell ID
PS	10/2/2020 09:06	02:11	(914) 555-2389	(914) 553-4870	15678931	59487023
PS	10/2/2020 09:17	05:56	(914) 555-2389	(212) 555-9020	58230944	34598723
SMS	10/2/2020 13:22	00:38	(914) 555-2389	(516) 555-0012	12894232	98735834
CS	10/2/2020 16:01	12:29	(914) 555-2389	(516) 555-3927	58320321	35897345
PS	10/2/2020 21:39	01:31	(914) 555-2389	(646) 555-8901	94899917	34589344

FIGURE 9.5 BTS data

To obtain evidence, law enforcement can contact the network carrier and explain the user information that is needed as part of an ongoing investigation. The investigator should also explain to the provider that the customer in question should not be notified about the investigation. Under U.S.C. 2703(f), "Requirements for Court Order", law enforcement can request that the suspect's records are preserved for 90 days, pending their acquisition of a search warrant. This court order can be extended for an additional 90 days. As previously noted, applying for a court order does not require approval from a judge or magistrate or necessitate the need to show probable cause – in other words, there is a lower burden of proof.

Subscriber Evidence

In addition to BTS evidence, law enforcement can obtain subscriber information, call detail records (CDR), and PUK codes. **Subscriber records** are personal details maintained by the carrier about their customers and can include their name, address, alternative phone numbers, social security number, and credit card information. **Call detail records (CDR)** are details used for billing purposes and can include phone numbers called, duration, dates and times of calls, and cell sites used. It is of course important to verify the data that you receive from the carrier with the evidence found on the device, that is, corroborating evidence. **PIN Unblocking Key (PUK)** is an unlock reset code used to bypass the SIM PIN protection; some carriers use the word "unlock" or "unlocking" as an alternative to "unblocking" with PUK.

Mobile Station

The **Mobile Station** is comprised of Mobile Equipment (handset) and, in the case of a GSM network, a Subscriber Identity Module (SIM). An **International Mobile Equipment Identity (IMEI)** number uniquely identifies the mobile equipment or handset. The initial six or eight digits of the IMEI are the Type Allocation Code (TAC). The **Type Allocation Code (TAC)** identifies the type of wireless device. The website http://www.nobbi.com/tacquery.php allows an investigator to enter a TAC or IMEI to discover details about a specific device.

The IMEI is generally found by removing the back of the cellphone and then looking under the battery, as shown in Figure 9.6.

FIGURE 9.6   IMEI on a cellphone

Let's Get Practical!   Locate the IMEI Through the Keypad

When looking for the IMEI, it is proper procedure to look under the battery. However, the IMEI can be displayed through the keypad.

1. Power on your cellphone.

2. On your keypad, type *#06#

The IMEI number should display on your GSM cellphone.

A **Universal Integrated Circuit Card (UICC)** is a smart card used to uniquely identify a subscriber on a GSM or UMTS network. With a GSM network, the smart card is a SIM, whereas with a UMTS the smart card is a USIM (Universal Subscriber Identity Module).

A **Mobile Equipment Identifier (MEID)** is an internationally unique number that identifies a CDMA handset (mobile equipment). The MEID was previously referred to as an Electronic Serial Number (ESN) before being replaced by a global MEID standard around 2005. An **Electronic Serial Number (ESN)** is an 11-digit number used to identify a subscriber on a CDMA cellular network. The ESN contains a manufacturer code and a serial number that identifies a specific handset. Both the ESN and the MEID are noted on the handset in a decimal format as well as a hex format. The website www. meidconverter.com allows users to convert between ESN and MEID and also view both decimal and hex values of an ESN or MEID. Some providers provide a lookup feature for subscriber details using the MEID.

Many CDMA cellphones have a subsidy lock. A **subsidy lock** confines a subscriber to a certain cellular network so that a cellphone can be sold for free or at a subsidized price. From a forensics perspective, this means that the phone's file system often cannot be acquired with an active subsidy. For example, an iPhone may be available for as little as $99 but you are locked into a particular carrier and a specific contract. The unlocked iPhone may actually cost over $1,000 (depending on the model) but the user can easily switch carriers and is not locked into a two-year agreement. Prepaid cellphone plans, offered by AT&T and others, where the subscriber paid full price for the phone, can be unlocked. An investigator should understand this because the (unlocked) handset may have been used internationally with a SIM card purchased abroad.

Locked cellphones (with a subsidy lock) are less widely available in some European countries, and carrier handset subsidies are less frequently offered. Prepaid or pay as you go are generally more popular. In fact, in some countries it is illegal for a cellphone carrier to sell a locked phone. Generally, in Italy a passport is required to obtain a SIM card and service, whereas in Ireland no identification is necessary. In Italy, a carrier will add a PIN to the SIM by default, whereas this is not the case in Ireland. These rules will vary from country to country and of course impact forensic investigations. Recently introduced European Union (EU) regulations mean that a consumer with a cellphone plan purchased in an EU country cannot be charged roaming fees when traveling to another EU country.

All cellphones sold in the United States have an FCC-ID. An **FCC-ID** is a number issued by the Federal Communication Commission (FCC) that indicates that the handset is authorized to operate on radio frequencies within the FCC's control. Figure 9.7 shows a sample FCC-ID on a handset.

FCC-ID

FIGURE 9.7   FCC ID

Once the back of a cellphone has been removed and the battery has been taken out, the FCC-ID can be viewed. The FCC-ID can be entered on the FCC website (http://transition.fcc.gov/oet/ea/fccid/). Once you enter the FCC-ID, you can download a manual for the cellphone. This is important for an investigator who may need to know about the features of the cellphone and, more importantly, how to remove the cellphone from all networks and external communications for proper containment.

Additional information about cellphones and cellphone carriers can be obtained from the websites www.phonescoop.com and www.gsmarena.com.

SIM Card

The **SIM card** identifies a user on a cellular network and contains an IMSI. SIM cards are found in cellphones that operate on GSM cellular networks and usually in iDEN network cellphones. A user can simply add a SIM card to an unlocked cellphone. Not all US cellphone carriers will allow a user to purchase a SIM card and use their handset on another network.

The **International Mobile Subscriber Identity (IMSI)** is an internationally unique number on the SIM card that identifies a user on a network. The **mobile country code (MCC)** is the first three digits of the IMSI. The proceeding two to three digits are the mobile network code (MNC). For example, MNC 026 for MCC 310 represents the carrier T-Mobile USA. The final part of the IMSI is the MSIN, which is comprised of up to 10 digits. A **mobile subscriber identity number (MSIN)** is created by a cellular telephone carrier and identifies the subscriber on the network. The **mobile subscriber ISDN (MSISDN)** is essentially the phone number for the subscriber. The MSISDN is a maximum of 15 digits and is comprised of the country code (CC), the numbering plan area (NPA) and the subscriber number (SN). Country codes are relatively easy to find. For example, in the Americas the CC is "1" because it is in Zone 1. For Trinidad and Tobago all telephone numbers begin with "1-868". European countries are in Zone 3 and Zone 4. For example, Ireland, in Zone 3, is "353" while the United Kingdom in Zone 4 is "44". The numbering plan area for Nassau County, New York, is "516" and is also referred to as the "Area Code".

The SIM card also includes an ICCID. The **Integrated Circuit Card ID (ICCID)** is a 19- to 20-digit serial number physically located on the SIM card, as shown in Figure 9.8.

FIGURE 9.8 SIM card

The first two digits of the ICCID are referred to as the major industry identifier (MII). ISO/IEC 7812-1:2017 is a standard for "Identification cards — Identification of issuers", which was published by the International Organization for Standardization (ISO) in 1989. As its name suggests, this is a numbering standard for identification cards. The first digit indicates the industry and "8" indicates "Healthcare, telecommunications and other future industry assignments". The first two digits indicate "Telecommunications administrations and private operating agencies". The ICCID on a SIM card will begin with "89". The proceeding two numbers will indicate the Country Code (CC). The next two numbers are the Issuer Identifier (II), which will indicate the telecommunications company. Understanding the ICCID will help you to identify the origins of a SIM card. The ICCID can be accessed, via the SIM card, in the EF_ICCID file.

There are of course mobile devices, like 4G-enabled iPads and Android tablets, that contain an eSIM (embedded SIM). The eSIM is soldered onto the device's printed circuit board.

International Numbering Plans

The website www.numberingplans.com is a tremendous resource for mobile forensics examiners working with GSM cellphones. The website provides "number analysis tools", which allow the user to conduct an analysis of the following:

- Phone number analysis

- IMSI number analysis

- IMEI number analysis

- SIM number analysis

- ISPC number analysis

An **International Signaling Point Code (ISPC)** is a standardized numbering system used to identify a node on an international telecommunications network.

Authenticating a Subscriber on a Network

The Mobile Switching Center is where user information passes to the Home Location Register, Visitor Location Register, and Authentication Center. The **Home Location Register (HLR)** is a database of a carrier's subscribers and includes their home address, IMSI, telephone number, SIM card ICCID, and services used by the subscriber. The **Visitor Location Register (VLR)** is a database of information about a roaming subscriber. A subscriber can only be found on one HLR but can be found in multiple VLRs. The current location of a mobile station (handset) can be found on a VLR. The VLR also contains the Temporary Mobile Subscriber Identity. The **Temporary Mobile Subscriber Identity (TMSI)** is a randomly generated number that is assigned to a mobile station, by the VLR, when the handset is switched on, and is based on the geographic location.

The **Equipment Identity Register (EIR)** is used to track IMEI numbers and decide whether an IMEI is valid, suspect, or perhaps stolen. The **Authentication Center (AuC)** is a database that contains the subscriber's IMSI, authentication, and encryption algorithms. The Authentication Center will issue the subscriber an encryption key, which will encrypt wireless communications between the mobile equipment and the network.

Cellular Network Types

There are two types of cellular service carriers. A **mobile network operator (MNO)** owns and operates a cellular network. The following companies are MNOs:

- Verizon
- T-Mobile/Sprint/Nextel
- AT&T/Cingular

A **mobile virtual network operator (MVNO)** does not own its own cellular network but operates on the network of a mobile network operator. For example, Altice Mobile has its own cellular service but operates on the AT&T network. This means that two warrants may be needed for an investigation – one for AT&T (the MNO) and one for Altice Mobile (the MVNO) to obtain a suspect's records. The following companies are Mobile Virtual Network Operators:

- Altice Mobile
- Net10 Wireless
- Consumer Cellular
- H2O Wireless

Evolution of Wireless Telecommunications Technologies

Cellular telecommunication technologies include 2G (second generation), 3G (third generation), 4G (fourth generation), and 5G (fifth generation) communications. It is important to note that the term "cellular telephone network" was not used because 3G and 4G cellular networks also support mobile broadband Internet services. Consumers utilizing these services can operate on cellular networks with either a MiFi router or a plug and play USB device. **My Wireless Fidelity (MiFi)** is a portable wireless router that provides Internet access for several Internet-enabled devices and communicates via a cellular network.

4G is a wireless telecommunications standard and supports high-speed large data transmission rates. **4G Long Term Evolution (LTE) Advanced** is a high-mobility broadband communication protocol that is suitable for use on trains and in other vehicles. Motorola Mobility, which was purchased by Google in 2011 but then sold to Lenovo in 2014, holds the patent for this technology. 4G LTE was first implemented in Oslo (Norway) and Stockholm (Sweden).

5G

5G is a transmission protocol developed by the 3rd Generation Partnership Project (3GPP). This enhanced protocol will allow telecom carriers to transmit data, via radio signals, at an extremely high frequency (EHF) or "millimeter wave". This new protocol will support the transmission of more data at much faster speeds than 4G in an age, which should address the exponential growth of wireless data transmission; more cellular devices and the Internet of Things (IoT) have put immense pressure on networks. More information about 5G is available in Chapter 14, "Internet of Things (IoT) Forensics and Emergent Technologies".

The **International Telecommunication Union (ITU)** is an agency of the United Nations that produces standards for information and communication technologies. The ITU is comprised of 193 members and more than 700 private sector and academic institutions.

Time Division Multiple Access (TDMA)

Time Division Multiple Access (TDMA) is a radio communication methodology that enables devices to communicate on the same frequency by splitting digital signals into time slots or "bursts". Bursts are data packets that are transmitted on the same frequency. 2G GSM networks use the TDMA method of communication.

Global System for Mobile Communications (GSM)

Global System for Mobile communications (GSM) is an international standard for signal communications, which uses TDMA and FDD (Frequency Division Duplex) communication methods. Thus, GSM cellular telephones use bursts. GSM is a standard created by the European Telecommunications Standards Institute (ETSI), which was primarily designed by Nokia and Ericsson. The most pervasive GSM standard is 4G LTE Advanced. 3G GSM networks use UMTS (Universal Mobile Telecommunications System) and WCDMA (Wide Band CDMA) for communication. **Wide Band CDMA (WCDMA)** is a high-speed signal transmission method based on CDMA and FDD methods. TDMA is often described as the precursor to the GSM protocol, although these two networks are incompatible. T-Mobile and AT&T use GSM networks in the United States.

GSM handsets, when unlocked, can be used on international networks by simply purchasing a SIM card locally and activating the SIM card with a local carrier. This is important to know because a suspect could have used a GSM cellphone internationally, which could have removed evidence when the SIM card was switched.

3GP is an audio/video file format found on mobile phones operating on 3G GSM cellular networks. This standard was developed by the 3rd Generation Partnership Project (3GPP). **3rd Generation Partnership Project (3GPP)** is a collaboration of six telecommunications standards bodies and a large number of telecommunications corporations worldwide that provide telecommunication standards. The scope of their work includes Global System for Mobile Communication (GSM), General Packet Radio Service (GPRS) and Enhanced Data rates for GSM Evolution (EDGE). More information about 3GPP can be found here: www.3gpp.org. **General Packet Radio Service (GPRS)** is packet switching wireless communication found on 2G and 3G GSM networks. **Enhanced Data rates for GSM Evolution (EDGE)** is a high data transfer technology, which is found on GSM networks. EDGE provides up to three times the data capacity of GPRS.

Universal Mobile Telecommunications System (UMTS)

Universal Mobile Telecommunications System (UMTS) is a 3G cellular network standard, which is based upon GSM and was developed by 3GPP. As previously noted, UMTS cellphones utilize a USIM smart card to identify the subscriber on a network. From a forensics perspective, a USIM can store more files than a SIM card. Communication across the network is via the wideband WCDMA protocol.

Code Division Multiple Access (CDMA)

Code Division Multiple Access (CDMA) is a spread-spectrum communication methodology that uses a wide bandwidth for transmitting data. This technology, developed by Qualcomm, does not share channels. It uses multiplexing techniques. **Multiplexing** is a communication protocol whereby multiple signals are transmitted simultaneously across a shared medium. A fiber optic is an example of a shared medium that can support multiplexing. **CDMA2000** is a 3G technology that uses the CDMA communications protocol. CDMA technology is used by Verizon and Sprint on their US nationwide cellular networks. With the merger of Sprint and T-Mobile, Sprint may move to GSM communications.

3GP2 is an audio/video file format found on mobile phones operating on 3G CDMA cellular networks. This standard was developed by the 3rd Generation Partnership Project 2 (3GPP2). **3rd Generation Partnership Project 2 (3GPP2)** is a partnership of North American and Asian 3G telecommunications companies that develop standards for third generation mobile networks, including CDMA. More information about the work of 3GPP2, its partners and its members, can be found here: www.3gpp2.org.

Integrated Digital Enhanced Network (iDEN)

Integrated Digital Enhanced Network (iDEN) is a wireless technology developed by Motorola, which combines two-way radio capabilities with digital cellphone technology. iDEN is based on TDMA. Nextel introduced "Push-to-talk", which used iDEN, in 1993. The service enabled subscribers to use their cellphones like a walkie-talkie (or two-way radio). When using the cellphone with the Push-to-talk feature, cell towers are not used. iDEN is a proprietary protocol, unlike all other major cellular networks, which use standard open protocols.

SIM Card Forensics

The two primary functions of a SIM card are (a) to identify the subscriber to a cellular network and (b) to store data. We have already discussed the mechanism by which the IMSI on the SIM is used to identify a user on a GSM or iDEN network. What is perhaps more important to the investigator is the SIM card's storage of important evidence. A SIM is essentially a smart card that is comprised of a processor and memory.

SIM Hardware

A SIM card varies in size based on the mobile device, although a standard SIM is 25mm x 15mm. The latest iPhones (iPhone 5 and later) use a nano-SIM card, which is 12.3mm x 8.8mm. A Samsung Galaxy S20, for example, supports both a nano SIM and an eSIM. Printed on the outside is a unique serial number called an ICCID. The serial interface is the area where the SIM Card communicates with the handset, as shown in Figure 9.9.

FIGURE 9.9   Serial interface

SIM File System

The Electronically Erasable Programmable Read Only Memory (EEPROM) is where the hierarchical file system exists. The operating system, user authentication, and encryption algorithms are found on the SIM card's Read Only Memory (ROM).

There are three primary areas of the SIM card file system:

1. Master File (MF): the root of the file system
2. Dedicated Files (DF): basically file directories
3. Elementary Files (EF): where the data is stored.

The Elementary Files (EF) are where the subscriber information is stored, which we shall now describe in detail. **Abbreviated Dialing Numbers (ADN)** contain the contact names and numbers entered by the subscriber. On the SIM, these contacts are located in the folder EF_ADN. **Forbidden Public Land Mobile Network (FPLMN)** refers to cellular networks that a subscriber attempted to connect to but was not authorized to connect; this data can be found in EF_FPLMN. This data can assist investigators who want to know where a suspect was located, even if they were unsuccessful in connecting to a network. **Last Numbers Dialed (LND)** refers to a list of all outgoing calls made by the subscriber; the folder EF_LND holds this information. EF_LOCI contains the Temporary Mobile Subscriber Identity (TMSI), which is assigned by the Visitor Location Register (VLR). The TMSI represents the location where the mobile equipment was last shut down. The TMSI is four octets long and will make no sense to the investigator. However, the investigator could contact the carrier for assistance with determining the location represented by the TMSI.

For easy reference, the acronyms in the SIM file system are as follows:

- **EF_ADN:** Abbreviated Dialing Numbers (ADN)
- **EF_FPLMN:** Forbidden Public Land Mobile Network (FPLMN)
- **EF_LND:** Last Numbers Dialed (LND)
- **EF_LOCI:** Area where user last powered down the phone
- **EF_SMS:** Short Message Service (SMS)

Figure 9.10 shows the SIM directory structure

FIGURE 9.10   SIM directory structure

Access to the SIM

Gaining access to the data on a SIM is challenging if the SIM card has been PIN-protected. A PIN on a SIM is usually four digits long but can be up to 8 digits. An investigator will have three attempts to get the PIN correct before the SIM is locked. After that, you are prompted to enter a PUK (PIN Unblocking Key) or a PUC (Personal Unblocking Code); these terms and acronyms will vary but are technically the same. An investigator can request a PUC from the carrier. A **Personal Unblocking Code (PUC)** is a code that is available from the carrier and allows a user to remove the PIN protection from the SIM card. The number of possible attempts varies, but generally after 5–10 incorrect PIN entry attempts, the SIM card will be permanently locked.

> **Note**
>
> A user can go online and change his or her PUK in which case the investigator would be unable to access the contents of the SIM without the cooperation of the subscriber.

SIM Card Cloning

Similar to hard disk drive cloning, an investigator will often choose to clone a SIM card, rather than examine the original SIM card. As a best practice, a SIM card clone should be used in the investigation rather than the original. Most cellphone forensic tools enable the investigator to clone a SIM card.

Types of Evidence

The range of evidence available from a cellphone is quite different from what can be acquired from a laptop or desktop. One of the primary differences is the existence of SMS, MMS, and RCS messages, which the following sections explain in detail.

Short Message Service (SMS)

Short Message Service (SMS) is a text message communication service found on mobile devices. These text messages can be found in memory on a mobile handset or on a SIM card in the handset. SMS is primarily saved on the handset but when stored on the SIM they can be found in the DF_ TELECOM file.

An investigator can determine whether an SMS message has been read, deleted, has not been read, sent or unsent, based upon the status flag. The byte value will change based on the status of the message. Table 9.1 identifies the values of the status flag and indicates their meaning.

TABLE 9.1   SMS Status Flags

Status Flag Value (Binary)	Description
00000000	Deleted message
00000001	Read message

Status Flag Value (Binary)	Description
00000011	Unread message
00000101	Sent message
00000111	Unsent message

When viewing the text message with a hex editor, an unread SMS message will begin with "11", a deleted message with "00", and so forth.

Multimedia Messaging Service (MMS)

Multimedia Messaging Service (MMS) is a messaging service, found on most cellphones, which allows the user to send multimedia content, including audio, video, and images. Using a cellphone forensics tool, the investigator can carve this multimedia content out of the user's messages.

Rich Communication Services (RCS)

Rich Communication Services (RCS) is an advanced messaging standard that aims to be a cross-platform mobile device solution for SMS, MMS, and other consumer communications. This standard is supported by smartphone manufacturers, telecommunications companies, and other companies, including Google. RCS is sometimes referred to as "Chat". The idea is that RCS will broaden the capabilities of traditional SMS and possess the functionality of other messaging apps, such as WhatsApp, iMessage, etc. RCS will be available through the Android Messages app. Forensics investigators should understand that Chat (RCS) (1) is becoming more popular, (2) is a protocol and not an app, (3) does not support end-to-end encryption, like Signal or iMessage, and (4) maintains the same legal intercept standards as SMS.

Handset Specifications

Knowledge of handset hardware will assist an investigator with knowing how to safely secure the device after it has been seized. As previously noted, the FCC-ID on the handset can be researched online to identify the features of the mobile device.

Memory and Processing

Cellphones contain a microprocessor, Read Only Memory (ROM) chip, and Random Access Memory (RAM). Secure Digital cards, particularly microSD cards, are less likely to be found in smartphones today, although an investigator should check to see if there is removable storage—especially with older phones. Memory cards can contain the following data:

- Photos
- Videos

- Apps

- Maps

Most smartphones today do not contain a removable SD card but instead will use an internal Embedded Multimedia Card (eMMC). This memory uses FAT32. Many tablets still maintain the ability to upgrade memory with an SD card.

Battery

There are primarily four types of cellphone batteries: (a) Lithium ion (Li-ion), (b) Lithium Polymer (Li-Poly), (c) Nickel Cadmium (NiCd), and (d) Nickel Metal Hydride (NiMH). The iPhone and Black-Berry Curve, for example, uses a Lithium Ion battery, which is a lightweight battery compared to other batteries.

Other Hardware

Cellphones will vary from model to model, but they will also generally have a radio module, digital signal processor, liquid crystal display (LCD), microphone, and speaker. Some models will also have a built-in keyboard.

Accelerometer and Sensors

Another feature, which is also frequently found on cellphones today, is an accelerometer. An **accelerometer** is a hardware device that senses motion or gravity and reacts to these changes. An accelerometer measures changes in velocity along an axis; on an iPhone there are three axes where this is measured. An accelerometer will facilitate a screen flipping when the device is turned sideways or upside-down. Moreover, the accelerometer is used to enhance the gamer's experience by allowing the user to turn and move in a game by changing the angle of the device. The accelerometer has become popular with its integration into the iPad and iPhone. An iOS developer can access raw data from an accelerometer using the Core Motion framework, and more specifically the CMMotionManager class. From a forensics perspective, access to this type of data could be extremely helpful in certain types of cases. There are also analog sensors on an iPhone that can measure gas, voltage, temperature, light, magnetism, and vibrations. With the introduction of a recent exploit for the iPhone, and the ability to acquire a full file system, we have learned more and more about the use of sensors and their potential in investigations. More information about this can be found in Chapter 12, "Mac Forensics".

Camera

Most cellphones today come with a digital camera, with still photo and video capabilities. Most smartphones possess features that allow the user to take a photo and quickly upload that picture to a social networking site, like Facebook. In terms of video, many smartphones enable the user to upload their content directly to sites like YouTube. Many smartphones will also embed the latitude and longitude of where the photograph was taken. Most Android cellphones will do this by default.

Mobile Operating Systems

As noted in earlier chapters, the purpose of an operating system (OS) is to manage the resources of an electronic device—usually a computer. From a computer forensics perspective, knowledge of an operating system helps an investigator understand what type of evidence can be retrieved, the tools required to retrieve the evidence, and an understanding of where to find the evidence. The problem for investigators is that there are so many different operating systems when it comes to mobile devices when compared to traditional computers.

Android OS

Android is an open source operating system based on the Linux 2.6 kernel. In 2005, Google acquired Android. Android is maintained by the Open Handset Alliance (OHA), which is a collaborative group of telecom companies, mobile phone manufacturers, semiconductor, and software companies.

The Android OS can be found on smartphones, tablets, and many other consumer electronics. Smartphones running on the Android platform can be found on the GSM, CDMA, and iDEN cellular networks. Android phones have tremendous capabilities, which stem from the numerous apps available from Google Play. However, this wealth of functionality comes at a price when it comes to battery life—something that an investigator should be aware of. It should also be borne in mind that a tablet could also have cellular capabilities. Numerous tablets run on Android OS, including Samsung's popular Galaxy Tab and eReaders, like Amazon's Kindle.

Android is widely found in the auto industry. The Shanghai Automotive Industry Corporation (SAIC) integrated Android into its media entertainment systems. Audi, Ford Motor Company, Renault, General Motors, and numerous other car manufacturers have done the same. The Nevada Department of Vehicles approved Android for use in its self-driving cars.

Android Auto

Android Auto is a system that is integrated into a vehicle dashboard or run from an Android smartphone. Android Auto supports a range of applications, including Google's voice-activated, artificial intelligence, Google Assistant. Google Assistant, through Android Auto, allows the user to use voice-activated navigation with Google Maps and Waze. The driver can also use the hands-free communication options of cellular service calls, WhatsApp, Kik, Telegram, WeChat, Hangouts, Skype, Webex, and other applications. The user can also play music with supported apps, like Spotify, Pandora, and Google Play Music. More than 500 car models currently support Android Auto.

Android can also be found in home appliances, like ovens for example, which can operate based on recipes from a tablet. Android has been integrated into refrigerators, which can scan the barcode on food labels and monitor the freshness of items left in the refrigerator; they can assist consumers with a diet application and can help complete a grocery list. Some air conditioners run on the Android OS and allow for remote control and operation. There are washing machines and dryers that also run on Android. The proliferation of IoT (Internet of Things) devices, including appliances, thermometers, televisions, artificial intelligence speakers and so forth, have created an Android ecosystem.

Android File System

There are two types of memory on an Android device: (a) RAM and (b) NAND. Like a regular computer, RAM is volatile memory and may contain evidence that includes the user's passwords. NAND is non-volatile flash memory. A page or a chunk on NAND can be anywhere from 512K to 2048K. Android supports several file systems, including EXT4, FAT32, and YAFFS2 (Yet Another Flash File System 2). The EXT4 file system can be found on numerous Android devices and has supplanted the YAFFS2 file system. YAFFS2 is an open source file system that was developed for use with NAND flash memory. Currently a forensic analyst must download the YAFFS2 source code and review the files in a Hex editor.

Microsoft's FAT32 file system can be found on Android devices. The FAT32 file system is found on microSD cards, which are commonplace in many Android handsets. The Linux file system driver for FAT32 is called VFAT. Often Android apps are run from the microSD card.

The most valuable evidence on an Android is in the libraries and especially in the SQLite databases. A **SQLite database** is an open source relational database standard, which is frequently found on mobile devices. The development and maintenance of SQLite is sponsored by the SQLite Consortium, which includes Oracle, Nokia, Mozilla, Adobe, and Bloomberg.

Android Partitions

While each Android device manufacturer may make modifications, we can describe some of the common partitions that an investigator will encounter on an Android, which are as follows:

- **/boot:** Contains the boot code for the device. It includes the kernel and a RAM disk, which is associated with an unmodified; mkbootimg is a Linux line-command tool for developers. It can allow a developer to create a new boot image. It is possible to access the boot partition by pressing certain keys on the device.

- **/system:** Contains the Android framework.

- **/recovery:** Stores the recovery image.

- **/cache:** Stores temporary data.

- **/misc:** Used by the recovery partition.

- **/userdata:** Contains user-installed apps and data. This is the most important partition from a forensics perspective because it contains all the user activity associated with mobile applications—applications like Facebook.

- **/metadata:** Used when the device is encrypted.

There are also several data partitions on an Android device, which are as follows:

- **Dalvik Cache**: .dex (Dalvik executable file) that were run.

- **Applications**: .apk Android application package files.

- **Data**: Subdirectory for each application with SQLite DB.

- **Misc**: DHCP, Wi-Fi, etc.

- **System**: packages.xml

When initially examining an Android device, it is helpful to identify what apps are installed on the device. One place to start is packages.list (data\system\packages.list), which will display the apps installed.

Samsung Galaxy

Apple may have the lion's share of the tablet market, but Samsung Galaxy is the top selling smartphone worldwide. Less than a month after its release, Galaxy S4 sales surpassed the 10 million units sold marker, which translated to four units sold every second. The S4 included a feature called *Dual Shot*, which enabled the user to simultaneously take a picture with the front and rear cameras on the device.

Spring 2014 saw the release of the Samsung S5. What is impressive about this device is its 16-megapixel camera with UHD 4K video recording at 30 fps. The device also came with a fingerprint scanner, which may pose accessibility issues for investigators. The device also had a heart rate monitor, which may help with personalization and proving ownership of the smartphone. Like its predecessor, the device also synced to a smart watch called Gear 2 Neo.

In August 2019, Samsung released the Samsung Galaxy Note 10/+. In 2020, the company released its Samsung Galaxy S20/+.

The Samsung Galaxy Fold was released in 2019, and the company has sold millions of units. This device features a folding screen.

Challenges with Mobile Forensics and Evidence Admissibility

Gaining access to the evidence on a suspect's device is a major challenge, given advances in encryption. However, it is important to distinguish how mobile forensics differs from computer forensics in terms of evidence admissibility. First, advances in encryption mean that experimental techniques may be the only course of action for the investigator and those techniques might not be documented in previous cases. Secondly, forensics is a science, which means that the experimentation and results should be repeatable. It is possible that an investigator gets lucky once with accessing data on a device. However, that technique might not be repeatable. For example, by the time a case comes to trial, Apple or Android may have patched a vulnerability that was used by the investigator to access data on a device. Furthermore, a device is often rendered unusable after certain types of forensic examinations, including chip-off.

An important consideration for an investigator is the importance of explaining the risks associated with experimental and invasive techniques associated with mobile devices. Circumventing encryption often means destroying the device, beyond repair, to access the data. Even then, it is possible that the user data cannot be retrieved from the device. The prosecutor should be aware of these risks before a mobile device is examined.

Computer forensics examinations often means imaging a storage drive, which has been removed from the computer, while a write-blocker may have been used to ensure the integrity of the examination. Generally, an MD5 hash of that drive is created and a second copy is then created with a matching MD5. However, following these steps and protocols is not possible with a mobile device. With a mobile device, we typically need to perform forensics on an entire system and may not be able to separate the volume during an examination. Moreover, write-blockers are generally not an option. Furthermore, creating two copies of the volume and obtaining two matching MD5 hashes is unlikely.

Android Evidence

There are five ways to extract evidence from an Android smartphone:

1. Logical (using hardware/software)

2. Physical (using hardware/software)

3. Joint Test Action Group (JTAG)

4. Chip-Off

5. In-System Programming (ISP)

Some mobile forensics software supports a logical acquisition of a smartphone, which means that only user data can be recovered and not system files. Optimally, the investigator will acquire a physical image when possible. To retrieve the user files on an Android, the Data partition must be accessed by rooting the device.

Joint Test Action Group (JTAG) is an IEEE standard (IEEE 1149.1) for testing, maintenance, and support of assembled circuit boards. JTAG has become increasingly important as a way to bypass security and encryption, on a smartphone, to obtain a physical dump of the device's data.

The RIFF Box in Figure 9.11 is used to acquire the data from the circuit board on the cellphone. A full dump of NAND memory can be obtained by extracting the contents of eMMC. The connectors are carefully soldered onto the JTAG points on the circuit board. Voltage can be applied to the circuit board using a cellphone battery and can be monitored using a voltmeter.

FIGURE 9.11   JTAG acquisition with a RIFF Box

Chip-Off

When mobile forensics tools, like Cellebrite UFED, cannot be used, then JTAG is the next course of action. The last resort available to the investigator, when all else fails, is chip-off. Very few computer forensics labs conduct chip-off because of the high costs involved, and skills required, which creates a significant barrier to entry. This method is also not always successful. Chip-off can be used to circumvent encryption on many different circuit boards or used to access data on a chip when a printed circuit board (PCB) has been damaged. The chip can be removed from the board by applying hot air or infrared to the soldered pins. The chip can then be added to an adaptor (see Figure 9.12) and read.

FIGURE 9.12 Chip adaptors

In-System Programming (ISP)

In-System Programming (ISP), in digital forensics, is the practice of connecting to an eMMC or eMCP flash memory chip to access files stored on the chip. This is a lot less invasive than chip-off since the chip does not need to be removed from the printed circuit board (PCB) because wires are attached to the protruding connections surrounding the chip.

Emergency Download (EDL) Mode

Emergency Download (EDL) mode is a technical recovery feature found on Android devices with Qualcomm chipsets. During the boot process, if there are any errors or faults detected, then the device will boot into EDL. Most importantly, EDL mode can be used to access and forensically image an Android device, if it supports this mode. If the device is unencrypted, you can typically read directly from the eMMC chip. If the Android device is encrypted, then EDL mode can be used to modify the bootloader to bypass the integrity check on a boot image, which maintains a rooted ADB shell. As a reminder, ADB (Android Debug Bridge) is a command-line utility that, if enabled on an Android, allows the device to receive instructions, from a computer, via a USB cable. A **bootloader** is a program that automatically runs when a device is powered on and it engages the operating system.

There are several ways to access EDL mode and no single method works on all devices. Methods to access EDL include the following:

- Use of a specialized cable (or EDL cable).
- Shorting pins on the printed circuit board (PCB).
- Device button combinations.

Using an EDL cable is the least invasive. The cable contains a toggle switch, which shorts a data pin, to force the device into EDL mode. These cables are relatively inexpensive to purchase or you can even create your own with a USB cable. You can then verify if the device is in EDL mode by searching for Qualcomm devices in Windows Device Manager. An acquisition using EDL may be helpful if the device screen is locked, USB debugging is disabled, the device is not rooted, In-System Programming (ISP) or chip-off is not possible (or not a preferred method), or if there is no existing forensic tool (professional solution).

If the EDL cable fails to force the device into EDL mode, then you can try another method – shorting two pins on the PCB. The second option may involve shorting the CMD pin on the PCB but check online to determine the most appropriate method for your specific Android device. There are several online websites, like alephsecurity.com, which provide information about exploiting Qualcomm EDL programmers. However, not all devices have test ports, which means that you may need to use another option.

If the device is turned on, it can be unlocked and ADB is enabled, then you can simply send the following command to the device: `adb reboot edl`. The device will then reboot into EDL mode.

Finally, there are a limited number of devices where you can use a combination of button push options to enter EDL mode. One example is while powering on the device, press and hold the volume + and volume – buttons simultaneously, and you can then access EDL mode.

Android Security

There are several ways that a user can secure his or her Android smartphone:

- **PIN-Protection**: This is a numeric PIN number.
- **Password**: This is an alpha-numeric password.
- **Pattern Lock**: A finger is used to secure the device with gestures (swiping motion).
- **Biometrics**: This could be an iris or retina scan or perhaps facial recognition.

The pattern lock is also referred to as a *gesture*. The user swipes a 3 x 3 grid (9 dots) on the smartphone screen and no dot can be swiped more than once. This means that it is not all that difficult to work out the user's gesture. This pattern lock can be found in `gesture.key`. The 20-byte hex value, found in gesture.key, can be added to a free tool produced by NowSecure, called viaExtract, to determine what the pattern lock is. The path to this gesture can be found here: `data/system/gesture.key`. The file is encrypted with SHA-1 hash algorithm.

Password protection can be the most difficult to crack. The file where the password is stored can be found here: `data/system/pc.key`. An investigator can attempt to crack the password using brute force or use a dictionary attack.

A PIN on an Android has a maximum of eight digits. After the user unsuccessfully enters the PIN several times, then the user is requested to enter the Gmail login and password.

Android Forensics Tools

There are many different Android forensics tools. NowSecure is one organization that produces several free tools. Santoku is one of these tools that enables the examiner to image an Android. The company also produces AFLogical, which performs a logical acquisition of Android 1.5 or later. The data acquired is stored on a blank SD card.

Andriller is a forensic suite of tools for Android devices. The tool can be used to crack PIN codes, passwords, and pattern locks, as well as extract mobile app data. It is available for both Windows PC and Ubuntu Linux. Like other Android forensic tools, USB debugging must be enabled on the device to extract files from the device. Enabling **USB debugging** allows a computer to communicate with an Android device via a USB cable. The location will vary, depending on the device, but you may be able to allow this function by accessing these screens:

Settings > Developer Options > USB Debugging

Android Debug Bridge (ADB) is a command-line utility that enables the user to send requests from a computer to an Android device. ADB is part of the Android Platform-Tools package, which is available for free from `developer.android.com`. Utilities, including BusyBox and nanddump, can then be used with ADB to pull an image of memory.

Whatever tool you decide to use, you will need to have root access to the device to access, or image, the user files. To gain root privileges we need to use an exploit, which is what tools, like Cellebrite UFED, use. An exploit is often specific to the make, model, and version of Android. An exploit is a small piece of code. It is important to remember that an exploit, used to root an Android device, will modify the device and may need to be later explained in court. However, the changes will be relatively small and can be accounted for. An exploit takes advantage of a known vulnerability in an operating system. Some exploits can be used when booting the device into Recovery Mode. ClockwordMod is an Android custom recovery image that can allow the investigator to access data on the device.

Magnet ACQUIRE is a free tool (magnetforensics.com) that allows an investigator to acquire an image from an iOS device, an Android mobile device, a hard drive, or removable media.

Android Resources

There are many great resources available online for investigators encountering Android devices, including:

- **ALEAPP – Android Logs Events and Protobuf Parser**: https://github.com/abrignoni/ALEAPP

- **Magnet Forensics, who produce AXIOM**: www.magnetforensics.com/blog

- **Cellebrite UFED**: www.cellebrite.com/en/blog

Android Applications (Apps)

Android applications are developed in Java and have an *.apk* file extension. For an Android application to be accepted by Google Play, there must be a signed certificate associated with the application. Applications run in a Dalvik Virtual Machine (DVM) and have a unique user ID and process. This enforces application security and prevents data sharing with other apps. What is helpful for the investigator is that the date and time of when an app is executed is stored on the device. It is the developer that decides what data will be shared, and therefore the data that the examiner can retrieve is only as good as what the developer has made available.

There are four choices available to the developer for data storage:

1. Preference

2. Files

3. SQLite database

4. Cloud

SQLite databases can be a great source of evidence for the investigator. The following tools can be used to retrieve data from these relational databases and include the following:

- SQLite Database Browser

- SQLite Viewer

- SQLite Analyzer

Every time an Android user walks past a Wi-Fi hotspot, that hotspot is recorded on that device—regardless of whether the user attempted to connect to that device or not. This information can be retrieved from `Cache.wifi` on the mobile device. The data retrieved from this file can be used to map out where a user was moving from and to.

Facebook is one of the most popular apps found on smartphones. It is important to know that just about all the information stored in a user's online profile can be found in their smartphone or tablet. Fb.db is the SQLite database that contains a user's Facebook contacts, chat logs, messages, photos, and searches.

A user's login and password for Exchange can be found in plaintext at the following path: /data/data/com.android.email/databases/EmailProvider.db. A user's Gmail login and password can also be found in plaintext here: com.google.android.gm.

Android smartphones come with Google Maps. A history of saved searches can be found here: /data/data/com.google.android.apps.maps/databases/search_history.db.

There is of course the cellular telephone evidence. SMS and MMS can be found here: /data/data/com.android.providers.telephony. This file will contain the sender, the recipient, read status, pictures, and audio/video files. MMS specifically can be found here: /data/data/com.android.mms.

Magnet Forensics App Simulator is a free tool that allows the forensics investigator to emulate an app in a virtualized environment. Before downloading the tool (magnetforensics.com), simply install Oracle VirtualBox and then install an Android VM.

Symbian OS

Symbian is a mobile device operating system developed by Nokia, which was later purchased by Accenture. At the beginning of 2012, Symbian was the most popular mobile operating system, although Android maintains the greatest market share. Symbian OS could be found on Nokia, Sony Ericsson, Samsung, and Hitachi handsets to name but a few. Symbian OS has now been discontinued, although an investigator may still encounter some older handsets running this operating system.

BlackBerry 10

RIM OS was the operating system, developed by Research in Motion, for use on BlackBerry smartphones and tablets. The BlackBerry OS is now open source. The operating system later became BlackBerry OS and was subsequently replaced by BlackBerry 10. Some BlackBerry models support an Android runtime, which can execute and support Android apps. We do not know how long BlackBerry 10 operating system will continue to be supported but investigators may still encounter these devices. In February 2020, TCL Communication announced that its partnership ended with BlackBerry and that it would end manufacturing BlackBerry devices but would continuing supporting customers with service contracts through 2022. TCL manufactured BlackBerry KEYonne Motion, KEY2 and KEY2 LE devices.

Windows Phone

Windows 10 Mobile was a Microsoft operating system that could be found on personal computers, mobile phones, and tablets. This operating system could be found on mobile phones manufactured by HTC, Samsung, Nokia, and others.

Standard Operating Procedures for Handling Handset Evidence

It is important for laboratories, and their investigators, to use best practices for cellphone examinations. Luckily, there are guidelines available for these best practices that they can use as the basis for the laboratory's standard operating procedures (SOP). An organization's SOP will vary from place to place primarily because of differences in organizational budgets, which in turn impacts the resources (equipment, personnel, training, etc.) that they have available.

National Institute of Standards and Technology (NIST)

NIST provides standard operating procedures for a variety of scientific practices, including cellphone forensics. NIST Special Publication 800-101 issued guidelines on cellphone forensics in 2014, NIST is a well-recognized organization, and computer forensics investigators should be familiar with their guidelines; 2014 appears to be the latest version of this document.

According to NIST Special Publication 800-101, there are four steps involved in a forensic examination:

1. Preservation

2. Acquisition

3. Examination and Analysis

4. Reporting

It is important to be aware of these guidelines when handling mobile evidence. Preservation involves other types of forensic examination for a mobile device, including preserving fingerprint and DNA evidence. This is certainly a best practice but, in reality, many agencies do not have the resources to perform these analyses. The document is very educational in its explanations of various concepts in mobile forensics and device identification. Therefore, for someone who is interested in mobile forensics, yet is new to the subject, it is a recommended read.

NIST Resources for Tool Validation

The first point that should be made is that, like every other forensic tool in a computer forensics lab, all tools should be validated prior to their use in investigations. It is essential to use test data and follow a set of investigative protocols to determine the data that can be extracted. There should also be comparisons made to other cellphone tools. Questions about this validation process may arise during a court trial. Validation also incorporates the usage of cryptographic hashes, like MD5 or a SHA-1 or SHA-256 hash, to ensure that the results from using a particular tool can be reproduced with the exact same outcome. During the validation process, error rates should be clearly documented.

NIST provides examiners with tremendous resources to assist with testing tools. The *Computer Forensic Tool Testing (CFTT)* project provides guidelines for testing computer forensics tools, which includes test criteria, test sets, and test hardware. More information can be found here: http://www.cftt.nist.gov/.

The National Software Reference Library (NSRL) provides guidance on effectively using technology in investigations that require the examination of digital evidence. More information can be found here: http://www.nsrl.nist.gov/.

NIST has provided test datasets of digital evidence. The Computer Forensic Reference Data Sets (CFReDS) for digital evidence are test data that can be used to validate forensic tools, test equipment and train investigators. More information can be found here: http://www.cfreds.nist.gov/.

Computer forensics investigators should also be familiar with the US Department of Justice's NIJ report—*Electronic Crime Scene Investigation: A Guide to First Responders*. This is a general guide to computer forensic investigations.

The Association of Chief Police Officers (ACPO) and other standards have noted the importance of evidence not changing after being subjected to an examination. According to the ACPO:

No actions performed by investigators should change data contained on digital devices or storage media that may subsequently be relied upon in court.

With mobile forensics, there is a fundamental problem when it comes to forensics. Mobile devices generally have smaller onboard memory capacity. Therefore, memory utilization and compression are essential. This, coupled with the fact that these devices are continually connected to a cellular network, means that the data on a cellphone is continually changing. When a computer forensics examiner attempts to extract evidence from a cellphone, changes can be made to the cellphone. What is important to remember is that the user-created data can remain unaltered when using best practices. Therefore, the evidence is admissible when the process is documented appropriately. Some investigators will still contend that "mobile forensics" does not exist and there are only "mobile examinations".

Preparation and Containment

Containing a cellphone should be a careful but expeditious process. According to the U.S. Department of Justice (NIJ) guidelines, in the *Electronic Crime Scene Investigation – A Guide for First Responders* book, the following steps should be followed:

Step 1. **Securing and evaluating the scene**: Steps should be taken to ensure the safety of individuals and to identify and protect the integrity of potential evidence.

Step 2. **Documenting the scene**: Create a permanent record of the scene, accurately recording both digital-related and conventional evidence.

Step 3. **Evidence collection**: Collect traditional and digital evidence in a manner that preserves their evidentiary value.

Step 4. **Packaging, transportation, and storage**: Take adequate precautions when packaging, transporting, and storing evidence, maintaining chain of custody.

Therefore, the investigator should first document the crime scene, including taking notes and taking photographs. The investigator should then properly contain the cellphone. Proper containment means removing the device from the network. The following containers can be used to remove the device from wireless networks:

- Faraday box

- Paraben StrongHold bag (see Figure 9.13)

- Arson can

Interestingly, placing three layers of tinfoil around a cellphone will prevent the device from connecting with any network. Of course, your lab must conduct your testing for this and any other containment protocols that you implement. One type of Faraday box is the Ramsey Box, which also includes a power source to keep devices in the box charging. Some models also allow the investigator to record voice and video, while performing an examination of the device in the Ramsey Box.

FIGURE 9.13   Paraben StrongHold bag

A Faraday box can be expensive, whereas an arson can may serve as a cheaper option, while being highly effective. Some investigators will place a cellphone in a Faraday box but leave a cable hanging out to continue charging the phone. The problem is that a charging cable can operate like an aerial. The issue with containment of a cellphone is that the device will boost the signal in an attempt to connect to the cellular network, which in turn will drain the battery faster. Smartphones, like the iPhone and Android phones, will require frequent charging because of the number of applications that simply drain the battery faster. Once the phone shuts down, there is the risk of encountering a user's handset PIN or a SIM card PIN (or both).

Wireless Capabilities

There are a number of wireless capabilities found in today's cellphones. Apart from cellular communications, many cellphones have infrared (IrDA), Wireless Fidelity (Wi-Fi) or Bluetooth wireless capabilities built in. This is important to remember when containing a cellphone device.

A cellphone can also be properly contained by taking the following steps:

Step 1. Remove the SIM card (if it has one).

Step 2. Change setting to "Airplane Mode".

Step 3. Disable the wireless connection.

Step 4. Disable the Bluetooth connection.

Using the FCC-ID and finding the cellphone's manual can assist with finding the wireless capabilities of the device and help in understanding how to remove the device from all potential wireless connections.

Let's Get Practical!   Identify the Features of a Cellular Phone

Detailed information about all devices operating on frequencies controlled by the FCC is available online. You will need Adobe Reader installed to complete this practical feature.

1. **Start** your web browser and then navigate to http://transition.fcc.gov/oet/ea/fccid/.

Ensure that any Pop-Up Blocker feature on your web browser is disabled.

2. Search for the FCC-ID on the back of a mobile device (an iPhone or an Android device).

3. Enter the **FCC-ID** in **Grantee Code** box and in the **Product Code** box as shown in Figure 9.14.

4. Click the **search** button.

5. Review the displayed documents and then document the features of the device, including wireless features and the type of network that it operates on, i.e. CDMA or GSM.

6. Submit the report as directed by your instructor.

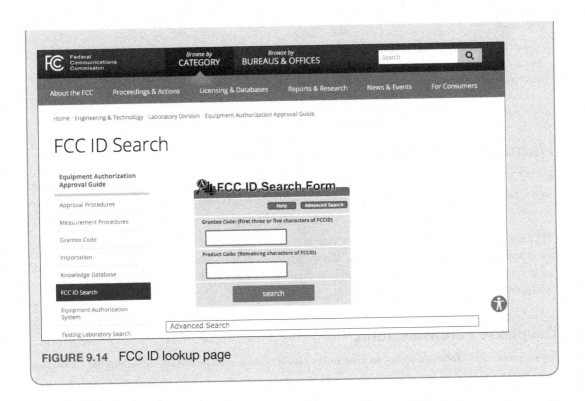

FIGURE 9.14 FCC ID lookup page

Some organizations have used signal jammers in their computer forensics labs to block all radio trans-missions and interference with cellphones. The FCC has however reiterated that these devices are illegal to use, even for law enforcement to use, because, in an emergency situation, a person in distress might not be able to contact emergency services if signal jammers are being used in the vicinity.

The cellphone carrier can also be contacted to ensure that the phone is removed from the network. Criminals will often report a cellphone lost to erase the contents of the cellphone. Thus, moving quickly to remove the device from the network is critical.

Charging the Device

It is critical to keep a cellphone's battery charged. Smartphones, especially Android and iPhones, can possess poor battery life because of the plethora of applications that quickly consume the phone's charge—especially older devices. Given that many smartphones are PIN-protected, in addition to the fact that containing a phone in a Faraday box will boost the signal and battery usage, finding a charger quickly is vital.

> **Note**
>
> Never keep a cellphone in a container, like a Faraday box, with a charging cable sticking out because a charging cable can act as an aerial. Never charge a seized cellphone via a computer or you are likely to change evidence on the phone.

Handset Forensics

A SIM card can provide a tremendous amount of evidence. However, examining the onboard memory on the handset itself is even more important. There are both software and hardware forensic solutions available.

NIST and NIJ provide detailed reports on their testing of cellphone forensic tools. The results of these tests, which include a number of forensic tools mentioned in this section, can be found online: https://www.nist.gov/itl/ssd/software-quality-group/computer-forensics-tool-testing-program-cftt/cftt-technical/mobile.

Cellphone Forensics Tools

Several innovative forensic tools can effectively perform cellphone forensics, including the following:

- GrayKey
- BitPim
- MOBILedit Forensic
- Device Seizure
- Cellebrite

The sections that follow describe these in more detail.

GrayKey

GrayKey is a forensics tool, from GrayShift, which is used to unlock iOS devices (iPhones and iPads). The device, which is only available to law enforcement, can bypass both four-digit and six-digit passcodes on a variety of iPhone models. The device can also recover the full file system, decrypted keychain, and process memory.

BitPim

BitPim is an open source tool that allows you to view and manipulate files on a many CDMA phones. Mobile phones supported by BitPim include Samsung, LG, and Sanyo, as well as many other cellphones that contain Qualcomm CDMA chipsets. The software can be downloaded for free from www. bitpim.org.

MOBILedit! Forensic

MOBILedit is an organizational tool for a smartphone user's contacts, messages, media, and other files, which are installed on the user's computer. There is also a forensic edition that can be used to extract cellphone files and generate investigation reports.

E3

Developed and distributed by Paraben Corporation, there are various E3 labeled tools for mobile forensic examiners. Figure 9.15 shows the user interface for Paraben's Device Seizure.

Paraben also supplies device containment supplies such as their StrongHold bag, StrongHold Tent (Faraday box) and Project-A-Phone (PAP) FLEX for manual examinations.

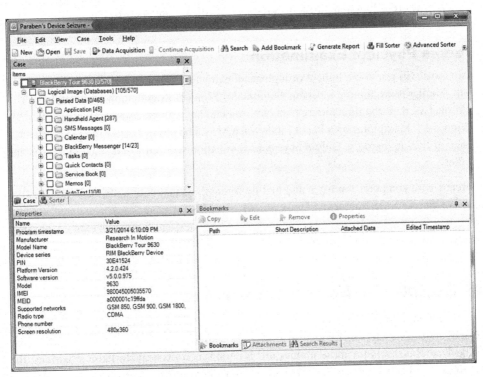

FIGURE 9.15   Device Seizure user interface

There are several other reputable cellphone forensic tools currently available, all with their unique strengths and features:

- **Oxygen**: Oxygen Forensic Suite
- **MSAB**: XRY
- **Susteen**: Secure View
- **Belkasoft:** Evidence Center

Cellebrite

Cellebrite's Universal Forensics Extraction Device (UFED) can be used for logical and physical extractions from cellphones and GPS devices. UFED is very well-regarded in the industry and the device can be found in many law enforcement computer forensics laboratories. Part of the UFED success is the wide range of phones that are supported by Cellebrite, which includes iOS and Android devices. The UFED can be used in either a laboratory or in the field, which appeals to law enforcement. In 2020, Cellebrite acquired BlackBag Technologies—the producer of BlackLight and MacQuisition.

Logical Versus Physical Examination

Mobile forensic tools will provide a logical or a physical extraction of evidence from a cellphone or sometimes both. Similar to examining a personal computer, a logical examination of a cellphone will provide a traditional view of the directories, files, and folders, and can be compared to the interface we see with Windows File Explorer on a PC or Finder on a Mac. The physical view refers to the actual location and size of files in memory. Only a physical examination will retrieve deleted messages and other deleted files.

A major difference with computer forensics and mobile forensics is that with a physical view of files on a computer we can find file fragments. However, when an SMS text message is deleted you can generally be certain that the message has been removed and no message fragments exist. A physical extraction can however resurrect some deleted files.

Manual Cellphone Examinations

In the absence of a mobile forensic imaging tool, the investigator is forced to make a manual examination of the cellphone. This happens frequently, especially with lower-end prepaid phones offered by companies, like Tracfone. Tools for these phones are generally non-existent. In these situations, the investigator will act as what is known as a "field jockey" and will thumb through the phone's contents, while taking photos as she goes. Project-a-Phone (see Figure 9.16) and Fernico ZRT 3 are two tools designed for photographing cellphone screens, although using a regular digital camera can suffice. Documenting the process in detail is critical, nevertheless. The reason for using a solution, like Project-A-Phone, is that the tool comes with a reporting tool to make the process easier.

FIGURE 9.16   Project-A-Phone

Flasher Box

In the absence of a cellphone forensic imaging solution, one might expect to perform a manual examination using Project-A-Phone or a similar device. Consider what happens when an examiner cannot bypass the cellphone's PIN or if the phone is damaged. As a last resort, some investigators will use a flasher box. A **flasher box** is a device used to make physical dump of a cellphone.

There are disadvantages though to using a flasher box. Using the device may change the data on the cellphone. Additionally, an examiner using such a device should have proper training. The device will not create a helpful MD5 hash for you. Nevertheless, NIJ and ACPO do discuss the use of flasher boxes in their standard operating procedures. Moreover, flasher boxes were initially a solution before we had other advanced cellphone forensic tools.

Global Satellite Service Providers

Wireless telephones do not always operate on a cellular network. In fact, the majority of the world's surface area does not have cellular service. Thus, a ship in the middle of the ocean or an expedition to the Antarctic cannot rely on a local cell site to route calls. Instead, these telephones communicate with other telephones through satellites. Just ask any military veteran, who has served in Iraq or Afghanistan, and she can tell you the importance of a satellite phone. These telephones can also be used by emergency personnel during a crisis situation, like an earthquake.

Satellite Communication Services

Iridium Communications Inc. maintains a large group of satellites called the Iridium Satellite Constellation. These satellites operate in a low orbit of approximately 485 miles into the Earth's atmosphere. The company also provides global satellite phones that go beyond traditional terrestrial cellphones. These cellphones can provide direct communications via satellite linkages in areas without cell site coverage, such as in the middle of the Atlantic Ocean or in the Artic. Globestar is another similar satellite phone provider. SkyWave Mobile Communications provides satellite and General Packet Radio Service for transportation, mining (oil and gas), heavy equipment, and utility companies.

Inmarsat PLC, a British satellite company, provides similar phone service through its geostationary telecommunications satellites. The company provides Global Maritime Distress & Safety Services (GMDSS).

Legal Considerations

As noted in Chapter 7, "Admissibility of Digital Evidence", under the Fourth Amendment, a government agent must obtain a warrant to conduct a search. This is true in the case of cellphones. However, there are exceptions to this rule, including consent, incident to arrest, or exigent circumstances. Exigent circumstances imply that a warrantless search was required to save a life—for example in the case of a kidnapping.

When applying for a search warrant, the investigator should describe the cellphone and include the following details:

- Make

- Model

- Manufacturer

- Telephone number

- Location of the device (address and specific location)

If available, the investigator should also include the IMEI or MEID of the phone. The investigator should also detail the type of evidence that she wishes to acquire, e.g. SMS, MMS, Contacts and so forth.

National Crime Information Center (NCIC)

The **National Crime Information Center (NCIC)** is a clearinghouse of crime data that is managed by the Federal Bureau of Investigations (FBI). The NCIC database contains 21 files, which are as follows:

- **Article File:** Records on stolen articles and lost public safety, homeland security, and critical infrastructure identification.

- **Gun File:** Records on stolen, lost, and recovered weapons and weapons used in the commission of crimes that are designated to expel a projectile by air, carbon dioxide, or explosive action.

- **Boat File:** Records on stolen boats.

- **Securities File:** Records on serially numbered stolen, embezzled, used for ransom, or counterfeit securities.

- **Vehicle File:** Records on stolen vehicles, vehicles involved in the commission of crimes, or vehicles that may be seized based on federally issued court order.

- **Vehicle and Boat Parts File:** Records on serially numbered stolen vehicle or boat parts.

- **License Plate File:** Records on stolen license plates.

- **Missing Persons File:** Records on individuals, including children, who have been reported missing to law enforcement and there is a reasonable concern for their safety.

- **Foreign Fugitive File:** Records on persons wanted by another country for a crime that would be a felony if it were committed in the United States.

- **Identity Theft File:** Records containing descriptive and other information that law enforcement personnel can use to determine if an individual is a victim of identity theft or if the individual might be using a false identity.

- **Immigration Violator File:** Records on criminal aliens whom immigration authorities have deported and aliens with outstanding administrative warrants of removal.

- **Protection Order File:** Records on individuals against whom protection orders have been issued.

- **Supervised Release File:** Records on individuals on probation, parole, or supervised release or released on their own recognizance or during pre-trial sentencing.

- **Unidentified Persons File:** Records on unidentified deceased persons, living persons who are unable to verify their identities, unidentified victims of catastrophes, and recovered body parts. The file cross-references unidentified bodies against records in the Missing Persons File.

- **Protective Interest:** Records on individuals who might pose a threat to the physical safety of protectees or their immediate families. Expands on the the U.S. Secret Service Protective file, originally created in 1983.

- **Gang File:** Records on violent gangs and their members.

- **Known or Appropriately Suspected Terrorist File:** Records on known or appropriately suspected terrorists in accordance with HSPD-6.

- **Wanted Persons File:** Records on individuals (including juveniles who will be tried as adults) for whom a federal warrant or a felony or misdemeanor warrant is outstanding.

- **National Sex Offender Registry File:** Records on individuals who are required to register in a jurisdiction's sex offender registry.

- **National Instant Criminal Background Check System (NICS) Denied Transaction File:** Records on individuals who have been determined to be "prohibited persons" according to the Brady Handgun Violence Prevention Act and were denied as a result of a NICS background check. (As of August 2012, records include last six months of denied transactions; in the future, records will include all denials.)

- **Violent Person File**: Once fully populated with data from our users, this file will contain records of persons with a violent criminal history and persons who have previously threatened law enforcement.

- **Violent Person File:** Once fully populated with data from our users, this file will contain records of persons with a violent criminal history and persons who have previously threatened law enforcement.

Source: https://www.fbi.gov/services/cjis/ncic

Therefore, law enforcement will often perform a search through NCIC to determine if items seized have been reported as being stolen.

Carrier Records

The investigator will also obtain corroborating evidence from the cellular carrier, in the form of subscriber records and call detail records (CDR). The subscriber records are used by the carrier for billing, while the call detail records will provide information about the location and time that a cellphone was used to make calls. Remember, a call can be traced to multiple cell sites and identify a route taken by the suspect. Call detail records identify the location of the handset at a location. It is up to the investigator to link the suspect to that handset. When obtaining call detail records, the investigator should request the data in a particular format (e.g. CSV), and should request information about how to interpret any cell site codes that are provided. The carrier can also send the investigator a voicemail reset code when requested. Once 5G becomes more pervasive, call detail records are likely to change and probably contain more precise details about the location of a mobile subscriber when making or receiving a call.

Other Mobile Devices

There are numerous other mobile devices that can be of evidentiary value to investigations. These devices include tablets, GPS devices, and other devices, like GoPro cameras, and smart watches.

Tablets

Like cellphones, there are many different types of tablets on the market and in fact the software and operating systems running on these devices are very similar. iOS and Android are the most widely found operating systems running on tablets. Some tablets also come with a cellular service. Computer forensic tools, like Cellebrite and BlackLight, will support a number of tablets.

GPS Devices

GPS devices can be used for maritime, driving, and aviation. Handheld devices are used for recreation, like biking and hiking, or can be used by emergency services during disasters. A number of these devices, like TomTom, can be imaged by forensic tools. Many of these devices come with an SD card, which can be valuable to an investigator. Similar to a cellphone, an investigator may also find evidence on a user's synced computer.

There are four primary sources of evidence available from a GPS device: trackpoints, track log, waypoint, and a route. More recent GPS devices may also contain data about cellphones that were connected via Bluetooth or even Internet searches. MotoNav is one example of the expanded services now available. Devices like MotoNav may possess data from the synced cellphone, such as user contacts. General Motors' (GM) OnStar service is another potential source of data for investigators. GM stores GPS data from vehicles with the built-in OnStar service. GM's monitoring has sparked controversy because they can disclose this information to third parties, even when the subscriber has terminated their services. The TomTom SatNav navigation system also caused controversy when it was discovered that the company was sending historical driver GPS routing data to police in the Netherlands. The user data from the TomTom was used to assist police with setting up speed traps based on driver habits.

A **trackpoint** is a geo-locational record that is automatically captured and stored by a GPS device. Trackpoints are not created by the user. For example, when a GPS device is turned on, a trackpoint, recording the current location, is made and then subsequent trackpoints are created at predetermined intervals. A **track log** is a list of trackpoints that can be used to recreate a route.

A **waypoint** is a geo-locational point of interest created by a user. Waypoints are often created by a user to note places of interest, like a restaurant or a hotel, as part of a longer route. Finally, a **route** is a series of user-created waypoints on a trip.

GPS Tracking

Since 2009, all cellphones are federally mandated to have a GPS chip embedded in the device. The U.S. Federal Communications Commission's E-911 Mandate of 2003 requires that manufacturers facilitate location tracking. **Enhanced 911** is a federal mandate that stipulates that all handset manufacturers must ensure that caller ID and locational data can be obtained from a cellphone subscriber making a 911 call. Therefore, the police can locate a person in distress using **Assisted GPS**, which uses the GPS chip in your cellphone and triangulation rather than simply relying on cell site data. A **public safety access point (PSAP)** is a call center that receives emergency requests from the public for police, medical, or firefighter services.

To Catch a Murderer – A Case Study

A PSAP can assist police by tracking a subscriber's cellphone in real time. In October 2004, the body of Fred Jablin was found dead in his home on Hearthglow Lane in Richmond, Virginia. Detective Coby Kelley quickly suspected Jablin's ex-wife, Piper Rountree, and quickly obtained a warrant for Rountree's cellphone records. Fred Jablin, Distinguished Chair at the University of Richmond, had suffered through a very nasty divorce and custody battle with Rountree, with Jablin winning sole custody. By September 2004, Rountree was in trouble—owing $10,000 in back alimony.

Detective Kelley obtained the cellphone records for Piper Rountree's cellphone, which placed the phone at the scene of the crime. Kelley tracked the cellphone going east on I-64 towards Norfolk Airport. There was then a brief interruption in locating a signal before it could be tracked again in Baltimore, Maryland. Piper Rountree of course stated that she was not in Virginia at the time of the murder but was actually in Houston, Texas. She also stated that her sister, Tina Rountree, often used her cellphone.

Piper Rountree called her son, 14 hours prior to the murder, and mentioned that she was in Texas, although her cellphone was pinging towers in Virginia. It was discovered that on October 21 (a few days prior to the murder) Piper purchased a wig on the Internet, using her own account, but had the wig delivered to her former boyfriend's P.O. Box in Houston. Piper was attempting to use the wig to pose as her sister Tina. A Southwest Airlines employee later testified that he had witnessed Piper Rountree boarding a plane to Virginia. On May 6, 2005, Piper Roundtree was sentenced to life in prison plus three years for use of a firearm in a crime. This case clearly illustrates how cellphone evidence was important corroborating evidence that was used at trial.

Documenting the Investigation

Most forensic tools, like BlackLight, have a built-in report feature. The investigator's report should ultimately include the following details:

- Device specifications, including details about the SIM card;

- Where the device was seized;

- How the device was seized (copies of consent form or warrant);

- Preparation techniques, including removing the device from the network;

- Forensic tools used to acquire the evidence;

- Evidence acquired (SMS, MMS, images, video, contacts, call history, etc.);

- Carrier evidence (subscriber details and call detail records); and

- Application service evidence (e.g., Gmail from Google's e-mail servers).

Naturally, photographs of the location where the device was seized, the device itself and all relevant numbers (ICCID, IMEI, etc.) should be taken.

Summary

Mobile forensics has become extremely important for investigations because of the wealth of evidence that they can provide. They can even be more important than a traditional computer because they are always on and we carry them everywhere. Forensic tools have improved over the past five years, but we still have many devices that are not supported. With the growing importance of cellphone forensics, investigators are reaching out beyond the cellphone to the cellular carrier and cloud computing service providers.

Cellphones are problematic to analyze because they possess different operating systems, there are numerous device models available, while the data on these devices continually changes because of network connections and their relatively small onboard memory. The contents of a smartphone cannot be analyzed as one mass media device because of removable memory and SIM cards (GSM phones).

There are a variety of cellular networks, with GSM and CDMA being the predominant network protocols. Understanding these networks helps to understand where the evidence is located. Mobile network operators, like T-Mobile and Verizon, own and operate networks, while a mobile virtual network operator provides service but does not own the cellular network infrastructure.

Several mobile devices, like tablets and GPS electronics, are important to investigators. A tablet can have Internet service through a cellular network. Broadband USB and mobile broadband devices also use cellular networks.

Investigators should always test forensic tools prior to their use. Many cellphones are not supported by forensic tools and therefore a manual investigation must be conducted. Investigators should also be aware of NIST, NIJ and ACPO standard operating procedures for investigating digital devices. Proper care should be afforded, by the investigator, in terms of containing the device, charging the device, and ensuring isolation from a variety of wireless networks.

Key Terms

3GP: An audio/video file format found on mobile phones operating on 3G GSM cellular networks.

3GP2: An audio/video file format found on mobile phones operating on 3G CDMA cellular networks.

3rd Generation Partnership Project (3GPP): A collaboration of six telecommunications standards bodies and several telecommunications corporations worldwide that provide telecommunication standards.

3rd Generation Partnership Project 2 (3GPP2): A partnership of North American and Asian 3G telecommunications companies that develop standards for third-generation mobile networks, including CDMA.

4G Long Term Evolution (LTE) Advanced: A high mobility broadband communication that is suitable for use on trains and in other vehicles.

Abbreviated Dialing Numbers (ADN): The contact names and numbers entered by the subscriber.

accelerometer: A hardware device that senses motion or gravity and reacts to these changes.

Android: An open source operating system based on the Linux 2.6 kernel.

Android Debug Bridge (ADB): A command-line utility that enables the user to send requests from a computer to an Android device.

Assisted GPS: A system that uses the GPS chip in a cellphone and triangulation rather than simply relying on cell site data.

Authentication Center (AuC): A database that contains the subscriber's IMSI, authentication and encryption algorithms.

Base Station Controller (BSC): manages the radio signals for base transceiver stations, in terms of assigning frequencies and handoffs between cell sites.

Base Transceiver Station (BTS): The equipment found at a cell site that facilitates the communication of a cellphone user across a cellular network.

bootloader: A program that automatically runs when a device is powered on and engages the operating system.

call detail records (CDRs): Details used for billing purposes, such as phone numbers called, duration, dates and times of calls, and cell sites used.

CDMA2000: A 3G technology that uses the CDMA communications protocol.

cell: A geographic area within a cellular network.

cell site: A cell tower located in a cell.

cellular network: A group of cells in a cellular communications network.

Code Division Multiple Access (CDMA): A spread-spectrum communication methodology that uses a wide bandwidth for transmitting data.

Electronic Serial Number (ESN): An 11-digit number used to identify a subscriber on a CDMA cellular network.

Emergency Download (EDL) Mode: A technical recovery feature found on Android devices with Qualcomm chipsets.

Enhanced 911: A federal mandate that stipulates that all handset manufacturers must ensure that caller ID and locational data can be obtained from a cellphone subscriber making a 911 call.

Enhanced Data rates for GSM Evolution (EDGE): A high data transfer technology on GSM networks. EDGE provides up to three times the data capacity of GPRS.

Equipment Identity Register (EIR): Registry used to track IMEI numbers and decide whether an IMEI is valid, suspect, or perhaps stolen.

FCC ID: A number issued by the Federal Communication Commission (FCC) which indicates that the handset is authorized to operate on radio frequencies within the FCC's control.

flasher box: A device used to make physical dump of a cellphone.

Forbidden Public Land Mobile Network (FPLMN): A cellular network that a subscriber attempted to connect to but was not authorized to connect to.

General Packet Radio Service (GPRS): A packet switching wireless communication found on 2G and 3G GSM networks.

Global System for Mobile communications (GSM): An international standard for signal communications, which uses TDMA and FDD (Frequency Division Duplex) communication methods.

hard handoff: Means that the communication is only handled by one base transceiver station at a time with no simultaneous communication.

Home Location Register (HLR): A database of a carrier's subscribers and includes their home address, IMSI, telephone number, SIM card ICCID, and services used by the subscriber.

In-System Programming (ISP): In digital forensics, this is the practice of connecting to an eMMC or eMCP flash memory chip to access files stored on the chip.

Integrated Circuit Card ID (ICCID): A 19- to 20-digit serial number physically located on a SIM card.

Integrated Digital Enhanced Network (iDEN): A wireless technology developed by Motorola, which combines two-way radio capabilities with digital cellphone technology.

International Mobile Equipment Identity (IMEI): A number that uniquely identifies the mobile equipment or handset.

International Mobile Subscriber Identity (IMSI): An internationally unique number on a SIM card that identifies a user on a network.

International Signaling Point Code (ISPC): A standardized numbering system used to identify a node on an international telecommunications network.

International Telecommunication Union (ITU): An agency of the United Nations that produces standards for information and communication technologies.

Joint Test Action Group (JTAG): An IEEE standard (IEEE 1149.1) for testing, maintenance, and support of assembled circuit boards.

Last Numbers Dialed (LND): A list of all outgoing calls made by a subscriber.

mobile country code (MCC): The first three digits of the IMSI.

Mobile Equipment Identifier (MEID): An internationally unique number that identifies a CDMA handset (mobile equipment).

mobile network operator (MNO): A cellular service carrier that owns and operates a cellular network.

Mobile Station: Term used to describe Mobile Equipment (handset) and a Subscriber Identity Module (SIM).

Mobile Subscriber Identity Number (MSIN): Created by a cellular telephone carrier and identifies the subscriber on the network.

Mobile Subscriber ISDN (MSISDN): Essentially the phone number for the subscriber.

Mobile Switching Center (MSC): Responsible for switching data packets from one network path to another on a cellular network.

mobile virtual network operator (MVNO): A cellular service carrier that does not own its own cellular network but operates on the network of a mobile network operator.

Multimedia Messaging Service (MMS): A messaging service, found on most cellphones, which allows the user to send multimedia content, like audio, video, and images.

multiplexing: A communication protocol whereby multiple signals are transmitted simultaneously across a shared medium.

My Wireless Fidelity (MiFi): A variety of portable wireless router that provides Internet access for a number of Internet-enabled devices and communicates via a cellular network.

National Crime Information Center (NCIC): A clearinghouse of crime data that is managed by the Federal Bureau of Investigations (FBI).

Personal Unblocking Code (PUC): A code that is available from the carrier and allows a user to remove the PIN protection from the SIM card

PIN Unblocking Key (PUK): An unlock reset code used to bypass the SIM PIN protection.

public safety access point (PSAP): A call center that receives emergency requests from the public for police, medical, or firefighter services.

Public Switched Telephone Network (PSTN): An aggregate of all circuit-switched telephone networks.

Rich Communication Services (RCS): An advanced messaging standard that aims to be a cross-platform mobile device solution for SMS, MMS, and other consumer communications.

RIM OS: The operating system developed by Research in Motion for use on BlackBerry smartphones and tablets.

route: A series of user-created waypoints on a trip.

Short Message Service (SMS): A text message communication service found on mobile devices.

SIM card: A smart card that identifies a user on a cellular network and contains an IMSI.

soft handoff: A cell system handoff in which a cellular communication is conditionally handed off from one base station to another, and the mobile equipment is simultaneously communicating with multiple base transceiver stations.

SQLite database: An open source relational database standard, which is frequently found on mobile devices.

subscriber records: Personal details maintained by the carrier about their customers and can include their name, address, alternative phone numbers, Social Security number and credit card information.

subsidy lock: A code that confines a subscriber to a certain cellular network so that a cellphone can be sold for free or at a subsidized price.

Symbian: A mobile device operating system developed by Nokia and currently maintained by Accenture.

Temporary Mobile Subscriber Identity (TMSI): A randomly generated number that is assigned to a mobile station, by the VLR, when the handset is switched on, and is based on the geographic location.

Time-Division Multiple Access (TDMA): A radio communication methodology that enables devices to communicate on the same frequency by splitting digital signals into time slots, or "bursts."

track log: A list of trackpoints that can be used to re-create a route.

trackpoint: A geolocational record that is automatically captured and stored by a GPS device.

Type Allocation Code (TAC): A number that identifies the type of wireless device.

Universal Integrated Circuit Card (UICC): A smart card used to uniquely identify a subscriber on a GSM or UMTS network.

Universal Mobile Telecommunications System (UMTS): A 3G cellular network standard, which is based upon GSM and was developed by 3GPP.

USB debugging: A process that allows a computer to communicate with an Android device via a USB cable.

Visitor Location Register (VLR): A database of information about roaming subscribers.

waypoint: A geolocational point of interest created by a user.

Wide Band CDMA (WCDMA): A high-speed signal transmission method based on CDMA and FDD methods.

Windows 10 Mobile: A Microsoft operating system that can be found on personal computers, mobile phones, and tablets.

Assessment

CLASSROOM DISCUSSIONS

1. You have just received a mobile device with an FCC-ID of BEJVM670. You have been told that the cellphone has an MEID. Using this information, answer the following questions:

   a. What U.S. cellular carrier(s) could be providing service for the cellphone?

   b. Does this cellphone possess Bluetooth?

   c. Could this cellphone have been used to take photographs and, if so, could the photos have GPS data associated with them?

   d. Where on this device could there be potential evidence? For example, does the handset use a SIM card or an SD card?

2. Detail best practices for containing and analyzing a cellular telephone.

3. In what ways could the cellphone carrier assist you in your investigation?

4. Describe how cellphone forensics is different from traditional computer forensics.

MULTIPLE-CHOICE QUESTIONS

1. The equipment found at a cell site that facilitates the communication of a cellphone user across a cellular network is best described as which of the following?

   A. Cellular network

   B. Base Transceiver Station

   C. Public Switched Telephone Network

   D. Home Location Register

2. Which of the following best describes the role of the Base Station Controller?

   A. Manages the radio signals for base transceiver stations

   B. Assigns frequencies and handoffs between cell sites

   C. Both A and B are correct

   D. Neither A nor B is correct

3. Which of the following are details used by telecommunications carriers for billing purposes and can include phone numbers called, call duration, dates and times of calls, and cell sites used?

   A. Equipment Identity Register

   B. Mobile network operator

   C. Temporary Mobile Subscriber Identity

   D. Call detail records

4. Which of the following will typically not be found on a GSM cellphone?

    A. SIM card

    B. IMEI

    C. FCC-ID

    D. MEID

5. The first three digits of the IMSI are referred to as which of the following?

    A. Mobile country code

    B. Mobile Subscriber Identity Number

    C. Mobile network operator

    D. Integrated Circuit Card ID

6. Which of the following is a portable wireless router that provides Internet access for up to five Internet-enabled devices and communicates via a cellular network?

    A. Office hub

    B. Public safety access point

    C. Mobile Station

    D. MiFi

7. Which of the following is a high mobility broadband communication that is suitable for use on trains and in other vehicles?

    A. 2G

    B. 3G

    C. 3GPP

    D. 4G LTE

8. Which of the following is an international standard for signal communications, which uses TDMA and FDD (Frequency Division Duplex) communication methods?

    A. GSM

    B. CDMA

    C. UMTS

    D. WCDMA

9. Which one of the following directories contains a list of contacts (names and telephone numbers) saved by a subscriber on a SIM card?

    A. EF_SMS

    B. EF_LOCI

    C. EF_LND

    D. EF_ADN

10. Which of the following mobile operating systems is an open source operating system based on the Linux 2.6 kernel and is owned by Google?

    A. Symbian

    B. Android

    C. RIM

    D. Windows

FILL IN THE BLANKS

1. A(n) _____ is the geographic area within a cellular network.

2. A Mobile _____ Center is responsible for switching data packets from one network path to another on a cellular network.

3. A(n) _____ handoff is when a cellular communication is conditionally handed off from one base station to another and the mobile equipment is simultaneously communicating with multiple base transceiver stations.

4. A(n) _____ Mobile Equipment Identity number uniquely identifies the mobile equipment or handset.

5. The database that contains information about a roaming subscriber is referred to as a(n) _____ Location Register.

6. The _____ Identity Register is used to track IMEI numbers and decide whether an IMEI is valid, suspect, or perhaps stolen.

7. Integrated _____ Enhanced Network is a wireless technology developed by Motorola, which combines two-way radio capabilities with digital cellphone technology.

8. A(n) _____ Public Land Mobile Network is a cellular network that a subscriber attempted to connect to but was not authorized to connect to.

9. A PIN Unblocking _____ (PUK) is a code that is available from the carrier and allows a user to remove the PIN protection from the SIM card.

10. A public safety _____ point is a call center that receives emergency requests from the public for police, medical, or firefighter services.

PROJECTS

Mobile Forensics Case Study

Find an investigation where cellphone forensics was used in a criminal investigation and then write an essay about the importance to successfully convict a suspect.

Standard Operating Procedures for Mobile Forensics

Find a smartphone and then write standard operating procedures for examining that cellphone. Include in your essay forensic tools that will work with that particular model.

Mobile Operating Systems

Select a mobile operating system and write a forensic examiner's guide to working with that operating system.

CDMA and GSM Telecommunication Protocols

Write an essay describing the differences from an examination of a CDMA cellphone and a GSM cellphone.

Experimenting with Emergency Download Mode

Create an EDL cable and then image an Android cellphone/tablet. There are numerous online resources available to determine which type of Android device this will work on. Try using the cable on an old, unused, Android device.

Chapter | **10**

Mobile App Investigations

Learning Outcomes

After reading this chapter, you will be able to understand the following:

- The importance of mobile apps in investigations;
- How to perform a static and dynamic analysis;
- The digital evidence available from dating, rideshare, and other popular apps;
- The value of deep-linking in investigations; and
- Analyzing SQLite databases.

Mobile applications (apps) are extremely important today in investigations for a variety of reasons. Interestingly, the databases associated with many apps, are unencrypted and are not too difficult to analyze. Furthermore, if a mobile device is locked or inaccessible, there are many other options available, which may include analyzing a linked desktop version of the app or sending a subpoena, or court order, to a third-party provider to obtain a suspect's data. Third-party companies collect, and store, a tremendous amount of data on their customers. Finally, many users opt to back up their data to cloud storage. For example, WhatsApp has the option for Apple iPhone/iPad users to back up their chats to iCloud, and that backup can be requested from Apple. Nevertheless, organized criminals and terrorist groups largely use mobile apps that utilize strong encryption or proprietary encryption, which can seriously hamper the work of law enforcement. Compounding these concerns is the fact that many apps maintain their servers in countries like Russia, which is beyond the reach of law enforcement in the West. Popular communication apps that use strong encryption include Telegram, Signal, Wickr, and Threema to name but a few. Nevertheless, zero-day exploits are frequently found in mobile apps, including Telegram, which can help investigators to gain access to an encrypted app. A **zero-day exploit** is a security vulnerability that is a threat on the day that it is discovered because a software patch, to fix the exploit, does not yet exist.

Static Versus Dynamic Analysis

During app installation, typically a SQLite database will be installed on the user device. This is a relational database that is comprised of tables. The data stored in these tables may or may not be encrypted. A table may contain a user's contacts, while a related table may store communications with contacts, for example. It is important to understand that these databases contain an extraordinary amount of personal information and, when unencrypted, can put an individual at risk for social engineering. Additionally, we should always consider the possibility to subpoena a third-party service provider for evidence.

When analyzing mobile apps, there are several approaches that an investigator can take, in order to examine the user data. A static analysis includes an examination of the SQLite database associated with that app. A dynamic analysis of the app is an analysis of the behavior of the application once it has been executed (or run). The sections that follow examine static analysis and dynamic analysis in more detail.

Static Analysis

A SQLite database is a relational database that is the preferred storage for data associated with mobile apps. SQLite is a C-language library that is responsible for the SQL database. SQLite source code is source code that resides in the public domain. Forensic tools, like BlackLight, enable the user to easily browse through application SQLite databases but there are other standalone tools that can be used. One of these tools is SQLite Database Browser, which is freeware. Later in this chapter we shall detail the types of evidence available from a number of popular mobile apps. Figure 10.1 shows an example of a SQLite database for the Tinder app on an iPhone.

Name	Date Created	Date Modified
▼ com.cardify.tinder	2019-02-08 15:16:59 (UTC)	2019-02-08 15:17:13 (UTC)
▶ Documents	2019-02-08 15:16:59 (UTC)	2019-06-20 15:35:14 (UTC)
▼ Library	2019-02-08 15:16:59 (UTC)	2019-06-20 15:35:12 (UTC)
▼ Application Support	2019-02-08 15:17:26 (UTC)	2019-02-26 15:26:53 (UTC)
▶ com.crashlytics	2019-02-08 15:17:26 (UTC)	2019-02-08 15:17:26 (UTC)
▶ GoogleMobileAds	2019-02-26 15:26:53 (UTC)	2019-06-20 15:35:12 (UTC)
▶ io.branch	2019-02-08 15:17:30 (UTC)	2019-06-20 15:35:12 (UTC)
▼ Tinder	2019-02-08 15:17:27 (UTC)	2019-02-26 15:26:50 (UTC)
Tinder2.sqlite	2019-02-08 15:17:27 (UTC)	2019-06-20 15:33:18 (UTC)
com-accountkit-sdk-AppEvents...	2019-04-03 14:04:10 (UTC)	2019-04-03 14:04:10 (UTC)
com-accountkit-sdk-PersistedA...	2019-02-08 15:17:49 (UTC)	2019-02-08 15:17:49 (UTC)
com-facebook-sdk-AppEventsP...	2019-06-20 15:35:12 (UTC)	2019-06-20 15:35:12 (UTC)
com-facebook-sdk-AppEventsT...	2019-06-20 15:35:12 (UTC)	2019-06-20 15:35:12 (UTC)
com-facebook-sdk-PersistedAn...	2019-02-08 15:17:30 (UTC)	2019-02-08 15:17:30 (UTC)
▶ Cookies	2019-02-20 16:44:23 (UTC)	2019-06-20 15:35:13 (UTC)
▶ Preferences	2019-02-08 15:16:59 (UTC)	2019-06-20 15:35:23 (UTC)
▶ WebKit	2019-02-20 16:44:23 (UTC)	2019-02-20 16:44:23 (UTC)

FIGURE 10.1　Tinder SQLite database on iOS (iPhone)

A cursory view of the information in Figure 10.1 shows that there are many folders and files associated with a mobile app SQLite database. Ultimately, the database could have five tables or could have 100 tables, which means that a thorough examination can be a painstaking process. Within each SQLite database (*.sqlite*) you will find databases, which will contain the file extension *.db*; for example, *google_analytics.db*. You will often find recognizable files, like *.jpg* (picture images), *.vcf* (or vCard for your contacts), or *.mp3* (sound file).

The chart in Figure 10.2 provides a general outline of how an iOS application is stored on an iPhone or iPad.

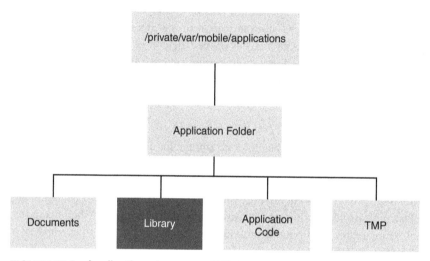

FIGURE 10.2   Application storage on iOS

The `Library` folder, which is highlighted in Figure 10.2, is where you will find the all-important user data, including cache, cookies, and other personal information. In the `Preferences` folder, which is displayed and highlighted in Figure 10.3, you may actually discover usernames and passwords that are stored in plaintext.

In Figure 10.4, we can view the name *com.cardify.tinder* and this is referred to as a bundle ID. A **bundle ID** is a uniform type identifier, which is comprised of alphanumeric characters, that uniquely identifies a specific app. The bundle ID for Microsoft's iOS Outlook app is *com.microsoft.Office.Outlook*. Thus, the format for the bundle ID is generally com.<*YourCompany*>.<*AppName*>, which is referred to as a reverse-domain name style string. When you visit the Apple App Store and search for the Microsoft Outlook app for iOS, then you will arrive at this URL in your web browser: https://apps.apple.com/us/app/microsoft-outlook/id951937596. Notice the "id951937596", which identifies this app on the App Store. An iOS app also has a unique identifier known as an App ID. An **App ID** is a two-part string that identifies a development team (Team ID) and an application (bundle ID). The Team ID is created and assigned by Apple, while the bundle ID is generated by the app developer.

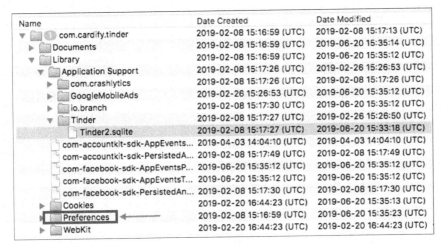

Name	Date Created	Date Modified
▼ com.cardify.tinder	2019-02-08 15:16:59 (UTC)	2019-02-08 15:17:13 (UTC)
▶ Documents	2019-02-08 15:16:59 (UTC)	2019-06-20 15:35:14 (UTC)
▼ Library	2019-02-08 15:16:59 (UTC)	2019-06-20 15:35:12 (UTC)
▼ Application Support	2019-02-08 15:17:26 (UTC)	2019-02-26 15:26:53 (UTC)
▶ com.crashlytics	2019-02-08 15:17:26 (UTC)	2019-02-08 15:17:26 (UTC)
▶ GoogleMobileAds	2019-02-26 15:26:53 (UTC)	2019-06-20 15:35:12 (UTC)
▶ io.branch	2019-02-08 15:17:30 (UTC)	2019-06-20 15:35:12 (UTC)
▼ Tinder	2019-02-08 15:17:27 (UTC)	2019-02-26 15:26:50 (UTC)
Tinder2.sqlite	2019-02-08 15:17:27 (UTC)	2019-06-20 15:33:18 (UTC)
com-accountkit-sdk-AppEvents...	2019-04-03 14:04:10 (UTC)	2019-04-03 14:04:10 (UTC)
com-accountkit-sdk-PersistedA...	2019-02-08 15:17:49 (UTC)	2019-02-08 15:17:49 (UTC)
com-facebook-sdk-AppEventsP...	2019-06-20 15:35:12 (UTC)	2019-06-20 15:35:12 (UTC)
com-facebook-sdk-AppEventsT...	2019-06-20 15:35:12 (UTC)	2019-06-20 15:35:12 (UTC)
com-facebook-sdk-PersistedAn...	2019-02-08 15:17:30 (UTC)	2019-02-08 15:17:30 (UTC)
▶ Cookies	2019-02-20 16:44:23 (UTC)	2019-06-20 15:35:13 (UTC)
▶ Preferences	2019-02-08 15:16:59 (UTC)	2019-06-20 15:35:23 (UTC)
▶ WebKit	2019-02-20 16:44:23 (UTC)	2019-02-20 16:44:23 (UTC)

FIGURE 10.3   Tinder SQLite database on iOS

Name	Date Created	Date Modified
▼ com.cardify.tinder	2019-02-08 15:16:59 (UTC)	2019-02-08 15:17:13 (UTC)
▶ Documents	2019-02-08 15:16:59 (UTC)	2019-06-20 15:35:14 (UTC)
▼ Library	2019-02-08 15:16:59 (UTC)	2019-06-20 15:35:12 (UTC)
▼ Application Support	2019-02-08 15:17:26 (UTC)	2019-02-26 15:26:53 (UTC)
▶ com.crashlytics	2019-02-08 15:17:26 (UTC)	2019-02-08 15:17:26 (UTC)
▶ GoogleMobileAds	2019-02-26 15:26:53 (UTC)	2019-06-20 15:35:12 (UTC)
▶ io.branch	2019-02-08 15:17:30 (UTC)	2019-06-20 15:35:12 (UTC)
▼ Tinder	2019-02-08 15:17:27 (UTC)	2019-02-26 15:26:50 (UTC)
Tinder2.sqlite	2019-02-08 15:17:27 (UTC)	2019-06-20 15:33:18 (UTC)
com-accountkit-sdk-AppEvents...	2019-04-03 14:04:10 (UTC)	2019-04-03 14:04:10 (UTC)
com-accountkit-sdk-PersistedA...	2019-02-08 15:17:49 (UTC)	2019-02-08 15:17:49 (UTC)
com-facebook-sdk-AppEventsP...	2019-06-20 15:35:12 (UTC)	2019-06-20 15:35:12 (UTC)
com-facebook-sdk-AppEventsT...	2019-06-20 15:35:12 (UTC)	2019-06-20 15:35:12 (UTC)
com-facebook-sdk-PersistedAn...	2019-02-08 15:17:30 (UTC)	2019-02-08 15:17:30 (UTC)
▶ Cookies	2019-02-20 16:44:23 (UTC)	2019-06-20 15:35:13 (UTC)
▶ Preferences	2019-02-08 15:16:59 (UTC)	2019-06-20 15:35:23 (UTC)
▶ WebKit	2019-02-20 16:44:23 (UTC)	2019-02-20 16:44:23 (UTC)

FIGURE 10.4   Tinder SQLite database on iOS

Static Analysis: Code Review

Another form of static analysis refers to performing a code review on a mobile app, which can help the investigator understand the type of evidence that is available. In terms of the evidence available for an Android app (.apk or Android Package) there is the manifest, which shows the permissions associated with a particular app. For example, the manifest may show that the app is collecting user location information ("COARSE_LOCATION" and/or "FINE_LOCATION"). ACCESS_COARSE_LOCATION is a permission that enables the app to access the approximate location of the user device, which is based on NETWORK_PROVIDER (cell sites, i.e. cell towers). ACCESS_FINE_LOCATION enables the app to determine the location of the user device based on NETWORK_PROVIDER and GPS (GPS_PROVIDER). An Android application contains a file at the root of the project source set, which is called *AndroidManifest.xml*. An **Android manifest file** contains the application's package name, its functionality, permissions, hardware, and software requirements for installation.

Understanding the permissions associated with an app allows the investigator to understand the type of evidence that can be requested from the provider and the type of evidence to look for when examining the SQLite database. The latter is important because examining one database can take many days, or even weeks, and therefore limiting the scope of your analysis is key. Example 10.1 shows a small extract from an Android manifest for WhatsApp.

EXAMPLE 10.1   Android Permissions Manifest for WhatsApp

```
<manifest xmlns:"http://schemas.android.com/apk/res/android"
android:versionCode="451048" android:versionName="2.12.550" package="com.whatsapp"
platformBuildVersionCode="23" platformBuildVersionName="6.0-2166767">
    <uses-sdk android:minSdkVersion="7" android:targetSdkVersion="23" />
    <uses-permission android:name="android.permission.ACCESS_COARSE_LOCATION" />
    <uses-permission android:name="android.permission.ACCESS_FINE_LOCATION" />
    <uses-permission android:name="android.permission.ACCESS_NETWORK_STATE" />
    <uses-permission android:name="android.permission.ACCESS_WIFI_STATE" />
    <uses-permission android:name="android.permission.AUTHENTICATE_ACCOUNTS" />
    <uses-permission android:name="android.permission.BLUETOOTH" />
    <uses-permission android:name="android.permission.BROADCAST_STICKY" />
    <uses-permission android:name="android.permission.CAMERA" />
    <uses-permission android:name="android.permission.CHANGE_WIFI_STATE" />
    <uses-permission android:name="android.permission.GET_ACCOUNTS" />
    <uses-permission android:name="android.permission.GET_TASKS" />
    <uses-permission android:name="android.permission.INSTALL_SHORTCUT" />
    <uses-permission android:name="android.permission.INTERNET" />
    <uses-permission android:name="android.permission.MANAGE_ACCOUNTS" />
    <uses-permission android:name="android.permission.MODIFY_AUDIO_SETTINGS" />
    <uses-permission android:name="android.permission.READ_CONTACTS" />
    <uses-permission android:name="android.permission.READ_PHONE_STATE" />
```

An understanding of the manifest is also important from a mobile security perspective. Many privacy policy statements are misleading or confusing and provide poor guidance about how trustworthy a mobile app is. The Federal Trade Commission (FTC), for example, investigated a popular free app for Android, called the Brightest Flashlight, after it was discovered that the app requested many more permissions from the user's device beyond the light function on the device. Therefore, some app permissions are high risk, while other permissions are low risk.

A Web search for the "Uber APK file", or any other APK file, quickly identifies where the application package can be downloaded. Once the APK has been downloaded, there are a number of applications that can be used to review the code and manifest for the APK. One tool for reviewing the APK developer code is dex2jar (dex compiler), which can be downloaded from SourceForge. Another application for viewing the APK is FileViewer Plus. One preferred tool is an online Java APK decompiler application, which is available from www.javadecompilers.com/apk. With this tool, you can decompile your APK in a web browser without downloading an APK decompiler to your computer. Therefore, you do not need to worry whether the application that you are downloading is from a trusted source because the application is being run from their web server and not from your computer. There are numerous other source code analytical tools that an investigator can use, including SourceMeter, JSLint, and FindBugs. Figure 10.5 shows the JSLint user interface.

FIGURE 10.5 JSLint user interface

Dynamic Analysis

A dynamic analysis of the app is an analysis of the behavior of the application once it has been executed (or run). An **Android emulator** is an application that simulates, or runs, the Android operating system in a virtual machine. These applications are generally developed for use with a personal computer and run as a virtual machine. App developers use an emulator to analyze how their apps will run before making them available to the public. However, an emulator can also benefit investigators who are interested in viewing the behavior of an app—especially if an app potentially contains malware. This is the benefit of using an emulator that operates as a virtual machine. An investigator may also be interested in monitoring the permissions and DNS connections associated with an executed mobile app. In terms of monitoring DNS connections (connections to servers), there is Wireshark (Windows) and Debookee (macOS), which are very effective at monitoring these connections over a wireless network. Figure 10.6 shows a screenshot of a pcap (packet capture) file from Wireshark. A **pcap file** is a wireless packet that contains user data and network data related to the sender and receiver of that data.

```
...0. .... .... = Truncated: Message is not truncated
.... ...1 .... .... = Recursion desired: Do query recursively
.... .... .0.. .... = Z: reserved (0)
.... .... ...0 .... = Non-authenticated data: Unacceptable
Questions: 1
Answer RRs: 0
Authority RRs: 0
Additional RRs: 0
Queries
   maps.googleapis.com: type A, class IN
      Name: maps.googleapis.com
      [Name Length: 19]
      [Label Count: 3]
      Type: A (Host Address) (1)
      Class: IN (0x0001)

0000   e6 a7 a0 31 9b 06 80 7a   bf 36 ca 10 08 00 45 00    ...1..z  .6....E.
0010   00 41 65 7f 40 00 40 11   89 d6 c0 a8 c9 04 c0 a8    .Ae.@.@. ........
0020   01 01 aa f9 00 35 00 2d   46 06 66 2f 01 00 00 01    .....5.- F.f/....
0030   00 00 00 00 00 00 04 6d   61 70 73 0a 67 6f 6f 67    .......m aps.goog
0040   6c 65 61 70 69 73 03 63   6f 6d 00 00 01 00 01       leapis.c om......
```

No. 20865 · Time: 453.434412 · Source: 192.168.201.4 · Destination: 192.168.1.1 · Protocol: DNS · Length: 79 · Info: Standard query 0x662f A maps.googleapis.com

```
3.402420
3.485637
3.487309
3.487310
3.488102
3.494230
3.506677
3.507137
3.509737
3.511118
...00 = Ex
Length: 65
fication: 0
0x02 (Don
.... = Re
.... = Do
.... = Mo
nt offset:
o live: 64
ol: UDP (1
checksum:
r checksum
: 192.168.
ation: 192
a0 31 9b
65 7f 40 00 40 11    89 d6 c0 a8 c9 04 c0 a8    .Ae.@.  ........
```

FIGURE 10.6   Google Maps API identified in a PCAP captured by Wireshark

Note

When performing any type of wireless monitoring, ensure that you have permission to be on a particular network and ensure that you are only monitoring your wireless traffic.

To remain safe and compliant, consider using a personal hotspot device, like a Verizon Jetpack, in a secure lab. A tool like Debookee also has the ability to encrypt some wireless traffic, which means that while app data may be encrypted on the device and on the server, often companies will implement poor encryption protocols, whereby the data in transmission can be intercepted and viewed in plaintext. Thus, tools like Debookee can also be used, by security professionals analyzing apps, to try to determine how secure apps are.

Introduction to Debookee

Debookee is a comprehensive wireless packet sniffer for macOS. The tool is not passive as it performs a man-in-the-middle (MITM) attack to intercept data from mobile and IoT devices. A **man-in-the-middle (MITM) attack** is an attempt to intercept electronic communications between two computing devices, with the intent to decipher encrypted messages. The tool also performs SSL/TLS decryption. Debookee supports numerous protocols, including HTTP, HTTPS, DNS, TCP, DHCP, SIP, and RTP (VoIP). The tool can be used to identify what data is being collected and shared by mobile apps. In other words, you can identify DNS connections to servers around the world and other companies that could be potentially subpoenaed for information. The data generated from one mobile app can be shared with fifty or more third-party companies, which are mostly analytics companies like Crashlytics, UXCam, Fabric, etc.

On the homepage of the Debookee website, click the **Download** button and install the software.

Note

You do not need to purchase the software but can begin by using the trial version. You may of course later decide to purchase the software, which is relatively inexpensive, and one license can be used on two different computers.

Once you install the software and start the program, you will see an interface, similar to Figure 10.8. The IP address, MAC address, and host name that are displayed provide information about your device.

Figure 10.9 shows a close-up of the information that we just discussed. Click the **Start LanScan** button as highlighted in Figure 10.9.

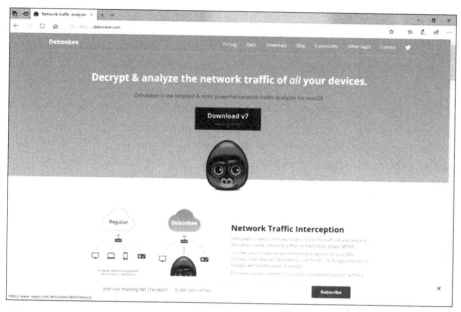

FIGURE 10.7   Debookee home page

FIGURE 10.8   Debookee user interface

You will then see a list of all devices that are connected to the same wireless access point as your computer. Once you select your target device, click the **Pcap** option, on the upper left of your screen, and then click **Save Pcap files**, as shown in Figure 10.10.

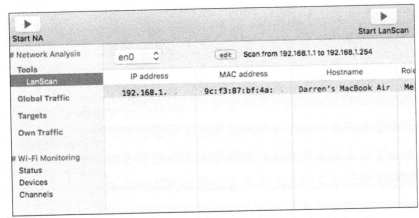

FIGURE 10.9 Debookee user interface with host computer information displayed

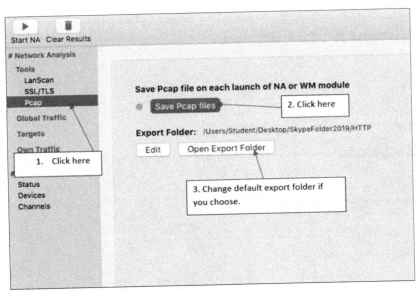

FIGURE 10.10 *Save Pcap files* option in Debookee

You can then click the **Open Export Folder** button to change the default export folder. There is an add-on tool in Debookee, which allows you to decrypt the contents of the pcap files. If you purchase this option, you can click the **SSL/TLS** button displayed in Figure 10.11.

The next step in the TLS decryption process is to install the certificate authority (CA) on the machine (see Figure 10-12). To start your NA, click the Play button ▶ in the very top left of your application screen (underneath it says, "Start NA"). Once the trust certificate has been installed, you should stop the NA (Network Analysis) by clicking the same button.

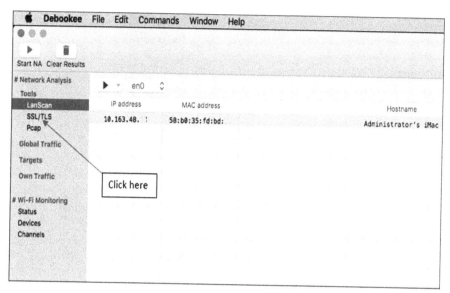

FIGURE 10.11   SSL/TLS decryption option in Debookee

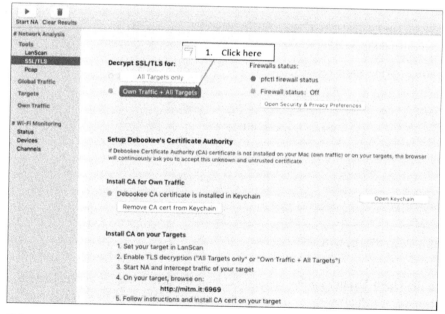

FIGURE 10.12   Decryption option in Debookee

From the screen in Figure 10.13, click the **Start NA ▶** button again. Open the webpage, or application, you want to analyze (or the device that you wish to monitor), and begin generating data packets by opening and closing different functions, sending messages, or just using the application.

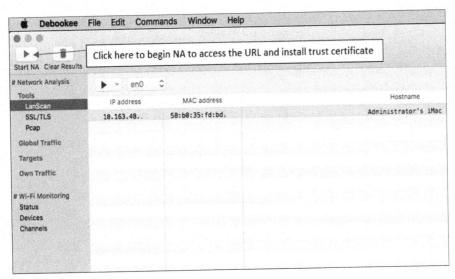

FIGURE 10.13   Start NA option in Debookee

On the left column in Figure 10.14, under **Own Traffic**, you will see that **DNS** and **HTTP** have populated. The NA will run continuously until you terminate it. When you are satisfied with the data collected, press the stop button. Remember that your pcap files are automatically exported to the folder that you previously selected.

Click **DNS** in the left column and you will see all DNS connections made during the NA (timestamped) with the hostname and/or IP address. These are the IP addresses and hosts that you can analyze, in addition to the pcaps.

It is recommended that you click **File > Export** and save this list as a .doc or a .txt file. You can then use some open source DNS analysis tools, including www.robtex.com and www.dnsdumpster.com.

Clicking the **HTTP** button, as shown in Figure 10.15, will display an itemized list of every packet transmitted over HTTP, HTTPS, TCP, SIP, IMAP, and other protocols. If you did not purchase the SSL/TLS decrypt module, HTTPS packets (transmitted over port 443 using TLSv1.2) will display in red, and you will not be able to read the data until you decrypt the packets. Port 443 is the port number for secure HTTP communications—in other words, Web traffic. If you did purchase the SSL/TLS decrypt module, HTTPS packets will display in black, and when you click on them, the data will be displayed in plaintext in the data field.

Click on a packet that you wish to examine. In the data field you will see some text populate underneath the tab labeled **Request**. Upon further inspection of the data field, you will see the full GET request along with the packet parameters and data, as displayed in Figure 10.16. **GET** is an HTTP method used to request data from a specific resource, like a web server.

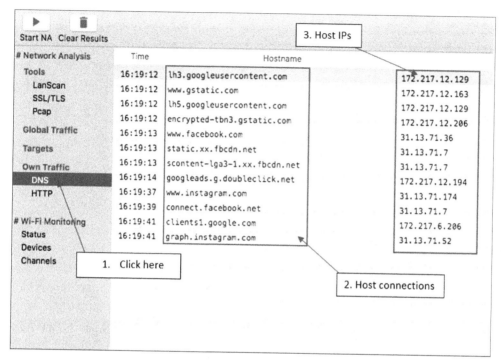

FIGURE 10.14   DNS connections captured

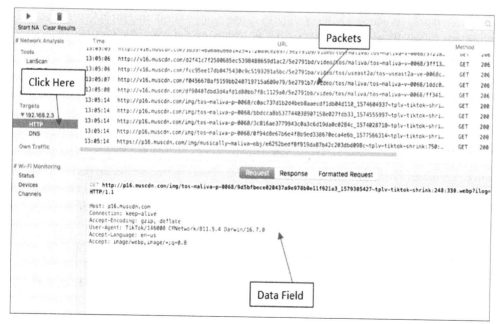

FIGURE 10.15   Decrypted TikTok packet (pcap)

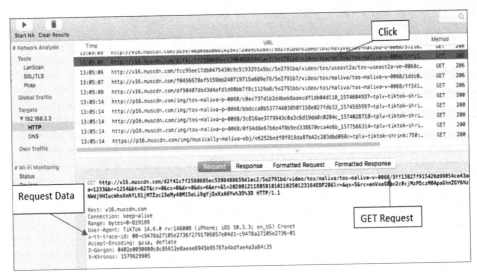

FIGURE 10.16   GET request data displayed

You may then click the **Response** tab to view the webpage or application response packet. Figure 10.17 displays a webpage response. Status code 200 means that it was successfully downloaded.

FIGURE 10.17   Response results

You can choose to export your packets so that they can be analyzed later. You can select to view your packet data in a text file or in a Word document. Figure 10.18 displays the option to export the packet data.

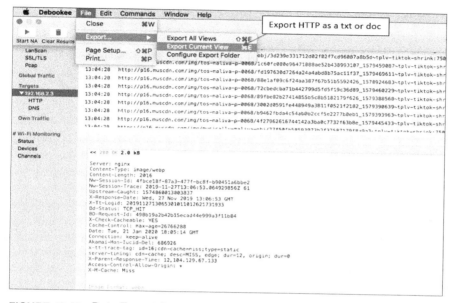

FIGURE 10.18   Data Export feature in Debookee

In Figure 10.19 and Figure 10.20 you can view the location and message data that was transmitted in plaintext while using the popular dating application Tinder. This data was observed while inspecting the entire packet in a text document.

```
{"status":200,"message":"Event batch accepted","time":0}
{
    "events": [
        {
            "event": {
                "IDFA": "00000000-0000-0000-0000-000000000000",
                "age": 21,
                "appBuild": "10050013",
                "appSessionId": "7C4F0F14AD784376A4743FD4D052F297",
                "appSessionTimeElapsed": 92.20265710353851,
                "appVersion": "10.5.0 (iOS)",
                "birthday": "859217222",
                "chatSessionId": "082FC369-5D81-4C7F-9A95-63C149373442",
                "city": "New York",
                "country": "US",
                "county": "New York",
                "dataProvider": "",
                "deviceId": "F4C88617-E5E2-4B7
                "didSuperLike": false,
                "gender": 0,
                "hasUnsentMessage": true,
                "heartbeatInMillis": 2000,
                "language": "en-US",
                "lastMessageFrom": "other",
                "lat": 40.71,
                "lon": -74.01,
                "manu": "Apple",
                "matchId": "5c5cf250309d391100d25e8c5c5d9e488bb5ba1100d4d8d5",
                "matchType": "solo",
                "model": "iPhone5,2",
                "neighborhood": "Manhattan",
                "numMessagesMe": 57,
                "numMessagesOther": 52,
                "osVersion": "10.3.3",
                "otherId": "5c5d9e488bb5ba1100d4d8d5",
                "platform": "1",
                "state": "NY",
                "superLike": false,
                "targetGender": 1,
```

- Explicit location data like:
  Country/City/State/Neighborhood/LatLong
- Device information (iPhone 5)
- Device OS Information (iOS 10.3.3)
- User information (age: 21)

FIGURE 10.19   Location, device, and user information from the Tinder app

```
"goingout": [],
"inbox": [],
"last_activity_date": "2019-03-21T15:28:35.757Z",
"liked_messages": [],
"lists": [],
"matches": [
    {
        "_id": "5c5cf250309d391100d25e8c5c5d9e488bb5ba1100d4d8d5",
        "is_new_message": true,
        "last_activity_date": "2019-03-21T15:28:35.757Z",
        "messages": [
            {
                "_id": "5c93ada33ae75815008049ae",
                "created_date": "2019-03-21T15:28:35.757Z",
                "from": "5c5cf250309d391100d25e8c",
                "match_id": "5c5cf250309d391100d25e8c5c5d9e488bb5ba1100d4d8d5",
                "message": "This is so confusing",
                "sent_date": "2019-03-21T15:28:35.757Z",
                "timestamp": 1553182115757,
                "to": "5c5d9e488bb5ba1100d4d8d5"
```

Message sent from one Tinder user to another while intercepting with Debookee

```
                "seen": "
                "last_seen_msg_id": "5c93a7e6335637150030d728",
                "match_seen": true
            }
        }
    ],
    "places": {
        "has_new": false
```

FIGURE 10.20   Message from the Tinder App Displayed in Plaintext

The pcaps generated by Debookee can then be exported and analyzed using the Wireshark application. Wireshark can also perform data capture and is recommended for Windows users.

Dating Apps

There were 3.6 million applications ("apps") on Google Play and 2.1 million iOS applications on Apple's App Store in 2017, and a mere 8.5% of those apps were cross-platform, meaning that they were available for both iOS and Android. Adults in the United States are using mobile devices in ways that could not be imagined just 15 years ago. According to Pew Research Center's report on mobile dating, 15% of adults (ages 18 and older), in the United States, have reported that they have used online dating sites or mobile dating apps. Dating site usage has nearly tripled for young adults (18 through 24) in just two years, from 10% to 27%. Therefore, it is important for investigators to understand the evidence available from mobile dating apps. Moreover, the prevalence of social engineering—using data derived from social media accounts—means that dating apps are a cause for concern in terms of organizational risk.

With the recent increase in online match-making connections, in a post-Snowden era where privacy has become a major concern, we might question whether dating applications are utilizing personal data ethically. In March 2018, a security flaw in the Grindr app disclosed user location data, which could have exposed app users to harassment; Grindr is a dating app, primarily used to connect gay men and unfortunately has facilitated numerous attacks against many gay men. Thus, understanding the available evidence from a dating app is extremely important because of the nature of the crimes being committed, the links to social media, the personal information available, and the location and communication capabilities of these apps.

Tinder

As of 2018, Tinder had 57 million users worldwide. Millions of Tinder subscribers pay for a premium service: Tinder Plus or Tinder Gold. Tinder is used in 190 countries and supports 40 languages. Owned by Match Group, Inc., Tinder is a location-based, social media, application for dating. The app connects singles and allows them to "Swipe Right", if they wish to connect with another individual, or they can "Swipe Left", if they are not interested. The user can also "Swipe Up" (called a "super like"), which notifies the user that they have been "Super Liked". The ability to passively block communication with someone, whom a user is not interested in, is what makes Tinder appealing for so many people.

Tinder gives the user the ability to chat with individuals who have both swiped right pseudo-anonymously. A user is not required to divulge his cellphone number, and a user can make his own judgment about how much personal information he wishes to share with another user when matched. Chats within the application are stored chronologically and can be deleted.

Tinder also offers a Web-based version of their service at gotinder.com and tinder.com (see Figure 10.21). The website gives users the ability to use Tinder's services without a smartphone. The user simply logs in with their credentials. However, location services must be turned on, in the browser application, to use the Web version of the application.

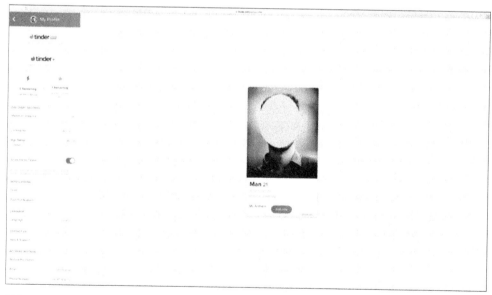

FIGURE 10.21   www.gotinder.com user profile

One of the most popular features of Tinder is the ability for users to synchronize their personal Instagram page with their Tinder profile (see Figure 10.22). This feature allows someone whom they have matched with (both parties swipe right) to have the ability to view the other user's Instagram profile. This allows a user to visit a Tinder user's Instagram profile, even if the Instagram account is set to private. Connecting social media accounts in this fashion is referred to as "deep-linking".

FIGURE 10.22 Tinder app linked to Instagram

A Spotify account can also be synchronized with a Tinder account, using deep-linking. This feature allows the users to share their personal playlists with individuals that they have matched with. A user can apply an "Anthem" to their profile, which can be the user's favorite song.

Using Robtex (robtex.com), we can quickly map out the domains associated with Tinder, some of which are displayed in Figure 10.23.

FIGURE 10.23 DNS data for gotinder.com (Source: Robtex.com)

Utilizing tools, like Robtex and traceroute, and whatismyipaddress.com, an investigator can determine where app user data is being stored and determining jurisdiction.

An analysis of Tinder's DNS connections shows that the Tinder app connects a user's profile with servers managed by Facebook, Leanplum, Appsflyer, DoubleClick, and many other companies. Using Debookee, it was possible to intercept Tinder messages, an example of which can be viewed in Figure 10.24. Figure 10.25 displays sample DNS connections associated with Tinder and captured with Debookee.

```
Host: api.gotinder.com
User-Agent: Tinder/10.5.0 (iPhone; iOS 10.3.3; Scale/2.00)
Accept: */*
Accept-Encoding: gzip, deflate
x-client-version: 10050013
platform: ios
Content-Type: application/json
os-version: 100000300003
Accept-Language: en-US;q=1
Connection: keep-alive
x-supported-image-formats: webp, jpeg
X-Auth-Token: 3e5e8de4-ab52-4b43-ba94-737cde82bfe8
Authorization: Token token="3e5e8de4-ab52-4b43-ba94-737cde82bfe8"
Content-Length: 34
app-version: 2665


{"message":"This is so confusing"}
```

FIGURE 10.24   Debookee HTTPS packet capture and decrypted chat message

```
11:28:27    api.gotinder.com 52.55.75.163       54.164.204.138
52.21.159.140 |    54.165.150.112    54.209.151.147    54.209.103.58
54.210.234.160    54.83.185.44
11:28:27    tinder-prod-pxy-1011891005.us-east-1.elb.amazonaws.com
      52.55.75.163       54.164.204.138    52.21.159.140
54.165.150.112    54.209.151.147    54.209.103.58    54.210.234.160
54.83.185.44
11:28:31    etl.tindersparks.com    34.201.194.172    34.203.141.28
35.169.148.27    34.200.209.241    34.225.218.222    34.206.163.185
34.230.239.87    34.204.222.14
11:28:31    a8030d69c412411e989e80a34354f837-948153997.us-east-
1.elb.amazonaws.com    34.201.194.172    34.203.141.28    35.169.148.27
34.200.209.241    34.225.218.222    34.206.163.185    34.230.239.87
34.204.222.14
11:29:28    api.gotinder.com 34.203.153.190    52.202.189.239
34.225.27.3       3.93.229.43       52.0.63.52       52.20.184.210
34.232.174.172    34.202.104.117
11:30:29    api.gotinder.com 34.203.153.190    52.202.189.239
34.225.27.3       3.93.229.43       52.0.63.52       52.20.184.210
34.232.174.172    34.202.104.117
11:30:31    etl.tindersparks.com    34.201.194.172    3.85.248.212
```

FIGURE 10.25   DNS sample traffic captured with Debookee

Using BlackLight, a static analysis of the user data, contained in the Tinder SQLite database on an iPhone, reveals that the data is stored in plaintext. Interestingly, a private Instagram account could be viewed during this analysis. Moreover, that (private) Instagram account stored Instagram photos from other users without that user's consent. User chat sessions, usernames, and Instagram data were all stored in plaintext on the iPhone test device. A URL can be found associated with each profile, which enables the user to access another user's profile page—even if it is marked private.

An examination of the Tinder SQLite database also revealed the location of other Tinder users in close proximity, as shown in Figure 10.26.

ZDISTANCEMILES
1.0
1.0
6.0
1.0
1.0
1.0
6.0
3.0
7.0
5.0
1.0

FIGURE 10.26   ZDISTANCEMILES displays the distances to other users

It is also possible to obtain more precise information about users' locations in the vicinity, as shown in Figure 10.27.

```
"city": "New York",
"country": "US",
"county": "New York",
"dataProvider": "",
"deviceId": "F4CB8617-E5E2-4B7A-8C46-CAFBFA75BE0F",
"didSuperLike": false,
"gender": 0,
"hasUnsentMessage": false,
"heartbeatInMillis": 2000,
"language": "en-US",
"lastMessageFrom": "other",
"lat": 40.71,
"lon": -74.01,
"manu": "Apple",
"matchId":
```

FIGURE 10.27   Location data from the Tinder app

Grindr

While there are many mobile apps that provide corroborating evidence in an investigation, Grindr is an app that has been used to perpetrate some of the most heinous crimes. Therefore, it is an app that warrants special attention for investigators. Stephen Port, from East London, U.K., was called the Grindr Serial Killer after he was charged with murdering four men that he met on Grindr. There are literally hundreds, if not thousands of cases, where Grindr has been used, by criminals, to lure victims and subsequently commit crimes, which include murder, assault, and robbery. The good news is that the Grindr app stores a wealth of information, in plaintext, which may help investigators and prosecutors.

Grindr was launched in 2009 and is the world's leading social networking application for gay, bisexual, trans and queer people. Grindr, unlike traditional dating apps, like Tinder and Bumble, is designed to find individuals in close proximity to the user. The smallest value for distance that Tinder/Bumble incorporates into their platform is one mile but Grindr will literally go to "zero feet away", and this is explicitly stated in the "About" section of their webpage. There is no "swipe left" or "dislike" and individuals are listed from closest to farthest away. There are no parameters to meet a certain type of user like with Tinder (age range, gender, etc.). If a user wants to engage with another user, they simply "Tap" that individual's profile, and they will be notified. The other user is then notified that they have been tapped. At this point, both users can immediately send an unlimited number of messages, which can be texts, images, and "GayMoji" stickers.

Popular dating applications, like Tinder and Bumble, require both users to explicitly indicate their willingness to engage with the other. However, Grindr does not require mutual consent to begin a chat session. There is a safeguard to protect from harassment, where the user can simply delete the "Tap" from a user they do not like, ending the message session. There are different types of "Taps" that give a visual representation of what the individual is looking for. There is a "Hi" icon tap for if the individual just wants to introduce himself or herself, or perhaps just chat. There is a "flame" icon tap for if the individual is interested in dating or sex. And finally, there is a "smiling devil Emoji" icon tap if the individual is looking for a "no strings attached" interaction. If the message is a text, then it will be previewed next to the user's profile. If it is a photo or video, it will have a small "Camera Icon" instead. A relatively new feature to the Grindr message function is "Read" receipts that will indicate whether the person a user messages has actually opened the message. Figure 10.28 shows the "Flame" tap and "Smiling Devil Tap" emojis.

Grindr has reached more than 196 countries with more than 3.6 million daily active users (2018). On average these users send 228 million messages and 20 million photos each day.

To date, there is no Web interface for Grindr, which supports user chat. However, the user can create a profile at www.grindr.com.

Grindr Evidence

Grindr does support deep-linking to social media services, which includes Facebook, Instagram, and Twitter. A feature of Grindr is the opportunity for a user to sync their personal Instagram page directly to their Grindr profile. This feature allows someone who has tapped on a user's Grindr profile to directly view the user's Instagram profile page. Grindr then gives the user the option to quickly switch directly to Instagram. This feature gives the user even more redundancy in deciding if the person they have matched with is someone they would still like to engage with. Both users still must go through the process of requesting to follow and allowing a follow through Instagram if the Instagram account is private. Like Instagram, a Facebook account can also be synced with a Grindr account, and it provides an easy one-click link directly to the Facebook profile on the Facebook app.

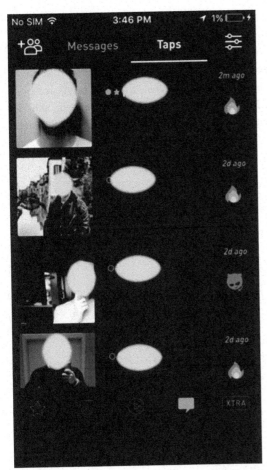

FIGURE 10.28 Grindr mobile user chat interface

Grindr appears to connect with a number of IP addresses, as displayed in Figure 10.29. A trace of these IP addresses goes back to San Francisco, California.

FIGURE 10.29 www.grindr.com.cdn.cloudfare.net DNS map (Source: Robtex.com)

Debookee could identify Grindr communication packets from iPhones, while they are being transmitted. The content is TLS/SSL encrypted. However, using the TLS decryption tool, offered by Debookee, it is possible to view a substantial amount of the DNS and HTTPS traffic, as shown in Figure 10.30. Messages are sent through *cdns.grindr.com* on port 443, using Amazon Web Services Inc. Although Grindr has made security updates to its platform since 2008, the third parties responsible for advertising, like Nexage, still pass sensitive PII, which includes exact location, sex, and age in plaintext, as shown in Figure 10.31. This means that anyone performing a man-in-the-middle attack could see that data.

```
GET
https://cdns.grindr.com/images/thumb/187x187/119ec148769261deac9753b958d1
05fa5c1b8047 HTTP/2.0

:authority: cdns.grindr.com:443
accept-language: en-us
accept: image/*;q=0.8
accept-encoding: gzip, deflate
user-agent: grindrx/5.5.2 (iPhone; iOS 10.3.3; Scale/2.00)


<< 403 213 B

date: Thu, 23 May 2019 16:27:28 GMT
content-type: application/xml
set-cookie: __cfduid=d368ff8b86152eab3a1603d1f3c3a02511558628848;
expires=Fri, 22-May-20 16:27:28 GMT; path=/; domain=.grindr.com; HttpOnly
x-amz-request-id: 482245E3F27DAC58
x-amz-id-2:
GqyrEWlEYPmGGfVE6WQvQEa2y6UQMGPEsksDfdfLXVjE6DdGXfzdr2NbBPSCIK1iCYHwW/hja
GU=
cf-cache-status: HIT
expect-ct: max-age=604800, report-uri="https://report-
uri.cloudflare.com/cdn-cgi/beacon/expect-ct"
vary: Accept-Encoding
server: cloudflare
cf-ray: 4db865c07cfb2214-EWR
content-encoding: gzip
```

FIGURE 10.30   Debookee HTTPS packet capture decryption

In a SQLite database, named *greventLog.sqlite*, you can find multiple latitude/longitude references stored in plaintext, as shown in Figure 10.32. Each message transaction is sent with updated location data. A latitude/longitude converter can then be used to find the address.

Messages in Grindr are unencrypted and are stored in plaintext. After viewing the data, a user has a unique identifier that is displayed in the "from" portion and in the "to" portion, which is a unique ID for the subject's iPhone, as shown in Figure 10.33. After combing through *PersistenceStore.bin*, it is possible to see all message data generated between two devices. Incoming messages can also be retrieved in plaintext as shown in Figure 10.33.

```
cb348162a0e4e8aafc96dd8259ba086,a9a6656256f74bb9979ed1c6e1cdda04,bae07051
d2a7499a9c394a84ff7028f6",
    "exclude_targeting_hash": "c8cce7cf889a841615a175ba5d9a59bd",
    "force_gdpr_applies": "0",
    "gdpr_applies": "0",
    "h": "1136",
    "id": "agltb3B1Yi1pbmNyDAsSBFNpdGUYorkhDA",
    "ll": "40.7106622970574,-74.00643135467496",
    "lla": "65",
    "llf": "446980",
    "llsdk": "1",
    "mr": "1",
    "nv": "5.4.1",
    "o": "p",
    "q": "app_version:5.5.2",
    "request_id": "ddcb6bc67b114f729164e97a7f5978a0_00be2cd300d5de54",
    "rtc": "4",
    "sc": "2.0",
    "tgr": "XObLdtR7RwsaIO9jOTZ2xgg9u2gcz0b4Wg8YOg",
    "udid": "mopub:788C666C-9774-4C3B-A9DD-D2535624C0E9",
    "user_data_q": "m_gender:m,m_age:20",
    "v": "8",
    "vv": "2",
    "w": "640",
    "z": "-0400"
}
```

FIGURE 10.31   Mopub banner ad including PII: Age, sex, and exact location

```
"carrier":null,"advertising_id":"00000000-0000-0000-0000-000000000000","cam
paign_id":null,"os_version":"iOS.10.3.3","notification_id":null,"timestamp"
:1554302044337.231,"notification_type":null,"latitude":"40.7105","longitude
":"-74.0065"},"name":"push_notification_clicked","timestamp":1554302044},{"
params":{},"name":"inbox_screen_viewed","timestamp":1554302045},{"params":{
"media_source":"None","campaign_name":"None","ad_set":"None"},"name":"link_
start","timestamp":1554302045},{"params":{"network_status":"WIFI","distance
_setting_enabled":false,"push_enabled":"true","advertising_id":"00000000-00
00-0000-0000-000000000000","launch_type":"resume","launch_from_push":"true"
,"location_permission":"true"},"name":"app_opened","timestamp":1554302046},
{"params":{},"name":"tap_receive","timestamp":1554302048},{"params":{},"nam
e":"tap_receive","timestamp":1554302048},{"params":{},"name":"tap_receive",
"timestamp":1554302049},{"params":{"source":"chat","type":"offline_photo","
time_passed_since_last_seen":null},"name":"chat_received","timestamp.Z..U [
..8A7BD6F8-007D-4B90-B9EE-42475C281B4F[{"params":{"source":"inputbar_text_v
iew_focus"},"name":"chat_inputbar_item_click","timestamp":1554302454},{"par
```

FIGURE 10.32   Latitude/longitude data from greventLog.sqlite

```
.DDDD.l..AAAA.........!"%&',":"21AAAAF...ĐA..Í..`F......AAAA.../56ce3ed6af
f806e98647af0b75aac46e7aa35879_0_0_0./AAAAF...È....<..AAAA.../617f4bd2a12de
4be0b6e5bf204abe78548bc799a_0_0_0..AAAA...f....mornin.bud..where.u.at?.seap
ort.at.work.here.Hello...Welcome!.Here's.how.to.start................Greeti
ngs.from.the.Lab!..Greetings.from.the.Lab.as.well!..MSG.#.1.Hey.how.are.you
?...MSG.#.2...MSG.#.3..MSG.#.4..MSG.#.5.ð...ð..ð..Oð..³.MSG.#.6.ð.¥.ð..¹ð.
.¿ð.ᴴº.https://www.google.com/?client=safari&channel=iphone_bm.MSG.#.7..Hey
.Looking?.MAG.#.8.MSG.#.9.reAAAAf....d..è...AAAA.../46c51b5686204422df139d7
c8aa6aae231417d81_0_0_0.@AAAA.../758efee8b5f128bb5c934320c3a0116b61ed7725_0
_0_0.@AAAA.../201af3684cf081252b2e9290a7cd9efb5a0ddafa_0_0_0..AAAA.../c8801
f2f83625579a979f93f469f6a52c2e83cb0_0_0_0.ÿAAAA.../ae7e050e37e5ea6f0dafbe6a
dfe00d0de614f714_0_0_0.ÿAAAA.../be53dcb817af7243721383061ee613011f4ee8f3_0_
0_0..AAAA.../02dc0246cf023c856d584682766df57d58cf5b26_0_0_0..AAAA....217345
133.......217345133.......217345133.......217345133......217345133.......2
17345133.......217345133.......217345133.......217345133.......217345133...
....217345133.......217345133.......217345133.......217345133......2173451
```

FIGURE 10.33   Text messages extracted in plaintext viewed in Hex Tab (BlackLight)

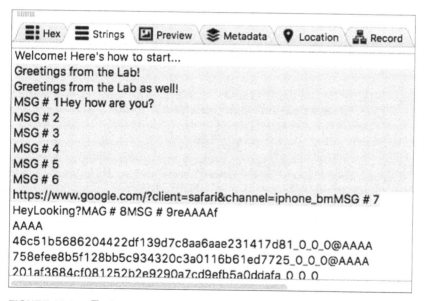

FIGURE 10.34   Text messages in plaintext viewed in Strings tab (BlackLight)

Rideshare Apps

Location information is always important in an investigation because an investigator does not just search for incriminating evidence but also needs to identify where a suspect was. As you will learn, rideshare apps, like Uber, contain extensive geolocation data that is easily accessible.

Uber

Uber is a service that enables drivers to act as flexible contractors and provide transportation services that compete with traditional taxi services. Consumers, using the Uber mobile app, can search for a car service in their area. The benefit to the consumer is that they are visually provided with the mapped location of Uber cars in their vicinity and are provided with an upfront quote for a specific journey (or "ride"). Uber operates in approximately 600 cities worldwide. In the past, Uber has received negative press about its geolocation tracking of users, which raised a number of concerns regarding its privacy policies and potentially invasive data collection practices. In April 2017, the *New York Times* published a story that documented a meeting, at Apple headquarters, in 2015, between Travis Kalanick, CEO of Uber, and Tim Cook, CEO of Apple. The article alleged that Mr. Cook scolded Mr. Kalanick for identifying and tagging iPhones after the Uber app had been uninstalled or the device had been wiped. Apparently, this type of user identity coding violated the Apple developer terms of service agreement.

An article in the *New York Times* detailed how Unroll.me, which purported to purge your device's email inbox of annoying advertising messages, was used to spy on competitors. The article documented how Unroll.me would scan a user's inbox, identify if there were service receipts, from competing companies like Lyft, and then sell that information to Lyft's competitor—Uber.

Since the introduction of iOS 5, Apple has been limiting app developer access to the iPhone's UDID (unique device identifier). A notice from Apple stated, "Starting May 1, the App Store will no longer accept new apps or app updates that access the UDID; please update your apps and servers to associate users with the Vendor or Advertising identifiers introduced in iOS 6." Apple now prefers that app developers utilize the official Apple advertising platform to track app users. Based on Apple's advertising and privacy policy, it appears that Apple does collect user data and then subsequently shares it with third parties. Nevertheless, developers can obtain extensive information about an app user through the integration of the UIDevice object. The UIDevice object can be used by an app developer to determine the assigned name of the device, device model and iOS version, orientation (orientation property) of the device, battery charge (batteryState property), and distance of the device to the user (proximityState property). Moreover, developers can integrate code, during app development, for third-party analytics. These third-party companies include Localytics, mixpanel, UXCam, and Fabric. Companies like Apptopia provide app developers with extensive, nay invasive, analytics on competitor apps.

The use of the user UDID has not always been employed for nefarious purposes. However, the UDID was often utilized to identify if an app user was legitimate and could block a customer's access if an account was compromised or potentially stolen. Fingerprinting is yet another methodology, used by third parties, to uniquely identify users, based on application configuration. Fingerprinting is best known for identifying online users based on user settings from their browser, which may include user cookies and browser plug-ins. The Electronic Frontier Foundation (EFF) created a project known as Panopticlick (panopticlick.eff.org) to raise awareness about how your browser is used by advertisers, and others, to identify and track you on the Web. The EFF announced that 84% of online users can be uniquely identified by their browser.

According to Uber's user privacy statement, there are two categories of information collected about users: (a) Information You Provide to Us, which can include name, email, phone number, postal address, profile picture, payment method, and (b) Information We Collect Through Your Use of Our Services, which can include location information, contacts, transactions, usage and preference, device information, call and SMS data, and log information. Of particular interest is the device information (hardware model, operating system and version, software and file names and versions, preferred language, unique device identifier, advertising identifiers, serial number, device motion information, and mobile network information). In terms of location information, Uber is not specific about the extent to which the user's location is being tracked but states that they "may also collect the precise location of your device when the app is running in the foreground or background." Uber provides more detailed information about the use of location services on its website under iOS App Permissions.

What is interesting is that during our installation of the Uber app, a dialog box appears and states that "Uber collects your location (i) when the app is open and (ii) from the time of the trip request through five minutes after the trip ends", as displayed in Figure 10.21.

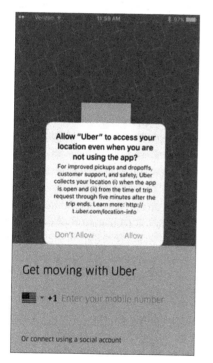

FIGURE 10.35   Uber dialog box during installation

Uber states in their FAQ that the reasoning behind this data collection is to "improve pickups, drop-offs, customer service, and to enhance safety." However, users reported seeing the Uber app using location services weeks after the app was used and certainly beyond the stated 5 minutes. Uber responded to these reports blaming Apple's iOS Maps extension that Uber uses to serve regional maps to their customers.

Perhaps unsurprisingly, Uber has invested heavily in data science to retain its competitive advantage, as evidenced by its aggressive recruitment of data scientists. We also know that Uber extensively uses a telematics pilot program, called Autohawk, to identify the location of its drivers and perform diagnostic testing on the vehicle to ensure passenger safety. In fact, Uber provides geolocation information, provided by its data visualization team, on its website at eng.uber.com/data-viz-intel. Uber integrates both Fabric and Localytics in its mobile app. Fabric provides companies, like Uber, with real-time information about the health of their app. These analytics include application crash analytics. Localytics provide location information.

As of November 2017, allegations abound about Uber's competitor spy programs. The *Waymo v. Uber* lawsuit appears to indicate that Uber may have been involved in illegal espionage. A letter, submitted as evidence in this lawsuit and penned by Richard Jacobs, former Uber security executive, details Uber's illegal practices of hiring actors to collect data and spy on their competitors. In the letter, Jacobs, who at the time had filed suit against Uber in the capacity of "whistleblower", detailed practices that would lead to the theft of trade secrets related to competitor fares and driver incentives. To settle, Uber paid Jacobs $4.3 million at the time. His allegations have now been made public and have been used in a related case, *Waymo v. Uber*. In this case, a former employee allegedly sold trade secrets to Uber, prior to the company being acquired by Uber.

Communication Apps

Communication apps, such as WhatsApp, Signal, Viber, and Skype, are arguably more important than traditional cellphone or landline calls for numerous reasons. The first reason is that it is a lot easier to obtain content from these apps than to obtain a Title III Wiretap. Secondly, the content is so much richer than a traditional call or a text message. For example, consumers will share rich content, while reacting to the comments of others. In other words, you can find group chats that can link individuals and see emoticons and other reactions to messages that demonstrate personalization and behavior.

Skype

Law enforcement today understands that cellular communications generally account for a minority of smartphone communications. In fact, criminal gangs will often prefer using mobile communication apps over traditional cellular calls. Therefore, it is essential to have a good understanding of applications like Skype, Viber, enLegion, and WhatsApp.

Skype is a peer-to-peer (P2P) communication application that facilitates free video, voice, and instant messaging (IM) using a Wi-Fi connection. Skype also allows for file transfer to other Skype contacts and fee-based voice calls to landline phones and cellular phones using VoIP. Skype can be used with Mac computers, personal computers, tablets, smartphones, smart televisions, smart Blu-ray players, and game systems that include Xbox One and Sony's PS Vita PlayStation.

There are close to 300 million active monthly users worldwide. The company was purchased by Microsoft Corporation in 2011 for $8.5 billion.

Skype Location

Location is important in terms of jurisdiction, when conducting an investigation. If the investigation is being conducted in the United States, then having a corporate location in the U.S. is helpful. However, even the presence of a server in the U.S. can enable law enforcement to subpoena that entity.

Skype is headquartered in Luxembourg but also has offices in London (U.K.), Palo Alto (U.S.A.) and Tallinn (Estonia), Prague (Czech Republic), Stockholm (Sweden), Moscow (Russia) and Singapore.

Skype Encryption

Instant messages (IM), between the Skype and chat service in the Cloud, are encrypted using TLS (transport-level security). IM between two Skype users are encrypted using AES (Advanced Encryption Standard). Voice messages are encrypted when sent to the recipient. However, when the voice message is downloaded and listened to, it is stored on the client's computer in an unencrypted way. Skype calls are also encrypted. When the user logs in, Skype will verify the user's public key using 1536 or 2048-bit RSA certificates.

Skype Evidence

The SQLite database file associated with Skype is `main.db`. The following files can be found within this SQLite database:

- `DbMeta`
- `Contacts`
- `Videos`
- `SMSes`
- `CallMembers`
- `ChatMembers`
- `Alerts`
- `Conversations`
- `Participants`
- `VideoMessages`
- `LegacyMessages`
- `Calls`
- `Accounts`
- `Transfers`

- Voicemails

- Chats

- Messages

- ContactGroups

- AppSchemaVersion

- MediaDocuments

- MessageAnnotations

- Translators

- tracker_journal

The Registry key associated with Skype is located here:

`HKEY_CURRENT_USER\Software\Skype.`

On a Windows PC, the file is located here:

`%localappdata%\Packages\Microsoft.SkypeApp_kzf8qxf38zg5c\LocalState\<Skype Name>`

On a Mac, the file is located here:

`~/Library/Application Support/Skype/YourSkypeName/main.db`

Table 10.1 and Table 10.2 display PLists associated with applications that may be of interest to investigators. More information about PLists can be found in Chapter 12, "Mac Forensics".

TABLE 10.1 Application PLists

Application	SQLite File	PList
Facebook	Friends.sqlite	com.facebook.Facebook.plist
LinkedIn		com.linkedin.LinkedIn.plist
Dropbox	Dropbox.sqlite	com.getdropbox.Dropbox.plist
Skype	main.db	com.skype.skype.plist
Amazon		com.amazon.Amazon.plist
eBay		com.ebay.iphone.plist
Google Maps	MapTiles.sqlitedb	
Tinder	Tinder2.sqlite	
WhatsApp	ChatStorage.sqlite	net.whatsapp.WhatsApp.plist

TABLE 10.2   Apple App `.db` Files

Apple App	SQLite File
Phone	`AddressBook.sqlitedb`
Calendar	`Calendar.sqlitedb`
Phone	`Voicemail.db`
Phone	`Call_history.db`
Messages	`Sms.db`
Safari	`Safari/History.db`
Maps	`Maps/History.plist`
Siri	`ManagedObjects.SQLite`

Summary

Mobile forensics has become extremely important for investigations because of the wealth of evidence available. The mobile apps found on a device are beneficial because of the fact that the data contained in the SQLite database is unencrypted for many mobile applications. Furthermore, deep-linking, which links one application to another application, enables an investigator to pull data from multiple sources while only examining one application. The data available during a static analysis can include contacts, chats, location data pictures, and other important evidence. As discussed, a SQLite database is a relational database that contains a series of tables. A static analysis is not limited to extracting evidence using forensics tools but also includes a review of the application manifest. The application manifest clearly identifies permissions associated with the application, which will help to guide the investigator to look for evidence related to those permissions. A dynamic analysis can assist an investigator in understanding potential third-party evidence, which is based on an app's connections to DNS servers when executed. Ultimately, these third-party companies can be subpoenaed for further evidence. A dynamic analysis can also determine the location of servers, associated with a mobile application, in terms of helping to identify jurisdiction. In this chapter, we spoke at length about mobile dating apps, which are important because of the extent of personal information available, primarily in the form of social media information. Dating apps are also important because we can also link people together. Grindr is particularly of interest to law enforcement because this dating app has actually been used to perpetrate crimes, especially hate crimes.

Key Terms

Android emulator: An application that simulates or runs the Android operating system in a virtual machine.

Android manifest file: A file that contains the application's package name, its functionality, permissions, hardware and software requirements for installation.

App ID: A two-part string that identifies a development team (Team ID) and an application (bundle ID).

bundle ID: A uniform-type identifier, which is comprised of alphanumeric characters, that uniquely identifies a specific app.

GET: An HTTP method used to request data from a specific resource, like a web server.

man-in-the-middle (MITM) attack: An attempt to intercept electronic communications between two computing devices with the intent to decipher encrypted messages.

pcap file: A wireless packet that contains user data and network data related to the sender and receiver of that data.

zero-day exploit: A security vulnerability that is a threat on the day that it is discovered because a software patch, to fix the exploit, does not yet exist.

Assessment

CLASSROOM DISCUSSIONS

1. Based on what you have learned in this chapter, from a security perspective, how can you determine if a mobile application is safe to use?

2. In what ways have mobile applications helped criminals and their criminal activities?

3. Under what circumstances is it legal to use wireless packet capture tools, like Wireshark or Debookee?

MULTIPLE-CHOICE QUESTIONS

1. An `.apk` file is associated with which of the following systems?

    A. Android

    B. iOS

    C. Wireshark

    D. Windows

2. Which of the following refers to a wireless packet that contains user data and network data related to the sender and receiver of that data?

    A. pcap file

    B. bundle ID

    C. Android manifest file

FILL IN THE BLANKS

1. An Android _____ file contains the application's package name, its functionality, permissions, hardware and software requirements for installation.

2. An Android _____ is an application that simulates or runs the Android operating system in a virtual machine.

3. A(n) _____ file is a wireless packet that contains user data and network data related to the sender and receiver of that data.

4. A(n) _____ ID is a uniform-type identifier, which is comprised of alphanumeric characters, that uniquely identifies a specific app.

5. A(n) _____ ID is a two-part string that identifies a development team (Team ID) and an application (bundle ID).

6. A(n) _____-day exploit is a security vulnerability that is a threat on the day that it is discovered because a software patch, to fix the exploit, does not yet exist.

7. A man-in-the-_____ attack is an attempt to intercept electronic communications between two computing devices with the intent to decipher encrypted messages.

8. _____ is an HTTP method used to request data from a specific resource, like a web server.

PROJECTS

Write an Essay about a Mobile Application

Select a popular mobile app of your choice, which is not covered in this chapter and then perform a static and dynamic analysis on the app, using the analytics tools discussed in this chapter. Describe the value of the evidence that you find from (a) a digital forensics investigator perspective and (b) an organizational security and privacy viewpoint.

Chapter | **11**

Photograph Forensics

Learning Outcomes

After reading this chapter, you will be able to understand the following:

- The use of photograph images by social media users;
- The metadata found in photograph images;
- Different types of digital photograph files;
- Admissibility of photographs in the courtroom; and
- Case studies involving the use of photographic evidence.

Photos are more pervasive than ever before and are therefore being used more frequently in the courtroom. Photographs have been used both to capture wanted criminals and to then convict criminal suspects.

The FBI's *Ten Most Wanted* list (www.fbi.gov/wanted/topten/) is the most infamous list of wanted criminals. The use of these photographs to find wanted suspects is so effective that many criminals admitted it was the kiss of death for them, when they were added to the list, and they felt that it was only a matter of time before they were caught. Thomas James Holden was the first criminal suspect to be added to the FBI's *Ten Most Wanted* list (see Figure 11.1). Holden was convicted of robbing a mail train in the 1920s and subsequently made a daring escape from Leavenworth Penitentiary in Leavenworth, Kansas. He was caught in 1932.

Law enforcement personnel have used photographs for years to track down missing people or identify victims. Advances in computing and social networking are even being used to reopen cold cases. In 2011, the Huntington Beach Police Department used Facebook to seek help from the public in identifying a murder victim from 1968 (Case No. 68-006079). After the picture of the young female was posted on Facebook (see Figure 11.2), the police received numerous tips. A purse found near the body that contained a number of photos was believed to belong to the victim, but when these photos were posted to Facebook, the police received numerous calls and emails indicating that this was a false lead.

FIGURE 11.1   Thomas James Holden

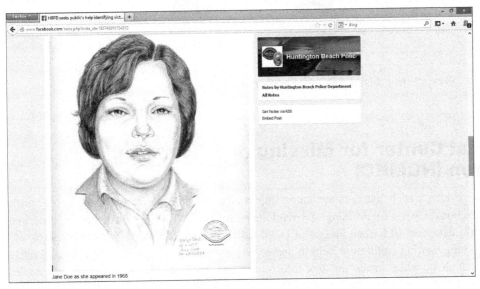

FIGURE 11.2   Huntington Beach Jane Doe, 1968

The Huntington Beach Police Department and many other police departments regularly use social media sites, like Facebook (www.facebook.com/HuntingtonBeachPolice), to ask the public for assistance with identifying suspects in photographs that are posted to the department's profile page.

Similarly, the Doe Network (www.doenetwork.org) is an organization that posts pictures and details pertaining to unidentified or missing persons.

The Royal Canadian Mounted Police (RCMP) in Canada's smallest province of Prince Edward Island (PEI) also actively uses Facebook (www.facebook.com/peicrimestoppers) to post photographs of wanted suspects (see Figure 11.3).

FIGURE 11.3   Prince Edward Island RCMP Facebook profile

National Center for Missing and Exploited Children (NCMEC)

Photographic evidence is obviously of the utmost importance in child exploitation cases. As previously noted, the National Center for Missing and Exploited Children (NCMEC) and other organizations maintain huge databases of hashed images of exploited children, in the hope that these images will assist in rescuing missing children or help to prosecute pedophiles. A hash of a photo is used rather than the actual photo, which means that law enforcement can search for photos and share information without having to view disturbing images. The MD5 algorithm can be used to create a unique identifier for each photo. Hash values can be run through NCMEC's Law Enforcement Services Portal (LESP), and law enforcement personnel send copies of images to NCMEC.

Law enforcement agencies are not the only entities to work with NCMEC. Voluntary industry initiatives have been set up to help NCMEC identify websites and users sharing child pornography. NCMEC maintains a list of URLs known to contain apparent child pornography in its URL Initiative. In 2009,

Microsoft collaborated with Dartmouth College to develop PhotoDNA, which companies and NCMEC use to identify child pornography on their servers. Although searching for illicit images is voluntary, many well-known companies use the software to support NCMEC. The Hash Value Sharing Initiative enables Electronic Service Providers to receive a list of MD5 hash values of abused children. In 2015, Microsoft made PhotoDNA, as a service, available on Azure, and it is available for free to law enforcement and other qualified organizations.

Project VIC

Project VIC is a collaboration between domestic law enforcement, international law enforcement, and private sector partners, with the goal of rescuing child abuse victims, apprehending sex offenders, and securing crime scenes. Project VIC is a huge database of child abuse photo hashes that is shared by law enforcement and the private sector, which can create links to other investigations. Many forensics tools today connect to Project VIC to quickly identify victims, using Photo DNA, and contribute to an existing database of victim images. Internet Crimes Against Children (ICAC) task forces across the nation connect to this database in an effort to locate missing children and investigate the criminals producing and/or distributing these illicit photos.

Case Studies

Photo evidence has been critical to solving cases and is frequently used as supporting evidence in a case. Digital photos can be enhanced and can include important metadata, called EXIF data. In the case of child exploitation investigations, items in the background are often used to try to determine where the photo was taken, in an effort to find a missing child. This section shows how important photographic evidence is.

Facebook Selfie

Cheyenne Rose Antoine, a 21-year-old from Canada, pled guilty to killing her friend, Brittney Gargol, in March 2015. A belt found near the teenager's body was a match to the same belt worn by Antoine, in a selfie posted on Facebook, just hours before the murder. The belt was used by Antoine to strangle Gargol. Antoine was sentenced to seven years in prison.

To Catch a Predator

A CNN report in March 2017 by Special Agent Jim Cole, Supervisor of Victim Identification at the Homeland Security Investigations' Cyber Crimes Center, and co-founder of Project VIC, described how a child predator took photos of his deplorable acts with a child in a bathroom. Using new advanced technology, Cole managed to identify a prescription medication bottle in one of the photos, enhance the writing on the prescription bottle, and identify the first name and first two letters of the last name on that bottle, along with the first three digits of the prescription number. Cole's team also managed to obtain the suspect's fingerprints from the photograph. The evidence was ultimately key in putting Stephen Keating behind bars for 110 years and resulted in 14 victims being rescued.

One cannot underestimate how much time law enforcement dedicates to child exploitation investigations and preventing the distribution of child abuse images. According to Special Agent Cole, in that CNN report, their task force was observing 500,000 child exploitation images a week, amounting to 25 million images annually, which is staggering.

Extortion

Unfortunately, sexually explicit images are often used to manipulate victims or extort money. Craig Britton, from Colorado Springs, created the website called IsAnybodyDown. The website was known to post revealing photographs of women on its site, including their names and telephone numbers, and then charged people $250 to have their photographs taken down. This site and others like it prompted California to institute a bill banning "revenge porn". Now anyone posting naked pictures online with the "intent to harass or annoy" faces six months in jail and a $1,000 fine.

In 2013, Jared Abrahams was arrested and accused of hacking a webcam in the home of Miss Teen USA Cassidy Wolf. Abrahams was charged with attempting to extort money from the model using nude photographs and videos he had captured. He was later sentenced to 18 months in prison.

Understanding Digital Photography

So what exactly is a digital photograph? A **digital photograph** is an image taken with a camera and stored as a computer file. Unlike older cameras that exposed photographic film to light, a digital camera creates an image with a light-sensitive lens. That camera can come in many different shapes and sizes, including a cellphone camera, webcam, or digital camera.

File Systems

Digital images are stored on a variety of storage media, including the following:

- Internal memory
- SD Card
- CompactFlash card
- MMC

The file system utilized by flash memory is FAT. As the resolution of digital photographs has increased over time, it has become necessary to use a more robust version of FAT. Therefore, higher-end cameras now use exFAT as the de facto file system.

The Design Rule for Camera File System

The **Design Rule for Camera file system (DCF)** was developed by the Japan Electronic Industry Development Association (JEIDA) to facilitate the exchange of images between digital still cameras and other devices for viewing digital photographs.

DCIM (Digital Camera IMages)

DCIM (Digital Camera IMages) is the root directory in the file system of a digital camera that contains a series of subdirectories containing digital images. This directory is part of DCF. Released in 1998, DCIM has become the standard protocol for digital cameras.

DSCN (Digital Still Capture Nikon)

DSCN (Digital Still Capture Nikon) is the prefix for digital images found on a Nikon camera. This is one way of connecting an image with a Nikon camera.

Digital Photography Applications and Services

This section explains how important digital photos have become. In particular, social media websites and smart devices running social media applications can act as huge repositories of photo images. These images can sometimes be incriminating or can simply help solve a crime or locate a missing person. Applications, like Facebook, maintain millions of its users' photographs, and the phrase "A picture tells a thousand words" is often true.

Facebook

Facebook is probably the world's most popular social networking service. Users create a profile and communicate with their network friends, family, and organizational contacts either online or through the Facebook mobile application. An important aspect of this communication is the sharing of digital photographs. The importance of this function to Facebook is evidenced by its purchase of Instagram for $1 billion. In 2012, Facebook also purchased Face.com, an Israeli company that specializes in facial recognition. According to Face.com, by 2011, the company had discovered and identified 18 billion faces across its APIs and Facebook apps. Consider the following quick facts about Facebook:

- Facebook has more than 2.3 billion active users;
- Facebook maintains more than 100 billion digital photos; and
- On average 350 million photos are uploaded daily.

Flickr

Flickr is a photo and video hosting company that enables users to organize and share their media. Access to Flickr is available to users through the Web and also as a mobile application on smart devices. Consider the following quick facts about Flickr:

- Flickr has millions of monthly users;
- Users have shared billions of photos on Flickr; and
- On average 1 million photos are shared daily.

Instagram

Kevin Systrom and Mike Krieger founded Instagram in 2010. In April 2012, Facebook purchased the company for $1 billion in cash and stock. This application allows the user to share photos and video content with his or her social network. Instagram is available for traditional computers, smartphones, and tablets. The application works with Windows, iOS, and Android. Consider the following quick facts about Instagram:

- Instagram has more than 1 billion users worldwide;
- Billions of photos have been uploaded; and
- Millions of photos are uploaded daily.

Snapchat

The service began in September 2011 and allows users to take photos and record videos. The sender can set a time limit for when the picture or video disappears (1 to 10 seconds). From a forensics perspective, these images are often still present on the user's device, even though the user thinks the file has been deleted. In fact, the Federal Trade Commission (FTC) has announced that the company made false privacy and security claims. Consider the following quick facts about Snapchat:

- Snapchat has millions of active daily and monthly users; and
- Users share billions of photos and videos (Snaps) daily.

Examining Picture Files

Three types of photo metadata exist: Extensible Metadata Platform (XMP), Information Interchange Model (IIM), and Exchangeable Image File Format (EXIF). We will focus on the most prevalent format—EXIF.

Exchangeable Image File Format (EXIF)

Exchangeable Image File Format (EXIF) is the metadata associated with digital pictures. The Japan Electronic Industries Development Association (JEIDA) released this format of photography metadata in 1995. Most smart devices today use the EXIF data format in the photographs they produce. EXIF data can include the following:

- Date and time;

- Make and model of camera;

- Thumbnail;

- Aperture, shutter speed, and other camera settings; and

- Optionally, longitude and latitude.

Naturally, it is important to verify that the date and time in the photo are correct.

BR Software produces a free tool called BR's EXIFextracter that can extract the EXIF data from a folder of photos and then save that metadata to a comma-separated values (CSV) file, as shown in some sample output from the EXIFextracter tool in Figure 11.4.

Filename	Date	Time	Camera Manufacturer & Model	Width x Height	Size of image file	Exposure (1/sec)	Aperture	ISO	Was flash used?	Focal length
DSCN0029.JPG	2012:09:09	13:10:00	NIKON COOLPIX L810	3456x4608	3507668	1/320	f4.2	80	No	13
DSCN0030.JPG	2012:09:09	13:10:08	NIKON COOLPIX L810	3456x4608	3731008	1/250	f4.2	80	No	13
DSCN0031.JPG	2012:09:09	13:10:25	NIKON COOLPIX L810	3456x4608	3397764	1/320	f4.2	80	No	13
DSCN0033.JPG	2012:09:09	13:10:57	NIKON COOLPIX L810	3456x4608	3659534	1/640	f3.4	80	No	6
DSCN0035.JPG	2012:09:09	14:20:17	NIKON COOLPIX L810	3456x4608	3468599	1/400	f4.0	80	No	11
DSCN0037.JPG	2012:09:09	14:20:42	NIKON COOLPIX L810	3456x4608	3714318	1/800	f3.3	80	No	5
DSCN0039.JPG	2012:09:09	14:21:07	NIKON COOLPIX L810	3456x4608	4021210	1/160	f10.6	80	No	5

FIGURE 11.4   Sample output from EXIFextracter

Note that EXIF data can be manipulated. Thus, to ensure the integrity of a digital photograph, an MD5 hash can potentially be used to determine that a copy has not been manipulated over time. ExifTool is free software that enables a user to change the metadata of a photo or an audio or video file. Jeffrey's Image Metadata Viewer is another free tool.

File Types

It is important for a forensics investigator to understand the difference between different types of images because the investigator might be questioned about image file formats and their properties or their ability to be edited. A raster image can allow for more color editing, whereas a vector image can retain quality regardless of whether the picture is blown up. A **raster graphic** is a pixelated image associated with pictures found on a computer or retrieved from a digital camera. A raster graphic consists of a grid of pixels. A **pixel** is the smallest element of a raster image, which may be either a dot or a square. A **megapixel** is a million pixels. There are so many pixels found in digital photos today that file sizes become very large. You can determine the file size for different photograph image types based on the size of the megapixels at http://web.forret.com/tools/megapixel.asp.

Compression algorithms are used to reduce the size of large digital images. JPEG and GIF are image formats that utilize compression. The following files are examples of raster graphics:

- Joint Photographic Experts Group (`.jpg` or `.jpeg`)
- RAW file
- Bitmap Image File (`.bmp`)
- Portable Network Graphics (`.png`)
- Graphics Interchange Format (`.gif`)
- Tagged Image File Format (`.tif`)

In contrast to a raster graphic, a **vector graphic** is comprised of curves, lines, or shapes based on mathematical formulae rather than pixels. An investigator is more likely to encounter raster graphics than vector graphics but mentioning vector graphic file types is worthwhile. The following files are examples of vector graphics:

- Adobe Illustrator File (`.ai`)
- Encapsulated PostScript File (`.eps`)
- Scalable Vector Graphics File (`.svg`)
- Drawing File (`.drw`)

Joint Photographic Experts Group (JPEG)

Joint Photographic Experts Group (JPEG) is both a committee and an image file format. The JPEG image file format is popular because of its compression and support for so many different colors. JPEG is a lossy format. Lossy means that compression causes some loss of quality to the image. A JPEG file often has one or more thumbnails embedded in it. File carving carves out these embedded files. In the case of TechTV's Cat Schwartz, the celebrity used Photoshop to crop photos of herself and then uploaded these photos online. Little did Schwartz know that Photoshop creates embedded thumbnails of the original photos—but a few viewers realized this and were able to recover thumbnails that showed the celebrity's breasts. Many smartphones, tablets, and digital cameras store photos as JPEGs.

RAW File

When you take a photograph with a high-end digital camera, the camera can either process the image as a JPEG file or save the data to a RAW file. A **RAW file** takes data from a digital camera's image sensor to create an unprocessed or minimally processed image. The user needs to spend time processing these images later but may choose this format to create a higher-quality photograph and have more control over how the image is processed. For example, the photographer can have more toning control with a RAW image file, instead of letting the camera perform that function in deciding on lighting and colors. Ultimately, more data is available for the photographer to manipulate because, when creating a JPEG, the camera discards a certain amount of data.

The manufacturers of these high-end digital cameras all have their own proprietary RAW file formats, and these formats can also vary between devices manufactured by the same company. The **Digital Negative (DNG)** is an open standard RAW image format developed by Adobe for digital photographs.

Bitmap Image File (BMP)

The **Bitmap Image File** (BMP) is a raster image file format that is generally associated with a Windows PC.

Portable Network Graphics (PNG)

A **Portable Network Graphics (PNG)** is a raster image file format that supports lossless compression. PNG images are often used on the Internet.

Graphics Interchange Format (GIF)

Graphics Interchange Format (GIF) is a raster image file format that was developed by CompuServe, Inc., in 1987. GIF images can be compressed using the Lempel–Ziv–Welch (LZW) lossless data compression algorithm.

Tagged Image File Format (TIFF)

Tagged Image File Format (TIFF) is a raster image file format that uses lossless data compression. Similar to a GIF, a TIFF uses the Lempel–Ziv–Welch (LZW) lossless data compression algorithm. It was developed by Aldus but is now controlled by Adobe Systems. TIFF was originally an ideal format for scanners.

thumbcache.db

thumbcache.db is a database of thumbnails, associated with digital photographs, which are found on Windows 10 computers. Each time an image is saved to a folder, a thumbnail of that photo is added to thumbcache.db. What is important for investigators is the fact that when a digital photo is deleted, the thumbnail will still exist in thumbcache.db. Additionally, if the user has a PowerPoint file (.ppt or .pptx) or a video file (MPG or AVI), then a thumbnail from the first slide will also be saved in thumbcache.db. In earlier versions of Windows, an investigator used to analyze the thumbs.db file.

thumbcache.db can be found in the following folder: **C:\Users\<user>\AppData\Local\Microsoft\ Windows\Explorer**. Forensics tools, like AccessData's FTK, can sort and display the thumbnails from thumbcache.db. There is also a free tool, called Thumbcache Viewer. This tool is available from Sourceforge and can also parse the contents of thumbcache.db.

Evidence Admissibility

Finding incriminating digital photographs is one thing yet admitting them as evidence is another. The law has changed to allow digital photographs as well as traditional photographs to be accepted as evidence.

The Scientific Working Group on Digital Evidence (SWGDE) has produced guidelines, which a forensics investigator should be aware of. In particular, the *SWGDE Technical Overview for Forensic Image Comparison* is a helpful guide for investigators. Another important publication is the *SWGDE Best Practices for Image Authentication*. There is also the *SWGDE Training Guidelines for Image Analysis, Video Analysis and Photography*.

Federal Rules of Evidence (FRE)

Article X of the Federal Rules of Evidence (FRE) relates to the "Contents of Writings, Recordings and Photographs". In Article X, the definition of "Photographs" includes "still photographs, X-ray films, video tapes, and motion pictures." An "original" can include a negative or a print from the negative. A "duplicate" is "a counterpart produced by the same impression as the original, or from the same matrix, or by means of photography, including enlargements and miniatures, or by mechanical or electronic re-recording".

Ultimately, an original must be used. In the absence of the original, a duplicate can be used if it is deemed a "genuine" copy. Using a duplicate of a digital photograph can be problematic because numerous applications can alter a digital photograph; Photoshop is one example. Therefore, an expert witness may be required to verify the authenticity of the original. Nevertheless, if a digital photograph is stored on a computer, then under Rule 1001, Article X, a printout or "other output readable by sight" is regarded as an original under FRE. Of course, each state also has its own rules of evidence, but when it comes to digital photographs, the state rules are often very similar to FRE, Article X.

An important question, then, is how can you tell if a copy of a digital photograph is the same as the original? One way to prove this is to create an MD5 hash of the original digital photograph and then an MD5 hash of the duplicate and see if they match.

Comparing photographic images can be important to see if someone was using digital photographs without the consent of the owner, or perhaps the prosecution wanted to prove that a suspect was distributing illicit photographs of minors to other pedophiles.

Analog vs. Digital Photographs

Interestingly, using digital photographs as evidence offers many benefits, compared to traditional photographs. With older photograph technology, detecting whether a photograph had been manipulated was often difficult. Although numerous applications are available to edit digital photographs, detecting those changes is possible. For example, an investigator can review a photograph's metadata and see whether changes were made and when. Additionally, certain tools can identify resolution mismatches and differences in noise signatures.

The other advantage of using digital images is that the investigator can perform improved enhancements to make background images or far away objects clearer because of higher-resolution photographs. The ability to remove noise from objects is greater than ever. There are numerous photo enhancement tools, like ClearID, which can deblur photographic and video evidence.

Image Enhancements

An investigator can use certain techniques to improve the clarity of an image. **Brightness adjustment** makes an image lighter or darker, to make the image easier to view. **Color balancing** describes the process of adjusting colors in an image so that they more accurately reflect the original scene when the photograph was taken. **Contrast adjustment** refers to improving the contrast of objects and backgrounds to make them more visible. **Cropping** is the process of removing unwanted portions of an image. Cropping is not always advisable unless the investigator can show a jury the original and demonstrate the need to crop a photograph. **Linear filtering** techniques can enhance edges and sharpen objects in an image, to make them less blurred.

In some cases, an image may not need an enhancement, but it might need to be restored. As digital photographs increase in resolution (and file size), the picture files are more likely to be fragmented across a volume rather than be stored in contiguous sectors. Restoration of an image may also include the reversal of edited or manipulated photographs. For example, a warping technique may have been used on an image, and that enhancement needs to be reversed.

More information about digital image evidence and manipulation can be found in the published work of the **Scientific Working Group on Imaging Technologies (SWGIT)**, an organization founded by the FBI that publishes standards on the use of digital and multimedia evidence in the justice system.

Discerning Fake or Altered Images

James O'Brien, University of California, Berkeley, in collaboration with Hany Farid and Eric Kee of Dartmouth University, has developed an algorithm to interpret whether light shadows throughout an image are consistent with a single light source. Unfortunately, the human eye cannot easily detect inconsistencies in light and shadows. Sometimes it is important for an investigator to show that a photo has or has not been tampered with.

Case Studies

Photographs have been used as evidence in all types of investigations. Photo evidence is, however, the basis for many child pornography investigations. Pictures are also often used in intellectual property cases and insurance fraud investigations.

Worldwide Manhunt

In 2007, INTERPOL reluctantly issued a worldwide hunt for a wanted pedophile. The reluctance stemmed from the fact that law enforcement did not wish to submit the suspect to public ridicule or demonstrate that INTERPOL could decipher a manipulated photographic image of a suspect.

Ultimately, the need to prevent further abuse to numerous children outweighed other factors. Figure 11.5 shows the masked photo of the suspect that INTERPOL needed to interpret. Figure 11.6 shows the original (recovered) photo image.

FIGURE 11.5   Swirled digital image (INTERPOL website)

FIGURE 11.6   Deciphered photo of Christopher Neil Paul (INTERPOL website)

The deciphered photo was sent to police and media outlets worldwide. After only 11 days of INTER-POL's worldwide manhunt, Royal Thai Police arrested Christopher Neil Paul, a Canadian national. He was later sentenced to three years and three months in prison.

NYPD Facial Recognition Unit

The New York Police Department's (NYPD) Facial Recognition Unit obtains sample photos, submitted by investigators, of wanted subjects. These sample photos can be obtained through social media, surveillance video, or other sources. These images are then compared to mug shots of people with prior arrests. Ultimately, this process helps find suspects. The unit has caught several suspects, including David Baez, a suspect found through an online photograph and arrested in connection with an assault in Bronx, New York. The unit also used photos from livery cabs to catch Alan Marrero—a suspect arrested in connection with the robbery of numerous livery cab drivers.

Summary

Law enforcement personnel have used photographs for about a century to find wanted criminals. Photographs have also been used to find missing persons. Digital photographs add a new proposition for investigators because they contain metadata, which may include the make and model of the camera, whether a flash was used, aperture, and longitude and latitude (if the user of the device that took the photo enabled location services). BR Software's EXIFextractor is one tool for quickly extracting digital photograph metadata. Most professional computer forensics tools carve out photographs embedded in emails and other documents, as well as standalone photographs. Computer operating systems and applications, like Microsoft Windows and Microsoft Office, come with many pictures, including logos. Luckily, computer forensics tools know the hash values associated with a variety of operating systems and applications and will filter out those images when conducting a search of a suspect's computer so that the investigator can focus on just the user's pictures.

Social media websites provide some of the most extensive databases of faces and give law enforcement opportunities to locate wanted criminals. The NYPD Facial Recognition Unit scours the Internet to find wanted criminals and bring them to justice. In London, U.K., there are approximately 500,000 closed-circuit television (CCTV) cameras, which indicates the growing importance of photo and video evidence.

Key Terms

Bitmap Image File (BMP): A raster image file format that is generally associated with a Windows PC.

brightness adjustment: An adjustment to make an image lighter or darker to make an image easier to view.

color balancing: The process of adjusting colors in an image to render them to more accurately reflect the original scene when the photograph was taken.

contrast adjustment: The process of improving the contrast of objects and backgrounds to make them more visible.

cropping: The process of removing unwanted portions of an image.

DCIM (Digital Camera IMages): The root directory in the file system of a digital camera, which contains a series of subdirectories containing digital images.

Design Rule for Camera file system (DCF): A format developed by the Japan Electronic Industry Development Association (JEIDA) to facilitate the exchange of images between digital still cameras and other devices for viewing digital photographs.

Digital Negative (DNG): An open standard RAW image format for digital photographs, developed by Adobe.

digital photograph: An image taken with a camera and stored as a computer file.

DSCN (Digital Still Capture Nikon): The prefix for digital images found on a Nikon camera.

Exchangeable Image File Format (EXIF): The metadata associated with most digital pictures.

Graphics Interchange Format (GIF): A raster image file format developed by CompuServe in 1987.

Joint Photographic Experts Group (JPEG): Both the name of a committee and an image file format.

linear filtering: Techniques that can enhance edges and sharpen objects in an image, to make them less blurred.

lossy: Means that compression causes some loss of quality to the image.

megapixel: A million pixels.

pixel: The smallest element of a raster image, which may be either a dot or a square.

Portable Network Graphics (PNG): A raster image file format that supports lossless compression.

raster graphic: A pixelated image associated with pictures found on a computer or retrieved from a digital camera.

RAW file: Takes data from a digital camera's image sensor, to create an unprocessed or minimally processed image.

Scientific Working Group on Imaging Technologies (SWGIT): An organization founded by the FBI that publishes standards for the use of digital and multimedia evidence in the justice system.

Tagged Image File Format (TIFF): A raster image file format that uses lossless data compression.

vector graphic: Comprised of curves, lines, or shapes based on mathematical formulae rather than pixels.

Assessment

CLASSROOM DISCUSSIONS

1. In what ways are digital photographs used by law enforcement?

2. What are some challenges associated with the admissibility of digital photographs in the courtroom?

3. In what kinds of cases are digital photographs extremely important?

MULTIPLE-CHOICE QUESTIONS

1. Which of the following takes data from a digital camera's image sensor to create an unprocessed or minimally processed image?

   A. PNG

   B. BMP

   C. JPEG

   D. RAW

2. Which of the following refers to the process of removing unwanted portions of an image?

   A. Cropping

   B. Linear filtering

   C. Color balancing

   D. Contrast adjustment

3. Which of the following is the prefix for digital images found on a Nikon camera?

   A. DCIM

   B. DSCN

   C. DCF

   D. DNG

4. A megapixel has how many pixels?

   A. 1,000

   B. 10,000

   C. 100,000

   D. 1,000,000

5. Which of the following is not an example of a raster graphic?

   A. `.jpg`

   B. `.bmp`

   C. `.eps`

   D. `.tif`

6. Which of the following is an open standard RAW image format for digital photographs that was developed by Adobe?

   A. DNG

   B. PNG

   C. GIF

   D. TIFF

7. Which of the following is the smallest element of a raster image, which may be either a dot or a square?

    A. Raster

    B. Vector

    C. Pixel

    D. Megapixel

8. Which of the following is a raster image file format that uses lossless data compression?

    A. Tagged Image File Format (TIFF)

    B. RAW

    C. Digital Negative (DNG)

    D. Scalable Vector Graphics (SVG)

9. Which of the following is an organization that was founded by the FBI and publishes standards for the use of digital and multimedia evidence in the justice system?

    A. InfraGard

    B. ASCLD/LAB

    C. SWDGE

    D. SWGIT

10. Which of the following is the root directory found in the file system of a digital camera that contains a series of subdirectories containing digital images?

    A. DNG

    B. DCF

    C. DCIM

    D. PNG

FILL IN THE BLANKS

1. The Joint Photographic _____ Group file format is the most common picture file found on a digital camera, smartphone, or tablet.

2. When compression causes a reduction in picture quality, this is referred to as _____.

3. A(n) _____ graphic is a pixelated image associated with pictures found on a computer or retrieved from a digital camera.

4. A(n) _____ graphic is comprised of curves, lines, or shapes based on mathematical formulae rather than pixels.

5. The Design Rule for _____ file system was developed by the Japan Electronic Industry Development Association (JEIDA) to facilitate the exchange of images between digital still cameras and other devices for viewing digital photographs.

6. Color _____ describes the process of adjusting colors in an image to enable them to more accurately reflect the original scene when the photograph was taken.

7. A(n) _____ Image File is a raster image file format that is generally associated with a Windows PC.

8. _____ adjustment is used to make an image lighter or darker, to make the image easier to view.

9. A(n) _____ photograph is an image taken with a camera and stored as a computer file.

10. Exchangeable _____ File Format is the metadata associated with digital pictures.

PROJECTS

Examine the Use of Digital Photography in Forensics

Describe the details of a case in which the use of digital photograph(s) was critical to the successful conviction of a suspect.

Use EXIFextractor to Examine EXIF Data

Download BR Software EXIFextractor and use it to create an Excel file of EXIF data from a photos folder on your computer.

Chapter | **12**

Mac Forensics

Learning Outcomes

After reading this chapter, you will be able to understand the following:

- The importance of Mac forensics;
- The history of Apple devices;
- Apple file systems: HFS, HFS+, and APFS;
- Apple software and hardware encryption;
- Virtual files on a Macintosh computer;
- Property lists (PLists) and their value to investigators;
- Applications and their associated files;
- Hardware and software forensics tools for Macintosh computers and iOS devices; and
- Examining Apple mobile devices.

Mac forensics has grown in importance in recent times. While Microsoft Windows-based computers still enjoy the majority of market share, especially in the corporate world, Macintosh computers have become more pervasive. The tremendous growth in sales of Apple Macintosh computers, iPads and iPhones has brought about the need for Mac forensics experts and specialized tools. Digital forensics software providers, including BlackBag Technologies (Cellebrite) and SUMURI, are specialists in developing Mac forensics solutions. Nevertheless, it is important to remember that Apple makes a large amount of technical resources available, primarily for developers, which are of great value to investigators.

A Brief History

Headquartered in Cupertino, California, Apple was formed by Steve Jobs, Steve Wozniak, and Ronald Wayne in 1976. Apple grew and flourished for many years until the mid-1990s when the company struggled with huge financial losses and a floundering stock price. In 1997, ironically,

Microsoft—Apple's longtime nemesis—came to the rescue of the company with a $150 million investment. By the end of 2001, the company was well on the road to success with its release of Mac OS X, the opening of its first retail store and, and the unveiling of the first iPod.

Macintosh

The Apple I was introduced in 1976, and it was not until 1984 that the first Macintosh computer was introduced. Apple released its PowerBook laptop in 1991. Between 1999 and 2006, Apple sold a range of laptops known as the iBook. The MacBook was then introduced in 2006.

In 1998 the iMac was introduced in a variety of cool-looking colors, which was a major departure from the choice of white or black desktop computers. In 2005, the Mac Mini was released, which was a smaller desktop version of the Macintosh computer. The computer weighed just less than three pounds. A server version of the Mac Mini was then released in 2009. The difference with the server edition is that it had no optical drive and had tremendous storage—a 1 terabyte hard drive. While Apple discontinued the Mac mini server in 2014, it does still produce the Mac mini. An investigator may still encounter the Mac mini Server.

Mac mini with OS X Server

The Mac mini Server basically had the same physical dimensions as the Mac mini. Even the ports on the back were the exact same (see Figure 12.1). The Mac mini Server is 0.2 pounds heavier, which is the only physical variation. The later server model did, however, have two 1 TB hard drives in the later model, unlike the Mac mini, which simply had one 500 GB or 1 TB hard drive. Therefore, an investigator should not assume that a seized Mac mini is a client computer—the suspect could be running a server from his home, which can completely change the complexion of an investigation and methods of examination. The Mac mini Server runs on OS X Server and includes the following:

- Server
- Xsan
- File Server
- Calendar Server
- Contacts Server
- Mail Server
- Web Server
- NetInstall
- DNS
- DHCP

- Open Directory
- Profile Manager
- VPN Server
- Wiki Server

Power   Power   Ethernet   HDMI   USB   SDXC Slot
Button   Supply   Port   Thunderbolt
                              FireWire

FIGURE 12.1   Mac Mini

Again, Apple moved away from developing servers and now focuses on Mac Mini (client).

iPod

The iPod was released in October 2001, and it was available in either a 5 GB or 10 GB model. This first-generation iPod was only compatible with Macintosh computers. The second generation of the iPod Classic was released in July 2002, and this model was compatible with Windows (2000). In 2004 the iPod Mini was released in a 4 GB model, and the Nano made its first appearance the following year. In 2005 the iPod Shuffle was released. The iPod Touch (see Figure 12.2) went on sale in September 2007, which was available in an 8, 16 or 32 GB model. The iPod Touch was basically an iPod with Wi-Fi capability, which enabled the user to surf the Internet with Safari, watch videos on YouTube or wirelessly download content from iTunes. In terms of an iPod, the only device being sold by Apple today is the iPod Touch, which now has a capacity storage of up to 256 GB.

FIGURE 12.2 iPod Touch

iPhone

In 2007 the world witnessed an even more remarkable product from Apple – the iPhone. This first-generation iPhone ran on iOS 1.0 and was available in a 4 GB model for $499 and an 8 GB model for $599. Close collaboration on the development of the iPhone between Apple and Cingular was successful, as evidenced by sales of the device and Cingular was rewarded by being the exclusive retailer of iPhones for the first four years of sales. The first-generation iPhone casing was made of plastic and aluminum. The iPhone 3G and 3GS had an all-plastic backing to improve the cellular signal.

The iPhone has changed dramatically since those early days. In September 2019, Apple announced its new iPhone 11, iPhone 11 Pro and iPhone 11 Pro Max. What is notable for investigators is how the storage capacity for iPhones has increased up to 512 GB. At time of writing, the latest version of iOS is 13.4.1. Figure 12.3 shows the iPhone 11.

Recently, consumers have been provided more choices with Apple's iOS devices, like a higher-end iPhone 11 Pro Max and a lower-end iPhone XR. The iPad Air was released in November 2013, which features an A7 chip, up to 128 GB of onboard memory and of course uses the Lightning pin connector.

A description of other iPhone models can be found later in this chapter.

FIGURE 12.3   iPhone 11

iPad

The first-generation iPad was released in 2010 and, like the iPhone and iPod, it ran on iOS. A year later, the iPad 2 was released, and consumers had a choice of a traditional iPad with Wi-Fi or a data plan operating on either CDMA or GSM.

Today, there are basically four different iPad models available: iPad, iPad Pro, iPad Air, and iPad Mini.

iPad Pro

The first iPad Pro was released in November 2015, it was 12.9 inches and featured LPDDR4 RAM. The third generation of iPad Pro, which was announced in October 2018, integrated Apple's FaceID technology and could be used while holding the tablet in either a portrait or in a landscape position. This third iteration also saw the home button being removed. In terms of memory, this version included storage options that reach 1TB. As with other iPad models, there are Wi-Fi or Wi-Fi and cellular versions of the tablet.

Apple Watch

Apple Watch is a smart watch that syncs with several apps from the user's iPhone, in addition to other Apple devices. Most importantly, the watch pairs with Apple's Health app, which tracks user activity, including calories burned, number of steps, and walking or running distance (kilometers or miles). The watch also monitors the user's vitals, such as heart rate. The Apple Watch can also be used to answer calls, reply to text messages (SMS) and can be used to answer incoming calls. The device can also pair with a Mac computer to unlock the device when in sleep mode. Originally introduced in 2015, subsequent versions have been introduced with the Series 1 and Series 2 in 2016, the Series 3 in 2017, the Series 4 in 2018, and the Series 5 in 2019.

Prior to the release of the Series 4 Apple Watch, Apple funded a heart study with Stanford University, focused on a cohort of 400,000 consumers with no pre-existing heart conditions. The goal of the study was to use the Apple Watch to identify heart arrhythmias (irregular heartbeats), which in turn can be used to diagnose serious heart conditions, like atrial fibrillation (aFib), which can cause stroke. Results from the study to date have been mixed due to numerous false-positive alerts.

Apple Watch: Series 4

The Series 4 featured a larger display and contained a much faster 64-bit dual-core processor. The device also contained an electrical heart sensor, while its ECG (electrocardiogram) was approved by the United States Food and Drug Administration. It also received the support of the American Heart Association (AHA). The device automatically calls emergency services if the device detects a fall.

The Series 4 Watch contains a GPS module, and there is an LTE chip on the cellular models. The cellular version contains an eSIM, which means that the user can make and receive calls without having their iPhone in close proximity. A separate cellular plan is required for this Apple Watch version. An eSIM (embedded SIM) is a Subscriber Identity Module that is soldered onto the Apple Watch's printed circuit board (PCB). This version supports Apple Pay

Apple Watch: Series 5

The Series 5 Watch introduced a new "Always-On Retina display", which means that the watch face now continually displays. There are also more customization options available for the display. The watch can also monitor your heart rhythm, which is an important development for investigators, who may use Apple Watch data as corroborating evidence to show that a suspect or a victim was sleeping or running, for example. There is also a built-in alert system to warn you about noise levels that may negatively impact your hearing. A new Cycle Tracking app can be used to track your menstrual cycle, which could perhaps be relevant to an investigation.

Similar to recent versions of the Apple Watch, the Series 5 does have a model that supports cellular service with the use of an eSIM. This version also supports Apple Pay, like its predecessor.

Contactless payments can be made with the Watch, which links to the Wallet app, at point of service (payment) terminals at retail stores. Person-to-person payments, facilitated by Siri, can be conducted on the Apple Watch. Transit cards can also be added to the Wallet app. This means that on some transit systems, such as the New York Subway system, a commuter can pass through an access turnstile using an iPhone or an Apple Watch.

Apple Health App

The Health app comes preinstalled on an iPhone, similar to Weather, Maps, Photos, and so forth. Much of the data stored by the Health app is derived from the Apple Watch, its sensors, and sensors on the iPhone. Therefore, it is appropriate to discuss the app in this section. Apple Health app data is often backed up to the user's iCloud account, which is certainly of interest to investigators. ElcomSoft offers a solution, called Phone Breaker (elcomsoft.com), which can pull this data from a user's iCloud account. Belkasoft Acquisition (belcasoft.com) Tool is another application that can acquire iCloud data; the data is subsequently analyzed with Belkasoft Evidence Center. The Health app data can include the following data points:

- Heart rate
- Sleeping habits
- Location points
- Workouts
- Steps
- Walking routines

Low-energy sensors are used to continually monitor the user's activity. More recently, Apple has been looking to integrate health-monitoring capabilities into their highly successful AirPods. Amazon and Google have also been investing in similar research. Figure 12.4 shows the iPad Air home screen.

FIGURE 12.4   iPad Air Home Screen

Apple Wi-Fi Devices

Apple has a number of wireless devices that enable consumers to create an integrated wireless "Apple Environment", meaning that a user's Apple devices are connected, and allow media and communications to be shared. For example, a website on Safari that is open on an iPhone can be opened on a synced MacBook. Another example is that an Apple consumer can also answer a phone call on her iPhone, on her Apple Watch or on her MacBook. Understanding this Apple Environment is important because evidence can be retrieved from multiple devices in the home or office.

Apple TV

Apple TV was introduced in 2007 as a device for streaming Internet content to a television. When it was first released, the device had a 40 GB hard drive, which later increased to 160 GB. The second-generation device was announced in September 2010, and this version allowed the user to download content from iTunes, through AirPlay, via computer or an iOS device. **AirPlay** is a proprietary protocol, developed by Apple, to wirelessly stream content from the Internet and between compatible devices. In March 2012, a third generation Apple TV was released, and this device provided the user with 1080p high definition video. From an investigator's perspective, only the second generation of Apple TV was of little forensics value because there was much smaller flash memory, which was inaccessible.

Released in September 2017, Apple TV 4K now allows users to experience movies in 4K HDR (High Dynamic Range). This version of Apple TV comes in either a 32 GB or 64 GB version. This version contains an A10X fusion chip with 64-bit processor. The operating system for the device is tvOS and is based on iOS. The model number for Apple TV 4K is A1842. The good news is that file stored on

Apple TV can now be accessed using an exploit called checkm8. We will discuss checkm8, in greater detail later in this chapter.

In September 2019, the company announced its new streaming service called Apple TV+, which would compete with other streaming services, like Netflix, Hulu, and Disney's new service (Disney+).

AirPort Express

AirPort Express is a Wi-Fi base station that allows a user to connect other Apple devices and wirelessly stream content on a simultaneous dual-band 802.11n Wi-Fi protocol. For example, this device can facilitate streaming audio from a computer to a music system via AirPlay. A user on the network can also wirelessly send print jobs to a networked printer. Using an Ethernet connection, AirPort Express can also function as a wireless access point and connect up to 50 users. AirPort Express can also extend the range of a Wi-Fi connection. This device is no longer sold by Apple, but investigators may still encounter these devices.

AirPort Extreme

AirPort Extreme is a Wi-Fi base station that possesses many of the same characteristics of AirPort Express but is designed for a larger home, small business, or a classroom. This device uses the 802.11ac Wi-Fi protocol. AirPort Extreme can also facilitate sharing an external hard drive. This device is no longer sold by Apple. However, investigators may still encounter these devices.

AirPort Time Capsule

AirPort Time Capsule is an automatic wireless backup drive for Mac users (see Figure 12.5). AirPort Time Capsule has many of the same features as the AirPort Extreme Wi-Fi base station but includes a 2 TB or 3 TB hard drive. It also operates on the 802.11ac Wi-Fi standard. Needless to say, the AirPort Time Capsule has tremendous potential for evidence in an investigation. This device was discontinued in April 2018. However, investigators may still encounter these devices.

FIGURE 12.5   Time Capsule

Macintosh File Systems

The **Macintosh File System (MFS)** is a flat file system that was introduced with Apple's Macintosh computer in 1984. The file system was developed to store files on floppy disks. As volumes grew in size, a new file system, called Hierarchical File System (HFS), was introduced. **Hierarchical File System (HFS)** is a file system that was developed by Apple in 1985 to support its hard disk drive. Introduced in 1998, **Hierarchical File System Extended (HFS+)** was another Apple proprietary file system that supported larger files and uses Unicode.

In general, Apple's operating system is based upon UNIX, and the HFS+ file system has been updated to function with macOS (previously called "Mac OS X"). Nevertheless, an Intel-based Macintosh could contain file systems like NTFS, FAT 32, EXT3, EXT4, because it can run multiple operating systems with their different file systems. **Boot Camp** is a tool that allows an Intel-based Macintosh to run Windows operating systems.

Hierarchical File System (HFS)

Earlier Mac operating systems were comprised of files with two parts. The first part was the **data fork**, which consisted of the data, while the **resource fork** stored the file metadata and associated application information. A resource fork is basically the equivalent of an Alternate Data Stream in NTFS. Use of the resource fork has been deprecated by the developers at Apple but can still be found in use. It is important to understand that files, containing a resource fork, will often lose the resource fork when copied to a volume with a different file system, like Windows NTFS. Sometimes, with other file systems, the resource fork will be a hidden file or simply be removed because of a lack of compatibility with resource forks.

HFS has a maximum of 65,536 blocks per volume; like NTFS, each block is 512 bytes.

HFS+

Also referred to as Mac OS Extended, HFS+ was introduced with Mac OS 8.1 in 1998. HFS+ provided improvements in the allocation of disk space. With HFS+, the maximum number of blocks is 2^{32} (4,294,967,296). More blocks meant less wasted space on a volume. Long file names can contain up to 255 characters in Unicode. The maximum file size is 2^{63} bytes. HFS+ is a case-sensitive file system, which means that files with the same name can co-exist in the same logical location, e.g. "File1" and "file1" in the same folder. NTFS is not a case-sensitive file system, and therefore there is a good argument for using a Mac to examine a Mac or iOS device. Otherwise, valuable files and metadata could be lost.

An **allocation block** is a unit of storage space and is typically 512 bytes for a hard drive. An **allocation block number** is a 32-bit number that identifies an allocation block. A **volume header** contains information about the volume, including the time and date of its creation and the number of files stored on that volume. The volume header is located 1024 bytes at the start of the volume. An **alternative volume header** is a copy of the volume header and is located 1024 bytes at the end of the volume. The **catalog file** contains detailed information about the file, including the file and folder name. The catalog file is structured as a B-tree. The **Catalog ID** is a unique sequential number that is created when a new file is created on a Mac. This is extremely important from a forensics perspective because an investigator can determine the sequence by which files were created and the Catalog ID cannot be manipulated by the user. Thus, the Catalog ID is dependable in determining when a file is created, whereas there are ways in which a user can manipulate file metadata associated with files. The Catalog ID is deleted when the file is deleted but the number is never repeated. In contrast, with NTFS, the MFT record identifier can be reused when a file is deleted.

Date and Time Metadata

The following date and time metadata can be found in an HFS+ file:

- **Created Date**: Time of creation
- **Last Accessed Date**: Time of creation
- **Modified Date**: Time of creation
- **Date Added**: Field is not populated

The HFS+ file system uses UNIX time, also referred to as Epoch time, for timestamps.

If a file is duplicated, then the following date and time metadata can be retrieved by the investigator:

- **Created**: Inherited from the original
- **Modified**: Inherited from the original
- **Accessed**: Time of duplication
- **Record Changed**: Time of duplication
- **Date Added**: Time of duplication

HFS+ maintains a link between the object (file) and its original source. This link can be found in kMDItemWhereFroms.

APFS

APFS (Apple File System) is a file system released by Apple, for use on its Macintosh computers as well as for mobile devices, like the iPhone. It was released with macOS Sierra in 2017. If you upgraded your iPhone or iPad to iOS 10.3 (or later) then APFS (Apple File System) was automatically installed on your device and replaced HFS+. macOS High Sierra installer offers non-destructive, in-place upgrades, from HFS+ to APFS. APFS can be found on devices running macOS, iOS, tvOS, and watchOS. This file system has been optimized for flash / solid state memory by increasing read/write speeds. HFS+ maintains no native support for encryption and instead relies on CoreStorage for encryption. Conversely, APFS does not rely on CoreStorage for encryption as it has encryption built into the file system; it encrypts data at the file systems level. CoreStorage and APFS both encrypt data with an XTS-AES-128 cipher. However, APFS-formatted volumes utilize randomly generated encryption keys, while CoreStorage uses the UUID as the secondary key. Since the CoreStorage UUID is not random and can be guessed, APFS may be viewed as possessing a superior encryption protocol.

APFS File Metadata

APFS is a 64-bit file system, with theoretical 2^{64} addressable blocks. Therefore, with APFS there are 9 quintillion addressable objects (files), compared to 4 billion in HFS+. There is greater accuracy with timestamps, which are now stored as 64-bit values; 1 nanosecond on APFS compared to 1 second in HFS+. In APFS, copy-on-write has replaced journaling. The **copy-on-write** feature creates a clone of files and only changes to the file are made to the file clone, which is more efficient when compared to journaling. Checksums are used for integrity of file metadata.

APFS uses a B-Tree data structure to store user data and file content information. The structure does differ from HFS+.

Data Cloning

Data cloning is an APFS feature, whereby when data is duplicated, within a container, regardless of the volume, the data content is not replicated and only the metadata is duplicated. This means that two files will have data content that is physically stored in the same blocks.

APFS Encryption

APFS also features strong encryption, which includes full-disk encryption with single or multi-key encryption. To summarize, here are the encryption options with APFS:

- No encryption;
- Single-key encryption; or
- Multi-key with per-file keys for file data, and a separate key for sensitive metadata.

Depending on the hardware, APFS uses AES-XTS or AES-CBC encryption.

Keybags store the encryption information, for an Apple Macintosh or iOS device, including the encryption keys. On a MacBook, keybags contain the keys to unlock a container and the keys to unlock a volume. The **Container Keybag** holds the Volume Keybags and the Volume Encryption Key (VEK). While the Container Keybag is encrypted, there are unencrypted data (plaintext) on the drive that will enable you to decrypt the Container Keybag. The **Volume Keybags** contains a series of Key Encryption Keys (KEK). The **Key Encryption Key (KEK)** is derived from each user's password on a system and the Recovery Key. The KEK is critical to decrypting a volume. An examiner only needs one user's password or the Recovery Key to open the Volume Keybag and access to the Volume Encryption Key (VEK), which will then be used to decrypt the volume. A **Volume Encryption Key (VEK)** is a file system key that is used to encrypt data blocks on a volume (disk). The good news is that tools, like BlackLight, can perform this decryption process for you. However, this process is not possible for more recent Mac computers that come with an Apple T2 chip.

iOS uses the following keybags: backup, device, escrow, iCloud Backup, and user. When the user enters her passcode, the *NSFileProtectionComplete* key is loaded from the *user keybag* and unwrapped. The *backup keybag* is generated when iTunes created an encrypted backup and this keybag is stored on the computer associated with the iOS device. The *escrow keybag* is used for mobile device management and iTunes syncing.

Apple T2 Chip

Beginning in 2017, most new Mac computers were manufactured with a T2 security chip, which are embedded in the disk controller. The T2 chip has effaceable storage for some encryption information and the chip also has a cryptographic engine to conduct hardware-enabled cryptographic operations. There are encryption keys stored on the chip, which are currently inaccessible (at time of writing). Therefore, decryption and access to the keybags is only possible by interfacing with the T2 chip. File data and metadata must be passed to the T2 chip to be decrypted. Prior to the T2 chip, the encryption was software-based and decryption could be performed after an acquisition. Decryption on a computer with a T2 chip must occur during acquisition, with the use of a password or recovery key, via the chip.

Encryption is enabled by default on these systems but FileVault is not activated by default. A user may add another layer of security by enabling FileVault. If FileVault is enabled, then you will need either the recovery key or the user password at acquisition time. MacQuisition can be used to acquire an AFF4 (compressed/uncompressed) image format. **AFF4 (Advanced Forensic File Format)** is an open, non-proprietary, image file format. **APFS Free Queue** refers to allocated blocks on a volume, not found in a logical acquisition, which are not referenced by the file system that can contain valuable evidence.

Space Sharing

APFS introduces the concept of space sharing. The **space sharing** feature allows multiple file systems to share the same underlying free space on a physical volume, which is unlike the rigid partitioning schemes that pre-allocate a fixed amount of space for each file system. APFS-formatted volumes can grow and shrink without volume repartitioning. This new system can be thought of as an APFS container. To clarify, a container is comprised of a series of logical APFS volumes, which all share blocks from the container; physical disks combine to form an APFS container. In Figure 12.6 you can see that the APFS container is a collection of logical APFS volumes, which share blocks on physical drives.

FIGURE 12.6   APFS Container

APFS Snapshots

A **snapshot** is a backup of an APFS volume, in a container, which can be used to restore files and data. For example, if files or data become corrupted, perhaps through a power outage or power surge, then the file system can be rolled back to an earlier checkpoint. This is a new feature with APFS and performs like a restore point on a Windows PC. This feature is comparable to Volume Shadow Copy (VSC) on Windows. APFS keeps track of snapshots through the use of a volume "checkpoint". Snapshots can also be found in other file systems, including reFS (Microsoft) and ZFS (Sun Microsystems). The contents of a snapshot are protected from deletion, although they will eventually be overwritten as new snapshots are created. A snapshot can also be created manually, from the Terminal on a Mac, using the following command:

`tmutil snapshot [enter]`

The `tmutil` command refers to the Time Machine utility. The Terminal can be accessed by going to **Applications** in the Finder, then click **Utilities** and then click **Terminal**. Then enter the **tmutil snapshot** command and then press [**enter**], and then compare your screen to Figure 12.7.

FIGURE 12.7 Terminal Utility with the `tmutil` Snapshot Command Run

Fusion Drive and CoreStorage

A **Fusion Drive** takes two drives, e.g. an SSD and HDD or SSD and SSD, and makes them seamlessly operate as one SSD. Fusion Drives are not compatible with APFS. However, Apple may release a solution in the future. **CoreStorage** forms the foundation for Fusion Drives and displays partitions on multiple drives as one drive. The idea is to store the most frequently used blocks on the most efficient storage, i.e. SSD (flash memory).

Forensic Examinations on a Mac

We have already noted that examining a Macintosh, using a Macintosh, is critical at some point in an investigation given that HFS+ supports a case-sensitive file system. Moreover, file metadata associated with HFS+, and especially APFS, is very different from FAT and NTFS and therefore using a Mac for a Mac investigation is vital. Furthermore, there are many extended attributes that can be lost when using a PC to examine a Mac computer. One example would be the origin of a file, i.e. how the file was transferred to a Mac, e.g. via AirDrop. In other words, if you just use a Windows PC for a Mac examination, you are at risk of losing critical files and evidence. **Quick Look** is a feature of macOS that allows the user to preview the contents of a file without opening the file or executing its associated application. For example, a PDF or a Keynote presentation or JPEG can be previewed using the Quick Look feature in Apple's Finder application.

Spotlight

Spotlight is a feature found in macOS that quickly finds files, folders, and applications as soon as the user starts typing a name in the Spotlight search field. Spotlight can also be used, by an investigator, to search through a .DMG image, although that image must be indexed first. A **DMG image** is an exact copy of a file, or a collection of files, or a volume, and has been the default image format for distributing applications for macOS. Indexing is a process of searching through an imaging and creating references to words in file names and within files. An investigator may choose to index an image so that a keyword search can be performed later. An investigator may choose not to since it is a long process. Spotlight contains a treasure trove of evidence for the investigator and includes file and app metadata. For example, an investigator can determine where an application, like AirPort Utility.app, came from, how many times the application has been used, etc. More specifically, *kMDItemUseCount* displays the number of times that an application was used. There are many third-party applications, like the Firefox.app, that can be found in Spotlight. This metadata can be found here:

```
/Users/.../Library/Metadata/CoreSpotlight/index.spotlightV3/.store.db
```

What is particularly interesting about Spotlight is that you can find a specific website that a user visited, searches performed on Safari, determine how many times the website was visited, search results that were displayed to the user, etc. This information can be found here:

```
com.apple.safari.history
```

You will, however, need a full file system to obtain this Spotlight metadata. Spotlight does not just store metadata but also stores cached data here:

```
/.Spotlight-V100/Store-V2/...
```

In the aforementioned folder, you will find metadata related to when a file was placed in a folder, how many times it was accessed, etc. Importantly, you may also find text from files here that were previously deleted by a user. In Spotlight Search History, you can find the text used, by the user, when performing a search and also view the search results that were originally displayed to the user.

Initialization

Initialization is the term used to refer to formatting a drive in macOS. Initializing a drive is performed with the Disk Utility tool on a Mac (Applications / Utilities), and there are six options:

- macOS Extended (Journaled)
- macOS Extended (Journaled, Encrypted)
- macOS Extended (Case-sensitive, Journaled)
- macOS Extended (Case-sensitive, Journaled, Encrypted)
- ExFAT
- MS-DOS (FAT)

IOReg Info

IOReg Info is a tool available from Cellebrite (formerly BlackBag Technologies) that can provide an investigator with information about devices connected to a Mac, like SATA Drives, FireWire devices and USB devices as illustrated in Figure 12.8. The tool is available from www.blackbagtech.com.

PMAP Info

PMAP Info is a tool available from Cellebrite (formerly BlackBag Technologies) that displays a map of a device's partition (see Figure 12.9). The partition map could be of the Mac's hard drive or could be an attached USB device. The tool is available from www.blackbagtech.com.

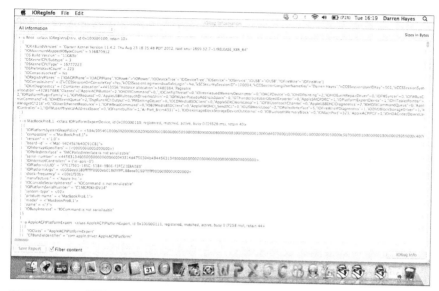

FIGURE 12.8   IOReg Info from Cellebrite

FIGURE 12.9   PMAP Info from Cellebrite

Epoch Time

As mentioned, UNIX time and Epoch time are the same. Like UNIX time, the file system date stamps times are recorded in seconds since January 1, 1970, 00:00:00 UTC (Epoch time). Date and time values are stored as a 32-bit integer. Unlike a UNIX system, when a file is moved from one location to another, the creation date does not change. The maximum date supported by HFS+ is February 6, 2040, at 06:28:15 GMT. Epoch (zero) time for macOS is January 1, 1904, 00:00:00 UTC. Epoch time is different for different web browsers and for other systems. Thus, converting timestamps can be challenging when working with a Mac or an iOS device. Epoch Converter can assist the examiner with this precarious conversion. The website www.epochconverter.com can assist with this daunting task. To summarize, timestamps from macOS must be translated into a human readable format.

Epoch Convertor

An Epoch Convertor is a tool, available from Cellbrite (BlackBag), which enables the user to convert epoch times on a macOS 10.5.8 or higher to both local and UTC times.

Let's Get Practical!

Converting Epoch Time on a Mac

1. Download the Epoch Converter program from the following URL:

   https://www.blackbagtech.com/resources/freetools/epochconverter.html

   Note that you need to register as a new user before you can begin the download.

2. Open Epoch Converter.

3. In the Epoch box, type **3471422400** and then click the **Convert** button, and then compare your screen to Figure 12.10.

FIGURE 12.10   Epoch Converter

Deleted Files

Files that are moved to Trash, and then the Trash is emptied, cannot be recovered because the operating system no longer maintains a link to reference that file's physical location on the hard drive, i.e., the Catalog ID no longer exists. There will still be a .ds_store file available in Trash, which can provide an indication of files that had been moved to the Trash.

Journaling

As noted earlier in this book, journaling is a file system feature that maintains a backup of user files so that if a system crashes the last saved copy of that file can be made available to the user. HFS+ has case-sensitive journaling. Window NTFS has journaling functionality, but NTFS is not case sensitive when it comes to file names. In other words, the file xyz.docx and XYZ.docx cannot co-exist in the same directory in NTFS, but they could co-exist with HFS+ or APFS. Therefore, an investigator should ensure that the destination drive for files from a Mac should be formatted with HFS+ (or APFS) and not NTFS. When examining files from a Mac computer, an investigator should perform the analysis with a Mac computer.

When a file is created, it is assigned a Catalog ID, which is similar to an inode in Linux. Catalog IDs have sequential numbers, and therefore it is possible to determine the order in which a user created files.

DMG

As discussed, a DMG image is an exact copy of a file, or a collection of files, or a volume, and has been the default image format for distributing applications for macOS. Files within the DMG can be encrypted. When installing an application on a MacBook, we typically install a DMG. From a forensics perspective, a DMG is the equivalent of a dd image and can be viewed as a mountable virtual disk. The logical size of a DMG can be larger than the sum of files physically contained in the DMG. A 1GB DMG might also have no files contained within the image. There are other virtual file systems available on a Mac, and these include sparse images (.sparseimage) and sparse bundles (.sparsebundle). Unlike a DMG, a **sparse image** is a virtual file for macOS that will grow in size as more files are added. A **sparse bundle** is a virtual file, introduced with macOS 10.5 for use with FileVault, which will grow in size as more files are added. To view the technical contents of a sparse bundle, the user can simply right-click over the image file and then click "Show Package Contents". However, normal usage is to double-click a sparse bundle in the Finder, and it will mount like other virtual disks.

PList Files

PList (Property List) Format files are configuration files found on a computer running the Mac operating system. PLists are found in macOS and in iOS systems. PLists are used by Cocoa and Core Foundation. **Cocoa** is a framework for developers of macOS and contains APIs (application programming interface), libraries and runtimes, and is largely based on Objective-C. **Objective-C** is an object-oriented programming language that is based on the C language and was developed in the early 1980s by NeXT. **Core Foundation (CF)** is a framework that provides useful fundamental software services to developers building applications for macOS and iOS.

These files can be thought of as similar to registry files found on a Windows computer. PLists will contain user settings and provide a wealth of information for investigators. PLists are used to store user and application preferences. They are an efficient way for a developer to store small blocks of data consisting primarily of numbers and strings. These PLists files are binary or XML formats and require a special PList viewer to see the data in a meaningful manner. A binary PList is a smaller file than an XML PList and can be accessed by macOS faster, and therefore are more prevalent than the XML format. Binary PLists need to be converted into a different format for the examiner to view the file. macOS contains a tool, which is available from the Terminal window, called "plutil". **plutil (property list utility)** is a tool found in macOS that can check the syntax of PList files or can be used to convert a PList to another format. For example, you may wish to convert a binary PList to an XML format, which is more readable and easily searchable (see Figure 12.11). The plutil tool is available from macOS 10.2 onwards. One can also use the Quick Look function in macOS to view the contents of any PLIST file.

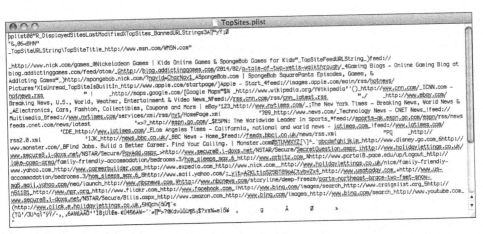

FIGURE 12.11 Sample PList

Let's Get Practical!

Working in the Terminal Window on a Mac

1. **Start** the *Finder* application.

2. On the menu bar, click **Go**, and then click **Utilities**.

3. In the *Utilities* folder, scroll down, and then double-click the **Terminal** icon.

4. At the prompt, type **say I want to be a forensics examiner** and then press **return**.

   If your sound is enable, then you will hear the sentence you just typed.

5. At the prompt, type **date** and then press **return**.

   The system date and time will display.

6. At the prompt, type **date -u** and then press **return**.

   The date and time in UTC will display.

7. At the prompt, type **hdiutil partition /dev/disk0** and then press **return**.

   A map of the boot drive partition will display. If Boot Camp has been used to install a Windows NTFS partition then it will display here.

8. At the prompt, type **system_profiler SPHardwareDataType** and then press **return**.

   A profile of the computer system displays, including the number of processors, RAM size, serial number and UUID.

9. At the prompt, type **system_profiler SPSoftwareDataType** and then press **return**.

   The version of macOS will display and also the computer name and username.

10. At the prompt, type **man plist** and then press **return**.

    An explanation of what a plist is displays on the screen.

11. Press **return** to scroll down through the explanation until *(END)* displays.

12. On the Menu bar, click **Terminal**, and then click **Quit Terminal**.

13. In the displayed dialog box, click **Close**.

A PList file will contain a header, which will indicate the type of PList file. With PLists, there are several abstract types as documented in Table 12.1.

TABLE 12.1   PList Abstract Types

Abstract Type	XML
Array	<array>
Dictionary	<dict>
String	<string>
Data	<data>
Date	<date>
Number—integer	<integer>
Number—floating point	<real>
Boolean	<true/> or <false/>

SQLite Databases

SQLite databases are generally associated with mobile devices. However, since many users synchronize these devices to the computer, it is quite common to see these databases resident on a Macintosh computer. As noted earlier in this book, these are relational databases that contain both application and user data in related tables. If deleted, these files can generally be recovered if the Trash on the dock (or desktop) has not been emptied. Nevertheless, some SQLite databases have a vacuuming feature. **Vacuuming** is a cleanup feature, associated with SQLite databases, that will permanently erase deleted records or tables. Currently, vacuuming is not found to be enabled on Apple devices.

Email Files

Email files on a Mac computer are an EMLX format (.emlx, .emlxpart, .partial.emlx). EMLX files are associated with Apple's Mail application, which is the default email program with macOS. Simple Carver Suite has a tool called Eml2HTML that can convert .eml and .emlx messages to a readable format. This tool is a cheap alternative if an investigator does not have access to more extensive professional tools, like EnCase or BlackLight.

Hibernation File

In macOS there is a sleepimage file. **sleepimage** is a file that is a copy of the contents of RAM that has been copied to the computer's hard drive, to protect a user in the event that battery power runs out. The file size is generally equivalent to the size of the RAM on the local computer. If the power has drained completely from a running Mac computer, when power is applied and the device is powered on, the contents of the sleepimage file is read and moved back into active memory. The following command in Terminal will show you the size of the sleepimage file on a computer:

```
ls -lh /private/var/vm/sleepimage
```

Macintosh Operating Systems

The classic macOS was introduced to the public in 1984 and was developed for use with the earliest Macintosh computers. This operating system was a dramatic departure from other personal computers at the time, which ran MS-DOS – a line-command interface. Instead, this operating system was characterized by a friendlier graphical user interface (GUI) that featured icons that you could click on with the use of a mouse. Initially the early macOS supported a flat file system called Macintosh File System (MFS), but this file system was replaced by Hierarchical File System (HFS) in 1985 to support its hard disk drive.

The macOS operating system was released to the public in 2002 and is still used today, although it has changed considerably since then. The following operating systems were subsequently released:

- **Version 10.0 (Cheetah):** Released in March 2001
- **Version 10.1 (Puma):** Released in September 2001
- **Version 10.2 (Jaguar):** Released in August 2002
- **Version 10.3 (Panther):** Released in October 2003
- **Version 10.4 (Tiger):** Released in April 2005
- **Version 10.5 (Leopard):** Released in October 2007
- **Version 10.6 (Snow Leopard):** Released in August 2009
- **Version 10.7 (Lion):** Released in July 2011
- **Version 10.8 (Mountain Lion):** Released in July 2012
- **Version 10.9 (Mavericks):** Released in October 2013
- **Version 10.10 (Yosemite):** Released in October 2014
- **Version 10.11 (El Capitan):** Released in September 2015
- **Version 10.12 (Sierra):** Released in September 2016
- **Version 10.13 (High Sierra):** Released in September 2017
- **Version 10.14 (Mojave):** Released Din: September 2018
- **Version 10.15 (Catalina):** Released in October 2019

macOS Catalina

macOS Catalina was released in October 2019, and with this version of the operating system we see iTunes phased out and replaced with three apps: Music, Podcasts and TV. Apple devices are now managed through the Finder, while media syncing is performed by Apple TV, Podcasts or Music. A new Sidecar feature enables users to use their iPad as a display for their Mac. macOS now includes

Gatekeeper. **Gatekeeper** is a macOS security feature that enforces code signing for downloaded apps before executing those applications. macOS now verifies the Developer ID signature and notarization status to check that the Mac apps and plug-ins that you download from the Internet come from a recognized developer and that the app has not been altered. The Find My app and Find My Friends app can also be used to track your Mac and other Apple devices—even when they are offline, which will be of particular interest to investigators. Also, of interest is the new Photos app, which organizes user photos by day, month, and year. Only 64-bit apps will work with this version of macOS. The Notes app has also changed and a new gallery displays. Similarly, the Reminders app has changed and was completely redesigned with iOS 13. In fact, Reminders are now organized into different lists that can be color-coded.

File Vault

FileVault is a volume encryption tool, developed by Apple for use with Macintosh computers. The version of this feature for macOS Lion or later is called FileVault 2. FileVault 2 utilizes XTS-AES 128 full disk encryption. When the user enables FileVault the user is asked to select the user accounts that may decrypt the encrypted drive.

In terms of investigations, if FileVault is enabled then there is virtually no helpful evidence that can be retrieved. It is important to understand that when FileVault is set up that the user is provided with a "recovery key", which is a safety net in case the user loses his password and cannot decrypt the hard drive. The recovery key is long and difficult for the user to remember but can decrypt the hard drive. The user is prompted to print or email or write down this recovery key. Additionally, the user is provided with the option to store the recovery key with Apple. Thus, contacting Apple is certainly worth a try.

Disk Utility

Disk Utility is an Apple Mac tool for conducting a variety of disk functions, including verifying and repairing disks, formatting disks, mounting disks, and creating disk images. These functions can be accessed through the Terminal with the commands `diskutil` or `hdiutil`.

macOS Keychain

The Keychain is a password management system in macOS. The Keychain contains passwords, session keys, private keys, and certificates. Importantly, there are a lot of unencrypted data that can be retrieved from the Keychain. The System Keychain can be found in /Library/Keychains and in /private/var/db/SystemKey. You need root access to access the SystemKey and therefore need a full file system image. There is also a user keychain found in the user's home directory (~/Library/Keychains). This can be unlocked with the user's password. In terms of security, the Keychain is based on the Common Security Services Manager (CSSM). CSSM was officially deprecated with macOS 10.7. You can find additional information about the Keychain at opensource.apple.com. With CSSM on a Mac, each record has a finite set of attributes, which includes record names and services names, and this information is generally unencrypted.

iCloud Keychain

iCloud Keychain stores all user online passwords, using 256-bit AES encryption, on approved Macs and iOS devices registered to the user. This utility also stores user credit card information.

Multiple Displays

macOS supports the use of multiple displays with a Mac. The user can also use a smart television as a display for the Mac using AirPlay and Apple TV.

Notifications

Notifications are a convenient way for the Apple Mac user to see incoming messages and respond to FaceTime requests or website alerts, without exiting an application.

Tags

Tags are a feature of macOS that enables the user to organize files with keywords. Therefore, Tags are valuable to an investigator as they can demonstrate the personalization and organization of files by a suspect. Multiple keywords can be added to a single file to associate it with multiple categories. These categories, with associated files, are easily accessible through the Finder application.

Safari

As you may know, Safari is the browser that comes bundled with the Mac operating system. If a user has activated private browsing, then there will be a limited amount of browser history available. From a forensics perspective, the most valuable files will be found in the user directory here:

```
~/Library/Safari/
```

Safari may be a lot more valuable to investigators given its new social networking features. Recent versions of Safari come with a sidebar that contains Shared Links posted by people that the user follows on LinkedIn and Twitter. This sidebar may of course help the investigator to build up a picture of the user's network of friends and interests.

History.plist

Safari browser history is stored in a binary PList called `History.plist` in the user directory. Every URL is recorded, as is the date and time of the last visit, and the number of times that the website has been visited, which can be extremely helpful for an investigator. The date and time values are a floating point value with the number of seconds since January 1, 2001 00:00:00 UTC, and therefore need to be translated. DCode is a tool that can convert this value to a readable date and time. When a website is visited, Safari creates a thumbnail of the site visited, as shown in Figure 12.12.

FIGURE 12.12 Webpage Previews

The JPEG and PNG files for these thumbnails can be retrieved from the following location:

`~/Library/Caches/com.apple.Safari/Webpage Previews`

Downloads.plist

Any downloads from the Internet are stored in the PList file `Downloads.plist`.

Cache.db

Safari cache can be retrieved from the SQLite database called `Cache.db`. This database contains a history of websites visited, images, dates, and access times. The file is located here:

`~/Library/Caches/com.apple.Safari`

Cookies.plist

The `Cookies.plist` file is another source of information about websites visited. The location of this file is found here:

`~/Library/Cookies/ subfolder`

TopSites.plist

The websites that are most frequently visited by a user are stored in TopSites.plist. A user may "pin" a website to this list so that it is saved to the gallery of top sites, or may be manually removed from the list, by the user, as shown in Figure 12.13. A user deleting his Web history is provided with the option to reset their top sites.

Safari for Windows

There is of course a version of Safari available for use with Windows. Safari browser history is generally found here on a Windows 7 or Windows 10 PC:

```
\AppData\Roaming\Apple Computer\Safari\
```

FIGURE 12.13   Top sites

Target Disk Mode and Device Cloning

The fastest method of cloning a computer's hard drive forensically is to use a cloning device, like a Disk Jockey Pro (Forensic Edition) or perhaps an Image MASSter Solo Forensic Hand-Held Duplicator. Mac devices can, however, be problematic when it comes to removing the hard drive. Target Disk Mode (TDM) allows an investigator to acquire a hard drive image using FireWire. **FireWire**, also referred to as IEEE 1394, allows for high-speed data transfer. With more recent Mac computers, you can use the Thunderbolt to perform an acquisition using Target Disk Mode. Thunderbolt 3 was developed by Intel and utilizes a USB-C interface. This interface has transfer speeds of up to 40 Gbps. Thunderbolt 3 can be used for data transfer, video output and power.

When booting the computer, pressing the "T" key will prevent the Mac operating system from loading and its firmware will enable the computer's drives to behave as FireWire mass storage devices. However, if the suspect's computer has a firmware password, then you will not be able to shift to Target Disk Mode and you will likely see a black screen. Therefore, your first step as an investigator should be to check to see if there is a firmware password. You can discern this by holding down the *option* key when booting and if a firmware password has been added by the user then a dialog box will display. Hopefully, the suspect will supply you with that password. It should be noted that you should use a write-blocker with TDM.

It should be noted that a lot of MacBooks sold by Apple today do not have a FireWire connection and a MacBook Air will only have one USB-C connection. When it comes to extracting data from an iPad, it is not easy to crack open the device, and then remove and clone the memory. The MacBook Air is also considerably difficult when it comes to acquiring a clone or an image of the hard drive.

FIGURE 12.14   Target Disk Mode (TDM) on a MacBook Pro

Apple Mobile Devices

Apple mobile devices, particularly the iPhone, are potentially more important than a MacBook or an iMac because they are more personalized and capture a greater variety of evidence than a traditional computer. The benefit for the investigator is that these devices are often interconnected in an Apple environment, so that the same evidence can be retrieved from multiple devices. Another benefit for the investigator is that the operating system on mobile devices (iOS) is very similar to macOS, and therefore there is more predictability about what to expect. Furthermore, unlike Android, where there are numerous manufacturers using the Android platform, Apple is in control of the device manufacture, operating system, iCloud backups for the user, and many of the applications. This means that there is a standardization of devices and that should make it easier to predict how to deal with each device, and consequently have standard protocols for working with these devices. It also means that investigators can request user data and assistance from Apple in Cupertino, California.

It all sounds very simple for law enforcement investigations but there are major challenges. Many Android mobile devices cannot be upgraded to the latest version of the Android OS, which is different with Apple devices. In fact, Apple encourages their users to upgrade to the latest version of iOS. Each new version of iOS introduces significant improvements in security, which creates more problems for law enforcement retrieving evidence from an iPhone or another iOS device.

iOS

iOS is the mobile operating system that has been developed by Apple and has been in existence since 2007. There are now more than 1.4 billion active Apple devices. iOS is a proprietary operating system that is found on the iPhone, iPad, and iPod. iOS uses APFS, which is a case-sensitive file system. The **root partition** is the first partition found in an iOS device and it contains the operating system. The root partition is also referred to as the system partition. After the root partition, the remainder of volume is the media partition. The **media partition** is the data partition on an iOS device and contains both user and some system files. Typical user data found in the media partition can include videos, contacts, and SMS.

Users of iOS devices are strongly encouraged by Apple to upgrade to the latest version of iOS, when available and when compatible, so as to enable the latest security fixes. **System Software Personalization** is a process, developed by Apple, which prevents a user from downgrading an iOS device to an earlier version of iOS firmware.

iOS 13 Features

iOS 13 provides some important enhancements to security from earlier versions of iOS, which investigators should be aware of. For example, the user has more options in terms allowing a mobile app to access the user's location. A user can select "Allow Once", permission to access the user's location information. Figure 12.15 shows the iOS location permissions that can be added later under **Settings**. As with earlier versions, iOS 13 comes with a feature called Control Center. The user accesses this function by swiping upward on the screen to display controls that include a flashlight, camera, stopwatch, and calculator. The Control Center may also be a fast way for an investigator to activate *Airplane Mode* so that the cellular and Wi-Fi connections are disabled. As with previous versions, **AirDrop** is a feature of iOS 13 that allows the user to share photos, videos, contacts, and other data, via Bluetooth, to another user in close proximity. This may be important to consider as defense counsel may question whether an investigator checked to see if this type of data transfer may have occurred.

FIGURE 12.15   Location permissions for an iOS app under Settings

Mobile apps will again need permission to access your Contacts. What has changed is that access to any notes, associated with a user's contact, will not be accessible to an app. In response to the deluge of robo-callers, iOS 13 maintains a feature that allows you to "Silence Unknown Callers", One feature that is a disadvantage to investigators is that a user can strip location data from a photo before sharing it.

The user may also receive notifications alerting the user to the fact that an app is tracking a user's location. The user will also likely receive notifications about allowing an app access to Bluetooth.

Security and Encryption

In terms of encryption, Apple uses Advanced Encryption Standard algorithm (AES) and more specifically AES-256. Encryption is at the block level. The **unique device identifier (UDID)** is a 40-digit alphanumeric identifier that uniquely identifies each Apple iOS device. The device's unique identifier (UID), and a device group identifier (GID), are AES 256-bit keys that are hard-coded into the application processor during manufacturing. Neither Apple nor its suppliers keep a record of this UID but this identifier allows data to be cryptographically linked to a specific device. Therefore, attempting chip-off of an iPhone or another iOS device would be worthless. Chip-off is however sometimes an option with Android smartphones.

We are all familiar with the six-digit passcode but the user can also opt to use a password, which is significantly more difficult to brute-force. Apple discourages brute-force attacks on the passcode with an increasing time delay every time an incorrect passcode is entered. More importantly for the investigator, the user may have set the device to wipe after a certain number of incorrect tries so the cooperation of a suspect may be imperative.

Data Protection was developed by Apple to keep all files encrypted in flash memory while allowing the user to receive phone calls, text messages and emails when the device is locked. Therefore, the device can react to an incoming phone call without decrypting sensitive data. Each time a file is created, Data Protection generates a new 256-bit key for that file, which in turn is sent to the AES engine. Adding a passcode to a device automatically enables the Data Protection feature.

USB Restricted Mode is a security feature, introduced with iOS 11.4.1, which prevents a trusted computer from unlocking an iOS device. For example, if you synchronize your iPhone with your computer, then it is a trusted device and you could connect your iPhone and share data, through the Apple Lightning cable, through the USB that was plugged into your computer. With USB Restricted Mode, the user will be forced to re-enter the iPhone passcode after an iPhone has been disconnected for one hour. There is however a workaround for investigators (at time of writing), which is to connect an Apple Lightening cable as soon as an iPhone is seized, to hopefully prevent USB Restricted Mode being enabled.

Apple ID

An Apple ID is the email address and password that is used by the user. When a user enters her Apple ID and downloads content from the Apple App Store or iCloud, then other devices registered to that user will also add that purchase. Apple requires a minimum of 8 characters, must include a number, a lowercase letter, an uppercase letter, and it cannot have more than three consecutive identical characters. Special characters may also be used in the password.

Every application (app) that comes with iOS 13 is encrypted with AES-256 and all third-party apps sold through App Store are also encrypted by default. The data associated with these apps are also tangled (encrypted) with the passcode. Therefore, iOS 13 can be a nightmare for law enforcement to gather information if the suspect is unwilling to provide his passcode and the judge deems the defendant to be protected by the Fifth Amendment (self-incrimination by supplying a passcode or password). Apple does not store these passcodes, which are stored locally on the device. Unfortunately, many users do not bother to ever synchronize these mobile devices with a computer, which eliminates the potential to unlock the device using a pairing file.

Before a logical acquisition can occur, the investigator must enter the passcode. Of course, there is always the risk that the suspect has set the device to wipe after a specific number of unsuccessful attempts. Alternatively, the lockdown file from a computer can be used if that device was synced to the user's computer. GrayKey is a tool, which is only available to law enforcement, that can acquire an image from a locked or unlocked iPhone. Grayshift is the developer of GrayKey. That image can be subsequently analyzed with a tool, like Magnet AXIOM.

iPod

Apart from the iPod Shuffle, all iPods contain a hard disk drive. Therefore, they can be more than just a music player but can be a source of valuable evidence.

The iPod PList locations are as follows:

- **Pictures:** `iPodName/Photos/Thumbs/...`

- **Contacts:** `iPodName/Contacts/iSync.vcf`

- **Calendars:** `iPodName/Calendars/iSync-CalendarName.ics`

- **Voice Memos:** `iPodName/iPod_Control/Music/...m4a`

- **Notes:** `iPodName/Notes/...rtf`

- **Music:** `iPodName/iPod_Control/Music/...m4a`

- **Trash:** `.Trashes/502/FileName.extension`

- **Date/Time/Name:** `VolumeName/Users/UserName/Library/Logs/iPod Updater Logs/iPodUpdater.log`

- **Serial #:** `VolumeName/Users/UserName/Library/Preferences/com.apple.iPod.plist`

- **Pictures:** `VolumeName/Users/UserName/Pictures/iPod Photo Cache/F00/`

iPad

The first-generation iPad was released in April 2010. Unlike the iPhone, it could not be charged by connecting it to a computer but had to be charged through an electrical outlet. The iPad is very similar to the iPhone in terms of functionality, although cellular Wi-Fi was optional. Today, there are four basic models, each of which has different options in terms of memory and cellular (4G):

- iPad Air
- iPad Pro
- iPad
- iPad mini

All of these iPad models use the Lightning connector for charging and data transfer.

iPhone

The iPhone operating system, known as iOS, is derived from macOS. Since the initial release of the iPhone in June 2007, Apple has sold millions of units. Some of the potential evidence available, which an investigator might not immediately think of, includes the following:

- Keyboard cache for autocorrect.
- Screenshots from last state of applications (KTX files, which are noted below)
- Current and deleted photos, searches, call history, email, voicemail, contacts, and application data
- Map tiles and routes and GPS fix

Imaging Software

There are many different iPhone forensics tools available. Here is a list of some tools for an investigator to select from:

- BlackBag Technologies (acquired by Cellebrite)—BlackLight
- SUMURI—Paladin
- Oxygen Forensics for iPhone
- MSAB—XRY
- Vaughn S. Cordero—MobileSyncBrowser
- opentext—EnCase Neutrino
- Cellebrite—UFED
- iPhone Analyzer (access via SourceForge)
- Compelson Laboratories—MOBILedit Forensic Express
- SubRosaSoft—MacLockPick
- Jonathan Zdziarski—Physical DD
- Belkasoft—Evidence Center
- Magnet Forensics—ACQUIRE

Modes of Operation

There are several modes of operation that an investigator should be aware of when examining an iPhone. Generally, the most important mode is DFU Mode, which is required when pushing an exploit to an iPhone—in other words, jailbreaking the device to get root access and obtaining a full file system, which includes system files in addition to user data.

DFU Mode

Device Firmware Upgrade (DFU) Mode enables the user to select the firmware version that they wish to install on the device. Later in the chapter we will learn about the *checkm8* exploit, which requires that the user place the device in DFU Mode. Enabling DFU Mode on an iPhone will vary depending on the model that you are investigating. On an iPhone X, for example, you would follow these instructions:

1. Ensure that iTunes is running on your Mac (or PC), and then connect your iPhone to your computer;

2. Press and release the volume up button;

3. Press and release the volume down button; and

4. Press and hold the side button until a black screen appears;

5. Once the black screen appears, continue pressing the side button and then press and hold the volume down button for about five seconds.

Recovery Mode

Recovery Mode enables the user to restore his iPhone settings to the original factory settings.

iBoot

When an iPhone is powered on, boot code is executed from the device's read-only memory (ROM). An Apple Root CA public key is located in this boot code to ensure that the Low-Level Bootloader (LLB) is signed by Apple, and then the bootloader runs. After the LLB finishes, the next phase of the boot-loader is executed, and this is called iBoot. **iBoot** is the second phase of the bootloader that verifies and mounts the iOS kernel. If an iOS device fails to load or verify during the boot process, then a message displays stating that the user must connect with iTunes; then this signifies that the device is now in recovery mode. If the initial boot fails or the LLB is not loaded, then the device goes into DFU mode and the user must connect the device to a computer, via USB.

Unlocking the SIM

Some iPhones are sold with the SIM card locked, thereby limiting the user to one cellular telephone carrier. AT&T used to be the exclusive carrier for iPhones in the U.S., but other companies, like Verizon, became resellers. For AT&T and Sprint users, this device operates on the GSM network. If the iPhone SIM is locked, then many companies will generally not divulge the code to unlock the device. Apple maintains information about this code when the iPhone is activated. There are, however, a number of hackers who have made tools available to unlock the iPhone and enable iPhone users to swap out the SIM card for another SIM card, thereby allowing users to avail themselves of lower calling rates when traveling internationally.

Original iPhone

Release Date: January 2007

The original iPhone was released with iPhone OS 1.0 but can support an operating system as high as iPhone OS 3.1.3.

iPhone 3G

Release Date: July 2008

This iPhone was released with iPhone OS 2.0 but can support an operating system as high as iPhone iOS 4.2.

iPhone 3GS

Release Date: June 2009

This iPhone was released with iPhone OS 3.0 but can support an operating system as high as iPhone iOS 4.2.

iPhone 4

Release Date: June 2010

This iPhone was released with iPhone OS 3.0 but can support an operating system as high as iPhone iOS 4.2. Its physical appearance is different from its predecessor given the flat aluminosilicate glass panel on the front and back of the device. This model came in a CDMA model (model number A1349). The CDMA model came with iOS 4.2.5. A GSM model (model number A1332) was also available and came with iOS 4.0. The GSM model has a SIM tray on the side for a micro SIM, while the CDMA version did not have a SIM tray.

iPhone 5

Release Date: September 2012

In 2012, Apple released the iPhone 5 with iOS 6.0.

Then, in 2013, the company, for the first time, released two versions of the iPhone at the same time: iPhone 5C and iPhone 5S. Both versions come with iOS 7. The Lightning cable was introduced with the iPhone 5.

iPhone 5C and iPhone 5S

The iPhone 5C (model number A1532) was different in appearance from the iPhone 5 and was available in the following colors: green, blue, yellow, pink, and white.

The iPhone 5S (model number A1532) was available in the following colors: silver, gold and gray. The IMEI was engraved on the back of the device. The iPhone 5C (see Figure 12.16) was only available with an A6 chip and a 16 GB or 32 GB model, while the 5S had an A7 chip and a 64 GB model. The charger did change with the iPhone 5C and 5S, and also required the "Lightning" 19-pin connector for power and wired data transfer. This replaced the 30-pin connector. In terms of weight and dimensions, the models have negligible differences.

iPhone 6 and iPhone 6 Plus

The iPhone 6 and the iPhone 6 Plus were very similar in specifications except for size . The Retina HD display on the iPhone 6 is 4.7 inches, whereas the screen on the iPhone 6 Plus was 5.5 inches long. Its rounded edges and thinner profile made it easier to distinguish from earlier models. The iPhone 6 is 6.9mm, and the iPhone 6 Plus had a thickness of 7.1mm. The iPhone 6 and 6 Plus have larger screens and are thinner than their predecessors.

FIGURE 12.16 iPhone 5C

The iPhone 6 was built on a 64-bit architecture and came with an A8 chip, which was advertised as faster and more energy efficient. The battery life was apparently longer, which benefited investigators who needed to maintain power to the device. This smartphone also came with an M8 coprocessor, which measures data from the compass, accelerometer, gyroscope, and the new barometer.

Touch ID

For investigators, a critical difference between older iPhone models and newer models is the biometric authentication sensor. **Touch ID** is the name of the fingerprint sensor used to unlock the iPhone. Touch ID can also be used, instead of entering an Apple ID, to make purchases from the Apps Store. The problem for an investigator is that if a user uses this biometric sensor, the hash value associated with this is stored on the device and Apple cannot assist. Apple cannot access the iPhone if the user has used Touch ID because a fingerprint map is stored in an encrypted format in the "Secure Enclave" section of the device's A7 processor and cannot be extracted by an examiner. Nevertheless, if the reader cannot authenticate the user with her fingerprint, then the user is asked to enter her passcode. Of course, an investigator today is more likely to encounter Face ID on an Apple device, as opposed to Touch ID.

Notice in Figure 12.17 that there is a metal ring around the fingerprint reader and that this iPhone does not have the distinctive rounded square that we found on the Home button for the older iPhone and iTouch.

iPhone 11/11 Pro/11 Pro Max

After the iPhone 6 / 6 Plus came the iPhone SE (1st), iPhone 7 / 7 Plus, iPhone 8 / 8 Plus, iPhone X, iPhone XS / XS Max, and then the iPhone XR. The iPhone 11, iPhone 11 Pro, and 11 Pro Max were announced in September 2019. As with the iPhone X, these models support Face ID. These iPhones were shipped with iOS 13. The iPhone 11 Pro and Pro Max both come with an 18W Lightning to USB-C fast charger, which may benefit investigators. These models also have storage that ranges from 64 GB to 256 GB to 512 GB. The iPhone SE (2nd) was released in April 2020.

FIGURE 12.17   Touch ID

Face ID

Face ID is a facial recognition technology, developed by Apple, used to unlock recent models of the iPhone and iPad. Face ID can also be used to install apps, make payments with Apple Pay, and access sensitive data, including app and online passwords. The iPhone collects a series of infrared dots and creates a pattern based on the user's face. This pattern is stored in the iPhone's Secure Enclave. According to Apple, the *Secure Enclave is a coprocessor fabricated within the system on chip (SoC). It uses encrypted memory and includes a hardware random number generator. The Secure Enclave provides all cryptographic operations for Data Protection key management and maintains the integrity of Data Protection even if the kernel has been compromised.* Basically, the Secure Enclave is a hardware-based key manager on the iPhone, where biometrics and encryption keys are securely stored, and is separate from the iPhone's main processor. More information can be found on the Apple website, including at developer.apple.com. Face ID replaced the fingerprint recognition technology associated with Touch ID.

Although the volume of data retrieved from a MacBook may be a lot larger, than from an iOS device, the nature of evidence retrieved from an iPhone may be considerably more important. Location information, the personal nature of the device, the fact that it is usually always turned on, and recording data make it undeniably rich in terms of incriminating evidence. As we shall see, exploits, like checkm8 and checkra1n, and GrayKey, now make it possible for law enforcement to access an iPhone and gather critical evidence.

iPhone Backup

Interestingly, you can access a wealth of iPhone evidence from a synced computer. Originally, Apple required all iOS devices to be synced to a Windows Personal Computer or to a Mac computer. Today that is not the case and a user may never sync their iPhone or iPod to a computer. The user has the option to backup files from his iPhone to either the computer or to iCloud. Encrypted backups are only permitted to the user's computer (if that option is enabled by the user), but not to iCloud. Nevertheless, an iTunes backup may be password-protected. If the user has synced their iPhone to a MacBook, then the backup location may be as follows:`~/Library/ApplicationSupport/MobileSync/ Backup/`.

When an iPhone has been synced to a Windows Vista machine, or a later version of Windows, then the location of the backup folder may be located here:`\Users\<username>\AppData\Roaming\ Apple Computer\MobileSync\Backup`.

iCloud

iCloud is Apple's cloud service that is available to Apple device owners. To use the service with an iPhone, the user needs to have at a minimum iOS 5, or later. Consumers will get 5 GB for free but must pay for any additional iCloud storage. All devices belonging to the user, including a MacBook, can be backed up to iCloud and are associated through the user's Apple ID. Up to 10 devices can be registered to one iCloud account. The benefit for the investigator is that Apple can be subpoenaed for iCloud evidence. User data from apps installed on the user's iOS device is frequently backed up to iCloud. By default, some user app data is backed up to iCloud although the user may later select which apps to be backed up. Moreover, a user's apps, and associated content, are synced across devices, and therefore just having one device can provide you with evidence of what exists on another user device. The investigator should understand that 5 GB of free iCloud space is not a lot. Thus, the iCloud backup, available through Apple, will be quite limited, unless the consumer has chosen to pay for additional space.

Safari

Safari Internet browser evidence from the backup on a synced computer can be found here:

```
/private/var/mobile/Library/Safari/Bookmarks.plist
/private/var/mobile/Library/Safari/History.plist
/private/var/mobile/Library/Safari/SuspendState.plist
/private/var/mobile/Library/Safari/SMS/sms.db
/private/var/mobile/Library/Cookies/Cookies.plist
```

Mail

Email evidence from the iPhone can be retrieved from the synced computer at these locations:

```
/private/var/mobile/Library/Mail/Accounts.plist
/private/var/mobile/Library/Mail/(mail account name)/Deleted Messages
/private/var/mobile/Library/Mail/(mail account name)/Sent Messages
/private/var/mobile/Library/Mail/<account name>/Inbox
```

Photographs

Photos on the iPhone can provide a treasure trove of information about events and about the user. Like other smartphones, the iPhone will record the longitude and latitude of where a photo was taken, as EXIF data (metadata), if Location Services (under Settings > Privacy) has been enabled by the user. Using BlackLight, the investigator can use this geolocation information to plot where a suspect or a victim was.

Location Services

The iPhone has a user function called Location Services. **Location Services** is a user preference that allows an iOS device, and a variety of applications running on the device, to determine your location based on cell sites, GPS, and Wi-Fi hotspots. According to Apple, Location Services uses the aforementioned sources for location, in addition to iBeacons. An **iBeacon** uses Bluetooth Low Energy (BLE) to identify the location of a user. An iPhone, and other Bluetooth devices, can act as iBeacons, which in turn can provide Location Services with your exact location, thereby reducing the reliance on identifying a device's location based on GPS or a cell site. An iBeacon can also be used to target shoppers in a micro-location or validate that a user is present at a location where a Wallet application is being used. The commercial benefits of using iBeacons are tremendous because the location of the device can be more accurately determined.

The file path of this information will vary based on the version of iOS. Forensic evidence, related to where the user has been, can be derived from Wi-Fi and cell sites (towers/antenna), and may be found here:

```
/private/var/root/Library/Caches/location/cache_encryptedB.db
    WifiLocation
    LteCellLocation
/private/var/root/Library/Caches/com.apple.wifid/ThreeBars.sqlite
/private/var/root/Library/Caches/com.apple.routined/Cache.sqlite
    ZRTWIFIACCESSPOINTMO
    ZRTCLLOCATIONMP
```

With regard to Wi-Fi connections, it is important to understand that the SSID (network name) of access points are captured on an iPhone but does not necessarily mean that the user actually connected to a router on that network. In fact, most SSIDs recorded on smartphones are access points that a user passed by without actually connecting. Once you view the SSIDs that were logged by an iPhone, you can further research these access points on wigle.net, as shown in Figure 12.18.

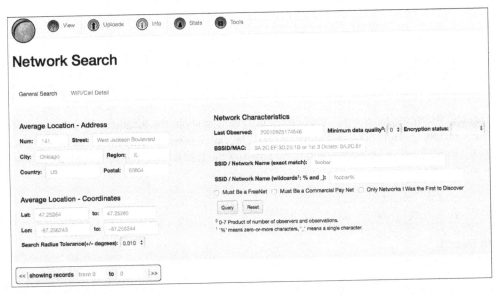

FIGURE 12.18   Wigle.net user interface

Obviously, obtaining this type of data can be extremely helpful for an investigator because you can determine the route that a user took, and even ascertain the speed at which someone was traveling. If a user disables Location Services, and then re-enables this function, the historical data will be lost. Regardless of whether Location Services is enabled or not, law enforcement can access the location of an iPhone during an emergency, and this information is based on cell site data.

When we examine the `ThreeBars.sqlite` database, we can retrieve the following SSID information: BSSID (MAC address of access point), longitude, latitude, and other helpful information.

Figure 12.19 shows a screenshot of the ThreeBars.SQLite database using a free tool called *DB Browser for SQLite* (sqlitebrowser.org).

FIGURE 12.19   View of ThreeBars.sqlite

There are several websites that can provide helpful information about the location of wireless access points (SSID), including wigle.net (see Figure 12.20). You can register for a free account at wigle.net and then you can perform an advanced search, by entering the BSSID or other information from the ThreeBars.sqlite database.

FIGURE 12.20   Wigle.net website

The ZCREATED field, in the ThreeBars.sqlite database, displays a number, which is actually an Apple Cocoa Core data timestamp. This date format is found in many SQLite databases on an iPhone. In our ThreeBars.sqlite database, we found the number *604847205*. We then visited epochconverter.com and converted that time to a human-readable format, as shown in Figure 12.21.

Enter your Core Data timestamp below (seconds or nanoseconds):

| 604847205 | × | Convert Core Data timestamp to human date |

Converting timestamp (604847205) in seconds:
GMT: Monday, March 2, 2020 1:06:45 PM
Your time zone Monday, March 2, 2020 8:06:45 AM GMT-05:00

FIGURE 12.21   Epoch Converter translates Apple Cocoa Core Data timestamp

Another forensics gem is Significant Locations, which records a list of locations where the user frequents. You will notice in Figure 12.22 that Significant Locations is connected with Photos that were taken with the user's iPhone. It is located here:

Settings > Privacy > Location Services > System Services > Significant Locations

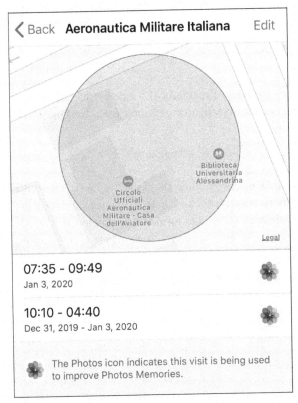

FIGURE 12.22   Significant Locations example on an iPhone

Apple states that it does collect user location information in an anonymous and encrypted manner so that the user is not identified. The data is used to create crowd-sourced Wi-Fi hotspot and cell tower locations. Apple also collects location information pertaining to traffic. They will monitor your speed on roads for a crowd-sourced road traffic database. Your location is also used to determine where you download apps, places that you frequent, and to target you for "geographically relevant iAds".

You can also find important Bluetooth information on an iPhone, which can be retrieved from here:

```
com.apple.MobileBluetooth.ledevices.other.db-wal
```

checkm8 and checkra1n

As with any mobile forensics examination, a full file system extraction is required to examine system files. An independent researcher, axi0mX, discovered an iOS exploit that works on the iPhone 4S up to and including the iPhone X. The exploit is a bootrom vulnerability, which means that it cannot be remotely patched by Apple. This exploit makes a full file system extraction possible on millions of iPhones. It is important to understand that implementing this exploit does mean jailbreaking an iPhone. Utilizing the checkm8 exploit in forensics is achieved using checkra1n. checkra1n is integrated into many iOS forensics tools, including Cellebrite UFED, or else it can be downloaded separately. A full file system extraction is possible using checkra1n when the iPhone passcode is known. A partial file system (BFU – Before First Unlock) extraction is possible using the exploit when the iPhone passcode is unknown.

iPhone Backups

iPhone backups can be very important in an investigation, especially if a suspect has attempted to remove incriminating evidence from his device. An investigator can look for a backup in the following file:

```
/private/var/mobile/Library/Preference/com.apple.mobile.ldbackup.plist
```

Within this file, there will exist a *LastCloudBackupDate*. As its name suggests, the investigator will be able to view this file to determine when the iPhone was last backed up to iCloud and then request a copy of that backup from Apple. There is just one snag – the date format is an Apple Cocoa Core Data timestamp. There are some free online converters, like epochconverter.com, where you can easily change that number to a human-readable date and time.

If you are interested in viewing the iPhone backup files on your computer, yet do not have the budget to purchase a professional digital forensics tool, like BlackLight, then you can download Decipher Backup Browser (deciphertools.com) for free (see Figure 12.23).

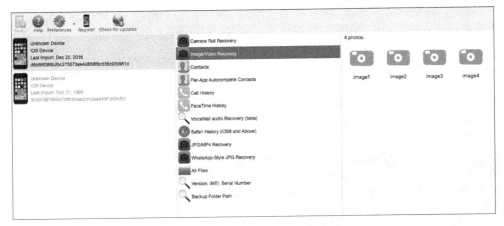

FIGURE 12.23 Decipher Backup Browser user interface

iPhone Notes

The Notes application on the iPhone can also be an important source of evidence and that data can be found in the following file:

```
NoteStore.sqlite-wal
```

Chapter 10, "Mobile App Investigations", provides further details about apps of interest to investigators.

iPhone Photos

Chapter 11, "Photograph Forensics", provides an in-depth look at photo forensics. However, it is important to mention one key source of evidence. It is not uncommon for a suspect to delete photographic evidence from her iPhone. Nevertheless, when this happens, thumbnails of those images will still exist on the device at the following location:

```
/private/var/mobile/Media/PhotoData/thumbnails/
```

Typically, an investigator will find numerous JPEG files in the Photos folder on an iPhone or on a Mac. However, sometimes there will be photos with a .HEIC file extension. **High Efficiency Image Format (HEIF)** is a container of one or more photos that is commonly found on smartphones. There are a number of free tools online that will enable you to convert the HEIC file format to JPEG. There is native support for this file format with the introduction of High Sierra (macOS 10.13). Microsoft also supports this file format in Windows 10.

KTX Snapshots

A user of an iPhone X or an iPhone 11 knows that in order to quickly access a running application you can swipe up on the screen, and then select an app based on a picture of the last state of the app, as shown in Figure 12.24. KTX files cannot be examined natively on a Windows PC and only on a Mac. An investigator can actually view these application snapshots in the following file:

```
/private/var/mobile/Library/Splashboard/Snapshots/com.apple.mobileslideshow/sceneID_
com.apple...
```

Several tools that are available to investigators who wish to examine these KTX Snapshots, including iOS Snapshot Triage Parser and SnapshotImageFinder.py.

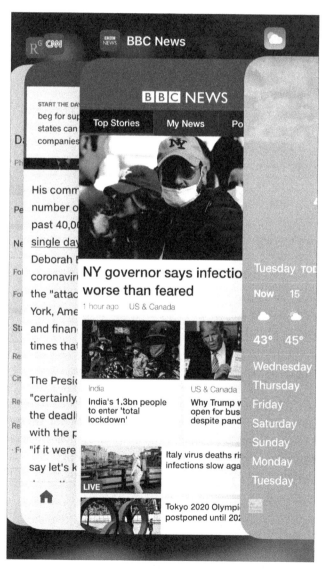

FIGURE 12.24   Snapshot of running apps on an iPhone

iPhone User Events

As we already learned, system files, including events, are not available with a traditional (logical) image of an iPhone. If we use checkm8 (checkm8.info) and checkra1n (checkra.in), then we can obtain a full file system extraction. Understanding when a suspect did something on his iPhone can be just as important as the evidence itself. Therefore, the `KnowledgeC.db` is tremendously important as it provides information about when particular events took place. On an iPhone, the database can be found here:

```
/private/var/mobile/ library/CoreDuet/Knowledge/KnowledgeC.db
```

Within `KnowledgeC.db`, if you want to get information about when the iPhone camera was used, you can access the following file:

```
com.apple.camera
```

You could also use the `KnowledgeC.db` to identify when a search was performed with Apple Maps. Within the `KnowledgeC.db`, an examination of the ZOBJECT and ZSTRUCTUREMETADATA tables will show when an application was installed by the user. An investigator can also determine the device lock states in the `KnowledgeC.db`. For example, after a car accident, an investigator could determine if a user's device was locked or unlocked at the time of an accident.

The `KnowledgeC.db` file is also available on the Mac, in the following location:

```
~/Library/Application Support/Knowledge/
```

Other files of interest that relate to network locations on an iPhone, which can be retrieved with a full file system extraction, after using checkra1n, include the following:

```
SMS Folder
sms-temp.db
 /private/var/db/dhcp_leases
 /private/var/db/dhcpclient/leases
 /private/var/mobile/Library/preferences/com.apple.MobileSMS.plist
 /private/var/mobile/Library/preferences/com.apple.locationd.plist
 /private/var/mobile/Library/preferences/com.apple.wifi.plist
 /private/var/mobile/Library/Caches/location/cache.plist
```

Apple Pattern of Life Lazy Output'er APOLLO

Apple Pattern of Life Lazy Output'er (APOLLO) is a tool that pulls from a number of iPhone SQLite databases to provide an in-depth picture of a user's interaction with a device over time. The benefit of using the tool is that the investigator does not have to examine dozens of app databases but rather can use one tool to automate the process of seeing most of the user's activities. The tool pulls data from the following databases:

- `KnowledgeC.db`
- `routined` databases

- `netusage.db`

- `locationd` databases

- `InteractionsC.db`

- `PowerLogs`

- `ADDataStore.sqlite.db`

- `healthdb_secure.sqlite`

As you can imagine, integrating health information with location data and other simultaneously gathered data can be extremely helpful to an investigator. For example, if a suspect shot a person and then ran away. Having location information tied to heart rate and steps is clearly advantageous. As previously mentioned, a full file system extraction, using checkra1n, is necessary to obtain system information in addition to user data.

Enterprise Deployment of Apple Devices

Apple Configurator is the framework for enterprise deployment of the iPhone, iPad, or Apple TV. Apple Configurator 2 is now available to users. It is a free download from the App Store, and it is available for iOS 5 and above. The Configurator allows for tremendous control of devices in the enterprise. For example, the enterprise administrator can configure the user lock-screen or prevent the user from syncing the device with a computer. The administrator can also restrict applications being installed on the device, restrict voice calls, use of Siri, and can control/restrict a variety of other functions on the user device.

A home user may also choose to use it to control use of Apple devices in the home. For example, a device used by a child can have restrictions placed on that device by a parent. It is therefore important to identify whether a device is under the control of the enterprise, in order to determine what types of activities a suspect may have carried out. Moreover, you are likely to need the support of the Apple Configurator administrator during your investigation. The profiles for Configuration can be found in the following path:

`/root/mobile/Library/ConfigurationProfiles`

There are three parts to Configurator:

- **Prepare Devices:** This function of Configurator allows an administrator to set up each device with a profile, which could be standardized across the organization. The administrator may choose to update the device to the latest iOS version, install apps, and so on.

- **Supervise Devices:** This function in Configurator gives the administrator control over groups of devices that have apps, profiles, and settings in common. This function enforces configuration standards imposed by the administrator. A supervised device cannot be configured or supervised by other computers running Configurator.

■ **Assign Devices:** This function allows the administrator to set up users and groups. The administrator can utilize this function to assign devices to users.

Battery

The iPhone 11 battery is a lithium ion (Li-ion) battery. If the battery on an iPhone dies, the time on the device will default to epoch time (January 1, 1970).

Performing a Mac Forensics Examination

As with any examination of a digital device, it is important for the investigator to understand the type of MacBook (or Mac computer) that will be examined. Each MacBook model has different ports, like a USB or a USB-C, or a FireWire connection, and this will determine the options that you have available in terms of how the device can be imaged and whether the hard drive can be easily removed or not. Determining the operating system will provide some guidance about what security features the examiner may encounter. Finally, the hardware and software running on the computer will also impact the investigator, including whether it has a T2 chipset with Secure Boot, has FileVault (encryption) running, and whether the system has APFS. The FCC-ID and serial number, often found at the bottom of the computer, can help the investigator to understand the type of Mac that they encounter (or will encounter) and the hardware and software potentially running on the device. The FCC-ID is a number, assigned by the Federal Communications Commission (FCC), to a device. An investigator can take the device FCC-ID and find out more about that device on the FCC website (fcc.gov). Apple maintains a website (checkcoverage.apple.com) where an investigator can enter a serial number and determine the MacBook or Mac's technical specifications. Although not forensically sound, you can click the Apple menu, and then click **About This Mac** to find out more information about the computer, as shown in Figure 12.25.

FIGURE 12.25   About This Mac

Given that encryption is arguably the biggest hurdle that law enforcement faces with Mac computers, if an investigator sees that a Mac is powered on and a password-enabled screensaver is not displayed, then perhaps this may be the only opportunity to image the device—especially if a suspect is uncooperative in providing a password.

An investigator can check System Preferences > Security and Privacy > FileVault to see if FileVault is enabled, as shown in Figure 12.26.

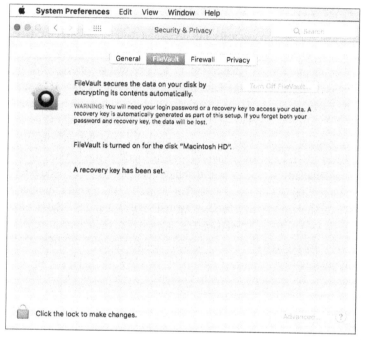

FIGURE 12.26   Security & Privacy dialog box

An investigator could then use a forensics tool, like RECON TRIAGE, from SUMURI, to perform live imaging. This tool can also be used to image RAM (virtual memory). Most importantly, as with any computer, always check the system time and document it and the actual time in your time zone. Ultimately, you will want to obtain a .DMG image of the Mac hard drive and then mount that image to view with a (read-only) forensics tool.

In terms of screen capture, the follow options are available on a Mac:

- Full-screen capture: **command + shift** +3
- User-defined screen capture: **command + shift + 4**
- Window screen capture: **command + shift + 4 + spacebar**

Case Studies

From its initial release in 2007 to 2018, Apple has sold 2.2 billion iPhones, which is staggering. Apple announced in November 2018 that it will no longer report its iPhone unit sales figures. Sales of the company's popular iPads have also been astounding. Therefore, iOS devices are being used as a source of evidence more and more to successfully convict criminals. The following are just a few ways that criminals have been brought to justice using evidence from iOS devices.

Find My iPhone

Police in Astoria, Oregon, were contacted by a victim of iPhone theft. The victim used the Find My iPhone app to locate where the iPhone was and subsequently informed police of the location. Police were on the scent and ended up in a convenience store and then dialed the number of the iPhone. Scott Simons, 23 years old of Oysterville, Washington, was found in possession of the iPhone. Simons was not only found in possession of the stolen iPhone but also had drug paraphernalia and heroin residue on his person. Additionally, Simons was already on probation for aggravated theft.

Wanted Hactevist

Higinio O. Ochoa III, the suspected CabinCr3w hacktivist, and computer programmer, was wanted in the United States in connection with hacking into at least four U.S. law enforcement websites. Ochoa used his iPhone to take a picture of his girlfriend who was wearing a sign that taunted law enforcement. Unfortunately for Ochoa, and fortunately for the FBI, the photo that was posted online contained location information in the image's EXIF data. The longitude and latitude data in the photo metadata led police to the exact house in Wantirna South, Melbourne, Australia, where Ochoa was hiding.

Michael Jackson

One of the most publicized murder trials of 2011 was that of Dr. Conrad Murray, Michael Jackson's personal physician. Dr. Murray recorded Michael Jackson's last words, as Jackson was dying, on his iPhone. Prosecutors were successfully able to admit this audio file, from Murray's iPhone as evidence and play it to the jury. This evidence was certainly important in successfully convicting Murray.

Stolen iPhone

Katy McCaffrey had her iPhone stolen on a Disney Wonder Cruise. Unbeknownst to the thief, a backup of all McCaffrey's photos were stored in her iCloud account. Once the suspect took photos of himself and his co-workers, McCaffrey retrieved these photos from her iCloud account and posted these images to her Facebook page in an album called "Stolen iPhone Adventures". Many of the photos featured an employee with the nametag "Nelson". She also sent the photos to Disney. It is unclear what Disney actually did in the end with the evidence that they received.

Drug Bust

Palo Alto Police tracked a stolen iPad to an apartment complex using GPS. Police officers did not have a search warrant, but the occupants agreed to allow police to enter the apartment. Police found 780 pounds of crystal methamphetamine and $35 million in cash, which is one of the largest drug busts in history.

Murder Trial

Hussein Khavari was put on trial in Germany for the rape and murder of Maria Ladenburger in 2016. Evidence from the Apple Health app was used as corroborating evidence to prove that he walked down to a riverbank with the victim's body and subsequently climbed back up the stairs.

Summary

Mac forensics is a relatively new field of study, yet it has rapidly grown in importance over the past few years. macOS, and its HFS+ and APFS file systems, are very different from Microsoft Windows and NTFS because they are based on the UNIX operating system. It is advisable for an investigator to use a Macintosh computer when examining either a Mac or an iOS device because the HFS+ and APFS are case-sensitive file systems and because you will need a Mac to open and view certain files.

iOS is a scaled-down version of macOS, which is certainly a benefit for investigators. Unfortunately, as new versions of iOS are released and consumers are prompted to upgrade their devices, security and encryption have also improved dramatically, so retrieving evidence is becoming more and more difficult. Additionally, fewer people are now syncing their iOS devices to a Mac or PC because it is no longer required as part of the activation process and devices are now synced through a user's iCloud account.

Understanding the Apple Environment is important because evidence can be found on a range of inter-connected, synced, devices in the home or office. Overlapping evidence can be found on an iPhone, Mac, AirPort Time Capsule, and iCloud.

SQLite databases, associated with mobile applications are usually unencrypted and have grown in importance. One reason for their growing importance is the fact that many users (and criminals) are using multiple applications for communication with friends (or co-conspirators) instead of making traditional cellular voice calls.

checkm8 and checkra1n can now be used to acquire a full file system image from an iPhone, which has significantly benefited investigations in recent times. A full file system image will include vital system data, including Health app data.

Key Terms

AFF4 (Advanced Forensic File Format): An open (non-proprietary) image file format.

AirDrop: A feature of iOS 7 and above that allows a user to share photos, videos, contacts, and other data via Bluetooth with other users in close proximity.

AirPlay: An Apple-proprietary protocol for wirelessly streaming content from the Internet and between compatible devices.

AirPort Express: A Wi-Fi base station that allows a user to connect other Apple devices and wirelessly stream content on a simultaneous dual-band 802.11n Wi-Fi protocol.

AirPort Extreme: A Wi-Fi base station that possesses many of the same characteristics as AirPort Express but is designed for a larger home, a small business, or a classroom.

AirPort Time Capsule: An automatic wireless backup drive for Mac users.

allocation block: A unit of space that is typically 512 bytes for a hard drive.

allocation block number: A 32-bit number that identifies an allocation block.

alternative volume header: A copy of the volume header located 1024 bytes at the end of the volume.

APFS (Apple File System): A file system released by Apple, for use on its Macintosh computers as well as for mobile devices, like the iPhone.

APFS Free Queue: Allocated blocks on a volume, not found in a logical acquisition, which are not referenced by the file system but can contain valuable evidence.

Apple Configurator: The framework for enterprise deployment of the iPhone, iPad, and Apple TV.

Boot Camp: A tool which allows an Intel-based Macintosh to run multiple operating systems.

catalog file: A file that contains detailed information about a file, including the filename and folder name.

Catalog ID: A unique sequential number that is created when a new file is created on a Mac.

Cocoa: A framework for developers of macOS that contains APIs (application programming interfaces), libraries, and runtimes and is largely based on Objective-C.

Container Keybag: An encryption feature in APFS that maintains the Volume Keybags and the Volume Encryption Key (VEK) on a Mac.

copy-on-write: A feature that creates a clone of files, whereby only changes to the file are made to the file clone, which is more efficient compared to journaling.

Core Foundation (CF): A framework that provides useful fundamental software services to developers building applications for macOS and iOS.

CoreStorage: A feature that forms the foundation for Fusion Drives and displays partitions on multiple drives as one drive.

data cloning: An APFS feature, whereby when data is duplicated, within a container, regardless of the volume, the data content is not replicated and only the metadata is duplicated.

data fork: Part of files from older Macintosh file system that consist of data.

Data Protection: A feature developed by Apple to keep all files encrypted in flash memory while allowing the user to receive phone calls, text messages, and emails when the device is locked.

Device Firmware Upgrade (DFU) Mode: A mode that enables the user to select the firmware version that they wish to install on the device.

DMG: An exact copy of a file, or a collection of files, or a volume, which has been the default image format for distributing applications for macOS.

Face ID: A facial recognition security feature, developed by Apple, used to unlock recent models of the iPhone and iPad.

FileVault: A volume encryption tool, developed by Apple, for use with Macintosh computers.

FireWire: Also referred to as IEEE 1394, which allows for high-speed data transfer.

Fusion Drive: A Mac technology takes two drives, e.g., an SSD and HDD or SSD and SSD, and makes them seamlessly operate as one SSD. Fusion Drives are not compatible with APFS.

Gatekeeper: A macOS security feature that enforces code signing for downloaded apps before executing those applications.

Hierarchical File System (HFS): A file system that was developed by Apple in 1985 to support its hard disk drive.

Hierarchical File System Extended (HFS+): An Apple proprietary file system that supports larger files that uses Unicode.

High Efficiency Image Format (HEIF): A container of one or more photos that is commonly found on smartphones.

iBeacon: An Apple feature for app developers that uses Bluetooth Low Energy (BLE) for identifying the location of a user.

iBoot: The second phase of the bootloader that verifies and mounts the iOS kernel.

iCloud: Apple's Cloud service that is available to Apple device owners.

iCloud Keychain: An area on a disk that stores all of the user's online passwords, using 256-bit AES encryption, on approved Macs and iOS devices registered to the user.

initialization: The term used to refer to formatting a drive in macOS.

Key Encryption Key (KEK): A cryptographic key in APFS that is derived from each user's password on a system and the Recovery Key.

keybags: The area on a disk that stores encryption information for an Apple Macintosh or iOS device, including the encryption keys.

Location Services: A user preference that allows an iOS device and a variety of applications running on the device to determine user location based on cell sites, GPS, and Wi-Fi hotspots.

Macintosh File System (MFS): A flat file system that was introduced with Apple's Macintosh computer in 1984.

Media partition: The data partition on an iOS device; contains both user data and some system files.

Notifications: A convenient way for the Apple Mac user to be notified about incoming messages, respond to FaceTime requests or Website alerts without exiting an application.

Objective-C: An object-oriented programming language that is based on the C language and was developed in the early 1980s by NeXT.

PList (property list) Format files: Configuration files found on a computer running the Mac operating system.

plutil (property list utility): A tool found in macOS that can check the syntax of PList files or can be used to convert a PList to another format.

Quick Look: A feature of macOS that allows the user to preview the contents of a file without opening the file or starting its associated application.

Recovery Mode: enables the user to restore his iPhone settings to the original factory settings.

resource fork: In an older Mac file system, the part of a file that consists of the file metadata and associated application information.

root partition: The first partition in an iOS device, which contains the operating system.

sleepimage: A copy of the contents of RAM that is copied to the computer's hard drive when the computer goes into hibernate mode.

snapshot: A backup of an APFS volume, in a container, which can be used to restore files and data.

space sharing: A feature that allows multiple file systems to share the same underlying free space on a physical volume, which is unlike rigid partitioning schemes that pre-allocate a fixed amount of space for each file system; APFS-formatted volumes can grow and shrink without volume repartitioning.

sparse bundle: A virtual file, introduced with macOS 10.5 for use with FileVault, which will grow in size as more files are added.

sparse image: A virtual file for macOS that grows in size as more files are added.

Spotlight: A feature found in macOS that quickly finds files, folders, applications as soon as the user starts typing a name in the Spotlight search field.

System Software Personalization: A process, developed by Apple, which prevents a user from downgrading an iOS device to an earlier version of iOS firmware.

Tags: A feature of macOS that enables the user to organize files with keywords.

Touch ID: The name of the fingerprint sensor used to unlock the iPhone.

unique device identifier (UDID): A 40-digit alpha-numeric identifier that uniquely identifies each Apple iOS device.

USB Restricted Mode: A security feature, introduced with iOS 11.4.1, which prevents a trusted computer from unlocking an iOS device.

Vacuuming: A cleanup feature associated with SQLite databases that permanently erases deleted records or tables.

volume header: A header that contains information about the volume, including the time and date of its creation and the number of files stored on that volume.

Volume Encryption Key (VEK): A file system key that is used to encrypt data blocks on a volume (disk).

Volume Keybags: An encryption feature in APFS that maintains a series of Key Encryption Keys (KEK) on a Mac.

Assessment

CLASSROOM DISCUSSIONS

1. How is Mac forensics different from forensics on a Windows personal computer?

2. When working with an "Apple Environment" at a suspect's home, what Apple devices are of potential value for an investigator?

3. What type of help can Apple potentially provide law enforcement in an investigation involving Apple devices?

MULTIPLE-CHOICE QUESTIONS

1. Which of the following devices includes a hard drive for backing up data?

   A. AirPort Express

   B. AirPort Time Capsule

   C. AirPort Express

   D. AirPort Extended

2. Which of the following is also referred to as IEEE 1394 and allows for high-speed data transfer?

   A. FireWire

   B. Thunderbolt

   C. USB 3

   D. Ethernet

3. Which of the following is a feature of macOS that enables the user to organize files with keywords?

   A. Cocoa

   B. iCloud

   C. iBeacon

   D. Tags

4. Which of the following uses Bluetooth Low Energy (BLE) to identify the location of a user?

   A. Cocoa

   B. iCloud

   C. iBeacon

   D. Tags

5. Which of the following enables the user to restore his iPhone settings to the original factory settings?

    A. Recovery Mode

    B. Device Firmware Upgrade Mode

    C. iBoot

    D. Restoration Mode

6. Which of the following stores all of the user's online passwords, using 256-bit AES encryption, on approved Macs and iOS devices registered to the user?

    A. FileVault

    B. DMG

    C. Root partition

    D. iCloud Keychain

7. Which of the following is a virtual file for macOS that grows in size as more files are added?

    A. Media partition

    B. Sleepimage

    C. PList

    D. Sparse image

8. Which of the following is a feature for the Apple Mac user to see incoming messages, respond to FaceTime requests or website alerts without exiting an application?

    A. Quick Look

    B. Notifications

    C. Apple Configurator

    D. Spotlight

9. Which of the following is an object-oriented programming language that is based on the C language and was developed in the early 1980s by NeXT?

    A. Python

    B. Java

    C. C++

    D. Objective-C

10. Which of the following is a feature found in macOS that quickly finds files, folders, applications as soon as the user starts typing a name in the search field?

    A. Spotlight

    B. AirDrop

    C. plutil

    D. Quick Look

FILL IN THE BLANKS

1. Apple _____ is the framework for enterprise deployment of the iPhone, iPad, and iPod.

2. _____ is a volume encryption tool developed by Apple for use with Macintosh computers.

3. _____ File System is the file system that was developed by Apple in 1985 to support its hard disk drive.

4. _____ Services is a user preference that allows an iOS device and a variety of applications running on the device to determine your position based on cell sites, GPS, and Wi-Fi hotspots.

5. _____ Mode enables the user to restore his iPhone settings to the original factory settings.

6. _____ is the name of the file that is a copy of the contents of RAM that is copied to the computer's hard drive when the computer goes into hibernate mode.

7. _____ is a cleanup feature associated with SQLite databases that will permanently erase deleted records or tables.

8. Boot _____ is a tool which allows an Intel-based Macintosh to run multiple operating systems.

9. A(n) _____ uses Bluetooth Low Energy (BLE) for identifying the location of a user.

10. _____ Lists are configuration files found on computers running the Mac operating system.

PROJECTS

iPhone App Tutorial

Using BlackLight, perform an examination of a mobile app and write an investigator's guide to retrieving evidence from that app.

iOS Forensics Tools

Create a user manual detailing information about various iOS forensics tools.

APFS

Create a user manual that discusses how APFS has changed Mac and iOS investigations and detail how to conduct an examination on a Mac and iPhone with APFS and a Macintosh with macOS Catalina (or higher).

Chapter | **13**

Case Studies

Learning Outcomes

After reading this chapter, you will be able to understand the following:

- Investigating Dark Web marketplaces;
- The importance of computer forensics in proving intent to commit a crime;
- How computer forensics is used at trial and the types of objections that may arise;
- The role of a computer forensics examiner as an expert witness;
- How digital forensics can potentially be used in any type of investigation or court proceeding;
- The problem of cyberbullying and digital evidence used to investigate these types of crimes;
- Anti-cyberbullying legislation; and
- How the use of digital files was challenged in the investigation of steroid use by Major League Baseball players.

Case studies that effectively illustrate the use of computer forensics at trial, or in investigations, are often hard to find. Exhibits from trial often are simply unavailable to the public. This happens in child abuse trials or trials that are subject to appeal. In other situations, the trial exhibits might be available from a court system but have a charge associated with access to them.

This chapter provides very different examples of cases involving digital forensics, from attempted murder, to serial killings, to bullying, to drug abuse in sports.

Silk Road

Ross Ulbricht, later known as "Dread Pirate Roberts", was a self-proclaimed libertarian, Graduate Research Assistant, from Austin, Texas, who was studying at Pennsylvania State University (see Figure 13.1). He decided to create a Dark Web marketplace called Silk Road. The marketplace was home to numerous criminal retailers who sold a plethora of narcotics and many other illegal products, including fake government documents, like drivers' licenses and passports, weapons and ammunition, and other illegal goods. At one point, there were 13,000 listings of controlled substances and more than 100,000 buyers. Over a period of two and a half years, 9.5 million Bitcoin were transacted, which at the time of trial was the equivalent of $1.3 billion USD. Silk Road allegedly pocketed $85 million in commissions.

FIGURE 13.1   LinkedIn profile of Ross Ulbrict

During the trial, Ulbricht's defense team argued that their client began the Silk Road as a class experiment, which he ultimately abandoned years before he was arrested. Thus, the use of digital evidence in this case was of the utmost importance to federal prosecutors.

Genesis of the Silk Road

In 2011, Ulbricht registered the website silkroad420.wordpress.com. During this time, Ulbricht created a user account on shroomery.org, with the username "Altoid" and submitted a post promoting Silk Road (see Figure 13.2):

> I came across this website called Silk Road. It's a Tor hidden service that claims to allow you to buy and sell anything online anonymously. I'm thinking of buying off it, but wanted to see if anyone here had heard of it and could recommend it.
>
> I found it through silkroad420.wordpress.com, which, if you have a tor browser, directs you to the real site at http://tydgccykixpbu6uz.onion.
>
> Let me know what you think…

FIGURE 13.2   Shroomery.org website with Ulbricht posting

Ulbricht also created a user account on Bitcointalk Forum and then posted an advertisement for an employment opportunity, as follows:

> the best and brightest IT pro in the bitcoin community [to] be the lead developer in a venture-backed bitcoin startup company

Those interested were asked to contact rossulbricht@gmail.com (see Figure 13.3).

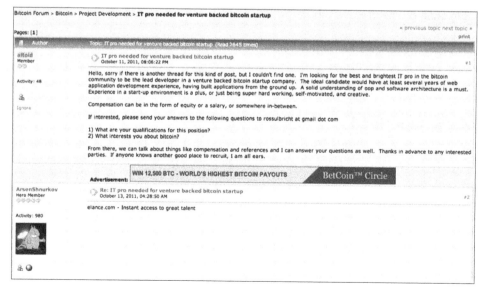

FIGURE 13.3   Bitcointalk Forum with Ulbricht posting

Investigators linked Ulbricht's email to his Google+ account (see Figure 13.4), and Google was later subpoenaed for information related to his Google accounts. In April 2012, Ulbricht posted on Google+, "anybody know someone that works for UPS, FedEX, or DHL?"

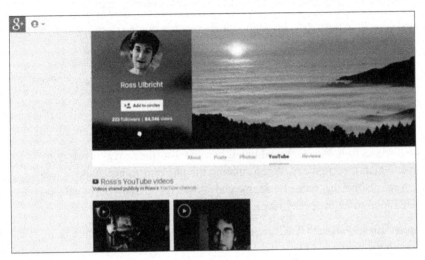

FIGURE 13.4   Ulbricht's Google+ account

Ross Ulbricht also posted a question under the name "Ross Ulbricht" on the website Stack Overflow:

How can I connect to a Tor hidden service using curl in php?

I'm trying to connect to a tor hidden service using the following php:

$url = 'http://jhiwjjlqpyawmpjx.onion/'

$ch = curl_init();

curl_setopt($ch, CURLOPT_URL, $url);

curl_setopt($ch, CURLOPT_RETURNTRANSFER, true);

curl_setopt($ch, CURLOPT_PROXY, "http://127.0.0.1:9050/");

curl_setopt($ch, CURLOPT_PROXYTYPE, CURLPROXY_SOCKS5);

$output = curl_exec($ch);

$curl_error = curl_error($ch);

curl_close($ch);

print_r($output);

print_r($curl_error);

when I run it I get the following error:

Couldn't resolve host name

However, when I run the following command from my command line in ubuntu:

curl -v --socks5-hostname localhost:9050 http://jhiwjjlqpyawmpjx.onion

I get a response as expected

the php cURL documentations says this:

--socks5-hostname

Use the specified SOCKS5 proxy (and let the proxy resolve the host name).

I believe the reason it works from the command line is because Tor (the proxy) is resolving the .onion hostname, which it recognizes. When running the php above, my guess is that cURL or php is trying to resolve the .onion hostname and doesn't recognize it. I've searched for a way to tell cURL/php to let the proxy resolve the hostname, but can't find a way.

There is a very similar question here: CURL request using socks5 proxy fails when using PHP but works through the command line

Death Threat

According to court records, in March 2013, a Silk Road seller, with the username "Friendly Chemist", threatened to reveal the real name of DPR (Dread Pirate Roberts) unless hush money, in the amount of $300,000 (later $500,000), was paid. DPR then allegedly asked a user on the Silk Road, called "redandwhite", to execute FriendlyChemist, in exchange for $150,000 (1,760 Bitcoins). DPR subsequently provided the real name and address for FriendlyChemist.

Silk Road Takedown

Ulbricht decided to order some fake drivers' licenses from a criminal retailer on the Silk Road (see Figure 13.5). In June 2013, U.S. Border Control agents at the Canadian border interdicted these fake licenses. In July 2013, Homeland Security visited the residence to where these licenses were being shipped, and they encountered Ross Ulbricht. Ulbricht himself actually informed Homeland Security about a great website called the Silk Road, where he made the purchase.

Ultimately, federal investigators tracked Ulbricht to the Bay Area (San Francisco, CA). They determined that his Gmail account was accessed from a computer in the area and also realized that the Silk Road server had been accessed from an Internet café beside the residence of Ulbricht's friend. Investigators had subpoenaed Comcast for information related to the secure server that had been accessed via a virtual private network (VPN).

FIGURE 13.5   Fake drivers' licenses sent to Ulbricht

The Takedown of Ulbricht

DHS Special Agent, Jared Der-Yeghiayan, managed to infiltrate the Silk Road by posing as a site administrator, with the username "cirrus". Investigators had two major concerns: (1) that Ulbricht likely had encryption running on his laptop, which would later be problematic for forensics investigators and (2) that he would later deny involvement in the Silk Road site.

At one point, Ulbricht was staying at his friend's place in the San Francisco Bay Area. When the Internet connection was cut to the apartment, Ulbricht decided to use the free Wi-Fi at the Glen Park Library, where investigators planned an undercover operation to take down Ulbricht. At 15:08, Ulbricht opened his laptop and logged into the staff chat for the Silk Road site (see Figure 13.6). Special Agent Der-Yeghiayan contacted Ulbricht, who had logged in as "dread" and the following chat transpired:

> cirrus: hey
>
> can you check out one of the flagged messages for me?
>
> dread: you did bitcoin exchange before you worked for me, right?
>
> cirrus: yes, but just for a little bit
>
> dread: not any more then?

cirrus: no, I stopped because of reporting requirements

dread: damn regulators, eh?

ok, which post?

cirrus: lol, yep

there was the one with the atlantis

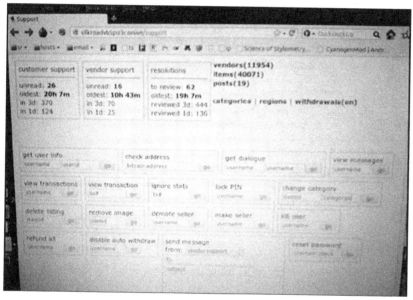

FIGURE 13.6   Screenshot of the Silk Road support page (administrator view)

Once Ulbricht ("dread") said "ok, which post?", Special Agent Der-Yeghiayan knew that Ulbricht was on the flagged message page and therefore had administrator access. Two undercover agents, male and female, feigned an argument near Ulbricht, in the Science Fiction section of the library. Ulbricht stood up and turned around. The woman held onto Ulbricht while the male agent grabbed Ulbricht's laptop, so that the computer remained on, and so that any potential encryption would not be implemented. Ultimately, it was determined that the seized Samsung 700z laptop was in fact running TrueCrypt (full disk encryption software). The agents could then show that Ulbricht was still logged into the Silk Road and he was using TorChat with backups, which would later assist investigators.

Ross Ulbricht Pre-trial

The defense counsel argued that the FBI hacked into a server in Iceland without a warrant. The defense subsequently filed a motion to suppress the evidence from that server. This server was supposedly used to host the Silk Road Dark Web marketplace. On June 12, 2013, a request was made to the Icelandic authorities to:

> (1) obtain subscriber information associated with the Subject Server; (2) collect routing information for communications sent to and from the Subject Server, including historical routing data from the prior 90 days; and (3) covertly image the contents of the Subject Server

Subsequently, the Reykjavik Metropolitan Police (the "RMP") acted upon this request. It appears that these results, by the RMP, were shared with U.S. authorities on July 29, 2013. Going back to the motion to suppress, the judge ruled that Ulbricht "failed to submit anything establishing that he has a personal privacy interest in the Icelandic server or any of the other items imaged and/or searched and/or seized." The issue for Ulbricht's defense counsel is that showing a personal privacy interest in the Icelandic server could imply that he was in fact still involved with the Silk Road at that time and they wanted to argue that he created the idea of the Silk Road but then abandoned the site.

The U.S. government did not just rely on digital evidence at trial but could also rely on the testimony of a number of people, including a narcotics dealer associated with the Silk Road. His name was Cornelis Jan Slomp, aged 22, from Woerden, the Netherlands (see Figure 13.7). Also known as "SuperTrips", Jan Slomp was the largest vendor on the site and was responsible for 10,000 transactions, which were worth 385,000 Bitcoin. Jan Slomp was arrested at Miami Airport, as he was about to get into his rented Lamborghini. Investigators found his fingerprints on DVD cases that he used to ship the drugs. In a plea deal, he offered to testify about his activities during the Ulbricht case, but he was never called to testify. His plea led to a more lenient sentence of 10 years, instead of potentially 40 years behind bars.

FIGURE 13.7 LinkedIn profile of Cornelis Jan Slomp, a.k.a. SuperTrips

Unfortunately, prior to testimony, the U.S. government inadvertently leaked a list of exhibits online that they intended to use at trial, which included potential objections by defense counsel. Figure 13.8 shows some of the leaked exhibits and potential objections.

103A	Screenshot: walk-through of UC purchase of "Brown Heroin No3 0.2 Gram"	No venue; Foundation (no date); No unilateral conspiracy; Not part of charged conspiracy, Rules 401/402, Fed.R.Evid.; Rule 403, Fed.R.Evid.
103B	Screenshot: walk-through of UC purchase of "0,5Gr Uncut Crack Cocaine"	No venue; Foundation (no date); No unilateral conspiracy; Not part of charged conspiracy, Rules 401/402, Fed.R.Evid.; Rule 403, Fed.R.Evid.
104	Picture of approximately 30 boxes of drug shipments seized from Chicago O'Hare	No venue; No unilateral conspiracy; Not part of charged conspiracy, Rules 401/402, Fed.R.Evid.; Rule 403, Fed.R.Evid.
104A	Sample box containing approximately 47 seized envelopes	No venue; No unilateral conspiracy; Not part of charged conspiracy, Rules 401/402, Fed.R.Evid.; Rule 403, Fed.R.Evid.

FIGURE 13.8   U.S. government leaked exhibits with potential objections

Ross Ulbricht on Trial

Special Agents Chris Tarbell and Illhwan Yum, CY2 (Cyber Crimes Squad), FBI, both worked on the case and gave testimony at trial. Illhwan Yum testified that investigators had tracked 3,760 Bitcoin transactions to Ulbricht after the time that Ulbricht had claimed that he had abandoned to site. Yum cross-checked transactions on the public ledger (Blockchain) with data pulled from Ulbricht's laptop and the Silk Road web server. Evidence was also presented that showed Bitcoin transfers from servers located in Philadelphia, Pennsylvania, and from Reykjavik, Iceland.

According to the "Declaration of Christopher Tarbell", the location of the Silk Road server was a result of the login interface, for the site, leaking its IP address. During the login process, some packets sent by the web server contained an IP address that was different from the IP addresses of known Tor nodes. It appears as though the IP address for the web server was leaked as a result of a misconfigured CAPTCHA, which was an application used to prevent automated bots from logging into the site.

Laptop Evidence

A logbook was found on Ulbricht's laptop, which detailed his day-to-day activities. Ulbricht's PGP private key was also recovered from the laptop, and this key was used for signing messages from DPR (Dread Pirate Roberts). Numerous .php files, used to create the Silk Road website, were also retrieved from his laptop (see Figures 13.9–13.11). Investigators also discovered an application for economic citizenship in Dominica. Ulbricht perhaps thought that he would become a legend because of his marketplace and therefore kept a journal on his laptop. In one entry he wrote the following:

I am creating a year of prosperity and power beyond what I have ever experienced. Silk Road is going to become a phenomenon and at least one person will tell me about it, unknowing that I was its creator

His entry in December 2011 stated the following:

I felt compelled to reveal myself to her. It was terrible. I told her I have secrets. She already knows I work with bitcoin wich [sic] is terrible. I'm so stupid. Everyone knows I am working on a bitcoin exchange. I always thought honesty was the best policy and now I don't know what to do. I should have just told everyone I am a freelance programmer or something, but I had to tell half-truths. It felt wrong to lie completely so I tried to tell the truth without revealing the bad parts, but now I am in a jam. Everyone knows too much, dammit.

FIGURE 13.9   FTK image from Ross Ulbricht's laptop

FIGURE 13.10   FTK image from Ross Ulbricht's laptop, showing files related to the Silk Road

FIGURE 13.11   Screenshot of bitcoin transactions from Ulbricht's laptop

Trial Verdict

The trial of Ross Ulbricht lasted 13 days and was followed by 3.5 hours of jury deliberations. Ulbricht was found guilty on the following charges:

- Narcotics trafficking conspiracy
- Computer hacking conspiracy
- Money laundering conspiracy

Las Vegas Massacre

On October 1, 2017, 64-year-old, Stephen Craig Paddock, from Babbling Brook, Mesquite, Nevada, who was staying at the Mandalay Bay in Las Vegas, shot and killed 58 people and injured 700 others in the largest massacre in U.S. history. The motive for the attack still remains a mystery, although an investigation of his digital devices does provide some indication of his intent. The Las Vegas Metropolitan Police Department (LVMPD) released a report that provided some preliminary findings about the crime and evidence that was obtained from his digital devices. According to the report, 21,560 hours of video were reviewed, 251,099 images were analyzed, while four laptops and three cellphones were also examined.

The following Google searches were discovered on one of Paddock's laptops – an HP laptop:

- **On 05-18-17:** Searches: "summer concerts 2017," "grant park functions," "biggest bear," "La Jolla Beach," "open air concert venues," "biggest open air concert venues in USA," and "how crowded does Santa Monica Beach get."

- **On 09-04-17:** Searches: "Las Vegas rentals," "Las Vegas condo rentals," "Las Vegas high rise condos rent," and "Las Vegas Ogden for rent."

- **On 09-05-17:** Searches: "life is beautiful expected attendance," "life is beautiful single day tickets," and "life is beautiful Vegas lineup."

- **On 09-15-17:** Searches: "swat weapons," "ballistics chart 308," "SWAT Las Vegas," "ballistic," and "do police use explosives."

A Google search can of course be performed using any type of web browser. On a Windows PC, when a user uses the Google Chrome web browser, there is a wealth of Web artifacts that can be retrieved from the following directory:

```
%root%\Users\%username%\AppData\Local\Google\Chrome\User Data\Default
```

On an Android you will find the evidence here:

```
data\data\com.android.chrome\app_chrome\Default
```

For iOS devices, the Web-related artifacts can be found here:

```
%root%\Library\Application Support\Google\Chrome\Default
```

A Bing search was also found:

- **On 09-05-17:** Search: "Mandalay Bay Las Vegas," "Route 91 harvest festival 2017 attendance", and "Route 91 harvest festival 2017."

Digital forensics evidence, from Paddock's laptop, did not yield a motive but, as you can see from the aforementioned searches, Paddock did use his laptop to identify a venue, with a lot of people in attendance when planning his attack.

A Dell laptop, Model E5570, belonging to Paddock, was also recovered from his room at Mandalay Bay. Hundreds of child exploitation images were retrieved from this laptop. He also performed numerous searches for open air venues. Police found a laptop, which was placed on a food service cart, which was connected to cameras that he had mounted to view anyone coming near his room (see Figure 13.12).

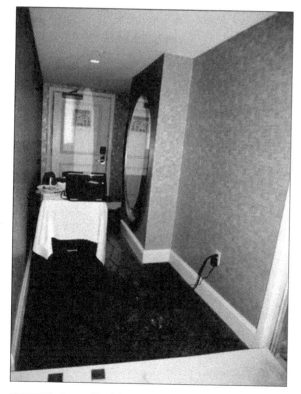

FIGURE 13.12   Paddock's laptop, found in his hotel room, connected to cameras in the hallway

Zacharias Moussaoui

Only one terrorist stood trial for the atrocities of September 11, 2001. That person was Zacharias Moussaoui. As a case study, his trial provides a valuable insight into the various types of digital evidence examined by law enforcement investigators. Additionally, the case demonstrates how this type of evidence is admitted to court and shows the arguments by the defense counsel against its use. Finally, this case illustrates how both defense attorneys and prosecution attorneys use expert witness testimony.

Background

Zacharias Moussaoui was born on May 30, 1968, in France and was of Moroccan descent. Moussaoui received his master's degree from South Bank University in London. During his time in Britain, he frequented the Brixton Mosque, which the "Shoe Bomber", Richard Reid, also attended. Moussaoui also attended the more radical Finsbury Park Mosque in London. He connected with Islamist extremists in England and subsequently trained with Al Qaeda in 1998 at Khalden, Derunta, Khost, Siddiq, and Jihad Wal training camps in Afghanistan. He also lived in Hamburg between 1998 and 1999 and shared an apartment with Mohammed Atta, one of the 9/11 co-conspirators who crashed American Airlines Flight 11 into the North Tower of the World Trade Center.

In August 2001, Moussaoui attended flight school in Minneapolis and trained on 747 flight simulators. The Federal Bureau of Investigation (FBI) had Moussaoui under surveillance and wanted to search his Toshiba laptop in early 2001. Unfortunately, the FBI agent requests from the bureau office in Minnesota were apparently rejected by FBI headquarters.

Table 13.1 shows a timeline of Moussaoui's actions leading up to the events of 9/11/01, as noted in the Virginia grand jury indictment (/www.vaed.uscourts.gov/notablecases/moussaoui/exhibits/).

TABLE 13.1   Moussaoui Events Timeline

Date	Event
September 29, 2000	Moussaoui sends an email to Airman Flight School in Norman, Oklahoma.
February 23, 2001	Moussaoui flies from London to Chicago and then on to Oklahoma City.
May 23, 2001	Moussaoui sends an email to Pan Am International Flight Academy in Miami.
June 20, 2001	Moussaoui purchases flight deck videos for Boeing 747 from Sporty's Pilot Shop.
July 10–11, 2001	Moussaoui makes a credit card payment to Pan Am International Flight Academy for flight simulation training.
August 13–15, 2001	Moussaoui attends Boeing 747 Model 400 simulator training at Pan Am International Flight Academy in Minneapolis.
August 17, 2001	Moussaoui is interviewed by federal agents in Minneapolis.
September 11, 2001	Four hijacked commercial jets crash into the World Trade Centers; the Pentagon; and a field in Somerset County, Pennsylvania.
December 11, 2001	Moussaoui is charged.
April 22, 2005	Moussaoui pleads guilty to all six charges.

Moussaoui was indicted by a federal grand jury, in the Eastern District of Virginia, to stand trial on six felony charges:

- Conspiracy to commit acts of terrorism transcending national boundaries

- Conspiracy to commit aircraft piracy

- Conspiracy to destroy aircraft

- Conspiracy to use weapons of mass destruction

- Conspiracy to murder United States employees

- Conspiracy to destroy property of the United States

Digital Evidence

Government investigators examined numerous computers in the wake of 9/11. The computer that Mukkarum Ali owned, in the apartment where Moussaoui lived in Norman, Oklahoma, was seized. The apartment was owned by the University of Oklahoma, and a computer from the University of Oklahoma computer lab was also seized.

The FBI also visited a Kinko's in Eagan, Minnesota, to examine a computer that the suspect used to access the Internet. FBI agents became aware of his use of a computer at Kinko's after examining Kinko's firewall logs. They discovered that Moussaoui had used the computer to access Hotmail. One of the email addresses the suspect used was xdesertmen@hotmail.com; the suspect listed it as one of his accounts in one of his *pro se* pleadings in July 2002. (**Pro se** refers to someone who advocates for him- or herself and does not use legal representation. Moussaoui requested to represent himself at trial.) The computer at Kinko's was not seized because agents were informed that the data on the computer would have been scrubbed every 24 hours, as part of standard operating procedures, and 44 days had now passed.

Prosecutors had failed to link the computer's Internet Protocol (IP) address at Kinko's with Moussaoui's Hotmail account because so much time had elapsed. After 30 days, the company deletes IP connection data and email content. Email account registration information is maintained for an additional 60 days, but this information then is deleted, and the account username once again becomes available to the public. Once investigators discovered the suspect's claim that he had used xdesertmen@hotmail.com, they contacted Hotmail (Microsoft). Alas, Hotmail had no saved information for this account.

The FBI found Moussaoui's receipt from Kinko's, related to his paid use of the Internet on a computer in the Eagan, Minnesota, store on August 12, 2001. The investigation concluded that the suspect had been connected to MSN/Hotmail for eight minutes. It also discovered that the other 19 9/11 hijackers had accessed the Internet on Kinko's computers at other locations across the country.

Government agents were aware of Moussaoui before 9/11. INS (Immigration and Naturalization Service) agents in Minnesota had arrested him on August 16, 2001, and actually seized his laptop and a floppy disk. Moussaoui had been staying in a Residence Inn in Eagan, Minnesota, while attending the Pan Am International Flight Academy. The FBI subsequently obtained and executed a warrant on September 11, 2001, to seize these items again. On the floppy disk, they found Moussaoui's emails to flight schools. He had contacted these flight schools from pilotz123@hotmail.com.

The FBI appears to have been a lot luckier when examining Moussaoui's pilotz123@hotmail.com records. Investigators were able to match Hotmail IP address connection logs to determine that he had accessed his email account from an address in Malaysia, from the computer lab at the University of Oklahoma, from Mukkarum Ali's apartment (in Norman, Oklahoma), and from Kinko's (in Eagan, Minnesota). Al Qaeda operatives had met in Kuala Lumpur in January 2000. The discovery of the IP address for Kinko's prompted investigators to search the computer at this location.

Standby Counsel Objections

Standby counsel argued that the government had failed to provide the defense with evidence recovered from the xdesertmen@hotmail.com account or from computers at Oklahoma University, at Kinko's, or at Mukkarum Ali's apartment. **Standby counsel** is a lawyer who assists a client who has invoked his right to self-representation.

Donald Eugene Allison provided computer forensics expert witness testimony for the defense in an affidavit dated September 4, 2002.

In this same court document, standby counsel questioned methods by which the prosecution authenticated digital evidence. They noted the following:

> [The] authentication information (such as the MD5 message digest and other accepted computer forensic methods) is critical as without it, it is impossible to verify that the duplicate hard drives are an exact copy of those that exist on the original systems. Likewise, without such information it is impossible to determine if the material retrieved from the hard drives is accurate.

In the same document, standby counsel argued that more than 200 hard drives were produced during discovery, yet the defense lacked the resources to thoroughly examine the drives to the same extent as the prosecution.

Standby counsel then asserted that the hard drive from the University of Oklahoma must have been contaminated. The defense contended that evidence from the Hotmail account should have been available from temporary Internet files. This again relates to the lack of evidence concerning the xdesertmen@hotmail.com account. Additionally, the defense argued that there was a mismatch of IP addresses used as evidence by the prosecution. The defense contended that even though Kinko's appeared to have erased data every 24 hours, investigators could theoretically have examined the computer for files that still existed, but they failed to attempt to retrieve any files. Moreover, the defense argued that the prosecution had not examined the file slack on Mukkarum Ali's computer.

Prosecution Affidavit

Dara K. Sewell was a supervisory special agent for the FBI and a computer forensics investigator who worked on this case. Sewell submitted an affidavit rebutting the assertions made by defense counsel, particularly Donald Eugene Allison. Sewell noted that the FBI uses three methods of duplicating or imaging a hard drive: (1) Linux dd, (2) SafeBack, and (3) Logicube handheld disk duplicator. All of these tools had undergone validation testing.

Sewell responded to Allison's assertion that NIST approves only one method of making duplicates by stating, "NIST does not 'approve' any computer forensic tools. Instead, it merely reports the results of its testing. Moreover, Mr. Allison wrongly identifies Linux dd as the 'only one method. . . . approved by [NIST].'"

Interestingly, Allison questioned the lack of a Message Digest Sum Version 5 (md5sum) or Secure Hash Algorithm Version 1 (SHA-1) hash verification being produced by the prosecution. Sewell responded by noting that a number of verification hashes can be used, including Cyclical Redundancy Checksum (CRC). Sewell continued that SafeBack and Logicube disk duplicators were used. They used an internal CRC and were tested by the FBI's CART. Therefore, "there would not ordinarily be any MD5 or SH-1 hash values to disclose to the defense for any computer drives imaged with SafeBack or a Logicube disk duplicator." However, even with confidence in SafeBack's CRC verification process, Sewell went back and generated an md5sum for the original evidence and the duplicates, and they were a match.

Exhibits

Hundreds of exhibits were submitted at trial. In terms of digital evidence, the prosecution presented numerous emails, wire transfers, receipts, and other exhibits.

The following email demonstrates Moussaoui's interest in learning how to fly:

From:	zuluman tangotango <pilotz123@hotmail.com>
To:	flights@flightsafety.com
Sent:	Monday, May 21, 2001 2:42 AM
Subject:	Simulator training

Hi, I would like some information on if I can get a full Simulator Training on a Boeing or Airbus even if I am not a Commercial Pilot. I am doing my PPL, but my dream is to fly one of these big Bird (of course in a simulator). Will you consider me even if I have not pass all the exam, I know it is a bit peculiar, but I am 33 years so a bit late to start a pilot career and the school where I do my ppl now told me he will take me two year before being a full qualified atp pilot. But for the moment I just want the experience to Fly.

Ultimately, it was the Pan Am International Flight Academy that provided Moussaoui with training on a flight simulator:

From:	xxx@panamacademy.com
To:	zuluman tangotango <pilotz123@hotmail.com>
Sent:	Wednesday, July 11, 2001 5:57 PM
Subject:	Home address for 747 manuals

Zac;

I need the shipping address for your manuals. Operations want to send on thursday, July 12.

Please email or call with the address on thursday.

Thank you

The Pan Am International Flight Academy still provides flight simulator training today, according to its website (www.panamacademy.com).

A copy of a receipt from a store called Sporty's, located in Batavia, Ohio, was also admitted into evidence. The receipt indicates that two VHS video tutorial tapes on the Boeing 747-200 and Boeing 747-400 were shipped to Moussaoui in Norman, Oklahoma, in June 2001. Receipts detailing payments to the Pan Am International Flight Academy were also produced at trial.

In August 2001, Moussaoui traveled to Eagan, Minnesota, to attend the Pan Am International Flight Academy. A hotel receipt for Moussaoui's stay at the Residence Inn, from August 11 to August 17, 2001, in Eagan, Minnesota, was admitted into evidence.

From a computer forensics perspective, this case is important because much of the prosecution's declarations depended on digital evidence. The case is interesting because it also highlights the types of objections that defense counsel can raise. Ultimately, the judge dismissed the objections made by Moussaoui's defense counsel relating to the digital evidence provided by the prosecution.

BTK (Bind Torture Kill) Serial Killer

When reviewing cases involving digital evidence, it is important to understand that these cases also rely on traditional investigative techniques. The BTK (bind torture kill) case clearly illustrates how old-fashioned investigative skills were supported by digital evidence in capturing and convicting the perpetrator of these heinous crimes.

Profile of a Killer

Dennis Lynn Rader was born in Pittsburg, Kansas, on March 9, 1945. Rader grew up in Wichita, Kansas and attended Wichita Heights High School. After a brief stint at Wichita State University, he joined the U.S. Air Force. He left the Air Force to study at a couple of colleges, but he ultimately returned to Wichita State University. Ironically, he graduated with a major in the administration of justice, in 1979. Rader's employment history included a part-time position in the meat department at an IGA grocery store and a job as an assembler at the Coleman Company, and he spent time working as an installation manager at ADT Security, where he had access to many homes, from 1974 to 1988. From 1990 to 2005, he was a supervisor for the Compliance Department at Park City.

Rader was also a father of two and, for three decades, was a member of the Christ Lutheran Church, where he was later elected president of the Congregation Council. Rader was even a Cub Scout leader. Yet even as he taught many kids how to tie knots, he plied his own trade when he bound, tortured, and killed his victims.

Rader began his serial killing on January 15, 1974, when he killed four members of the Otero family in Wichita, Kansas. He went on to kill another six people. He strangled his final victim, Dolores Davis, age 62, with pantyhose on January 19, 1991.

Evidence

In March 2004, Rader began sending letters and packages to the local media describing his victims. Some of the packages actually included items belonging to the victims, to prove that he was the killer but still remained anonymous. Rader left one of these packages, a cereal box, in the bed of a pickup truck at a Home Depot. However, the owner of the vehicle discarded the box as trash. When Rader asked members of the media about the evidence, they had no knowledge. He subsequently went back to the Home Depot and retrieved the box from the trash. Investigators were later able to review surveillance footage from the Home Depot and noticed a black Jeep Cherokee returning to the scene to retrieve the evidence. This became a clue in the case. In 2005, Rader left a Post Toasties cereal box on a dirt road north of Wichita.

Rader then asked the police if it was possible to trace information to a floppy disk. Police posted their response in the *Wichita Eagle* newspaper by stating that it was "OK" to use a floppy disk. On February 16, 2005, an envelope arrived at KSAS-TV in Wichita. The package contained a translucent purple Memorex 1.44MB floppy disk. Randy Stone, from the Forensics Computer Crime Unit of the Wichita Police Department, examined the contents of the disk using EnCase forensics software. The disk contained one file, called `Test A.rtf`. The file metadata showed "Dennis" and Wichita's "Christ Lutheran Church". An Internet search then quickly indicated Dennis Rader as the suspect they would now search for.

Law enforcement began to monitor Rader and his residence. They noticed a black Jeep Cherokee parked outside the Rader residence. Investigators were then able to retrieve DNA from a Pap smear belonging to Rader's daughter from a sample at the University of Kansas medical clinic. The DNA from the Pap smear was a match to the DNA found on one of the victims, thereby proving that the murderer was a member of the Rader family.

On February 25, 2005, Dennis Rader was arrested by a task force of agents from the FBI, the KBI, and the Wichita Police. In June 2005, Rader pleaded guilty and was sentenced to 10 life sentences. He is currently serving time at the El Dorado Correctional Facility.

Cyberbullying

Cyberbullying has become an epidemic in the United States and many other countries. The difference between cyberbullying and traditional bullying is that, years ago, when a child was bullied in the schoolyard, he or she could go home at the end of the day and escape the taunts of peers. Today, however, the taunting continues with the use of the Internet and cellphones. Unfortunately, many states have been slow to enact anti-cyberbullying laws, and much of this legislation has come as a result of a suicide. Statistics infer that the issue is a bigger problem with girls than with boys.

Federal Anti-harassment Legislation

47 USC § 223 is an anti-harassment act aimed to prevent those who use telecommunications from transmitting "any comment, request, suggestion, proposal, image, or other communication which is obscene or child pornography, with intent to annoy, abuse, threaten, or harass another person."

State Anti-harassment Legislation

HB 479, *The Offense of Stalking*, is an act passed by the state of Florida that explicitly prohibits cyberstalking. It defines the term *cyberstalk* to mean communication by means of electronic mail or electronic communication that causes substantial emotional distress and does not serve a legitimate purpose. It includes within the offenses of stalking and aggravated stalking the willful, malicious, and repeated cyberstalking of another person. It also provides penalties and revises the elements of the offense of aggravated stalking to include placing a person in fear of death or bodily injury of the person or the person's child, sibling, spouse, or dependent.

Numerous states, including Alabama, Arizona, Connecticut, Hawaii, Illinois, New Hampshire, and New York, prohibit harassing electronic, computer, or email communications.

Warning Signs of Cyberbullying

Warning signs generally arise when a child is being bullied. Signs can include the following:

- Feelings of anxiety, sadness, or hopelessness;
- A decline in school grades;
- Diminishing interest in social and recreational activities;
- Upset behavior after leaving a computer or cellphone;

- Excessive use of digital devices;

- Irregular sleep patterns; and

- Changes in weight or loss of appetite.

What Is Cyberbullying?

Cyberbullying is not simply sending harassing emails or nasty text messages. Many forms of intimidating communications fall under this category:

- **Images and video:** Cyberbullies commonly use social media sites such as Facebook to post images and videos in attempts to embarrass other children.

- **Sexting:** In **sexting**, an individual illegally shares a sexually explicit image, usually via MMS from a cellphone. If an adult becomes involved and images of minors are being shared, charges of possession or distribution can ensue.

- **Outing: Outing** occurs when an individual publishes confidential personal information online or shares it in an email to embarrass another individual.

- **Flaming: Flaming** is online arguing, often including vulgar and offensive language to denigrate another person.

- **Bash boards: Bash boards** are online bulletin boards used to post hateful comments about peers or teachers that people dislike. Twoo.com, formerly Spring.me, is a website often connected with Facebook that has been used as a bash board.

- **Tricking: Tricking** is the process of duping an individual into divulging personal comments, with the intent to publicly publish those secrets to humiliate another individual.

- **Happy slapping: Happy slapping** occurs when people organize to physically harm another person and also video the abuse and later post the content online or send it to others. The proliferation of smartphones has facilitated a disturbing growth in these types of attacks.

- **Online polls: Online polls** are used to get classmates to vote on certain topics, such as the ugliest student in class.

- **Impersonation: Impersonation** is when a person either illegally breaks into another person's account and pretends to be that person or sets up a fake page purporting to be someone else.

Phoebe Prince

On January 14, 2010, Phoebe Prince, a 15-year-old who had immigrated to South Hadley in Massachusetts, from the West of Ireland, committed suicide after being consistently bullied by other teenagers. Unbelievably, highly disrespectful comments were posted to her Facebook memorial page after her death. Six teenagers were charged as adults with a variety of felony charges, including statutory rape, stalking, and assault with a deadly weapon. Like so many other cyberbullying cases, the perpetrators got off lightly—some with probation or community service. Nevertheless, the state legislature enacted Senate No. 2404, an anti-bullying law.

Ryan Halligan

Ryan Halligan, a middle school student from Vermont, was another victim of cyberbullying who committed suicide. Many of the nasty messages sent to him were inadvertently archived on his computer through an application known as DeadAIM. In the aftermath of his death, in 2004, Vermont enacted a Bullying Prevention Policy Law and, later, the Suicide Prevention Law (Act 114) in 2005.

Megan Meier

Megan Meier was a 13-year-old student from Ostmann Elementary School, in Missouri, who committed suicide by hanging herself. Lori Drew, a 47 year old, posed as a boy named Josh Evans. She created a fake MySpace page and befriended Megan. In the case of *United States vs. Lori Drew*, Drew was charged with the following:

- Indicted on Charge of Conspiracy (Violation of 18 U.S.C. § 371)
- Infliction of emotional distress (Violation of 18 U.S.C. §1030(a)(2)(c))
- Computer Fraud & Abuse Act (CFAA)
- Breach of MySpace Terms of Service Agreement

After becoming good friends online, "Josh Evans" (Lori Drew) began to send hurtful comments to Meier, which many believed led Megan to commit suicide. Josh Evans sent comments such as "everybody hates you" and the "world would be a better place without you". Evans communicated first via MySpace but later through AOL IM. The trial culminated with Lori Drew ultimately being acquitted, without serving any jail time.

In the wake of Meier's death, the City of Florissant, Missouri, changed the cyber-harassment law from a misdemeanor to a Class D felony. Proving that cyberbullying ultimately led to suicide is always challenging.

Tyler Clementi

On September 22, 2010, a distraught 18-year-old Rutgers student ended his life by throwing himself off the George Washington Bridge. The unfortunate case of Tyler Clementi highlights the importance of digital evidence in bullying cases. Clementi was from Ridgewood, New Jersey. Just before committing suicide, Clementi checked Dharun Ravi's Twitter account for the 59th time. Sadly, he then posted one last message on his Facebook profile: "Jumping off the gw bridge, sorry".

Ravi was Clementi's roommate, and he had secreted a webcam in their dorm room to capture Clementi's intimate encounters with another man, intending to stream the video over the Internet on September 19. He then viewed the video from a friend's dorm room across the hall. Ravi apparently encouraged others to invade Clementi's privacy and watch the video. Prosecutors contended that Ravi intended to use the video to humiliate his gay roommate. Ravi's tweets on Twitter clearly illustrated his intent to do just that, with Twitter messages informing his friends that he was in a dorm mate's room, watching a video of Clementi "making out with a dude". Ravi intended to set up yet another video of an intimate encounter of Clementi when he tweeted, "Anyone with iChat I dare you to video chat me between the hours of 9:30 and 12. Yes, it's happening again".

Digital Evidence Used at Trial

Gary Charydczak, a computer forensics examiner from the Middlesex County Prosecutor's Office, gave testimony at the trial. Charydczak had examined the hard drive from Clementi's blue laptop, seized from his dorm room. He discovered tweets on his laptop with the names `untitled.jpg` and `secondtime.jpg`.

Text message exchanges were also discussed at trial. Michelle Huang texted Ravi, "Watch out, he may come for you when you're sleeping". Ravi responded that his computer would alert him if anyone used his bed, noting, "It keeps the gays away".

Charydczak also noted a number of Internet searches conducted by Ravi between August 21 and 23 to determine whether his new roommate was homosexual. Ravi searched YouTube and Facebook to determine his sexual orientation, and there were 20 AOL instant messages discussing the topic. This evidence was important to support the charge of a bias crime.

Prosecutors also disclosed evidence that they had uncovered related to the videos streamed across the Internet. An examination of Molly Wei's computer produced video chat files and AOL IMs relating to the tryst; Molly Wei's computer was used by Ravi to view Tyler Clementi in his dorm on that fateful night. Under oath, Wei had confirmed the events that had occurred with the webcam. Timothy Hayes, an IT administrator at Rutgers, affirmed the claim that Ravi's computer was used for two video chats on September 21. Charydczak testified that the computers of Molly Wei and Dharun Ravi contained video chat evidence from the same time that Wei stated she had witnessed Tyler Clementi kissing another man.

The Verdict

In March 2012, Dharun Ravi was found guilty of invasion of privacy and four counts of bias intimidation. He was also found guilty of tampering with evidence, tampering with a witness, and hindering apprehension. After declining a plea deal, Ravi was imprisoned, with the added potential of deportation. Molly Wei was granted leniency in return for her cooperation with the investigation, but she was still ordered to perform 300 hours of community service, undergo counseling, and obtain training in cyberbullying and alternative lifestyles.

> **Note**
>
> **Doxing** is the process of gathering personal information about an individual and then making that information publicly available. The word *doxing* is derived from *documents* (.doc). For example, in the Occupy L.A. protests, some protesters felt that they were manhandled by the Los Angeles police. In response, the hacktivist group CabinCr3w posted the personal information of more than two dozen police officers, including political contributions, property records, names of children, and other very personal information.

Sports

One might wonder how computer forensics could be linked to sports and, more specifically, Major League Baseball (MLB). In 2006, the government initiated a highly publicized investigation involving the alleged use of steroids by a large number of high-profile players. Player David Wells stated that many players were using steroids, and Jose Canseco, Alex Rodriguez, Mark McGwire, Barry Bonds, Jason Giambi, and others came under the spotlight for use of performance-enhancing drugs (PEDs).

Former Senator George Mitchell was appointed to lead an investigation into the use of steroids in professional baseball. The report indicated that the use of PEDs was rampant among players in MLB. Naturally, if you want to find out who is using steroids, you go to the source. Thus, federal investigators focused largely on one particular supplier to MLB players: the Bay Area Lab Cooperative (BALCO). The MLB Players Association agreed to allow "suspicionless drug testing" of its players, with the names of the players to remain anonymous. Comprehensive Drug Testing (CDT) conducted the urine tests of the players. Under the program, federal investigators learned of 10 players who had tested positive. The government then obtained a grand jury subpoena seeking all drug testing records and specimens. The players' union sought to quash the subpoena. Subsequently, the government obtained a warrant to search CDT's premises. The search was limited to the records of the 10 players for whom probable cause had been established. However, when government agents executed the warrant, they seized and reviewed the records of hundreds of MLB players. The records seized were computer records that were at the heart of a rehearing of the case *en banc* by the Ninth Circuit Court of Appeals. The term *en banc* refers to all members of an appellate court hearing an argument rather than just the required quorum.

Government agents seized computers, hard drives, and other storage media. They argued that they could not decide, on the spot, which computers or storage media contained evidence pertaining to the 10 players in question, and therefore they had seized all storage devices. They also argued that because information pertaining to the players in question could be in non-descript files or folders, they would need to review all the files.

The three-judge panel opined:

> We disapproved the wholesale seizure of the documents and particularly the government's failure to return the materials that were not the object of the search once they had been segregated. Id. at 596-97. However, we saw no reason to suppress the properly seized materials just because the government had taken more than authorized by the warrant.

Furthermore, government agents refused the offer of CDT to provide information directly related to the 10 suspects. Government investigators also failed to redact evidence seized on the players who were not a part of the investigation. However, the judges did acknowledge the challenges associated with electronic evidence and the potential of suspect data to be intermingled with those not party to an investigation.

Summary

Digital evidence was key to the successful prosecution of Ross Ulbricht, who made millions in commissions from sales on the Dark Web marketplace called Silk Road. The evidence included investigators analyzing Bitcoin transactions from Ulbricht's laptop and matching those transactions to the Blockchain (public ledger). Additionally, the laptop evidence indicated that Ulbricht had not abandoned the site, as the defense had claimed, and even maintained a journal that recorded his daily activities.

Computer forensics is clearly not limited to computer crime or cybercrime but encompasses a host of criminal investigations. The use of digital evidence in the Zacarias Moussaoui trial was necessary as corroborating evidence on both his intentions and the events that led up to 9/11. Documents from the trial provide tremendous insight into the use of expert witness testimony by computer forensics experts. Moreover, the objections by defense counsel and the rebuttal by the government investigator clearly illustrated how important the process by which digital evidence is acquired, handled, and analyzed is to the successful admittance as evidence at trial.

Murder investigations often rely on digital evidence to catch and convict suspects. The case of the BTK Killer is an excellent example of how digital evidence and old-fashioned investigative skills are equally important in apprehending and successfully convicting a criminal.

Sadly, cyberbullying is here to stay, and growth in the use of computers and cellphones will continue to make it a priority for many investigators. The case of Tyler Clementi underscores how multiple sources of digital evidence are pivotal to the successful conviction of perpetrators who use technology to facilitate their ambitions to humiliate and denigrate others. Computers and devices belonging to Clementi and other students were examined, records from online service providers were gathered, and even the university's IT administrator was called upon to provide corroborating evidence at trial. Although cyberbullying continues to menace many people, the good news is that the scope of the digital evidence trail is far reaching, and states have enacted more laws to bring the perpetrators to justice.

Finally, the investigation by federal agents into MLB player use of performance-enhancing drugs clearly illustrates how computers and digital evidence are now used in every type of investigation imaginable. The case study also highlights how difficult cases that involve digital evidence can be highly problematic, given the narrow scope of a warrant garnered to investigate a computer or device on which only a few files out of millions of files might actually pertain to a suspected criminal act.

Key Terms

bash board: An online bulletin board used to post hateful comments about peers or teachers that people dislike.

doxing: The process of gathering personal information about an individual and then making that information publicly available.

*en banc***:** Refers to all members of an appellate court, rather than just the required quorum.

flaming: Online arguing, often used with vulgar and offensive language, to denigrate another person.

happy slapping: People organizing to physically harm another person and also video the abuse and later post the content online or send to others.

impersonation: When a person either illegally breaks into another person's account and pretends to be that person or sets up a fake page purporting to be someone else.

online polls: Polls used to get classmates to vote on certain topics, such as the ugliest student in class.

outing: Publishing confidential personal information about others online or in an email, to embarrass another individual.

pro se: Refers to someone who advocates for him- or herself and does not use legal representation.

sexting: Illegally sharing a sexually explicit image, usually via MMS from a cellphone.

standby counsel: A lawyer who assists a client who has invoked his right to self-representation.

tricking: The process of duping an individual into divulging personal comments, with the intent to publicly publish those secrets to humiliate another individual.

Assessment

CLASSROOM DISCUSSIONS

1. What objections did Ross Ulbricht's defense counsel raise before and during trial?

2. Why were there quite a number of supporters of Ross Ulbricht during his trial?

3. How can you recognize a child who is a victim of cyberbullying, and how can you help?

4. What type of digital evidence can be used in a cyberbullying investigation?

MULTIPLE-CHOICE QUESTIONS

1. Which of the following best describes sending a sexually explicit MMS on a cellphone?

    A. Flaming

    B. Happy slapping

    C. Tricking

    D. Sexting

2. Which of the following refers to someone who advocates for him- or herself and does not use legal representation?

   A. Pro se

   B. En banc

   C. Impersonation

   D. Certiorari

3. Which of the following describes convincing a person to provide confidential information, with the intention of later publicizing the information to embarrass the person?

   A. Tricking

   B. Happy slapping

   C. Online polls

   D. Flaming

4. Much like a blog, this online service is specifically used to post hateful comments about peers or teachers that some people dislike.

   A. Online poll

   B. Bash board

   C. User group

   D. Social media

5. Which of the following terms refers to all members of an appellate court hearing an argument rather than just the required quorum?

   A. *En banc*

   B. *Certiorari*

   C. *Per curiam*

   D. *Per se*

FILL IN THE BLANKS

1. When an individual publishes confidential personal information with others online or in an email to embarrass another individual, it is known as _____.

2. A group that organizes to physically harm another person and then video the event to share with others is involved with _____ _____.

3. _____ occurs when a person breaks into another person's account and pretends to be that person.

4. Arguing online with another person using obscenities is called _____.

5. When peers are asked to rank who they believe to be the ugliest in the class online, the peers are asked to contribute to an online _____.

PROJECT

Analyze a Cyberbullying Case

The following is a made-up cyberbullying case study for you to read, analyze, and discuss in your class. Although the case is not real, you could very well imagine something like this taking place.

Scenario

A 16-year-old girl by the name of Jenny Foster was found hitchhiking along the Adirondack Mountains Highway in upstate New York. Mr. David Sykes, a driver on the highway, stopped to pick up the prospective passenger. Realizing that the hitchhiker was a scared, shivering young girl who had just run away from home, he drove Jenny to the local police station, where his brother-in-law was a police officer. The officer, Lt. Todd Gallagher, provided Jenny with a blanket and a mug of hot cocoa. While recuperating, Jenny told the officer that she had run away from home and was on her way to New York, where she knew an old school friend was now living. She was going to stay with her for a few weeks while she found a job as a waitress. The police officer asked for Jenny's home telephone number to call her parents. After a few attempts the officer was able to reach Jenny's parents, who were frantically searching for her and calling her friends' houses.

The officer assumed that she had a disagreement with her parents, but in Jenny's case, it was quite the opposite: Jenny loved her parents but felt that nobody else loved her. When questioned why she had left home, Jenny cried and said, "I wish I was dead. I have been thinking about killing myself because my so-called friends told me that I'd be better off dead". She also confided in them that Rachel, one of her former friends, had posted a message on Facebook stating that she would be happy to push Jenny into oncoming traffic to help her end her "pathetic life". The police officer was startled by this and asked Jenny if she minded if he took notes. She responded that she had no problem with this. The police officer then said that he wanted to bring in another police officer, Det. Margaret Schultz, to accompany them. Jenny did not object, and Det. Schultz joined them. Jenny continued to talk about herself. She felt that she was different from everyone else in the class. She had no brothers or sisters, and her family had recently relocated to the area after her father had been laid off from his job as an electrician. She explained that her mother had a part-time job at Target and that her father was only getting handyman jobs here and there; it was a real struggle in their house to make ends meet.

The police officer asked why Jenny was so upset and felt so alone in the world. She explained that she was continually taunted by friends at school, but it had not always been like that.

She proceeded to tell them that her mother used to be a secretary, but when her old company's regional dealership folded, her boss had allowed her to take home the office computer. Luckily for Jenny (or unluckily, as it turned out), the family was able to access a Wi-Fi Internet connection. Therefore, like many teenagers, Jenny used Facebook after doing her homework, eating dinner, and washing up. She admitted that she spent a lot of time on the computer complaining about homework and chatting about boys in the class, mainly those on the school's football team. She had befriended a group of girls who were cheerleaders for the team. However, Jenny was not part of the cheerleading squad. Jenny explained that another big difference between her and these girls was their economic situation. These girls all came from affluent homes, yet Jenny's family was struggling to make ends meet.

According to Jenny, everything was great when she first started school, but then for no apparent reason, her friends started tormenting her. Everything started to go wrong after Jenny brought one of her friends over for dinner. Her friend was very surprised that Jenny lived in a small one-bedroom apartment and did not seem too happy that meatloaf and water was the menu for dinner. From that day on, Jenny noticed that things changed between her and her so-called friends. Gradually, the other girls began to say really hurtful things to Jenny. Now they knew that her family did not have a lot of money, so they purposely planned outings to expensive shops to buy clothes and made arrangements to go skiing, knowing that Jenny could not afford to join them. But things got worse when Jenny started going out with Brad Smalls, an 18-year-old senior who was the captain of the football team. Jenny explained to the officers that they had dated for a little while, but she had broken up with him because he had taken an inappropriate photograph of her with his BlackBerry and refused to delete it, despite her requests.

One of the cheerleaders, Charlene Davis, found out that he had this picture and asked Brad to forward it to her cellphone and email, which he did. Soon the picture was all around the school. In fact, Jenny saw Charlene and Jillian making copies of the photograph in the school's library but was too afraid to confront them or report them. (Students were allocated 150 copies every semester through their student ID card.) Within days, the picture was posted in the girls' bathroom and in the boys' football changing room. Jenny removed the picture from the girls' bathroom but heard that the picture in the boys' changing room stayed up for weeks. Jenny had hoped the football coach would take the picture down, but that was not the case. Eventually, the photo ended up on Facebook. Jenny told the officers she had been so embarrassed and humiliated that she had worn a hat and glasses to school so that people would not recognize her. She dreaded going to school so much that she would get physically ill in the mornings. She had always been an honor student, but because of all the terrible things that were happening to her, she could not focus on her school work and even avoided going to class. She often ended up in detention on purpose so that she did not have to deal with those heartless cheerleaders.

Jenny shared with the officers that, one day, the cheerleaders asked her if she wanted to be friends with them again and go to the local diner for a milkshake. Jenny reluctantly agreed. Her initial instinct to not go with them had been correct: The trip to the diner had been a setup. She recounted the events of that afternoon: "They were all smoking, and the next thing I heard was 'Now' and then they stubbed my head and arms with their cigarettes. I cried, ran home, and luckily didn't have to answer any questions because my parents were still at work. I couldn't sleep that night and cried all night. The next day, I saw the nurse. She asked me about the marks on my body, and I told her what had happened. I also asked her not to say anything. She agreed, and as far as I know, she never said anything to anyone."

Jenny told the officers that, the day after the diner, she had received taunting text messages and emails about the incident. When she got home, there were messages on Facebook about how she should kill herself and how they would help her do it. "That's when I read Rachel's posting about pushing me into oncoming traffic", Jenny told the officers. Her mother had come home one night and found Jenny in tears. Jenny had told her mother about the emails, cellphone texts, and postings on Facebook. She had showed her mother her Facebook page and the emails she had received through her Yahoo! account. Her mother had taken a screenshot of the Facebook messages and printed the emails. After her mother printed the emails, Jenny deleted all of them because she did not want to see them ever again. Jenny could not show her mother all the harassing text messages because she had deleted them as soon as she had received them. "Anyway, my mother wouldn't understand some of them because kids have a different language when texting—a language that adults simply don't understand", Jenny explained to the officers. She then proceeded to tell them that Brad had created a Facebook page about her, with that infamous photograph, and said Jenny liked to sleep around. Jenny broke down in tears as she said, "He even said that I was open to visits at my home and listed my address. I was sickened and very frightened."

Jenny then continued with her story and said her mother had given the screenshots and printed emails to the assistant principal. At the meeting with the AP, Jenny not only mentioned the incident with the cigarettes, but also related how these students would trip her in the hallway, put chilies in her food, and pull her hair. "My mother was surprised and upset to hear all of this because I had never mentioned any of this before", Jenny shared with the officers. Jenny also told them that she had been disappointed with the meeting because the assistant principal was not particularly interested in what had been happening to her. His response to Jenny's allegations had been dismissive, to say the least: "I agree that these kids have been misbehaving, but this is 2010 and the world has changed—kids will say anything on Facebook. Look, they don't have access to Facebook in the school, so we cannot be held responsible. What students do on their own time is not my business, and it's actually your responsibility." Jenny told the officers that her mother had shown the AP a couple of emails in which her life had been threatened. Jenny remembered very clearly the AP's response: "This isn't really evidence because these are not actual emails. How do I know that someone didn't edit these? Tell me the truth—when you were a kid, did you ever say 'I wish so-and-so was dead'? Frankly, Mrs. Foster, I'm more concerned about your daughter, who keeps ending up in detention every other day." Jenny also remembered that her mother was annoyed with her because she did not know about her frequent visits to detention, since she was working most evenings.

At that point, Jenny's parents arrived at the police station. They were happy to see Jenny and thankful to the police officers, but when Jenny's father heard that they had interviewed Jenny and taken notes, he was very upset and said to the officers, "You have no right to take a statement from my daughter. I know my rights, and you need the consent of her parents before questioning my daughter." The detective explained to Jenny's father that the conversation had been very informal, that she had just talked and they had listened. They reassured him that they only wanted to help. The detective told Jenny's parents that she believed they should refer the matter to the district attorney's office to determine whether there was a case against the students or the school.

Scenario Considerations and Discussion

1. Did the police act appropriately by taking notes while they waited for Jenny's parents to arrive?

2. Did the police require parental consent before speaking to Jenny?

3. Were Jenny's Miranda rights violated? Research what the Miranda warning is.

4. Was it a good idea to bring a detective into the same room?

5. Are the email printouts made by Jenny's mother admissible as evidence in this case?

6. How could the emails be authenticated?

7. What, if any, objections could be raised regarding the admissibility of the emails?

8. Is the snapshot of the Facebook page admissible as evidence in this case?

9. Did the school act appropriately? Could they be found negligent?

10. Are Brad's and the cheerleaders' actions protected under the First Amendment?

Legal Action Taken by the Prosecution

The Farmville County District Attorney has decided to prosecute the following people:

- Brad Smalls, senior (former boyfriend)

- Charlene Davis, sophomore (and football cheerleader)

- Rachel Vasquez, sophomore (and football cheerleader)

- Jillian Kopley, sophomore (and football cheerleader)

The district attorney has also taken an extraordinary move to prosecute the school and its administrators.

Defendant Statements to the Media

School Spokesman Statement

"The school is shocked by the unprecedented charges against the school and its administration. The school is not responsible for the actions of its students after school hours. The incident of injury to the student occurred outside the school. The intimidating emails, text messages, and Facebook postings noted in this case were beyond our control and were never reported by the victim. It was only when we spoke to the victim's mother that these transgressions came to light. We did issue a warning to the perpetrating students. With regard to the issue of a photo being posted in the football changing room, the football coach did not post any photos and is not liable for the posting of such images. The victim never mentioned this in our conversation, otherwise, we would have removed the image, and the student responsible would have been suspended from school.

The school's administration now feels that they are the ones being bullied. The school has very strict policies when it comes to bullying and has zero tolerance for this kind of behavior. In summary, we were never a part of this bullying and should not be singled out. In time, it will become clear that respect, honesty, and integrity are three principles that we live by. We will be proved innocent and our reputation will remain untarnished."

Defense Attorney (Brad Smalls)

"My client's name and reputation have been smeared. It will soon become apparent that Jenny Foster is a misguided child. Foster is relatively new to the area. Her poor parents were out working most evenings and were unable to supervise their daughter's use of the Internet. This is a girl who simply wanted some attention. This case will demonstrate that Jenny Foster, a student who spends more time in detention and on Facebook than studying, needs some guidance and direction in her life, and I really hope that she gets better and gets the professional help that she needs. This case will never go to trial, and I hope that my client, an honors student, can get back to focusing on his studies as quickly as possible."

Case and Evidence Considerations

1. Jenny Foster deleted her emails, and the email printouts are in some file in the assistant principal's office. Can anything be done?

2. Could the school be found negligent? On what basis?

3. What charges do you think the district attorney would make against the school?

4. What charges do you think the district attorney would make against Brad Smalls?

5. What charges do you think the district attorney would make against Charlene Davis, Rachel Vasquez, and Jillian Kopley?

Assignment

Create two teams: (a) Prosecution and (b) Defense. A judge should preside over the case. Reenact the ensuing court case as you anticipate it would happen.

ASSESSMENT OF CASES BY JUDGES

Each team will be adjudicated by a panel of judges who have technical and legal expertise. The panel will judge the teams based on the following criteria.

I. Technical Ability

1. Detailing the evidence to be used in the case

2. Detailing the admissibility of the evidence

3. Detailing how the evidence was acquired and handled

4. Warrants issued

5. Subpoenas issued

II. Legal and Presentation Skills

1. Detailing the charges being brought by the prosecution

2. Detailing the prosecution's arguments

3. Detailing the defense's arguments

4. Detailing the prosecution's objections and cross-examinations

5. Detailing the defense's objections and cross-examinations

6. The judge's facilitation of court proceedings

Chapter | **14**

Internet of Things (IoT) Forensics and Emergent Technologies

Learning Outcomes

After reading this chapter, you will be able to understand the following:

- The importance of IoT devices in an investigation;
- IoT devices with artificial intelligence capabilities;
- The impact of 5G on investigations;
- Police safety;
- Police vehicle technologies;
- Evidence derived from wearable technologies; and
- Action camera evidence used in investigations.

An **Internet of Things (IoT)** device is an Internet-enabled electronic device that can include a smart television, thermostat, refrigerator, or a speaker with artificial intelligence (AI) built-in. These IoT devices are different from traditional devices or appliances because their ability to connect to the Internet means that they can often be controlled using a smartphone app, which generally means that IoT devices can be remotely controlled. For example, a Nest thermostat can be remotely controlled from your smartphone so that you can turn on the heat in your house on the way home from work. Some estimate that by the end of 2020 there will be more than 30 billion IoT devices globally. The revenue generated by sales of these devices is well in excess of $1 billion annually. While the local storage capacity, associated with many of these devices is relatively negligible, they are hugely important to investigators because the producers of these devices collect vast amounts of user data, and we are seeing more and more IoT developers being subpoenaed for IoT user data during criminal investigations.

This new field of forensics has tremendous potential for investigators. However, there are many challenges that need to be overcome first. As a new field of study, existing forensic solutions (tools) are very limited. Secondly, there are thousands of different IoT devices, each with different proprietary firmware and often with non-standard file formats. There are literally hundreds of different video file formats for example, and therefore finding a tool that can support video analysis can be problematic.

While many IoT devices cannot be directly forensically imaged, much of the data derived by these devices resides in the Cloud, and therefore considering the use of a subpoena for cloud storage can be critical.

In 2016, Japan's National Center for Incident Readiness and Strategy for Cybersecurity (NISC) released Japan's *General Framework for Secured IoT Systems*. This framework provides guidance on the requirements for securing IoT devices on a network. The *U.K. Code of Practice for Consumer Internet of Things Security* was introduced in 2018 and provides best practices for security by design for IoT devices. In 2019, the U.S. Senate introduced a bill requiring federal government agencies, and also contractors and vendors providing IoT services to the federal government, to be transparent about vulnerabilities associated with IoT devices. We certainly expect more legislation to be introduced worldwide with the proliferation of IoT devices, which are largely unregulated and many of which are inherently unsecured.

5G

The introduction of 5G will change our lives dramatically, especially for those who live and work in major cities. 5G will create smart cities, which will be heavily dependent on IoT, a reality. **5G** is the fifth generation of cellular technologies. 1G cellular service allowed us to talk and then 2G gave us the ability to text (SMS). With the advent of 3G, we could now access the Web on our mobile devices. Then came 4G LTE, which increased data speed by about 10-fold. Speed has increased exponentially with the introduction of 5G. **Latency** is the delay between sending and receiving data. With 5G, latency has been dramatically reduced. While 5G-ready mobile devices are prohibitively expensive for many, 5G will certainly grow in popularity once the carriers make 5G more pervasive.

5G is not just about improving cellular communications. People are excited about its impact on so many other technologies, from virtual reality to self-driving cars to remote-controlled factories as well as an impact on emergency responders. IoT devices will benefit greatly from the change. We will see 5G integrated into cars, thereby making self-driving vehicles more of a reality. 5G will be important for industrial robotics, where robots will communicate with one another and drones will have the ability to coordinate their activities in groups. The technology still has obstacles that need to be overcome, like walls and bad weather. 5G uses millimeter waves and therefore a new infrastructure—with new transmitters in closer proximity—needs to be built. Thus, major cities will see 5G well before suburban and rural areas. Hundreds of thousands of new towers will need to be constructed. Consumer concerns have been raised about the impacts of 5G technology on health, given that 5G towers need to be closer to subscribers and due to fears that the frequency of the waves transmitted from these towers and antenna could impact humans. In the electromagnetic spectrum, the radio waves from 5G and other mobile phone technology are on the low frequency end of the spectrum. In fact, it is less powerful than visible light.

In the United States, tower operators such as SBA Communications, Crown Castle, and American Tower will be huge beneficiaries as they lease 5G towers to wireless carriers like Verizon and AT&T.

The costs of implementing 5G are huge, and therefore it is possible that there will be changes to the structure of the mobile network operators (MNOs). We have already witnessed the merger of T-Mobile with Sprint, which has reduced competition and should bring about savings through economies of scale. Minimization of Drive Testing (MDT) is not a 5G concept yet it is being discussed as an important way to measure consumer satisfaction on a cellular network, including new 5G networks. For example, instead of Verizon or AT&T engineers driving around and measuring network signals and performance, the cellular providers have sought to gather performance metrics directly from consumer cellular devices, thereby minimizing the need to drive and test signal strength. Thus, MDT may create a new, rich source of evidence for law enforcement.

The path that traffic takes in a network will change with 5G, which means that the sources of digital evidence and the nature of evidence will change. Two key concepts associated with 5G are Multi-access Edge Computing (MEC) and CUPS (Control and User Plane Separation). **Multi-access Edge Computing (MEC)** is a networking protocol, whereby mobile users can establish direct connections, using available network infrastructure, at the edge of the network, rather than being routed through the mobile network operator's core network. **CUPS (Control and User Plane Separation)** is a 3GPP specification that facilitates Multi-access Edge Computing (MEC), whereby control functions, like establishing a connection with another device, take a different route through a network. The goal of MEC and CUPS is to create more bandwidth for users and significantly reduce latency by facilitating connections at the network edge, while moving away from a centralized network. Multi-access Edge Computing (MEC) will also benefit virtual reality gaming and self-driving cars.

Another element of 5G is D2D. **Device-to-device (D2D)** communication is technology that enables user equipment (UE) to communicate with one another, with or without a network infrastructure. The UE can be a mobile device or can be vehicle-to-vehicle communication. The primary benefit of D2D communication is ultra-low latency. Another benefit of D2D is the reduction of network capacity issues, thereby enabling devices to communicate with each other without the need to connect with a network.

IEEE 802.11p is part of the dedicated short-range communications (DSRC) system and is a standard for adding wireless access in vehicle environments (WAVE). With the proliferation of 5G, we shall see more vehicles communicate with one another, especially in corporate fleets and potentially in fleets of police squad cars. We have already seen vehicle-to-vehicle communications with Tesla cars for example.

With the development of 5G, there have been many discussions about security and privacy. The CTIA, which represents America's wireless communications industry, has stated that enhanced privacy protections have been integrated into 5G and this includes encrypting the device's IMSI (international mobile subscriber identity). As discussed earlier in the book, an IMSI uniquely identifies a subscriber on a GSM cellular network. There are numerous law enforcement agencies that have used "IMSI-catchers" to catch wanted criminals and suspects. The Harris Corporation produces StingRays, which are IMSI-catchers, for law enforcement only. A StingRay acts as a fake cell tower. If law enforcement knows the cellphone number, or the number of a MiFi device, of a criminal but is unsure of the exact location of a suspect, then law enforcement can use the device to locate the suspect. A carrier can provide the

IMSI number, associated with a telephone number, to law enforcement. There have also been reports of ICE (Immigration and Customs Enforcement) using IMSI-catchers to locate undocumented residents in the United States. These devices have been effective in catching criminals. However, some privacy advocates have raised concerns about StingRays capturing the location information for hundreds or even thousands of innocent citizens. According to the CTIA, on a 5G network, the IMSI will be encrypted to protect the privacy of a mobile subscriber. This will potentially create an issue for law enforcement agencies using StingRay devices. Furthermore, virtualization will increase in importance with 5G while replacing legacy hardware—sometimes on the fly in a cellular network. This is also likely to impact the retention of data related to the subscriber and the availability of evidence to law enforcement.

The GSMA represents the telecommunications industry and they have developed a digital authentication standard called Mobile Connect. This standard will allow a subscriber to create a universal digital identity with a single sign-on (SSO). **Mobile Connect** is a 5G technology that matches a user's mobile number to an account, thereby allowing the user to login to websites and applications, without remembering the login and password.

Huawei, a Chinese telecommunications company that has invested heavily in 5G, published a white paper about Vo5G. **Vo5G (Voice over 5G)** is a standard for voice/video on the fifth generation of mobile technologies and approved by 3GPP. Vo5G will use Voice over New Radio (VoNR) for calls on a 5G network. VoNR will use a 5G network and replace VoLTE (Voice over LTE).

Wi-Fi 6

Wi-Fi 6 is a recent wireless fidelity (Wi-Fi) standard that has been developed by the Wi-Fi Alliance. We have so many Internet-enabled devices today, and therefore we need to ensure that Wi-Fi can handle all of these additional devices. It is not just the addition of more devices that we need to consider but also the increase in data with advances in technology. For example, 4K video has double the bit rate of high definition (HD) video. In 2020, it is estimated that more than 70% of the global population (equal to 5.7 billion) will have mobile devices and there will be an estimated 12.3 billion devices. Therefore, we need new technologies, like Wi-Fi 6, to handle all of these devices—especially on public networks, where a lot of devices are serviced on a single network. Samsung Galaxy and the iPhone 11 support this new standard, which was previously called 802.11ax. Incidentally, 802.11ac has been retroactively renamed Wi-Fi 5.

Wi-Fi 6 operates on 2.4 GHz or 5GHz and has a theoretical maximum throughput of 10.53 Gbps, but in reality we should experience about a 30% increase in speed. **Quadrature Amplitude Modulation (QAM)** is a modulation scheme in digital telecommunication systems, like Wi-Fi. Transmitting data wirelessly is achieved by modulating radio waves. Wi-Fi 6 is 1024-QAM and can transmit 10 bits at a time, which is 2 bits more than Wi-Fi 5. Thus, QAM increases the performance associated with Wi-Fi 6 by pushing out more bits in each transmission.

Companies, like Netgear, are already manufacturing Wi-Fi 6 routers but the Internet service providers (ISPs) still need to catch up with this latest technology. Wi-Fi 6 routers will now have a label with "Wi-Fi 6 Certified" on them. Wi-Fi 6 routers can deliver up to 12 simultaneous Wi-Fi streams, which reduces latency. Wi-Fi 6 routers use OFDMA technology. **Orthogonal frequency-division multiple access (OFDMA)** enables an 802.11ax router to send and receive data to multiple devices simultaneously by splitting a transmission channel into a number of transmission sub-channels. Wi-Fi 7 is already under development.

Wi-Fi Mesh Networks

A **Wi-Fi mesh network** is a network comprised of a series of nodes, or computing devices, which help to propagate a wireless signal. This type of configuration was developed to support numerous IoT devices in a home network. For example, while an access point (router) repeater can help with providing Wi-Fi access to dead zones, the data throughput rate is dramatically reduced.

There are many types of mesh networks, which is a growing trend with some car manufacturers, including Tesla and Mercedes. In a mesh network, nodes will share data with one another, and that data is often derived from sensors. Thus, one node (or vehicle) can potentially detect problems that are being encountered by another node and report that information back to a central repository, like a database.

Shodan

Shodan (shodan.io) is a search engine for the Internet of Things (IoT), as shown in Figure 14.1. This free tool simply requires that a user registers for an account on their website. The website allows a user to look for unsecured IoT devices, which are primarily IP cameras, and Shodan users can (illegally) connect to those cameras. The tool shows how ubiquitous IoT devices are and also demonstrates how many unsecured devices there are across the world. Investigators may find Shodan helpful. For example, if an investigator wants to search for CCTV, in a particular area, Shodan could display video evidence that could benefit an investigation.

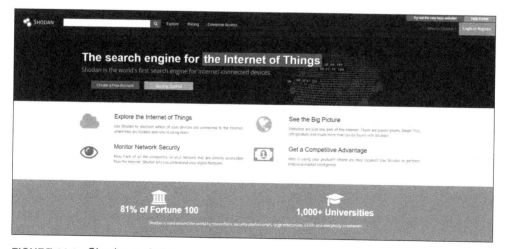

FIGURE 14.1   Shodan website

Shodan can also be used to identify if an organization has any vulnerable IoT devices on their network. Security practitioners can also learn about IoT hardware vulnerabilities in an effort to improve their organization's security profile. The website also provides helpful information for those looking to learn how to use the tool, including filter cheat sheets, as displayed in Figure 14.2.

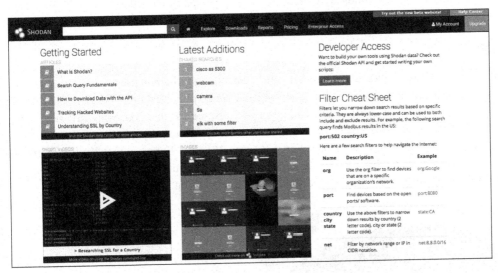

FIGURE 14.2 Shodan filter cheat sheets

Mirai Botnet

Mirai was malware that infected Internet-enabled devices, running on Linux, and the malware enrolled those devices into a Botnet. The malware surfaced in 2016. The infected devices included routers and IP cameras. Basically, hackers scanned large segments of the Internet for open Telnet ports and then attempted to login with default logins and passwords. The Mirai Botnet was ultimately responsible for a massive distributed denial of service (DDoS) attack, which left many on the East Coast of the United States without Internet access. In general, many IoT devices are vulnerable to attack because they are rarely patched, if ever. The Mirai Botnet incident clearly demonstrates how IoT devices often possess poor security protocols and provide a new vector of attack, at home and in the workplace, for hackers.

Cryptocurrency Mining

Cryptocurrency, like Bitcoin, requires that a crypto miner solve a complex mathematical algorithm when facilitating a transaction between the sender and receiver of the currency. Solving these mathematical problems gradually becomes more difficult over time and, more importantly, requires a tremendous amount of computing power. **Cryptojacking** is the unauthorized use of a computing device to mine a crytocurrency. Cryptojacking generally works when a user clicks on a link, sent in an email, for example, or visits a website with embedded malware scripts. From the user's perspective, she is generally unaware of the malware running in the background, which allows cryptomining, and the computer may experience a slight degradation in performance. More recently, Avast tested a proof a concept to show that IoT devices could be compromised and used to mine Monero (cryptocurrency). Thus, IoT devices can be compromised by malware and become part of a botnet.

Alexa

Alexa is a virtual assistant, with artificial intelligence capabilities, which is used to answer questions, interact with smart home devices (IoT), like The Ring and Wemo plugs and light switches, play games, play music and perform many other tasks (see Figure 14.3). Apple's Home Pod (with Siri) and Google Home are similar devices to Amazon's Alexa Echo, whereby the user speaks requests to a virtual assistant and then receives an answer or action via a speaker. The Echo continually listens for the "wake word", which is generally "Alexa", then records the user's request and then sends the request to a processor for analysis to either fulfill a request or answer a question.

FIGURE 14.3   Echo speaker with Alexa AI

In 2019, it was revealed that some Amazon employees are tasked with listening to consumers' audio clips of requests made to Alexa to improve device performance. However, many consumers do not realize that they can opt-out of sharing their voice recordings with Amazon, via the Amazon app, under "Alexa Privacy".

Amazon's Alexa (Echo) audio files have been used by law enforcement in investigations. James Bates, from Bentonville, Arkansas, was arrested on suspicion of murder. The prosecutor sought audio recordings related to the suspect's Echo device, but Amazon refused to assist, and their lawyers released the following statement in response to the request:

> Given the important First Amendment and privacy implications at stake, the warrant should be quashed unless the Court finds that the State has met its heightened burden for compelled production of such materials.

The suspect's attorney subsequently gave permission for Amazon to release the information requested by the prosecutor. The prosecutor then decided to drop murder charges against James Bates. Bates subsequently filed a lawsuit against the police in Bentonville, alleging that the police tried to frame him for the murder of another man.

Micro-Chipping

Micro-chips are placed under the skin of people and, while this is RFID technology rather than IoT, its growth is important to discuss in this chapter. Furthermore, micro-chip data is likely to be a valuable supplement to IoT evidence and, in particular, to wearable technology.

Micro-chipping humans has become popular in Sweden, where the technology enables people to enter an apartment, access a workplace, make purchases from vending machines and stored emergency contact information. The technology first became popular with pet dogs. Implanting a chip would allow dog owners to quickly locate their pets. In fact, in Ireland micro-chipping dogs became a legal requirement in response to incidents where people who were mauled by some breeds of dogs. Since March 2016, it is a legal requirement for all dogs to be chipped. Mexico's attorney general and 160 people in his office were implanted with micro-chips to allow employees access to restricted areas of the attorney general's headquarters.

Fitness Trackers

In November 2017, an application called Strava was released, which was a data visualization map that displayed the user activity of fitness tracking apps, including Fitbit (see Figure 14.4). In fact, more than three trillion GPS data points for its users were mapped across the globe. Interestingly, the release of this information proved to be an operational security hazard as anyone could view the movements of active U.S. military at bases around the world. More importantly, the maps showed military personnel on operational tours in Syria and assigned to other countries, which created an inadvertent threat, as adversaries could now track U.S. soldiers strategically placed in war zones around the world. Strava could also inadvertently provide information about secret bases and other sensitive locations.

The Strava app has been used at trial. NFL tight end, Kellen Winslow II, was charged on 12 counts, from indecent exposure to rape. It is Winslow's biking activity, and his use of the Strava app, that was used against the suspect in this case. Investigators in San Diego visited Winslow's public Strava account and captured screenshots of the routes he had traveled prior to his account being deleted. These Strava screenshots allegedly indicated that the suspect was in the vicinity of a person that he allegedly exposed his body to.

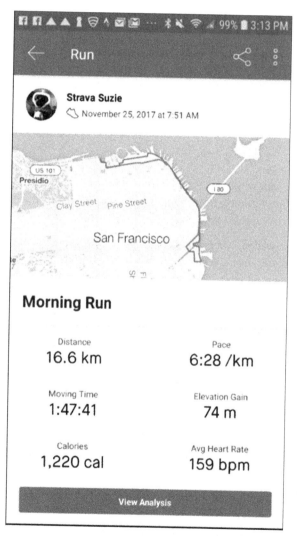

FIGURE 14.4   Strava app user interface

Apple Watch

The Apple Watch (see Figure 14.5) monitors a user's heart rate and the user can view his resting, walking, workout heart rate throughout the day. The user can also enable notifications if his heart rate drops too low or is too high when at rest. A user's heart rate is monitored continuously during a workout and three minutes after the conclusion of a workout to monitor the user's workout recovery.

FIGURE 14.5   Health Rate App

The Apple Watch uses an optical heart sensor to monitor heart rate. The technology used to monitor heart rate is photoplethysmography (PPG), whereby the Watch uses LED lights, combined with light-sensitive photodiodes, to determine blood flow in the wrist. **Photoplethysmography (PPG)** is the use of light to determine blood flow based on rates of light absorption. This technology is based on the premise that blood is red because it reflects red light but absorbs green light. The optical heart sensor flashes its LED lights hundreds of times a second. With each heartbeat, there is more blood flow in the wrist, and therefore a higher absorption of green light, which is recorded by the Watch. The optical heart sensor uses infrared light to measure heart rate in the background and to provide heart rate notifications. Figure 14.6 shows the (green) lights on the underside of the Apple Watch after a workout.

The Apple Watch Series 4 has built-in electrodes that monitor electrical signals from your heart, while using the ECG or Heart Rate functions. The electrodes are located at the back of Watch and on the Digital Crown as illustrated in Figure 14.7.

FIGURE 14.6   Apple Watch (green) LED lights

FIGURE 14.7   Rear view of Apple Watch

When the user touches the Digital Crown, it creates a circuit between your arms and your heart and measures electrical impulses across your chest.

While there is some digital evidence stored locally on the Watch, the investigator must largely rely on extracting Apple Watch data from the iPhone that it is synchronized with. Much of the data from the Watch is found in Apple's Health app, as there is no real backup for the device. An investigator can find Apple Health data, associated with an iPhone, at the following file path:

/private/var/mobile/Library/Health/

There may also be relevant data located in iTunes backups:

/HealthDomain/Health/

The folder contains two SQLite databases: **healthdb.sqlite** and **healthdb_secure.sqlite**.

With the necessary court approvals, law enforcement can also request Apple to provide Health app data, which is synced to iCloud. The user may also use another app that complements the Health app, like Strava, and this data may also be accessible to law enforcement. ElcomSoft Phone Breaker can extract Health app data, as can the Apple Pattern of Life Lazy Output'er (APOLLO) tool. APOLLO is an iOS forensics tool that pulls data from numerous SQLite databases on an iPhone and correlates that information with the investigator. In other words, data from the Health app, like steps and heart rate, are correlated with location information, weather, and other user activity to provide a more holistic view of what a user was doing during a particular timeframe. Pulling data from multiple databases means that the investigator now has one tool that can show that a person was running in Central Park, New York City, while listening to music, on a sunny day, at 17:53 on May 4, 2021.

Action Cameras

Digital video evidence has been used at trial in many cases worldwide, including in the United States. This evidence includes files extracted from action cameras, like GoPro. In 2016, Richard Hammond was arrested by Sussex police, in the United Kingdom, after popping a wheelie on his Honda motorcycle at 80 mph and performing dangerous maneuvers at speeds that reached 153 mph. The video evidence was extracted from the secure digital (SD) card, which was installed in the suspect's helmet camera. In this case, there were 150 video clips, which included views of the suspect's speedometer. By viewing the suspect's speedometer and by examining the frame rate in the video, police determined how fast the suspect was traveling. The suspect was found guilty and was sentenced to two years in prison.

There have been numerous cases prosecuted that involved video evidence from action cameras, which involved motorcyclists traveling at high speed. In a few cases, video clips have been uploaded to YouTube by suspects or their friends. Law enforcement has then been able to subpoena Google for additional information about the video posting, including the IP address, which would lead investigators to the location where the suspect uploaded the video. In 2015, a man from the United Kingdom, Jamie Simmonds, 21, was jailed for six months for doing wheelies on his moped at high speed. Video from his helmet camera was used as evidence at trial. Interestingly, Simmonds wore a sweatshirt with the phrase "CAN'T CATCH ME", yet he posted the video footage on YouTube with his real name. A search of his home by police revealed the moped, helmet camera, and infamous sweatshirt.

Police Safety

There have been many discussions about how IoT can help protect the health and welfare of police officers. Of course, some may have privacy implications, including data captured by the Apple Watch. The Apple Watch can monitor the health of its officers, primarily by monitoring ECG levels, which could alert their departments about the stress levels of their officers. Furthermore, a police department could check to see if their officers are getting enough sleep at night. Stress, and even suicide, is a major problem for police officers around the world. There have been some NYPD (New York Police Department) officers who have taken their own lives, for example. In 2018, there were 166 police officers killed in the line of duty. In 2019, there were 228 police suicides, including 27 in New York. This number was actually higher than the 132 officers killed in the line of duty in 2019.

Drones are being used more and more by law enforcement. For example, drones are currently being used by SWAT (Special Weapons And Tactics) teams, to gather aerial reconnaissance prior to, and during, an operation. The benefit of using drones is that they can be stealthier, less costly, and safer than using a police helicopter. Drones have also been used in hostage situations, for manhunts, missing persons, and post incidents.

Today we have smart holster sensors. A **smart holster sensor**, which is built into a gun holster, is used to detect when a firearm has been removed from its holster, which in turn activates a body camera. This eliminates the need for an officer to manually activate her body camera. The sensor will also send real-time alerts to dispatch an officer in the vicinity. We now have connected firearms. This small device attaches to a gun and has a built-in accelerometer and magnetometer, which can detect the location of the firearm, whether the firearm is holstered, when it is loaded, and the video when it is discharged.

A **body worn camera (BWC)** is a digital video camera that can be clipped onto clothing or can be built into a vest and worn on the torso. Many police agencies, across the United States and in other countries, use body cameras. Some body worn cameras can be automatically activated when a police officer removes his gun from its holster. Manufacturers of BWCs include Axon, Coban, Data911, FlyWIRE, and many more producers. Some BWCs collect video, audio, date and timestamps, and GPS coordinates, and the video can be later used for facial recognition.

Companies, such as Yardarm, have developed gun sensors that utilize three-axis telemetry to monitor the position of a police officer's gun. Thus, the direction that the gun is held in, and the direction of fire, can be recorded. Each gunfire event is captured via a Bluetooth device, and that event information is sent to the officer's smartphone. An alert can also be automatically sent to dispatch in addition to other officers in close proximity.

Police in China have been using smart glasses, which have facial recognition capabilities. These spectacles are connected to a handheld device, and facial images are captured in crowded public spaces. Subsequently, these facial images are scanned against a database of suspected criminals. According to Chinese state media reports, law enforcement has been successful in capturing wanted criminals using this technology. There are approximately 200 million CCTV cameras in China, many of which have facial recognition capabilities. We have heard reports of smart glasses being used by police during the Hong Kong Protests in 2019 and 2020. Student protestors, in Hong Kong, were so fearful of law enforcement's use of facial recognition that they wore masks and used lasers to prevent the police from recognizing protest participants. It may be only a matter of time before law enforcement in the USA, and other regions, begin using smart glasses. As smart glasses evolve, they may be used by law enforcement to improve situational awareness, i.e. use augmented reality to navigate certain terrain, understand potential hazards, and perhaps locate a criminal suspect.

Amazon has partnered with more than 400 law enforcement agencies to share data from the Ring doorbell to help investigators solve burglaries, using Ring video footage. Some legislators have expressed privacy concerns about this partnership in the absence of consumer consent. It is clear, however, that doorbell cameras and home cameras can be effective in the successful capture of criminal suspects, including crimes like kidnapping. In May 2019, a Ring doorbell captured the abduction of eight-year-old Salem Sabatka, in Fort Worth, Texas. Video of the abduction was shared with neighbors, and Fort Worth police were able to use the Ring video to identify the suspect who abducted the girl.

Police Vehicles

IoT has made it possible for law enforcement to have smart connected vehicles. **Cellular Vehicle-to-Everything (C-V2X)** is a 3GPP standard for use with smart vehicles on 4G and 5G networks. This is an alternative standard to the IEEE 802.11p standard for V2V (vehicle-to-vehicle) communications.

Police vehicles are now fitted with dash cameras. These vehicles are also fitted with GPS so that dispatch will always know where their officers are at all times. The vehicle may also have a Cradlepoint router, which connects first responders on a 4G LTE network. Firefighters use Cradlepoint to remotely access building blueprints and maps, aerial views of a fire from on-scene drones, and coordinate fire trucks and personnel. Similarly, Cradlepoint assists law enforcement with situational awareness and coordinates law enforcement resources. Pepwave is a 5G-ready technology that provides law enforcement, firefighters, and emergency medical services (EMS) with public safety network capabilities.

Today's police cruiser may also incorporate automatic number plate recognition. **Automatic number plate recognition (ANPR)** is a technology that uses optical character recognition to read vehicle registration plates and record the location of the vehicle. In the United States, this technology is referred to as License Plate Recognition (LPR), while in the U.K. ANPR is used to describe the same thing. Grafton Thomas, 37, of Greenwood Lake, in Orange County, New York, was charged with federal hate crimes after allegedly attacking a Jewish community in Monsey, New York. A license plate reader, on the George Washington Bridge, was critical to his capture.

Geotab GO is a device used for vehicle telematics. **Telematics** is a technology in which a telecommunications device sends real-time data, over a network, to a centralized computer system. Often that device is a mobile phone or can be a device like Geotab. Geotab GO has the ability to collect location data, engine idling times, engine data to determine potential issues, acceleration, braking, cornering, and other important information that could be used in an accident investigation or be used to improve police safety. Uber is one company that uses telematics to keep track of their drivers and determine if their drivers are driving safely.

Vehicle Forensics

Vehicle forensics has grown in importance because of advancements in vehicle technology, including applications like Apple CarPlay, which links and synchronizes with an Apple iPhone. These connections, coupled with other telematics, can provide important, or even critical, digital evidence for an investigator. Berla is arguably the leading provider of vehicle forensics solutions with its iVe forensic tool. There are also a number of online tools available to investigators searching for information on a vehicle, when in possession of a VIN:

- **National Insurance Crime Bureau**: https://www.nicb.org/vincheck

- **Reverse Genie**: http://www.reversegenie.com/plate.php

- **VINDECODERZ**: https://www.vindecoderz.com/

A **vehicle identification number (VIN)** is a unique code, used by the automotive industry, to identify a specific vehicle and is defined by ISO 3779 and ISO 4030. A VIN will include a manufacturer identifier, vehicle descriptor (vehicle attributes), and vehicle identifier (model year, plant code, manufacturer number and sequential number). Let us take a look at the following VIN example: 1GKKVRED3CJ315078

The first number, 1, shows the world manufacturer number and "1" means that the vehicle was manufactured in the USA. A VIN beginning with 4 or 5 would have also been manufactured in the USA. The first three digits of the VIN is the world manufacturer identifier (WMI). In our VIN example, "1G" is assigned to General Motors (USA).

The fourth to ninth numbers of the VIN are the vehicle descriptor section (VDS) and often references the model type, body style or sometimes the engine type. The last 5 digits of a VIN in North America must be numeric so the VIN noted above is definitely a North American vehicle. However, the 10th digit of a VIN is always consistent and represents the year that the vehicle was produced. In our example VIN, the "C" shows that the vehicle is a 2012 vehicle. "D" is 2013, "E" is 2014, and so on. Thus, we know that the VIN is a GM vehicle, manufactured in the USA in 2012. A search on VINDECODERZ (https://www.vindecoderz.com/) shows that the vehicle is a 2012 GMC Acadia SLT 1 (AWD). Additional information about this vehicle could then be found at carvertical.com, carfax.com or on a number of other websites.

Low-Tech Solution for High-Tech Seizures

When it comes to search and seizure, there are so many different electronic devices that a crime scene investigator must think about. The problem is compounded when a suspect decides to hide devices, like a flash drive. A number of police departments, like Westchester County Police Department, have a "cyber dog". Harley (see Figure 14.8) is an electronic storage detection (ESD) dog. The average dog possesses a sense of smell that is fifty times that of humans. **TPPO (triphenylphosphine oxide)** is a chemical found in all electronics, and some dogs can be trained to locate devices with TPPO. This means that dogs, like Harley, can find thumb drives, cellphones, laptops, and other electronics that a suspect may have hidden in the home.

FIGURE 14.8   Harley the cyber dog with Detective Brett Hochron

Summary

IoT (Internet of Things) devices are ubiquitous in society today and will only continue to grow in number in the foreseeable future. These devices can include speakers with integrated artificial intelligence (AI), like Amazon's Echo (with Alexa AI). Traditional forensics tools cannot image most IoT devices, and therefore we rely on the mobile devices that IoT devices synchronize with, or else associated evidence stored in the Cloud. We have already witnessed Amazon being issued with subpoenas to turn over sound files, stored in the Cloud, which are derived from their Echo speaker/listening devices. IoT devices, unlike traditional computers, are infrequently patched by manufacturers to shore up security vulnerabilities and are therefore susceptible to malware. IoT devices are also a target for cryptocurrency miners.

Wearable IoT devices, like the Apple Watch, and fitness trackers have been used at trial to prove innocence or to successfully prosecute suspects. These devices can be used to prove the activity or inactivity of the user, which can be critical in many cases.

The exponential growth of IoT devices and new technologies, like 4K video, have created immense demands on home network bandwidth and also in public areas that seek to offer efficient wireless communications. Wi-Fi 6 and 5G have been developed to address the changing needs of our interconnected society and will change the nature of digital evidence. For example, the implementation of new transmitters to support 5G will change the nature of traditional cell site analysis, while networked devices, like cars and drones, will share more data in a more decentralized manner. 5G will promote the growth of mesh networks and smart cities.

Key Terms

5G: The fifth generation of cellular technologies.

automatic number plate recognition (ANPR): A technology that uses optical character recognition to read vehicle registration plates and record the locations of vehicles.

body worn camera (BWC): A digital video camera that can be clipped onto clothing or built into a vest and worn on the torso.

Cellular Vehicle-to-Everything (C-V2X): A 3GPP standard for use with smart vehicles on 4G and 5G networks.

cryptojacking: The unauthorized use of a computing device to mine a crytocurrency.

CUPS (Control and User Plane Separation): A 3GPP specification that facilitates Multi-access Edge Computing (MEC), whereby control functions, like establishing a connection with another device, take a different route through a network.

device-to-device (D2D): A technology that enables user equipment (UE) to communicate with one another or with a network infrastructure.

Internet of Things (IoT): Device that is Internet-enabled and can include a smart television, thermostat, refrigerator, or a speaker with artificial intelligence (AI) built-in.

latency: The delay between when data is sent and when it is received.

Mobile Connect: A 5G technology that matches a user's mobile number to an account, thereby allowing the user to log in to websites and applications without remembering the login and password information.

Multi-access Edge Computing (MEC): A networking protocol, whereby mobile users are able to establish direct connections, using network infrastructure at the edge of the network, rather than being routed through the mobile network operator's core network.

orthogonal frequency-division multiple access (OFDMA): Enables an 802.11ax router to send and receive data to multiple devices simultaneously by splitting a transmission channel into a number of transmission subchannels.

photoplethysmography (PPG): The use of light to determine blood flow based on rates of light absorption.

Quadrature Amplitude Modulation (QAM): A modulation scheme in digital telecommunication systems, like Wi-Fi.

smart holster sensor: A sensor built into a gun holster that is used to detect when a firearm has been removed from its holster and then activates a body camera.

telematics: A technology in which a telecommunications device sends real-time data, over a network, to a centralized computer system.

TPPO (triphenylphosphine oxide): A chemical found in all electronics, and some dogs can be trained to locate devices with TPPO.

vehicle identification number (VIN): A unique code used by the automotive industry to identify a specific vehicle and is defined by ISO 3779 and ISO 4030.

Vo5G (Voice over 5G): A standard for voice/video on the fifth generation of mobile technologies and is approved by 3GPP.

Wi-Fi 6: A wireless fidelity (Wi-Fi) standard that has been developed by the Wi-Fi Alliance.

Wi-Fi mesh network: A network comprised of a series of nodes, or computing devices, which help to propagate a wireless signal.

Assessment

CLASSROOM DISCUSSIONS

1. What is a mesh network, and why are these networks growing in importance?

2. While IoT devices can be cheap and provide convenience, we should consider improving the security of these devices. How can we improve IoT device security?

3. What will the impact of 5G be on digital evidence?

4. What will a smart city with integrated IoT and 5G technologies look like in the future?

5. How can IoT and wearable technologies be used to protect law enforcement officers?

MULTIPLE-CHOICE QUESTIONS

1. Which of the following can be used to search for a specific vehicle?

    A. CUPS

    B. Vo5G

    C. VIN

    D. D2D

2. Which of the following is a modulation scheme in digital telecommunication systems, like Wi-Fi?

    A. QAM

    B. VIN

    C. CUPS

    D. PPG

3. Which of the following refers to the delay between sending and receiving data?

    A. Cryptojacking

    B. Telematics

    C. OFDMA

    D. Latency

4. Which of the following is technology that enables user equipment (UE) to communicate with one another with or with a network infrastructure?

    A. D2D

    B. OFDMA

    C. CUPS

    D. MEC

5. Which of the following is a 5G technology that matches a user's mobile number to an account, thereby allowing the user to log in to websites and applications without having to remember login and password information?

   A. Control and User Plane Separation

   B. Apple CarPlay

   C. Mobile Connect

   D. Multi-access Edge Computing

6. Which of the following is a 3GPP standard for use with smart vehicles on 4G and 5G networks?

   A. VoLTE

   B. Vo5G

   C. C-V2X

   D. VIN

7. Which of the following is a standard for voice/video on the fifth generation of mobile technologies and is approved by 3GPP?

   A. VoLTE

   B. Vo5G

   C. C-V2X

   D. VIN

8. Which of the following defines the use of light to determine blood flow based on rates of light absorption?

   A. Photophosphorylation

   B. Photoplethysmography (PPG)

   C. Tryptophan (TTO)

   D. Triphenylphosphine oxide (TTPO)

9. Which of the following is a chemical found in all electronics, and some dogs can be trained to locate devices with this chemical?

   A. Photophosphorylation

   B. Photoplethysmography (PPG)

   C. Tryptophan (TTO)

   D. Triphenylphosphine oxide (TTPO)

10. Which of the following enables an 802.11ax router to send and receive data to multiple devices simultaneously by splitting a transmission channel into a number of transmission subchannels?

   A. D2D

   B. OFDMA

   C. CUPS

   D. MEC

FILL IN THE BLANKS

1. The unauthorized use of a computing device to mine a cryptocurrency is referred to as _____.

2. 802.11ax is also referred to as Wi-Fi _____.

3. Multi-access _____ Computing (MEC) is networking protocol, whereby mobile users are able to establish direct connections, using network infrastructure at the edge of the network, rather than being routed through the mobile network operator's core network.

4. An Internet of _____ device is Internet-enabled and can include a smart television, thermostat, refrigerator, or a speaker with artificial intelligence (AI) built-in.

5. Quadrature _____ Modulation (QAM) is a modulation scheme in digital telecommunication systems, like Wi-Fi.

6. A Wi-Fi _____ network is a network comprised of a series of nodes, or computing devices, which help to propagate a wireless signal.

7. A smart holster _____ is built into a gun holster and is used to detect when a firearm has been removed from its holster, and then activates a body camera.

8. Automatic _____ plate recognition (ANPR) is a technology that uses optical character recognition to read vehicle registration plates and record the location of the vehicle.

9. Voice over 5G is a standard for voice/video on the fifth generation of mobile technologies and approved by _____

10. _____ is a technology in which a telecommunications device sends real-time data, over a network, to a centralized computer system.

PROJECTS

5G Smart Cities

Create a research project describing how a 5G smart city of the future will look. Include information about how public Wi-Fi hotspots will benefit the future of IoT, robotics, and vehicle technology. Consider how 5G will change digital forensics investigations.

The Future of Policing

Write a research paper about how policing will be impacted by 5G and other new technologies. Include a graphical representation of police wearable technologies and technologies that will be integrated into police vehicles. You may also want to discuss how crime scene investigations will change over time and how IoT and smart devices in the home may benefit investigators.

Answer Key

MULTIPLE-CHOICE QUESTIONS

Chapter 1

1. B
2. C
3. D
4. D
5. D

6. B
7. A
8. B
9. D
10. A

Chapter 2

1. A
2. B
3. B
4. D
5. D

6. D
7. D
8. C
9. D
10. C

Chapter 3

1. C
2. D
3. A
4. A
5. D

6. C
7. D
8. A
9. C
10. D

Chapter 4

1. D
2. C
3. A
4. A
5. D

6. C
7. D
8. B
9. A
10. D

Chapter 5

1. A
2. D
3. C
4. B
5. A

6. D
7. C
8. B
9. A
10. A

Chapter 6

1. A
2. D
3. B
4. D
5. B

6. B
7. A
8. D
9. C
10. A

Chapter 7

1. B
2. D
3. A
4. B
5. D

6. C
7. D
8. B
9. A
10. A

Chapter 8

1. C
2. A
3. D
4. B
5. D
6. B
7. C
8. C
9. B
10. C

Chapter 9

1. B
2. C
3. D
4. D
5. A
6. D
7. D
8. A
9. D
10. B

Chapter 10

1. A
2. A

Chapter 11

1. D
2. A
3. B
4. D
5. C
6. A
7. C
8. A
9. D
10. C

Chapter 12

1. B
2. A
3. D
4. C
5. A
6. D
7. D
8. A
9. D
10. A

Chapter 13

1. D
2. A
3. A

4. B
5. A

Chapter 14

1. C
2. A
3. D
4. A
5. C

6. C
7. B
8. B
9. D
10. B

FILL IN THE BLANKS

Chapter 1

1. An algorithm is a set of steps used to solve a problem.

2. Computer forensics is the use of digital evidence in a criminal investigation.

3. Computer security is the prevention of unauthorized access to computers and their associated resources.

4. A defendant can prove his innocence with the use of exculpatory evidence.

5. The process of scrambling plain text into an unreadable format using a mathematical formula is called encryption.

6. The world's largest international police organization is called INTERPOL.

7. Short-term, volatile memory, the contents of which disappear when a computer is powered down, is called Random Access Memory.

8. A skimmer is a device used to capture the information stored in the magnetic strip of an ATM, credit, or debit card.

9. A web server delivers HTML documents and related resources in response to client computer requests.

10. InfraGard is a public–private agency of the FBI, which promotes the exchange of information between the private and public sectors on issues related to terrorism, intelligence, and security matters.

Chapter 2

1. A bit can possess one of two values: 1 or 0.

2. Hexadecimal is the base 16 numbering system, which includes numbers 0 to 9 and letters A to F.

3. A byte is comprised of eight bits and is the smallest addressable unit in memory.

4. The Master Boot Record is used by the BIOS to start the boot process.

5. Disk Geometry refers to the structure of a hard disk in terms of platters, tracks, and sectors.

6. FAT12 file system was introduced in 1980 as the first version of FAT and is the file system found on floppy disks.

7. The journal uses tracked changes to files for fast and efficient restoration of files when there is a system failure or power outage.

8. Windows Registry is a hierarchical database that stores system configuration information. The Registry is comprised of two elements, keys and values.

9. Defragmentation is the process of eliminating the amount of fragmentation in a file system to make file chunks (512KB blocks) closer together and increase free space areas on a disk.

10. Event Viewer is a Windows application used to view event logs.

Chapter 3

1. Boot Camp is a utility included with Mac OS X 10.6 (Snow Leopard) that enables the user to run a Windows operating system on an Intel-based Mac.

2. Integrated Drive Electronics is a drive interface, connector, and controller that is largely based on IBM PC standards for devices such as hard disk drives, tape drives, and optical drives.

3. Serial ATA is an interface that connects devices such as hard disk drives to host bus adapters.

4. A disk image is actually one file or a group of files that contain bit-for-bit copies of a hard drive but cannot be used for booting a computer or for other operations.

5. The Host Protected Area is a region on a hard disk that often contains code associated with the BIOS for booting and recovery purposes.

6. Garbage collection is a memory management process that involves removing unused files to make more memory available.

7. Fault tolerance means that if one component in a system, such as a hard disk drive, fails, the system will continue to operate.

8. A write-blocker is a hardware device that allows an individual to read data from a device such as a hard drive without writing to that device.

9. The less reflective surfaces on a CD that have not been burned by a laser are called pits.

10. A floppy disk is a thin, flexible plastic computer storage disk that is housed in a rigid plastic rectangular casing.

Chapter 4

1. The open source file format developed by Simson Garfinkel and supported by Autopsy and The Sleuth Kit forensics software is called Advanced Forensics Format.

2. An ATM skimmer is used to capture data from the magnetic strip on credit cards or ATM cards.

3. A cellphone jammer is a device that prevents cellular telephone users from connecting with other cellular telephones by blocking all radio signals.

4. The programming language developed by Guidance Software that allows EnCase users to create their own customized function and features in EnCase is called EnScript.

5. File carving is the process of identifying a file by certain characteristics, such as a file header or footer, rather than by the file extension or metadata.

6. When unneeded data is eliminated from a photo, this is referred to as lossless compression.

7. A virtual machine is a computer running software that allows for an instance of an operating system, or multiple operating systems, without making any changes to the user's computer.

8. Uninterruptable power supply is a power supply containing a battery that will maintain power in the event of a power outage.

9. A parasite is a point-of-sale skimmer.

10. An evidence locker is a metal cabinet with compartments that can be locked individually.

Chapter 5

1. An undercover investigation is the process used to acquire information without the individual or suspect knowing the true identity of the investigator.

2. Tails (short for theamnesicincognitolivesystem) is a live operating system that provides anonymity for the user using virtualized sessions with Tor.

3. Fiat currency is legal tender that is backed by a government or governments.

4. Sometimes referred to as newsgroups, a usenet is an online distributed discussion board that allows users to post messages and read postings.

5. The Real Time Crime Center is a data warehouse developed and used by the New York Police Department's more than 35,000 police officers to track and apprehend known and suspected criminals.

6. The Homeland Security Data Network is a network developed by Northrup Grumman that contains top-secret, classified, and unclassified information.

7. A flash cookie is also referred to as a local shared object (LSO). It stores data on a user's system and is pushed out by websites running Adobe Flash.

8. An Application Programming Interface is a computer program that facilitates the interaction between two computer applications or programs.

9. An Internet Protocol address is a 32-bit or 128-bit number that uniquely identifies a host on the Internet.

10. A session cookie is a text file sent to a browser that is stored on a computer and used to identify and authenticate an Internet user; it is removed when the user's browser is closed.

Chapter 6

1. Predictive coding is a scientific methodology used to find keywords, patterns, or relevant content on a computer.

2. The time recorded at 0 degrees longitude is called Greenwich Mean Time.

3. The practice of advancing time by one hour in spring and then decrementing time by one hour in fall is called Daylight Saving Time.

4. A lay witness testifies about personal experience and knowledge.

5. A leap second is added to clocks to allow for inconsistencies between the Earth's rotation and the time recorded by our everyday devices.

6. An expert witness may create an investigative report or review the findings of an investigative report and provide an interpretation of those findings based on specialized education, training, and knowledge.

7. Mountain Standard Time is the time zone in the United States that includes Arizona, Utah, Colorado, New Mexico, Wyoming, Idaho, and Montana.

8. The computer glitches that can occur as a result of a leap second that is added to atomic clocks in order to coordinate with the Earth's rotation is referred to as the leap second bug.

9. Universal Time Coordinated is an international time standard that is based on longitude and uses a 24-hour clock format.

10. A preservation order is a request by law enforcement to maintain the records of a suspect, pending the approval of a subpoena or warrant.

Chapter 7

1. A group of people put under oath to hear arguments at trial and render a verdict of guilty or not guilty is referred to as a(n) jury.

2. The Bill of Rights refers to the first 10 amendments to the U.S. Constitution.

3. The Fifth Amendment states that a defendant is not required to take the witness stand.

4. Fruit of the poisonous tree is a metaphorical expression for evidence acquired from an illegal search.

5. Probable cause is the condition under which law enforcement may obtain a warrant for a search or arrest when it is evident that a crime has been committed.

6. A statement other than one made by the declarant while testifying at the trial or hearing, offered in evidence to prove the truth of the matter asserted, is called hearsay.

7. The Daubert test means that evidence does not necessarily need to have general acceptance by the scientific community but does need to meet the requirements of FRE 702.

8. Discovery is the pretrial phase in which both parties in a civil lawsuit must share evidence when requested, by means of interrogations, depositions, documents, and subpoenas from parties not part of the lawsuit.

9. Curtilage is the name given to the property surrounding a house.

10. Stingray is the generic name given to a device that acts like a cellphone tower to locate criminal suspects, but can also be used to locate people in disaster areas, such as earthquake zones.

Chapter 8

1. A packet is a block of data used in communications across the Internet.

2. Transmission Control Protocol is a communication standard that is used in conjunction with the Internet.

3. An intrusion detection system is hardware or software used to monitor network traffic for malicious activity.

4. User Datagram Protocol is a connectionless communication protocol that has limited packet recovery functionality and operates at the Transport Layer.

5. Address Resolution Protocol is a method by which the Network Layer (Layer 3) of the OSI Model is linked to the Data Link Layer (Layer 2).

6. A Browser Help Object is used to add functionality to a web browser. The object starts every time the user opens the browser.

7. Dynamic Link Library files are Windows system files that contain procedures and drivers that are executed by a program.

8. An advanced persistent threat is a sophisticated, relentless, coordinated attack on a computer network, with the goal of stealing intellectual property.

9. Packet sniffers are used to capture data packets on a wireless or wired network.

10. HyperText Transfer Protocol is a standard for requests and responses between a client and a server.

Chapter 9

1. A cell is the geographic area within a cellular network.

2. A Mobile Switching Center is responsible for switching data packets from one network path to another on a cellular network.

3. A soft handoff is when a cellular communication is conditionally handed off from one base station to another and the mobile equipment is simultaneously communicating with multiple base transceiver stations.

4. An International Mobile Equipment Identity number uniquely identifies the mobile equipment or handset.

5. The database that contains information about a roaming subscriber is referred to as a(n) Visitor Location Register.

6. The Equipment Identity Register is used to track IMEI numbers and decide whether an IMEI is valid, suspect or perhaps stolen.

7. Integrated Digital Enhanced Network is a wireless technology developed by Motorola, which combines two-way radio capabilities with digital cellphone technology.

8. A Forbidden Public Land Mobile Network is a cellular network that a subscriber attempted to connect to but was not authorized to connect to.

9. A Personal Unblocking Key (PUK) is a code that is available from the carrier and allows a user to remove the PIN protection from the SIM card.

10. A public safety access point is a call center that receives emergency requests from the public for police, medical or firefighter services.

Chapter 10

1. An Android manifest file contains the application's package name, its functionality, permissions, hardware, and software requirements for installation.

2. An Android emulator is an application that simulates or runs the Android operating system in a virtual machine.

3. A pcap file is a wireless packet that contains user data and network data related to the sender and receiver of that data.

4. A bundle ID is a uniform type identifier, which is comprised of alphanumeric characters, that uniquely identifies a specific app.

5. An App ID is a two-part string that identifies a development team (Team ID) and an application (bundle ID).

6. A zero-day exploit is a security vulnerability that is a threat on the day that it is discovered because a software patch, to fix the exploit, does not yet exist.

7. A man-in-the-middle attack is an attempt to intercept electronic communications between two computing devices with the intent to decipher encrypted messages.

8. GET is an HTTP method used to request data from a specific resource, like a web server.

Chapter 11

1. The Joint Photographic Experts Group file format is the most common picture file found on a digital camera, smartphone, or tablet.

2. When compression causes a reduction in picture quality, this is referred to as lossy.

3. A raster graphic is a pixelated image associated with pictures found on a computer or retrieved from a digital camera.

4. A vector graphic is comprised of curves, lines, or shapes based on mathematical formulae rather than pixels.

5. The Design Rule for Camera file system was developed by the Japan Electronic Industry Development Association (JEIDA) to facilitate the exchange of images between digital still cameras and other devices for viewing digital photographs.

6. Color balancing describes the process of adjusting colors in an image to render them to more accurately reflect the original scene when the photograph was taken.

7. A Bitmap Image File is a raster image file format that is generally associated with a Windows PC.

8. Brightness adjustment is used to make an image lighter or darker, to make the image easier to view.

9. A digital photograph is an image taken with a camera and stored as a computer file.

10. Exchangeable Image File Format is the metadata associated with digital pictures.

Chapter 12

1. Apple Cocoa is the framework for enterprise deployment of the iPhone, iPad, and iPod.

2. FileVault is a volume encryption tool developed by Apple for use with Macintosh computers.

3. Hierarchical File System is the file system that was developed by Apple in 1985 to support its hard disk drive.

4. Location Services is a user preference that allows an iOS device and a variety of applications running on the device to determine your position based on cell sites, GPS, and Wi-Fi hotspots.

5. Recovery Mode enables the user to restore his iPhone settings to the original factory settings.

6. Sleepimage is the name of the file that is a copy of the contents of RAM that is copied to the computer's hard drive when the computer goes into hibernate mode.

7. Vacuuming is a cleanup feature associated with SQLite databases that will permanently erase deleted records or tables.

8. Boot Camp is a tool which allows an Intel-based Macintosh to run multiple operating systems.

9. An iBeacon uses Bluetooth Low Energy (BLE) for identifying the location of a user.

10. Property Lists are configuration files found on computers running the Mac operating system.

Chapter 13

1. When an individual publishes confidential personal information with others online or in an email to embarrass another individual, it is known as outing.

2. A group that organizes to physically harm another person and then video the event to share with others is involved with happy slapping.

3. Impersonation occurs when a person breaks into another person's account and pretends to be that person.

4. Arguing online with another person using obscenities is called flaming.

5. When peers are asked to rank who they believe to be the ugliest in the class online, the peers are asked to contribute to an online poll.

Chapter 14

1. The unauthorized use of a computing device to mine a cryptocurrency is referred to as cryptojacking.

2. 802.11ax is also referred to as Wi-Fi 6.

3. Multi-access Edge Computing (MEC) is a networking protocol whereby mobile users are able to establish direct connections, using network infrastructure at the edge of the network, rather than being routed through the mobile network operator's core network.

4. An Internet of Things device is Internet-enabled and can include a smart television, thermostat, refrigerator, or a speaker with artificial intelligence (AI) built-in.

5. Quadrature Amplitude Modulation (QAM) is a modulation scheme in digital telecommunication systems, like Wi-Fi.

6. A Wi-Fi mesh network is a network comprised of a series of nodes, or computing devices, which help to propagate a wireless signal.

7. A smart holster sensor is built into a gun holster and is used to detect when a firearm has been removed from its holster, and then activates a body camera.

8. Automatic number plate recognition (ANPR) is a technology that uses optical character recognition to read vehicle registration plates and record the location of the vehicle.

9. Voice over 5G is a standard for voice/video on the fifth generation of mobile technologies and approved by 3GPP.

10. Telematics is a technology in which a telecommunications device sends real-time data, over a network, to a centralized computer system.

Index

Symbols

Numbers

A

B

Register Your Product at pearsonITcertification.com/register

Access additional benefits and **save 35%** on your next purchase

- Automatically receive a coupon for 35% off your next purchase, valid for 30 days. Look for your code in your Pearson IT Certification cart or the Manage Codes section of your account page.

- Download available product updates.

- Access bonus material if available.*

- Check the box to hear from us and receive exclusive offers on new editions and related products.

Registration benefits vary by product. Benefits will be listed on your account page under Registered Products.

Learning Solutions for Self-Paced Study, Enterprise, and the Classroom

Pearson IT Certification delivers training materials that address the learning, preparation, and practice needs of a new generation of certification candidates, including the official publishing programs of Adobe Press, Cisco Press, and Microsoft Press. At pearsonITcertification.com, you can:

- Shop our books, eBooks, practice tests, software, and video courses
- Sign up to receive special offers
- Access thousands of free chapters and video lessons

Visit **pearsonITcertification.com/community** to connect with Pearson IT Certification

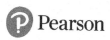

Addison-Wesley • Adobe Press • Cisco Press • Microsoft Press • Pearson IT Certification • Que • Sams • Peachpit Press